RECONSTRUCTING GENDER

RECONSTRUCTING GENDER
A Multicultural Anthology

Fifth Edition

Estelle Disch
University of Massachusetts Boston

McGraw-Hill
Higher Education

Boston   Burr Ridge, IL   Dubuque, IA   New York   San Francisco   St. Louis
Bangkok   Bogotá   Caracas   Kuala Lumpur   Lisbon   London   Madrid   Mexico City
Milan   Montreal   New Delhi   Santiago   Seoul   Singapore   Sydney   Taipei   Toronto

McGraw-Hill
Higher Education

Published by McGraw-Hill, an imprint of The McGraw-Hill Companies, Inc., 1221 Avenue of the Americas, New York, NY 10020. Copyright © 2009, 2006, 2003, 2000, 1997. All rights reserved. No part of this publication may be reproduced or distributed in any form or by any means, or stored in a database or retrieval system, without the prior written consent of The McGraw-Hill Companies, Inc., including, but not limited to, in any network or other electronic storage or transmission, or broadcast for distance learning.

This book is printed on acid-free paper.

1 2 3 4 5 6 7 8 9 0 DOC/DOC 1 0 9 8

ISBN: 978-0-07-338006-3
MHID: 0-07-338006-7

Editor in Chief: *Michael Ryan*
Publisher: *Frank Mortimer*
Sponsoring Editor: *Gina Boedeker*
Executive Marketing Manager: *Leslie Oberhuber*
Developmental Editor: *Kate Scheinman*
Editorial Coordinator: *Evan Bock*
Production Editor: *Karol Jurado*
Production Service: *Anne Draus, Scratchgravel Publishing Services*
Manuscript Editor: *Pat Tompkins*
Cover Designer: *Laurie Entringer*
Production Supervisor: *Richard DeVitto*
Composition: *10/12 Book Antiqua by ICC Macmillan Inc.*
Printing: *45# New Era Matte Plus, R. R. Donnelley & Sons*
Cover image: Luz-Ines Mercier. *Down to Earth,* 1996. Mixed Media on Canvas, 41 × 60."
   © Luz-Ines Mercier

Library of Congress Cataloging-in-Publication Data

Reconstructing gender : a multicultural anthology/[edited by] Estelle Disch.—5th ed.
   p. cm.
Includes bibliographical references and indexes.
ISBN-13: 978-0-07-338006-3 (alk. paper)
ISBN-10: 0-07-338006-7 (alk. paper)
1. Sex role. 2. Masculinity. 3. Femininity. 4. Women—Psychology. 5. Socialization.
I. Disch, Estelle.

HQ1075.R43 2009
305.3—dc22   2007032975

The Internet addresses listed in the text were accurate at the time of publication. The inclusion of a Web site does not indicate an endorsement by the authors or McGraw-Hill, and McGraw-Hill does not guarantee the accuracy of the information presented at these sites.

www.mhhe.com

◆ About the Editor

Estelle Disch is professor of sociology at the University of Massachusetts Boston where she has been active in curricular transformation, general education reform, and faculty development. She has written extensively on pedagogical issues in diverse classrooms. Her research focuses on the effects of sexual abuse by professionals and on assessing learning in university courses. She has served as a consultant and trainer related to creating more open and accepting campus climates and has run many workshops for professionals related to maintaining appropriate professional boundaries.

◆ Contents

PART II: GENDER SOCIALIZATION   107

PART III: EMBODIMENT   156

PART IV: COMMUNICATION 221

PART V: SEXUALITY 262

PART VI: FAMILIES 297

x   *Contents*

◆ Preface

About a decade ago in my undergraduate Sociology of Gender course,[1] I asked the class to sit in small groups and identify gender-related problems that each student was currently facing and that were not too personal to discuss in the class. I then asked the students to assess to what extent their problems were personal troubles, that is, specific to themselves as individuals, or public issues, reflective of wider issues in the social order and experienced by many people.[2] When the groups reported back, two men responded, "We were raised never to hit girls, and now with the women's movement, we want to know whether or not that's OK." Their question was serious, and the class exploded. Many women in the room became very upset and started yelling at the two men. (I later learned that at least a third of the women in the room had been raped.) I was caught off guard and realized that the course was not designed to effectively address the various issues embedded in the men's question. I did not have nearly enough material on men's socialization and behavior. I was particularly concerned about providing students with enough information to help them begin to make sense of the high rates of men's violence toward women and toward each other.

In my search for better materials about men's socialization, I found a growing literature in men's studies to accompany the already huge literature in women's studies and the sociology of gender. But my favorite articles were scattered in a wide range of sources. Although some excellent anthologies were available about and by women and men separately, no one volume available at that time and appropriate for use in a social science course gave substantial attention to both genders. Although the choice of texts has grown considerably since 1996, I have chosen to revise this one four times to keep it current. Thus, this book is designed to meet the needs of faculty who want to teach about both women and men from a multicultural perspective but who want to use one anthology instead of two. I define multicultural broadly to include the perspectives and experiences of a wide range of people within the context of power and inequality.

The explosion of work by and about people of color, people of various ethnicities, gay men, lesbians, bisexuals, transgendered people, people with disabilities, and working-class people has made the creation of this book possible. Most of the readings included here are ones that colleagues and I have used in classrooms with success. By success, I mean that many students have become engaged with the material in various ways: becoming excited or angered by the ideas expressed, talking with friends and family about the material, making sense of their own experience in relation to the authors' experiences, feeling excited to learn more about a particular issue, or becoming politically involved in response to what they are learning. I teach in a way that encourages interaction among students,[3] and I am particularly committed to using articles that stimulate discussion. I welcome readers' feedback about what works in classrooms and what doesn't.

This book also emerges, in part, from questions and concerns that I've experienced in my own life, especially my own experience growing up in a sexist, racist, anti-Semitic, white, economically privileged, Protestant family. With three older brothers and a sports-oriented father who was a physician, I often felt like I was immersed in a male club. This club demanded rigid gender conformity of my brothers. My least-athletic brother was brutally teased and called a sissy because of his lack of athletic ability, his pain while watching my father and my other brothers shoot ducks, his interest in music, his ability to cry, and his chubby body. I watched my father rage when my aunt bought that particular brother a pink shirt. My survival strategy in this system was to attempt to fit into the male club. By about age seven I had learned to shoot frogs with a .22 rifle, to clean fish, to brace myself against the pain I felt watching a duck thrash in the water after being shot, to enjoy watching baseball games (or to pretend that I did), and to be otherwise tough and strong.

I also learned about racist and anti-Semitic attitudes in my family. I can remember my grandmother expressing disapproval that my best friend was Jewish and my father telling me an anti-Semitic "joke" that I repeated to my best friend, who didn't find it funny. Unfortunately, we had no skills at age 10 or so to discuss what was wrong with the "joke." And I can remember my father complaining about the presence of Black baseball players, actors, and newscasters on TV—"That man's got a white man's job." Luckily, my mother provided a contrast to my father's views. She did not participate in his racist and anti-Semitic discussions, spoke freely about her poverty-stricken origins, and allowed me to question his values.

I am impressed to this day at the contradictions embedded in what my father expected of boys and men. On the one hand, he seemed at his happiest in the all-male hunting and fishing cultures in which he spent as much free time as he could. When these men went hunting, they slept in close quarters, spent days together in tiny gunning boats or hiding in duck blinds, cooked elaborate meals at the end of the day, and kept house—all with no women present. (I begged to go on these trips but was barred.) On the other hand, his homophobia was always there, levying disrespect at any boy or man who might be "too feminine," who might acknowledge his love for a man, or who might choose to make a life with men doing much of what my father, his friends, and my brothers did on hunting trips.

Another personal interest that informs my selections for this anthology is my knowledge about male violence and sexual abuse toward boys, girls, women, and men. I continue to be baffled at our inability to effectively prevent that abuse. I am shocked not so much by the facts (I have accepted them after years of awareness) but by the entrenched system of violence and domination that teaches new generations of people, especially men, how to be violent and oppressive. For 12 years, I worked with survivors of sexual abuse committed by health care and mental health care providers and clergy and have been struck by the fact that the vast majority of offenders—against both men and women—are men.[4] Although offenses of this type are brutally damaging when perpetrated by members of either gender, the overwhelming imbalance toward male perpetrators has led me to wonder what has caused so many of them to be so exploitative or violent. I am reminded of a very disturbing photo essay of men who had attended a residential religious school in which male clergy physically and sexually abused many of the boys.[5] One of the men shown tells of the abuse he suffered as a child and reports that when he learned that his younger brother was about to be put in the same school, he killed his brother to save him from the abuse. It appears that the only way he had learned to address brutal situations was to be brutal himself.

I am also informed here by 25 years of working collectively with others: 10 years working with white, mostly middle-class, almost exclusively heterosexual women and men in alternative mental health centers; 10 years in a feminist therapy collective where a group of mixed-class white heterosexual women and lesbians learned to work closely together; and in working groups at the University of Massachusetts Boston, where faculty, students, and staff built a multicultural, broad-based coalition to win the passage of a diversity requirement for undergraduate students.[6] I have learned that diverse women and men can work together using decision-making processes in which conflict is discussed, compromises are negotiated, and leadership and rewards are shared. If people are committed to communicating and cooperating and working on their prejudices, then differences of gender, race, culture, class, sexual orientation, disability, and age can be addressed and dealt with to accomplish common goals.

I am also concerned in this anthology with the entrenchment of privilege. I have observed how much time and attention it has taken me to unravel my own prejudices and become aware of my privileges, and I wonder how we will ever construct a humane social order when it is so difficult for those with privilege to see how caught we are in its cushioned web. Even with an education that communicated democratic values, a mother who worked full time and talked extensively about growing up poor, an older brother who mentored me into liberal/radical views, and a feminist movement and support system that has especially supported my anti-racist and multicultural activism, I still find it difficult to stay fully conscious of some of the oppressive attitudes I have learned. Although I have analyzed enough of my socialization to feel fully capable of working on my attitudes and am able to openly apologize for any lingering insensitivities, I believe that I will be working on this for the rest of my life. I hope the readings that follow will help those with more privilege become clear about what that means for them, that those with less privilege will find inspiration for empowerment, and that both groups will find ways to work toward a more egalitarian social order—one in which all people will have an opportunity to work with others in shared ways, in which real community can evolve from positions of equal respect, and in which all people enjoy basic human rights free of poverty, violence, preventable illness, and discrimination.

I have chosen to include increasingly more material on international issues with each revision of this book, always centering on issues with a direct connection to the United States. The events of September 11, 2001, followed by the wars in Afghanistan and Iraq, led me to include more essays aimed at helping readers understand some of the issues embedded in and surrounding those events.

Many people have helped with this book. Serina Beauparlant, my former editor at Mayfield Publishing, approached this project with enthusiasm and support throughout its birth and development and saw the book through two editions. My editors at McGraw-Hill—Gina Boedeker and Kate Scheinman—energetically embraced the current edition and moved the project to completion. Becky Thompson (Simmons College) convinced me that I should do the book in the first place and provided support, feedback, and creative suggestions for the first four editions. Our ongoing discussions about racism and teaching over the years have contributed to my thinking in many ways.

Reviewers were also very helpful as I grappled with major changes in this edition: Chris Duncan, DePaul University; Geraldine M. Hendrix, Southern Illinois University, Carbondale; Diane Kayongo-Male, South Dakota State University; Michele Lee Kozimor-King, Elizabethtown College; and Nivedita Vaidya, California State University, Los Angeles.

Other friends, family, colleagues, and students provided direct or indirect support for this edition, such as suggestions for readings or helpful conversations. They include Peggy Barett, Larry Blum, Chris Bobel, Jorge Capetillo-Ponce, Connie Chan, Robert Disch, Linda Dittmar, Cynthia Enloe, Susan Gore, Laura Hansen, Jean Hardisty, Katie Hartley, Muna Kangsen, Kathleen Kelley, Esther Kingston-Mann, Winston Langley, Elaine Morse, Mickaella Perina, Emmett Schaefer, Tim Sieber, Susan Tomlinson, Mariamne Whatley, Nancy Worcester, Raul Ybarra, and Vivian Zamel. Janet DiPaolo, UMass Boston librarian par excellence, deserves my highest praise and deepest thanks for her many last-minute rescue operations. Pat Aron provided essential technical assistance, proofreading help, and emotional support. The production staff at McGraw-Hill—Karol Jurado, Project Manager—kept the project moving smoothly and on schedule. My compañera and intellectual colleague Rita Arditti talked with me extensively about all five editions of the book as they evolved, helped me to clarify my thinking, and suggested new readings for me to consider. She read most of what I have added to this edition and assessed many other pieces as well. Finally, thanks go to my best teachers—the terrific students at the University of Massachusetts Boston, who frequently challenge and always engage me. I especially thank the 50 students whom I accompanied on a bus trip to New Orleans in January 2008 to gut houses damaged by hurricane Katrina.

Supplements

Visit our book-specific Web site at www.mhhe.com/disch5 for robust student and instructor resources. Student study tools include on-line multiple-choice and true-false quizzes. The password-protected instructor portion of the Web site includes the instructor's manual and test bank. For each reading and part introduction, there are multiple-choice, true-false, and short answer/essay questions. There are also questions for classroom discussion, journal reading, and take-home exams.

NOTES

1. This was a course at the University of Massachusetts Boston, a public urban university with about 12,000 students, all of whom commute.
2. The class had read an excerpt from C. Wright Mills, *The Sociological Imagination* (New York: Oxford University Press, 1959), in which Mills discusses personal troubles and public issues.
3. This teaching method is described in Estelle Disch, "Encouraging Participation in the Classroom," in Sara Davis et al., eds., *Coming Into Her Own: Educational Success for Girls and Women* (Jossey-Bass, 1999); Becky Thompson and Estelle Disch, "Feminist, Anti-Racist, Anti-Oppression Teaching: Two White Women's Experience," *Radical Teacher* 41 (Spring 1992), pp. 4–10.
4. In a study of survivors of sexual professional abuse, for which I am the principal investigator, 88 percent of the women and 94 percent of the men were abused by men.
5. Photo essay by E. Jan Mundy, "Wounded Boys, Courageous Men," displayed at the Linkup Conference, Chicago, September 1–4, 1995.
6. I have documented this work in an essay, "The Politics of Curricular Change: Establishing a Diversity Requirement at the University of Massachusetts at Boston," in Becky W. Thompson and Sangeeta Tyagi, eds., *Beyond a Dream Deferred: Multicultural Education and the Politics of Excellence* (Minneapolis: University of Minnesota Press, 1993), pp. 195–213.

General Introduction

The system of patriarchy . . . seems to have nearly run its course—it no longer serves the needs of men or women and in its inextricable linkage to militarism, hierarchy, and racism it threatens the very existence of life on earth.

GERDA LERNER[1]

As a Black lesbian feminist comfortable with the many different ingredients of my identity, and a woman committed to racial and sexual freedom from oppression, I find I am constantly being encouraged to pluck out some one aspect of myself and present this as a meaningful whole, eclipsing or denying the other parts of self. But this is a destructive and fragmenting way to live.

AUDRE LORDE[2]

No one is simply a man or a woman. Each of us embodies intersecting statuses and identities, empowered and disempowered, including physical and demographic traits, chosen and unchosen. In any discussion of gender, serious students of the social order need to be prepared to ask, Which men? Which women? If students of gender studies choose to be conscious of the complexity of human life, much of the literature on human nature and gender needs to be read carefully and any generalizations made with extreme caution. Sometimes findings about men are generalized to describe people in general. Sometimes data from racially mixed populations are combined and analyzed as a whole, leaving out the details and differences between groups. And sometimes when there are only small numbers of, say, women or people of color in a study, those respondents are excluded from analysis for lack of a large enough group. In any of these cases, the voices of the few are obscured by those of the many. Unless we focus on the few alongside the many, we not only lose the voices of the few, but we also lose any meaningful understanding of the relationship between the few and the many, particularly in terms of power, privilege, disempowerment, and empowerment. The readings in this book invite you to hear the perspectives of many women and men whose voices have been ignored, marginalized, or silenced in the past.

This collection of readings focuses on power, addressing the conditions under which the gender system intersects with other factors to create various kinds of power and powerlessness. The readings also address how people empower themselves, both personally and collectively. This book is grounded in several important intellectual perspectives that support the acquisition of inclusive knowledge as a prerequisite to empowerment. These perspectives are based on the assumption that we need to understand the complexity of human experience in order to develop effective strategies for humane, inclusive social change.

Gender in Historical Perspective—Using a Sociological Imagination

An important sociological knowledge seeker, C. Wright Mills, argued in 1959 that it is possible to understand human lives only if we can understand the connections between those lives and the social and historical contexts in which they exist. He further argued that people need to understand the sources of their problems in order to fully understand why their lives are difficult. Thus, he encouraged people to distinguish between problems that affect only themselves and perhaps a few others from those problems that large numbers of people experience and that have their cause in social structures beyond particular individuals or families. He referred to the former as "personal troubles" and to the latter as "public issues." Mills urged people to develop a "sociological imagination" so that they could place themselves in social context and identify how public issues affect them at the personal level, arguing that people need to know the source of their difficulties in order to make sense of their lives.[3] Understanding the source of one's difficulties opens the possibility of shifting the blame off of oneself and onto the social order, when appropriate. It also opens the possibility of working with others to change aspects of the social order that create difficulties for many individuals. Our mental health and our effective resistance to social structures that we find oppressive depend upon our possession of a sociological imagination.

The second wave of the feminist movement in the United States, which started in the mid-1960s, incorporated a sociological imagination when it adopted the phrase "the personal is political." Arguing that larger political realities were felt at the personal level, women were encouraged to look beyond themselves for the sources of their problems in order to feel less alone and less to blame for the difficulties they faced. Analysis of the real sources of problems allowed women both to understand their personal situations better and to devise individual and collective means of resistance. In many situations, women have used the link between the political and the personal to help each other understand sexism as it is played out in the political structure, the community, the workplace, schools, families, and bedrooms. In response to this awareness, women have established a national network of services for women, such as shelters for battered women, rape crisis centers, and health centers, and have worked for legal changes to help end discrimination on the basis of sex or gender.[4]

A sociological imagination is essential for helping us to understand both ongoing realities—such as gender discrimination—and events such as the attacks on the World Trade Center and the Pentagon on September 11, 2001, and the subsequent U.S.-initiated wars in Afghanistan and Iraq. Without an understanding of the historical context, the September 11 attacks might be comprehensible only in terms of individual psychopathology. A look at other factors, however, offers both plausible explanations and suggestions for how future attacks might be rendered less likely. The history of U.S. policy toward Saudi Arabia, the Gulf War, the Israeli-Palestinian conflict, religious fundamentalism, and recent history in Afghanistan all help to set the stage for making sense of the attacks and their gendered nature. People caught up in these events or their aftermaths are finding their personal lives deeply affected. Apart from the horrendous grief and turmoil in families who lost loved ones in the September 11 attacks and the wars that followed, the personal implications are wide ranging. Consider, for example, the effects of the U.S. counterattack on the people of Afghanistan, most of whom had nothing to do with the conflict but were caught in the cross fire, often forced to flee for their lives. Consider women in Afghanistan, free of Taliban rule but now living under a government controlled by a regime that has its own record of violence. Consider U.S. soldiers mobilized for war, pulled out of school or careers and away from their loved ones in response to government mandates, possibly coming home disabled or dead. Consider the partners of the men and women called to combat, worrying about their loved ones and coping at home without the support of their partners. Consider Arab American men, targeted now for racial profiling because men from Arab countries perpetrated the attacks on September 11. Consider innocent dark-skinned men from any cultural group, ordered off of planes because they "look Arabic." Consider men and women detained under the new antiterrorism legislation without the ordinary due process of law that U.S. citizens and residents expect. Consider a U.S. citizen who criticizes the U.S. government's response to September 11 and finds his or her job threatened because of the criticism. Consider the rise in Christian white supremacist hate group activity following September 11. Or consider the costs to social programs when a huge proportion for the federal budget is spent on war.

A sociological imagination helps us see that the personal problems that evolve from the events of September 11 are by no means personal troubles in Mills's use of that term. They are public issues, shared by many others, reflective of realities that go way beyond individual motivation or control, and that stretch, in fact, into the highly complex realms of international trade, foreign policy, the quest for oil, and religious values; these problems cannot be addressed by individuals alone. Some of the readings in this book will attempt to put September 11 and the current wars in Iraq and Afghanistan in perspective. A major goal of this book generally is to help readers explore many of the social realities and events that surround and explain individual experiences.

The material in this book was written primarily in the United States in the late twentieth and early twenty-first centuries, when many gender-related trends and events were occurring. This period of history has seen growing scholarship and activism among women, especially women of color. This period of history also saw conflict among white women, including writings and activism by those who object to feminism and by those who critique what mainstream feminism has stood for.[5] Third wave feminism emerged in the 1990s and continues.[6] This time also saw an increase in research and writing by profeminist men, especially those working for changes in men's usual roles, often working for a cessation of violence against women.[7] During this period, other groups of men also became increasingly public about their various disenchantments with either their own roles or those of women. A men's rights movement emerged to protest the kinds of power its members perceived women to have. A Christian men's movement emerged calling for men to take back the power they had lost as women began to develop more public power. A "mythopoetic" men's movement began to hold men-only retreats at which primarily white, middle-class men attempted to contact their "essential masculinity." The Million Man March in 1995 provided an empowering experience for many Black men, highlighted some of the tensions and conflicts over men's roles and responsibilities in the Black community, and elicited a range of responses from Black women and men, which continue today.[8]

Increased attention to the situations of boys emerged in the 1990s, matching to some extent the attention to girls that began in the 1980s. Some authors attended to boys in general, looking at everyday violence and school failure, calling for more careful attention to boys' emotional and educational needs.[9] Others addressed the needs of boys in urban contexts, considering the impact of poverty and racism.[10] Others decried the lack of attention to boys in the context of criticizing the feminist-driven attention to girls.[11] A balanced look at these concerns calls for attention to the needs of both girls and boys, in all contexts, including those of lesbian, gay, bisexual, or transgender (LGBT) youth.

A series of school shootings, such as the one at Columbine High School in Littleton, Colorado, brought particular attention to the potential for violence of seemingly normal white, middle-class boys.[12] Sociologist Michael Kimmel, critical of the media discussion of "youth violence," emphasized that what had occurred was male, rather than youth, violence, encouraging a discussion of masculinity: "In a way, Eric Harris and Dylan Klebold weren't deviants, but over-conformists to norms of masculinity that prescribe violence as a solution. Like real men, they didn't just get mad, they got even."[13] Standard masculinity, many authors argue, can be detrimental. Embedded in the attention to boys is a concern by some authors that expected standards of behavior do not fit boys and men and that we might, in fact, be attempting to impose on males the standards of expression of feeling, open communication, and "good behavior" that are more likely to occur in girls and women.[14] The lesson from this is that boys as well as girls need serious attention, within the various contexts in which they attempt to live satisfying lives.

The past decade or so also brought increased attention to men, particularly men who felt left out of major trends in the wider society. Some men felt left out of the economic boom in the nineties; others felt alienated by the increase in attention to women; some white men felt troubled by the increasing diversification of U.S. society. Some books focused specifically on men of color, including gay and bisexual Black men, while others simply explored more deeply who various men are and what they want (often with race unnamed).[15]

Another recent trend is growing public awareness of transgender issues. Media and scholarly attention to this issue has grown substantially in the 12 years since I assembled the first edition of this book. The literature includes writings by scholars documenting third and fourth genders in Native American and other cultures[16] as well as writings by people who are stretching gender boundaries and challenging the two-gender system as it is currently constructed in mainstream U.S. culture. Attention to transgender rights (and breaches thereto) is an essential aspect of this work.[17] Leslie Feinberg, a central spokesperson for what she calls "Trans liberation," describes the participants in this movement:

> We are masculine females and feminine males, cross-dressers, transsexual men and women, intersexuals born on the anatomical sweep between female and male, gender blenders, many other sex and gender-variant people, and our significant others. All told, we expand understanding of how many ways there are to be a human being.[18]

The *Utne Reader* brought attention to this issue with a cover in 1998: "It's 2 AM. Do you know what sex you are? Does anybody?" Even *Cosmopolitan* ran a story in November 1998 entitled "The man I married was really a woman."[19] The editors of *Utne Reader* summed up the issue this way:

> Queer theorists call gender a social construct, saying that when we engage in traditional behaviors and sexual practices, we are nothing but actors playing ancient, empty roles. Others suggest that gender is performance, a collection of masks we can take on and off at will. So are we witnessing the birth of thrilling new freedoms, or the disintegration of values and behaviors that bind us together? Will we encounter new opportunities for self-realization, or hopeless confusion? Whatever the answers, agreeing that our destinies aren't preordained will launch a search that will profoundly affect society, and will eventually engage us all. [p. 45]

In an unusual twist, a female same-gendered couple in Texas was allowed to marry because one of them was transgendered and was genetically male.[20] How transgender issues will intersect with other issues of oppression is yet to be defined, although Leslie Feinberg is deeply committed to seeing Trans liberation in the context of other social justice struggles and is herself actively engaged in social justice struggles for all oppressed people.

The writings in this book have also emerged in a virulent political era in which attacks on feminists, people of color, poor people, Jewish people, and gay men, lesbians, and transgendered people have been and continue to be common. The hate murders of James Earl Byrd, Jr., a Black man in Texas, and Matthew Shepard, a gay man in Wyoming, are recent examples.[21] Even more recently, Sakia Gunn, a 15-year-old lesbian in Newark, New Jersey, was stabbed to death in May 2003 after telling her assailant that she was a lesbian. In October 2002, Gwen Araujo, a transgendered 17-year-old, was beaten and strangled to death by a group of men. Fred Martinez, a two-spirit Native American teen, was murdered in 2001 in Colorado. In 2002, two black transgendered girls, Ukea Davis and Stephanie Thomas, were shot in Washington, DC. And in 2003, Nikki Nicholas, a black transgendered teen, was beaten and shot near Detroit. Although the National Coalition of Anti-Violence Programs reports a 3 percent decrease in incidents against LGBT individuals in 2006 (compared to 2005), incidents against transgendered individuals of African or Native American descent rose 7 percent and 133 percent, respectively.[22] According to FBI statistics for 2005, more than half of hate crimes are motivated by racial bias (54.7 percent), 17.1 percent were triggered by religious bias, and 14.2 percent were triggered by sexual orientation bias.[23] Reports of bias against Muslims are up since September 11, 2001, in a context laden with fear and hostility.[24] Issues of affirmative action remain on the table as universities struggle with how to legally address the need for a diverse student body. Assaults on people with disabilities, including sexual assaults on more than 75 percent of mentally disabled women according to some studies, continue seemingly unchecked.[25] Also on the disability front, the Supreme Court struck a serious blow to the 1990 Americans with Disabilities Act in February 2001 by supporting a state's right to not provide reasonable accommodations in a case in Alabama in which a man with asthma was not assured a smoke-free environment and a woman with breast cancer was demoted.[26] A recent Supreme Court decision makes it very difficult to sue in cases of wage and salary discrimination. In a case in which a woman realized she was earning much less than her male counterparts, the court ruled that she should have caught the salary discrepancy within 180 days of its first occurrence.[27]

This period of history has also been characterized by an increase in poverty in the United States. Changes in welfare policy in 1996 created major challenges for poor women.[28] Wealth is increasingly concentrating in the hands of a small number of individuals[29] while many families struggle to pay their essential bills, often causing adults to work more than one job.

Another recent trend that sets the stage for an analysis of gender is increased awareness of globalization. Major shifts in the world's economy that favor industrialized nations over developing ones have provoked international protests against the World Trade Organization, the World Bank, the

G-8 nations (the world's most economically powerful countries), and the International Monetary Fund. Growing awareness of structural adjustment policies that increasingly impoverish developing nations has provoked these protests, such as those in Seattle, Montreal, Genoa, and most recently in Germany, as people (many of them young) attempt to right the wrongs they see occurring. As U.S. corporations establish factories overseas to take advantage of inexpensive labor, women have begun to organize for better wages and working conditions (see Enloe, Part VIII). Mexican border factories (maquiladoras) where the products of U.S. corporations are assembled or built, primarily by women, have provoked outrage due to poor working conditions and sweatshop wages. And sweatshop conditions within the United States persist, in part because workers are afraid that corporations will move the factories to other countries if they fight too hard for better wages or working conditions.[30] Poverty around the globe, especially in Mexico and Central America, leads people to seek more economically secure lives in the United States. The current debate about immigration is immersed in conflict, with corporations implicitly supporting the presence of a cheap labor force; with families torn apart by immigration hoping to be safely and legally united; and with some people committed to punishing those who have entered the U.S. illegally (see Marchevsky and Theoharis in Parts I and VIII).

Increased attention to human rights is another trend that characterizes the current era. A worldwide movement is attempting to bring a human rights perspective into people's everyday consciousness. Rights to such essential things as food, shelter, education, health care, and physical safety are frequently ignored in many places in both the United States and the rest of the world. The recruitment of children—primarily boys but girls as well— into militias is a major breach of children's rights. The use of child labor and the selling of children into slavery are gaining worldwide attention.[31] The sexual trafficking of women and girls is finally getting some of the attention that this brutal reality deserves, following the signature and ratification of the Protocol to Prevent, Suppress and Punish Trafficking in Persons, Especially Women and Children (which the United States signed in 2000 and ratified in 2005).[32] An effort to demonstrate the link between women's rights and human rights is happening in many countries. The United Nations' Convention on the Elimination of All Forms of Discrimination Against Women (CEDAW), accepted by 179 countries, serves as a basis for examining women's rights as human rights. Efforts to establish CEDAW at the local level in the United States are under way since the United States has not signed CEDAW (see Arditti, Part XI). An early definition of feminism in the contemporary women's movement connects to this issue: Feminism is the radical notion that women are human. There remains a lot of work to do to convince both women and men of this fact.

In the context of human rights abuses, international ethnic conflicts and genocides—such as those in Bosnia-Herzegovina, Rwanda, and currently in Darfur, Sudan—are attracting the attention of many concerned people around the world. The use of rape and other sexual torture of women as a weapon of war has been widely documented, as have the effects on women and girls following rape or forced impregnation by enemy combatants, provoking outrage in many circles. Even when the conflict ends, the fallout from the abuse is difficult to heal, especially in situations where raped women and girls are defined as unmarriageable and not accepted back into their families or communities.[33]

Since George W. Bush took office in 2001, several major issues have emerged against the backdrop of what I have just described. These include the war against terrorism in Afghanistan, Iraq, and the United States; the eroding of women's reproductive rights; the backlash against same-sex marriage; and the merging of church and state. All of these have deep implications for the gendered aspects of people's lives.

The aftermath of September 11, 2001, has drawn thousands of U.S. citizens, primarily men who are disproportionately poor and working class, into combat or preparation for combat. At home, the Patriot Act and its accompanying subversion of civil liberties has primarily affected dark-skinned men and women who wear head scarves. Racial profiling, a long-standing problem in law enforcement that has been subject to periodic reviews, has attracted much recent attention.[34] A spokesperson for Amnesty International concluded that "Racial profiling is to the 21st century what Jim Crow laws were to the last, turning entire groups of people into second-class citizens and denying them the rights to which we are all due."[35] Accompanying the war in Iraq and other terrorism battles are the costs of these efforts—both direct costs in terms of dollars and indirect costs in terms of potential negative effects, often called "blowback." The direct costs have increased the federal deficit to record levels, leaving less money available for public services such as education, affordable housing, and health care. The attacks on September 11 were one example of blowback—retaliation for the United States policy in the Middle East. Time will tell what else is in store for the United States as we forge ahead with scant international support in the seemingly interminable war in Iraq and against terrorism more generally.

Related to any discussion of the war on terrorism is our understanding of what security means. National security—the attempt to protect the United States from future attacks—needs to be distinguished from human security—protection of the human individual from breaches of their human rights. Human rights activist Charlotte Bunch argues, "It is imperative to maintain focus on human rights as a crucial component of human security." She emphasizes that the right to bodily integrity, reproductive rights, and freedom from violence are essential components of security for women.[36]

Abortion rights have been under attack since President Bush took office. A bill banning so-called partial birth abortion that was passed by Congress and signed by President Bush in 2003 was deemed constitutional in April 2007.[37] President Bush also imposed the "Global Gag Rule" in January 2001, blocking funds to the United Nations Population Fund because the money might possibly go to clinics that make referrals for abortions.[38] An effect of his decision has been a worldwide cutback of health services to women and children. In response to policies like these, in April 2004 more than a million people, representing a broad coalition of groups, gathered in Washington, DC, in support of reproductive rights in what was most likely the largest women's rights demonstration in history.

There is substantial backlash to efforts to institute gay marriage in the United States, as evidenced by voters' rejection of same-sex marriage by large margins on referendums in both the 2004 and the 2006 elections. In fact, the high turnout of those opposed to gay marriage may have helped President Bush win the election.[39] Resistance to same-sex marriage is part of the larger issue of the relationship between church and state. The idea of civil rights for same-sex couples conflicts with the religious "sanctity" of marriage in many peoples' minds, leading some advocates of same-sex rights to advocate for the establishment of civil unions for *all* couples while eliminating civil marriage and leaving marriage to religious institutions. That option would provide legal equality for all committed couples without requiring marriage of anyone, although the likelihood of doing this is not high, given the general blurring of the boundaries between church and state under President Bush.

Although a majority of people in the United States object to allowing same-sex couples to marry, a majority supports some sort of legal recognition such as civil unions.[40] Same-sex couples have gained some sort of relationship recognition in Washington, DC, and 10 U.S. states: marriage in Massachusetts; civil unions or domestic partnerships in Vermont, Connecticut, California, New Jersey, New Hampshire, Oregon, and Washington, DC; and beneficiary systems in Hawaii, Maine, and Washington. Marriage has been legalized in several countries (Canada, Belgium, The Netherlands, South Africa, and Spain), and legal arrangements that provide some or all of marriage's benefits are available in many others. Lesbian and gay parents in the United States who want to coadopt each other's children may do so in many states. The American Academy of Pediatrics has recommended legalizing same-sex adoption, arguing that children "deserve the security of two legally recognized parents."[41] Various court rulings have acknowledged the legitimacy of same-sex couples related to child support, visitation, and other issues.[42]

The struggle for lesbian, gay, bisexual, and transgender rights exists in a complex social and political climate. Even President George W. Bush and former Secretary of State Colin Powell have been accused of being too pro-gay because of allowing gay men to serve the current administration in various ways.[43] Following the Supreme Court's support in June 2000 of the Boy Scouts' policy of barring gays as scout leaders and members, objection to the policy began to grow not only in the ranks of scout members and leaders (with membership reportedly down 4.5 percent in 2001) but also in the schools and other institutions in which scouts tend to recruit new members, making recruitment more difficult. A Boston-area Boy Scout council voted to adopt a "don't ask, don't tell" policy so that gay leaders and members could remain in the Scouts without technically breaching the national ban on gays.[44] The National Education Association recently adopted a plan to make schools more respectful, and hopefully safer, for lesbian, gay, bisexual, and transgendered students and school employees.[45] And in Japan, a youth center was found guilty of discrimination when it banned a gay youth group from using the center. The discrimination occurred in 1990, and the Tokyo High Court handed down its decision seven and a half years later.[46]

Resistance to same-sex marriage is part of the larger issue of the relationship between church and state. Other church-state issues that are currently being debated are abortion rights mentioned earlier and federally funded faith-based initiatives. The latter become especially controversial when, based on religious principles, institutions receiving federal funds are allowed to discriminate in hiring, violating various antidiscrimination laws. The debate about the separation of church and state takes place in a wider context as well, as we watch France grapple with the fallout of its policy to not allow children to wear head coverings or other ostensible religious symbols in public schools.[47] Although Muslim women interviewed in France have wide-ranging attitudes about head scarves, the public association of head scarves with fundamentalists has overshadowed their perspectives.[48]

These changes are occurring in a context in which it appears to some observers that many people in the United States are increasingly less likely to engage with each other in mutually supportive ways, leading to what sociologist Robert Putnam calls a decline in "social capital," which in turn seems to lead to less safety, declining health, and less civic engagement.[49] Writers and activists, however, continue to promote and to engage in progressive social change. A large and growing antiwar movement objects to the wars in Iraq and Afghanistan. Young feminists have established magazines to address girls' and young women's needs. *Teen Voices, New Moon* (for girls 8 to 14), *Bitch, Bust,* and *Fabula* join an array of books by third wave feminists.[50] Membership in the Third Wave Foundation, an organization that supports young women and transgendered people, stood at about 5,000 members in 2004.[51] How all this activism will evolve is unpredictable, but I am heartened by this clarity of thought and continuing struggle for justice in an era of war, racial profiling, hate crimes, backlash, and economic conservatism.

People committed to democracy and pluralism will especially need the knowledge that inclusive scholarship provides, both now and in the future, as people formerly silenced make themselves heard and suffer the anger and violence of those who would prefer them to be invisible or at least silent. For example, as the U.S. population became more multicultural and less white, white supremacist and militia activity increased. As gay, lesbian, bisexual, and transgendered people have increasingly refused to be labeled and closeted, more resistance to freedom of sexual and affectional expression has been mounted. Continued resistance to the same-sex marriage movement in spite of small gains provides a powerful example. And as wealth in the United States has been moving increasingly into the hands of a small proportion of very rich people, poor women and children, especially those on public assistance or removed from public assistance because of time limits imposed by the new Temporary Aid to Needy Families (TANF) program, continue to suffer. Even though the cost of the now-defunct Aid to Families with Dependent Children (AFDC) constituted less than 1 percent of the federal budget, welfare under the Clinton presidency was treated as if it were a major cause of the national deficit, and few voices called for a more family-friendly policy.[52]

Dissident Voices

Hearing from a wide range of men and women across many disciplines is crucial to an effective understanding of what is going on about gender. Sociology; women's studies; men's studies; African American studies; Asian American studies; Latin American and Latino studies; Native American studies; gay, lesbian, bisexual, transgender, and queer studies; disability studies; studies of aging; and American studies have welcomed the voices and experiences of previously silenced people into scholarly discourse. The expansion of work by people in these fields has provided a rich, exciting base of new information that continues to grow. This book includes research, essays, and autobiographical material from this literature.

By including men's studies in this book, I do not mean to imply that the situations of men are equivalent to those of women. Although women are almost all oppressed in one way or another by some men and by patriarchal structures, the reverse is not true. Thus, while men might suffer from detrimental aspects of male socialization such as participation in war, premature death, increased exposure to violence, and higher rates of suicide, it is generally not women who control the outcome of men's lives. Male-dominated institutions and powerful individual men control both women and less-empowered men. And powerful men reap great benefits from our male-dominant structure even if they do tend to die younger than women and suffer other difficulties related to being male.

Many of the writers in men's studies are dissatisfied with male-dominated society, having personally experienced the painful aspects of male socialization. This perspective puts these writers in a good position to analyze masculinities from within. Their voices are dissident within the ranks of powerful men, and many would not be particularly welcome in boardrooms, locker rooms, or faculty meetings. They are outsiders as they critique the bastions of hegemonic masculinity—the dominant, white, heterosexual, patriarchal, privileged masculinity that still controls many aspects of people's lives.

Hegemonic masculinity, which promotes the tough, take-charge, don't-feel image of men, frequently dominates the socialization process in spite of increasing efforts to develop other masculinities and femininities.[53] The writers referred to earlier who are concerned with the fate of boys are particularly attuned to the damage that hegemonic masculinity can do.

An examination of masculinity in male-dominated society is a crucial aspect of both women's studies and men's studies, especially if we try to understand how to work toward a social order in which there is less violence. A look at the literature on men violently abused as children, for example, suggests that about a third of them grow up to violently abuse others.[54] An understanding of adult male abusers leads us to examine how children are socialized and helps us to understand the process by which many baby boys grow into violent or controlling men. Another perspective suggests that circumstances at any point in life can contribute to violent responses, lending support to the sociological perspective that propensity to violence is socialized rather than inherent (for example, citizens become soldiers when a country is involved in war, as is currently the case in the United States). Many of the men included in this book critique the gender system and are committed to working to end a social system that teaches men to be violent and that leaves boys and men frequently victimized and revictimized by other violent men.

There are some potential conflicts between women's studies and men's studies. One basic question concerns the extent to which men can effectively criticize a system in which they have experienced various amounts of privilege. Another question is the issue of crossover—can men effectively study women or women effectively study men?[55] The study of women by men raises the larger question of whether it is possible for someone from a more-empowered group to study, effectively understand, and analyze the experiences of people from a less-empowered group. Certainly there is a long history of "scholarship" by men distorting or ignoring the lives of women and by white people distorting or ignoring the lives of people of color. A third area of conflict is the use of the term "feminist" when applied to men. Both sides of this question have passionate proponents, including those who claim that the term "feminist man" is an inherent contradiction and others who claim that it isn't.[56] Finally, limited resources in academia are an issue. The development of gender studies and men's studies poses a potential threat to women's studies on some campuses, just as multicultural studies can pose a threat to Black or Africana studies in some situations. These threats include both possible cutbacks in resources and the potential for these programs to be placed in a larger structure controlled by someone from another discipline. Philosopher and men's studies professor Harry Brod concludes that the men's studies field is a necessary addition to academe but that resources for the development of this relatively new field should not come from women's studies.[57]

Intersecting Identities

Another recent effort at truth seeking is the attention now paid to the complex combination of identities each individual holds.[58] The readings included here address the concerns of Patricia Hill Collins, Audre Lorde, Gloria Anzaldúa, James Baldwin, W. E. B. Du Bois, Suzanne Pharr, and others who ask us to acknowledge such complexities. Sociologist W. E. B. Du Bois, writing in 1903, called for awareness of what he named the "double-consciousness" of African Americans—the awareness that they can't simply be Americans, working toward whatever goals they might have; rather, they are simultaneously forced to deal with racism, seeing themselves through the eyes of hateful others. Thus, Du Bois says, African American men and women can never experience themselves as simply men or women because they are constantly hated or pitied.[59]

The importance of acknowledging multiple aspects of identity is also powerfully stated by Patricia Hill Collins, who addresses the complex combination of oppression and privilege held by each individual. She argues that individuals can simultaneously be members of both privileged and oppressed groups, citing the example of white women who are "penalized by their gender but privileged by their race."[60] Collins also argues that there is a matrix of domination, compelling us to look at the intersecting aspects of oppression in individuals and groups. She names race, class, and gender as the three axes of oppression that typically characterize Black women's experiences, and she lists other axes of oppression as well that may or may not affect particular individuals, such as sexual orientation, religion, and age. Collins further argues that domination occurs at several levels, including personal biography, group-community interaction, and social institutions.[61] The readings in this volume have been chosen to reflect experience in and analysis of oppression, privilege, or both at all three levels, as well as reflecting people's empowerment struggles at these various levels.

Naming and Owning Privilege

This book is also grounded in the tradition of scholars and activists who struggle to bring privilege into focus.[62] In her well-known essay on white privilege, women's studies scholar Peggy McIntosh names her professional white privilege and heterosexual privilege and discusses how difficult it was to hold onto her awareness of her privileges as she worked on the essay; ideas about how she was privileged kept slipping away unless she wrote them down.[63] Sociologist Michael S. Kimmel tells about his difficulty in naming and owning his race and gender. Before attending a seminar on feminist theory in which race and gender were discussed, when he looked in the mirror, Kimmel saw "a human being . . . universally generalizable . . . the generic person." As a middle-class, white man, he had difficulty identifying how gender and race had affected his experience.[64] Antiviolence and antiracist activist Paul Kivel, in a recent guide for white people who want to work for racial justice, provides a "white benefits checklist" that addresses the intersections of class and race. He also provides a checklist of the "costs of racism for white people."[65]

In addition to the matrix of domination argued for by Patricia Hill Collins, we might also conceive of a matrix of privilege. Assuming that most people and groups possess some degree of privilege, however limited, we can frequently examine oppression and privilege together. We can identify where privilege lies and analyze how it smoothes the way for those who possess it and simultaneously makes life more difficult for those who don't. The issue here, however, is not simply to identify privilege. Rather, as the late writer Audre Lorde said, we should make it available for wider use. Thus, a white person who opposes racism might use his or her contacts with groups of white people as opportunities to educate them about racism. A man who opposes sexism might use his contacts with other men to educate them about sexism.

Privilege is a difficult concept for many of those who have it because it is frequently unnamed in wider U.S. society. In a social order whose mainstream values include individual achievement and competition, many people with privilege are supported to assume that they deserve the "luck" or "normalcy" they experience, whereas those who lack privilege are encouraged to blame themselves.[66] Thus, an able-bodied person might experience the ability to walk up a flight of stairs as simply a normal thing to do, rather than seeing the expectation that all people walk as part of a system that treats stair climbing as normal and thus fails to build ramps for those on wheels. A white person might assume that white is "normal," might feel lucky to be white, and might fail to see that the alleged superiority of whiteness is part of a racist system that keeps people of color from moving freely in the social order. A person born wealthy is likely to be taught that he or she deserves the wealth rather than to be taught how wealth is related to poverty in U.S. society. Although people with less privilege are usually astute analysts of how privilege works, those who enjoy it are frequently less conscious of its impact.[67] Thus, a challenge for progressive people with privilege, especially for those with substantial privilege, is to become aware of the nuances of privilege and to learn how to use it in ways that raise consciousness about oppression and promote fairness.

Another possibility for those with privilege is to identify some of the liabilities that accompany privilege and to use that awareness to work toward changing the system. For example, many white professional men lead highly stressful, dissatisfying lives with restricted access to their feelings and a limited capacity for intimacy. Writer Mark Gerzon, a white professional man, convincingly criticizes the roles and role models available to men like himself and calls for new roles to replace them. After describing what he believes are archetypal roles for men, he asks men to reject these roles in exchange for more democratic and humane ones. Instead of frontiersmen, he wants men to be healers—of both people and the earth; instead of breadwinners, men should be companions; instead of soldiers, mediators; instead of experts, colleagues; and instead of lords, nurturers. Gerzon's work emerged from his dissatisfaction with being male in spite of his race and class privilege.[68]

A denial of privilege can greatly limit our understanding of how our worlds work and how losing that privilege might affect us. White people who are not conscious of their white privilege, or who simply accept the system around them without question, spend their lives in what I think of as powerful denial—knowing at some unconscious level that they do not deserve and did not earn the skin-color privilege they enjoy, yet pretending at some level that they deserve it. Many temporarily able-bodied people are thrown into deep shock when they become disabled because they have structured their lives in ways that avoided people with disabilities and that allowed them to pretend that disability would never affect them. They therefore have no framework in which to combine personhood and disability and have suddenly become something that they have previously despised. I have heard many of my students, especially male students, say that they'd rather be dead than physically disabled.

The Reconstruction of Knowledge

Based on the kinds of truth telling identified thus far—the importance of a sociological imagination and the need to hear marginalized voices, acknowledge intersecting identities, and name privilege—numerous scholars have called for the reconstruction of knowledge.[69] Philosopher Elizabeth Minnich, for example, argues convincingly that four basic errors in knowledge need to be corrected as we move toward more inclusive knowing.[70] The first error is overgeneralization based on information gathered from small sectors of the population throughout history—primarily empowered male writers and the people they chose to acknowledge in their writing. Philosopher Harry Brod argues assertively that the study of men as men, in all the nuances of their experiences with masculinity, is crucial to the study of human beings. He asserts that to generalize from male experience to human experience not only distorts what human experience is but also distorts what is specifically male.[71] Historian Gerda Lerner calls for a restructuring of thought and for an analysis that acknowledges that half the people in the world are women. She argues that all generalizations about human beings need to acknowledge this fact.[72] The selections in this book should help readers challenge inaccurate generalizations about men and women and develop new, more limited generalizations.

A second error in knowledge cited by Elizabeth Minnich is circular reasoning, which justifies traditional knowledge based on the standards embedded in that knowledge. In sociology, for example, for many years certain topics were not studied at all, particularly women's experiences. Students, especially women students, who couldn't relate to the material presented were seen as inadequate. Ultimately, women sociologists began studying gender, and the field of sociology was forced to become more inclusive. Joyce Ladner, for example, in *Tomorrow's Tomorrow,* not only studied Black adolescent girls, but also refused to accept the standard sociological definition of their lives as "deviant." Rather, she identified some of the ways in which her respondents found empowerment in an economically limited, racist context.[73] Ladner studied and redefined a population that usually had no direct voice in the sociological literature.

The third knowledge error that Minnich identifies is our attachment to what she calls mystified concepts—concepts that are frequently used but seldom carefully defined and often not particularly applicable to real people. Minnich argues that if we can let go of such concepts, new questions and new avenues for research can emerge. Masculinity and femininity are two such concepts. As we examine the literature in women's studies and men's studies, we find that many men and women do not conform to the dominant Anglo ideals of femininity and masculinity. Many men, for instance, do not fit the strong, tough, take-charge mode; do not enjoy fighting; and would like more freedom to express their feelings. And, in fact, many men do express themselves openly.[74] Martín Espada (Part I), Tommi Avicolli (Part II), Phil Petrie (Part IV), Robert Jensen (Part V), Don Sabo (Part V), and Mark Anthony Neal (Part XI) all provide examples of men breaking ranks with the masculine norms presented in mainstream U.S. culture. Many women also do not fit the stereotypical visions of women presented in mainstream culture, especially in the media. Christy Haubegger (Part III), Martha Coventry (Part III), bell hooks (Part VII), and Melanie Kaye/Kantrowitz (Part IX), among others, provide examples of women who refuse narrow and limited ideas about gender.

Gender itself is a mystified concept for the many people who see it as biologically determined. Recent scholars in gender studies argue convincingly, however, that there is nothing necessary or predictable about gender. In fact, it is becoming more commonly known that human bodies do not come in just two sexes but rather fall along a continuum between female and male, as argued convincingly by biologist Anne Fausto-Sterling in her widely read article entitled "The Five Sexes."[75] Gender, then, rather than being dictated by body types, is socially determined, or "constructed" in various contexts. Sociologist Judith Lorber, in her book *Paradoxes of Gender,* encourages us to "challenge the validity, permanence, and necessity of gender."[76]

Heterosexuality is another mystified concept related to masculinity and femininity that has proven hard to even question. So "normal" is heterosexuality that it is difficult to imagine a world without this expectation.[77] The "sissy" and "lezzie" insults levied at boys and girls who do not conform to heterosexist expectations have a lot to teach us about how charged and compelling the heterosexual mandate is. In spite of fashion trends toward androgynous clothing in the mainstream media at times, individuals who choose to express themselves through androgynous presentations risk ridicule and ostracism in many circles. Some of the ridicule stems from standards of masculinity and femininity; some of it relates more directly to homophobia. But even those most masculine of men—gay professional team athletes such as football players—are terrified of coming out of the closet in the context of the heteronormative world of men's sports and female athletes are pressured to look feminine, lest they be seen as lesbians.[78] Those who love someone of the same sex know at deeply painful levels the costs of breaking with the heterosexual ideal. This ideal is also tightly bound up with the requirement to match gender with sex. For example, an ironic twist of fate occurred in a tragic atrocity; the man who massacred 13 women in Montreal because they were studying engineering spared one of the women present because he perceived her to be a man.[79]

Many new questions emerge if we examine the heterosexual ideal: What would life be like without the insults and labels aimed at boys who are gentle, at girls who are athletes, at women who study engineering, or at men who study nursing? What explains the discomfort of the majority of us who want or need people to fit into gender categories? How does this affect the lives of girls, boys, men, and women who express love for someone of the same sex or live their lives in the gender to which they have not been assigned? How does it affect the social order when bisexual women and men who could choose to relate sexually/affectionally to members of the opposite gender choose to do so with the same gender instead? We cannot begin to address these questions without careful attention to the heterosexual ideal and its accompanying homophobia. I often ask myself how gender roles might look without homophobia. Would there even be gender roles as we know them?

Finally, the fourth knowledge error identified by Minnich is our inability, without new knowledge systems, to discard or correct prior ones. If, however, we can embrace new models of knowledge, we can discard or adapt the old ones. Sociologist Charles Lemert's edited volume, *Social Theory: The Multicultural and Classic Readings,* provides an excellent example of this. By expanding the definition of who is considered a social theorist, Lemert allows new voices to enter sociological discourse and invites readers to consider a wide range of contemporary thinkers not usually included in texts on sociological theory.[80] Ronald Takaki's *A Different Mirror: A History of Multicultural America* provides another very good example of a new knowledge system. Takaki focuses on the lives of ordinary people, including those in various racial and ethnic groups, rather than on the lives of politicians and other famous people. He examines class and gender within the groups he studies.[81] Currently, people looking for alternatives to the mainstream media's discussion of the war in Iraq, breaches of civil liberties, and other political issues can easily find Web and TV sources of news that offer more critical analyses.[82]

Empowerment—Challenging the Patriarchal System

The need for inclusive knowledge has broad implications for empowerment at the interpersonal, community, and policy levels. Without inclusive knowledge, we cannot develop comprehensive empowerment strategies or inclusive social policy. Without seeing the complexity of human experience and the complexity of human oppression, we cannot begin to address the real needs of human beings caught in systematically oppressive social structures. Marilyn Frye makes this point effectively and graphically with the metaphor of the bird cage in her essay "Oppression."[83] She argues that when someone is caged, or oppressed, it is crucial to examine all the bars of the cage to get a full understanding of the inability to escape; close, myopic examination of just one bar will not give a full understanding of why the person is trapped. For example, if we look at gender discrimination on the job, we might wonder why women can't just work harder to overcome the prejudice and discrimination they experience and get on with their lives, even if they make less money, are passed over for promotions, and can support their families only marginally. But if we simultaneously look at other factors, such as sexual harassment within the workplace, racism, fat phobia, heterosexism, ableism, the exit of many formerly higher-paying jobs to countries where labor costs are very low, and violence against women and children, we will come to a clearer understanding of how certain people and groups are caught in a web that they often can't escape; barriers, the bars of the cage, are erected everywhere they turn.

Another metaphor I find useful in making sense of oppression and privilege to frame social change is the idea of being tied down. If a person is tied by one oppression rope, say, sexual harassment, it's likely that she or he has some movement, can see how the knots are tied, and may be able to maneuver to untie the knots, slide under the rope, or move in and out of the rope at different times, depending on the context. If a rope is light, she or he might even break it. But if someone is tied by several ropes, such that she or he cannot move enough to clearly see the sizes and quality of the ropes or the configurations of the knots, there is little possibility for escape. If we imagine that each oppression is a different rope and that the power of oppressions might vary, creating light ropes and heavy ones, a person could be tied down by an almost infinite combination of ropes of different sizes and strengths. And occasionally there will be people tied by no ropes at all at various moments, such as wealthy, white, Anglo-Saxon, Protestant, heterosexual, married, able-bodied, muscular, normal-weight, physically attractive, tall (but not too tall) men in their middle years who are in good health and are seen as mentally stable.

The presence or absence of ropes is a public, not a private, matter. The vast majority of people do not tie themselves down; they are born with limitations due to the structure of the socioeconomic system in which they are situated. German social theorist Max Weber called this system of possibilities "life chances," referring to the array of opportunities, however limited or plentiful, with which a person is born.[84] Although we live in an alleged democracy that offers the potential for upward mobility for anyone, the probability of that happening is severely limited, especially for those born under multiple ropes. Equal access to wealth and other privileges is not structurally guaranteed, even for white, able-bodied men; and many white people in the middle class are currently experiencing downward mobility.[85]

There is no systematic training for untying or breaking the ropes of oppression. Those held by fewer ropes are usually not encouraged to share their privilege by helping others to escape their ropes. Those tied down often learn survival, resilience, resistance, and liberation skills from their families, cultures, and communities but are offered little systematic support from the wider social order. Instead, those tied by many ropes are likely to attend poor schools in which race, class, gender, disability, and sexual orientation interact to produce high rates of failure or marginal functioning.

The oppressive social structure surrounding many people sets in place some probabilities for success or failure. It is important to acknowledge, however, how groups and individuals blocked from success in the privileged, wealthy centers of power find ways to empower themselves, solve problems, and survive against very difficult odds. They do, at times, escape from multiple ropes. For example, some people from highly dysfunctional families have grown up to establish healthy relationships for themselves. The strength and resilience found in poor communities, especially in communities of color, also portray empowerment within otherwise very trying circumstances.[86] Many of the readings in this book report on resilience and personal agency in response to various oppressions.

A look at the web of ropes that surrounds us or the structure of the cages we are in can help us understand how our lives are limited and how to develop institutional, community, and individual strategies for empowerment. An understanding of multiple oppressions helps us see how people can resist oppression at both individual and collective levels and helps us understand why people don't usually escape from multiple ropes. This understanding is especially important in a patriarchal social order in which some variety of gender oppression ties down virtually every woman.

Patriarchy, defined in various ways by various theorists, has as its core male control of women. The pervasiveness of the effects of gender oppression and gender socialization has led sociologist Judith Lorber to call gender a social institution (see Part II of this book). Feminist historian Gerda Lerner names an array of ways in which women are socialized, indoctrinated, and coerced into cooperation with patriarchal systems. For example, women are prevented from fully participating in such empowering activities as education (including learning women's history), politics, and the use of economic resources. Lerner names several dynamics particular to women that make this cooperation with patriarchy especially difficult to resist or subvert. First, she argues, women have internalized the idea of their own inferiority. Second, historically, wives and daughters have lived under male domain where they exchange submission for protection and unpaid labor for economic maintenance. Third, women with substantial class privilege have a more difficult time seeing themselves as deprived and subordinated, thus making it especially hard for women of different classes to work together. Fourth, women are separated by their differences in sexual expression and sexual activities.[87] When we add race, age, and ability differences to these class and sexual divisions, the likelihood of women uniting against patriarchy becomes even less probable.

In spite of these extremely powerful structures that conspire to limit the roles and options of both genders and render those who are multiply oppressed close to powerless at times, there is a long history of resistance to patriarchy.[88] Although a unified revolt against patriarchy will probably not occur in the forseeable future, people are fighting back in various ways and struggling to change the systems that support inequality. Many of the writers in this book have struggled for empowerment of one sort or another and provide hopeful exceptions to this often-oppressive picture. The pages that follow contain examples of people finding their voices, telling unpopular truths, taking charge of their own needs, offering concrete advice for improving the lives of women and men, and organizing for change. Don Sabo, for example, critiques male sports culture (Part V); Christy Haubegger embraces her round body (Part III); Jackson Katz and Robert Allen work to prevent male violence (Part VII).

I define power broadly to include a range of personal and collective actions. At a personal level, empowerment includes the ability to name and assert one's identity in all its complexity, including the naming of one's privilege and oppression. Related to this is the refusal to accept someone else's definition of who one is. Possessing a sociological imagination is another form of personal power; this allows us to know where we fit historically in the world, to know what our options are likely to be, and to know how to determine whether our pain stems from a personal trouble or from a public issue felt at the personal level. A sociological imagination contributes to the ability to challenge dominant ideas and to develop a healthy skepticism about how the world works. Based on informed analyses of what is wrong with the social order, people can use the power of knowledge to determine what kinds of social changes to work toward. Finally, people can empower themselves by taking political action, both individually and collectively.

Empowerment develops in stages. The first stage is awareness that something is not right. To conceptualize what's wrong, people need inclusive knowledge to develop a case for what feminist writer Elizabeth Janeway calls "disbelief," which includes the refusal to accept the definition of oneself that is put forward by those with more power.[89] Janeway argues that in order to mistrust or disbelieve the messages of those in power, validation from others is necessary. Speaking of women, she argues, "The frightening experience of doubting society's directives and then doubting one's right to doubt them is still very recent."[90] Thus, if one's mistrust of the system is not solid, the presence of other disbelievers is likely to strengthen one's position. The role of Black churches in validating this mistrust has been well documented; congregants name how the racist power structure perpetuates itself, and they support each other to work to lessen its onslaught.[91] Women's consciousness-raising groups have also served this purpose.[92] The civil rights movement served to do this for its members in the 1960s as organizations such as the National Association for the Advancement of Colored People and the Student Nonviolent Coordinating Committee supported their members to define the system of racism as unacceptable and to fight against it as they registered voters, engaged in sit-ins and boycotts, and integrated formerly white establishments and institutions in the face of virulent opposition.

Once people are convinced that something is wrong or unfair in their lives, they can consider taking steps toward making it right at several levels. At the individual level, people can practice personal acts of passive resistance, direct confrontation, or other actions such as telling the truth about how they really feel; challenging someone who said something hurtful or insulting; leaving an abusive relationship; insisting on not always being in a particular role in a relationship; avoiding contact with people whose attitudes are disrespectful, including refusing to frequent certain places; and making a public statement. On a collective level, people can resist oppressive arrangements by joining forces. This might happen in small or large ways, including movements for social change in communities, institutions, legislative bodies, other governmental structures, and international forums. All of these levels of resistance to oppressive structures and relationships are necessary if we are to create, in Gerda Lerner's words, "a world free of dominance and hierarchy, a world that is truly human."[93]

Regarding Language

A white student from a university other than my own e-mailed me to complain that I had capitalized Black but not white in the previous edition of this text. I considered various alternatives, including capitalizing both White and Black, putting the word black in lowercase, or varying the capitalization—using black as an adjective (for example, black individuals) and Black as a noun when referring to a group (for example, Blacks in the United States). I examined how various other writers handled this issue and discovered that some capitalize Black and others do not. Out of respect, especially, for Black writers who choose to capitalize Black, and with awareness that the nature of racism confers a version of ethnic status on all people who appear to be of

African descent even though they belong to a wide range of ethnicities, I have chosen to continue to capitalize the word Black and leave white in lowercase except when referring to white ethnic groups (for example, French or Italian).

The term *race* is itself so problematic that many scholars regularly put the word in quotation marks to remind readers that it is a social construction rather than a valid biological category. Genetically, there is currently no such thing as "race" and the category makes little or no sense from a scientific standpoint.[94] What is essential, of course, is the meaning that people in various cultural contexts attribute to differences in skin color or other physical characteristics. Thus, when a study of women with breast cancer reveals that although white women have higher rates of breast cancer, Black women are 34 percent more likely than white women to die of the disease, it is important to be cautious in attributing the differences to alleged "racial" differences of a biological nature as if the differences were genetically determined. In fact, studies of people living in polluted environments show that chromosomal aberrations caused by pollution can make people more vulnerable to illnesses, including cancer. When being Black correlates with being exposed to higher levels of pollution, the environmental question needs to be addressed before conclusions about causes of high death rates are attributed to "race."[95]

I have chosen not to put the word *race* in quotation marks but I encourage readers to keep in mind that when I or other authors in this book discuss race, we are addressing the sociocultural aspects of skin color, including some of the ways in which various social groups are privileged and/or oppressed in various social contexts. We do not intend to imply that differences between groups are genetic, immutable, or innate. In fact, if we were to imagine a world without prejudice and discrimination, we might begin to imagine a world in which skin color made little or no difference.

NOTES

1. Gerda Lerner, *The Creation of Patriarchy* (New York: Oxford, 1986), pp. 228–29.
2. Audre Lorde, "Age, Race, Class, and Sex: Women Defining Difference," in *Sister Outsider* (Freedom, CA: Crossing Press, 1984), p. 120.
3. C. Wright Mills, *The Sociological Imagination* (New York: Oxford University Press, 1959).
4. For a review of legal changes and challenges ahead, see Jo Freeman, "The Revolution for Women in Law and Public Policy," in Jo Freeman, ed., *Woman: A Feminist Perspective*, 5th ed. (Mountain View, CA: Mayfield, 1995), pp. 365–404. For a summary of the development of the contemporary women's movement, including a review of women's activism from the nineteenth century to the present, see Margaret Andersen, *Thinking about Women: Sociological Perspectives on Sex and Gender*, 7th ed. (New York: Macmillan, 2005).
5. For objections to feminism, see writings by Beverly LaHaye (Concerned Women for America) and Phyllis Schlafly; for critiques of mainstream feminism, see Camille Paglia, *Sexual Personae: Art and Decadence from Nefertiti to Emily Dickinson* (London: Penguin, 1990); Christina Sommers, *Who Stole Feminism?* (New York:

Simon & Schuster, 1994); Katie Roiphe, *The Morning After: Sex, Fear, and Feminism* (London: H. Hamilton, 1994).

6. A sample of recent third wave feminist books includes Barbara Findlen, ed., *Listen Up: Voices from the Next Feminist Generation* (Emeryville, CA: Seal Press, 2001); Daisy Hernández and Barbara Rehman, eds., *Colonize This! Young Women of Color on Today's Feminism* (Emeryville, CA: Seal Press, 2002); Megan Seely, *Fight Like a Girl: How to Be a Fearless Feminist* (New York: New York University Press); Jessica Valenti, *Full Frontal Feminism: A Young Woman's Guide to Why Feminism Matters* (Emeryville, CA: Seal Press, 2007); Rebecca Walker, ed., *To Be Real* (New York: Anchor Books/Doubleday, 1995).

7. For a representative look at some of the issues confronted by profeminist men, see Michael S. Kimmel and Michael A. Messner, eds., *Men's Lives*, 7th ed. (Boston: Allyn & Bacon, 2006); Jackson Katz, *The Macho Paradox: Why Some Men Hurt Women and How All Men Can Help* (Naperville, IL: Sourcebooks, 2006); Mark Anthony Neal, *New Black Man* (New York: Routledge, 2006).

8. For an overview of public masculinity movements and politics, see Michael A. Messner, *Politics of Masculinities: Men in Movements* (Thousand Oaks, CA: Sage, 1998). For a critique of the mythopoetic men's movement, see Michael S. Kimmel and Michael Kaufman, "The New Men's Movement: Retreat and Regression with America's Weekend Warriors," *Feminist Issues*, Fall 1993, pp. 3–21. For a look inside Promise Keepers, one of the large evangelical men's organizations, from the perspective of a feminist woman observer, see Donna Minkowitz, "In the Name of the Father," *Ms.*, November/December 1995, pp. 64–71. For a discussion of the Million Man March and the O. J. Simpson case, see Henry Louis Gates, Jr., "Thirteen Ways of Looking at a Black Man," *The New Yorker*, 23 October 1995, pp. 56ff; Mark Anthony Neal, *New Black Man* (New York: Routledge, 2006). For a presentation of various men's movement positions not represented in this book, see Robert Bly, *Iron John* (New York: Random House, 1990); Stephen B. Boyd, *The Men We Long to Be: Beyond Domination to a New Christian Understanding of Manhood* (New York: HarperCollins, 1995); Warren Farrell, *The Myth of Male Power: Why Men Are the Disposable Sex* (New York: Berkeley Books, 1993); Sam Keen, *Fire in the Belly: On Being a Man* (New York: Bantam, 1991); Harvey C. Mansfield, *Manliness* (Binghamton, NY: Vail-Ballou Press, 2006); Keith Thompson, ed., *To Be a Man: In Search of the Deep Masculine* (New York: Putnam, 1991).

9. William Pollock, *Real Boys: Rescuing Our Sons from the Myths of Boyhood* (New York: Random House, 1998); Daniel Kindlon and Michael Thompson, *Raising Cain: Protecting the Emotional Life of Boys* (New York: Ballantine Books, 1999).

10. Geoffrey Canada, *Reaching Up for Manhood: Transforming the Lives of Boys in America* (Boston: Beacon Press, 1998); Ann Arnett Ferguson, *Bad Boys: Public Schools and the Making of Black Masculinity* (Ann Arbor: University of Michigan Press, 2000); James Garbarino, *Lost Boys: Why Our Sons Turn Violent and How We Can Save Them* (New York: Free Press, 1999).

11. Christina Hoff Sommers, *The War Against Boys: How Misguided Feminism Is Harming Our Young Men* (New York: Simon & Schuster, 2000).

12. James Garbarino, "Some Kids Are Orchids," *Time*, 20 December 1999, p. 51.

13. Michael S. Kimmel, *The Gendered Society* (New York: Oxford University Press, 2000).

14. Kimmel, *The Gendered Society*; William Pollock, *Real Boys*.

15. Susan Faludi, *Stiffed: The Betrayal of Modern Man* (New York: Harper Collins, 1999); Michelle Fine, Lois Weis, Judi Addelston, and Julia Marusza, "(In) Secure Times: Constructing White Working-Class Masculinities in the Late 20th Century," in Theodore F. Cohen, ed., *Men and Masculinity: A Text Reader* (Belmont,

CA: Wadsworth, 2001), pp. 422–435; Sally Robinson, *Marked Men: White Masculinity in Crisis* (New York: Columbia University Press, 2000); Neil Chethik, *VoiceMale* (New York: Simon & Schuster, 2006); Daniel Jones, ed., *The Bastard on the Couch* (New York: HarperCollins Perennial Currents, 2004); Mark Anthony Neal, *New Black Man* (New York: Routledge, 2006); Keith Boykin, *One More River to Cross: Black & Gay in America* (New York: Doubleday Anchor Books, 1996); Keith Boykin, *Beyond the Down Low: Sex, Lies, and Denial in Black America* (New York: Carroll & Graf, 2005); Scott Poulson-Bryant, *Hung: A Meditation on the Measure of Black Men in America* (New York: Doubleday, 2005).

16. Sabine Lang, *Men as Women, Women as Men: Changing Gender in Native American Cultures* (Austin: University of Texas Press, 1998); Stephen O. Murray and Will Roscoe, *Boy-Wives and Female Husbands: Studies in African Homosexualities* (New York: St. Martin's Press, 1998); Will Roscoe, *Changing Ones: Third and Fourth Genders in Native North America* (New York: St. Martin's Press, 1998).

17. Phyllis Burke, *Gender Shock* (New York: Anchor/Doubleday, 1996); Cheryl Chase, "Hermaphrodites with Attitude: Mapping the Emergence of Intersex Political Activism," *GLQ* 4, no. 2 (1998), pp. 189–211; Leslie Feinberg, *Transgender Warriors: Making History from Joan of Arc to Ru Paul* (Boston: Beacon Press, 1996); Leslie Feinberg, *Trans Liberation: Beyond Pink or Blue* (Boston: Beacon Press, 1998); Susan Stryker and Stephen Whittle, eds., *The Transgender Studies Reader* (New York: Routledge, 2006); Joan Nestle, Clare Howell, and Riki Wilchins, eds., *GenderQueer* (Los Angeles: Alyson Books, 2002); Paisley Currah, Richard M. Juang, and Shannon Price Minter, eds., *Transgender Rights* (Minneapolis: University of Minnesota Press, 2006).

18. Feinberg, *Trans Liberation,* p. 5.

19. *Utne Reader,* September–October 1998; "The Man I Married Was Really a Woman," as told to James Oliver Cury, *Cosmopolitan,* November 1998, pp. 176ff.

20. Michelle Koidin, "Transsexual Union Sanctioned: Chromosomes Key as Couple Is Granted Texas Marriage License," *The Boston Globe,* 7 September 2000, p. A18.

21. For ongoing lists of bias-related murders, assaults, arson attacks, bombings, threats, cross burnings, harassment, intimidation, and vandalism, see *Klanwatch Intelligence Report,* published by the Southern Poverty Law Center, Montgomery, AL. For reports on right-wing political activity in general, see *The Public Eye,* published by Political Research Associates, Somerville, MA. See also Patricia Wong Hall and Victor M. Hwang, *Anti-Asian Violence in North America* (Lanham, MD: Rowman & Littlefield, 2001); Helen Zia, *Asian American Dreams: The Emergence of an American People* (New York: Farrar, Straus and Giroux, 2000).

22. Daisy Hernández, "Young and Out: Anything but Safe," *ColorLines,* Winter 2004, pp. 26–29.

23. http://www.fbi.gov/ucr/ucr.htm. Search Hate Crime Statistics.

24. Diane E. Lewis, "Workplace Bias Claims Jump after Sept. 11," *The Boston Globe,* 22 November 2001, p. B1; also see a recent report by the Council on American-Islamic Relations http://www.cair.com/cair2006report/.

25. David Crary, "Assaults on Disabled People Called Epidemic, 'Invisible,'" *The Boston Globe,* 26 December 2000, pp. A20, A21.

26. Derrick Z. Jackson, "High Court Makes a Case for Discrimination," *The Boston Globe,* 28 February 2001, p. A19.

27. AP, "High Court Limits Pay-Discrimination Claims," http://www.msnbc.msn.com/id/18920357/.

28. Sharon Hays, *Flat Broke with Children: Women in the Age of Welfare Reform* (New York: Oxford University Press, 2003).

29. John Iceland, *Poverty in America: A Handbook* (Berkeley: University of California Press, 2003).

30. Altha J. Cravy, *Women and Work in Mexico's Maquiladoras* (Lanham, MD: Rowman & Littlefield, 1998); Miriam Ching Yoon Louie, *Sweatshop Warriors: Immigrant Women Workers Take on the Global Factory* (Cambridge, MA: South End Press, 2001); Crista Wichterich, *The Globalized Woman: Reports from a Future of Inequality* (New York: Zed Books, 2000).

31. Videorecording "Stolen Childhoods" (Vineyard Haven, MA: Galen Films, 2003).

32. The home page of the U.N. High Commission on Human Rights is a good source of news and information about trafficking: http://www.ohchr.org/english/. Among many books on trafficking, an excellent one is *Sex Trafficking: The Global Market in Women and Children* by Kathryn Farr (New York: Worth, 2004).

33. Farr, *Sex Trafficking*. For a report on rape in Sudan by Amnesty International, see http://web.amnesty.org/library/index/engafr540762004.

34. Nancy Murray et al., *Mass Impact: The Domestic War Against Terrorism—Are We on the Right Track?* (Boston: American Civil Liberties Union of Massachusetts, 2004).

35. Benjamin Jealous, "Profiles of the Profiled," *Amnesty International*, no. 4 (Winter 2004), p. 18.

36. Charlotte Bunch, "A Feminist Human Rights Lens on Human Security," Center for Women's Global Leadership, Rutgers University (2004), p. 4, Web version. http://www.cwgl.rutgers.edu/globalcenter/charlotte/humansecurity.pdf.

37. For the full court decision, see http://www.supremecourtus.gov/opinions/06pdf/05-380.pdf.

38. For effects of the Global Gag Rule on women's health, see http://www.globalgagrule.org/.

39. Scott S. Greenberger, "Gay-Marriage Ruling Pushed Voters: Mobilized Bush, Left Kerry Wary," *The Boston Globe*, 7 November 2004, p. B1.

40. David W. Moore and Joseph Carroll, "Support for Gay Marriage/Civil Unions Edge Upward," Gallup News Service, 17 May 2004, Web version. http://www.galluppoll.com/content/?CI=11689.

41. American Academy of Pediatrics Press Release, "AAP Supports Adoption by Same-Sex Parents," 4 February 2002, http://www.aap.org/advocacy/releases/febsamesex.htm.

42. Randall Chase, "Estranged Lesbian Partner Is Told to Pay Child Support," *The Boston Globe*, 18 March 2002, p. A3.

43. See, for example, "Jobs and Money: A Small Step Forward for Same-Sex Couples," *The Guardian* (London), 7 April 2001, p. 7; Ben White, "Conservative Group Assails White House 'Trend' on Gays," *The Washington Post*, 30 September 2001, p. A04.

44. Catherine Holahan, "Mass. Scout Unit Allows Gay Leaders," *The Boston Globe*, 1 August 2001, pp. A1, A15; Claudia Kolker, "Scouts Divided: A Fixture under Seige," *The Boston Globe*, 26 November 2000, p. A25.

45. National Education Association, "NEA Board Adopts Plan to Make Schools Safer," 8 February 2002, http://www.nea.org/nr/nr020208.html.

46. Barbara Summerhawk, Cheiron McMahill, and Darren McDonald, eds. and trans., *Queer Japan: Personal Stories of Japanese Lesbians, Gays, Bisexuals and Transsexuals* (Norwich, VT: New Victoria Publishers, 1998).

47. Jane Kramer, "Taking the Veil: How France's Public Schools Became the Battleground in a Culture War," *The New Yorker*, 22 November 2004, pp. 58ff.

48. Caitlin Killian, "The Other Side of the Veil: North African Women in France Respond to the Headscarf Affair," *Gender & Society* 17, no. 4 (August 2003): 567–590.

49. Robert D. Putnam, *Bowling Alone: The Collapse and Revival of American Community* (New York: Simon & Schuster, 2000).

50. Jennifer Baumgardner and Amy Richards, *Manifesta: Young Women, Feminism, and the Future* (New York: Farrar, Straus and Giroux, 2000); Barbara Findlen, ed., *Listen Up: Voices from the Next Feminist Generation* (Seattle: Seal Press, 2001); Rebecca Walker, ed., *To Be Real: Telling the Truth and Changing the Face of Feminism* (New York: Anchor Books, 1995); Uphira Edut, ed., *Body Outlaws: Young Women Write about Body Image and Identity* (Seattle: Seal Press, 1998 and 2000).

51. Anastasia Higginbotham, "Alive and Kicking," *The Women's Review of Books* 18, no. 1 (October 2000): 1ff. Personal communication with Third Wave Foundation staff, November 2004. http://www.thirdwavefoundation.org/about.

52. Randy Albelda and Chris Tilly, "It's a Family Affair: Women, Poverty, and Welfare" in Diane Dujon and Ann Withorn, eds., *For Crying Out Loud: Women's Poverty in the United States* (Boston: South End Press, 1996), p. 79.

53. For a discussion of hegemonic masculinity, see R. W. Connell, *Gender and Power* (Palo Alto, CA: Stanford University Press, 1987) and *Masculinities* (Palo Alto, CA: Stanford University Press, 1995); and Sharon R. Bird, "Welcome to the Men's Club: Homosociality and the Maintenance of Hegemonic Masculinity," *Gender & Society* 10, no. 2 (April 1996): 120–32.

54. Bella English, "Looking Horror in the Eye," *The Boston Globe,* 27 July 2000, p. F1. For related work, see Paul Miller and David Lisak, "Associations between Childhood Abuse and Personality Disorder Symptoms in College Males," *Journal of Interpersonal Violence,* 14, no. 6 (1999): 642(1); for a look at men and women who do not repeat destructive patterns from their families, see Steven J. Wolin and Sybil Wolin, *The Resilient Self: How Survivors of Troubled Families Rise above Adversity* (New York: Villard Books, 1994).

55. For examples of crossover research, see Todd W. Crosset, *Outsiders in the Clubhouse: The World of Women's Professional Golf* (Albany: State University of New York Press, 1995); Elliot Liebow, *Tell Them Who I Am: The Lives of Homeless Women* (New York: Penguin, 1993); Kathleen Gerson, *No Man's Land: Men's Changing Commitments to Family and Work* (New York: Basic Books, 1993); and Christine L. Williams, *Still a Man's World: Men Who Do "Women's Work"* (Berkeley: University of California Press, 1995).

56. See Renate Duelli Klein, "The 'Men-Problem' in Women's Studies: The Expert, the Ignoramus and the Poor Dear," *Women's Studies International Forum* 6, no. 4 (1983): 413–21; Michael Awkward, "A Black Man's Place(s) in Black Feminist Criticism," in Marcellus Blount and George P. Cunningham, eds., *Representing Black Men* (New York: Routledge, 1996), pp. 3–26.

57. Harry Brod, "Scholarly Studies of Men: The New Field Is an Essential Complement to Women's Studies," *The Chronicle of Higher Education,* 21 March 1990, p. B2.

58. Gloria Anzaldúa, *Borderlands/La Frontera: The New Mestiza* (San Francisco: Spinsters/Aunt Lute, 1987); Gloria Anzaldúa, ed., *Making Face, Making Soul/Haciendo Caras: Creative and Critical Perspectives by Women of Color* (San Francisco: Spinsters/Aunt Lute, 1987); Patricia Hill Collins, *Black Feminist Thought: Knowledge, Consciousness, and the Politics of Empowerment* (New York: Routledge, 1990); Audre Lorde, *Sister Outsider* (Freedom, CA: Crossing Press, 1984); Audre Lorde, *A Burst of Light* (Ithaca, NY: Firebrand Books, 1988); Cherríe Moraga and Gloria Anzaldúa, eds., *This Bridge Called My Back: Writings by Radical*

Women of Color (Watertown, MA: Persephone Press, 1981); Rebecca Walker, ed., *To Be Real: Telling the Truth and Changing the Face of Feminism* (New York: Anchor Books, 1995). See also W. E. B. Du Bois, *The Souls of Black Folk* (New York: Penguin, 1989).

59. Du Bois, *Souls of Black Folk,* p. 5.

60. Collins, *Black Feminist Thought,* p. 225.

61. Collins, *Black Feminist Thought,* p. 227.

62. See, for example, Elly Bulkin, Minnie Bruce Pratt, and Barbara Smith, *Yours in Struggle: Three Perspectives on Anti-Semitism and Racism* (Ithaca, NY: Firebrand Books, 1984); Judith Katz, *White Awareness: Handbook for Anti-Racist Trainings* (Norman, OK: Oklahoma University Press, 1978); Jane Lazarre, *Beyond the Whiteness of Whiteness: Memoir of a White Mother of Black Sons* (Durham, NC: Duke University Press, 1996); Peggy McIntosh, "White Privilege and Male Privilege: A Personal Account of Coming to See Correspondences through Work in Women's Studies," in Margaret L. Andersen and Patricia Hill Collins, *Race, Class, and Gender, An Anthology* (Belmont, CA: Wadsworth, 1995), pp. 76–87; Ruth Frankenberg, *White Women, Race Matters: The Social Construction of Whiteness* (Minneapolis: University of Minnesota Press, 1993); Paul Kivel, *Uprooting Racism: How White People Can Work for Racial Justice* (Philadelphia: New Society Publishers).

63. McIntosh, "White Privilege and Male Privilege."

64. Michael S. Kimmel, "Invisible Masculinity," *Society* 30, no. 6 (September/October 1993): 29–30.

65. Paul Kivel, *Uprooting Racism: How White People Can Work for Racial Justice* (Philadelphia: New Society, 1996), pp. 30–32 and 37–39.

66. For a critique of competition, see Alfie Kohn, *No Contest: The Case against Competition* (Boston: Houghton Mifflin, 1986).

67. In the 1970s, I had difficulty teaching the concept of social class to students at an elite private college, whereas the working class and poor students I taught at a nearby public college grasped this concept with ease. For a discussion of people with less power as astute observers of those with more power, see Jean Baker Miller, *Toward a New Psychology of Women* (Boston: Beacon Press, 1977).

68. Mark Gerzon, *A Choice of Heroes: The Changing Face of American Manhood* (Boston: Houghton Mifflin, 1992), pp. 235–62.

69. Harry Brod, ed., *The Making of Masculinities: The New Men's Studies* (Boston: Allen & Unwin, 1987); Patricia Hill Collins, *Black Feminist Thought: Knowledge, Consciousness, and the Politics of Empowerment* (New York: Routledge, 1990); Patricia Hill Collins, *Fighting Words: Black Women and the Search for Social Justice* (Minneapolis: University of Minnesota Press, 1998); Sandra Harding, *The Science Question in Feminism* (Ithaca, NY: Cornell University Press, 1986); bell hooks, *Feminist Theory from Margin to Center* (Boston: South End Press, 1984); Evelyn Fox Keller, *Reflections on Gender and Science* (New Haven, CT: Yale University Press, 1985); Kimmel and Messner, *Men's Lives;* Lerner, *The Creation of Patriarchy* (New York: Oxford University Press, 1986); Elizabeth Kamarck Minnich, *Transforming Knowledge* (Philadelphia: Temple University Press, 1990); Joseph H. Pleck and Jack Sawyer, eds., *Men and Masculinity* (Englewood Cliffs, NJ: Prentice Hall, 1974); Ronald Takaki, *A Different Mirror: A History of Multicultural America* (Boston: Little, Brown, 1993).

70. Minnich, *Transforming Knowledge,* pp. 185–87.

71. Harry Brod, "Scholarly Studies of Men: The New Field Is an Essential Complement to Women's Studies," *The Chronicle of Higher Education,* 21 March

1990, p. B2. Reprinted in Karin Bergstrom Costello, ed., *Gendered Voices: Readings from the American Experience* (New York: Harcourt Brace, 1996), pp. 333–36.

72. Lerner, *Creation of Patriarchy*, p. 220.

73. For some early work on gender by women sociologists, see Jessie Bernard, *Women, Wives, Mothers: Values and Options* (Chicago: Aldine, 1975); Joyce Ladner, *Tomorrow's Tomorrow* (Garden City, NY: Doubleday, 1995); Marcia Millman and Rosabeth Moss Kanter, eds., *Another Voice* (Garden City, NY: Doubleday, 1975); Alice Rossi, ed., *Essays on Sex Equality* (Chicago: University of Chicago Press, 1970); Alice Rossi, ed., *The Feminist Papers* (New York: Columbia University Press, 1973); Anne Oakley, *The Sociology of Housework* (London: Mertin Robertson, 1974).

74. For a discussion of research on this issue, see Joseph H. Pleck, "The Gender Role Strain Paradigm: An Update" in Ronald F. Levant and William S. Pollack, eds., *A New Psychology of Men* (New York: Basic Books, 1995), pp. 11–32.

75. Anne Fausto-Sterling, "The Five Sexes: Why Male and Female Are Not Enough," *The Sciences,* March/April 1993, pp. 20–24.

76. Judith Lorber, *Paradoxes of Gender* (New Haven: Yale University Press, 1994), p. 5.

77. Suzanne Pharr, *Homophobia: A Weapon of Sexism* (Inverness, CA: Chardon Press, 1988); Adrienne Rich, "Compulsory Heterosexuality and Lesbian Existence," *Signs* 5 (Summer 1980): 631–60.

78. Eric Anderson, *In the Game: Gay Athletes and the Cult of Masculinity* (Albany: State University of New York Press, 2005); Pat Griffin, "Changing the Game: Homophobia, Sexism, and Lesbians in Sport," *Quest* 44 (1992): 251–265.

79. Minnie Bruce Pratt, *S/HE* (Ithaca, NY: Firebrand Books, 1995), p. 186.

80. Charles Lemert, *Social Theory: The Multicultural and Classic Readings,* 3rd ed. (Boulder, CO: Westview Press, 2004). Lemert includes Audre Lorde, Gloria Anzaldúa, Cornell West, and Virginia Woolf, among many others.

81. Ronald Takaki, *A Different Mirror: A History of Multicultural America.*

82. Democracy Now (www.democracynow.org); Independent Media (www .indymedia.org); Free Speech Radio News (www.fsrn.org); Women's International News Gathering Service (www.wings.org); Between the Lines (www .btlonine.org); and Women's eNews (www.womensenews.org).

83. Marilyn Frye, "Oppression," in *The Politics of Reality: Essays in Feminist Theory* (Freedom, CA: Crossing Press, 1983), pp. 1–16.

84. Max Weber, "Class, Status, Party," in S. M. Miller, ed., *Max Weber: Selections from His Work* (New York: Crowell, 1963), p. 43.

85. See Katherine S. Newman, *Falling from Grace: The Experience of Downward Mobility in the American Middle Class* (New York: Free Press, 1988) and *Declining Fortunes: The Withering of the American Dream* (New York: Basic Books, 1993).

86. For discussions of individual survival after painful childhoods, see Linda T. Sanford, *Strong at the Broken Places: Overcoming the Trauma of Childhood Abuse* (New York: Random House, 1990) and Stephen J. Wolin and Sybil Wolin, *The Resilient Self: How Survivors of Troubled Families Rise above Adversity* (New York: Villard Books, 1994). For a review of past and current literature on strategies for coping with poverty and racism as well as some new qualitative data documenting creative responses to poverty among single African American women on AFDC, see Robin L. Jarrett, "Living Poor: Family Life among Single Parent, African-American Women," in *Social Problems* 41, no. 1 (February 1994): 30–49.

87. Lerner, *Creation of Patriarchy,* pp. 217–19.

88. Sandra Morgen and Ann Bookman, "Rethinking Women and Politics: An Introductory Essay," in Ann Bookman and Sandra Morgen, eds., *Women and the Politics of Empowerment* (Philadelphia: Temple University Press, 1988), p. 4.

89. Elizabeth Janeway, *Powers of the Weak* (New York: Knopf, 1980), p. 167.

90. Janeway, *Powers of the Weak*, p. 168.

91. James Blackwell, *The Black Community: Diversity and Unity* (New York: HarperCollins, 1991).

92. Hester Eisenstein, *Contemporary Feminist Thought* (Boston: G. K. Hall, 1983) cited in Andersen, *Thinking about Women*.

93. Lerner, *Creation of Patriarchy*, p. 229.

94. Audrey Smedley and Brian D. Smedley, "Race as Biology Is Fiction, Racism as a Social Problem Is Real: Anthropological and Historical Perspectives on the Social Construction of Race," *The American Psychologist* 60, no. 1 (January 2005): 16(ff); Gerda Lerner, *Why History Matters: Life and Thought* (New York: Oxford University Press, 1997), p. viii.

95. Rita Arditti, "Breast Cancer Rates Differ by Race," *BCA Newsletter* no. 84 (December 2004/January 2005), p. 3ff., http://www.bcaction.org; Frederica Perera et al. "DNA Damage from Polycyclic Aromatic Hydrocarbons (PAHs) in Mothers and Newborns from Northern Manhattan, the World Trade Center Area, Poland, and China," *Cancer Epidemiology, Biomarkers & Prevention* 14, no. 3, (March 2005): 709–14.

PART I
It's Not Just about Gender

The gender system is socially constructed. Political, educational, occupational, and religious institutions, along with the family, create and enforce expectations for how women and men should behave in all known societies. Although the gender rules vary from one cultural setting to another, all settings have such rules, and most of these rules are rooted in patriarchy—the control or dominance of women by men, and the control of less-empowered men by men with more power. Within these institutions, people are systematically socialized to become women or men via complex processes of learning and are frequently bombarded with gender rules from many sources simultaneously.

Although individuals can break or stretch the rules without changing the structures surrounding human lives, individual change will not have much impact on the structures. For example, many individual women in the United States are committed to holding jobs requiring high levels of responsibility and competence but are blocked from promotion for such reasons as sexism, racism, ageism, and homophobia. Men who want to be involved in their children's lives often find it difficult. For some, the need to hold more than one job in order to make ends meet severely limits their time at home. For those with more economic privilege, work often demands long, inflexible hours at the office. Men who are unemployed and might have more time to spend with their children frequently find their inability to provide economic support to their families humiliating and thus stay away. And men who do find the time to get involved are often met with disbelief and disapproval from health care and educational systems accustomed to dealing only with mothers. Thus, even when individuals are motivated to stretch the boundaries of gender, social structures often impede them.

How we express our maleness or femaleness varies widely from one social context to another. Sociologists, anthropologists, biologists, and others argue convincingly that it is not reproductive biology alone that determines how a person develops. Rather, there is an interaction between one's genetic, biological makeup, usually referred to as sex, and the expectations for male and female behavior in the social contexts in which a person lives, usually referred to as gender.[1] People who change genders provide compelling evidence of the difference between sex and gender. David Beuchner, a famous concert pianist, decided to change his gender and become Sara Beuchner. As Sara, she had a much more difficult time finding work and booking agents, and university hiring committees were unprepared and unaccepting of the gender switch, even though her skills at the piano remained unchanged. On the other hand, when women become men, they seem to fare better, receiving the advantage of gender stereotypes relating to men's authority and competence in the workplace. A recent study of 29 female-to-male transsexuals

31

found that the majority fared well at work after transitioning to their new gender, even if they stayed at the same workplace while transitioning. Men who were white and tall had the most success, underlining the reality of stereotypes and discrimination on the basis of race and physical stature.[2]

Expectations for what constitutes femininity and masculinity along with the options available to different women and men are deeply affected by sexism, poverty, racism, homophobia, heterosexism, and other cultural constraints and expectations. To understand people's identities and opportunities, we need to understand the privilege or oppression that they experience, the historical times and the circumstances in which they are currently living, the structural arrangements that surround their lives, and the possibilities for empowerment that they encounter or create.

This part of the book includes eight essays that address the experiences and concerns of people from various groups: African American (Patricia Hill Collins), Asian American (Helen Zia), Latino (Martín Espada and Alejandra Marchevsky & Jeanne Theoharis), Native American (Paula Gunn Allen), Jewish (Ruth Atkin and Adrienne Rich), Muslim (Farida Shaheed) and white Euro American (Peggy McIntosh). Though prejudice, marginality, overt discrimination, and privilege are described in these essays, they are experienced somewhat differently by members of each group. And the historical contexts, including such issues as broken treaties, immigration policy, poverty, the structure of various societies, and attitudes and prejudices, vary enough to create different kinds of men and women in each of these groups. The other two essays in this section look at the larger structural picture. First, Chandra Talpade Mohanty provides a conceptual framework that helps us understand the complexities of how gender and globalization intersect. Going beyond the concept of multiracial feminism that has sensitized feminists to the disparate realities of women in different social locations in the United States,[3] Mohanty calls upon us to attend to the global realities surrounding women's lives. Next, Allan Johnson discusses the system of patriarchy.

The authors in Part I identify intersecting oppressions in various combinations and encourage us to think in more complex ways about how people become who they are. They help us to look at what ties people down and what provides unearned privilege. These writers ask for a humane world in which economic and social injustice would not exist. You might want to reflect on how what these authors say affects you: Do the issues presented ring true to your own experience? Have you observed or directly experienced any of the oppressive situations or privileges that these authors describe? Have you thought about patriarchy as a system? What are your thoughts about immigration and immigration reform? What images do you hold of Muslim women and men?

NOTES

1. For more about this issue, see Margaret Andersen, *Thinking about Women: Sociological Perspectives on Sex and Gender,* 3rd ed. (New York: Macmillan, 1993), ch. 2, pp. 21–51; Marion Lowe and Ruth Hubbard, eds., *Woman's Nature* (New

York: Pergamon Press, 1983); Anne Fausto-Sterling, *Myths of Gender* (New York: Basic Books, 1985); Ruth Hubbard, M. S. Henifin, and B. Fried, eds., *Women Look at Biology Looking at Women* (Cambridge, MA: Schenckman, 1979).

2. Kristen Schilt, "Just One of the Guys? How Transmen Make Gender Visible at Work," *Gender & Society* 20 no. 4 (August 2006): 465–90.

3. Maxine Baca Zinn and Bonnie Thornton Dill, "Theorizing Difference from Multiracial Feminism," *Feminist Studies* 22, no. 2 (Summer 1996): 321–31. Becky Thompson, "Multiracial Feminism: Recasting the Chronology of Second Wave Feminism," *Feminist Studies* 28, no. 2 (Summer 2002): 337–62.

1

THE PUERTO RICAN DUMMY AND THE MERCIFUL SON

MARTÍN ESPADA

Martín Espada has published eight books of poems, the latest of which is *The Republic of Poetry* (2006). *Imagine the Angels of Bread* (1997) won an American Book Award. A former tenant lawyer, Espada is a Professor of English at the University of Massachusetts, Amherst.

I have a four-year-old son named Clemente. He is not named for Roberto Clemente, the baseball player, as many people are quick to guess, but rather for a Puerto Rican poet. His name, in translation, means "merciful." Like the cheetah, he can reach speeds of up to sixty miles an hour. He is also, demographically speaking, a Latino male, a "macho" for the twenty-first century.

Two years ago, we were watching television together when a ventriloquist appeared with his dummy. The ventriloquist was Anglo; the dummy was a Latino male, Puerto Rican, in fact, like me, like my son. Complete with pencil mustache, greased hair, and jawbreaking Spanish accent, the dummy acted out an Anglo fantasy for an Anglo crowd that roared its approval. My son was transfixed; he did not recognize the character onscreen because he knows no one who fits that description, but he sensed my discomfort. Too late, I changed the channel. The next morning, my son watched Luis and María on *Sesame Street*, but this is inadequate compensation. *Sesame Street* is the only barrio on television, the only neighborhood where Latino families live and work, but the comedians are everywhere, with that frat-boy sneer, and so are the crowds.

However, I cannot simply switch off the comedians, or explain them (how do you explain to a preschooler that a crowd of strangers is angrily laughing at the idea of *him?*). We live in western Massachusetts, not far from Springfield and Holyoke, hardscrabble small cities that, in the last generation, have witnessed a huge influx of Puerto Ricans, now constituting some of the poorest Puerto Rican communities in the country. The evening news from Springfield features what I call the "Puerto Rican minute." This is the one minute of the newscast where we see the faces of Puerto Rican men, the mug shot or the arraignment in court or witnesses pointing to the blood-stained sidewalk, while the newscaster solemnly intones the mantra of gangs, drugs, jail. The notion of spending the Puerto Rican minute on a teacher or a health care worker or an artist in the community never occurs to the television journalists who produce this programming.

The Latino male is the bogeyman of the Pioneer Valley, which includes the area where we live. Recently, there was a rumor circulating in the atmosphere that Latino gangs would be prowling the streets on Halloween, shooting anyone in costume. My wife, Katherine, reports that one Anglo gentleman at the local swimming pool took responsibility for warning everyone, a veritable Paul Revere in swim trunks wailing that "The Latinos are going to kill kids on Halloween!" Note how 1) Latino gangs became "Latinos" and 2) Latinos and "kids" became mutually exclusive categories. My wife wondered if this warning contemplated the Latino males in her life, if this racially paranoid imagination included visions of her professor husband and his toddling offspring as gunslingers in full macho swagger, hunting for "gringos" in Halloween costumes. The rumor, needless to say, was unfounded.

Then there is the national political climate. In 1995, we saw the spectacle of a politician, California Governor Pete Wilson, being seriously considered for the presidency on the strength of his support for Proposition 187, the most blatantly anti-Latino initiative in recent memory. There is no guarantee, as my son grows older, that this political pendulum will swing back to the left; if anything, the pendulum may well swing farther to the right. That means more fear and fury and bitter laughter.

Into this world enters Clemente, which raises certain questions: How do I think of my son as a Latino male? How do I teach him to disappoint and disorient the bigots everywhere around him, all of whom have bought tickets to see the macho pantomime? At the same time, how do I teach him to inoculate himself against the very real diseases of violence and sexism and homophobia infecting our community? How do I teach Clemente to be Clemente?

My son's identity as a Puerto Rican male has already been reinforced by a number of experiences I did not have at so early an age. At age four, he has already spent time in Puerto Rico, whereas I did not visit the island until I was ten years old. From the time he was a few months old, he has witnessed his Puerto Rican father engaged in the decidedly nonstereotypical business of giving poetry readings. We savor new Spanish words together the same way we devour mangoes together, knowing the same tartness and succulence.

And yet, that same identity will be shaped by negative as well as positive experiences. The ventriloquist and his Puerto Rican dummy offered

Clemente a glimpse of his inevitable future: not only bigotry, but his growing awareness of that bigotry, his realization that some people have contempt for him because he is Puerto Rican. Here his sense of maleness will come into play, because he must learn to deal with his own rage, his inability to extinguish the source of his torment.

My father has good reason for rage. A brown-skinned man, he learned rage when he was arrested in Biloxi, Mississippi, in 1950, and spent a week in jail for refusing to go to the back of the bus. He learned rage when he was denied a college education and instead struggled for years working for an electrical contractor, hating his work and yearning for so much more. He learned rage as the political triumphs of the 1960s he helped to achieve were attacked from without and betrayed from within. My father externalized his rage. He raged at his enemies and he raged at us. A tremendous ethical and cultural influence for us nonetheless, he must have considered himself a failure by the male career-obsessed standards of the decade into which I was born: the 1950s.

By adolescence, I had learned to internalize my rage. I learned to do this, not so much in response to my father, but more in response to my own growing awareness of bigotry. Having left my Brooklyn birthplace for the town of Valley Stream, Long Island, I was dubbed a spic in an endless torrent of taunting, bullying, and brawling. To defend myself against a few people would have been feasible; to defend myself against dozens and dozens of people deeply in love with their own racism was a practical impossibility. So I told no one, no parent or counselor or teacher or friend, about the constant racial hostility. Instead, I punched a lamp, not once but twice, and watched the blood ooze between my knuckles as if somehow I could leech the poison from my body. My evolving manhood was defined by how well I could take punishment, and paradoxically I punished myself for not being man enough to end my own humiliation. Later in life, I would emulate my father and rage openly. Rarely, however, was the real enemy within earshot, or even visible.

Someday, my son will be called a spic for the first time; this is as much a part of the Puerto Rican experience as the music he gleefully dances to. I hope he will tell me. I hope that I can help him handle the glowing toxic waste of his rage. I hope that I can explain clearly why there are those waiting for him to explode, to confirm their stereotypes of the hot-blooded, bad-tempered Latino male who has, without provocation, injured the Anglo innocents. His anger—and that anger must come—has to be controlled, directed, creatively channeled, articulated—but not all-consuming, neither destructive nor self-destructive. I keep it between the covers of the books I write.

The anger will continue to manifest itself as he matures and discovers the utter resourcefulness of bigotry, the ability of racism to change shape and survive all attempts to snuff it out. "Spic" is a crude expression of certain sentiments that become subtle and sophisticated and insidious at other levels. Speaking of crudity, I am reminded of a group organized by white ethnics in New York during the 1960s under the acronym of SPONGE: The Society for the Prevention of the Niggers Getting Everything. When affirmative action is criticized today by Anglo politicians and pundits with exquisite diction and erudite vocabulary, that is still SPONGE. When and if my son is admitted to school or obtains a job by way of affirmative action, and is resented for it by his colleagues, that will be SPONGE, too.

Violence is the first cousin to rage. If learning to confront rage is an important element of developing Latino manhood, then the question of violence must be addressed with equal urgency. Violence is terribly seductive; all of us, especially males, are trained to gaze upon violence until it becomes beautiful. Beautiful violence is not only the way to victory for armies and football teams; this becomes the solution to everyday problems as well. For many characters on the movie or television screen, problems are solved by *shooting* them. This is certainly the most emphatic way to win an argument.

Katherine and I try to minimize the seductiveness of violence for Clemente. No guns, no soldiers, and so on. But his dinosaurs still eat each other with great relish. His trains still crash, to their delight. He is experimenting with power and control, with action and reaction, which brings him to an imitation of violence. Needless to say, there is a vast difference between stegosaurs and Desert Storm.

Again, all I can do is call upon my own experience as an example. I not only found violence seductive; at some point, I found myself enjoying it. I remember one brawl in Valley Stream when I snatched a chain away from an assailant, knocked him down, and needlessly lashed the chain across his knees as he lay sobbing in the street. That I was now the assailant with the chain did not occur to me.

I also remember the day I stopped enjoying the act of fistfighting. I was working as a bouncer in a bar, and found myself struggling with a man who was so drunk that he appeared numb to the blows bouncing off his cranium. Suddenly, I heard my fist echo: *thok.* I was sickened by the sound. Later, I learned that I had broken my right ring finger with that punch, but all I could recall was the headache I must have caused him. I never had a fistfight again. Parenthetically, that job ended another romance: the one with alcohol. Too much of my job consisted of ministering to people who had passed out at the bar, finding their hats and coats, calling a cab, dragging them in their stupor down the stairs. Years later, I channeled those instincts cultivated as a bouncer into my work as a legal services lawyer, representing Latino tenants, finding landlords who forgot to heat buildings in winter or exterminate rats to be more deserving targets of my wrath. Eventually, I even left the law.

Will I urge my son to be a pacifist, thereby gutting one of the foundations of traditional manhood, the pleasure taken in violence and the power derived from it? That is an ideal state. I hope that he lives a life that permits him pacifism. I hope that the world around him evolves in such a way that pacifism is a viable choice. Still, I would not deny him the option of physical self-defense. I would not deny him, on philosophical grounds, the right to resistance in any form that resistance must take to be effective. Nor would I have him deny that right to others, with the luxury of distance. Too many people in this world still need a revolution.

When he is old enough, Clemente and I will talk about matters of justification, which must be carefully and narrowly defined. He must understand that abstractions like "respect" and "honor" are not reasons to fight in the street, and abstractions like "patriotism" and "country" are not reasons to fight on the battlefield. He must understand that violence against women is not acceptable, a message which will have to be somehow repeated every time another movie trailer blazes the art of misogyny across his subconscious mind. Rather than sloganizing, however, the best way I can communicate that message is by the way I treat his mother. How else will he know that jealousy is not love, that a lover is not property?

Knowing Katherine introduced me to a new awareness of many things: compassion and intimacy, domestic violence and recovery. Her history of savage physical abuse as a child—in a Connecticut farming community—compelled me to consider what it means to heal another human being, or to help that human being heal herself. What small gestures begin to restore humanity?

WHEN THE LEATHER IS A WHIP

At night,
with my wife
sitting on the bed,
I turn from her
to unbuckle
my belt
so she won't see
her father
unbuckling
his belt

Clemente was born on December 28, 1991. This was a difficult birth. Katherine's coccyx, or tailbone, broken in childhood, would break again during delivery. Yet only with the birth could we move from gesture to fulfillment, from generous moments to real giving. The extraordinary healing that took place was not only physical but emotional and spiritual as well. After years of constant pain, her coccyx bone set properly, as if a living metaphor for the new opportunity represented by the birth of this child.

WHITE BIRCH

Two decades ago rye whiskey
scaled your father's throat,
stinking from the mouth
as he stamped his shoe
in the groove between your hips,
dizzy flailing cartwheel down the stairs.
The tail of your spine split,
became a scraping hook.

For twenty years a fire raced
across the boughs of your bones,
his drunken mouth a movie
flashing with every stabbed gesture.

Now the white room of birth is throbbing:
the numbers palpitating red on the screen of machinery
tentacled to your arm; the oxygen mask wedged
in a wheeze on your face; the numbing medication
injected through the spine.
The boy was snagged on that spiraling bone.

Medical fingers prodded your raw pink center
while you stared at a horizon of water
no one else could see, creatures leaping silver
with tails that slashed the air
like your agonized tongue.

You were born in the river valley,
hard green checkerboard of farms,
a town of white birches
and a churchyard from the workhorse time,
weathered headstones naming women
drained of blood with infants coiled inside
the caging hips, hymns swaying
as if lanterns over the mounded earth.

Then the white birch of your bones,
resilient and yielding, yielded again,
root snapped as the boy spilled out of you
into hands burst open by beckoning
and voices pouring praise like water,
two beings tangled in exhaustion,
blood-painted, but full of breath.
After a generation of burning
the hook unfurled in your body,
the crack in the bone dissolved:
One day you stood, expected again
the branch of nerves
fanning across your back to flame,
and felt only the grace of birches.

Obviously, my wife and son had changed me, had even changed my poetry. This might be the first Puerto Rican poem swaying with white birch trees
instead of coconut palms. On the other hand, Katherine and I immediately set
about making this a Puerto Rican baby. I danced him to sleep with blaring
salsa. Katherine painted *coquís*—tiny Puerto Rican frogs—on his pajamas. We
spoon-fed him rice and beans. He met his great-grandmother in Puerto Rico.

The behavior we collectively refer to as "macho" has deep historical roots, but the trigger is often a profound insecurity, a sense of being threatened. Clemente will be as secure as possible, and that security will stem in large part from self-knowledge. He will know the meaning of his name.

Clemente Solo Vélez was a great Puerto Rican poet, a fighter for the independence of Puerto Rico who spent years in a prison as a result. He was also our good friend. The two Clementes met once, when the elder Clemente was eighty-seven years old and the younger Clemente was nine months. Fittingly, it was Columbus Day, 1992, the five-hundredth anniversary of the conquest. We passed the day with a man who devoted his life and his art to battling the very colonialism personified by Columbus. The two Clementes traced the topography of one another's faces. Even from his sickbed, the elder Clemente was gentle and generous. We took photographs, signed books. Clemente Solo Vélez died the following spring, and eventually my family and I visited the grave in the mountains of Puerto Rico. We found the grave unmarked but for a stick with a number and letter, so we bought a gravestone and gave the poet his name back. My son still asks to see the framed photograph of the two Clementes, still asks about the man with the long white hair who gave him *his* name. This will be family legend, family ritual, the origins of the name explained in greater and greater detail as the years pass, a source of knowledge and power as meaningful as the Book of Genesis.

Thankfully, Clemente also has a literal meaning: "merciful." Every time my son asks about his name, an opportunity presents itself to teach the power of mercy, the power of compassion. When Clemente, in later years, consciously acts out these qualities, he does so knowing that he is doing what his very name expects of him. His name gives him the beginnings of a moral code, a goal to which he can aspire. "Merciful": Not the first word scrawled on the mental blackboard next to the phrase "Puerto Rican male." Yet how appropriate, given that, for Katherine and me, the act of mercy has become an expression of gratitude for Clemente's existence.

BECAUSE CLEMENTE MEANS MERCIFUL
—for Clemente Gilbert-Espada
    February 1992

At three AM, we watched
the emergency room doctor
press a thumb against your cheekbone
to bleach your eye with light.
The spinal fluid was clear, drained
from the hole in your back,
but the X ray film
grew a stain on the lung,
explained the seizing cough,
the wailing heat of fever:
pneumonia at the age

of six weeks, a bedside vigil.
Your mother slept beside you,
the stitches of birth still burning.
When I asked, "Will he be OK?"
no one would answer: "Yes."
I closed my eyes and dreamed
my father dead, naked on a steel table
as I turned away. In the dream,
when I looked again,
my father had become my son.

So the hospital kept us: the oxygen mask,
a frayed wire taped to your toe
for reading the blood,
the medication forgotten from shift to shift,
a doctor bickering with radiology over the film,
the bald girl with a cancerous rib removed,
the pediatrician who never called, the yawning intern,
the hospital roommate's father
from Guatemala, ignored by the doctors
as if he had picked their morning coffee,
the checkmarks and initials at five AM,
the pages of forms flipping like a deck of cards,
recordkeeping for the records office,
the lawyers and the morgue.

One day, while the laundry
in the basement hissed white sheets,
and sheets of paper documented dwindling breath,
you spat mucus, gulped air, and lived.
We listened to the bassoon of your lungs,
the cadenza of the next century, resonate.
The Guatemalan father
did not need a stethoscope to hear
the breathing, and he grinned.
I grinned too, and because Clemente
means merciful, stood beside the Guatemalteco,
repeating in Spanish everything
that was not said to him.

I know someday you'll stand beside
the Guatemalan fathers,
speak in the tongue
of all the shunned faces,
breathe in a music
we have never heard, and live
by the meaning of your name.

Inevitably, we try to envision the next century. Will there be a men's movement in twenty years, when my son is an adult? Will it someday alienate and exclude Clemente, the way it has alienated and excluded me? The counterculture can be as exclusive and elitist as the mainstream; to be kept out of both is a supreme frustration. I sincerely do not expect the men's movement to address its own racism. The self-congratulatory tone of that movement drowns out any significant self-criticism. I only wish that the men's movement wouldn't be so *proud* of its own ignorance. The blatant expropriation of Native American symbols and rituals by certain factions of the movement leaves me with a twitch in my face. What should Puerto Rican men do in response to this colonizing definition of maleness, particularly considering the presence of our indigenous Tanío blood?

I remember watching one such men's movement ritual, on public television, I believe, and becoming infuriated because the drummer couldn't keep a beat. I imagined myself cloistered in a tent with some Anglo accountant from the suburbs of New Jersey, stripped to the waist and whacking a drum with no regard for rhythm, the difference being that I could hear Mongo Santamaría in my head, and he couldn't. I am torn between hoping that the men's movement reforms itself by the time my son reaches adulthood, or that it disappears altogether, its language going the way of Esperanto.

Another habit of language that I hope is extinct by the time Clemente reaches adulthood is the Anglo use of the term "macho." Before this term came into use to define sexism and violence, no particular ethnic or racial group was implicated by language itself. "Macho," as employed by Anglos, is a Spanish word that particularly seems to identify Latino male behavior as the very standard of sexism and violence. This connection, made by Anglos both intuitively and explicitly, then justifies a host of repressive measures against Latino males, as our presence on the honor roll of many a jail and prison will attest. In nearby Holyoke, police officers routinely round up Puerto Rican men drinking beer on the stoop, ostensibly for violating that city's "open container" ordinance, but also as a means of controlling the perceived threat of macho volatility on the street. Sometimes, of course, that perception turns deadly. I remember, at age fifteen, hearing about a friend of my father's, Martín "Tito" Pérez, who was "suicided" in a New York City jail cell. A grand jury determined that it is possible for a man to hang himself with his hands cuffed behind him.

While Latino male behavior is, indeed, all too often sexist and violent, Latino males in this country are in fact no worse in that regard than their Anglo counterparts. Arguably, European and European-American males have set the world standard for violence in the twentieth century, from the Holocaust to Hiroshima to Vietnam.

Yet, any assertiveness on the part of Latino males, especially any form of resistance to Anglo authority, is labeled macho and instantly discredited. I can recall one occasion, working for an "alternative" radio station in

Wisconsin, when I became involved in a protest over the station's refusal to air a Spanish-language program for the local Chicano community. When a meeting was held to debate the issue, the protesters, myself included, became frustrated and staged a walkout. The meeting went on without us, and we later learned we were *defended*, ironically enough, by someone who saw us as acting macho. "It's their culture," this person explained apologetically to the gathered liberal intelligentsia. We got the program on the air.

I return, ultimately, to that ventriloquist and his Puerto Rican dummy, and I return, too, to the simple fact that my example as a father will have much to do with whether Clemente frustrates the worshippers of stereotype. To begin with, my very *presence*—as an attentive father and husband—contradicts the stereotype. However, too many times in my life, I have been that Puerto Rican dummy, with someone else's voice coming out of my mouth, someone else's hand in my back making me flail my arms. I have read aloud a script of cruelty or rage, and swung wildly at imagined or distant enemies. I have satisfied audiences who expected the macho brute, who were thrilled when my shouting verified all their anthropological theories about my species. I served the purposes of those who would see the Puerto Rican species self-destruct, become as rare as the parrots of our own rain forest.

But in recent years, I have betrayed my puppeteers and disappointed the crowd. When my new sister-in-law met me, she pouted that I did not look Puerto Rican. I was not as "scary" as she expected me to be; I did not roar or flail. When a teacher at a suburban school invited me to read there, and openly expressed the usual unspoken expectations, the following incident occurred, proving that sometimes a belly laugh is infinitely more revolutionary than the howl of outrage that would have left me pegged, yet again, as a snarling, stubborn macho.

MY NATIVE COSTUME

When you come to visit,
said a teacher
from the suburban school,

don't forget to wear
your native costume.

But I'm a lawyer,
I said.
My native costume
is a pinstriped suit.

You know, the teacher said,
a Puerto Rican costume.

Like a guayabera?
The shirt? I said.

But it's February.
The children want to see
a native costume,
the teacher said.

So I went
to the suburban school,
embroidered guayabera
short sleeved shirt
over a turtleneck,
and said, Look kids
cultural adaptation.

The Puerto Rican dummy brought his own poems to read today. *Claro que sí.* His son is always watching.

2

FROM NOTHING, A CONSCIOUSNESS

HELEN ZIA

Helen Zia, the daughter of Chinese immigrants, grew up in the fifties when there were only 150,000 Chinese Americans in the entire country. An award-winning journalist, Zia has covered Asian American communities and social and political movements for more than twenty years. She lives in the San Francisco Bay Area.

Despite my deference to traditional Chinese behavior, the day finally came when I had to disobey my father. I had received several offers of full scholarships to attend college. Like the Chinese who lined up for the imperial civil service examinations in hopes of a new life, I viewed college as my means of escape from the narrow life of making flower shop baby novelties in our dull New Jersey town.

Though my father was proud of my educational achievement, he didn't want me to leave for college. He had already stated his desire for me to attend the closest school to home. When the time came for him to sign the college registration forms, he refused. "The proper place for an unmarried daughter is at home with her parents," he insisted. He wanted to keep me out of trouble until I found a husband to do the overseeing.

I could see the doors to my future slamming shut. At age seventeen, I had never knowingly disobeyed my father. I policed myself, turning down dates, invitations to parties, and even educational opportunities away from home, because I thought Dad would disapprove. I was caught between two conflicting Asian ideals. The Three Obediences* demanded subservience from females, but the primacy of education taught me to seek advancement through study. My American side told me to heed my own call.

Somehow I mustered the courage to shout, "No! I'm going to college." I don't know who was more surprised by my outburst, my father or me. He said nothing more about the subject, and I continued my preparations to leave. I also finally learned that the world wouldn't end if I challenged authority, a lesson I would take with me to college.

My father was right on one account—I intended to look for trouble in the campus political and social movements that appeared on the news each night. The call for civil rights was all around me, beginning in my own high school. Women's liberation offered an alternative to the Three Obediences. Then there was the war in Vietnam, involving yet another Asian enemy. My father was against the war because he saw U.S. involvement in Southeast Asia as a continuation of American domination over the people of Asia. At the dinner table my father lectured us about the immorality of the war; the next day I'd go to school and sit through government propaganda films and civics teachers condemning the Communist scourge and extolling the importance of the war effort to democracy.

For an Asian American kid, the worst part about the Vietnam War was watching the carnage on the news every night, with people who looked like my mom and dad machine-gunned from U.S. helicopters, scorched by American-made napalm, executed at point-blank range, igniting themselves with gasoline in protest, being massacred in their homes and ridiculed on TV shows. It seemed that we had killed the entire population of Vietnam many times over for all the dead who were reported in the body counts each night.

The constant barrage aimed at stirring up patriotic zeal against the Vietnamese enemy took its toll on Asian Americans, in the same way that the previous hostilities with Japan, China, and North Korea had. Many kids in my school had relatives fighting—and dying—in Vietnam. One classmate could barely look at me because I reminded her of the war that killed her older brother. Encountering her in gym class was awkward and sad. At the dry cleaner's and the doughnut shop where I worked in the summers, plenty

---

*[The daughter obeys the father, the wife obeys the husband, and, eventually, the widow obeys the son.]

of GIs would stop in, and some would have to comment. "They're every-where, aren't they?" a soldier customer said to his buddy as I handed him his laundered and starched fatigues. I had become the local personification of a war nearly ten thousand miles away. Since I looked like the enemy, I must be the enemy.

At the same time, there was no place for me in the debates over national issues like the war or racial equality. People like me were absent from every-thing that was considered to be "American"—from TV, movies, newspapers, history, and everyday discussions that took place in the school yard. It was hard to feel American when I wasn't treated like one. Yet I didn't feel Asian, either: I couldn't speak Chinese and I hardly knew Chinatown, let alone China. The void left me with many questions.

In the spring of my senior year in high school, the small group of Asian American undergraduates at Princeton University invited me to an orienta-tion meeting. My incoming first-year class had the largest number of Asian Americans ever—sixteen men and four women, nearly as many as the three upper classes combined. I was excited to be part of this tiny but growing Asian student body, coming to Princeton on a full scholarship, part of the wave that drove the university to open its doors to women for the first time in more than two hundred years. In the decades before my arrival, Princeton and the other Ivy League schools accepted only a few Asian students a year, most likely from Asia, not American-born Asians. Though I graduated from high school at the top of my class, I knew that I never would have been admitted to Princeton were it not for the civil rights movement. I was eager to find this movement, as soon as I could escape the watchful eyes of my parents.

The day of my orientation program happened to coincide with a massive student protest and strike at Princeton. The common areas were a sea of young people with placards, banners, and peace signs. Some were locked in earnest debate; others were simply playing Frisbee in the sun. Excited to have found my element, I headed to the Little Hall dormitory to meet the Asian American students.

When I and the handful of other visiting high school seniors knocked on the door that afternoon, we were shocked to find that our hosts were still asleep. About a half-dozen or so Asian American undergraduates were sprawled in various parts of the dorm suite. Strewn around them were beer cans, liquor bottles, ashtrays full of cigarette butts, and other paraphernalia. I was glad that my non-smoking, teetotaler parents had not come along, or I might never have made it to college after all. Our student mentors had been up all night, protesting, partying, debating the role that Asian American stu-dents should play in the Third World liberation movement and antiwar student strikes. They regaled us with tales of their lives as Asian American student protesters. I was on the road to discovering my own identity as an Asian American.

I wasn't alone in my quest. The Asian American baby boomers were all approaching college age. For the first time in American history, we were being admitted into colleges and universities in visible numbers as racial barriers began to come down. Some students were from immigrant families like mine, while others were multi-generation Americans.

The foreign-born Chinese students called us American-born types "jock sings," or "hollow bamboo"—Chinese on the outside, but empty inside. The kids from Hawaii were so much more secure in both their Asianness and their Americanness, having grown up in an Asian American majority; they called Japanese Americans from the mainland "katonks"—empty coconuts. The Chinatown kids seemed streetwise and hip, while students from places such as Phoenix, Buffalo, and Columbus were more like me, having grown up without seeing many faces like our own. Some Asian Americans I met called for Yellow Power, in the same spirit as Black Power advocates; others were so assimilated that they were called "bananas."

For the first time in my life, I heard about the internment of 120,000 Japanese Americans from third-generation—Sansei—Japanese American students. The experience of being incarcerated for presumed disloyalty was so painful that many of their parents refused to discuss it with them. I heard about Chinese "paper sons" who were "adopted" by Chinese men living in the United States after all immigration records were destroyed in the San Francisco earthquake of 1906. And about the Filipino "manongs"—old uncles—who worked the farms of California and the West, moving from harvest to harvest. We taught ourselves much of this information, using dog-eared mimeographed course syllabi gathered from Asian American courses in California and elsewhere like a new Holy Grail.

I began to make the connections between past history and my own life, understanding, for example, how the effort to deport my father in the early 1950s was linked to Chinese Americans of the 1800s. When the Immigration and Naturalization Service debated whether to permit my underemployed father to stay in the United States, the fact that he was the sole breadwinner for two infant U.S. citizens by birth swayed their decision. Henry and I were Americans thanks to an 1898 Supreme Court decision in response to a lawsuit by Wong Kim Ark.

I imagined people with Asian faces taking part in American life in a way that I had never before dreamed possible. A new generation of Asian Americans was injecting itself into national debates on civil rights, equality for women, poverty, workplace and labor issues, South African apartheid—we didn't limit the breadth of our vision. Just like the other baby boomers of all races in that 1960s and 1970s era, we knew we were making history. The excitement of that historical sweep added an element of grandeur to our activities; we weren't afraid to think big.

In the spring of 1971, a joint committee of the black, Latino, and Asian American students decided it was time to make the university address the racial inequities on campus. Princeton had very few students of color then, about a hundred in an undergraduate student body of nearly four thousand. We agreed that life at Princeton for students of color was akin to being stuck in a vast snowdrift, and it was time to thaw the university out. Our small numbers didn't deter us.

The leadership wanted to make a bold, definitive statement, so they decided that our loose grouping of minority students—Third World students—should seize and occupy Firestone Library and call for a massive rally at the University Chapel. We would denounce racism at Princeton and the racist war in Vietnam. We would demand an end to the war, as well as the creation of programs, courses, and a center for Third World students. To a first-year student from a sheltered Confucian home in New Jersey, this was the big time.

Princeton in 1971 was almost entirely male, having admitted its first women undergraduates in 1969. I was one of the half-dozen Asian American women students on campus, and the only one involved in this grandiose plan. Until then I assisted the guys by taking on useful "female" chores like learning to run a mimeograph machine. But this ambitious library plan caught us shorthanded, and somehow I was assigned the task of handling security for the takeover.

Firestone Library is bigger than most castles—and built like one. In my one previous attempt at security, I had installed a padlock on my bedroom door so my brothers wouldn't trash my room; that failed when they screwed the latch off the door. But I took my job very seriously and ran through all of Firestone, getting a good aerobic workout. Our little band of Third World men and a few women entered Firestone one afternoon and refused to come out. We secured the building and declared it occupied. I missed the main action, if there was any, because I was so busy running around and checking all the doors and windows.

The next day, we marched out of Firestone and declared victory before a huge rally at the chapel. My brush with student activism changed my life. Not just because of my successful tenure as security czar, during which I protected our sit-in from Princeton's wild squirrels, but because of the rally that followed. In the days leading up to our library takeover, it was somehow decided that several Asian Americans should speak about the racism of the Vietnam War. This was an important moment, because, as relative political newcomers, we would often defer to the more numerous black and Latino students. But we had a lot to say about racism and the war, and our Asian faces would make a powerful statement. It was also decided that an Asian woman should be among the speakers.

This idea posed a certain logistical problem, since there were so few Asian American female undergraduates. None of us would do it. I had never spoken to a group larger than my fifth-grade class, and the very idea made my stomach churn. Yet the thought that no one would talk about women of Vietnam and the war seemed terribly wrong. In the course of my patrol runs through Firestone the night before the rally, I decided that someone had to do it, even if it had to be me.

During our triumphant march out of the library and into the crowded chapel, packed with a thousand or more people, I fought nausea and panic. I had never met a Vietnamese woman, and what did I know about war? But my mother's stories rescued me: stories of the war that she had witnessed from her childhood spent fleeing Japanese soldiers, of the terrible brutality, of rape, torture, mutilation, and murder, and of the tremendous will to survive. I managed to walk through the long chapel without stumbling, and to speak of my mother's experiences and the inhumanity of this war.

After the rally, an undergraduate student from Vietnam thanked me. Marius Jansen, one of my professors and a distinguished scholar of Japanese history, gave me a puzzled look and told me I didn't sound like myself at all. His comment made me pause to think, for the first time, about the images I must project as an Asian American woman, and the images that might be projected back on me. Most of all, I was relieved and astonished that I, who a year earlier couldn't correct my teacher's pronunciation of my name, had spoken out loud. This Asian American movement was transforming me in a way such that I might transform others. Through it, I began to find my voice.

Finding my voice didn't always mean that my words were welcome, even among my Asian American pals. One day early in my second year, I was walking across campus with my classmate Alan, a street-smart Chinatown boy from California. We were headed to the newly established Third World Center—the prize from our student strike and occupation of the library. On the way, we argued over the relative importance of race and gender. "The revolution must fight racism first," Alan said to me. "Race is primary. Only after we eliminate racism can we fight sexism. Women will have to wait." It was like being at home with my brothers. I called Alan a male chauvinist; a pig, even.

Furious at such attitudes from our "revolutionary" Asian American brothers, the Asian American women at Princeton organized a seminar on Asian American women. Our numbers had grown enough to establish the first course on this topic on the East Coast, perhaps in the country. We didn't ask the men *not* to participate, but they didn't anyway. In our own space, we explored the social, historical, and political context of our mothers' and grandmothers' lives in Asia, their journeys to America, their experiences in sweatshops, on plantations, at home. We discussed our lives as Asian American women. I began to understand the Confucian hierarchy that forced women and girls into perpetual subordination. We, on the other hand, vowed never to accept being less than equal to our brothers.

But our class on Asian American women didn't explore the silences that our newly created Asian American "family" imposed on us. We didn't talk about sexual harassment or date rape within our own community. The language and the concepts didn't quite exist yet. But the incidents did. My academic adviser, a distinguished Chinese professor, gave unsolicited advice—about sex—to his female students during their faculty consultations. When the professor added such tidbits to the discussion of my thesis, my newly discovered voice failed me. I had run headlong into the quandary common to women of color and others from beleaguered communities: if we air our dirty laundry, we bring shame on ourselves and our community. With the status of Asian Americans so fragile, why drag down one of the few respected Asian American professors? Years later, I learned that another female student, a European American, had filed a report with the university. The esteemed professor had been disgraced—but, at least, not by one of "his own."

Women's liberation didn't offer much help at the time. I felt alienated after my visits to the campus women's center. The women I met were more interested in personal consciousness raising than social consciousness raising. I wanted to do both, but their lives as white women were so removed from mine, which was entwined with my life as an Asian American. Yet this distance didn't prove that race was primary, either. Other experiences made that clear, such as the time I met Gus Hall, a perennial candidate for president, on the ticket of the American Communist Party. He was speaking at Princeton with his running mate, Herbert Aptheker. Some Third World students were invited to a small luncheon for them; Alan and I went as representatives of the newly formed Asian American Students Association. Throughout the entire reception and luncheon, Hall and Aptheker, who were both white, spoke primarily to the African American students, pointedly ignoring Alan and me. To these American Communists, Asian Americans had no political currency; in their eyes, we didn't exist, or perhaps they assumed from our Asian faces that we were predisposed to support China, a bitter foe of the Soviets. It was the first time I witnessed such a blatant race ploy by political "progressives," but it wouldn't be the last.

A whole generation of Asian Americans was getting an education about our identity. We couldn't wait to leave the safe confines of our campuses, to share our lessons and our pride in this newfound heritage. Many of us went into Asian American enclaves as community organizers, intent on making changes there. Our campus experiences made it abundantly clear that if Asian Americans were to take our rightful place in American society, we would have to scratch and dig and blast our way in, much as the railroad workers had through the Rockies one hundred years earlier.

Few in America, or even in our own communities, paid much attention to these young Asian Americans. Among the separate—and expanding—Asian immigrant groups, the vision of pan-Asian unity was not compelling; survival was their main focus.

Still, a dynamic process was set in motion: we were reclaiming our stake in a land and a history that excluded us, transforming a community that was still in the process of becoming. We were following our destinies as Asian Americans.

3

THE PAST IS EVER PRESENT
Recognizing the New Racism

PATRICIA HILL COLLINS

Patricia Hill Collins is professor of sociology at the University of Maryland, College Park, and author of *Black Feminist Thought: Knowledge, Consciousness, and the Politics of Empowerment* (2000); *Black Sexual Politics: African Americans, Gender, and the New Racism* (2004); and *From Black Power to Hip Hop: Racism, Nationalism, and Feminism* (2006).

> *It's just me against the world, baby, me against the world.*
> *I got nothin' to lose—it's just me against the world.*
>
> —*TUPAC SHAKUR*

Black youth born after the great social movements of the 1950s and 1960s should have faced a bright future. Social movements of the past fifty years celebrated victories over historical forms of racism, perhaps naively believing that they were creating a new foundation for this new generation. The end of colonialism and dismantling of racial apartheid within the United States and in South Africa signaled the possibilities for antiracist, democratic societies in which Blackness would no longer serve as a badge of inferiority. Yet the actual social conditions that confront this global cohort and their responses to it have turned out to be quite different. When it comes to Black youth, poor housing, inferior education, precarious health status, and dwindling job prospects reoccur across diverse societies. Whether in newly democratic nation-states such as South Africa, African nation-states that have had formal independence for over thirty years, advanced industrial societies such as the United States, Great Britain, France, and Germany, or historically independent states of the Caribbean and Latin America, youth who are noticeably of African descent fare worse than their lighter-skinned counterparts. For many, Tupac Shakur's words, "I got nothin' to lose—it's just me against the world," ring true.

Victory over one form of racism has not, apparently, ensured triumph over others. How is it that social conditions can change so dramatically yet still relegate Black youth to the bottom of the social hierarchy?[1] As hip-hop social critic Bakari Kitwana points out, "now more than ever . . . divided generations must begin to understand the ways that the new Black youth culture both empowers and undermines Black America. As brilliant a moment in history as the civil rights and Black power eras were, the older generation must realize they cannot claim any real victory if the hip-hop generation cannot build significantly on those gains."[2] The emergence of a new Black youth culture in the United States that simultaneously empowers and undermines African American progress signals a new phase in the contours of racism itself as well as antiracist initiatives that will be needed to counter it.

What's new about this new racism? First, new patterns of corporate organization have made for an increasingly global economy. In particular, the concentration of capital in a few corporations has enabled them to shape many aspects of the global economy. One outcome is that, on a global scale, wealth and poverty continue to be racialized, with people of African descent disproportionately poor.[3] Second, local, regional, and national governmental bodies no longer yield the degree of power that they once did in shaping racial policies. The new racism is transnational.[4] One can now have racial inequality that does not appear to be regulated by the state to the same degree. For example, the legal support given racial segregation in the United States has been abandoned yet African Americans remain disproportionately at the bottom of the social hierarchy. Third, the new racism relies more heavily on the manipulation of ideas within mass media. These new techniques present hegemonic ideologies that claim that racism is over. They work to obscure the racism that does exist, and they undercut antiracist protest.[5] Globalization, transnationalism, and the growth of hegemonic ideologies within mass media provide the context for a new racism that has catalyzed changes within African, Black American, and African-Diasporic societies. From one society to the next, Black youth are at risk, and, in many places, they have become identified as problems to their nation, to their local environments, to Black communities, and to themselves.[6]

This new racism reflects the juxtaposition of old and new, in some cases a continuation of long-standing practices of racial rule and, in other cases, the development of something original. In the United States, the persistence of poor housing, poor health, illiteracy, unemployment, family upheaval, and social problems associated with poverty and powerlessness all constitute new variations of the negative effects of colonialism, slavery, and traditional forms of racial rule. The new racism reflects sedimented or past-in-present racial formations from prior historical periods.[7] Some elements of prior racial formations persist virtually unchanged, and others are transformed in response to globalization, transnationalism, and the proliferation of mass media. Each racial formation reflects distinctive links among characteristic forms of economic and political exploitation, gender-specific ideologies developed to justify Black exploitation, and African American men's and women's reactions both to the political economy and to one another. Each also generated distinctive African American political responses that aimed to provide a better life for each generation of Black youth.

• • •

The Closing Door: The Post–Civil Rights Era

Many accounts of the vanishing color line make little room for the Tupac Shakurs among contemporary Black youth. Instead, they celebrate a new multicultural America that seems bent on sweeping Tupac's nihilism under the rug and relegating racism to the dustbins of the past. For example, in *Love's Revolution,* Maria Root points to increased rates of interracial marriage, especially for Black men, as evidence of a "revolution" in values that is ushering in a new nonracial America.[8] Identifying the growth of a new Black middle class as evidence of racial uplift, well-respected social scientist William Julius Wilson argues that racism diminishes the further up the economic ladder African Americans climb.[9] In this regard, he joins other scholars who view the racial ideologies and practices of Latin American nations where "money whitens" as applicable for American race relations. All of these factors matter—mass media, marital rates, and a changing social class structure all indicate that former patterns of racial segregation have given way to something new. But what?

For all Americans, the political, economic, and social reorganization of American society that began in the 1970s and took shape during the 1980s and 1990s suggested that a more democratic, multicultural America was at hand. Politically, much changed in the United States. Social movements by Blacks, Latinos, women, and gays and lesbians, among others, catalyzed a changing legal climate in the United States. In a span of less than twenty-five years, legal reforms set the stage for the erosion of a wide array of mechanisms for reproducing social inequality in American society. In addition to the 1954 *Brown v. Board of Education* Supreme Court decision, in the decades that followed, the Civil Rights Act of 1964 prohibited discrimination on the basis of race, color, religion, sex, age, ethnicity, or national origin; the Fair Housing Law of 1968 prohibited discrimination against people seeking housing on the basis of race, color, religion, or national origin; and the Voting Rights Act of 1965 repealed local discriminatory practices against African American voters, an act amended in 1975 and 1982 to include linguistic minorities. The Immigration Act of 1965 removed barriers to immigration for people from primarily non-White nations. The 1967 *Loving v. Virginia* Supreme Court decision removed all legal barriers to interracial marriage. In 2003, in *Lawrence and Garner v. Texas,* the Supreme Court struck down an antisodomy law that made it illegal for same sex partners to engage in sexual conduct that was allowed for different sex partners. In essence, the court ruled that the sexual practices of LGBT people were covered under privacy laws. Collectively, this new legal infrastructure provided a legal context for challenging deep-seated customs across virtually all segments of American society.

In contrast to the victories in the legal system, the changing contours of residential racial segregation during the twenty-year period from 1980 to 2000 suggested that, for many African Americans, this new multicultural America would remain elusive. In 1999, African Americans (55.1 percent) were far more likely than non-Hispanic Whites (21.7 percent) to live inside the central city boundaries of metropolitan areas.[10] This overarching framework of disproportionately Black central cities and disproportionately White greater metropolitan areas produced new patterns of residential racial segregation. While residential racial segregation declined overall, for large segments of the Black population, especially poor and working-class African Americans, residential racial resegregation within urban areas persisted.[11] The concentration of poor and working-class Black people in racially segregated neighborhoods has been so severe in metropolitan areas with large Black populations, that it is often described as "hypersegregation."[12]

By the 2000 census, the African American population numbered 36.4 million people and was characterized by clear social class differences that took geographic form within patterns of racial segregation.[13] For middle-class African Americans and for those working-class African Americans who were able to move into the middle class, the Black political movements of the 1960s and 1970s delivered tangible, albeit tenuous, gains. The proportion of African Americans in the middle class clearly grew in this new legal climate, spurred by new opportunities that allowed many African Americans to join the middle class for the first time.[14] Women and men who acquired jobs as managers in corporations and government agencies, as well as certain staff and line positions in these sectors, benefited from the changed political climate. African American physicians, lawyers, teachers, university professors, engineers, journalists, and other professionals typically procured sufficient job security, job autonomy, decision-making power, and good salaries and benefits that enabled them to move into or up within a growing Black middle class.[15]

An increasingly heterogeneous Black middle class emerged, based in part on the paths that they followed to get there.[16] Some well-off African Americans were positioned to take advantage of the opportunities created by the civil rights movement. Their families had been middle-class for generations, had participated in Black community politics, and had functioned as a Black bourgeoisie or leadership class.[17] Far more African Americans arrived via the route of individual social mobility from the working class. This upward mobility typically required access to higher education; the protections provided by strong antidiscrimination and affirmative action programs in education and employment; the assimilation of White norms and values, including those concerning gender and sexuality; as well as the social skills needed to handle increasing contact with White people as colleagues and friends. No matter how they arrived in the Black middle class, many well-off Blacks engaged in yet another migration, this time out of African American inner-city neighborhoods into racially integrated urban and suburban neighborhoods. The Census Bureau reports that from 1980 to 2000 residential racial segregation declined for African Americans (although it was still higher than any other group).[18] Although these communities routinely resegregated and often became all-Black enclaves, they did provide better housing, schools, and facilities for African American children.[19]

Ideally, African American children growing up in middle-class neighborhoods would retain the class benefits provided by their parents. There is some evidence that passing on middle-class economic gains in the post–civil rights era may be far more difficult than originally thought, in part, due to the proximity of Black middle-class neighborhoods to working-class and poor Black communities. Mary Patillo-McCoy's study of the difficulties faced by Black youth in the fictional Chicago neighborhood of Groveland illustrates the pressures facing middle-class Black youth. For one, they are often mistaken for delinquents by security guards and other officials because they mimic the dress, walk, and talk of working-class Black youth. In this way, stylistic choices often have tangible material consequences. For another, in a community in which the influences of ghetto life permeate everyday life, embracing ghetto styles takes on different meaning than for youth who are in predominantly White middle-class neighborhoods: "sometimes, when you dress like a gangsta, talk like a gangsta, and rap like a gangsta, soon enough you *are* a gangsta."[20]

Many poor and working-class African Americans need not assume the trappings of gangstas—the lack of economic options in their neighborhoods pressures them to become gangstas. For Black youth who feel they have "nothin' to lose" because they lack access to the housing, education, health care, and jobs needed for upward social mobility, the political victories of the civil rights and Black power movements failed to produce the promised economic development envisioned by civil rights activists. The hope was that the opportunities for Black working-class children would continue after the victories of the civil rights and Black power movements. But four back-to-back recessions in the 1970s, a growing White backlash against equal opportunity, and the ascendancy of conservative Republican administrations under Ronald Reagan (1980–1988) and George Bush (1988–1992) as well as the election of George W. Bush to the presidency in 2000 combined to shatter this expectation. In the 1980s, Republican administrations set about dismantling enforcement efforts for equal opportunity, cutting funding for urban programs, incarcerating growing numbers of African Americans in the burgeoning prison industry, shrinking the social welfare budget through punitive measures, and endorsing historical labor market patterns.[21] Fearful of losing conservative White voters who had traditionally supported the Democratic Party, party leaders shifted the party to the right. For example, in 1996, Democratic president Bill Clinton signed the Personal Responsibility and Work Opportunity Reconciliation Act, a law that, despite its lofty title, effectively shifted social welfare programs back to the states and signaled a retrenchment from federal social welfare programs.[22]

Participants in civil rights and Black Nationalist struggles saw their activism as providing opportunities for the next generation of Black youth to live better lives. They reasonably expected that, as did earlier generations of African Americans, Black youth living in inner-city areas might use routes for upward social mobility to better themselves. Instead, as the music of Tupac Shakur and other hip-hop artists reminds us, the door of economic opportunity closed and routes for upward social mobility seem distant memories. For far too many Black youth, inner-city neighborhoods have become dumping grounds, as one observer describes it, "jobless, crime-ridden ghettos [that] have become glorified, modern-day concentration camps."[23] Within inner-city neighborhoods, public schools are dilapidated, teachers are underpaid and overwhelmed, guns and the informal drug economy have made African American neighborhoods dangerous, and jobs have vanished.[24] Gone are the sports programs, music, debate clubs, and other elements of public school education that helped poor and working-class youth stay in school.

Poor and working-class Black youth who grew up in the 1980s and 1990s, often within racially segregated, inner-city neighborhoods, encountered markedly different economic, political, and social conditions than those that faced their parents or those provided to middle-class youth of all races. Despite coming of age during a time of unprecedented social change, regardless of gender, opportunities for poor Black youth eroded. For example, for children under age eighteen the poverty rate is consistently three times higher for Black children than for White children—in 1998, it was 37 percent for Black children versus 11 percent for non-Hispanic White children.[25] When it comes to poverty among Black children, gender did not make a significant difference. Black males under age eighteen had a poverty rate of 36 percent and Black females a rate of 37.3 percent.[26] With over one-third of all Black youth living in poverty, mainly in inner-city, racially segregated neighborhoods, young Black men and women *both* face limited prospects for quality education, well-paid employment, and stable family life. At the same time, poor and working-class Black youth also face gender-specific challenges in two main areas: (1) eroding work and family structures within urban Black working-class neighborhoods; and (2) the changing contours of Black working-class culture assaulted by drugs, crime, and guns.

The most noteworthy structural changes within African American working-class neighborhoods in the post–World War II period concern work and family.[27] Joblessness fosters family disruption for both men and women, and the effects on each have taken gender-specific forms. In this regard, the rapid growth of a criminal justice system that ensnares large numbers of young, working-class, urban African American men has separated them from their families and left many with slim prospects for stable family life. There appears to be no place for young Black men in urban labor markets, but there is one in jails and prisons. Since 1980, whatever measures are used—rates of arrest, conviction, jail time, parole, or types of crime—African American men are more likely than White American men to encounter the criminal justice system. For example, in 1990, the non-profit Washington, D.C. based Sentencing Project released a survey suggesting that, on an average day in the United States, one in every four African American men aged 20–29 was either in prison, jail, or on probation/parole.[28] Incarcerating young Black men is profitable. The privatized prison industry capitalizes on the growth of prisons. This industry consists of a network of private corporations that provide every service imaginable to prisons and inmates, from prison construction and operation to telecommunications services, food, clothing, and medicine. Corporations also capitalize on cheap prison labor.[29] Jobless Blacks collecting unemployment insurance are unprofitable. In contrast, "the inroads that have been made in privatizing the prison industry have created a profit motive for keeping young Blacks locked up."[30]

In this context, women are left to head families, a structural change with great implications for African American youth and for Black working-class neighborhoods. By 1999, less than one-half (47 percent) of all Black families were married-couple families, 45 percent were maintained by women with no spouses present, while only 8 percent were maintained by men with no spouses present.[31] Families maintained by Black women are not inherently worse than those maintained by married couples but a sizeable majority of Black families that are maintained by women live in poverty.[32] Family income, however, is greatly affected by having a male earner in the household, primarily because men on average earn far more than women when they are able to find work. Family composition affects family income. For example, in 1998, 20.8 percent of Black families maintained by married couples had incomes less than $25,000. The corresponding percentage for Black families maintained by men with no spouse present was 43.1 percent and by Black women with no spouse present was 66.8 percent.[33] The lowest percentage of families with income under $25,000 was found among married couple families (20.8), the highest among families headed by single mothers (66.8), and the middle by single fathers heading families (43.1).

These structural changes in work and family affected the quality of life in Black urban neighborhoods, and they catalyzed changes within Black working-class culture. During the onslaught of drugs and guns in the 1980s, Black working-class neighborhoods simply became more dangerous. Residents of working-class, urban Black communities increasingly beset by drugs and crime used the terms "decent" and "street" families to distinguish stable yet vulnerable working-class families from working-class families in crisis.[34] In this context, the "decent" families, those where members had some connection to traditional jobs in the formal blue-collar labor market or the secondary labor markets, struggled to get by. Plagued by chronic unemployment, these families confronted uncertain industrial jobs, underpaid clerical work, and low-paid service work. Such families may move in and out of the social welfare system and individuals within these "decent" families may have difficulties with the police. In contrast, "street" families, those who have largely fallen out of the formal labor market and whose fate is linked to the informal economy of the global drug industry, have more tenuous connections to school, employment, and other markers of citizenship. They too may move in and out of the social welfare and penal systems, but they hold little hope of ever being "decent' or even wanting to become "decent."

Gender matters in this working-class variation of the tension between Black respectability and Black authenticity, between being "decent" and "street." The growth of the prison culture in the 1980s greatly influenced African American social organization, especially for young African American men. In particular, the arrest and imprisonment of Black street gangs in the 1970s and 1980s fostered more pronounced and organized gang structures within prisons that became conduits for hierarchies of masculinity. Prison gangs inevitably became connected to their street gang counterparts (in fact, many join gangs while in prison, primarily for protection). As the line between street gangs and prison gangs blurred, so did the distinctions between prison culture, street culture, and some aspects of Black youth culture. More important, this growing interconnectedness of prison, street, and youth culture, with the importance given to hierarchies of masculinity, affects African American neighborhoods and families. The valorization of thug life within Black youth culture, the growing misogyny within heterosexual love relationships, and the increased visibility (and some would say the increased virulence) of homophobic violence targeted to gay, lesbian, and bisexual African Americans all seem to be casualties of the incarceration of African American men and the ceaseless need to prove one's "manhood."[35]

Black women have often found themselves on the front line in dealing with issues that affect Black men. As girlfriends and wives, Black women are often the ones who bear the brunt of Black men's anger at a racism that has and continues to operate so thoroughly through gendered practices and ideologies. Reflecting the realities of street culture, some forms of rap music may serve the purpose of political expression concerning racism, but they also now operate as an important site for the spread of sexism and homophobia. Male artists who refer to Black girls and women as "bitches," "hos," "freaks," "skeezers," "gold diggers," and "chickenheads" malign Black women, "decent" and "street" alike. Protesting this misogyny in rap, Johnnetta Cole and Beverly Guy-Sheftall contend: "We are concerned because we believe that hip-hop is more misogynist and disrespectful of Black girls and women than other popular music genres. The casual references to rape and other forms of violence and the soft-porn visuals and messages of many rap music videos are seared into the consciousness of young Black boys and girls at an early age."[36]

Despite the misogyny that takes the form of Black women-blaming that permeates American culture, Black mothers who struggle to retain "decent" families remain justifiably worried about the effects of "street culture" on their sons. Black daughters often misunderstand this concern until they become mothers. Several African American autobiographies, especially those written by Black women, identify this theme of Black mothers who treat their sons differently from their daughters. For example, in her memoir *An American Story,* journalist Debra Dickerson describes her childhood as one of five siblings, four girls and one boy. Despite her academic achievements, her mother ignored her whereas her brother, who routinely did poorly, was repeatedly forgiven for his misdeeds.[37] In her aptly titled volume, *Mama's Girl,* Veronica Chambers reports similar differential treatment: "my brother . . . was the only person I ever met who almost flunked kindergarten. He was smart—eventually he would test better in math than I did—but he was badly behaved. As he got older, his behavior got worse, until it reached the point where he was always talking back to the teachers and never bothered to do any of the work."[38] Chambers's mother was so worried about her son that his actions formed the subject of many conversations with her women friends. Chambers felt neglected: "there was never any talk about me or what I needed. I was just a quick rest stop in their marathon conversations."[39]

Dickerson and Chambers viewed their mothers' behavior through the lens of childhood, and they came to the conclusion that a certain inequality stemmed from this differential treatment. But Black mothers who worry about the fate of their sons because they are single parents living in dangerous neighborhoods may also be reacting to bona fide threats to their sons' well-being. African American women are often particularly afraid for their sons, fearing that their son's race and size might get them killed for no reason. Marita Golden captures this fear for her son Michael growing up in Washington, D.C.:

> My son careened into adolescence. I heard the deepening of Michael's voice, witnessed the growth spurts that propelled him to a height that echoed his father's, saw the sudden appearance of muscles. . . . I was flushed with trepidation. Soon Michael would inhabit that narrow, corrupt crawl space in the minds of whites and some black people too, a space reserved for criminals, outcasts, misfits, and black men. Soon he would become a permanent suspect. [40]

Golden knew that her son must leave boyhood behind, but she sees all too clearly the costs of doing so. She does not want to join the legions of Black women who attend funerals, burying children who are far younger than they are.

These new social relations that disrupt Black families, incarcerate young men, leave Black women as single mothers, and foster new forms of Black working-class culture constitute yet another racial formation that builds upon and changes those of the past. Chattel slavery as a distinct form of bondage, the labor exploitation of rural Southern agriculture, and urban industrialization and the racial segregation of Black populations through ghettoization have all left their mark on today. These three racial formations may have peaked during specific periods of African American history, but now they overlap, draw strength from one another, and continue to contribute to the new racism. For example, reflecting this past-in-present racism, pockets of rural poverty in the contemporary American South are a direct consequence of sharecropping and other agricultural policies and technologies of the postemancipation South. Similarly, African American hyper-ghettos in Baltimore, Philadelphia, Detroit, Chicago, and other large metropolitan areas as well as urban/suburban housing patterns that make many cities *de facto* Black ghettos, are direct descendents of policies of *de facto* racial segregation developed during the height of urban industrialization. Even slavery persists, but not in the form of chattel slavery experienced by enslaved Africans in the American South. If one defines slavery as "the total control of one person by another for the purpose of economic exploitation,"[41] children and young women and men involved in prostitution and the situation of illegal immigrants held in debt bondage to pay off the cost of their passage constitute reworked versions of slavery.

Just as emerging structures of the new racism constitute a reformulation of former racial formations, the closing door of racial opportunity of the post—civil rights era also invokes ideas and practices about class, gender, and sexuality associated with those prior periods. All three past-in-present racial formations have effects that endure into the present and are likely to persist, regardless of changes in ideology. In *The Debt*, African American social critic Randall Robinson describes the legacy of these prior racial formations: "No nation can enslave a race of people for hundreds of years, set them free bedraggled and penniless, pit them, without assistance in a hostile environment, against privileged victimizers, and then reasonably expect the gap between the heirs of the two groups to narrow. Lines, begun parallel and left alone, can never touch."[42]

The contemporary closing door of opportunity must be judged in the context of prior racial formations dedicated to maintaining the "parallel lines" of separate and unequal opportunities and outcomes. Legal changes are necessary, but they are far from sufficient in responding to a new seemingly colorblind racism where the past is ever present. Contemporary ideas about race, gender, and sexuality did not drop from the sky. In this context, neither Black men nor women can win an oppression contest, because both face different challenges raised by the new racism. Both suffer from different expressions of the disappearing hope that the closing door of opportunity represents.

NOTES

1. For a comprehensive analysis of this same theme as it applies to African American women, see my discussion of the new politics of containment in Chapter 2 of *Fighting Words* (Collins 1998, 11–43).

2. Kitwana 2002, 23.

3. For discussions of various aspects of globalization, race, and inequality, see Bales 1999; Lusane 1997; Bauman 1998; Mohanty 1997.

4. For a general overview of how race operates in a transnational framework, see Winant 2001. The framework of transnationalism is less often applied to African American experiences than those of Latinos.

5. For representative works on new racist ideologies, see Crenshaw 1997; Guinier and Torres 2002; Bonilla-Silva 2001; and Goldberg 1993. For race and media, see Entman and Rojecki 2000. For representative works in the field of Black cultural studies, consult Kelley 1994; Kelley 1997; Gates 1992; Neal 2002; Dent 1992b; Hall 1992; Dyson 1996.

6. For example, much attention has been given to the important issue of the poor school performance of African American youth (Fordham 1996), and Black males in particular (Arnett Ferguson 2000). Afro-Caribbean immigrants to the United Kingdom express similar concerns with their children's performance. This theme of Black youth being denied access to education and/or receiving differential treatment by schools run by dominant groups reappears across societies. Despite similar disadvantages among Black youth worldwide, a transnational discourse addressing issues peculiar to Black youth has not yet surfaced.

7. For a comprehensive treatment of racial formation theory, see Omi and Winant 1994.

8. Root 2001.

9. Wilson 1978.

10. McKinnon and Humes 2000, 2.

11. Five measures of racial residential segregation are typically used. Evenness measures the differential distribution of the population. Exposure measures potential contact among racial groups. Concentration refers to the relative amount of physical space occupied by a racial group. Centralization indicates the degree to which a racial group is located near the center of an urban area. Clustering measures the degree to which racial groups live disproportionately in contiguous areas (Iceland, Weinberg, and Steinmetz 2002, 7–10). The literature reports declines in residential racial segregation for African Americans across all five measures. However, the largest metropolitan areas (1 million or more population) had higher residential segregation than the middle-sized ones (500,000 to 999,999), which in turn had higher rates than smaller ones. The size of the metropolitan area and the size of the Black population within it seem to matter. Three of the five indexes showed a pattern of higher segregation in places with a higher percentage of Blacks in 2000, while two showed the reverse. In particular, as the percentage of the population that is Black increased, Blacks were (1) less likely to be evenly spread across the metropolitan area; (2) less likely to share common neighborhoods with Whites (isolation index); and (3) more likely to live near other Blacks (spatial proximity index) (Iceland, Weinberg, and Steinmetz 2002, 63).

12. For an analysis of racial segregation, see Massey and Denton 1993. Also, see Oliver and Shapiro 1995, 15–23. In 2000, the five most segregated metropolitan areas for Black people were Milwaukee, Detroit, Cleveland, St. Louis, and Newark. Cincinnati, Buffalo, and New York were roughly tied for sixth place, and the top ten was rounded out by Chicago and Philadelphia (although Philadelphia was roughly tied with Kansas City, New Orleans, and Indianapolis) (Iceland, Weinberg, and Steinmetz 2002, 68). By 2000, African Americans constituted a sizeable percentage of the populations of large American cities. Of the ten largest areas in the United States, Detroit had the largest proportion of Black

people (83 percent), followed by Philadelphia (44 percent), and Chicago (38 percent). Two places—New York and Chicago—together accounted for nine percent of the total Black population. The ten largest places for Blacks accounted for 20 percent of the total Black population (McKinnon 2001, 7).

13. McKinnon 2001.

14. The criteria used to define social class, for example, educational attainment, occupational level, and income, affect estimates of the size of the Black middle class. Here I emphasize occupational characteristics because these demonstrate race/gender patterns that are central to the arguments in this essay.

15. Race and gender differences characterize this movement of African Americans into professional and managerial jobs. In 1999, the proportion of employed non-Hispanic White men (32 percent) in managerial and professional occupations was almost twice that of Black men (17 percent). Non-Hispanic White women (35 percent) were more likely than Black women (24 percent) to be in these positions. In this regard, White men and women were far closer in occupational status (32 and 35 percent) than Black men and women (17 and 24 percent) (McKinnon and Humes 2000).

16. This heterogeneity within the Black middle class should not obscure the major differences between middle-class Blacks and Whites. For an analysis of these differences in income and wealth, see Oliver and Shapiro 1995, 91–125.

17. Graham 2000.

18. Iceland, Weinberg, and Steinmetz 2002, 3–4.

19. Patillo-McCoy 1999.

20. Patillo-McCoy 1999, 123.

21. Race and gender also influenced the continued concentration of Black men and women in less desirable jobs. For example, Black men (17 percent) are more than twice as likely as White men (8 percent) to work in service occupations and almost twice as likely (31 percent compared to 17 percent) to be operators, fabricators, and laborers. Black women (27 percent) were more likely than non-Hispanic White women (15 percent) to be employed in service occupations (McKinnon and Humes 2000, 4). In essence, gender-segmented jobs of laborers and service work continued to characterize the occupational experiences of poor and working-class African Americans.

22. Much has been written about the PRWOR Act. For a discussion of how this act fits into a frame of "welfare racism," see Neubeck and Cazenave 2001, 115–144.

23. Kitwana 2002, 48.

24. Squires 1994.

25. McKinnon and Humes 2000, 5.

26. McKinnon and Humes 2000, 6.

27. Franklin 1997, 153–214.

28. Miller 1996, 1–9.

29. Kitwana 2002, 71–76.

30. Kitwana 2002, 76.

31. McKinnon and Humes 2000, 2.

32. Definitions of poverty seem to matter greatly in who gets counted as poor. In 1998, the official poverty threshold for a family of four was $16,600, leaving a sizeable gap between the $25,000 income threshold reported here and official poverty. Whatever the family composition, Black families are poorer than White ones, with families headed by Black women with no spouse present poorer than all. In 1998, poverty was highest in families maintained by women with no

spouse present: 41 percent for Blacks compared to 21 percent for non–Hispanic Whites (McKinnon and Humes 2000, 6).

33. Varying explanations have been given for these patterns. William Julius Wilson's research links patterns of family organization to the changing contours of economic opportunities in Black urban neighborhoods (Wilson 1996; Wilson 1987). Wilson's research highlights how growing joblessness among African American men in the 1960s and 1970s correlates with (but does not necessarily cause) increasing rates of African American mother-child families. His work documents how the emergence of mother-child families among working-class African Americans can be attributed, in part, to a changing political economy that disadvantaged U.S. Blacks. Others criticize capitalist development itself (Squires 1994).

34. Anderson 1999.

35. The crisis within contemporary gender politics sparked Cole and Guy-Sheftall to write their book: "Now is a particularly critical time for *Gender Talk* because of what we perceive to be an embattled Black, mostly male leadership, a deepening crisis in Black male-female relationships, an embrace of patriarchal family values, and a backlash against feminism and Black feminists" (Cole and Guy-Sheftall 2003, xxxii).

36. Cole and Guy-Sheftall 2003, 186.

37. Dickerson 2000.

38. Chambers 1996, 44.

39. Chambers 1996, 46.

40. Golden 1995, 68.

41. Bales 1999, 6.

42. Robinson 2000, 74.

REFERENCES

Anderson, Elijah. 1999. *Code of the Street: Decency, Violence and the Moral Life of the Inner City*. New York: W. W. Norton.

Arnett Ferguson, Ann. 2000. *Bad Boys: Public Schools in the Making of Black Masculinity*. Ann Arbor: University of Michigan Press.

Bales, Kevin. 1999. *Disposable Slavery: New Slavery in the Global Economy*. Berkeley: University of California Press.

Bauman, Zygmunt. 1998. *Globalization: The Human Consequences*. New York: Columbia University Press.

Bonilla-Silva, Eduardo. 1996. "Rethinking Racism: Toward a Structural Interpretation." *American Sociological Review* 62 (June): 465–480.

Chambers, Veronica. 1996. *Mama's Girl*. New York: Riverhead Books.

Cole, Johnnetta Betsch, and Beverly Guy-Sheftall. 2003. *Gender Talk: The Struggle for Women's Equality in African American Communities*. New York: Ballantine.

Collins, Patricia Hill. 1998. *Fighting Words: Black Women and the Search for Justice*. Minneapolis: University of Minnesota Press.

Crenshaw, Kimberlé Williams. 1997. "Color Blindness, History, and the Law." *The House That Race Built*. Ed. Wahneema Lubiano, 280–288. New York: Pantheon.

Dent, Gina, ed. 1992b. *Black Popular Culture*. Seattle: Bay Press.

Dickerson, Debra J. 2000. *An American Story*. New York: Anchor.

Dyson, Michael. 1996. *Between God and Gangsta Rap: Bearing Witness to Black Culture*. New York: Oxford University Press.

Entman, Robert M., and Rojecki Andrew. 2000. *The Black Image in the White Mind: Media and Race in America*. Chicago: University of Chicago Press.

Fordham, Signithia. 1996. *Blacked Out: Dilemmas of Race, Identity, and Success at Capital High.* Chicago: University of Chicago Press.

Franklin, Donna L. 1997. *Ensuring Inequality: The Structural Transformation of the African-American Family.* New York: Oxford University Press.

Gates, Henry Louis. 1992. *Loose Canons: Notes on the Culture Wars.* New York: Oxford University Press.

Goldberg, David Theo. 1993. *Racist Culture: Philosophy and the Politics of Meaning.* Cambridge, Mass.: Blackwell.

Golden, Marita. 1995. *Saving Our Sons: Raising Black Children in a Turbulent World.* New York: Doubleday.

Graham, Lawrence Otis. 2000. *Our Kind of People: Inside America's Black Upper Class.* New York: HarperPerennial.

Guinier, Lani, and Gerald Torres. 2002. *The Miner's Canary: Enlisting Race, Resisting Power, Transforming Democracy.* Cambridge, Mass.: Harvard University Press.

Hall, Stuart. 1992. "What Is This 'Black' in Black Popular Culture?" *Black Popular Culture.* Ed. Gina Dent, 21–33. Seattle: Bay Press.

Iceland, John, Daniel H. Weinberg, and Erika Steinmetz. 2002. *Racial and Ethnic Residential Segregation in the United States: 1980–2000,* U.S. Census Bureau, Series CENSR-3. Washington, D.C.: U.S. Government Printing Office.

Kelley, Robin D. G. 1994. *Race Rebels: Culture, Politics, and the Black Working Class.* New York: Free Press.

———. 1997. *Yo' Mama's DisFUNKtional!: Fighting the Culture Wars in Urban America.* Boston: Beacon Press.

Kitwana, Bakari. 2002. *The Hip Hop Generation: Young Blacks and the Crisis in African-American Culture.* New York: Basic Books.

Lusane, Clarence. 1997. *Race in the Global Era: African Americans at the Millennium.* Boston: South End Press.

Massey, Douglas S., and Nancy A. Denton. 1993. *American Apartheid: Segregation and the Making of the Underclass.* Cambridge, Mass.: Harvard University Press.

McKinnon, Jesse. 2001. *The Black Population: 2000.* Vol. C2KBR/01–5. U.S. Census Bureau. Washington, D.C.: U.S. Government Printing Office.

McKinnon, Jesse, and Karen Humes. 2000. *The Black Population in the United States: March 1999.* Current Population Reports, Series P20–530. U.S. Census Bureau. Washington, D.C.: U.S. Government Printing Office.

Miller, Jerome G. 1996. *Search and Destroy: African-American Males in the Criminal Justice System.* New York: Cambridge University Press.

Mohanty, Chandra Talpade. 1997. "Women Workers and Capitalist Scripts: Ideologies of Domination, Common Interests, and the Politics of Solidarity." *Feminist Genealogies, Colonial Legacies, Democratic Futures.* Ed. M. Jacqui Mohanty Chandra and Talpade Alexander, 3–29. New York: Routledge.

Neal, Mark Anthony. 2002. *Soul Babies: Black Popular Culture and the Post-Soul Aesthetic.* New York: Routledge.

Neubeck, Kenneth J., and Noel A. Cazenave. 2001. *Welfare Racism: Playing the Race Card against America's Poor.* New York: Routledge.

Oliver, Melvin L., and Thomas M. Shapiro. 1995. *Black Wealth/White Wealth: A New Perspective on Racial Inequality.* New York: Routledge.

Omi, Michael, and Howard Winant. 1994. *Racial Formation in the United States: From the 1960s to the 1990s.* New York: Routledge.

Patillo-McCoy, Mary. 1998. "Church Culture as a Strategy of Action in the Black Community." *American Sociological Review* 63 (December): 767–784.

———. 1999. *Black Picket Fences: Privilege and Peril among the Black Middle Class.* Chicago: University of Chicago Press.

Robinson, Randall. 2000. *The Debt: What America Owes to Blacks.* New York: Plume.

Root, Maria P. P. 2001. *Love's Revolution: Interracial Marriage.* Philadelphia: Temple University Press.

Wilson, William Julius. 1978. *The Declining Significance of Race.* Chicago: University of Chicago Press.

———. 1987. *The Truly Disadvantaged: The Inner City, the Underclass, and Public Policy.* Chicago: University of Chicago Press.

———. 1996. *When Work Disappears: The World of the New Urban Poor.* New York: Knopf.

Winant, Howard. 2001. *The World Is a Ghetto: Race and Democracy since World War II.* New York: Basic Books.

4

ANGRY WOMEN ARE BUILDING
Issues and Struggles Facing American Indian Women Today

PAULA GUNN ALLEN

Paula Gunn Allen, Laguna, Sioux, and Lebanese, is a poet, novelist, and critic. She retired from her position as professor of English/creative writing/American Indian studies at the University of California at Los Angeles in 1999.

The central issue that confronts American Indian women throughout the hemisphere is survival, *literal survival,* both on a cultural and bio-logical level. According to the 1980 census, the population of American Indians is just over one million. This figure, which is disputed by some American Indians, is probably a fair estimate, and it carries certain implications.

Some researchers put our pre-contact population at more than 45 million, while others put it around 20 million. The U.S. government long put it at 450,000—a comforting if imaginary figure, though at one point it was put around 270,000. If our current population is around one million; if, as some researchers estimate, around 25 percent of Indian women and 10 percent of

Indian men in the United States have been sterilized without informed consent; if our average life expectancy is, as the best informed research presently says, 55 years; if our infant mortality rate continues at well above national standards; if our average unemployment for all segments of our population—male, female, young, adult, and middle-aged—is between 60 and 90 percent; if the U.S. government continues its policy of termination, relocation, removal, and assimilation along with the destruction of wilderness, reservation land, and its resources, and severe curtailment of hunting, fishing, timber harvesting, and water-use rights—then existing tribes are facing the threat of extinction, which for several hundred tribal groups has already become fact in the past five hundred years.

In this nation of more than 200 million, the Indian people constitute less than one-half of one percent of the population. In a nation that offers refuge, sympathy, and billions of dollars in aid from federal and private sources in the form of food to the hungry, medicine to the sick, and comfort to the dying, the indigenous subject population goes hungry, homeless, impoverished, cut out of the American deal, new, old, and in between. Americans are daily made aware of the worldwide slaughter of native peoples such as the Cambodians, the Palestinians, the Armenians, the Jews—who constitute only a few groups faced with genocide in this century. We are horrified by South African apartheid and the removal of millions of indigenous African black natives to what is there called "homelands"—but this is simply a replay of nineteenth-century U.S. government removal of American Indians to reservations. Nor do many even notice the parallel or fight South African apartheid by demanding an end to its counterpart within the border of the United States. The American Indian people are in a situation comparable to the imminent genocide in many parts of the world today. The plight of our people north and south of us is no better; to the south it is considerably worse. Consciously or unconsciously, deliberately as a matter of national policy, or accidentally as a matter of "fate," *every single government,* right, left, or centrist, in the western hemisphere is consciously or subconsciously dedicated to the extinction of those tribal people who live within its borders.

Within this geopolitical charnel house, American Indian women struggle on every front for the survival of our children, our people, our self-respect, our value systems, and our way of life. The past five hundred years testify to our skill at waging this struggle: for all the varied weapons of extinction pointed at our hands, we endure.

We survive war and conquest; we survive colonization, acculturation, assimilation; we survive beating, rape, starvation, mutilation, sterilization, abandonment, neglect, death of our children, our loved ones, destruction of our land, our homes, our past, and our future. We survive, and we do more than just survive. We bond, we care, we fight, we teach, we nurse, we bear, we feed, we earn, we laugh, we love, we hang in there, no matter what.

Of course, some, many of us, just give up. Many are alcoholics, many are addicts. Many abandon children, the old ones. Many commit suicide. Many become violent, go insane. Many go "white" and are never seen or heard from again. But enough hold on to their traditions and their ways so that even after almost five hundred brutal years, we endure. And we even write songs and poems, make paintings and drawings that say "We walk in beauty. Let us continue."

Currently our struggles are on two fronts: physical survival and cultural survival. For women this means fighting alcoholism and drug abuse (our own and that of our husbands, lovers, parents, children);[1] poverty; affluence—a destroyer of people who are not traditionally socialized to deal with large sums of money; rape, incest, battering by Indian men; assaults on fertility and other health matters by the Indian Health Service and the Public Health Service; high infant mortality due to substandard medical care, nutrition, and health information; poor educational opportunities or education that takes us away from our traditions, language, and communities; suicide, homicide, or similar expressions of self-hatred; lack of economic opportunities; substandard housing; sometimes violent and always virulent racist attitudes and behavior directed against us by an entertainment and education system that wants only one thing from Indians: our silence, our invisibility, and our collective death.

A headline in the *Navajo Times* in the fall of 1979 reported that rape was the number one crime on the Navajo reservation. In a professional mental health journal of the Indian Health Services, Phyllis Old Dog Cross reported that incest and rape are common among Indian women seeking services and that their incidence is increasing. "It is believed that at least 80 percent of the Native Women seen at the regional psychiatric service center (5 state area) have experienced some sort of sexual assault."[2] Among the forms of abuse being suffered by Native American women, Old Dog Cross cites a recent phenomenon, something called "training." This form of gang rape is "a punitive act of a group of males who band together and get even or take revenge on a selected woman."[3]

These and other cases of violence against women are powerful evidence that the status of women within the tribes has suffered grievous decline since contact, and the decline has increased in intensity in recent years. The amount of violence against women, alcoholism, and violence, abuse, and neglect by women against their children and their aged relatives have all increased. These social ills were virtually unheard of among most tribes fifty years ago, popular American opinion to the contrary. As Old Dog Cross remarks:

> Rapid, unstable and irrational change was required of the Indian people if they were to survive. Incredible loss of all that had meaning was the norm. Inhuman treatment, murder, death, and punishment was a typical experience for all the tribal groups and some didn't survive.

The dominant society devoted its efforts to the attempt to change the Indian into a white-Indian. No inhuman pressure to effect this change was overlooked. These pressures included starvation, incarceration, and enforced education. Religious and healing customs were banished.

In spite of the years of oppression, the Indian and the Indian spirit survived. Not, however, without adverse effect. One of the major effects was the loss of cultured values and the concomitant loss of personal identity. . . . The Indian was taught to be ashamed of being Indian and to emulate the non-Indian. In short, "white was right." For the Indian male, the only route to be successful, to be good, to be right, and to have an identity was to be as much like the white man as he could.[4]

Often it is said that the increase of violence against women is a result of various sociological facts such as oppression, racism, poverty, hopelessness, emasculation of men, and loss of male self-esteem as their own place within traditional society has been systematically destroyed by increasing urbanization, industrialization, and institutionalization, but seldom do we notice that for the past forty to fifty years, American popular media have depicted American Indian men as bloodthirsty savages devoted to treating women cruelly. While traditional Indian men seldom did any such thing—and in fact among most tribes abuse of women was simply unthinkable, as was abuse of children or the aged—the lie about "usual" male Indian behavior seems to have taken root and now bears its brutal and bitter fruit.

Image casting and image control constitute the central process that American Indian women must come to terms with, for on that control rests our sense of self, our claim to a past and to a future that we define and that we build. Images of Indians in media and education materials profoundly influence how we act, how we relate to the world and to each other, and how we value ourselves. They also determine to a large extent how our men act toward us, toward our children, and toward each other. The popular American media image of Indian people as savages with no conscience, no compassion, and no sense of the value of human life and human dignity was hardly true of the tribes—however true it was of the invaders. But as Adolf Hitler noted a little over fifty years ago, if you tell a lie big enough and often enough, it will be believed. Evidently, while Americans and people all over the world have been led into a deep and unquestioned belief that American Indians are cruel savages, a number of American Indian men have been equally deluded into internalizing that image and acting on it. Media images, literary images, and artistic images, particularly those embedded in popular culture, must be changed before Indian women will see much relief from the violence that destroys so many lives.

To survive culturally, American Indian women must often fight the United States government, the tribal governments, women and men of their tribe or their urban community who are virulently misogynist or who are threatened by attempts to change the images foisted on us over the centuries by whites. The colonizers' revisions of our lives, values, and histories have devastated us at the most critical level of all—that of our minds, our own sense of who we are.

Many women express strong opposition to those who would alter our life supports, steal our tribal lands, colonize our cultures and cultural expressions, and revise our very identities. We must strive to maintain tribal status; we must make certain that the tribes continue to be legally recognized entities, sovereign nations within the larger United States, and we must wage this struggle in many ways—political, educational, literary, artistic, individual, and communal. We are doing all we can: as mothers and grandmothers; as family members and tribal members; as professionals, workers, artists, shamans, leaders, chiefs, speakers, writers, and organizers, we daily demonstrate that we have no intention of disappearing, of being silent, or of quietly acquiescing in our extinction.

NOTES

1. It is likely, say some researchers, that fetal alcohol syndrome, which is serious among many Indian groups, will be so serious among the White Mountain Apache and the Pine Ridge Sioux that if present trends continue, by the year 2000 some people estimate that almost one-half of all children born on those reservations will in some way be affected by FAS. (Michael Dorris, Native American Studies, Dartmouth College, private conversation. Dorris has done extensive research into the syndrome as it affects native populations in the United States as well as in New Zealand.)
2. Phyllis Old Dog Cross, "Sexual Abuse, A New Threat to the Native American Woman: An Overview," *Listening Post: A Periodical of the Mental Health Programs of Indian Health Services,* vol. 6, no. 2 (April 1982), p. 18.
3. Old Dog Cross, p. 18.
4. Old Dog Cross, p. 20.

5

"J.A.P."-SLAPPING
The Politics of Scapegoating

RUTH ATKIN • ADRIENNE RICH

Ruth Atkin is a middle-class, Ashkenazi Jewish feminist activist born in the Midwest. She has been involved in progressive Jewish publishing since 1979 and is a founding editor of *Gesher's* successor, *Bridges: A Journal for Jewish Feminists and Our Friends.*

Adrienne Rich, the daughter of a Jewish father and a non-Jewish mother, is a poet and nonfiction writer and an activist. A founding editor of *Bridges: A Journal for Jewish Feminists and Our Friends,* Rich is the author of more than twenty-five books, the most recent of which is *Telephone Ringing in the Labyrinth: Poems 2004–2006* (2007).

Those who remember World War II may well recall the racist imagery and language levelled at Japanese people. The Japanese, formerly ideal- ized as giving us exquisite art, magical paper toys, flower arranging, swiftly became the "Japs," to be "slapped" by American military force: yellow, toothy torturers with a genetic flair for cruelty, the dastardly bombers of Pearl Harbor: the people who would deserve the genocidal bombings of Hiroshima and Nagasaki. The word "Jap" held its own in the monosyllabic language of "kike," "wop," "spic," "chink," "bitch," "slut"—short, brutal sounds like the impact of a fist. "Slap That Jap" was a familiar wartime slogan.

These memories of the 1940s are part of the background some of us bring to the recent explosion of "Jewish-American Princess" stereotypes on Eastern college campuses. The Jewish feminist magazine *Lilith* first reported the phenomenon in its Fall 1987 issue (#17); since then, articles have ap- peared in the *New York Times* and the Jewish press. A column, "No Laughing Matter," by Suzanne Messing, appeared in the feminist paper *New Directions for Women.* On December 9, [1987], National Public Radio broadcast a segment on the spread of "J.A.P.-baiting," interviewing Evelyn Torton Beck, Professor of Women's Studies at the University of Maryland and editor of *Nice Jewish Girls: A Lesbian Anthology.*

"J.A.P."-baiting has taken a range of forms: novels by post–World War II American Jewish writers such as Herman Wouk's *Marjorie Morningstar;* the routines of Jewish comedians; negative stereotyping of middle-class Jewish

---

Ruth Atkin and Adrienne Rich, "'J.A.P.'-Slapping: The Politics of Scapegoating" from *Gesher* (January 1988). Reprinted with the permission of the authors.[1]

women in greeting cards, jewelry, T-shirts, graffiti; and ritualized verbal assaults on Jewish women on college campuses. The Jewish woman is stereotyped as rich, spoiled, avidly materialistic, and solely out for herself. Most
of the negative attributes are, of course, familiar anti-Jewish stereotypes: here
they are pushed onto the Jewish woman. *Lilith* reported that at Syracuse
University basketball games, the pep band would point at certain women
who stood up and chant "JAP, JAP, JAP." On other campuses have appeared
such graffiti as: "I tolerate JAPS for sex"; "All JAPS are sluts"; "Solution to
the JAP question: when they go for their nose jobs, tie their tubes as well."
(This last graffito is packed with implications: the "J.A.P." is trying to assimilate, to pass; Jewish women should be sterilized [as thousands were under
Hitler]. It implies a knowledge of Nazi vocabulary and practice that belies
the theory of "J.A.P"-baiting as ignorant fun and games.)

A different kind of hostility identifies the "J.A.P." not as a "slut" but as a
"frigid" woman, unwilling to "put out" sexually. Messing quotes a greeting
card (published by Noble Press, New York): "Why do JAPS close their eyes
while having sex? So they can pretend they're shopping." National Public
Radio reports a fun-fair booth: "Make Her Prove She's Not a JAP—Make Her
Swallow."

"J.A.P." imagery has been acceptable in the Jewish community and
continues to be. According to the Chicago *Jewish Sentinel*, the National
Federation of Temple Sisterhoods adopted a resolution at their national
convention this fall condemning "J.A.P." jokes and images, since what began
as an object of sexist humor has now become a tool of the anti-Semite. The
resolution called on member sisterhoods to discontinue the sale of "J.A.P.
items" in their Judaica shops. But if the sisterhoods had challenged the
stereotyping of Jewish women from the first, it might have stood less chance
to become the tool of the anti-Semite, and within the Jewish community "JAP
items" would not have received the endorsement of the National Federation.
The issue is sometimes trivialized as a matter of humor ("we can laugh at
ourselves"), or on the grounds that the negative stereotypes contain a "ker-
nel of truth." We need to examine these responses.

The semiotics, or signifying power, of the "J.A.P." stereotype is complex.
A clear feminist perception is needed to decipher the scapegoating of the
women within a historically scapegoated group. Within the Jewish community, scapegoating and negative labeling of Jewish women may reflect tensions over gender roles and conflicts specific to the group. They also reveal
how Jews participate in the sexism of the society at large.

"Kaleidoscopic" is Susan Schnur's term (in *Lilith*) for the "JAP theme."
Rarely have two forms of social hatred—misogyny and anti-Semitism—
been so explicitly joined: the "materialistic, pushy" Jew and the "princess,"
the selfish, privileged rich woman. Conflate these two identities and you
have an easy target in a time when the presence of women on campuses is
threatening to men, when jobs after college are at a premium, and any
woman can be perceived by any man as a competitor for his future job. In

fact, "J.A.P." is a conflation of three hated identities: Jew, woman, and those people who are seen, in a society of vast inequalities and injustice, as having "made it."

But to understand the "J.A.P."-baiting phenomenon fully we need an understanding of how the mechanisms of anti-Jewish thought operate. The "Jewish Mother" stereotype—of a too-assertive, domineering woman, devouring the lives of her children—a leftover of the community-building, survival orientation of immigrant culture, is followed by the "Jewish American Princess." The next generation of epithets directed at Jewish women reflects the assimilation of the daughters into American society. As with any stereotype, a complex social pattern is crudely and simplistically caricatured. Young Jewish women are scapegoated for the material "success" of their parents' (usually their fathers') earning power. Scapegoating young Jewish women fits into the historic cyclical pattern of Jewish oppression, whereby some Jews have been allowed a limited access to power (as tax-collectors, money-lenders, etc.), creating the illusion of Jews overall having power. Every period of toleration of Jews in host countries has been followed by periods of economic and social unrest when ruling interests have withdrawn "protection" and support of Jews, and have encouraged the general population to direct their resentments against Jews. This phase has been brutal in the extreme: Eastern European pogroms; the Nazi camps.

Increasing numbers of people in America today are without basic necessities and comforts. The current atmosphere of growing resentment of material success is fully justified. But its historic precedents, for Jews, are troubling. As the economic situation in the U.S. widens the gap between rich and poor, we need to be on the alert for expressions of anger and frustration which divert attention from the real sources of economic hardship—the prioritizing of death over life, of profit over the basic needs of people. This hardship is shared by many Jews, especially older Jewish women. It is not a coincidence that "J.A.P."-baiting is occurring on college campuses, perceived as places of privilege.

Jews have been perceived, and to a certain extent correctly, as a "successful" minority group in America. Writing in *Lilith*, Francine Klagsbrun asks: "Isn't it odd that the term JAP, referring to a spoiled, self-indulgent woman, should be so widely used at a time when women are working outside their homes in unprecedented numbers, struggling to balance their home lives and their work lives, to give as much of themselves as they can to everybody— their husbands, their kids, their bosses?" In the same issue, Susan Schnur notes that "the characterizations of JAPs and Yuppies are often identical." She sees the label of Yuppies as "neutral or even positive," but many a bitter, long-stored anti-Yuppie joke was heard when Wall Street crashed last October. And it is perhaps not coincidental that the acronym "JAP" fits so neatly into a growing anti-Asian racism that has accompanied the increased perception of Asians as a "successful" minority. Insofar as a fraternity house booth inviting passers-by to "Slap a JAP" echoes the "Slap That Jap: Buy War

Bonds" posters of World War II, it legitimizes anti-Semitism, misogyny, and anti-Asian racism simultaneously.

As the U.S. economy wavers, as American national identity itself wavers, anti-Semitism is one time-honored escape from critical thinking and political responsibility. Young Jewish women on college campuses may have received little in their education to help them interpret this double assault—especially since the "JAP" label can be applied to non-Jews as well. Some older Jewish women, too, as articles in both *Lilith* and *New Directions for Women* indicate, have reacted by accepting stereotyping, by suggesting that "We should be able to laugh at ourselves." Both Jewish men and women tell "J.A.P." jokes. But, according to Messing, "No one refers to herself as a JAP." Francine Klagsbrun observes, "When we put down other Jewish women, that is a form of self-hatred."

And yes, we do need to laugh at ourselves. But our humor cannot—for our own health—be founded on self-hatred. When we delight in ourselves as women, delight in ourselves as Jews, we can laugh out of the fullness of recognizing ourselves as necessarily flawed and sometimes ridiculous human beings. Our humor need not come out of the arsenal of those who would deny us our humanity.

NOTE

1. Thanks to *Lilith: The Jewish Women's Magazine,* 250 W. 57th Street, New York, NY 10107; *New Directions for Women,* 108 Palisade Ave., Englewood, NJ 07631; the Chicago *Jewish Sentinel,* 323 S. Franklin St., Rm. 501, Chicago, IL 60606.

6

LATINAS ON THE FAULT LINES
OF CITIZENSHIP

ALEJANDRA MARCHEVSKY • JEANNE THEOHARIS

Alejandra Marchevsky is associate professor of Liberal Studies at California State University, Los Angeles.

Jeanne Theoharis is associate professor of Political Science at Brooklyn College of CUNY. She is co-editor of *Groundwork: Local Black Freedom Movements* and *Freedom North: Black Freedom Struggles Outside the South, 1940–1980.*

Myrna Cardenas and her three children live in a one-bedroom garden apartment in central Long Beach. With its collection of single-story row apartments organized around a communal courtyard landscaped with flowering bushes and imported palms, the "garden apartment complex" is a quintessential Southern California architectural form. Regional developers and architects of the early twentieth century drew upon the California landscape as a metaphor for the transformative power of this new American city, a classless society where newcomers could reinvent themselves and where even the most modest apartment renters, shut out of the dream of the single-family home, could enjoy a small patch of green outside their front door.[1]

The courtyard complex where Myrna lives is located on the outskirts of Long Beach's renovated downtown shopping district and a few miles from one of the nation's busiest ports. This Spanish-style apartment complex was likely built to house sailors during the navy's heydays in Long Beach in the 1920s. Now, all of Myrna's neighbors in this apartment complex are migrants from Mexico, Guatemala, and El Salvador. During the weekdays, the courtyard feels abandoned; the muffled sounds of *rancheras* or midday *telenovelas* the only signs of life behind bolted doors and drawn curtains. In the evenings, however, the concrete walkway comes alive as residents open their doors to let in the ocean air, and sit on their front steps watching young children ride tricycles up to the front gate and back again.

Alejandra Marchevsky and Jeanne Theoharis, "Introduction: Latinas on the Fault Lines of Citizenship" from *Not Working: Latina Immigrants, Low-Wage Jobs, and the Failure of Welfare Reform* (New York: New York University Press, 2006). Reprinted with permission.

In the 500-square-foot apartment that Myrna rents for $650 a month, a full-sized mattress is pushed up against the far wall of the living room for twelve-year-old Ana and five-year-old Jasmine. Their brother, James, a fourth-grade "citizen of the month" at Jefferson Elementary School, sleeps on a cot under the front window. Working 40-hour weeks at an Orange County plastics factory, along with a part-time graveyard shift stocking inventory at a discount department store, Myrna is lucky when she can sleep for three or four hours in a 24-hour period. Usually she crashes out alongside her daughters for the few hours that separate her night shift from her day shift. Myrna is saving to buy a dresser at a second-hand furniture store; in the meantime, the family sofa is piled high with clothing. At the beginning of the week, the sofa is neatly stacked with pressed and folded clothing fresh from the laundromat. By Thursday morning at 5 a.m., as Myrna frantically rushes to get her children dressed and to her mother's house all in time to make her 9 a.m. shift at the factory 25 miles east in Orange County, the apartment has devolved into what Myrna calls a "un desmadre" (slang for a mess, literally translated as "unmotherly").

If we looked into most homes in America, we might find this same tangled mess of socks, jeans, and sweaters on the sofa, and perhaps a pile of dirty dishes in the sink. But, in Myrna's case, a messy home or an empty refrigerator could cost her her children because Myrna is on welfare. Twice, in fact, the government has inspected her home, checking for food in the refrigerator and men's clothing in the closet. There are only three populations in the United States whose privacy is not protected under "probable cause" rules: prisoners, undocumented immigrants, and welfare recipients. As one of the latter, Myrna must allow government inspectors into her home, or she will be labeled "non-compliant," a designation that strips her of her welfare benefits and possibly results in criminal prosecution. While Myrna had little choice but to cooperate with welfare officials during these surprise inspections, she did not passively accept the system's criminalization of her as a welfare cheat and unfit mother. Rather, like most of the Mexican immigrant women interviewed in Long Beach, she agreed to participate in a nationwide ethnographic study of welfare reform because she saw it as an opportunity to refute the stereotypes that society imposes on her and other welfare mothers.

"They can't say that people on welfare are lazy, because I do work. When there's hours, I work over 40 hours." With this statement Myrna opened her first interview for this study in March 1997, directly disputing the notion that people on welfare do not want to work or that they do not know how to get and keep a job. At thirty-five years old, Myrna Cardenas has worked nearly continuously for the past 12 years but has never earned enough to lift her family above the poverty line. For five of those years, Myrna worked *and* was on welfare. She first applied for AFDC in 1991 after her husband returned to Mexico, leaving her behind with three young children. At the time, Myrna did not qualify for aid because she was not a lawful permanent resident. Myrna had always known that she was born two months premature while her mother, a lawful U.S. resident, was visiting an aunt in Tijuana. Yet, she had always believed that her mother had "fixed" her paperwork soon upon returning to Los Angeles. While she was growing up in Long Beach, Myrna's immigration status was never under question. Her unaccented English and light complexion led public schoolteachers and, later, employers to presume that she was a U.S. citizen. Myrna had lived her entire life in the United States, attended American public schools, and given birth to two U.S. citizens, yet she could be deported at any moment. When the caseworker at the welfare office demanded to see Myrna's green card and she could not produce one, Myrna was deemed ineligible for public assistance. Still, her U.S. citizen children were eligible, and Myrna began receiving cash assistance and food stamps on their behalf. For two years, she cut corners and worked odd jobs to stretch a welfare check for three into a livelihood for a family of four.

When her residency application was approved by the INS, Myrna returned to the welfare office to be added to her family's welfare grant. The caseworker took one look at her newly issued green card, and "she said, 'No, no, it's a fake. What you need to do is look for a job.'" Myrna spent the next four years trying to track down a caseworker that would take the time to call the INS to verify that her green card was valid. In the meantime, she found a part-time job at Target, counting and reshelving inventory from 10 p.m. to 6 a.m. for $4.25/hour. Because Myrna and her coworkers were classified as part-time employees, despite the fact that some months they worked over 40 hours per week, Target did not pay their medical benefits or overtime pay. Myrna was working and reported her wages to the welfare office, yet it did not take long for her to realize that this job was not a pathway off welfare. During the holiday rush season, from late September through December, Myrna worked 30 to 40 hours per week and earned a monthly paycheck of $760. However, once the store's Christmas decorations came down, her work hours dwindled to as few as ten per week and her monthly paycheck shrunk to less than $170, which was only marginally corrected by a slight increase in her children's food stamps and cash assistance.

In November 1997, Myrna's persistence finally paid off as she managed to convince a new caseworker that her green card was legitimate and that she was eligible for welfare. She was officially added to her family's case the following month, which raised their monthly benefits by a total of $100—enough to get their phone reconnected and buy an extra bag of groceries. But as Myrna explained,

> I didn't get no check in the following year, in February [two months later]. And I called my [caseworker], "Why am I not getting a check? You told me that if I could get more money, that I could get childcare, and this and that. And now you're cutting me off?" [. . .] And so I called her and she told me, "Oh it's because you work and you made more than $790, that's more than enough. So you're not getting nothing."

Encouraged by the welfare system to get a job, Myrna was now told she no longer qualified for aid because her December paycheck was slightly above the County's eligibility threshold (but still below the poverty line for a family of four). By the time she secured a face-to-face meeting with a caseworker three weeks later, Myrna had already registered with a temporary employment agency and had been assigned to an assembly line, where she attached handles onto plastic buckets for $6.50/hr. with no benefits. At this meeting, yet a different caseworker explained to Myrna the new welfare rules that had been imposed by Congress in August 1996. Each day that she received welfare (even if she was also working) would be counted against a five-year lifetime maximum. Because Myrna was already working the required 35 hours per week, she was advised not to apply for welfare and to "save those five years for a rainy day, when things get really bad."

By March 1998, Myrna was off welfare and juggling two jobs—a full-time shift at the plastics factory along with a few nights per week on the graveyard shift at Target—yet her family's economic security was shakier than ever before. It had been over a year since the family had health insurance, because their Medi-Cal coverage had been cancelled when their TANF file closed. She had lost over 25 pounds because some of the factories she works at are "like 10 to 20 degrees hotter than what it is outside" but was trying to avoid having to go to the doctor. And, with a monthly income of $900, or a yearly income of $15,600, Myrna and her children continued to fall below the poverty line. Moreover, working an average of 50 hours per week, Myrna was lucky when she could spend an hour or two each day with her children. The morning of the interview, Myrna had even more reason to worry. The supervisor of the temp agency had called to say that she and several other employees had been placed on a week-long suspension, punishment for their refusal to work on Labor Day. As Myrna explained, "She said that if I kept up this bad attitude, I wouldn't get no more work." Less than a year later, Myrna was laid off at the factory and had reapplied for welfare.

NOTE

1. Robert Fogelson was one of the earliest scholars to write about this relationship between architectural design and ideologies of urbanism in Los Angeles. See chapter 7 of his now classic 1967 work, *The Fragmented Metropolis* (Berkeley, 1967). For a lucid social history of architecture in Los Angeles, also see Merry Ovnick, *Los Angeles: End of the Rainbow* (Los Angeles, 1994).

7
———————

WHITE PRIVILEGE
Unpacking the Invisible Knapsack

PEGGY McINTOSH

Peggy McIntosh, associate director of the Wellesley College Center for Research on Women, is founder and co-director of the United States S.E.E.D. Project on Inclusive Curriculum (Seeking Educational Equity and Diversity). She is best known for her work on curricular revision, privilege systems, and feelings of fraudulence.

> *I was taught to see racism only in individual acts of meanness, not in invisible systems conferring dominance on my group.*

T hrough work to bring materials from Women's Studies into the rest of the curriculum, I have often noticed men's unwillingness to grant that they are overprivileged, even though they may grant that women are disadvantaged. They may say they will work to improve women's status, in the society, the university, or the curriculum, but they can't or won't support the idea of lessening men's. Denials which amount to taboos surround the subject of advantages which men gain from women's disadvantages. These denials protect male privilege from being fully acknowledged, lessened or ended.

Thinking through unacknowledged male privilege as a phenomenon, I realized that since hierarchies in our society are interlocking, there was most likely a phenomenon of white privilege which was similarly denied and protected. As a white person, I realized I had been taught about racism as something which puts others at a disadvantage, but had been taught not to see one of its corollary aspects, white privilege, which puts me at an advantage.

I think whites are carefully taught not to recognize white privilege, as males are taught not to recognize male privilege. So I have begun in an untutored way to ask what it is like to have white privilege. I have come to see white privilege as an invisible package of unearned assets which I can count on cashing in each day, but about which I was "meant" to remain oblivious.

White privilege is like an invisible weightless knapsack of special provisions, maps, passports, codebooks, visas, clothes, tools, and blank checks.

Describing white privilege makes one newly accountable. As we in Women's Studies work to reveal male privilege and ask men to give up some of their power, so one who writes about having white privilege must ask, "Having described it, what will I do to lessen or end it?"

After I realized the extent to which men work from a base of unacknowledged privilege, I understood that much of their oppressiveness was unconscious. Then I remembered the frequent charges from women of color that white women whom they encounter are oppressive. I began to understand why we are justly seen as oppressive, even when we don't see ourselves that way. I began to count the ways in which I enjoy unearned skin privilege and have been conditioned into oblivion about its existence.

My schooling gave me no training in seeing myself as an oppressor, as an unfairly advantaged person, or as a participant in a damaged culture. I was taught to see myself as an individual whose moral state depended on her individual moral will. My schooling followed the pattern my colleague Elizabeth Minnich has pointed out: whites are taught to think of their lives as morally neutral, normative, and average, and also ideal, so that when we work to benefit others, this is seen as work which will allow "them" to be more like "us."

I decided to try to work on myself at least by identifying some of the daily effects of white privilege in my life. I have chosen those conditions which I think in my case *attach somewhat more to skin-color privilege* than to class, religion, ethnic status, or geographical location, though of course all these other factors are intricately intertwined. As far as I can see, my African American coworkers, friends and acquaintances with whom I come into daily or frequent contact in this particular time, place, and line of work cannot count on most of these conditions.

1. I can if I wish arrange to be in the company of people of my race most of the time.
2. If I should need to move, I can be pretty sure of renting or purchasing housing in an area which I can afford and in which I would want to live.
3. I can be pretty sure that my neighbors in such a location will be neutral or pleasant to me.
4. I can go shopping alone most of the time, pretty well assured that I will not be followed or harassed.
5. I can turn on the television or open to the front page of the paper and see people of my race widely represented.
6. When I am told about our national heritage or about "civilization," I am shown that people of my color made it what it is.
7. I can be sure that my children will be given curricular materials that testify to the existence of their race.

8. If I want to, I can be pretty sure of finding a publisher for this piece on white privilege.

9. I can go into a music shop and count on finding the music of my race represented, into a supermarket and find the staple foods which fit with my cultural traditions, into a hairdresser's shop and find someone who can cut my hair.

10. Whether I use checks, credit cards, or cash, I can count on my skin color not to work against the appearance of financial reliability.

11. I can arrange to protect my children most of the time from people who might not like them.

12. I can swear, or dress in second hand clothes, or not answer letters, without having people attribute these choices to the bad morals, the poverty, or the illiteracy of my race.

13. I can speak in public to a powerful male group without putting my race on trial.

14. I can do well in a challenging situation without being called a credit to my race.

15. I am never asked to speak for all the people of my racial group.

16. I can remain oblivious of the language and customs of persons of color who constitute the world's majority without feeling in my culture any penalty for such oblivion.

17. I can criticize our government and talk about how much I fear its policies and behavior without being seen as a cultural outsider.

18. I can be pretty sure that if I ask to talk to "the person in charge," I will be facing a person of my race.

19. If a traffic cop pulls me over or if the IRS audits my tax return, I can be sure I haven't been singled out because of my race.

20. I can easily buy posters, postcards, picture books, greeting cards, dolls, toys, and children's magazines featuring people of my race.

21. I can go home from most meetings of organizations I belong to feeling somewhat tied in, rather than isolated, out-of-place, outnumbered, unheard, held at a distance, or feared.

22. I can take a job with an affirmative action employer without having coworkers on the job suspect that I got it because of race.

23. I can choose public accommodation without fearing that people of my race cannot get in or will be mistreated in the places I have chosen.

24. I can be sure that if I need legal or medical help, my race will not work against me.

25. If my day, week, or year is going badly, I need not ask of each negative episode or situation whether it has racial overtones.

26. I can choose blemish cover or bandages in "flesh" color and have them more or less match my skin.

I repeatedly forgot each of the realizations on this list until I wrote it down. For me white privilege has turned out to be an elusive and fugitive subject. The pressure to avoid it is great, for in facing it I must give up the myth of meritocracy. If these things are true, this is not such a free country; one's life is not what one makes it; many doors open for certain people through no virtues of their own.

In unpacking this invisible knapsack of white privilege, I have listed conditions of daily experience which I once took for granted. Nor did I think of any of these perquisites as bad for the holder. I now think that we need a more finely differentiated taxonomy of privilege, for some of these varieties are only what one would want for everyone in a just society, and others give license to be ignorant, oblivious, arrogant and destructive.

I see a pattern running through the matrix of white privilege, a pattern of assumptions which were passed on to me as a white person. There was one main piece of cultural turf; it was my own turf, and I was among those who could control the turf. *My skin color was an asset for any move I was educated to want to make*. I could think of myself as belonging in major ways, and of making social systems work for me. I could freely disparage, fear, neglect, or be oblivious to anything outside of the dominant cultural forms. Being of the main culture, I could also criticize it fairly freely.

In proportion as my racial group was being made confident, comfortable, and oblivious, other groups were likely being made inconfident, uncomfortable, and alienated. Whiteness protected me from many kinds of hostility, distress, and violence, which I was being subtly trained to visit in turn upon people of color.

For this reason, the word "privilege" now seems to me misleading. We usually think of privilege as being a favored state, whether earned or conferred by birth or luck. Yet some of the conditions I have described here work to systematically overempower certain groups. Such privilege simply *confers dominance* because of one's race or sex.

I want, then, to distinguish between earned strength and unearned power conferred systematically. Power from unearned privilege can look like strength when it is in fact permission to escape or to dominate. But not all of the privileges on my list are inevitably damaging. Some, like the expectation that neighbors will be decent to you, or that your race will not count against you in court, should be the norm in a just society. Others, like the privilege to ignore less powerful people, distort the humanity of the holders as well as the ignored groups.

We might at least start by distinguishing between positive advantages which we can work to spread, and negative types of advantages which unless rejected will always reinforce our present hierarchies. For example, the feeling that one belongs within the human circle, as Native Americans say, should not be seen as privilege for a few. Ideally it is an *unearned entitlement*. At present, since only a few have it, it is an *unearned advantage* for them. This paper results from a process of coming to see that some of the power which I originally saw as attendant on being a human being in the U.S. consisted in *unearned advantage* and *conferred dominance*.

I have met very few men who are truly distressed about systemic, unearned male advantage and conferred dominance. And so one question for me and others like me is whether we will be like them, or whether we will get truly distressed, even outraged, about unearned race advantage and conferred dominance and if so, what we will do to lessen them. In any case, we need to do more work in identifying how they actually affect our daily lives. Many, perhaps most, of our white students in the U.S. think that racism doesn't affect them because they are not people of color; they do not see "whiteness" as a racial identity. In addition, since race and sex are not the only advantaging systems at work, we need similarly to examine the daily experience of having age advantage, or ethnic advantage, or physical ability, or advantage related to nationality, religion, or sexual orientation.

Difficulties and dangers surrounding the task of finding parallels are many. Since racism, sexism, and heterosexism are not the same, the advantaging associated with them should not be seen as the same. In addition, it is hard to disentangle aspects of unearned advantage which rest more on social class, economic class, race, religion, sex and ethnic identity than on other factors. Still, all of the oppressions are interlocking, as the Combahee River Collective Statement of 1977 continues to remind us eloquently.

One factor seems clear about all of the interlocking oppressions. They take both active forms which we can see and embedded forms which as a member of the dominant group one is taught not to see. In my class and place, I did not see myself as a racist because I was taught to recognize racism only in individual acts of meanness by members of my group, never in invisible systems conferring unsought racial dominance on my group from birth.

Disapproving of the systems won't be enough to change them. I was taught to think that racism could end if white individuals changed their attitudes. [But] a "white" skin in the United States opens many doors for whites whether or not we approve of the way dominance has been conferred on us. Individual acts can palliate, but cannot end, these problems.

To redesign social systems we need first to acknowledge their colossal unseen dimensions. The silences and denials surrounding privilege are the key political tool here. They keep the thinking about equality or equity incomplete, protecting unearned advantage and conferred dominance by making these taboo subjects. Most talk by whites about equal opportunity seems to me now to be about equal opportunity to try to get into a position of dominance while denying that *systems* of dominance exist.

It seems to me that obliviousness about white advantage, like obliviousness about male advantage, is kept strongly inculturated in the United States so as to maintain the myth of meritocracy, the myth that democratic choice is equally available to all. Keeping most people unaware that freedom of confident action is there for just a small number of people props up those in power, and serves to keep power in the hands of the same groups that have most of it already.

Though systemic change takes many decades, there are pressing questions for me and I imagine for some others like me if we raise our daily consciousness on the perquisites of being light-skinned. What will we do with
such knowledge? As we know from watching men, it is an open question
whether we will choose to use unearned advantage to weaken hidden systems of advantage, and whether we will use any of our arbitrarily awarded
power to try to reconstruct power systems on a broader base.

8

CONTROLLED OR AUTONOMOUS: IDENTITY AND THE EXPERIENCE OF THE NETWORK, WOMEN LIVING UNDER MUSLIM LAWS

FARIDA SHAHEED

Farida Shaheed is a sociologist and activist who works with Shirkat Gah—Women's
Resource Centre in Lahore, Pakistan and the Women Living Under Muslim Laws
(WLUML) International Solidarity Network.

The international network Women Living under Muslim Laws
(WLUML) was initially formed in response to several incidents ur-
gently requiring action in 1984, all of which related to Islam, laws, and
women. In Algeria, three feminists were arrested and jailed without trial,
then kept incommunicado for seven months. Their crime was having discussed with other women the government's proposal to introduce a new set
of laws on the family (Code de la Famille) that severely reduced women's
rights in this field. In India, a Muslim woman filed a petition to the Supreme
Court arguing that the application of religious minority law denied her
rights otherwise guaranteed all citizens under the Constitution of India. In
Abu Dhabi, for the alleged crime of adultery a pregnant woman was sentenced to be stoned to death two months after giving birth. In Europe, the

Farida Shaheed, "Controlled or Autonomous: Identity and the Experience of the
Network, Women Living under Muslim Laws" from *Signs: Journal of Women in
Culture and Society* 19, no. 4 (1994): 997–1019. Copyright © 1994 by The University of
Chicago Press. Reprinted with permission.

Mothers of Algiers (a group formed by women divorced from Algerian men) were seeking access to or custody of their children.[1] Excepting the condemned woman, on whose behalf others initiated action, those concerned in each incident asked for international support. Starting as an action committee, WLUML coalesced into a network between 1984 and 1986, when it formulated its first Plan of Action.

Geographically scattered, these first incidents were symptomatic of the much wider problem confronting women in the Muslim world, who increasingly find that, in the tussle for political pre-eminence, political forces (in and out of office) are increasingly formulating legal, social, or administrative measures justified by reference to Islam that militate against women's autonomy and self-actualization.

To understand the logic underpinning WLUML's creation and in order to assess the possible impact of its actions and strategies, it is essential to first locate women in the complex web of Islam, law, and society in the Muslim world and to clarify some basic issues in this respect. First, the essential components of patriarchal structure in Muslim societies do not differ from those enumerated by non-Muslim feminists, and, like elsewhere, women's subordination occurs at multiple levels (kinship structures, state-building projects, anti-imperialist and populist ideologies, and national and international policies). Nor should women be viewed as passive victims, as "they are fully fledged social actors, bearing the full set of contradictions implied by their class, racial, and ethnic locations as well as gender" (Kandiyoti 1989, 8)[2]—all being factors that in turn moderate women's interaction with both the state and religion.

Second, the idea of one homogeneous Muslim world is an illusion and, in fact (as Deniz Kandiyoti puts it),

> So-called Islamic societies embody widely differing histories of state and class formation. The relationships between state and religion have correspondingly varied as they have evolved. . . . [But] all have had to grapple with the problems of establishing "modern" nation-states. This meant forging of citizenship, and finding new legitimizing ideologies and power bases. . . . Most Muslim states have failed to generate ideologies capable of coping realistically with social change. This and their histories of dependence vis-à-vis the West have led them to rely on Islam not only as the sole coherent ideology at their disposal but also as a symbol of their cultural identity and integrity. [1989, 5]

Third, when identity is transformed into a set of beliefs and behavioral patterns ordering community life, existing socioeconomic and political structures play a major role in shaping the transformation. Consequently, while it is frequently claimed that any given state, society, or community is Islamic, it is in fact not *Islamic* (i.e., that which is ordained) but *Muslim* (i.e., of those who adhere to Islam) and reflects the assimilation of Islam into prevailing structures, systems, and practices—hence the many significantly different varieties of Muslim societies that exist today. And, finally, the diversity of Muslim societies and the differing realities of women within them have produced a plethora of feminist responses in the political arena that range from the exclusively secular to the exclusively theological, with many permutations in between.

[…]

Formation of the Network

It is against this backdrop that the network Women Living under Muslim Laws was created to break women's isolation and to provide linkages and support to all women whose lives may be affected by Muslim laws.

[…]

The formulation of the network's name is an acknowledgment of both the complexity and diversity of women's realities in the Muslim world. A less obvious concern that went into the choice of name is that women affected by Muslim laws may not be Muslim, either by virtue of having a different religion or by virtue of having chosen another marker of political or personal identity. The emphasis in the title and in the group is therefore on the women themselves and their situations and not on the specific politicoreligious option they may exercise. As a network, WLUML therefore extends to women living in countries where Islam is the state religion as well as those from Muslim communities ruled by religious minority laws, to women in secular states where a rapidly expanding political presence of Islam increasingly provokes a demand for minority religious law, as well as to women in migrant Muslim communities in Europe, the Americas, and Australasia, and further includes non-Muslim women who may have Muslim laws applied to them directly or through their children.

Propelled by concrete, on-the-ground issues rather than the outcome of merely theoretical discourse, WLUML's objectives are to create and reinforce linkages between women and women's groups within Muslim communities, to increase their knowledge about both their common and diverse situations, and to strengthen their struggles by creating the means and channels needed to support their efforts internationally from within and outside the Muslim world. In essence, the purpose of WLUML is to increase the autonomy of women affected by Muslim laws by encouraging them to analyze and reformulate the identity imposed on them through the application of Muslim laws, and by so doing to assume greater control over their lives. The WLUML aims to achieve this by building a network of mutual solidarity and information flow; by facilitating interaction and contact between women from Muslim countries and communities, on the one hand, and between them and progressive and feminist groups at large, on the other; by promoting the exposure of women from one geographical area to another in and outside the Muslim world; and by undertaking common projects identified by and executed through network participants. The WLUML's initial Plan of Action clearly states that "its purpose is simply to facilitate access to information and to each other. Its existence therefore depends on our links and not on the specific activities undertaken or positions held by any group or individual involved in this process" (1986, 1).

Women Living under Muslim Laws believes that the seeming helplessness of a majority of women in the Muslim world in effectively mobilizing against and overcoming adverse laws and customs stems not only from their being economically and politically less powerful but also from their erroneous belief that the only existence possible for a Muslim woman that allows her to maintain her identity—however that may be defined—is the one delineated for her in her own national context. In fact, the common presumption both within and outside the Muslim world that there exists one homogeneous Muslim world is fallacy. Interaction between women from different Muslim societies proves that, while some similarities may stretch across cultures, classes, sects, schools, and continents, the diversities are at least equally striking. The different realities of women living under Muslim laws, according to WLUML, "range from being strictly closeted, isolated and voiceless within four walls, subjected to public floggings and condemned to death for presumed adultery (which is considered a crime against the state) and forcibly given in marriage as a child, to situations where women have a far greater degree of freedom of movement and interaction, the right to work, to participate in public affairs and also exercise a far greater control over their own lives" (1986, 5).

Dreaming of an alternative reality is not simply a matter of inspiration but, to a large extent, depends on accessing information on the sources of law and *customary practices* and on the political and social forces that determine women's current reality. Beyond this is the need to belong to a social collectivity. As mentioned above, the fear of being cut off from one's collective identity militates against women challenging "Muslim laws." Therefore, taking initiative against such laws is facilitated if women can be sure of the support of another collectivity that functions as an alternative reference group and, by so doing, may also help women redefine the parameters of their current reference group(s). In this, contacts and links with women from other parts of the Muslim world—whose very existence speaks of the multiplicity of women's realities within the Muslim context—provide an important source of inspiration. Likewise, information on the diversity of existing laws within the Muslim world gives material shape to alternatives. Both encourage women to dream of different realities—the first step in changing the present one.

In contrast, an inability to unravel the various strands of an apparently inseparable but actually composite identity presented in the name of Islam serves to silence and immobilize women. This silence is deepened by women's isolation in specific environments and their lack of knowledge about their official legal rights—both in terms of Muslim personal laws

and/or civil codes and of the source of these laws. Most women remain ignorant of even the basic disparities between customary laws applied to them
and the official version of Muslim laws. Action is likewise impeded by
women's negligible access to information enabling them to challenge the
validity of either type of law, including information about the strategies and
struggles of other women in the Muslim world and the discussions and debates that flow from these.

Then there is the political use of Islam. In most of the Muslim world
Islam has been used by those in power and those out of it, more often by
right-wing elements than progressive forces but inevitably in a bid for political power: for consolidating support or legitimizing force (Mumtaz and
Shaheed 1987, 1). This practice is so widespread as to provoke one feminist to
conclude that "not only have the sacred texts always been manipulated, but
manipulation of them is a structural characteristic of the practice of power in
Muslim societies" (Mernissi 1992, 8–9). For women living under Muslim
laws, one of the dangers is that politicoreligious groups find it convenient to
cite so-called Islamic laws already being applied in different Muslim countries in support of their own demands for more stringent, essentially unde-
mocratic or discriminatory "Islamic" laws. For their part, when women can
cite examples of positive legislation or their demands are supported from
within the Muslim world (though not necessarily from within a religious
framework), their effectiveness is strengthened.

Women Living under Muslim Laws posits that it is only when women
start assuming the right to define for themselves the parameters of their own
identity and stop accepting unconditionally and without question what is
presented to them as the "correct" religion, the "correct" culture, or the "correct" national identity that they will be able effectively to challenge the
corpus of laws imposed on them. The WLUML is convinced that while controlling women through identity has multiple ramifications—in which religion, nationality, ethnicity, and class all come into play—"depriving
[women] of even dreaming of a different reality is one of the most debilitating forms of oppression [they] face" (WLUML 1986, 7). It is the vision of a
different reality that propels the reformulation of the present one, and it is
here, in opening the doors to a multiplicity of possible alternatives, that the
WLUML network hopes to make its most important contribution.

NOTES

1. In Algeria, the three feminists were released; however, the new Family Code was
enacted in 1984, negatively affecting women. In India, the Muslim Women
(Protection of the Rights on Divorce) Act 1986 allowed Muslim minority law to
supersede the Constitutional provisions, depriving Muslim women of rights
enjoyed by others. In Abu Dhabi, after a strong international campaign of numerous groups, the woman was repatriated to her own country, Sri Lanka. After
several years, the governments of Algeria and France signed a treaty providing
for visiting rights to divorced mothers of Algerian children.

2. For a more complete discussion on the subject of the cultural articulation of patriarchy, see Shaheed 1986; on the complexities of the situation, see Kandiyoti 1989.

REFERENCES

Kandiyoti, Deniz. (1989). "Women and Islam: What Are the Missing Terms?" *Dossier 5/6* (Grabels), December 1988/May 1989, 5–9.
Mernissi, Fatima. (1992). *The Veil and the Male Elite: A Feminist Interpretation of Women's Rights in Islam,* Mary Jo Lakeland, trans. New York: Addison-Wesley.
Mumtaz, Khawar, and Farida Shaheed. (1987). *Two Steps Forward, One Step Back? Women of Pakistan.* London: Zed Books.
Shaheed, Farida. (1986). "The Cultural Articulation of Patriarchy: Legal Systems, Islam and the Women in Pakistan." *South Asia Bulletin* 6(1): 38–44.
WLUML. (1986). *Plan of Action (Aramon).*

9

UNDER AND (INSIDE) WESTERN EYES: AT THE TURN OF THE CENTURY

CHANDRA TALPADE MOHANTY

Chandra Talpade Mohanty, Ph.D., is professor of women's studies at Syracuse University. In addition to writing *Feminism without Borders: Decolonizing Theory, Practicing Solidarity,* she coedited *Feminist Genealogies, Colonial Legacies, Democratic Futures (Thinking Gender)* (1996) as well as *Third World Women and the Politics of Feminism* (1991).

There have been a number of shifts in the political and economic landscapes of nations and communities of people in the last two decades. The intellectual maps of disciplines and areas of study in the U.S. academy have shifted as well during this time. The advent and institutional visibility of postcolonial studies for instance is a relatively recent phenomenon—as is the simultaneous rollback of the gains made by race and ethnic studies departments in the 1970s and 1980s. Women's studies is now a well-established field of study with over eight hundred degree-granting programs and departments in the U.S. academy.[1] Feminist theory

Chandra Talpade Mohanty, *Feminism Without Borders: Decolonizing Theory, Practicing Solidarity* (Durham, NC: Duke University Press, 2003). Reprinted with permission.

and feminist movements across national borders have matured substantially since the early 1980s, and there is now a greater visibility of transnational women's struggles and movements, brought on in part by the United Nations world conferences on women held over the last two decades.

Economically and politically, the declining power of self-governance among certain poorer nations is matched by the rising significance of transnational institutions such as the World Trade Organization and governing bodies such as the European Union, not to mention the for-profit corporations. Of the world's largest economies, fifty-one happen to be corporations, not countries, and Amnesty International now reports on corporations as well as nations (Eisenstein 1998b, 1). Also, the hegemony of neoliberalism, alongside the naturalization of capitalist values, influences the ability to make choices on one's own behalf in the daily lives of economically marginalized as well as economically privileged communities around the globe.

The rise of religious fundamentalisms with their deeply masculinist and often racist rhetoric poses a huge challenge for feminist struggles around the world. Finally, the profoundly unequal "information highway" as well as the increasing militarization (and masculinization) of the globe, accompanied by the growth of the prison industrial complex in the United States, poses profound contradictions in the lives of communities of women and men in most parts of the world. I believe these political shifts to the right, accompanied by global capitalist hegemony, privatization, and increased religious, ethnic, and racial hatreds, pose very concrete challenges for feminists. In this context, I ask what would it mean to be attentive to the micropolitics of everyday life as well as to the larger processes that recolonize the culture and identities of people across the globe. How we think of the local in/of the global and vice versa without falling into colonizing or cultural relativist platitudes about difference is crucial in this intellectual and political landscape. And for me, this kind of thinking is tied to a revised race-and-gender-conscious historical materialism.

The politics of feminist cross-cultural scholarship from the vantage point of Third World/South feminist struggles remains a compelling site of analysis for me.[2] Eurocentric analytic paradigms continue to flourish, and I remain committed to reengaging in the struggles to criticize openly the effects of discursive colonization on the lives and struggles of marginalized women. My central commitment is to build connections between feminist scholarship and political organizing. My own present-day analytic framework remains very similar to my earliest critique of Eurocentrism. However, I now see the politics and economics of capitalism as a far more urgent locus of struggle. I continue to hold to an analytic framework that is attentive to the micropolitics of everyday life as well as to the macropolitics of global economic and political processes. The link between political economy and culture remains crucial to any form of feminist theorizing—as it does for my work. It isn't the framework that has changed. It is just that global economic and political processes have become more brutal, exacerbating economic, racial, and gender inequalities, and thus they need to be demystified, reexamined, and theorized.

While my earlier focus was on the distinctions between "Western" and "Third World" feminist practices, and while I downplayed the commonalities between these two positions, my focus now . . . is on what I have chosen to call an anticapitalist transnational feminist practice—and on the possibilities, indeed on the necessities, of cross-national feminist solidarity and organizing against capitalism. While "Under Western Eyes" was located in the context of the critique of Western humanism and Eurocentrism and of white, Western feminism, a similar essay written now would need to be located in the context of the critique of global capitalism (on antiglobalization), the naturalization of the values of capital, and the unacknowledged power of cultural relativism in cross-cultural feminist scholarship and pedagogies.

"Under Western Eyes" sought to make the operations of discursive power visible, to draw attention to what was left out of feminist theorizing, namely, the material complexity, reality, and agency of Third World women's bodies and lives. This is in fact exactly the analytic strategy I now use to draw attention to what is unseen, undertheorized, and left out in the production of knowledge about globalization. While globalization has always been a part of capitalism, and capitalism is not a new phenomenon, at this time I believe the theory, critique, and activism around antiglobalization has to be a key focus for feminists. This does not mean that the patriarchal and racist relations and structures that accompany capitalism are any less problematic at this time, or that antiglobalization is a singular phenomenon. Along with many other scholars and activists, I believe capital as it function now depends on and exacerbates racist, patriarchal, and heterosexist relations of rule.

Feminist Methodologies: New Directions

What kinds of feminist methodology and analytic strategy are useful in making power (and women's lives) visible in overtly nongendered, nonracialized discourses? The strategy discussed here is an example of how capitalism and its various relations of rule can be analyzed through a transnational, anticapitalist feminist critique, one that draws on historical materialism and centralizes racialized gender. This analysis begins from and is anchored in the place of the most marginalized communities of women—poor women of all colors in affluent and neocolonial nations; women of the Third World/South or the Two-Thirds World.[3] I believe that this experiential and analytic anchor in the lives of marginalized communities of women provides the most inclusive paradigm for thinking about social justice. This particularized viewing allows for a more concrete and expansive vision of universal justice.

This is the very opposite of "special interest" thinking. If we pay attention to and think from the space of some of the most disenfranchised communities of women in the world, we are most likely to envision a just and democratic society capable of treating all its citizens fairly. Conversely, if we begin our analysis from, and limit it to, the space of privileged communities, our visions of justice are more likely to be exclusionary because privilege nurtures blindness to those without the same privileges. Beginning from the lives and interests of marginalized communities of women, I am able to access and make the workings of power visible—to read up the ladder of privilege. It is more necessary to look upward—colonized peoples must know themselves and the colonizer. This particular marginalized location makes the politics of knowledge and the power investments that go along with it visible so that we can then engage in work to transform the use and abuse of power. The analysis draws on the notion of epistemic privilege as it is developed by feminist standpoint theorists (with their roots in the historical materialism of Marx and Lukacs) as well as postpositivist realists, who provide an analysis of experience, identity, and the epistemic effects of social location.[4] My view is thus a materialist and "realist" one and is antithetical to that of postmodernist relativism. I believe there are causal links between marginalized social locations and experiences and the ability of human agents to explain and analyze features of capitalist society. Methodologically, this analytic perspective is grounded in historical materialism. My claim is not that all marginalized locations yield crucial knowledge about power and inequity, but that within a tightly integrated capitalist system, the particular standpoint of poor indigenous and Third World/South women provides the most inclusive viewing of systemic power. In numerous cases of environmental racism, for instance, where the neighborhoods of poor communities of color are targeted as new sites for prisons and toxic dumps, it is no coincidence that poor black, Native American, and Latina women provide the leadership in the fight against corporate pollution. Three out of five Afro-Americans and Latinos live near toxic waste sites, and three of the five largest hazardous waste landfills are in communities with a population that is 80 percent people of color (Pardo 2001, 504–11). Thus, it is precisely their critical reflections on their everyday lives as poor women of color that allow the kind of analysis of the power structure that has led to the many victories in environmental racism struggles.[5] Herein lies a lesson for feminist analysis.

Feminist scientist Vandana Shiva, one of the most visible leaders of the antiglobalization movement, provides a similar and illuminating critique of the patents and intellectual property rights agreements sanctioned by the World Trade Organization (WTO) since 1995.[6] Along with others in the environmental and indigenous rights movements, she argues that the WTO sanctions biopiracy and engages in intellectual piracy by privileging the claims of corporate commercial interests, based on Western systems of knowledge in agriculture and medicine, to products and innovations derived from indigenous knowledge traditions. Thus, through the definition of Western scientific epistemologies as the only legitimate scientific system, the WTO is able to underwrite corporate patents to indigenous knowledge (as to the Neem tree in India) as their own intellectual property, protected through intellectual property rights agreements. As a result, the patenting of drugs derived from indigenous medicinal systems has now reached massive proportions. I quote Shiva:

> [T]hrough patenting, indigenous knowledge is being pirated in the name of protecting knowledge and preventing piracy. The knowledge of our ancestors, of our peasants about seeds is being claimed as an invention of U.S. corporations and U.S. scientists and patented by them. The only reason something like that can work is because underlying it all is a racist framework that says the knowledge of the Third World and the knowledge of people of color is not knowledge. When that knowledge is taken by white men who have capital, suddenly creativity begins. . . . Patents are a replay of colonialism, which is now called globalization and free trade. (2000, 32)

The contrast between Western scientific systems and indigenous epistemologies and systems of medicine is not the only issue here. It is the colonialist and corporate power to define Western science, and the reliance on capitalist values of private property and profit, as the only normative system that results in the exercise of immense power. Thus indigenous knowledges, which are often communally generated and shared among tribal and peasant women for domestic, local, and public use, are subject to the ideologies of a corporate Western scientific paradigm where intellectual property rights can only be understood in possessive or privatized form. All innovations that happen to be collective, to have occurred over time in forests and farms, are appropriated or excluded. The idea of an intellectual commons where knowledge is collectively gathered and passed on for the benefit of all, not owned privately, is the very opposite of the notion of private property and ownership that is the basis for the WTO property rights agreements. Thus this idea of an intellectual commons among tribal and peasant women actually excludes them from ownership and facilitates corporate biopiracy.

Shiva's analysis of intellectual property rights, biopiracy, and globalization is made possible by its very location in the experiences and epistemologies of peasant and tribal women in India. Beginning from the practices and knowledges of indigenous women, she "reads up" the power structure, all the way to the policies and practices sanctioned by the WTO. This is a very clear example then of a transnational, anticapitalist feminist politics.

However, Shiva says less about gender than she could. She is after all talking in particular about women's work and knowledges anchored in the epistemological experiences of one of the most marginalized communities of women in the world—poor, tribal, and peasant women in India. This is a community of women made invisible and written out of national and international economic calculations. An analysis that pays attention to the everyday experiences of tribal women and the micropolitics of their ultimately anticapitalist struggles illuminates the macropolitics of global restructuring.

It suggests the thorough embeddedness of the local and particular with the global and universal, and it suggests the need to conceptualize questions of justice and equity in transborder terms. In other words, this mode of reading envisions a feminism without borders, in that it foregrounds the need for an analysis and vision of solidarity across the enforced privatized intellectual property borders of the WTO.

These particular examples offer the most inclusive paradigm for understanding the motivations and effects of globalization as it is crafted by the WTO. Of course, if we were to attempt the same analysis from the epistemological space of Western, corporate interests, it would be impossible to generate an analysis that values indigenous knowledge anchored in communal relationships rather than profit-based hierarchies. Thus, poor tribal and peasant women, their knowledges and interests, would be invisible in this analytic frame because the very idea of an intellectual commons falls outside the purview of privatized property and profit that is a basis for corporate interests. The obvious issue for a transnational feminism pertains to the visions of profit and justice embodied in these opposing analytic perspectives. The focus on profit versus justice illustrates my earlier point about social location and analytically inclusive methodologies. It is the social location of the tribal women as explicated by Shiva that allows this broad and inclusive focus on justice. Similarly, it is the social location and narrow self-interest of corporations that privatize intellectual property rights in the name of profit for elites.

Shiva essentially offers a critique of the global privatization of indigenous knowledges. This is a story about the rise of transnational institutions such as the WTO, the World Bank, and the International Monetary Fund, of banking and financial institutions and cross-national governing bodies like the MAI (Multinational Agreement on Investments). The effects of these governing bodies on poor people around the world have been devastating. In fundamental ways, it is girls and women around the world, especially in the Third World/South, that bear the brunt of globalization. Poor women and girls are the hardest hit by the degradation of environmental conditions, wars, famines, privatization of services and deregulation of governments, the dismantling of welfare states, the restructuring of paid and unpaid work, increasing surveillance and incarceration in prisons, and so on. And this is why a feminism without and beyond borders is necessary to address the injustices of global capitalism.

Women and girls are still 70 percent of the world's poor and the majority of the world's refugees. Girls and women comprise almost 80 percent of displaced persons of the Third World/South in Africa, Asia and Latin America. Women own less than one-hundredth of the world's property, while they are the hardest hit by the effects of war, domestic violence, and religious persecution. Feminist political theorist Zillah Eisenstein says that women do two-thirds of the world's work and earn less than one-tenth of its income. Global capital in racialized and sexualized guise destroys the public spaces of democracy, and quietly sucks power out of the once social/public spaces of nation-states. Corporate capitalism has redefined citizens as consumers—and global markets replace the commitments to economic, sexual, and racial equality (Eisenstein 1998b, esp. ch. 5).

It is especially on the bodies and lives of women and girls from the Third World/South—the Two-Thirds World—that global capitalism writes its script, and it is by paying attention to and theorizing the experiences of these communities of women and girls that we demystify capitalism as a system of debilitating sexism and racism and envision anticapitalist resistance. Thus any analysis of the effects of globalization needs to centralize the experiences and struggles of these particular communities of women and girls.

Drawing on Arif Dirlik's notion of "place consciousness as the radical other of global capitalism" (Dirlik 1999), Grace Lee Boggs makes an important argument for place-based civic activism that illustrates how centralizing the struggles of marginalized communities connects to larger antiglobalization struggles. Boggs suggests that "[p]lace consciousness . . . encourages us to come together around common, local experiences and organize around our hopes for the future of our communities and cities. While global capitalism doesn't give a damn about the people or the natural environment of any par-ticular place because it can always move on to other people and other places, place-based civic activism is concerned about the heath and safety of people and places" (Boggs 2000, 19). Since women are central to the life of neighbor-hood and communities they assume leadership positions in these struggles. This is evident in the example of women of color in struggles against envi-ronmental racism in the United States, as well as in Shiva's example of tribal women in the struggle against deforestation and for an intellectual com-mons. It is then the lives, experiences, and struggles of girls and women of the Two-Thirds World that demystify capitalism in its racial and sexual dimensions—and that provide productive and necessary avenues of theorizing and enacting anticapitalist resistance.

I do not wish to leave this discussion of capitalism as a generalized site without contextualizing its meaning in and through the lives it structures. Disproportionately, these are girls' and women's lives, although I am com-mitted to the lives of all exploited peoples. However, the specificity of girls' and women's lives encompasses the others through their particularized and contextualized experiences. If these particular gendered, classed, and racial-ized realities of globalization are unseen and undertheorized, even the most radical critiques of globalization effectively render Third World/South women and girls as absent. Perhaps it is no longer simply an issue of Western eyes, but rather how the West is inside and continually reconfigures globally, racially, and in terms of gender. Without this recognition, a necessary link between feminist scholarship/analytic frames and organizing/activist projects is impossible. Faulty and inadequate analytic frames engender ineffective political action and strategizing for social transformation.

What does the above analysis suggest? That we—feminist scholars and teachers—must respond to the phenomenon of globalization as an urgent site for the recolonization of peoples, especially in the Two-Thirds World. Globalization colonizes women's as well as men's lives around the world, and we need an anti-imperialist, anticapitalist, and contextualized feminist project to expose and make visible the various, overlapping forms of subjugation of women's lives. Activists and scholars must also identify and reenvision forms of collective resistance that women, especially, in their different communities enact in their everyday lives. It is their particular exploitation at this time, their potential epistemic privilege, as well as their particular forms of solidarity that can be the basis for reimagining a liberatory politics for the start of this century.

NOTES

1. In fact, we now even have debates about the "future of women's studies" and the "impossibility of women's studies." See the Web site "The Future of Women's Studies," Women's Studies Program, University of Arizona, 2000 at http://info-center.ccit.arizona.edu/~ws/conference; and Brown 1997.

2. See, for instance, the work of Ella Shohat, Lisa Lowe, Aihwa Ong, Uma Narayan, Inderpal Grewal and Caren Kaplan, Chela Sandoval, Avtar Brah, Lila Abu-Lughod, Jacqui Alexander, Kamala Kempadoo, and Saskia Sassen.

3. See the works of Maria Mies, Cynthia Enloe, Zillah Eisenstein, Saskia Sassen, and Dorothy Smith (for instance, those listed in the bibliography) for similar methodological approaches. An early, pioneering example of this perspective can be found in the "Black Feminist" statement by the Combahee River Collective in the early 1980s.

4. See discussions of epistemic privilege in the essays by Mohanty, Moya, and Macdonald in Moya and Hames-Garcia 2000.

5. Examples of women of color in the fight against environmental racism can be found in the organization Mothers of East Los Angeles (see Pardo 2001), the magazine *ColorLines,* and *Voces Unidas,* the newsletter of the SouthWest Organizing project, Albuquerque, New Mexico.

6. See Shiva, Jafri, Bedi, and Holla-Bhar 1997. For a provocative argument about indigenous knowledges, see Dei and Sefa 2000.

REFERENCES

Abu-Lughod, Lila. 1998. *Remaking Women: Feminism and Modernity in the Middle East.* Princeton: Princeton University Press.

Alexander, Jacqui M. 1991. "Redrafting Morality: The Postcolonial State and the Sexual Offenses Bill of Trinidad and Tobago." In *Third World Women and the Politics of Feminism,* edited by Chandra Talpade Mohanty, Ann Russo, and Lourdes Torres. Bloomington: Indiana University Press.

Alexander, Jacqui M., and Chandra Talpade Mohanty. 1997. *Feminist Genealogies, Colonial Legacies, Democratic Futures.* New York: Routledge.

Boggs, Grace Lee. 2000. "A Question of Place." *Monthly Review* 52, no. 2 (June): 18–20.

Brah, Avtar. 1996. *Cartographies of Diaspora: Contesting Identities.* London: Routledge.

Brown, Wendy. 1997. "The Impossibility of Women's Studies." *differences* 9, no. 3: 79–101.

ColorLines. 2000. "Global Brahmanism: The Meaning of the WTO Protests—An Interview with Vandana Shiva." *ColorLines* 3, no. 2 (summer): 30–32. *Gender and Global Restructuring: Sightings, Sites, and Resistances.*

Combahee River Collective. 1983. "A Black Feminist Statement." Reprinted in *All the Women are White, All the Blacks are Men, But Some of Us are Brave,* edited by Gloria Hull, Patricia Bell Scott, and Barbara Smith. Old Westbury, NY: Feminist Press.

Dei, George, and J. Sefa. 2000. "Rethinking the Role of Indigenous Knowledges in the Academy." *International Journal of Inclusive Education* 4, no. 2: 111–32.

Dirlik, Arif. 1999. "Place-Based Imagination: Globalism and the Politics of Place." In *Review, A Journal of the Ferdinand Braudel Center for the Study of Economics, Historical Systems, and Civilizations* 22, no. 2 (spring): 151–87.

Eisenstein, Zillah R. 2001. *Manmade Breast Cancers.* Ithaca: Cornell University Press.

———. 1998a. *The Female Body and the Law.* Berkeley: University of California Press.

———. 1998b. *Global Obscenities: Patriarchy, Capitalism, and the Lure of Cyberfantasy.* New York: New York University Press.

———. 1996. *Hatreds: Racialized and Sexualized Conflicts in the 21st Century.* New York: Routledge.

———. 1994. *The Color of Gender: Reimaging Democracy.* Berkeley: University of California Press.

———. 1990. "Feminism v. Neoconservative Jurisprudence: The Spring '89 Supreme Court." Unpublished manuscript. Ithaca, NY: Ithaca College.

———. 1984. *Feminism and Sexual Equality.* New York: Monthly Review Press.

———. 1981. *The Radical Future of Liberal Feminism.* New York: Longman, 1981.

———. 1978, editor. *Capitalist Patriarchy and the Case for Socialist Feminism.* New York: Monthly Review Press.

Enloe, Cynthia. 1993. *The Morning After: Sexual Politics at the End of the Cold War.* Berkeley: University of California Press.

———. 1990. *Bananas, Beaches, and Bases: Making Feminist Sense of International Politics.* Berkeley: University of California Press.

The Future of Women's Studies. 2000. Conference Proceedings. Tucson: University of Arizona Women's Studies Department. <http://info-center.ccit.Arizona.edu/~ws/conference/conference.html>.

Grewal, Inderpal, and Caren Kaplan, eds. 1994. *Scattered Hegemonies, Postmodernity and Transnational Feminist Practices.* Minneapolis: University of Minnesota Press.

Kempadoo, Kamala, and Jo Doezema, eds. 1999. *Global Sex Workers, Rights, Resistance, and Redefinition.* London: Routledge.

Lowe, Lisa. 1996. *Immigrant Acts: on Asian American Cultural Politics.* Durham, N.C.: Duke University Press.

———. 1994. *Globalization, Space, Difference.* Honolulu: East-West Center.

Lowe, Lisa, and David Lloyd. 1997. *The Politics of Culture in the Shadow of Capital.* Durham, N.C.: Duke University Press.

Mies, Maria. 1986. *Patriarchy and Accumulation on a World Scale: Women in the International Division of Labor.* London: Zed Press.

———. 1982. *The Lacemakers of Narsapur: Indian Housewives Produce for the World Market.* London: Zed Press.

Mies, Maria, and Vandana Shiva. 1993. *Ecofeminism.* London: Zed Press.

Mohanty, Chandra Talpade. 1984. "Under Western Eyes: Feminist Scholarship and Colonial Discourses." *Boundary* 2 12, no. 3/13, no. 1 (spring/fall): 338–358.

Moya, Paula, and Michael R. Hames-Garcia, eds. 2000. *Reclaiming Identity: Realist Theory and the Predicament of Postmodernism.* Berkeley: University of California Press.

Narayan, Uma. 1997. *Dislocating Cultures: Identities, Traditions, and Third-World Feminism.* New York: Routledge.

Ong, Aihwa. 1991. "The Gender and Labor Politics of Postmodernity." *Annual Review of Anthropology* 20: 279–309.

———. 1987. *Spirits of Resistance and Capitalist Discipline: Factory Women in Malaysia.* Albany: State University of New York Press.

Pardo, Mary. 2001. "Mexican-American Women Grassroots Community Activists: Mothers of East Los Angeles." *In Women's Lives: Multicultural Perspectives,* ed. Margo Okazawa-Rey and Gwyn Kirk, 504–11. Mountain View, CA: Mayfield Publishing Company.

Sandoval, Chela. 2000. *Methodology of the Oppressed.* Minneapolis: University of Minnesota Press.

———. 1991. "U.S. Third World: The Theory and Method of Oppositional Consciousness in the Postmodern World," *Genders* 10 (spring): 1–24.

———. 1983. "Women Respond to Racism: A Report on the National Women's Studies Association Conference, Storrs, Connecticut." Occasional Paper Series. Oakland, Calif.: Center for Third World Organizing, 1983.

Sassen, Saskia. 1998. "New Employment Regimes in Cities: The Impact on Immigrant Workers," *Journal of Ethnic and Minority Studies* 22, no. 4: 579–94.

———. 1991. *The Global City: New York, London, Tokyo.* Princeton: Princeton University Press.

———. 1988. *The Mobility of Labor and Capital.* New York: Cambridge University Press.

Shiva, Vandana, A. H. Jafri, G. Bedi, and R. Holla-Bhar. 1997. *The Enclosure and Recovery of the Commons: Biodiversity, Indigenous Knowledge and Intellectual Property Rights.* New Delhi: Research Foundation for Science and Technology.

Shiva, Vandana, Rebecca Gordon, and Bob Wing. 2000. "Global Brahminism: The Meaning of the WTO Protests: An Interview with Dr. Vandana Shiva," *ColorLines,* 3 (2): 30–32.

Shohat, Ella. 2001. "Area Studies, Transnationalism, and the Feminist Production of Knowledge." *Signs* 26, no. 4 (summer): 1269–72.

———. 2001. *Talking Visions: Multicultural Feminism in a Transnational Age.* Cambridge, Mass.: MIT Press.

Shohat, Ella, and Robert Stam. 1994. *Unthinking Eurocentrism: Multiculturalism and the Media.* London: Routledge.

Smith, Dorothy. 1987. *The Everyday World as Problematic: A Feminist Sociology.* Boston: Northeastern University Press.

10

PATRIARCHY, THE SYSTEM
An It, Not a He, a Them, or an Us

ALLAN G. JOHNSON

Allan G. Johnson, Ph.D., teaches sociology at Hartford College for Women. His books include *Power, Privilege and Difference,* 2nd ed. (2005); *The Gender Knot,* 2nd ed. (2005); *The Forest and the Trees: Sociology as Life, Practice and Promise* (1997); and *The Blackwell Dictionary of Sociology* (2000).

"When you say patriarchy," a man complained from the rear of the audience, "I know what you *really* mean—me!" A lot of people hear "men" whenever someone says "patriarchy," so that criticism of gender oppression is taken to mean that all men—each and every one of them—are oppressive people. Not surprisingly, many men take it personally if someone merely mentions patriarchy or the oppression of women, bristling at what they often see as a way to make them feel guilty. And some women feel free to blame individual men for patriarchy simply because they're men. Some of the time, men feel defensive because they identify with patriarchy and its values and don't want to face the consequences these produce or the prospect of giving up male privilege. But defensiveness more often reflects a common confusion about the difference between patriarchy as a kind of society and the people who participate in it. If we're ever going to work toward real change, it's a confusion we'll have to clear up.

To do this, we have to realize that we're stuck in a model of social life that views everything as beginning and ending with individuals. Looking at things in this way, we tend to think that if evil exists in the world, it's only because there are evil people who have entered into an evil conspiracy. Racism exists, for example, simply because white people are racist bigots who hate members of racial and ethnic minorities and want to do them harm. There is gender oppression because men want and like to dominate women and act out hostility toward them. There is poverty and class oppression because people in the upper classes are greedy, heartless, and cruel. The flip side of this individualistic model of guilt and blame is that race, gender, and class oppression are actually not oppression at all, but merely the sum of individual failings on the part of blacks, women, and the poor, who lack the right stuff to compete successfully with whites, men, and others who know how to make something of themselves.

What this kind of thinking ignores is that we are all participating in something larger than ourselves or any collection of us. On some level, most people are familiar with the idea that social life involves us in something larger than ourselves, but few seem to know what to do with that idea. When Sam Keen laments that "THE SYSTEM is running us all,"[1] he strikes a deep chord in many people. But he also touches on a basic misunderstanding of social life, because having blamed "the system" (presumably society) for our problems, he doesn't take the next step to understand what that might mean. What exactly *is* a system, for example, and how could it run us? Do *we* have anything to do with shaping *it*, and if so, how? How, for example, do we participate in patriarchy, and how does that link us to the consequences it produces? How is what we think of as "normal" life related to male dominance, women's oppression, and the hierarchical, control-obsessed world in which they, and our lives, are embedded? . . .

. . . If we see patriarchy as nothing more than men's and women's individual personalities, motivations, and behavior, for example, then it probably won't even occur to us to ask about larger contexts—such as institutions like the family, religion, and the economy—and how people's lives are shaped in relation to them. From this kind of individualistic perspective, we might ask why a particular man raped, harassed, or beat a woman. We wouldn't ask, however, what kind of society would promote persistent *patterns* of such behavior in everyday life, from wife-beating jokes to the routine inclusion of sexual coercion and violence in mainstream movies. We are quick to explain rape and battery as the acts of sick or angry men; but we rarely take seriously the question of what kind of society would produce so much male anger and pathology or direct it toward sexual violence rather than something else. We rarely ask how gender violence might serve other more "normalized" ends such as male control and domination. . . .

. . . If the goal is to change the world, this won't help us. We need to see and deal with the social roots that generate and nurture the social problems that are reflected in the behavior of individuals. We can't do this without realizing that we all participate in something larger than ourselves, something we didn't create but that we have the power to affect through the choices we make about *how* to participate.

That something larger is patriarchy, which is more than a collection of individuals (such as "men"). It is a system, which means it can't be reduced to the people who participate in it. If you go to work in a corporation, for example, you know the minute you walk in the door that you've entered "something" that shapes your experience and behavior, something that isn't just you and the other people you work with. You can feel yourself stepping into a set of relationships and shared understandings about who's who and what's supposed to happen and why, and all of this limits you in many ways.

And when you leave at the end of the day you can feel yourself released from the constraints imposed by your participation in that system; you can feel the expectations drop away and your focus shift to other systems such as family or a neighborhood bar that shape your experience in different ways. To understand a system like a corporation, we have to look at more than people like you, because all of you aren't the corporation, even though you make it run. If the corporation were just a collection of people, then whatever happened to the corporation would by definition also happen to them, and vice versa; but this clearly isn't so. A corporation can go bankrupt, for example, or cease to exist altogether without any of the people who work there going bankrupt or disappearing. Conversely, everyone who works for the corporation could quit, but that wouldn't necessarily mean the end of the corporation, only the arrival of a new set of participants. We can't understand a corporation, then, just by looking at the people who participate in it, for it is something larger and has to be understood as such.

So, too, with patriarchy, a kind of society that is more than a collection of women and men and can't be understood simply by understanding them. *We are not patriarchy,* no more than people who believe in Allah *are* Islam or Canadians *are* Canada. Patriarchy is a kind of society organized around certain kinds of social relationships and ideas. As individuals, we participate in it. Paradoxically, our participation both shapes our lives and gives us the opportunity to be part of changing or perpetuating it.[2] But *we are not it,* which means that patriarchy can exist without men having "oppressive personalities" or actively conspiring with one another to defend male privilege. To demonstrate that gender oppression exists, we don't have to show that men are villains, that women are good-hearted victims, that women don't participate in their own oppression, or that men never oppose it. If a society is oppressive, then people who grow up and live in it will tend to accept, identify with, and participate in it as "normal" and unremarkable life. That's the path of least resistance in any system. It's hard not to follow it, given how we depend on society and its rewards and punishments that hinge on going along with the status quo. When oppression is woven into the fabric of everyday life, we don't need to go out of our way to be overly oppressive in order for an oppressive system to produce oppressive consequences. As the saying goes, what evil requires is simply that ordinary people do nothing.

Patriarchy

The key to understanding any system is to identify its various parts and how they're arranged to form a whole. To understand a language, for example, we have to learn its alphabet, vocabulary, and rules for combining words into meaningful phrases and sentences. With a social system such as patriarchy, it's more complicated because there are many different kinds of parts, and it is often difficult to see just how they're connected. Patriarchy's defining elements are its male-dominated, male-identified, and male-centered character, but this is just the beginning. At its core, patriarchy is a set of symbols and ideas that make up a culture embodied by everything from the content of everyday conversation to literature and film. Patriarchal culture includes ideas about the nature of things, including men, women, and humanity, with manhood and masculinity most closely associated with being human and womanhood and femininity relegated to the marginal position of "other." It's about how social life is and how it's supposed to be; about what's expected of people and about how they feel. It's about standards of feminine beauty and masculine toughness, images of feminine vulnerability and masculine protectiveness, of older men coupled with young women, of elderly women alone. It's about defining women and men as opposites, about the "naturalness" of male aggression, competition, and dominance and of female caring, cooperation, and subordination. It's about the valuing of masculinity and maleness and the devaluing of femininity and femaleness. It's about the primary importance of a husband's career and the secondary status of a wife's, about child care as a priority in women's lives and its secondary importance in men's. It's about the social acceptability of anger, rage, and toughness in men but not in women, and of caring, tenderness, and vulnerability in women but not in men.

Above all, patriarchal culture is about the core value of control and domination in almost every area of human existence. From the expression of emotion to economics to the natural environment, gaining and exercising control is a continuing goal of great importance. Because of this, the concept of power takes on a narrow definition in terms of "power over"—the ability to control others, events, resources, or oneself in spite of resistance—rather than alternatives such as the ability to cooperate with others, to give freely of oneself, or to feel and act in harmony with nature.[3] To have power over and to be prepared to use it are defined culturally as good and desirable (and characteristically "masculine"), and to lack such power or to be reluctant to use it is seen as weak if not contemptible (and characteristically "feminine").

The main use of any culture is to provide symbols and ideas out of which people construct their sense of what is real. As such, language mirrors social reality in sometimes startling ways. In contemporary usage, for example, the words "crone," "witch," "bitch," and "virgin" describe women as threatening, evil, or heterosexually inexperienced and thus incomplete. In prepatriarchal times, however, these words evoked far different images.[4] The crone was the old woman whose life experience gave her insight, wisdom, respect, and the power to enrich people's lives. The witch was the wise-woman healer, the knower of herbs, the midwife, the link joining body, spirit, and Earth. The bitch was Artemis-Diana, goddess of the hunt, most often associated with the dogs who accompanied her. And the virgin was merely a woman who was unattached, unclaimed, and unowned by any man and therefore independent and autonomous. Notice how each word has been transformed from a positive cultural image of female power, independence, and dignity to an insult or a shadow of its former self so that few words remain to identify women in ways both positive and powerful.

Going deeper into patriarchal culture, we find a complex web of ideas that define reality and what's considered good and desirable. To see the world through patriarchal eyes is to believe that women and men are profoundly different in their basic natures, that hierarchy is the only alternative to chaos, and that men were made in the image of a masculine God with whom they enjoy a special relationship. It is to take as obvious the idea that there are two and only two distinct genders; that patriarchal heterosexuality is "natural" and same-sex attraction is not; that because men neither bear nor breast-feed children, they cannot feel a compelling bodily connection to them; that on some level every woman, whether heterosexual or lesbian, wants a "real man" who knows how to "take charge of things," including her; that females can't be trusted, especially when they're menstruating or accusing men of sexual misconduct. To embrace patriarchy is to believe that mothers should stay home and that fathers should work out of the home, regardless of men's and women's actual abilities or needs.[5] It is to buy into the notion that women are weak and men are strong, that women and children need men to support and protect them, all in spite of the fact that in many ways men are not the physically stronger sex, that women perform a huge share of hard physical labor in many societies (often larger than men's), that women's physical endurance tends to be greater than men's over the long haul, that women tend to be more capable of enduring pain and emotional stress.[6] And yet such evidence means little in the face of a patriarchal culture that dictates how things *ought* to be and, like all cultural mythology,

> will not be argued down by facts. It may seem to be making
> straightforward statements, but actually these conceal another
> mood, the imperative. Myth exists in a state of tension. It is not
> really describing a situation, but trying by means of this description
> to *bring about* what it declares to exist.[7]

To live in a patriarchal culture is to learn what's expected of us as men and women, the rules that regulate punishment and reward based on how we behave and appear. These rules range from laws that require men to fight in wars not of their own choosing to customary expectations that mothers will provide child care, or that when a woman shows sexual interest in a man or merely smiles or acts friendly, she gives up her right to say no and control her own body. And to live under patriarchy is to take into ourselves shared ways of feeling—the hostile contempt for femaleness that forms the core of misogyny and presumptions of male superiority, the ridicule men direct at other men who show signs of vulnerability or weakness, or the fear and insecurity that every woman must deal with when she exercises the right to move freely in the world, especially at night and by herself. . . .

The prominent place of misogyny in patriarchal culture, for example, doesn't mean that every man and woman consciously hates all things female. But it does mean that to the extent that we don't feel such hatred, it's *in spite of* paths of least resistance contained in our culture. Complete freedom from such feelings and judgments is all but impossible. It is certainly possible for heterosexual men to love women without mentally fragmenting them into breasts, buttocks, genitals, and other variously desirable parts. It is possible for women to feel good about their bodies, to not judge themselves as being too fat, to not abuse themselves to one degree or another in pursuit of impossible male-identified standards of beauty and sexual attractiveness. All of this is possible; but to live in patriarchy is to breathe in misogynist images of women as objectified sexual property valued primarily for their usefulness to men. This finds its way into everyone who grows up breathing and swimming in it, and once inside us it remains, however unaware of it we may be. So, when we hear or express sexist jokes and other forms of misogyny we may not recognize it, and even if we do, say nothing rather than risk other people thinking we're "too sensitive" or, especially in the case of men, "not one of the guys." In either case, we are involved, if only by our silence. . . .

To understand patriarchy, we have to identify its cultural elements and see how they are related to the structure of social life. We must see, for example, how cultural ideas that identify women primarily as mothers and men primarily as breadwinners support patterns in which women do most domestic work at home and are discriminated against in hiring, pay, and promotions at work. But to do anything with such an understanding, we also must see what patriarchy has to do with us as individuals—how it shapes us and how we, in choosing how to participate, shape *it*.

The System in Us in the System

One of the most difficult things to accept about patriarchy is that we're involved in it, which means we're also involved in its consequences. This is especially hard for men who refuse to believe they benefit from women's oppression, because they can't see how this could happen without their being personally oppressive in their intentions, feelings, and behavior. For many men, being told they're *involved* in oppression can only mean they *are* oppressive. . . .

. . . Societies don't exist without people participating in them, which means that we can't understand patriarchy unless we also ask how people are connected to it and how this connection varies, depending on social characteristics such as race, gender, ethnicity, age, and class. Capitalism, for example, didn't just happen on its own but emerged as an economic system in a patriarchal world dominated by men and their interests, especially white

European men of the newly emerging merchant class. The same can be said of industrialization, which was bound up with the development of capitalism in eighteenth- and nineteenth-century Europe. This line of thinking might seem to undermine the argument I've made about including systems in our thinking—"It really comes down to individuals after all"—but it's more complicated than that. The problem isn't society and it isn't us. It's the relationship between the two that we have to understand, the nature of the thing we participate in and how we choose to participate in it and how both are shaped in the process. In this sense, it's a mistake to equate patriarchy with men; but it's also wrong to act as though systems like patriarchy or capitalism have nothing to do with gender and differences in power and interests that distinguish and separate men and women. It's equally wrong to act as though all men or all women are the same, as though dynamics such as racism and class oppression don't affect how patriarchy operates and affects people's lives in different ways.

One way to see how people connect with systems is to think of us as occupying social positions that locate us in relation to people in other positions. We connect to families, for example, through positions such as "mother," "daughter," and "cousin"; to economic systems through positions such as "vice president," "secretary," or "unemployed"; to political systems through positions such as "citizen," "registered voter," and "mayor"; to religious systems through positions such as "believer" and "clergy." How we perceive the people who occupy such positions and what we expect of them depend on cultural ideas—such as the belief that mothers are naturally better than fathers at child care or the expectation that fathers will be the primary breadwinners. Such ideas are powerful because we use them to construct a sense of who we and other people are. When a woman marries, for example, how people (including her) perceive and think about her changes as cultural ideas about what it means to be a wife come into play—ideas about how wives feel about their husbands, for example, what's most important to wives, what's expected of them, and what they may expect of others. . . .

We can think of a society as a network of interconnected systems within systems, each made up of social positions and their relations to one another. To say, then, that I'm white, male, college educated, and a writer, sociologist, U.S. citizen, heterosexual, middle-aged, husband, father, brother, and son identifies me in relation to positions which are themselves related to positions in various social systems, from the entire world to the family of my birth. In another sense, the day-to-day reality of a society only exists through what people actually do as they participate in it. Patriarchal culture, for example, places a high value on control and maleness. By themselves, these are just abstractions. But when men and women actually talk and men interrupt women more than women interrupt men, or men ignore topics introduced by women in favor of their own or in other ways control conversation,[8] or when men use their authority to sexually harass women in the workplace, then the reality of patriarchy as a kind of society and people's sense of themselves as female and male within it actually happen in a concrete way.

In this sense, like all social systems, patriarchy exists only through people's lives. Through this, patriarchy's various aspects are there for us to see over and over again. This has two important implications for how we understand patriarchy. First, to some extent people experience patriarchy as external to them; but this doesn't mean that it's a distinct and separate thing, like a house in which we live. Instead, by participating in patriarchy we are of patriarchy and it is *of* us. Both exist *through* the other and neither can exist without the other. Second, patriarchy isn't static; it's an ongoing *process* that's continuously shaped and reshaped. Since the thing we're participating in is patriarchal, we tend to behave in ways that create a patriarchal world from one moment to the next. But we have some freedom to break the rules and construct everyday life in different ways, which means that the paths we choose to follow can do as much to change patriarchy as they can to perpetuate it.

We're involved in patriarchy and its consequences because we occupy social positions in it, which is all it takes. Since gender oppression is, by definition, a system of inequality organized around gender categories, we can no more avoid being involved in it than we can avoid being female or male. *All* men and *all* women are therefore involved in this oppressive system, and none of us can control *whether* we participate, only *how.* . . .

NOTES

1. Sam Keen, *Fire in the Belly: On Being a Man* (New York: Bantam, 1991), 207.
2. This is one of the major differences between organisms like the human body and social systems. Cells and nerves cannot "rebel" against the body and try to change it into something else.
3. For a thorough discussion of this distinction, see Marilyn French, *Beyond Power: On Men, Women, and Morals* (New York: Summit Books, 1985).
4. For discussions of language and gender, see Jane Caputi, *Gossips, Gorgons, and Crones* (Santa Fe: Bear and Company, 1993); Mary Daly, *Gyn/Ecology: The Metaethics of Radical Feminism* (Boston: Beacon Press, 1978); Dale Spender, *Man Made Language* (London: Pandora, 1980); Barbara G. Walker, *The Woman's Encyclopedia of Myths and Secrets* (San Francisco: Harper and Row, 1983); idem, *The Woman's Dictionary of Symbols and Sacred Objects* (San Francisco: Harper and Row, 1988). For a very different slant on gender and language, see Mary Daly (in cahoots with Jane Caputi), *Webster's First New Intergalactic Wickedary of the English Language* (Boston: Beacon Press, 1987).
5. See Arlie Hochschild (with Anne Machung), *The Second Shift* (New York: Avon Books, 1989).
6. See, for example, Rosalyn Baxandall, Linda Gordon, and Susan Reverby, eds., *America's Working Women: A Documentary History—1600 to the Present* (New York: Vintage Press, 1976); Ashley Montagu, *The Natural Superiority of Women* (New York: Collier, 1974); Robin Morgan, ed., *Sisterhood Is Global* (New York: Anchor, 1990); and Marilyn Waring, *If Women Counted: A New Feminist Economics* (San Francisco: HarperCollins, 1988).

7. Elizabeth Janeway, *Man's World, Woman's Place: A Study in Social Mythology* (New York: Dell, 1971), 37.

8. See, for example, P. Kollock, P. Blumstein, and P. Schwartz, "Sex and Power in Interaction," *American Sociological Review* 50, no. 1 (1985): 34–46; N. Henley, M. Hamilton, and B. Thorne, "Womanspeak and Manspeak: Sex Differences and Sexism in Communication," in *Beyond Sex Roles,* ed. A. G. Sargent (New York: West, 1985), 168–185; and L. Smith-Lovin and C. Brody, "Interruptions in Group Discussions: The Effect of Gender and Group Composition," *American Sociological Review* 51, no. 3 (1989): 424–435.

PART II
Gender Socialization

The gender system, embedded in other institutions, ensures its continuance through systematic socialization of children, adolescents, and adults. Even though there is substantial variation in how different cultural groups and families within the United States and throughout the world teach their children to be girls or boys, and even though men and women are more alike than they are different, the presence of gender training persists, and larger institutional structures reinforce it. Sociologist Michael Messner, for example, in a telling account of white male socialization in childhood, describes the day he attended his first Little League practice and was told by his father that he threw like a girl. A week later, after careful coaching by his father and intense fear of being thought a sissy, he had learned to throw like a man.[1] In a study of Black and white elementary school children, Jacqueline Jordan Irvine concluded that teachers systematically encouraged Black girls to act submissive and that by upper elementary school, both Black and white girls are rendered relatively invisible in classrooms, receiving significantly less attention from teachers than boys of both races receive.[2]

From the time we are born until we die, gender socialization is a constant part of our lives. Although the genes that determine sex come in several combinations (not just two), and although the hormonal makeup and physical characteristics of human beings fall along a continuum defined as masculine at one end and feminine at the other, allowing for many combinations and permutations that define one's biological sex, the social contexts in which infants are assigned a gender do not allow for more than two categories in mainstream U.S. society. Based on examination of its genitalia, an infant will almost always be defined as female or male, whatever its chromosomal and hormonal makeup. Within this powerful system of gender assignment, women and men work to define their individual identities. Because gender is a socialized aspect of life rather than a purely genetic/biological one, and because it is largely "socially constructed" rather than instinctual, there is flexibility in how it is expressed.

In a distressing illustration of how girl and boy children are treated differently from very early in their lives, authors of a study of infants with abusive head trauma found that most of the infant victims were boys (60.3 percent). Both women and men tended to abuse boys more than girls in ways serious enough to inflict head injury via shaken baby syndrome or impact trauma. The majority of perpetrators were men in the infants' lives—most typically fathers, stepfathers, or the mother's partner. The authors of the study suggest that perhaps adults have different expectations of male and female infants. If the latter is the case, it could be that tolerance for crying in girl babies is higher than it is for boys. These authors and others call for better parenting training, especially focused on men and boys.[3] The resistance of parents to give dolls to boys seems to be part of the failure to teach boys to care for children. The fact that more women than ever before are involved in the paid workforce means that more men and boys are spending time with children, either because the parents are working split shifts, or because men and boys are serving as babysitters more often.

A push toward gender equality in recent years in some aspects of schooling has led to higher math scores and greater success in science among girls. It has also led to higher rates of smoking, drinking, and drug use according to a report sponsored by the National Council for Research on Women.[4]

The field of gender socialization is currently facing some redefinition related to the role of hormones and genitals in human development. Since 1972, many academics and medical professionals have been arguing that gender is primarily socialized, independent of genes and hormones—that infants are psychologically undifferentiated at birth. In short, they argued that any baby could be raised in either gender if the family and community gave the child consistent messages. This conclusion was based on a single case reported by psychologist John Money concerning a biological male whose penis was accidentally destroyed in a routine circumcision at seven months of age. The parents, following the advice of Money and his medical team, decided to raise the child as a girl a year or so later, and the child's testicles were surgically removed.[5] The early reports on this boy/girl's life claimed that "Joan" had made a successful adjustment as a girl. In 1997, however, psychologist Milton Diamond and psychiatrist Keith Sigmundson reported that Joan had rejected the sex reassignment treatments at age 14 and decided to live as a heterosexual male from then on. He eventually married a woman with children. Adamantly rejecting the notion that gender must be based on genital appearance, size, and function, he stated, "If that's all they think of me, that they gotta justify my worth by what I have between my legs, then I gotta be a complete loser."[6] Diamond and Sigmundson concluded that the early gender reassignment had been a mistake and later the same year offered guidelines for how to address situations in which children had unusual or injured genitals.[7] Later journalist John Colapinto wrote a book about this case, describing in detail the experiences of David Reimer (his real name) and exposing what he believed were serious ethical breaches in Money's treatment of both Reimer and the readers of his publications.[8] Sadly, David Reimer committed suicide in 2004. This case suggests that the extent to which gender is hardwired to physical sex is still unclear, especially because many people raised in a gender that matches their sex feel as though they are in the wrong body and choose to change genders.

Sex reassignment seems most successful when chosen by the person him- or herself. The negative aspects of forced gender reassignment surgery have been made especially clear by members of the Intersex Society of North America (www.isna.org) who argue that forced gender and sex assignments that contradicted their bodily truths have been destructive. They recommend assigning a gender to an infant, avoiding any unnecessary surgery, and allowing the child to choose how to express her/himself once s/he is old enough to understand what version of intersexuality or disorders of sexual development (DSD) are present. An example from the Dominican Republic illustrates how this is handled relatively successfully in one unusual situation. Children in three villages inherited a syndrome that produced somewhat ambiguous genitalia at birth but that later became male genitalia at puberty. These children were raised as girls who knew that they might become boys at puberty. They received a third gender label, "male genitalia at 12." Of 18 children originally raised as girls, 16 successfully assumed male genders after their penises developed.[9] At least one chose to remain female, even though her body had masculinized, because she enjoyed living as a girl/woman.

The potential for gender resocialization is clearly illustrated by adults who become transsexuals or transgendered, making a choice to resocialize themselves, to varying degrees, into the gender in which they were not raised. This resocialization process is often accompanied by a new sexual orientation as well. Many people who have gone through this kind of transition have written firsthand accounts describing what convinced them to do it and what it was like.[10] (See Ben Barres, Part VII.)

Research literature on adult development suggests that expressions of gender shift in various ways throughout the life cycle.[11] Men and women frequently grow more similar in midlife. Socialization patterns and expectations for male and female behavior also change over time, related to the historical context. For example, many women were needed in factories during World War II but were sent home when men, returning from the war, were given priority in hiring; these women were then encouraged to be housewives and mothers, forced to resocialize themselves to match prior expectations. Those who had to continue to work outside the home, however, ended up with lower-paying jobs because the jobs with higher wages were given to men returning from the war.

Socialization as soldiers or fighters, increasingly obvious to people in the United States as we grapple with the aftermath of September 11, 2001, affects millions of young men (especially) and women worldwide. Recruitment of boys and men into national armies or resistance movements has an impact on not only the young men themselves but also their families and communities.[12] Turning people into fighters takes an intensive socialization process for which state armies and militias are famous. The effects of militarism on women as well are widespread and well documented.[13] Both men and women returning from combat have high rates of post-traumatic stress disorder, making resocialization into civilian life particularly difficult. Recent attention to the mental health effects on soldiers returning from the war in Iraq has highlighted the different experiences of women and men and suggests that the combination of combat stress and sexual assault within the armed services make the war experience even more stressful for some women than it is for men.[14] (See Helen Benedict and Cynthia Enloe, Part IX.)

This part of the book looks at selected aspects of gender socialization. A recurring theme in the study of gender socialization is the presence of homophobia overtly expressed against boys and girls who don't fit gender stereotypes and internalized by gay men, lesbians, bisexuals, and transgendered people as fear of ostracism or as self-hatred. The essays included here address the social construction of gender and gender inequality (Judith Lorber), pressures for gender conformity (Tommi Avicolli, Linnea Due, and Michael Kimmel), and gender socialization in varied cultural/racial/class contexts in the United States (Michael Messner and Jill Nelson).

These articles urge us to become more conscious of various aspects of gender socialization and to consider ways to change what limits people of both genders from being fully human in their own right. There are policy implications here regarding how we accept people who don't fit the norms of masculinity and femininity, regarding the negative effects of limited economic options for poor and working-class children, and regarding the intersections of racism, homophobia, elitism, and sexism as they affect people's lives.

As you read the articles in this section, you might find it interesting to ask yourself what your life might have been like if you had been born a different sex. Then make your imagined experience more complex by varying your cultural group or your social class or your sexual orientation or all of these. Explore both pros and cons of these imagined new experiences as your invented self.

NOTES

1. Michael A. Messner, "Ah, Ya Throw Like a Girl!" in Michael A. Messner and Donald F. Sabo, eds., *Sex, Violence and Power in Sports: Rethinking Masculinity* (Freedom, CA: Crossing Press, 1994), pp. 28–32. Messner also reports that this way of throwing is so unnatural and injurious to the shoulder that few pitchers in childhood survive as pitchers into adulthood, having permanently injured their shoulders.

2. Jacqueline Jordan Irvine, "Teacher Communication Patterns as Related to the Race and Sex of the Student," *Journal of Educational Research* 78, no. 6 (1985): pp. 338–45; Jacqueline Jordan Irvine, "Teacher-Student Interactions: Effects of Student Race, Sex, and Grade Level," *Journal of Educational Psychology* 78, no. 1 (1986): pp. 14–21.

3. Suzanne P. Starling, James R. Holden, and Carole Jenny, "Abusive Head Trauma: The Relationship of Perpetrators to Their Victims," *Pediatrics* 95, no. 2 (February 1995): 259ff; Alisa Valdés-Rodríguez, "Shaken Baby Deaths Typically Involve Fathers: Young Males Need Infant-Care Training, Abuse Prevention Activists, Doctors Say," *The Boston Globe,* 22 September 1998, pp. B1, B8.

4. Lynn Phillips, *The Girls Report: What We Know & Need to Know about Growing Up Female* (New York: National Council for Research on Women, 1998).

5. John Money and Anke A. Ehrhardt, *Man & Woman, Boy & Girl: The Differentiation and Dimorphism of Gender Identity from Conception to Maturity* (Baltimore: Johns Hopkins University Press, 1972).

6. Milton Diamond and H. Keith Sigmundson, "Sex Reassignment at Birth," *Archives of Pediatric and Adolescent Medicine,* 151, no. 3 (March 1997): 301.

7. Milton Diamond and H. Keith Sigmundson, "Management of Intersexuality: Guidelines for Dealing with Persons with Ambiguous Genitalia," *Archives of Pediatric and Adolescent Medicine,* 151, no. 10 (October 1997): 1046–50.

8. John Colapinto, *As Nature Made Him: The Boy Who Was Raised as a Girl* (New York: Harper Collins, 2000).

9. Anne Fausto-Sterling, *Myths of Gender* (New York: Basic Books, 1985), pp. 86–87.

10. For discussions of the experiences of transsexuals and gender benders, see the *Journal of Gay, Lesbian, and Bisexual Identity;* Jennifer Finney Boylan, *She's Not There: A Life in Two Genders* (New York: Broadway Books, 2003); Paul Hewitt, *A Self-Made Man: The Diary of a Man Born in a Woman's Body* (London: Headline, 1995); Richard Ekins, *Blending Genders: Social Aspects of Cross-Dressing and Sex Changing* (New York: Routledge, 1995); Max Wolf Valerio, *The Testosterone Files: My Hormonal and Social Transformation from Female to Male* (Emeryville, CA: Seal Press, 2006); Dhillon Khosla, *Both Sides Now: One Man's Journey through Womanhood* (New York: Jeremy Tarcher/Penguin, 2006); Susan Stryker and Stephen Whittle, eds., *The Transgender Studies Reader* (New York: Routledge, 2006). For a critical look at solving gender confusion via transsexual surgery, see Janice Raymond, *The Transsexual Empire: The Making of the She-Male* (New York: Teachers College Press, 1994).

11. Margaret L. Andersen, *Thinking about Women: Sociological Perspectives on Sex and Gender,* 3rd ed. (New York: Macmillan, 1993), p. 44.

12. David Filipov, "Afghan Boys Take Up Rifles to Become Men," *Boston Sunday Globe,* 28 October 2001, p. A20.

13. Cynthia Enloe, *Manueuvers: The International Politics of Militarizing Women's Lives* (Berkeley, CA: University of California Press, 2000); Cynthia Enloe, *The Morning After: Sexual Politics at the End of the Cold War* (Berkeley: University of California Press, 1993); Dafna N. Izraeli, "Paradoxes of Women's Service in the Israel Defense Forces," in *Military, State and Society in Israel,* eds. Daniel Maman, Eyal Ben-Ari, and Zeev Rosenhek (New Brunswick, NJ: Transaction Publishers, 2001), pp. 203–38.

14. Helen Benedict, "The Private War of Women Soldiers," March 7, 2007, www.Salon.com; Sara Corbett, "The Women's War," *The New York Times Magazine,* 18 March 2007, 42ff.

11

THE SOCIAL CONSTRUCTION OF GENDER

JUDITH LORBER

Judith Lorber is professor emerita of sociology and women's studies at Brooklyn College and The Graduate School, City University of New York. Her most recent books are *Breaking the Bowls: Degendering and Feminist Change* (2005); *Gender Inequality: Feminist Theories and Politics, 2nd edition* (2001); *Gender and the Social Construction of Illness, 2nd edition,* coauthored with Lisa Jean Moore (2002); and *Gendered Bodies: Feminist Perspectives* (2007), also coauthored with Lisa Jean Moore.

Talking about gender for most people is the equivalent of fish talking about water. Gender is so much the routine ground of everyday activities that questioning its taken-for-granted assumptions and presuppositions is like thinking about whether the sun will come up.[1] Gender is so pervasive that in our society we assume it is bred into our genes. Most people find it hard to believe that gender is constantly created and re-created out of human interaction, out of social life, and is the texture and order of that social life. Yet gender, like culture, is a human production that depends on everyone constantly "doing gender" (West and Zimmerman 1987).

And everyone "does gender" without thinking about it. Today, on the subway, I saw a well-dressed man with a year-old child in a stroller. Yesterday, on a bus, I saw a man with a tiny baby in a carrier on his chest. Seeing men taking care of small children in public is increasingly common— at least in New York City. But both men were quite obviously stared at—and smiled at, approvingly. Everyone was doing gender—the men who were changing the role of fathers and the other passengers, who were applauding them silently. But there was more gendering going on that probably fewer people noticed. The baby was wearing a white crocheted cap and white clothes. You couldn't tell if it was a boy or a girl. The child in the stroller was wearing a dark blue T-shirt and dark print pants. As they started to leave the train, the father put a Yankee baseball cap on the child's head. Ah, a boy, I thought. Then I noticed the gleam of tiny earrings in the child's ears, and as they got off, I saw the little flowered sneakers and lace-trimmed socks. Not a boy after all. Gender done.

Gender is such a familiar part of daily life that it usually takes a deliberate disruption of our expectations of how women and men are supposed to act to pay attention to how it is produced. Gender signs and signals are so ubiquitous that we usually fail to note them—unless they are missing or ambiguous. Then we are uncomfortable until we have successfully placed the other person in a gender status; otherwise, we feel socially dislocated. In our society, in addition to man and woman, the status can be *transvestite* (a person who dresses in opposite-gender clothes) and *transsexual* (a person who has had sex-change surgery). Transvestites and transsexuals construct their gender status by dressing, speaking, walking, gesturing in the ways prescribed for women or men—whichever they want to be taken for—and so does any "normal" person.

For the individual, gender construction starts with assignment to a sex category on the basis of what the genitalia look like at birth.[2] Then babies are dressed or adorned in a way that displays the category because parents don't want to be constantly asked whether their baby is a girl or a boy. A sex category becomes a gender status through naming, dress, and the use of other gender markers. Once a child's gender is evident, others treat those in one gender differently from those in the other, and the children respond to the different treatment by feeling different and behaving differently. As soon as they can talk, they start to refer to themselves as members of their gender. Sex doesn't come into play again until puberty, but by that time, sexual feelings and desires and practices have been shaped by gendered norms and expectations. Adolescent boys and girls approach and avoid each other in an elaborately scripted and gendered mating dance. Parenting is gendered, with different expectations for mothers and for fathers, and people of different genders work at different kinds of jobs. The work adults do as mothers and fathers and as low-level workers and high-level bosses, shapes women's and men's life experiences, and these experiences produce different feelings, consciousness, relationships, skills—ways of being that we call feminine or masculine.[3] All of these processes constitute the social construction of gender.

Gendered roles change—today fathers are taking care of little children, girls and boys are wearing unisex clothing and getting the same education, women and men are working at the same jobs. Although many traditional social groups are quite strict about maintaining gender differences, in other social groups they seem to be blurring. Then why the one-year-old's earrings? Why is it still so important to mark a child as a girl or a boy, to make sure she is not taken for a boy or he for a girl? What would happen if they were? They would, quite literally, have changed places in their social world.

To explain why gendering is done from birth, constantly and by everyone, we have to look not only at the way individuals experience gender but at gender as a social institution. As a social institution, gender is one of the major ways that human beings organize their lives. Human society depends on a predictable division of labor, a designated allocation of scarce goods, assigned responsibility for children and others who cannot care for themselves, common values and their systematic transmission to new members, legitimate leadership, music, art, stories, games, and other symbolic productions. One way of choosing people for the different tasks of society is on the basis of their talents, motivations, and competence—their demonstrated achievements. The other way is on the basis of gender, race, ethnicity—ascribed membership in a category of people. Although societies vary in the extent to which they use one or the other of these ways of allocating people to work and to carry out other responsibilities, every society uses gender and age grades. Every society classifies people as "girl and boy children," "girls and boys ready to be married," and "fully adult women and men," constructs similarities among them and differences between them, and assigns them to different roles and responsibilities. Personality characteristics, feelings, motivations, and ambitions flow from these different life experiences so that the members of these different groups become different kinds of people. The process of gendering and its outcome are legitimated by religion, law, science, and the society's entire set of values.

Gender as Process, Stratification, and Structure

As a social institution, gender is a process of creating distinguishable social statuses for the assignment of rights and responsibilities. As part of a stratification system that ranks these statuses unequally, gender is a major building block in the social structures built on these unequal statuses.

As a *process*, gender creates the social differences that define "woman" and "man." In social interaction throughout their lives, individuals learn what is expected, see what is expected, act and react in expected ways, and thus simultaneously construct and maintain the gender order: "The very injunction to be given gender takes place through discursive routes: to be a good mother, to be a heterosexually desirable object, to be a fit worker, in sum, to signify a multiplicity of guarantees in response to a variety of different demands all at once" (J. Butler 1990, 145). Members of a social group neither make up gender as they go along nor exactly replicate in rote fashion what was done before. In almost every encounter, human beings produce gender, behaving in the ways they learned were appropriate for their gender status, or resisting or rebelling against these norms. Resistance and rebellion have altered gender norms, but so far they have rarely eroded the statuses.

Gendered patterns of interaction acquire additional layers of gendered sexuality, parenting, and work behaviors in childhood, adolescence, and adulthood. Gendered norms and expectations are enforced through informal sanctions of gender-inappropriate behavior by peers and by formal punishment or threat of punishment by those in authority should behavior deviate too far from socially imposed standards for women and men.

Everyday gendered interactions build gender into the family, the work process, and other organizations and institutions, which in turn reinforce gender expectations for individuals.[4] Because gender is a process, there is room not only for modification and variation by individuals and small groups but also for institutionalized change (J. W. Scott 1988, 7).

As part of a *stratification* system, gender ranks men above women of the same race and class. Women and men could be different but equal. In practice, the process of creating difference depends to a great extent on differential evaluation. As Nancy Jay (1981) says: "That which is defined, separated out, isolated from all else is A and pure. Not-A is necessarily impure, a random catchall, to which nothing is external except A and the principle of order that separates it from Not-A" (45). From the individual's point of view, whichever gender is A, the other is Not-A; gender boundaries tell the individual who is like him or her, and all the rest are unlike. From society's point of view, however, one gender is usually the touchstone, the normal, the dominant, and the other is different, deviant, and subordinate. In Western society, "man" is A, "wo-man" is Not-A. (Consider what a society would be like where woman was A and man Not-A.)

The further dichotomization by race and class constructs the gradations of a heterogeneous society's stratification scheme. Thus, in the United States, white is A, African American is Not-A; middle class is A, working class is Not-A, and "African-American women occupy a position whereby the inferior half of a series of these dichotomies converge" (P. H. Collins 1989, 770). The dominant categories are the hegemonic ideals, taken so for granted as the way things should be that white is not ordinarily thought of as a race, middle class as a class, or men as a gender. The characteristics of these categories define the Other as that which lacks the valuable qualities the dominants exhibit.

In a gender-stratified society, what men do is usually valued more highly than what women do because men do it, even when their activities are very similar or the same. In different regions of southern India, for example, harvesting rice is men's work, shared work, or women's work: "Wherever a task is done by women it is considered easy, and where it is done by [men] it is considered difficult" (Mencher 1988, 104). A gathering and hunting society's survival usually depends on the nuts, grubs, and small animals brought in by the women's foraging trips, but when the men's hunt is successful, it is the occasion for a celebration. Conversely, because they are the superior group, white men do not have to do the "dirty work," such as housework; the most inferior group does it, usually poor women of color (Palmer 1989).

Freudian psychoanalytic theory claims that boys must reject their mothers and deny the feminine in themselves in order to become men: "For boys the major goal is the achievement of personal masculine identification with their father and sense of secure masculine self, achieved through superego formation and disparagement of women" (Chodorow 1978, 165). Masculinity may be the outcome of boys' intrapsychic struggles to separate their identity from that of their mothers, but the proofs of masculinity are culturally shaped and usually ritualistic and symbolic (Gilmore 1990).

The Marxist feminist explanation for gender inequality is that by demeaning women's abilities and keeping them from learning valuable technological skills, bosses preserve them as a cheap and exploitable reserve army of labor. Unionized men who could easily be replaced by women collude in this process because it allows them to monopolize the better-paid, more interesting, and more autonomous jobs: "Two factors emerge as helping men maintain their separation from women and their control of technological occupations. One is the active gendering of jobs and people. The second is the continual creation of sub-divisions in the work processes, and levels in work hierarchies, into which men can move in order to keep their distance from women" (Cockburn 1985, 13).

Societies vary in the extent of the inequality in social status of their women and men members, but where there is inequality, the status "woman" (and its attendant behavior and role allocations) is usually held in lesser esteem than the status "man." Since gender is also intertwined with a society's other constructed statuses of differential evaluation—race, religion, occupation, class, country of origin, and so on—men and women members of the favored groups command more power, more prestige, and more property than the members of the disfavored groups. Within many social groups, however, men are advantaged over women. The more economic resources, such as education and job opportunities, are available to a group, the more they tend to be monopolized by men. In poorer groups that have few resources (such as working-class African Americans in the United States), women and men are more nearly equal, and the women may even outstrip the men in education and occupational status (Almquist 1987).

As a *structure*, gender divides work in the home and in economic production, legitimates those in authority, and organizes sexuality and emotional life (Connell 1987, 91–142). As primary parents, women significantly influence children's psychological development and emotional attachments, in the process reproducing gender. Emergent sexuality is shaped by heterosexual, homosexual, bisexual, and sadomasochistic patterns that are gendered—different for girls and boys, and for women and men—so that sexual statuses reflect gender statuses.

When gender is a major component of structured inequality, the devalued genders have less power, prestige, and economic rewards than the valued genders. In countries that discourage gender discrimination, many major roles are still gendered; women still do most of the domestic labor and child rearing, even while doing full-time paid work; women and men are segregated on the job and each does work considered "appropriate"; women's work is usually paid less than men's work. Men dominate the positions of authority and leadership in government, the military, and the law; cultural productions, religions, and sports reflect men's interests.

In societies that create the greatest gender difference, such as Saudi Arabia, women are kept out of sight behind walls or veils, have no civil rights, and often create a cultural and emotional world of their own (Bernard 1981).

But even in societies with less rigid gender boundaries, women and men spend much of their time with people of their own gender because of the way work and family are organized. This spatial separation of women and men reinforces gendered differences, identity, and ways of thinking and behaving (Coser 1986).

Gender inequality—the devaluation of "women" and the social domination of "men"—has social functions and social history. It is not the result of sex, procreation, physiology, anatomy, hormones, or genetic predispositions. It is produced and maintained by identifiable social processes and built into the general social structure and individual identities deliberately and purposefully. The social order as we know it in Western societies is organized around racial, ethnic, class, and gender inequality. I contend, therefore, that the continuing purpose of gender as a modern social institution is to construct women as a group to be the subordinates of men as a group.

The Paradox of Human Nature

To say that sex, sexuality, and gender are all socially constructed is not to minimize their social power. These categorical imperatives govern our lives in the most profound and pervasive ways, through the social experiences and social practices of what Dorothy Smith calls the "everday/evernight world" (1990, 31–57). The paradox of human nature is that it is *always* a manifestation of cultural meanings, social relationships, and power politics; "not biology, but culture, becomes destiny" (J. Butler 1990, 8). Gendered people emerge not from physiology or sexual orientations but from the exigencies of the social order, mostly, from the need for a reliable division of the work of food production and the social (not physical) reproduction of new members. The moral imperatives of religion and cultural representations guard the boundary lines among genders and ensure that what is demanded, what is permitted, and what is tabooed for the people in each gender is well known and followed by most (C. Davies 1982). Political power, control of scarce resources, and, if necessary, violence uphold the gendered social order in the face of resistance and rebellion. Most people, however, voluntarily go along with their society's prescriptions for those of their gender status, because the norms and expectations get built into their sense of worth and identity as [the way we] think, the way we see and hear and speak, the way we fantasy, and the way we feel.

There is no core or bedrock in human nature below these endlessly looping processes of the social production of sex and gender, self and other, identity and psyche, each of which is a "complex cultural construction" (J. Butler 1990, 36). *For humans, the social is the natural.* Therefore, "in its feminist senses, gender cannot mean simply the cultural appropriation of biological sexual difference. Sexual difference is itself a fundamental—and scientifically contested—construction. Both 'sex' and 'gender' are woven of multiple, asymmetrical strands of difference, charged with multifaceted dramatic narratives of domination and struggle" (Haraway 1990, 140).

NOTES

1. Gender is, in Erving Goffman's words, an aspect of "Felicity's Condition": "any arrangement which leads us to judge an individual's . . . acts not to be a manifestation of strangeness. Behind Felicity's Condition is our sense of what it is to be sane" (1983:27). Also see Bem 1993; Frye 1983, 17–40; Goffman 1977.
2. In cases of ambiguity in countries with modern medicine, surgery is usually performed to make the genitalia more clearly male or female.
3. See J. Butler 1990 for an analysis of how doing gender is gender identity.
4. On the "logic of practice," or how the experience of gender is embedded in the norms of everyday interaction and the structure of formal organizations, see Acker 1990; Bourdieu [1980] 1990; Connell 1987; Smith 1987.

REFERENCES

Acker, Joan. 1990. "Hierarchies, jobs, and bodies: A theory of gendered organizations," *Gender & Society* 4:139–58.

Almquist, Elizabeth M. 1987. "Labor market gendered inequality in minority groups," *Gender & Society* 1:400–14.

Bem, Sandra Lipsitz. 1993. *The Lenses of Gender: Transforming the Debate on Sexual Inequality.* New Haven: Yale University Press.

Bernard, Jessie. 1981. *The Female World.* New York: Free Press.

Bourdieu, Pierre. [1980] 1990. *The Logic of Practice.* Stanford, Calif.: Stanford University Press.

Butler, Judith. 1990. *Gender Trouble: Feminism and the Subversion of Identity.* New York and London: Routledge.

Chodorow, Nancy. 1978. *The Reproduction of Mothering.* Berkeley: University of California Press.

Cockburn, Cynthia. 1985. *Machinery of Dominance: Women, Men and Technical Know-how.* London: Pluto Press.

Collins, Patricia Hill. 1989. "The social construction of black feminist thought," *Signs* 14:745–73.

Connell, R. [Robert] W. 1987. *Gender and Power: Society, the Person, and Sexual Politics.* Stanford, Calif.: Stanford University Press.

Coser, Rose Laub. 1986. "Cognitive structure and the use of social space," *Sociological Forum* 1:1–26.

Davies, Christie. 1982. "Sexual taboos and social boundaries," *American Journal of Sociology* 87:1032–63.

Dwyer, Daisy, & Judith Bruce (eds.). 1988. *A Home Divided: Women and Income in the Third World.* Palo Alto, Calif.: Stanford University Press.

Frye, Marilyn. 1983. *The Politics of Reality: Essays in Feminist Theory.* Trumansburg, N.Y.: Crossing Press.

Gilmore, David D. 1990. *Manhood in the Making: Cultural Concepts of Masculinity.* New Haven: Yale University Press.

Goffman, Erving. 1977. "The arrangement between the sexes," *Theory and Society* 4:301–33.

Goffman, Erving. 1983. "Felicity's condition," *American Journal of Sociology* 89:1–53.

Haraway, Donna. 1990. "Investment strategies for the evolving portfolio of primate females," in *Jacobus, Keller, and Shuttleworth.*

Jacobus, Mary, Evelyn Fox Keller, & Sally Shuttleworth (eds.). (1990). *Body/politics: Women and the Discourse of Science.* New York and London: Routledge.

Jay, Nancy. 1981. "Gender and dichotomy," *Feminist Studies* 7:38–56.

Mencher, Joan. 1988. "Women's work and poverty: Women's contribution to household maintenance in South India," in *Dwyer and Bruce.*

Palmer, Phyllis. 1989. *Domesticity and Dirt: Housewives and Domestic Servants in the United States, 1920–1945.* Philadelphia: Temple University Press.

Scott, Joan Wallach. 1988. *Gender and the Politics of History.* New York: Columbia University Press.

Smith, Dorothy. 1987. *The Everyday World as Problematic: A Feminist Sociology.* Toronto: University of Toronto Press.

———. 1990. *The Conceptual Practices of Power: A Feminist Sociology of Knowledge.* Toronto: University of Toronto Press.

West, Candace, & Don Zimmerman. 1987. "Doing gender," *Gender & Society* 1:125–51.

12

BOYHOOD, ORGANIZED SPORTS, AND THE CONSTRUCTION OF MASCULINITIES

MICHAEL A. MESSNER

Michael A. Messner is a professor of sociology and gender studies at the University of Southern California. His most recent books are *Politics of Masculinities: Men in Movements* (1997), *Men's Lives* (2007, edited with Michael Kimmel); *Paradoxes of Youth and Sport* (2002, edited with Margaret Gatz and Sandra Rokeach), and *Taking the Field: Women, Men, and Sports* (2002).

The rapid expansion of feminist scholarship in the past two decades has led to fundamental reconceptualizations of the historical and contemporary meanings of organized sport. In the nineteenth and twentieth centuries, modernization and women's continued movement into public life created widespread "fears of social feminization," especially among middle-class men (Hantover, 1978; Kimmel, 1987). One result of these fears was the creation of organized sport as a homosocial sphere in which competition and (often violent) physicality was valued, while "the feminine" was devalued. As a result, organized sport has served to bolster a sagging ideology of male superiority, and has helped to reconstitute masculine hegemony (Bryson, 1987; Hall, 1988; Messner, 1988; Theberge, 1981).

The feminist critique has spawned a number of studies of the ways that women's sport has been marginalized and trivialized in the past (Greendorfer, 1977; Oglesby, 1978; Twin, 1978), in addition to illuminating the continued existence of structural and ideological barriers to gender equality within sport (Birrell, 1987). Only recently, however, have scholars begun to use feminist insights to examine men's experiences in sport (Kidd, 1987; Messner, 1987; Sabo, 1985). This article explores the relationship between the construction of masculine identity and boyhood participation in organized sports.

I view gender identity not as a "thing" that people "have," but rather as a *process of construction* that develops, comes into crisis, and changes as a person interacts with the social world. Through this perspective, it becomes possible to speak of "gendering" identities rather than "masculinity" or "femininity" as relatively fixed identities or statuses.

There is an agency in this construction; people are not passively shaped by their social environment. As recent feminist analyses of the construction of feminine gender identity have pointed out, girls and women are implicated in the construction of their own identities and personalities, both in terms of the ways that they participate in their own subordination and the ways that they resist subordination (Benjamin, 1988; Haug, 1987). Yet this self-construction is not a fully conscious process. There are also deeply woven, unconscious motivations, fears, and anxieties at work here. So, too, in the construction of masculinity. Levinson (1978) has argued that masculine identity is neither fully "formed" by the social context, nor is it "caused" by some internal dynamic put into place during infancy. Instead, it is shaped and constructed through the interaction between the internal and the social. The internal gendering identity may set developmental "tasks," may create thresholds of anxiety and ambivalence, yet it is only through a concrete examination of people's interactions with others within social institutions that we can begin to understand both the similarities and differences in the construction of gender identities.

In this study I explore and interpret the meanings that males themselves attribute to their boyhood participation in organized sport. In what ways do males construct masculine identities within the institution of organized sports? In what ways do class and racial differences mediate this relationship and perhaps lead to the construction of different meanings, and perhaps different masculinities? And what are some of the problems and contradictions within these constructions of masculinity?

Description of Research

Between 1983 and 1985, I conducted interviews with 30 male former athletes. Most of the men I interviewed had played the (U.S.) "major sports"—football, basketball, baseball, track. At the time of the interview, each had been retired from playing organized sports for at least five years. Their ages ranged from 21 to 48, with the median 33; 14 were black, 14 were white, and 2 were Hispanic; 15 of the 16 black and Hispanic men had come from poor or working-class families, while the majority (9 of 14) of the white men had come from middle-class or professional families. All had at some time in their lives based their identities largely on their roles as athletes and could therefore be said to have had "athletic careers." Twelve had played organized sports through high school, 11 through college, and 7 had been professional athletes. Though the sample was not randomly selected, an effort was made to see that the sample had a range of difference in terms of race and social class backgrounds, and that there was some variety in terms of age, types of sports played, and levels of success in athletic careers. Without exception, each man contacted agreed to be interviewed.

The tape-recorded interviews were semi-structured and took from one and one-half to six hours, with most taking about three hours. I asked each man to talk about four broad eras in his life: (1) his earliest experiences with sports in boyhood, (2) his athletic career, (3) retirement or disengagement from the athletic career, and (4) life after the athletic career. In each era, I focused the interview on the meanings of "success and failure," and on the boy's/man's relationships with family, with other males, with women, and with his own body.

In collecting what amounted to life histories of these men, my overarching purpose was to use feminist theories of masculine gender identity to explore how masculinity develops and changes as boys and men interact within the socially constructed world of organized sports. In addition to using the data to move toward some generalizations about the relationship between "masculinity and sport," I was also concerned with sorting out some of the variations among boys, based on class and racial inequalities, that led them to relate differently to athletic careers. I divided my sample into two comparison groups. The first group was made up of 10 men from higher-status backgrounds, primarily white, middle-class, and professional families. The second group was made up of 20 men from lower-status backgrounds, primarily minority, poor, and working-class families.

Boyhood and the Promise of Sports

Zane Grey once said, "All boys love baseball. If they don't they're not real boys" (as cited in Kimmel, 1990). This is, of course, an ideological statement; in fact, some boys do *not* love baseball, or any other sports, for that matter. There are millions of males who at an early age are rejected by, become alienated from, or lose interest in organized sports. Yet all boys are, to a greater or lesser extent, judged according to their ability, or lack of ability, in competitive sports (Eitzen, 1975; Sabo, 1985). In this study I focus on those males who did become athletes—males who eventually poured thousands of hours into the development of specific physical skills. It is in boyhood that we can discover the roots of their commitment to athletic careers.

How did organized sports come to play such a central role in these boys' lives? When asked to recall how and why they initially got into playing sports, many of the men interviewed for this study seemed a bit puzzled: after all, playing sports was "just the thing to do." A 42-year-old black man who had played college basketball put it this way:

> It was just what you did. It's kind of like, you went to school, you
> played athletics, and if you didn't, there was something wrong
> with you. It was just like brushing your teeth: it's just what you
> did. It's part of your existence.

Spending one's time playing sports with other boys seemed as natural as the cycle of the seasons: baseball in the spring and summer, football in the fall, basketball in the winter—and then it was time to get out the old baseball glove and begin again. As a black 35-year-old former professional football star said:

> I'd say when I wasn't in school, 95% of the time was spent in
> the park playing. It was the only thing to do. It just came as
> natural.

And a black, 34-year-old professional basketball player explained his early experiences in sports:

> My principal and teacher said, "Now if you work at this you might
> be pretty damned good." So it was more or less a community
> thing—everybody in the community said, "Boy, if you work hard
> and keep your nose clean, you gonna be good." Cause it was
> natural instinct.

"It was natural instinct." "I was a natural." Several athletes used words such as these to explain their early attraction to sports. But certainly there is nothing "natural" about throwing a ball through a hoop, hitting a ball with a bat, or jumping over hurdles. A boy, for instance, may have amazingly dexterous inborn hand-eye coordination, but this does not predispose him to a career of hitting baseballs any more than it predisposes him to life as a brain surgeon. When one listens closely to what these men said about their early experiences in sports, it becomes clear that their adoption of the self-definition of "natural athlete" was the result of what Connell (1990) has called "a collective practice" that constructs masculinities. The boyhood development of masculine identity and status—truly problematic in a society that offers no official rite of passage into adulthood—results from a process of interaction with people and social institutions. Thus, in discussing early motivations in sports, men commonly talk of the importance of relationships with family members, peers, and the broader community.

Family Influences

Though most of the men in this study spoke of their mothers with love, respect, even reverence, their descriptions of their earliest experiences in sports are stories of an exclusively male world. The existence of older brothers or uncles who served as teachers and athletic role models—as well as sources of competition for attention and status within the family—was very common. An older brother, uncle, or even close friend of the family who was a successful athlete appears to have acted as a sort of standard of achievement against whom to measure oneself. A 34-year-old black man who had been a three-sport star in high school said:

> My uncles—my Uncle Harold went to the Detroit Tigers, played pro ball—all of 'em, everybody played sports, so I wanted to be better than anybody else. I knew that everybody in this town knew them—their names were something. I wanted my name to be just like theirs.

Similarly, a black 41-year-old former professional football player recalled:

> I was the younger of three brothers and everybody played sports, so consequently I was more or less forced into it. 'Cause one brother was always better than the next brother and then I came along and had to show them that I was just as good as them. My oldest brother was an all-city ballplayer, then my other brother comes along he's all-city and all-state, and then I have to come along.

For some, attempting to emulate or surpass the athletic accomplishments of older male family members created pressures that were difficult to deal with. A 33-year-old white man explained that he was a good athlete during boyhood, but the constant awareness that his two older brothers had been better made it difficult for him to feel good about himself, or to have fun in sports:

> I had this sort of reputation that I followed from the playgrounds through grade school, and through high school. I followed these guys who were all-conference and all-state.

Most of these men, however, saw their relationships with their athletic older brothers and uncles in a positive light; it was within these relationships that they gained experience and developed motivations that gave them a competitive "edge" within their same-aged peer group. As a 33-year-old black man describes his earliest athletic experiences:

> My brothers were role models. I wanted to prove—especially to my brothers—that I had heart, you know, that I was a man.

When asked, "What did it mean to you to be 'a man' at that age?" he replied:

> Well, it meant that I didn't want to be a so-called scaredy-cat. You
> want to hit a guy even though he's bigger than you to show that,
> you know, you've got this macho image. I remember that at that
> young an age, that feeling was exciting to me. And that carried
> over, and as I got older, I got better and I began to look around me
> and see, well hey! I'm competitive with these guys, even though
> I'm younger, you know? And then of course all the compliments
> come—and I began to notice a change, even in my parents—
> especially in my father—he was proud of that, and that was very
> important to me. He was extremely important . . . he showed me
> more affection, now that I think of it.

As this man's words suggest, if men talk of their older brothers and uncles mostly as role models, teachers, and "names" to emulate, their talk of their relationships with their fathers is more deeply layered and complex. Athletic skills and competition for status may often be learned from older brothers, but it is in boys' relationships with fathers that we find many of the keys to the emotional salience of sports in the development of masculine identity.

Relationships with Fathers

The fact that boys' introductions to organized sports are often made by fathers who might otherwise be absent or emotionally distant adds a powerful emotional charge to these early experiences (Osherson, 1986). Although playing organized sports eventually came to feel "natural" for all of the men interviewed in this study, many needed to be "exposed" to sports, or even gently "pushed" by their fathers to become involved in activities like Little League baseball. A white 33-year-old man explained:

> I still remember it like it was yesterday—Dad and I driving up in
> his truck, and I had my glove and my hat and all that—and I said,
> "Dad, I don't want to do it." He says, "What?" I says, "I don't want
> to do it." I was nervous. That I might fail. And he says, "Don't be
> silly. Lookit: There's Joey and Petey and all your friends out there."
> And so Dad says, "You're gonna do it, come on." And in my
> memory he's never said that about anything else; he just knew
> I needed a little kick in the pants and I'd do it. And once you're out
> there and you see all the other kids making errors and stuff, and
> you know you're better than those guys, you know: Maybe I *do*
> belong here. As it turned out, Little League was a good experience.

Some who were similarly "pushed" by their fathers were not so successful as the aforementioned man had been in Little League baseball, and thus the experience was not altogether a joyous affair. One 34-year-old white man, for instance, said he "inherited" his interest in sports from his father, who started playing catch with him at the age of four. Once he got into Little League, he felt pressured by his father, one of the coaches, who expected him to be the star of the team:

> I'd go 0-for-four sometimes, strike out three times in a Little
> League game, and I'd dread the ride home. I'd come home and
> he'd say, "Go in the bathroom and swing the bat in the mirror for
> an hour," to get my swing level. . . . It didn't help much, though,
> I'd go out and strike out three or four times again the next game
> too [laughs ironically].

When asked if he had been concerned with having his father's approval, he responded:

> Failure in his eyes? Yeah, I always thought that he wanted me to get
> some kind of [athletic] scholarship. I guess I was afraid of him
> when I was a kid. He didn't hit that much, but he had a rage about
> him—he'd rage, and that voice would just rattle you.

Similarly, a 24-year-old black man described his awe of his father's physical power and presence, and his sense of inadequacy in attempting to emulate him:

> My father had a voice that sounded like rolling thunder. Whether
> it was intentional on his part or not, I don't know, but my father
> gave me a sense, an image of him being the most powerful being on
> earth, and that no matter what I ever did I would never come close
> to him. . . . There were definite feelings of physical inadequacy that
> I couldn't work around.

It is interesting to note how these feelings of physical inadequacy relative to the father lived on as part of this young man's permanent internalized image. He eventually became a "feared" high school football player and broke school records in weight-lifting, yet:

> As I grew older, my mother and friends told me that I had actually
> grown to be a larger man than my father. Even though in time I
> required larger clothes than he, which should have been a very
> concrete indication, neither my brother nor I could ever bring
> our-selves to say that I was bigger. We simply couldn't conceive of it.

Using sports activities as a means of identifying with and "living up to" the power and status of one's father was not always such a painful and diffi-cult task for the men I interviewed. Most did not describe fathers who "pushed" them to become sports stars. The relationship between their athletic strivings and their identification with their fathers was more subtle. A 48-year-old black man, for instance, explained that he was not pushed into sports by his father, but was aware from an early age of the community status his father had gained through sports. He saw his own athletic accomplishments as a way to connect with and emulate his father:

> I wanted to play baseball because my father had been quite a good baseball player in the Negro leagues before baseball was integrated, and so he was kind of a model for me. I remember, quite young, going to a baseball game he was in—this was before the war and all—I remember being in the stands with my mother and seeing him on first base, and being aware of the crowd. . . . I was aware of people's confidence in him as a serious baseball player. I don't think my father ever said anything to me like "play sports." . . . [But] I knew he would like it if I did well. His admiration was important . . . he mattered.

Similarly, a 24-year-old white man described his father as a somewhat distant "role model" whose approval mattered:

> My father was more of an example . . . he definitely was very much in touch with and still had very fond memories of being an athlete and talked about it, bragged about it. . . . But he really didn't do that much to teach me skills, and he didn't always go to every game I played like some parents. But he approved and that was important, you know. That was important to get his approval. I always knew that playing sports was important to him, so I knew implicitly that it was good and there was definitely a value on it.

First experiences in sports might often come through relationships with brothers or older male relatives, and the early emotional salience of sports was often directly related to a boy's relationship with his father. The sense of commitment that these young boys eventually made to the development of athletic careers is best explained as a process of development of masculine gender identity and status in relation to same-sex peers.

Masculine Identity and Early Commitment to Sports

When many of the men in this study said that during childhood they played sports because "it's just what everybody did," they of course meant that is was just what *boys* did. They were introduced to organized sports by older brothers and fathers, and once involved, found themselves playing within an exclusively male world. Though the separate (and unequal) gendered worlds of boys and girls came to appear as "natural," they were in fact socially constructed. Thorne's observations of children's activities in schools indicated that rather than "naturally" constituting "separate gendered cultures," there is considerable interaction between boys and girls in classrooms and on playgrounds. When adults set up legitimate contact between boys and girls, Thorne observed, this usually results in "relaxed interactions." But when activities in the classroom or on the playground are presented to children as sex-segregated activities and gender is marked by teachers and other adults ("boys line up here, girls over there"), "gender boundaries are heightened, and mixed-sex interaction becomes an explicit arena of risk" (Thorne, 1986; 70). Thus sex-segregated activities such as organized sports as structured by adults, provide the context in which gendered identities and separate "gendered cultures" develop and come to appear natural. For the boys in this study, it became "natural" to equate masculinity with competition, physical strength, and skills. Girls simply did not (could not, it was believed) participate in these activities.

Yet it is not simply the separation of children, by adults, into separate activities that explains why many boys came to feel such strong connection with sports activities, while so few girls did. As I listened to men recall their earliest experiences in organized sports, I heard them talk of insecurity, loneliness, and especially a need to connect with other people as a primary motivation in their early sports strivings. As a 42-year-old white man stated, "The most important thing was just being out there with the rest of the guys—being friends." Another 32-year-old interviewee was born in Mexico and moved to the United States at a fairly young age. He never knew his father, and his mother died when he was only nine years old. Suddenly he felt rootless, and threw himself into sports. His initial motivations, however, do not appear to be based on a need to compete and win:

> Actually, what I think sports did for me is it brought me into kind
> of an instant family. By being on a Little League team, or even just
> playing with all kinds of different kids in the neighborhood, it
> brought what I really wanted, which was some kind of closeness. It
> was just being there, and being friends.

Clearly, what these boys needed and craved was that which was most problematic for them: connection and unity with other people. But why do these young males find *organized sports* such an attractive context in which to establish "a kind of closeness" with others? Comparative observations of young boys' and girls' game-playing behaviors yield important insights into this question. Piaget (1965) and Lever (1976) both observed that girls tend to have more "pragmatic" and "flexible" orientations to the rules of games; they are more prone to make exceptions and innovations in the middle of a game in order to make the game more "fair." Boys, on the other hand, tend to have a more firm, even [in]flexible orientation to the rules of a game; to them, the rules are what protects any fairness. This difference, according to Gilligan (1982), is based on the fact that early developmental experiences have yielded deeply rooted differences between males' and females' developmental tasks, needs, and moral reasoning. Girls, who tend to define themselves primarily through connection with others, experience highly competitive situations (whether in organized sports or in other hierarchical institutions) as threats to relationships, and thus to their identities. For boys, the development of gender identity involves the construction of positional identities, where a sense of self is solidified through separation from others (Chodorow, 1978). Yet feminist psychoanalytic theory has tended to oversimplify the internal lives of men (Lichterman, 1986). Males do appear to develop positional identities, yet despite their fears of intimacy, they also retain a human need for closeness and unity with others. This ambivalence toward intimate relationships is a major thread running through masculine development throughout the life course. Here we can conceptualize what Craib (1987) calls the "elective affinity" between personality and social structure: For the boy who both seeks and fears attachment with others, the rule-bound structure of organized sports can promise to be a safe place in which to seek nonintimate attachment with others within a context that maintains clear boundaries, distance, and separation.

Competitive Structures and Conditional Self-Worth

Young boys may initially find that sports give them the opportunity to experience "some kind of closeness" with others, but the structure of sports and athletic careers often undermines the possibility of boys learning to transcend their fears of intimacy, thus becoming able to develop truly close and intimate relationships with others (Kidd, 1990; Messner, 1987). The sports world is extremely hierarchical, and an incredible amount of importance is placed on winning, on "being number one." For instance, a few years ago I observed a basketball camp put on for boys by a professional basketball coach and his staff. The youngest boys, about eight years old (who could barely reach the basket with their shots) played a brief scrimmage. Afterwards, the coaches lined them up in a row in front of the older boys who were sitting in the grandstands. One by one, the coach would stand behind each boy, put his hand on the boy's head (much in the manner of a priestly benediction), and the older boys in the stands would applaud and cheer, louder or softer, depending on how well or poorly the young boy was judged to have performed. The two or three boys who were clearly the exceptional players looked confident that they would receive the praise they were due. Most of the boys, though, had expressions ranging from puzzlement to thinly disguised terror on their faces as they awaited the judgments of the older boys.

This kind of experience teaches boys that it is not "just being out there with the guys—being friends" that ensures the kind of attention and connection that they crave; it is being *better* than the other guys—*beating* them—that is the key to acceptance. Most of the boys in this study did have some early successes in sports, and thus their ambivalent need for connection with others was met, at least for a time. But the institution of sport tends to encourage the development of what Schafer (1975) has called "conditional self-worth" in boys. As boys become aware that acceptance by others is contingent upon being good—a "winner"—narrow definitions of success, based upon performance and winning, become increasingly important to them. A 33-year-old black man said that by the time he was in his early teens:

> It was expected of me to do well in all my contests—I mean by my coaches, my peers, and my family. So I in turn expected to do well, and if I didn't do well, then I'd be very disappointed.

The man from Mexico, discussed above, who said that he had sought "some kind of closeness" in his early sports experiences, began to notice in his early teens that if he played well, was a *winner,* he would get attention from others:

> It got to the point where I started realizing, noticing that people were always there for me, backing me all the time—sports got to be really fun because I always had some people there backing me. Finally my oldest brother started going to all my games, even though I had never really seen who he was [laughs]—after the game, you know, we never really saw each other, but he was at all my baseball games, and it seemed like we shared a kind of closeness there, but only in those situations. Off the field, when I wasn't in uniform, he was never around.

By high school, he said, he felt "up against the wall." Sports hadn't delivered what he had hoped it would, but he thought if he just tried harder, won one more championship trophy, he would get the attention he truly craved. Despite his efforts, this attention was not forthcoming. And, sadly, the pressures he had put on himself to excel in sports had taken most of the fun out of playing.

For many of the men in this study, throughout boyhood and into adolescence, this conscious striving for successful achievement became the primary means through which they sought connection with other people (Messner, 1987). But it is important to recognize that young males' internalized ambivalences about intimacy do not fully determine the contours and directions of their lives. Masculinity continues to develop through interaction with the social world—and because boys from different backgrounds are interacting with substantially different familial, educational, and other institutions, these differences will lead them to make different choices and define situations in different ways. Next, I examine the differences in the ways that boys from higher- and lower-status families and communities related to organized sports.

Status Differences and Commitments to Sports

In discussing early attractions to sports, the experiences of boys from higher- and lower-status backgrounds are quite similar. Both groups indicate the importance of fathers and older brothers in introducing them to sports. Both groups speak of the joys of receiving attention and acceptance among family and peers for early successes in sports. Note the similarities, for instance, in the following descriptions of boyhood athletic experiences of two men. First, a man born in a white middle-class family:

> I loved playing sports so much from a very early age because of early exposure. A lot of the sports came easy at an early age, and because they did, and because you were successful at something, I think that you're inclined to strive for that gratification. It's like, if you're good, you like it, because it's instant gratification. I'm doing something that I'm good at and I'm gonna keep doing it.

Second, a black man from a poor family:

> Fortunately I had some athletic ability, and, quite naturally, once you start doing good in whatever it is—I don't care if it's jacks— you show off what you do. That's your ability, that's your blessing, so you show it off as much as you can.

For boys from both groups, early exposure to sports, the discovery that they had some "ability," shortly followed by some sort of family, peer, and community recognition, all eventually led to the commitment of hundreds and thousands of hours of playing, practicing, and dreaming of future stardom. Despite these similarities, there are also some identifiable differences that begin to explain the tendency of males from lower-status backgrounds to develop higher levels of commitment to sports careers. The most clear-cut difference was that while men from higher-status backgrounds are likely to describe their earliest athletic experiences and motivations almost exclusively in terms of immediate family, men from lower-status backgrounds more commonly describe the importance of a broader community context. For instance, a 46-year-old man who grew up in a "poor working class" black family in a small town in Arkansas explained:

> In that community, at the age of third or fourth grade, if you're a male, they expect you to show some kind of inclination, some kind of skill in football or basketball. It was an expected thing, you know? My mom and my dad, they didn't push at all. It was the general environment.

A 48-year-old man describes sports activities as a survival strategy in his poor black community:

> Sports protected me from having to compete in gang stuff, or having to be good with my fists. If you were an athlete and got into the fist world, that was your business, and that was okay—but you didn't have to if you didn't want to. People would generally defer to you, give you your space away from trouble.

A 35-year-old man who grew up in "a poor black ghetto" described his boyhood relationship to sports similarly:

> Where I came from, either you were one of two things: you were in sports or you were out on the streets being a drug addict, or breaking into places. The guys who were in sports, we had it a little easier, because we were accepted by both groups. . . . So it worked out to my advantage, cause I didn't get into a lot of trouble—some trouble, but not a lot.

The fact that boys in lower-status communities faced these kinds of realities gave salience to their developing athletic identities. In contrast, sports were important to boys from higher-status backgrounds, yet the middle-class environment seemed more secure, less threatening, and offered far more options. By the time most of these boys got into junior high or high school, many had made conscious decisions to shift their attentions away from athletic careers to educational and (nonathletic) career goals. A 32-year-old white college athletic director told me that he had seen his chance to pursue a pro baseball career as "pissing in the wind," and instead focused on education. Similarly, a 33-year-old white dentist who was a three-sport star in high school, decided not to play sports in college, so he could focus on getting into dental school. As he put it,

> I think I kind of downgraded the stardom thing. I thought it was small potatoes. And sure, that's nice in high school and all that, but on a broad scale, I didn't think it amounted to all that much.

This statement offers an important key to understanding the construction of masculine identity within a middle-class context. The status that this boy got through sports had been *very* important to him, yet he could see that "on a broad scale," this sort of status was "small potatoes." This sort of early recognition is more than a result of the oft-noted middle-class tendency to raise "future-oriented" children (Rubin, 1976; Sennett and Cobb, 1973). Perhaps more important, it is that the *kinds* of future orientations developed by boys from higher-status backgrounds are consistent with the middle-class context. These men's descriptions of their boyhoods reveal that they grew up immersed in a wide range of institutional frameworks, of which organized sports was just one. And—importantly—they could see that the status of adult males around them was clearly linked to their positions within various professions, public institutions, and bureaucratic organizations. It was clear that access to this sort of institutional status came through educational achievement, not athletic prowess. A 32-year-old black man who grew up in a professional-class family recalled that he had idolized Wilt Chamberlain and dreamed of being a pro basketball player, yet his father discouraged his athletic strivings:

> He knew I liked the game. I *loved* the game. But basketball was not recommended; my dad would say, "That's a stereotyped image for

black youth. . . . When your basketball is gone and finished, what
are you gonna do? One day, you might get injured. What are you
gonna look forward to?" He stressed education.

Similarly, a 32-year-old man who was raised in a white middle-class
family had found in sports a key means of gaining acceptance and connection in his peer group. Yet he was simultaneously developing an image
of himself as a "smart student," and becoming aware of a wide range of
non-sports life options:

> My mother was constantly telling me how smart I was, how good I
> was, what a nice person I was, and giving me all sorts of positive
> strokes, and those positive strokes became a self-motivating kind of
> thing. I had this image of myself as smart, and I lived up to that
> image.

It is not that parents of boys in lower-status families did not also encourage their boys to work hard in school. Several reported that their parents
"stressed books first, sports second." It's just that the broader social context—
education, economy, and community—was more likely to *narrow* lower-
status boys' perceptions of real-life options, while boys from higher-status
backgrounds faced an expanding world of options. For instance, with a different socioeconomic background, one 35-year-old black man might have
become a great musician instead of a star professional football running back.
But he did not. When he was a child, he said, he was most interested in music:

> I wanted to be a drummer. But we couldn't afford drums. My dad
> couldn't go out and buy me a drum set or a guitar even—it was just
> one of those things; he was just trying to make ends meet.

But he *could* afford, as could so many in his socioeconomic condition, to
spend countless hours at the local park, where he was told by the park
supervisor

> that I was a natural—not only in gymnastics or baseball—whatever
> I did, I was a natural. He told me I shouldn't waste this talent, and
> so I immediately started watching the big guys then.

In retrospect, this man had potential to be a musician or any number of
things, but his environment limited his options to sports, and he made the
best of it. Even within sports, he, like most boys in the ghetto, was limited:

> We didn't have any tennis courts in the ghetto—we used to have a
> lot of tennis balls, but not racquets. I wonder today how good
> I might be in tennis if I had gotten a racquet in my hands at an
> early age.

It is within this limited structure of opportunity that many lower-status
young boys found sports to be *the* place, rather than *a* place, within which to

construct masculine identity, status, the relationships. A 36-year-old white man explained that his father left the family when he was very young and his mother faced a very difficult struggle to make ends meet. As his words suggest, the more limited a boy's options, and the more insecure his family situation, the more likely he is to make an early commitment to an athletic career:

> I used to ride my bicycle to Little League practice—if I'd waited for someone to pick me up and take me to the ball park I'd have never played. I'd get to the ball park and all the other kids would have their dad bring them to practice or games. But I'd park my bike to the side and when it was over I'd get on it and go home. Sports was the way for me to move everything to the side—family problems, just all the embarrassments—and think about one thing, and that was sports. . . . In the third grade, when the teacher went around the classroom and asked everybody, "What do you want to be when you grow up?" I said, "I want to be a major league baseball player," and everybody laughed their heads off.

This man eventually did enjoy a major league baseball career. Most boys from lower-status backgrounds who make similar early commitments to athletic careers are not so successful. As stated earlier, the career structure of organized sports is highly competitive and hierarchical. In fact, the chances of attaining professional status in sports are approximately 4:100,000 for a white man, 2:100,000 for a black man, and 3:1 million for a Hispanic man in the United States (Leonard and Reyman, 1988). Nevertheless, the immediate rewards (fun, status, attention), along with the constricted (nonsports) structure of opportunity, attract disproportionately large numbers of boys from lower-status backgrounds to athletic careers as their major means of constructing a masculine identity. These are the boys who later, as young men, had to struggle with "conditional self-worth," and, more often than not, occupational dead ends. Boys from higher-status backgrounds, on the other hand, bolstered their boyhood, adolescent, and early adult status through their athletic accomplishments. Their wide range of experiences and life changes led to an early shift away from sports careers as the major basis of identity (Messner, 1989).

Conclusion

The conception of the masculinity-sports relationship developed here begins to illustrate the idea of an "elective affinity" between social structure and personality. Organized sports is a "gendered institution"—an institution constructed by gender relations. As such, its structure and values (rules, formal organization, sex composition, etc.) reflect dominant conceptions of masculinity and femininity. Organized sports is also a "gendering institution"—an institution that helps to construct the current gender order. Part of this construction of gender is accomplished through the "masculinizing" of male bodies and minds.

Yet boys do not come to their first experiences in organized sports as "blank slates," but arrive with already "gendering" identities due to early developmental experiences and previous socialization. I have suggested here that an important thread running through the development of masculine identity is males' ambivalence toward intimate unity with others. Those boys who experience early athletic successes find in the structure of organized sport an affinity with this masculine ambivalence toward intimacy: The rule-bound, competitive, hierarchical world of sport offers boys an attractive means of establishing an emotionally distant (and thus "safe") connection with others. Yet as boys begin to define themselves as "athletes," they learn that in order to be accepted (to have connection) through sports, they must be winners. And in order to be winners, they must construct relationships with others (and with themselves) that are consistent with the competitive and hierarchical values and structure of the sports world. As a result, they often develop a "conditional self-worth" that leads them to construct more instrumental relationships with themselves and others. This ultimately exacerbates their difficulties in constructing intimate relationships with others. In effect, the interaction between the young male's preexisting internalized ambivalence toward intimacy with the competitive hierarchical institution of sport has resulted in the construction of a masculine personality that is characterized by instrumental rationality, goal orientation, and difficulties with intimate connection and expression (Messner, 1987).

This theoretical line of inquiry invites us not simply to examine how social institutions "socialize" boys, but also to explore the ways that boys' already-gendering identities interact with social institutions (which, like organized sport, are themselves the product of gender relations). This study has also suggested that it is not some singular "masculinity" that is being constructed through athletic careers. It may be correct, from a psychoanalytic perspective, to suggest that all males bring ambivalences toward intimacy to their interactions with the world, but "the world" is a very different place for males from different racial and socioeconomic backgrounds. Because males have substantially different interactions with the world, based on class, race, and other differences and inequalities, we might expect the construction of masculinity to take on different meanings for boys and men from differing backgrounds (Messner, 1989). Indeed, this study has suggested that boys from higher-status backgrounds face a much broader range of options than do their lower-status counterparts. As a result, athletic careers take on different meanings for these boys. Lower-status boys are likely to see athletic careers as *the* institutional context for the construction of their masculine status and identities, while higher-status males make an early shift away from athletic careers toward other institutions (usually education and nonsports careers). A key line of inquiry for future studies might begin by exploring this irony of sports careers: Despite the fact that "the athlete" is currently an example of an exemplary form of masculinity in public ideology, the vast majority of boys who become most committed to athletic careers are never well rewarded for their efforts. The fact that class and racial dynamics lead boys from higher-status backgrounds, unlike their lower-status counterparts, to move into nonsports careers illustrates how the construction of different kinds of masculinities is a key component of the overall construction of the gender order.

REFERENCES

Birrell, S. (1987) "The woman athlete's college experience: knowns and unknowns." *J. of Sport and Social Issues* 11:82–96.

Benjamin, J. (1988) *The Bonds of Love: Psychoanalysis, Feminism, and the Problem of Domination.* New York: Pantheon.

Bryson, L. (1987) "Sport and the maintenance of masculine hegemony." *Women's Studies International Forum* 10:349–360.

Chodorow, N. (1978) *The Reproduction of Mothering.* Berkeley: Univ. of California Press.

Connell, R. W. (1990) "An iron man: the body and some contradictions of hegemonic masculinity," in M. A. Messner and D. F. Sabo (eds.) *Sport, Men and the Gender Order: Critical Feminist Perspectives.* Champaign, IL: Human Kinetics.

Craib, I. (1987) "Masculinity and male dominance." *Soc. Rev.* 38:721–743.

Eitzen, D. S. (1975) "Athletics in the status system of male adolescents: a replication of Coleman's *The Adolescent Society.*" *Adolescence* 10:268–276.

Gilligan, C. (1982) *In a Different Voice: Psychological Theory and Women's Development.* Cambridge, MA: Harvard Univ. Press.

Greendorfer, S. L. (1977) "The role of socializing agents in female sport involvement." *Research Q.* 48:304–310.

Hall, M. A. (1988) "The discourse on gender and sport: from femininity to feminism." *Sociology of Sport J.* 5:330–340.

Hantover, J. (1978) "The boy scouts and the validation of masculinity." *J. of Social Issues* 34:184–195.

Haug, F. (1987) *Female Sexualization.* London: Verso.

Kidd, B. (1987) "Sports and masculinity," pp. 250–265 in M. Kaufman (ed.) *Beyond Patriarchy: Essays by Men on Pleasure, Power, and Change.* Toronto: Oxford Univ. Press.

Kidd, B. (1990) "The men's cultural centre: sports and the dynamic of women's oppression/men's repression," in M. A. Messner and D. F. Sabo (eds.) *Sport, Men and the Gender Order: Critical Feminist Perspectives.* Champaign, IL: Human Kinetics.

Kimmel, M. S. (1987) "Men's responses to feminism at the turn of the century." *Gender and Society* 1:261–283.

Kimmel, M. S. (1990) "Baseball and the reconstitution of American masculinity: 1880–1920," in M. A. Messner and D. F. Sabo (eds.) *Sport, Men and the Gender Order: Critical Feminist Perspectives.* Champaign, IL: Human Kinetics.

Leonard, W. M. II and J. M. Reyman (1988) "The odds of attaining professional athlete status: refining the computations." *Sociology of Sport J.* 5:162–169.

Lever, J. (1976) "Sex differences in the games children play." *Social Problems* 23:478–487.

Levinson, D. J. et al. (1978) *The Seasons of a Man's Life.* New York: Ballantine.

Lichterman, P. (1986) "Chodorow's psychoanalytic sociology: a project half-completed." *California Sociologist* 9:147–166.

Messner, M. (1987) "The meaning of success: the athletic experience and the development of male identity," pp. 193–210 in H. Brod (ed.) *The Making of Masculinities: The New Men's Studies.* Boston: Allen & Unwin.

Messner, M. (1988) "Sports and male domination: the female athlete as contested ideological terrain." *Sociology of Sport J.* 5:197–211.

Messner, M. (1989) "Masculinities and athletic careers." *Gender and Society* 3:71–88.

Oglesby, C. A. (ed.) (1978) *Women and Sport: From Myth to Reality.* Philadelphia: Lea & Farber.

Osherson, S. (1986) *Finding our Fathers: How a Man's Life is Shaped by His Relationship with His Father.* New York: Fawcett Columbine.

Piaget, J. H. (1965) *The Moral Judgment of the Child.* New York: Free Press.

Rubin, L. B. (1976) *Worlds of Pain: Life in the Working Class Family.* New York: Basic Books.

Sabo, D. (1985) "Sport, patriarchy and male identity: new questions about men and sport." *Arena Rev.* 9:2.

Schafer, W. E. (1975) "Sport and male sex role socialization." *Sport Sociology Bull.* 4:47–54.

Sennett, R. and J. Cobb (1973) *The Hidden Injuries of Class.* New York: Random House.

Theberge, N. (1981) "A critique of critiques: radical and feminist writings on sport." *Social Forces* 60:2.

Thorne, B. (1986) "Girls and boys together . . . but mostly apart: gender arrangements in elementary schools," pp. 167–184 in W. W. Hartup and Z. Rubin (eds.) *Relationships and Development.* Hillsdale, NJ: Lawrence Erlbaum.

Twin, S. L. (ed.) (1978) *Out of the Bleachers: Writings on Women and Sport.* Old Westbury, NY: Feminist Press.

13

WHO'S THE FAIREST OF THEM ALL?

JILL NELSON

Jill Nelson's work has appeared in *Essence, The New York Times, The Nation, USA Weekend,* and *The Village Voice.* She is a columnist for *MSNBC Online* and a contributing editor for *USA Weekend.*

N early three decades after I turned eighteen in 1970, the issues that I struggled with as a girl and young woman coming of age still dominate, the trinity of hair, body, and complexion prevail. It is only their manifestations that have changed.

In a wonderful collection of essays called *Home,* published in 1966, Leroi Jones, now Amiri Baraka, commented about television that the best thing about it was that black people weren't on it. Nowadays, our faces are all over television. Most of the time we're being arrested, robbing, shooting, posturing on talk shows, writhing in music videos. Black women are most often seen in music videos, gyrating in sexually explicit pantomime, the close-up, more often than not, on our juggling butts, breasts, or open thighs, although you may see a yard or two of synthetic hair fly by now and then. I may have known the women on my parents' album covers only as singing heads without bodies, but at least I knew they had heads. What I know after an afternoon watching music videos is that black women's bodies can now be used to sell things too. What's in their heads is irrelevant. Sometimes I think that, overall, invisibility might have been better.

Aside from a brief period in the late 1950s and 60s when the "Afro" was in style, the natural texture of most black women's hair remains, as it has historically been, unacceptable. The apparently neverending popularity of a variety of straightening devices, from the hot comb to chemical straighteners—now euphemistically called "relaxers," as if the problem is that sister's hair is uptight and all we need to do is to get it to cool out—attests to this. The proliferation in the last decade of hair weaves and braided extensions is a manifestation of black women's desire for hair that is not only straight but long, the better to toss. To black women, the message sent by the culture of beauty remains the same, i.e., that we genetically lack a fundamental element of desirability. The difference is that now we have thousands of products marketed specifically to us, the vast majority of them produced by white companies. This has nothing to do with inclusion and everything to do with cash. Just as when I was growing up we all knew the answer to the refrain of the Clairol ads, "Is it true blondes have more fun?," today when the actress Cybill Shepherd, blonde, straight-haired, and hawking L'Oreal hair products, declares she uses them "Because I'm worth it," we all know the flip side is that those of us who don't are worth less.

Not much has changed. The infrequent times when black women are portrayed as objects of desire in popular culture, their hair is invariably long, their features usually more Caucasian than Negroid, their bodies, since most often they are models, skinny. Happy as I was to see the images of black models Naomi Sims, Pat Cleveland, Alva Chin, Iman, and Pat Johnson break onto the scene when I was a young woman, it was clear most black women did not—and could not—look like them with their narrow noses, high cheekbones, and long, silky manes. Thirty years later, the same can be said of Veronica Webb and Tyra Banks. Even the popularity of the dark-skinned, British-born Naomi Campbell, whose natural hair is often shrouded in wigs, represents merely an updated version of white beauty in blackface, but this time with a twist: the black woman as exotic, animalistic, sexualized dominatrix. Still, note Campbell's long hair and colored contact lenses, making it clear that she is not the loathed and dreaded authentic black woman.

Stephanie Berry is a brown-skinned woman in her early forties who has been acting for thirteen years, and has recently begun getting television roles.

Berry looks more like Every Sister than a model. "I have never been the love interest," she says. "I am always a single mother. I am always the parent of a male black child and he is always a victim or perpetrator of violence. I usually don't have a husband, and if I do, he dies too. I am always grieving." Berry tells the story of a recent audition. "I knew I was a grieving mother. I walked in and said, 'Okay, what happened to my baby this time? What did my boy do?' I was trying to make light. They didn't find it funny. I did not get the part."

In the last thirty years there has been little real alteration of the beauty industry's marketing of whiteness as the norm, the standard to which all the rest of us should aspire. For black girls and women this journey is as psychically devastating as it is omnipresent. Even if we manage to get rid of our hips, breasts, waistlines, grow our hair, get a weave or extensions, even if we go blonde, we will never possess the fundamental ingredient for female beauty in America, and that is whiteness.

In this climate, we conveniently forget that for most black Americans light skin is the result of rape and sexual exploitation during slavery; we are only interested in the proffered rewards or favor we believe come with lighter skin color. It is a psychological given that all people feel most immediately comfortable with those who look like them. It is not coincidence that the primary image of African American women we see in popular culture, particularly television and print advertisements, are light-skinned. It's gotten to the point that I often have to see a commercial two or three times to figure out if the green-eyed, crinkly-haired woman selling cereal or soda is black. If she's dark-skinned, chances are she's selling something that's a drag to use, like toilet bowl cleanser or a laxative. What we are witnessing is the rise of the biracial as favored black woman, even though it's stretching the point to suggest any of us are preferred. At the millennium, the culture has taken their contempt and our erasure one step further. Two of the most visible and acceptable images of black women in the eyes of the dominant culture are those offered by RuPaul and, occasionally, the Chicago Bulls' Dennis Rodman, black men in drag.

Black Americans twist the fruit of our enslavement into a prized possession. As much as black people don't like to talk about or admit it, a color caste system remains a dominant aspect of our communities, particularly for women. Put a truly beautiful chocolate-colored woman side by side with an average-looking beige one and I guarantee you that most black people will declare the lighter-skinned one prettier. Look at black couples and notice how often the woman's complexion is lighter than the man's, evidence that we continue, consciously or not, to find light-skinned women, and the increased chance that they will produce lighter-skinned children, more valuable. This is our version of "marrying up." Listen even to the language we use when talking about color. Light-skinned people are described as "fair"; language as value judgment. People are often described as "dark, *but* beautiful," as if their complexion were something to overcome. Too often, we hold darker children to behavioral standards that lighter children are not required to meet, as if their complexion confers upon them a state of grace that excuses or mitigates misbehavior, instant entitlement based upon color that extends, especially for women, into adulthood. In describing newborns, what black people always tell you is about the baby's color and the texture of their hair, even when they cannot recall the infant's name. We have a plethora of myths and folk wisdom relating to hair and complexion: A bald head on a baby means the child will have "good" hair, a thick head of hair means naps will follow, an infant's adult complexion can be judged by the color of the palms of its hands or soles of its feet, a clothespin on the nose will keep it from spreading, becoming a wide, Negroid nose.

Flip through an issue of *Vogue, Elle, Mademoiselle,* or any other women's magazine (a misnomer, since they should more accurately be called men's magazines, since their focus is on how men want to configure women), and black women are largely absent. When we are present, it is as images that conform to white notions of black beauty. There is no doubt that some of these women are beautiful, but Naomi Campbell is not most of us, any more than Kate Moss is most white women. The difference is that above and beyond the destructive myths of beauty, white women have a whole white culture that confers on them, in whatever twisted ways, the myriad rewards of whiteness. She is at least viewed as a woman, in the sweepstakes, and visible.

Most women, white and black, are not comforted by the dominant myths of beauty. The difference for black women is that we do not feel simply ugly, but totally outside, irrelevant, invisible. The significant and continuing success of *Essence,* the only fashion and beauty magazine targeted toward black women, is due in large part to the visibility it gives to black women in all our diversity of color, hair, and body. Almost three decades after its debut in 1970, *Essence* remains the only magazine that consistently recognizes and embraces the true range of black beauty. In the pages of *Essence,* our beauty is not dependent on our degree of whiteness or the subtle and overt racist and sexist fantasies of male photographers and art directors of black women as exotic, animalistic, overly sexualized objects of domination, degradation, and desire. In these pages, black women's beauty is normal, not aberrant. As a black woman, I have been trying to figure out what is beautiful, and functional, and comfortable for me and my sisters for most of my life.

Over the last ten years I've been having my hair cut shorter and shorter. In the late summer of 1996, when I am forty-four, I have my hair shaved to the scalp with an electric razor. When I leave my head is covered with a faint memory of brown and silver peach fuzz, I am as close to bald as I can get without lathering up and using a straight razor. I do this because I am tired of everything about hair—having it, combing it, thinking about it, plain feeling it. So, to test my theory that for me hair has finally become obsolete, I got rid of it. I want to see how people react to me, and how I react to myself, hairless. After the first few days, when I wake up startled by my own reflection in the mirror, I come to love it. I like the way it looks, the way it feels bristly when I run my hand over it from any direction, the fact that after four decades I have achieved hair that requires no maintenance.

The response of others is profound. Most black men's eyes skip over me rapidly, distastefully, as if they do not care to see someone who looks like me. I catch pure disdain in the eyes of several. A few stare, look intrigued, and rap to me, although most of these are young enough to be my children. Black women in general—with the exception of the few who are also either bald or wearing short naturals or dreadlocks, who give me a solidarity smile or compliment me—look at me as if I am totally unattractive, insane, and vaguely threatening. It is as if in deciding to be bald I am challenging our collective obsession with hair. Maybe I am. White people, women and men, look surprised and stare at me as I go by. Many people, across race, particularly women, give me a sympathetic smile, assuming, perhaps, that I am a cancer patient undergoing chemotherapy. Whatever a specific individual's response, the most interesting thing about being bald is that I am no longer invisible. Like it or not, everyone sees me. It is a wonderful sensation. Maybe a giant step in black women gaining visibility would be if we all shaved our heads. We would be both immediately visible and connected.

Barring such drastic action, a possible first step would be in acknowledging the commonality of our experiences as black girls and women in a hostile and alien culture. Sometimes that affirmation comes from simply making eye contact. Or talking to girls about self-image. Or teaching young women how to look at popular culture critically. Or telling another woman that she looks nice. That is sisterhood.

Several days after I cut my hair I walk to the subway station. The woman rapidly climbing the steps ahead of me has dark brown skin, a slim frame. I cannot see how old she is. A teenage girl walks slightly behind her. One of the girl's hands casually touches the woman's dreadlocks as she talks. As I close the distance between us I hear the girl say, "Really, Mom, you could go to the hairdresser and they twist them up right, fix up your locks, they'd look nice. People would notice you, people would be looking from across the street."

The woman turns slightly to look back at her daughter. She is smiling. "Forget it. This ain't no hairstyle," she says as I pull alongside her. She is probably in her early thirties. I reach out my hand and we slap five, briefly clasp hands, laugh. It is a moment of unspoken understanding, communion, knowing that hair, and so much of what we thought mattered to the business of our being women, doesn't matter at all, or much, or certainly not enough for her to go to a beauty salon and have her low-maintenance dreadlocks styled. It is obsolete. That there is too much work to be done and that she with her non–salon selected locks and me with my damn near bald head, and all the other sisters struggling for loving self-definition, are bad as we wanna be. At the bottom of the steps her daughter peels off, heading downtown. We climb the last flight of steps in tandem, going in the same direction.

14

HE DEFIES YOU STILL
The Memoirs of a Sissy

TOMMI AVICOLLI

Tommi Avicolli, who now goes by Tommi Avicolli Mecca, is a radical working-class Southern Italian queer writer, performer, and activist. He is author of *Between Little Rock and a Hard Place* (1993) and coeditor of *Hey Paesan: Writing by Lesbians and Gay Men of Italian Descent* (1999). He works by day helping tenants fight gentrification and eviction in San Francisco.

> You're just a faggot
> No history faces you this morning
> A faggot's dreams are scarlet
> Bad blood bled from words that scarred[1]

Scene One

A homeroom in a Catholic high school in South Philadelphia. The boy sits quietly in the first aisle, third desk, reading a book. He does not look up, not even for a moment. He is hoping no one will remember he is sitting there. He wishes he were invisible. The teacher is not yet in the classroom so the other boys are talking and laughing loudly.

Suddenly, a voice from beside him:

"Hey, you're a faggot, ain't you?"

The boy does not answer. He goes on reading his book, or rather pretending he is reading his book. It is impossible to actually read the book now.

"Hey, I'm talking to you!"

The boy still does not look up. He is so scared his heart is thumping madly; it feels like it is leaping out of his chest and into his throat. But he can't look up.

"Faggot, I'm talking to you!"

To look up is to meet the eyes of the tormentor.

Suddenly, a sharpened pencil point is thrust into the boy's arm. He jolts, shaking off the pencil, aware that there is blood seeping from the wound.

"What did you do that for?" he asks timidly.

Tommi Avicolli, "He Defies You Still: The Memoirs of a Sissy" from *Radical Teacher*, 24 (1986). Reprinted with permission.

"Cause I hate faggots," the other boy says, laughing. Some other boys begin to laugh, too. A symphony of laughter. The boy feels as if he's going to cry. But he must not cry. Must not cry. So he holds back the tears and tries to read the book again. He must read the book. Read the book.

When the teacher arrives a few minutes later, the class quiets down. The boy does not tell the teacher what has happened. He spits on the wound to clean it, dabbing it with a tissue until the bleeding stops. For weeks he fears some dreadful infection from the lead in the pencil point.

Scene Two

The boy is walking home from school. A group of boys (two, maybe three, he is not certain) grab him from behind, drag him into an alley and beat him up. When he gets home, he races up to his room, refusing dinner ("I don't feel well," he tells his mother through the locked door) and spends the night alone in the dark wishing he would die. . . .

These are not fictitious accounts—I *was* that boy. Having been branded a sissy by neighborhood children because I preferred jump rope to baseball and dolls to playing soldiers, I was often taunted with "hey sissy" or "hey faggot" or "yoo hoo honey" (in a mocking voice) when I left the house.

To avoid harassment, I spent many summers alone in my room. I went out on rainy days when the street was empty.

I came to like being alone. I didn't need anyone, I told myself over and over again. I was an island. Contact with others meant pain. Alone, I was protected. I began writing poems, then short stories. There was no reason to go outside anymore. I had a world of my own.

> In the schoolyard today
> they'll single you out
> Their laughter will leave your ears ringing
> like the church bells
> which once awed you. . . .[2]

School was one of the more painful experiences of my youth. The neighborhood bullies could be avoided. The taunts of the children living in those endless repetitive row houses could be evaded by staying in my room. But school was something I had to face day after day for some two hundred mornings a year.

I had few friends in school. I was a pariah. Some kids would talk to me, but few wanted to be known as my close friend. Afraid of labels. If I was a sissy, then he had to be a sissy, too. I was condemned to loneliness.

Fortunately, a new boy moved into our neighborhood and befriended me; he wasn't afraid of the labels. He protected me when the other guys threatened to beat me up. He walked me home from school; he broke through the terrible loneliness. We were in third or fourth grade at the time.

We spent a summer or two together. Then his parents sent him to camp and I was once again confined to my room.

Scene Three

High school lunchroom. The boy sits at a table near the back of the room. Without warning, his lunch bag is grabbed and tossed to another table. Someone opens it and confiscates a package of Tastykakes; another boy takes the sandwich. The empty bag is tossed back to the boy who stares at it, dumbfounded. He should be used to this; it has happened before.

Someone screams, "faggot," laughing. There is always laughter. It does not annoy him anymore.

There is no teacher nearby. There is never a teacher around. And what would he say if there were? Could he report the crime? He would be jumped after school if he did. Besides, it would be his word against theirs. Teachers never noticed anything. They never heard the taunts. Never heard the word, "faggot." They were the great deaf mutes, pillars of indifference; a sissy's pain was not relevant to history and geography and God made me to love honor and obey him, amen.

Scene Four

High school Religion class. Someone has a copy of *Playboy*. Father N. is not in the room yet; he's late, as usual. Someone taps the boy roughly on the shoulder. He turns. A finger points to the centerfold model, pink fleshy body, thin and sleek. Almost painted. Not real. The other asks, mocking voice, "Hey, does she turn you on? Look at those tits!"

The boy smiles, nodding meekly; turns away.

The other jabs him harder on the shoulder, "Hey, whatsamatter, don't you like girls?"

Laughter. Thousands of mouths; unbearable din of laughter. In the Arena: thumbs down. Don't spare the queer.

"Wanna suck my dick? Huh? That turn you on, faggot!"

The laughter seems to go on forever . . .

> Behind you, the sound of their laughter
> echoes a million times
> in a soundless place
> They watch you walk/sit/stand/breathe. . . .[3]

What did being a sissy really mean? It was a way of walking (from the hips rather than the shoulders); it was a way of talking (often with a lisp or in a high-pitched voice); it was a way of relating to others (gently, not wanting to fight, or hurt anyone's feelings). It was being intelligent ("an egghead" they called it sometimes); getting good grades. It means not being interested in sports, not playing football in the street after school; not discussing teams and scores and playoffs. And it involved not showing fervent interest in girls, not talking about scoring with tits or *Playboy* centerfolds. Not concealing naked women in your history book; or porno books in your locker.

On the other hand, anyone could be a "faggot." It was a catch-all. If you did something that didn't conform to what was the acceptable behavior of the group, then you risked being called a faggot. If you didn't get along with the "in" crowd, you were a faggot. It was the most commonly used putdown. It kept guys in line. They became angry when somebody called them a faggot. More fights started over someone calling someone else a faggot than anything else. The word had power. It toppled the male ego, shattered his delicate facade, violated the image he projected. He was tough. Without feeling. Faggot cut through all this. It made him vulnerable. Feminine. And feminine was the worst thing he could possibly be. Girls were fine for fucking, but no boy in his right mind wanted to be like them. A boy was the opposite of a girl. He was not feminine. He was not feeling. He was not weak.

Just look at the gym teacher who growled like a dog; or the priest with the black belt who threw kids against the wall in rage when they didn't know their Latin. They were men, they got respect.

But not the physics teacher who preached pacifism during lectures on the nature of atoms. Everybody knew what he was—and why he believed in the anti-war movement.

My parents only knew that the neighborhood kids called me names. They begged me to act more like the other boys. My brothers were ashamed of me. They never said it, but I knew. Just as I knew that my parents were embarrassed by my behavior.

At times, they tried to get me to act differently. Once my father lectured me on how to walk right. I'm still not clear on what that means. Not from the hips, I guess, don't "swish" like faggots do.

A nun in elementary school told my mother at Open House that there was "something wrong with me." I had draped my sweater over my shoulders like a girl, she said. I was a smart kid, but I should know better than to wear my sweater like a girl!

My mother stood there, mute. I wanted her to say something, to chastise the nun; to defend me. But how could she? This was a nun talking—representative of Jesus, protector of all that was good and decent.

An uncle once told me I should start "acting like a boy" instead of like a girl. Everybody seemed ashamed of me. And I guess I was ashamed of myself, too. It was hard not to be.

Scene Five

Priest: Do you like girls, Mark?
Mark: Uh-huh.
Priest: I mean *really* like them?
Mark: Yeah—they're okay.
Priest: There's a role they play in your salvation. Do you understand it, Mark?
Mark: Yeah.
Priest: You've got to like girls. Even if you should decide to enter the seminary, it's important to keep in mind God's plan for a man and a woman. . . .[4]

Catholicism of course condemned homosexuality. Effeminacy was tolerated as long as the effeminate person did not admit to being gay. Thus, priests could be effeminate because they weren't gay.

As a sissy, I could count on no support from the church. A male's sole purpose in life was to father children—souls for the church to save. The only hope a homosexual had of attaining salvation was by remaining totally celibate. Don't even think of touching another boy. To think of a sin was a sin. And to sin was to put a mark upon the soul. Sin—if it was a serious offense against God—led to hell. There was no way around it. If you sinned, you were doomed.

Realizing I was gay was not an easy task. Although I knew I was attracted to boys by the time I was about eleven, I didn't connect this attraction to homosexuality. I was not queer. Not I. I was merely appreciating a boy's good looks, his fine features, his proportions. It didn't seem to matter that I didn't appreciate a girl's looks in the same way. There was no twitching in my thighs when I gazed upon a beautiful girl. But I wasn't queer.

I resisted that label—queer—for the longest time. Even when everything pointed to it, I refused to see it. I was certainly not queer. Not I.

We sat through endless English classes, and history courses about the wars between men who were not allowed to love each other. No gay history was ever taught. No history faces you this morning. You're just a faggot. Homosexuals had never contributed to the human race. God destroyed the queers in Sodom and Gomorrah.

We learned about Michelangelo, Oscar Wilde, Gertrude Stein—but never that they were queer. They were not queer. Walt Whitman, the "father of American poetry," was not queer. No one was queer. I was alone, totally unique. One of a kind. Were there others like me somewhere? Another planet, perhaps?

In school, they never talked of the queers. They did not exist. The only hint we got of this other species was in religion class. And even then it was clouded in mystery—never spelled out. It was sin. Like masturbation. Like looking at *Playboy* and getting a hard-on. A sin.

Once a progressive priest in senior year religion class actually mentioned homosexuals—he said the word—but was into Erich Fromm, into homosexuals as pathetic and sick. Fixated at some early stage; penis, anal, whatever. Only heterosexuals passed on to the nirvana of sexual development.

No other images from the halls of the Catholic high school except those the other boys knew: swishy faggot sucking cock in an alley somewhere, grabbing asses in the bathroom. Never mentioning how much straight boys craved blow jobs, it was part of the secret.

It was all a secret. You were not supposed to talk about the queers. Whisper maybe. Laugh about them, yes. But don't be open, honest; don't try to understand. Don't cite their accomplishments. No history faces you this morning. You're just a faggot   faggot   no history   just a faggot

Epilogue

The boy marching down the Parkway. Hundreds of queers. Signs proclaiming gay pride. Speakers. Tables with literature from gay groups. A miracle, he is thinking. Tears are coming loose now. Someone hugs him.

> You could not control
> the sissy in me
> nor could you exorcise him
> nor electrocute him
> You declared him illegal illegitimate
> insane and immature
> But he defies you still.[5]

NOTES

1. From the poem "Faggot" by Tommi Avicolli, published in *GPU News,* Sept. 1979.
2. Ibid.
3. Ibid.
4. From the play *Judgment of the Roaches* by Tommi Avicolli, produced in Philadelphia at the Gay Community Center, the Painted Bride Arts Center and the University of Pennsylvania; aired over WXPN-FM, in four parts; and presented at the Lesbian/Gay Conference in Norfolk, VA, July, 1980.
5. From the poem "Sissy Poem," published in *Magic Doesn't Live Here Anymore* (Philadelphia: Spruce Street Press, 1976).

15

GROWING UP HIDDEN

LINNEA DUE

Linnea Due is a writer and managing editor of *Express,* an alternative weekly in Berkeley, California. She is the author of three novels, *High and Outside* (1989), *Give Me Time* (1987), and *Life Savings* (1992), and she was the coeditor of the anthology *Dagger: On Butch Women* (1994).

Growing up hidden—coming of age not only invisible but embattled in that invisibility—is hard to describe to someone who has not experienced it. A phrase like "a wolf in sheep's clothing" takes on special meaning to a gay kid—at least it did for me. Was I hiding because I was bad? Why didn't I feel bad if I was so bad I had to hide? What I should have asked—why do I have to hide?—was too obvious to require an answer, and yet it turned out to be the real question.

I don't remember ever not knowing who I was. For a while I revealed myself, saying I wanted to be strong ("Girls don't need to be strong"), that when I got married, my wife and I would have a wonderful house ("You won't have a wife, you'll have a husband"). By the time I went to summer camp, at age seven, I was already trying to tone myself down: people told me I was too raucous, too wild, and I had to drop that damn fool idea about getting married to a woman. I decided to shut up—not that I'd changed my mind, but it was easier than trying to explain myself to people who'd never met a girl like me.

In the closing days of camp, we were supposed to say who we were going steady with. No one was actually going with anybody—we were all too young—but I was still thrown into a quandary. If I were going to pledge my troth, it certainly would be to Stacy, with whom I'd been sneaking off all summer to plan our life together. Ken snagged me after dinner one night, just before campfire. "Look," he said bluntly, "you want to go with Stacy and I want to go with Roger. So what we'll do is tell everybody you're going with me and she's going with Rog."

God, what a mind! Such duplicity would never have occurred to me. It made me feel a little funny—wasn't it like lying?—but it wasn't a long stretch from the silence I'd been cultivating for a time anyway. As I became older,

I edited myself more and more, especially after I realized that it wasn't that people hadn't known about girls like me, but that those girls were so horrible no one wanted to ever talk about them.

By then, I knew what I was called. I'd been risking my life balancing on my father's office chair, snatching books off the uppermost shelf as I rolled by. Richard von Krafft-Ebing's *Psychopathia Sexualis.* Havelock Ellis's *Sexual Inversion.* Freud. Erikson. I'd also been haunting the paperback rack at my neighborhood grocery, ripping off the romances of the '50s—*Beebo Brinker,* Ann Bannon, *Women on the Edge of Twilight.* Krafft-Ebing made me popular on the playground—I was the Susie Bright of Hilltop Elementary School—but my knowledge was a mixed blessing. I was glad to know people like me existed, but I also knew from my dad that a psychopath was the worst thing you could be. Finding my sexuality among those who fucked chickens or corpses made me feel—well, a little queer.

Still, I figured I was hiding successfully until the day my Girl Scout troop leader threw me out for being "too masculine." My world fell apart. I had believed censoring my thoughts was enough; I hadn't realized my manner and my body—the very way I moved—were betraying me daily. Something drastic had to be done.

Something was. I dropped out of the athletics I loved, wore nylons and makeup, carried my books in front of me, shortened my stride. I developed an imperious persona to go along with my new look and pretended an interest in boys (a breach of ethics I tried to mitigate by not letting them come too close). It was like learning a foreign language—and not coincidentally, I began drinking to blackouts.

From seventh through twelfth grades, I functioned as another person, someone I became in the morning and shed in the evening when, safely in my room, I could pore over my romances and daydream about kissing my own raven-haired beauty. It never occurred to me to look for her; my dreams ranked alongside my classmates' fantasies of becoming famous actresses or politicians. That I was labeling illusory the most important stuff of life—my identity and my relationships—didn't seem odd. Staying undercover was job number one.

My life as a spy reached a pinnacle of the absurd during my first year at Sarah Lawrence. I received a visit from several of my elementary school friends; they had traveled from Smith, from Brandeis, from Boston University, certain that I, the amateur sexologist, could set their minds at ease. They were worried, they explained haltingly, about those sailor/whore games we had played at slumber parties. Wasn't it weird for thirteen-year-old girls to practice kissing each other? Was I concerned that we had lesbian tendencies? Not at all, I replied heartily, and proceeded to regale them with a lot of assurances they wanted to hear. They went back to Massachusetts much relieved, and I lay on my bed and stared at the ceiling, wondering who was the bigger fool. Two years later, I didn't lie when the college president asked if I was a lesbian, though it meant leaving the school I loved; I would never lie again—not about that anyway.

16

MASCULINITY AS HOMOPHOBIA

MICHAEL S. KIMMEL

Michael S. Kimmel is professor of sociology at SUNY at Stony Brook. His many books include: *Manhood in America* (2005, 2nd edition), *The Gendered Society* (2004), and, coedited with Michael A. Messner, *Men's Lives* (2006, 7th edition).

Even if we do not subscribe to Freudian psychoanalytic ideas, we can still observe how, in less sexualized terms, the father is the first man who evaluates the boy's masculine performance, the first pair of male eyes before whom he tries to prove himself. Those eyes will follow him for the rest of his life. Other men's eyes will join them—the eyes of role models such as teachers, coaches, bosses, or media heroes; the eyes of his peers, his friends, his workmates; and the eyes of millions of other men, living and dead, from whose constant scrutiny of his performance he will never be free. "The tradition of all the dead generations weighs like a nightmare on the brain of the living," was how Karl Marx put it over a century ago (1848/1964, p. 11). "The birthright of every American male is a chronic sense of personal inadequacy," is how two psychologists describe it today (Woolfolk & Richardson, 1978, p. 57).

That nightmare from which we never seem to awaken is that those other men will see that sense of inadequacy, they will see that in our own eyes we are not who we are pretending to be. What we call masculinity is often a hedge against being revealed as a fraud, an exaggerated set of activities that keep others from seeing through us, and a frenzied effort to keep at bay those fears within ourselves. Our real fear, "is not fear of women but of being ashamed or humiliated in front of other men, or being dominated by stronger men" (Leverenz, 1986, p. 451).

This, then, is the great secret of American manhood: *We are afraid of other men.* Homophobia is a central organizing principle of our cultural definition of manhood. Homophobia is more than the irrational fear of gay men, more than the fear that we might be perceived as gay. "The word 'faggot' has nothing to do with homosexual experience or even with fears of homosexuals," writes David Leverenz (1986). "It comes out of the depths of manhood: a label of ultimate contempt for anyone who seems sissy, untough, uncool"

(p. 455). Homophobia is the fear that other men will unmask us, emasculate us, reveal to us and the world that we do not measure up, that we are not real men. We are afraid to let other men see that fear. Fear makes us ashamed, because the recognition of fear in ourselves is proof to ourselves that we are not as manly as we pretend, that we are, like the young man in a poem by Yeats, "one that ruffles in a manly pose for all his timid heart." Our fear is the fear of humiliation. We are ashamed to be afraid.

Shame leads to silence—the silences that keep other people believing that we actually approve of the things that are done to women, to minorities, to gays and lesbians in our culture. The frightened silence as we scurry past a woman being hassled by men on the street. That furtive silence when men make sexist or racist jokes in a bar. That clammy-handed silence when guys in the office make gay-bashing jokes. Our fears are the sources of our silences, and men's silence is what keeps the system running. This might help to explain why women often complain that their male friends or partners are often so understanding when they are alone and yet laugh at sexist jokes or even make those jokes themselves when they are out with a group.

The fear of being seen as a sissy dominates the cultural definitions of manhood. It starts so early. "Boys among boys are ashamed to be unmanly," wrote one educator in 1871 (cited in Rotundo, 1993, p. 264). I have a standing bet with a friend that I can walk onto any playground in America where 6-year-old boys are happily playing and by asking one question, I can provoke a fight. That question is simple: "Who's a sissy around here?" Once posed, the challenge is made. One of two things is likely to happen. One boy will accuse another of being a sissy, to which that boy will respond that he is not a sissy, that the first boy is. They may have to fight it out to see who's lying. Or a whole group of boys will surround one boy and all shout "He is! He is!" That boy will either burst into tears and run home crying, disgraced, or he will have to take on several boys at once, to prove that he's not a sissy. (And what will his father or older brothers tell him if he chooses to run home crying?) It will be some time before he regains any sense of self-respect.

Violence is often the single most evident marker of manhood. Rather it is the willingness to fight, the desire to fight. The origin of our expression that one has a chip on one's shoulder lies in the practice of an adolescent boy in the country or small town at the turn of the century, who would literally walk around with a chip of wood balanced on his shoulder—a signal of his readiness to fight with anyone who would take the initiative of knocking the chip off (see Gorer, 1964, p. 38; Mead, 1965).

As adolescents, we learn that our peers are a kind of gender police, constantly threatening to unmask us as feminine, as sissies. One of the favorite tricks when I was an adolescent was to ask a boy to look at his fingernails. If he held his palm toward his face and curled his fingers back to see them, he passed the test. He'd looked at his nails "like a man." But if he held the back of his hand away from his face, and looked at his fingernails with arm outstretched, he was immediately ridiculed as a sissy.

As young men we are constantly riding those gender boundaries, checking the fences we have constructed on the perimeter, making sure that nothing even remotely feminine might show through. The possibilities of being unmasked are everywhere. Even the most seemingly insignificant thing can pose a threat or activate that haunting terror. On the day the students in my course "Sociology of Men and Masculinities" were scheduled to discuss homophobia and male-male friendships, one student provided a touching illustration. Noting that it was a beautiful day, the first day of spring after a brutal northeast winter, he decided to wear shorts to class. "I had this really nice pair of new Madras shorts," he commented. "But then I thought to myself, these shorts have lavender and pink in them. Today's class topic is homophobia. Maybe today is not the best day to wear these shorts."

Our efforts to maintain a manly front cover everything we do. What we wear. How we talk. How we walk. What we eat. Every mannerism, every movement contains a coded gender language. Think, for example, of how you would answer the question: How do you "know" if a man is homosexual? When I ask this question in classes or workshops, respondents invariably provide a pretty standard list of stereotypically effeminate behaviors. He walks a certain way, talks a certain way, acts a certain way. He's very emotional; he shows his feelings. One woman commented that she "knows" a man is gay if he really cares about her; another said she knows he's gay if he shows no interest in her, if he leaves her alone.

Now alter the question and imagine what heterosexual men do to make sure no one could possibly get the "wrong idea" about them. Responses typically refer to the original stereotypes, this time as a set of negative rules about behavior. Never dress that way. Never talk or walk that way. Never show your feelings or get emotional. Always be prepared to demonstrate sexual interest in women that you meet, so it is impossible for any woman to get the wrong idea about you. In this sense, homophobia, the fear of being perceived as gay, as not a real man, keeps men exaggerating all the traditional rules of masculinity, including sexual predation with women. Homophobia and sexism go hand in hand.

The stakes of perceived sissydom are enormous—sometimes matters of life and death. We take enormous risks to prove our manhood, exposing ourselves disproportionately to health risks, workplace hazards, and stress-related illnesses. Men commit suicide three times as often as women. Psychiatrist Willard Gaylin (1992) explains that it is "invariably because of perceived social humiliation," most often tied to failure in business:

> Men become depressed because of loss of status and power in
> the world of men. It is not the loss of money, or the material
> advantages that money could buy, which produces the despair that
> leads to self-destruction. It is the "shame," the "humiliation," the
> sense of personal "failure." . . . A man despairs when he has ceased
> being a man among men. (p. 32)

In one survey, women and men were asked what they were most afraid of. Women responded that they were most afraid of being raped and murdered. Men responded that they were most afraid of being laughed at (Noble, 1992, pp. 105–106).

Power and Powerlessness in the Lives of Men

I have argued that homophobia, men's fear of other men, is the animating condition of the dominant definition of masculinity in America, that the reigning definition of masculinity is a defensive effort to prevent being emasculated. In our efforts to suppress or overcome those fears, the dominant culture exacts a tremendous price from those deemed less than fully manly: women, gay men, nonnative-born men, men of color. This perspective may help clarify a paradox in men's lives, a paradox in which men have virtually all the power and yet do not feel powerful (see Kaufman, 1993).

Manhood is equated with power—over women, over other men. Everywhere we look, we see the institutional expression of that power—in state and national legislatures, on the boards of directors of every major U.S. corporation or law firm, and in every school and hospital administration. Women have long understood this, and feminist women have spent the past three decades challenging both the public and the private expressions of men's power and acknowledging their fear of men. Feminism as a set of theories both explains women's fear of men and empowers women to confront it both publicly and privately. Feminist women have theorized that masculinity is about the drive for domination, the drive for power, for conquest.

This feminist definition of masculinity as the drive for power is theorized from women's point of view. It is how women experience masculinity. But it assumes a symmetry between the public and the private that does not conform to men's experiences. Feminists observe that women, as a group, do not hold power in our society. They also observe that individually, they, as women, do not feel powerful. They feel afraid, vulnerable. Their observation of the social reality and their individual experiences are therefore symmetrical. Feminism also observes that men, as a group, are in power. Thus, with the same symmetry, feminism has tended to assume that individually men must feel powerful.

This is why the feminist critique of masculinity often falls on deaf ears with men. When confronted with the analysis that men have all the power, many men react incredulously. "What do you mean, men have all the power?" they ask. "What are you talking about? My wife bosses me around. My kids boss me around. My boss bosses me around. I have no power at all! I'm completely powerless!"

Men's feelings are not the feelings of the powerful, but of those who see themselves as powerless. These are the feelings that come inevitably from the discontinuity between the social and the psychological, between the aggregate analysis that reveals how men are in power as a group and the psychological fact that they do not feel powerful as individuals. They are the feelings of men who were raised to believe themselves entitled to feel that power, but do not feel it. No wonder many men are frustrated and angry.

This may explain the recent popularity of those workshops and retreats designed to help men to claim their "inner" power, their "deep manhood," or their "warrior within." Authors such as Bly (1990), Moore and Gillette (1991, 1992, 1993a, 1993b), Farrell (1986, 1993), and Keen (1991) honor and respect men's feelings of powerlessness and acknowledge those feelings to be both true and real. "They gave white men the semblance of power," notes John Lee, one of the leaders of these retreats (quoted in Ferguson, 1992, p. 28). "We'll let you run the country, but in the meantime, stop feeling, stop talking, and continue swallowing your pain and your hurt." (We are not told who "they" are.)

Often the purveyors of the mythopoetic men's movement, that broad umbrella that encompasses all the groups helping men to retrieve this mythic deep manhood, use the image of the chauffeur to described modern man's position. The chauffeur appears to have the power—he's wearing the uniform, he's in the driver's seat, and he knows where he's going. So, to the observer, the chauffeur looks as though he is in command. But to the chauffeur himself, they note, he is merely taking orders. He is not at all in charge.[1]

Despite the reality that everyone knows chauffeurs do not have the power, this image remains appealing to the men who hear it at these weekend workshops. But there is a missing piece to the image, a piece concealed by the framing of the image in terms of the individual man's experience. That missing piece is that the person who is giving the orders is also a man. Now we have a relationship *between* men—between men giving orders and other men taking those orders. The man who identifies with the chauffeur is entitled to be the man giving the orders, but he is not. ("They," it turns out, are other men.)

The dimension of power is now reinserted into men's experience not only as the product of individual experience but also as the product of relations with other men. In this sense, men's experience of powerlessness is *real*—the men actually feel it and certainly act on it—but it is not *true*, that is, it does not accurately describe their condition. In contrast to women's lives, men's lives are structured around relationships of power and men's differential access to power, as well as the differential access to that power of men as a group. Our imperfect analysis of our own situation leads us to believe that we men need more power, rather than leading us to support feminists' efforts to rearrange power relationships along more equitable lines.

Philosopher Hannah Arendt (1970) fully understood this contradictory experience of social and individual power:

> Power corresponds to the human ability not just to act but to act in concert. Power is never the property of an individual; it belongs to

a group and remains in existence only so long as the group keeps together. When we say of somebody that he is "in power" we actually refer to his being empowered by a certain number of people to act in their name. The moment the group, from which the power originated to begin with . . . disappears, his "power" also vanishes. (p. 44)

Why, then, do American men feel so powerless? Part of the answer is because we've constructed the rules of manhood so that only the tiniest fraction of men come to believe that they are the biggest of wheels, the sturdiest of oaks, the most virulent repudiators of femininity, the most daring and aggressive. We've managed to disempower the overwhelming majority of American men by other means—such as discriminating on the basis of race, class, ethnicity, age, or sexual preference.

Masculinist retreats to retrieve deep, wounded masculinity are but one of the ways in which American men currently struggle with their fears and their shame. Unfortunately, at the very moment that they work to break down the isolation that governs men's lives, as they enable men to express those fears and that shame, they ignore the social power that men continue to exert over women and the privileges from which they (as the middle-aged, middle-class white men who largely make up these retreats) continue to benefit—regardless of their experiences as wounded victims of oppressive male socialization.

Others still rehearse the politics of exclusion, as if by clearing away the playing field of secure gender identity of any that we deem less than manly—women, gay men, nonnative-born men, men of color—middle-class, straight, white men can reground their sense of themselves without those haunting fears and that deep shame that they are unmanly and will be exposed by other men. This is the manhood of racism, of sexism, of homophobia. It is the manhood that is so chronically insecure that it trembles at the idea of lifting the ban on gays in the military, that is so threatened by women in the workplace that women become the targets of sexual harassment, that is so deeply frightened of equality that it must ensure that the playing field of male competition remains stacked against all newcomers to the game.

Exclusion and escape have been the dominant methods American men have used to keep their fears of humiliation at bay. The fear of emasculation by other men, of being humiliated, of being seen as a sissy, is the leitmotif in my reading of the history of American manhood. Masculinity has become a relentless test by which we prove to other men, to women, and ultimately to ourselves, that we have successfully mastered the part. The restlessness that men feel today is nothing new in American history; we have been anxious and restless for almost two centuries. Neither exclusion nor escape has ever brought us the relief we've sought, and there is no reason to think that either will solve our problems now. Peace of mind, relief from gender struggle, will come only from a politics of inclusion, not exclusion, from standing up for equality and justice, and not by running away.

NOTE

1. The image is from Warren Farrell, who spoke at a workshop I attended at the First International Men's Conference, Austin, Texas, October 1991.

REFERENCES

Arendt, H. (1970). *On revolution*. New York: Viking.

Bly, R. (1990). *Iron John: A book about men*. Reading, MA: Addison-Wesley.

Farrell, W. (1986). *Why men are the way they are*. New York: McGraw-Hill.

Farrell, W. (1993). *The myth of male power: Why men are the disposable sex*. New York: Simon & Schuster.

Ferguson, A. (1992, January). America's new men. *American Spectator, 25* (1).

Gaylin, W. (1992). *The male ego*. New York: Viking.

Gorer, G. (1964). *The American people: A study in national character*. New York: Norton.

Kaufman, M. (1993). *Cracking the armour: Power and pain in the lives of men*. Toronto: Viking Canada.

Keen, S. (1991). *Fire in the belly*. New York: Bantam.

Leverenz, D. (1986, Fall). Manhood, humiliation and public life: Some stories. *Southwest Review, 71*.

Marx, K., & Engels, F. (1848/1964). The communist manifesto. In R. Tucker (Ed.), *The Marx-Engels reader*. New York: Norton.

Mead, M. (1965). *And keep your powder dry*. New York: William Morrow.

Moore, R., & Gillette, D. (1991). *King, warrior, magician lover*. New York: Harper Collins.

Moore, R., & Gillette, D. (1992). *The king within: Accessing the king in the male psyche*. New York: William Morrow.

Moore, R., & Gillette, D. (1993a). *The warrior within: Accessing the warrior in the male psyche*. New York: William Morrow.

Moore, R., & Gillette, D. (1993b). *The magician within: Accessing the magician in the male psyche*. New York: William Morrow.

Noble, V. (1992). A helping hand from the guys. In K. L. Hagan (Ed.), *Women respond to the men's movement*. San Francisco: HarperCollins.

Rotundo, E. A. (1993). *American manhood: Transformations in masculinity from the revolution to the modern era*. New York: Basic Books.

Woolfolk, R. L., & Richardson, F. (1978). *Sanity, stress and survival*. New York: Signet.

PART III

◆ Embodiment

Our relationships to our bodies and our decisions about how we present ourselves to the world are heavily influenced by the historical and cultural contexts in which we live. In U.S. society, these contexts are determined to a large
extent by the media. A brief look at the history of clothing and fashion or at
the history of women in sports, for example, shows changes in the ideal female
body image over time. Laced corsets, once very popular, are now used by few
women. Sports such as track and field, once considered taboo for women athletes, are now acceptable although the athletes are much more easily accepted
if they appear to be feminine.[1] Current media images of young women support hyper-sexualized, thin bodies with bare midriffs.[2] Many of the dominant
messages about bodies are tied to images of gender, race, and class, mandating
different expectations for various women and men. For example, in a study of
Asian American women and cosmetic surgery, Eugenia Kaw reports an
increase in the number of people from racial and ethnic minority groups in the
United States electing racially specific plastic surgery. Whereas white women
tend to choose liposuction, breast augmentation, or reduction of wrinkles,
Asian American women, for example, tend to choose eyelid surgery to make
their eyes wider, and nasal surgery to make their noses more prominent. Kaw
concludes that Asian American women do this to escape racial prejudice by
looking more Anglo. She further concludes that Asian American women are
heavily influenced by the "medicalization" of racial features; rather than seen
as normal, their eyelids and noses are seen as something to be fixed by medical
intervention.[3] Of the 11.5 million cosmetic surgery procedures performed in
2006, 22 percent were done on people of color.[4]

Criticism of Black hairstyles illustrates societal pressure toward conformity with a white model of hair, pressuring Black people to straighten
their hair. In an illustrative example from the mid-1990s, a junior high school
near Chicago established a hair policy that barred cornrows, dredlocks,
braids, and headcarvings that displayed patterns (for example, a zigzag
part), presumably because they were symbols of gang involvement. After
protest by a multiracial group of parents who argued that most of the banned
hairstyles were "Black," the school changed its policy to allow dredlocks,
braids and cornrows (but no zigzags or other designs).[5]

Physical appearance is often an obsession for people in U.S. society, especially for people privileged enough to have the time and money to attend to
their bodies. The pressure to look "right" can be internalized as profound self-
disapproval. It drives many people to spend long hours exercising and
preening and many years dieting. Even for people who would be considered
attractive within their own communities, the dominant culture's obsession
with youth, muscles, whiteness, blondness, and thinness can undermine
positive attitudes for many.[6] With rare exceptions, most of us will look

seriously "wrong" at some point if we have the privilege of growing old. People whose bodies don't match dominant images of what is defined as normal suffer immense discrimination, especially on the basis of skin color, weight, age, or disability.[7]

Weight is a major issue, leading many girls, especially, to go on diets at young ages, derailing energy that might otherwise be spent in more creative ways, and often developing full-blown eating disorders such as bingeing, bulimia, or anorexia. Data gathered from 38 states by the Centers for Disease Control shows use of illegal steroids by high school students at 4 percent for 2005, including 3.2 percent among girls (compared to 4.8 percent among boys); this is presumably a strategy to lose fat and become more muscular but carries serious health risks.[8] In a study of body image and depression among low-income middle school African American girls, the girls suffered more from both depression and poor body image than did their male counterparts, although many of the boys, too, were concerned about their weight.[9] In an examination of grade point average and obesity, white girls who were obese had lower grade point averages than white girls who were not; the relationship did not hold for girls of color or boys.[10]

Boys and men seem to be increasingly concerned with their looks. Muscles are a big issue, leading to obsessive weight lifting and/or steroid use.[11] Gay men, adopting the pressure to please men that is pervasive in mainstream heterosexual culture, also suffer from body image dissatisfaction, topping the dissatisfaction list in some studies (followed by heterosexual women). Heterosexual men and lesbians seem to feel the most accepting of their bodies when these various groups are compared.[12] The year 2003 saw wider use of a trendy new word—metrosexual—used to describe heterosexual urban men who attend carefully to their bodies and homes, stretching the gender boundaries that define hegemonic masculinity to include more typically feminine aspects.

Cosmetic surgery is very popular in spite of its high cost.[13] According to the American Society for Aesthetic Plastic Surgery, the 11.5 million procedures performed in 2006 cost just under $12.2 billion. Of these, 92 percent were performed on women; 1 percent were performed on young people age 18 and under.[14] A case in England illustrates the pressure on teenage girls to have "perfect" bodies. Intense debate ensued when parents gave their teenage daughter, Jenna Franklin, a gift of silicone breast implants for her 16th birthday. The parents run a plastic surgery clinic and were supportive of their daughter's decision to have implants (the news reports said that she had been wanting implants since age 12). Critics worried that surgery on someone that young could cause psychological damage and be done for the wrong reasons, and even the surgeon that Franklin's parents chose refused to do the surgery until she was at least 18 years old; he was apparently concerned about both psychological issues and doing surgery on immature breasts, so Franklin was made to wait.[15] The demand for inexpensive plastic surgery has apparently stimulated the growth of underground beauty treatments performed by unlicensed practitioners who typically inject liquid silicone into lips, faces, or breasts, frequently leaving a wide range of health problems in their wake. A woman in Massachusetts died in 2006 following liposuction at an illegal clinic.[16]

The requirement in some cultural, religious, and family contexts to maintain virginity until marriage provoked the development of hymen reconstruction surgery long ago, but the issue seems to be getting more attention lately. Women in these cultures can protect their "honor" by having the surgery done. A surgeon in Toronto reports that primarily Muslim women inquire about or have the surgery. In Brooklyn, NY, plastic surgery clinics advertise "reconstrucción del hymen" for Latina women.[17]

The pressure toward perfect male and female bodies is perhaps most powerfully expressed in the treatment of infants born neither male nor female but with disorders of sexual development (DSD), more commonly called intersex. In cases where medical teams cannot tell whether the infant is a boy or a girl, which is estimated to occur in about 1 in 1,500 or 1 in 2,000 births, the child is assigned to one sex or the other based on visual appearance of the genitals.[18] Then, typically, a series of surgical and hormonal treatments is done to bring the child's body into conformity with the assigned gender. The lack of tolerance for a body that does not conform with gender appears to be profound in medical settings. There is resistance to this pressure, however, on various fronts. The Intersex Society of North America (ISNA) (www.isna.org) has been organizing and educating around this issue for years, arguing against surgical and hormonal intervention until the child is old enough to decide for her/himself. Occasionally parents have also resisted the pressure for sex reassignment, creating serious frustration for medical professionals at times.[19] And in some unusual cases, children are allowed to choose for themselves whether to change their bodies physically, although all seem to be assigned a gender at birth.[20] Some professionals in the United States and Canada are supporting the recommendations of ISNA on the heels of the outrage expressed by many intersex people whose lives have been fraught with identity confusion, shame, and lack of sexual sensation as a result of medical treatment and the lies that frequently surround these cases.[21]

The need to convert bodies might not be so intense if third-gender options existed in mainstream U.S. society. Males who live as females in many societies (called berdaches, hijiras, or xaniths, and common in many Native American tribes) have a specific role that allows for a break from what is expected.[22] Other societies have female men—women who behave as men in terms of work, marriage, parenting, and possession of the economic resources to purchase a wife.[23] Societies with these options might be better equipped to deal with intersex people because such societies already have more than two genders.

The transgender liberation movement is paving the way for more flexible treatment of intersex children as people who refuse to fit into the gender binary fight for their rights to present themselves as they feel they truly are, rather than as society would like them to be. For example, the Sylvia Rivera Law Project (SRLP) in New York City fights for the rights of people who are transgendered in the public context—in prisons and juvenile justice facilities, in shelters, and in relation to what is covered and not covered by public and private health care. And although there is conflict at times within the trans community related to how people should present themselves—Dean Spade, an attorney with the SRLP was arrested for using a men's bathroom and then criticized by people in the trans community for not looking masculine enough to pass as male—the goals of changing societal expectations and eliminating discrimination and violence are central to this movement: "SRLP works to guarantee that all people are free to self-determine gender identity and expression, regardless of income or race, and without facing harassment, discrimination or violence" (http://www.srlp.org/).[24]

Sports-oriented culture intensifies the pressure for a perfect body. Sports themselves are also a problem for many athletes because sports are highly competitive, few participants are able to make a career of sports (see Michael Messner, Part II), sports injuries occur frequently, sexism pervades sports, and sports support heterosexism and homophobia. Homophobia is ever-present; male athletes are pressured to nurture their homophobia as they express their athletic masculinity in homoerotic contexts, and female athletes are pressured to be feminine, lest they look too much like men and challenge the division of the world into male and female.[25] The intersex/DSD issue plays a role here too. Genetic testing is sometimes required of athletes to ensure that no men are competing as women or vice versa. Occasionally (perhaps as often as 1 in 500 tested athletes), someone who has lived her life, say, as a woman is informed that she has a Y chromosome and is actually, in a genetic sense, male and therefore disqualified. In one such case, a woman with a Y chromosome was disqualified from competition but later gave birth to a child.[26]

Objectification pervades our understanding of gender. People are frequently seen not for who they are but for what they represent. People may become beauty objects, sex objects, racial objects, athletic objects, unattractive objects, disabled objects, or simply objects to abuse. The media feed this process by providing distorted messages about how people should look, what makes people happy, and how people spend their time: middle-class, white housewives excited over laundry detergent or toothpaste, white men buying cars and selling life insurance, Black men with muscular bodies playing sports, and so on. Few women believe they have acceptable bodies, and the media nurture this insecurity and self-hatred, pounding away at the expectation of perfection, leading people to see themselves as imperfect objects. Even men are now seeking plastic surgery in increasing numbers to mask the effects of aging or to lengthen or enlarge their penises.[27]

Women are raised to believe that they are just not adequate in many ways. In many contexts women are mandated to wear restrictive clothing and makeup. Menstruation, perhaps the most defining aspect of womanhood (in spite of challenges to that definition by some menstrual activists), is labeled as dirty and demeaning; women often live their entire lives embarrassed to buy sanitary napkins or tampons. A small movement of young feminists, however, is confronting this issue via menstrual activism, talking out loud about menstruation, about separating "womanhood" from the ability to menstruate, and leading protests against the use of toxic menstrual products, especially tampons.[28]

Related to concerns about toxic body care products, in May 2007 the Environmental Working Group released Skin Deep 3.0, a database with updated safety ratings for nearly 25,000 personal care products (http://www.cosmeticdatabase.com/). Its Web site states: "With no federal law requiring safety testing before selling products, Skin Deep is the original and best resource for consumers who want to avoid ingredients like mercury, lead, and human placenta extract." The Campaign for Safe Cosmetics is working to eliminate carcinogens from cosmetics. The European Union banned "the use of known or suspected carcinogens, mutagens and reproductive toxins (a.k.a. CMRs) from cosmetics." As of September 2004, products such as parabens cannot be added to products manufactured or sold in Europe. Lest you think this is only about cosmetics, check out what scientists are saying about body care products and troubled sperm (lower counts, decreased mobility, deformity) at http://www.safecosmetics.org/action/features/sperm.cfm.

According to a fairly recent television documentary, of 40,000 female applicants to a modeling agency, only four were selected as acceptable.[29] Despite the impossibility of ever looking like a model for the vast majority of women, the media message is so powerful that many women wish they did. Many will have face-lifts, get breast implants, or go on extreme diets in quest of the perfect body despite the health risks involved. According to a study by sociologists Diana Dull and Candace West, plastic surgery is a heavily gendered process. The plastic surgeons they interviewed readily supported plastic surgery to enhance a woman's appearance, but they did not support it to enhance a man's appearance.[30]

A few years ago, the National Institutes of Health lowered the point at which a person is defined as overweight, effectively affixing a stigmatizing label to an additional 29 million people who were not defined as overweight before the change in definition. Many of these newly "overweight" people can expect to suffer weight discrimination, including lectures about weight from their doctors and increased difficulty getting health insurance.[31] Author and nurse Pat Lyons, director of Free at Last: The Women's Body Sovereignty Project, asks people to help diminish fat discrimination by doing such things as not commenting about weight, accepting bodies as they are, not telling "fat jokes," and supporting healthy lifestyles for people of all sizes.[32] Author Natalie Kusz, in a powerful personal narrative about what it is like to be fat, lists an array of insults that she has experienced, such as unsolicited advice about dieting, being told to walk when she is driving, and being called "fatass." She discusses the courage it takes simply to leave her home and face the public. On a positive note, Kusz changes her approach to her body. Rather than spending about 70 percent of her energy on food, she decided to give up her lifelong dieting and food obsession, eat when she wanted to, let her body become the size it needed to be, and free her energies for more productive pursuits such as parenting, writing, and caring for an ailing father.[33]

The authors in this section address various aspects of embodiment, including women's everyday grooming practices (Sheila Jeffreys), eating troubles among women of color and white women (Becky Thompson), approaches to appearance and varieties of gender expression in Native American culture (Leslie Marmon Silko), the social cost of living in a Black male body (Brent Staples), the struggle for manhood in the face of disability (Leonard Kriegel), embracing a round woman's body in a Latino context (Christy Haubegger), and dealing with the impact of genital surgery on intersexuals (Martha Coventry).

The authors in this part argue either directly or indirectly for a world in which people are seen for who they are as people, rather than as physical objects to be liked, ridiculed, abused, or ignored. I am reminded here of a stranger who walked past my office one day. I couldn't tell whether the person was male or female, noticed only that the person was medium height, white, and solidly built with relatively short brown hair. I found myself thinking, "That person is in an interesting package." I have since then pondered the package image. In most circumstances, when given a package, our impulse is to open it to find out what's inside. In the case of bodies, however, the wrapping frequently has such an impact that we have no interest in opening the package—that is, finding out more about the person within it—simply because the person's packaging does not appeal to us for whatever reason. And as a result of external responses, the people inside risk incorporating those responses into their personalities, frequently as internalized oppression. Many of the authors in this section would like to see a world in which the person inside was more important than the packaging and in which the packaging would not become a cause for hatred, physical harm, or blocked access to opportunities.

As you read these essays, you might want to reflect upon your own responses to various forms of embodiment. What kinds of grooming do you practice and how do you feel about it? Do you have choices about how you present yourself to your various communities? What helps you find out who is home inside a body that you might find off-putting in some way? How do you feel about your own body? Can you name a few things that you like about it? Or that you don't like about it? Have you known any people who were sexually or physically abused? How did that affect their sense of their bodies? If you had been born into a different kind of body package, how might your life be different? Consider ability/disability, skin color, weight, "attractiveness," hair, height, and other characteristics.

NOTES

1. On the history of fashion and clothing, see Elayne A. Saltzberg and Joan C. Chrisler, "Beauty is the Beast: Psychological Effects of the Pursuit of the Perfect Female Body" in Jo Freeman, ed., *Women: A Feminist Perspective* (Mountain View, CA: Mayfield Publishing, 1994), pp. 306–315. For a discussion of clothing and identity, see Mary Ellen Roach-Higgins, Joanne B. Eichner, and Kim K. P. Johnson, eds., *Dress and Identity* (New York: Fairchild Publishers, 1995). For a history of women in sports, see Susan K. Cahn, *Coming on Strong: Gender and Sexuality in Twentieth-Century Women's Sport* (Cambridge, MA: Harvard University Press, 1994).

2. *Frontline* (Public Broadcasting System), *"The Merchants of Cool,"* video aired January 31, 2002; Gail Dines and Jean M. Humez, eds., *Gender, Race and Class in Media: A Text-Reader,* 2nd ed. (Thousand Oaks, CA: Sage, 2002).

3. Eugenia Kaw, "Medicalization of Racial Features: Asian-American Women and Cosmetic Surgery" in Rose Weitz, ed., *The Politics of Women's Bodies: Sexuality, Appearance, and Behavior* (New York: Oxford, 1998), pp. 167–183. See also Anupreeta Das, "The Search for Beautiful," *The Boston Globe Magazine*, 21 January 2007, pp. 23ff.

4. The American Society for Aesthetic Plastic surgery, "Cosmetic Surgery National Data Bank Statistics" (2006). http://www.surgery.org/download/2006stats.pdf.

5. Ayana D. Byrd and Lori L. Tharps, *Hair Story: Untangling the Roots of Black Hair in America* (New York: St. Martin's Griffin, 2001), pp. 178–179.

6. For an interesting discussion of the use of blue contact lenses by people with brown eyes, including women of color, see Susan Bordo, "'Material Girl'—The Effacements of Postmodern Culture," in *Unbearable Weight: Feminism, Western Culture and the Body* (Berkeley: University of California Press, 1993), pp. 245–249.

7. For discussions of the impact of looks, obesity, and various kinds of disabilities on employment and other aspects of life, see Susan E. Browne, Debra Connors, and Nanci Stern, eds., *With the Power of Each Breath* (Pittsburgh: Cleis Press, 1985); Lisa Schoenfielder and Barbara Wieser, eds., *Shadow on a Tightrope* (Iowa City: Aunt Lute, 1983); Irving Kenneth Zola, *Missing Pieces: A Chronicle of Living with a Disability* (Philadelphia: Temple University Press, 1982); Gwyneth Matthews, *Voices from the Shadows: Women with Disabilities Speak Out* (Toronto: Women's Educational Press, 1983); Lucy Grealy, *Autobiography of a Face* (Boston: Houghton Mifflin, 1994); Kennie Fries, ed., *Staring Back: The Disability Experience from the Inside Out* (New York: Plume, 1997).

8. CDC data can be found at: http://www.cdc.gov/HealthyYouth/yrbs/slides/2005YRBSslides-TobaccoDrug.ppt#407,61,Percentage of High School Students Who Reported Lifetime Illegal Steroid Use,* by Sex** and Race/Ethnicity,*** 2005.

9. Kathryn Grant, Aoife Lyons, Dana Landis, Mi Hyon Cho, Maddalena Scudiero, Linda Reynolds, Julie Murphy, and Heather Bryant, "Gender, Body Image, and Depressive Symptoms among Low-Income African American Adolescents," *Journal of Social Issues* 55, no. 2 (1999): 299–316.

10. Joseph J. Sabia, 'The Effect of Body Weight on Academic Performance," *Southern Economic Journal*, 73, no. 4 (2007): 871–900.

11. Barbara Meltz, "Boys and Body Image," *The Boston Globe,* 1 June 2000, pp. F1ff; Alan M. Klein, "Life's Too Short to Die Small: Steroid Use Among Male Bodybuilders," in Donald F. Sabo and David Frederick Gordon, eds., *Men's Health and Illness: Gender, Power and the Body* (Thousand Oaks, CA: Sage, 1995), pp. 105–120.

12. Dawn Atkins, "Introduction: Looking Queer," in Dawn Atkins, ed., *Looking Queer: Body Image and Identity in Lesbian, Bisexual, Gay, and Transgender Communities* (New York: Haworth Press, 1998), pp. xxix–li.

13. For a discussion of cultural aspects of cosmetic surgery, see Kathy Davis, *Dubious Equalities and Embodied Differences: Cultural Studies on Cosmetic Surgery* (Lanham, MD: Rowman and Littlefield, 2003).

14. For data on plastic surgery, see http://www.surgery.org/download/2006stats.pdf.

15. Chris Holme, "'You've Got to Have Breasts to Be Successful. Every Other Person You See on TV Has Had Implants': Teenager Justifies Decision in Face of Outrage from Experts," *The Herald* (Glasgow), (5 January 2001), p. 3.

16. Aime Parnes, "In Florida, Risky Shots at Being Beautiful," *The Boston Globe* (May 1, 2001), p. A1 ff; Liz Kowalczk, "A death after liposuction exposes busy illegal clinic," *The Boston Globe*, 1 August 2006, p. B1.

17. Sylvana Paternostro, "Northern Ladies," in *In the Land of God and Man: A Latin Woman's Journey* (New York: Penguin Putnam, Inc., 1999), pp. 270–288; Susan Oh, "Just Like a Virgin? Surgeons Restore Hymens for Cultural Reasons and Tighten Vagina Walls for Better Sex," *Maclean's,* June 12, 2000, p. 44ff.

18. Phyllis Burke, *Gender Shock: Exploding the Myths of Male and Female* (New York: Anchor, 1966); Cheryl Chase, "Hermaphrodites with Attitude: Mapping the Emergence of Intersex Political Activism," *GLQ* 4, no. 2 (1998): 189–211; Alice Domurat Dreger, "'Ambiguous' Sex—Or Ambivalent Medicine? Ethical Issues in the Treatment of Intersexuality," *The Hastings Center Report* 28, no. 3 (May–June 1998): 24–35. The estimate of number of cases is from Dreger.

19. Katherine Rossiter and Shonna Diehl, "Gender Reassignment in Children: Ethical Conflicts in Surrogate Decision-Making," *Pediatric Nursing* 24, no. 1 (January–February 1998): 59–62.

20. Froukje M. E. Slijper, Stenvert L. S. Drop, Jan C. Molenaar, and Sabine M. P. F. de Muinck Keizer-Schrama, "Long-Term Psychological Evaluation of Intersex Children," *Archives of Sexual Behavior* 27, no. 2 (April–May 1998): 125–44, p. 6, Internet version. William George Reiner, "Case Study: Sex Reassignment in a Teenage Girl," *Journal of the American Academy of Child and Adolescent Psychiatry* 35, no. 6 (June 1996), p. 799(5). The latter article describes an intersex Hmong child who was raised as a girl and decided she wanted to be a boy at age 14. Her doctors supported her decision and provided relevant medical treatment to help her body become more male.

21. Milton Diamond and H. Keith Sigmundson, "Management of Intersexuality: Guidelines for Dealing with Persons with Ambiguous Genitals," *Archives of Pediatric and Adolescent Medicine* 151, no. 10 (October 1997): 1046–1050.

22. Gary Mihalik, "More Than Two: Anthropological Perspectives on Gender," *Journal of Lesbian and Gay Psychotherapy*, no. 1 (1989): 105–118. John C. Wood, *When Men Are Women: Manhood among Gabra Nomads of East Africa* (Madison: Wisconsin University Press, 1999).

23. Judith Lorber, *Paradoxes of Gender* (New Haven: Yale University Press, 1994), pp. 17–18. Antonia Young, *Women Who Become Men: Albanian Sworn Virgins* (Oxford, U.K.: Berg, 2000).

24. Dean Spade, "Undermining Gender Regulation," in Mattilda, a.k.a. Matt Bernstein Sycamore, ed., *Nobody Passes: Rejecting the Rules of Gender and Conformity* (Emeryville, CA: Seal Press, 2006), pp. 64–70.

25. For research and critical analysis of gender and sports, see Greta Cohen, ed., *Women in Sports: Issues and Controversies* (Newbury Park, CA: Sage, 1993);

Susan K. Cahn, *Coming on Strong* (Toronto: Free Press, 1994); Pat Griffin, *Strong Women, Deep Closets: Lesbians and Homophobia in Sport* (Champaign, IL: Human Kinetics, 1998); Michael A. Messner, *Power at Play: Sports and the Problem of Masculinity* (Boston: Beacon Press, 1992); Michael A. Messner and Donald F. Sabo, *Sex, Violence and Power in Sport: Rethinking Masculinity* (Freedom, CA: Crossing Press, 1994).

26. Phyllis Burke, *Gender Shock* (New York: Anchor/Doubleday, 1996), p. 229.

27. Dale Koppel, "About Face: The Focus on Appearance Is Becoming a Male Obsession," *Your Health, The Boston Globe,* (23 April 1995), pp. 10, 23, 26. An ad in *The Boston Globe* announced plastic surgery for "male enhancement" in May 1995.

28. Chris Bobel, "Resistance with a Wink: Young Women, Feminism and the (Radical) Menstruating Body," in Judith Lorber and Lisa Jean Moore, *Gendered Bodies: Feminist Perspectives* (Los Angeles: Roxbury, 2007), pp. 87–91.

29. *The Famine Within,* Filmmakers Library, 124 E. 40th St., New York, NY (Winter 1995).

30. Diana Dull and Candace West, "Accounting for Cosmetic Surgery: The Accomplishment of Gender," *Social Problems* 38, no. 1 (February 1991): pp. 54–70.

31. Pat Lyons, "The Great Weight Debate: Where Have All the Feminists Gone?" *The Network News* 23, no. 5 (September–October 1998): pp. 1ff. (National Women's Health Network).

32. Lyons, p. 5.

33. Natalie Kusz, "The Fat Lady Sings," in Cathi Hanauer, ed., *The Bitch in the House: 26 Women Tell the Truth about Sex, Solitude, Work, Motherhood, and Marriage* (New York: Harper, 2003), pp. 239–247.

17

MAKING UP IS HARD TO DO

SHEILA JEFFREYS

Sheila Jeffreys is Associate Professor in the Department of Political Science at the University of Melbourne where she teaches sexual politics, international feminist politics and lesbian and gay politics. She is the author of five books on the history and politics of sexuality, and has been active in feminist and lesbian feminist politics since 1973.

Everyday beauty practices, such as the use of makeup or hair removal, were central to the feminist critique of beauty launched by Andrea Dworkin (1974) and Sandra Bartky in the 1970s (1990, collection of earlier writings). In the 1990s something very odd happened. Suddenly, in the writings of popular liberal feminists and in the writings of some feminists who adopted a postmodern approach, those very same practices gained a whole new credibility. They were promoted as "empowering" to women, the proof of the new power to choose that was the legacy of feminism (Lehrman, 1997; Walter, 1999; Frost, 1999). But the practices themselves did not change. In this chapter I consider whether everyday beauty practices deserve to be the subject of this new enthusiasm, and critically examine the claim that these everyday beauty practices are good and useful aspects of women's lives.

There is little research on the reasons why women wear makeup, or engage in other forms of "grooming", the effects that these practices have on women's feelings about themselves and others, and their interactions with the public world (Dellinger and Williams, 1997). This is a puzzle since the wearing of lipstick, for example, could be seen as a very strange practice in which women smear toxic substances on their lips several times a day, particularly before they encounter the public world, and take into their bodies an estimated 3 to 4.5 kilos in a lifetime's use (Erickson, 2002; Farrow, 2002). Lipstick wearing, like the other practices we look at in this chapter, consumes women's time, money and emotional space. The absence of interest in examining it suggests that it is seen as "natural" for women and therefore unworthy of examination. More extreme forms of beauty practice which endanger women's lives such as eating disorders (Fallon *et al.*, 1994), or require serious surgery such as breast implants (Davis, 1995), have been studied, perhaps because they are seen as less "natural", and so harder to understand. But I suggest here that the everyday grooming practices that women engage in—lipstick wearing, depilation, hair dyeing and perming—do need explanation and that they can be best explained by understanding them as harmful cultural practices. They fulfil the criteria of emerging from the subordination of women and being for the benefit of men, of creating gender stereotypes; that is, making a difference. They are justified by tradition as in being seen as natural to women, and it may be that they need to be recognized as harmful to the health of women and girls. Certainly, as we shall see, the chemicals and human and animal body products involved pose risks to physical health.

When beauty practices are carried to extremes they are the subject of research, however, as a form of mental illness. Thus 30 years after the publication of Andrea Dworkin's work (Dworkin, 1974) the anxious and obsessive beauty practices that she describes so well have been identified as symptomatic of a newly discovered and labelled mental health problem called "body dysmorphic disorder" or BDD. Katharine Phillips, an expert in the field, tells us that clues to the disorder are, "frequent mirror checking, excessive grooming, face picking, and reassurance seeking" (Phillips, 1998, p. 48). When she describes the clues in more detail they turn out to resemble quite precisely the ordinary everyday practices of femininity:

> Do you often check your appearance in mirrors or other reflecting surfaces, such as windows? Or do you frequently check your appearance without using a mirror, by looking directly at the disliked body part? . . . Do you spend a lot of time grooming—for example, combing or arranging your hair, applying makeup, or shaving? Do you spend too much time getting ready in the morning, or do you groom yourself frequently during the day? Do others complain that you spend too much time in the bathroom? . . . Do you often change your clothes, trying to find an outfit that covers or improves disliked aspects of your appearance? Do you take a long time selecting your outfit for the day, trying to find one that makes you look better?
>
> (Phillips, 1998, p. 49)

Phillips provides 27 clues which denote anxiety about appearance, none of which seem exceptional in terms of women's daily lives.

In Susan Brownmiller's book *Femininity* (1984) she describes very similar practices as simply the ordinary coming of age rituals of girls:

> At what age does a girl child begin to review her assets and count her deficient parts? When does she close the bedroom door and begin to gaze privately into the mirror at contortionist angles to get a view from the rear, the left profile, the right, to check the curve of her calf muscle, the shape of her thighs, to ponder her shoulder

blades and wonder is she is going to have a waistline? And pull in her stomach . . . making a mental note of what needs to be worked on, what had better develop, stay contained, or else?

(Brownmiller, 1984, p. 9)

But, interestingly, Phillips says that the patients that are referred to her include an equal number of men and women. The men are overwhelmingly concerned with not being sufficiently masculine and worried about having small penises. It seems very odd that a concern so ordinary among women, anxiety about appearance, should, in its extreme forms, be equally manifest among men. The explanation may be that something so normal for women would mostly go unnoticed, whereas a concern with appearance that is abnormal among men would lead to them coming to the attention of a psychiatrist more easily. The only distinction between women's ordinary concern with appearance and that which leads to a diagnosis of Body Dysmorphic Disorder does seem to be the extremity of the symptoms. Applying excessive makeup, for instance, is a sign of BDD, as is buying excessive numbers of hair products. But it might be hard to work out what was normal and what was excessive in women's behaviour in a beauty culture. Phillips explains that, "Hair removal may also be done to excess. People concerned about excessive body hair may spend lots of time tweezing it, removing it from their face, their arms, or other parts of their body . . . Eyebrows may be repeatedly plucked to create the right shape" (Phillips, 1998, p. 108). But how much time is "lots"? "Other people" she says, "apply and reapply makeup", and one of her patients remarks, "I use a lot of makeup, and I take a long time to put on my eyeliner and lipstick . . . I'm in agony if I can't do this. I need my fix!" (p. 108). But what is a "lot" of makeup, or excessive time in its application? "Most people with BDD", Phillips says, "actively think about their appearance problem for at least an hour a day" (1998, p. 76). Thus those who think about the defects of their appearance for half an hour might just be the victims of the construction of ordinary everyday beauty, and not representative of the syndrome.

Whether women engage in beauty practices for 30 minutes or for 1 hour, the practices are not "natural" but culturally prescribed and it is important to understand where beauty practices come from. The history of makeup, the fact that there have been times and places in which women were not required to be obsessed with makeup, makes it clear that this practice is peculiar to a time and place and most definitely cultural rather than emanating from any natural "femininity".

The History of Makeup

The work of the historian Kathy Peiss explains when and how the practice of making up originated (Peiss, 1998). Peiss is a historian of commerce and points out that writers on beauty rarely pay much attention to the industry that creates and profits from beauty practices (Peiss, 2001). She explains that the beauty industry as we understand it today developed in the first decades of the twentieth century, particularly in the 1920s: "Between 1909 and 1929 the number of American perfume and cosmetics manufacturers nearly doubled, and the factory value of their products rose tenfold, from $14.2 million to nearly $141 million" (Peiss, 1998, p. 97). In the nineteenth century there was no mass market of beauty products. Women might make some limited range of beauty aids at home according to traditional recipes, and some could be bought. There was no expectation, however, that women would paint their faces. Makeup was called "paint" and associated with prostitution and the theatre. It was not respectable. Peiss opens her book with the story of this most important change in social attitudes, in which the practice of prostitution was transformed into an expected part of feminine grooming. She gives as an example of the change the fact that a cosmetics firm in 1938 introduced two new lipsticks named "Lady" and "Hussy". She explains:

> For nineteenth-century Americans, lady and hussy were polar opposites—the best and worst of womanhood—and the presence or absence of cosmetics marked the divide. Reddened cheeks and darkened eyelids were signs of female vice, and the "painted woman" provoked disgust and censure from the virtuous. But by the 1930s, lady and hussy had become "types" and "moods".
>
> (Peiss, 1998, p. 3)

Language changed and consumerism won out so that, "Where 'paint' implied a concealing mask, the term 'makeup,' in common usage by the 1920s, connoted a medium of self-expression in a consumer society where identity had become a purchasable style . . . apparently Hussy outsold Lady five to one!" (Peiss, 1998, p. 4).

Lipstick is a beauty practice that seems to have strong historical links with prostitution. The sexologists Harry Benjamin and R.E.L. Masters describe in the book they wrote to justify and normalize prostitution in the early stages of the "sexual revolution" (1964) what they understand to be the origins of lipstick wearing. They say that it originated from prostituted women in the ancient middle east who used it to show that they would do oral sex: "lipstick was supposed to make the mouth resemble the vulva, and it was first worn by those females who specialized in oral stimulation of the penis" (Benjamin and Masters, 1964, p. 58).

As a historian of commerce Peiss is enthusiastic about the opportunities that the newly developing beauty industry offered women. As the industry developed between the 1890s and the 1920s it was largely in the hands of women entrepreneurs, "women formulated and organized 'beauty culture' to a remarkable extent" (Peiss, 1998, p. 4). Women founded "salons, beauty schools, correspondence courses, and mail-order companies". They did not need to advertise but used the "patterns of women's social life—their old customs of visiting, conversation, and religious observance, as well as their presence in shops, clubs and theaters". Many of these women were "immigrant, working-class or black" and they "played a surprisingly central role in redefining mainstream ideals of beauty and femininity in the twentieth century . . . they made the pursuit of beauty visible and respectable" (Peiss, 1998, p. 5). The history of these women, Peiss states, "flatly contradicts the view that the beauty industry worked only *against* women's interests", because they, "created job opportunities for women, addressed the politics of appearance, and committed their profits to their community". But the fact that women were involved in the development of beauty practices does not in any way contradict the notion that such practices are harmful. As Mary Daly points out in *Gyn/Ecology* (1979), women are frequently those who are responsible for carrying out what she calls "sado-rituals" on girls and women, as in the practices of female genital mutilation and footbinding. Women carry out the dictates of male dominance even to the extent of multilating female children. Men and male dominance escape indictment or responsibility because they are nowhere to be seen. The practices appear to originate with and be done by women alone. Industries which offer employment to women are not always beneficial: the sex industry being one example (Jeffreys, 1997b). Industries that employ women can arise directly from and serve to maintain women's subordination.

Peiss explains the rise of the beauty industry as resulting from a change in the way women thought of themselves as they moved into the public world in the 1920s. In the nineteenth century public women were understood to be prostituted women and they did paint their faces. In the late nineteenth century there was an opening up of public space to respectable women. The development of the department store was one example of this, and Judith Walkowitz has written interestingly on the way in which shopping enabled respectable middle-class Victorian women in London to come out onto the street (Walkowitz, 1992). In the same period the job market opened up to middle-class women with the birth of white-collar occupations such as office work and teaching. Peiss associates the new enthusiasm for cosmetics among women with this movement of women into the public world.

She says that "beauty culture" should be "understood not only as a type of commerce but as a system of meaning that helped women navigate the changing conditions of modern social experience" (Peiss, 1998, p. 6). Women, she says, were getting jobs in offices, stores and occupations where they had to engage in face-to-face interactions. There was a more public marriage market with the development of the dance hall and a new sense of sexual freedom: "Moving into public life, they staked a claim to public attention, demanded that others look. This was not a fashion dictated by Parisian or other authorities, but a new mode of feminine self-presentation, a tiny yet resonant sign of a larger cultural contest over women's identity" (1998, p. 55). But none of this precisely explains why women had to "put their face on" to be in the public world. Why did they need to wear masks, when men did not? There is an interesting similarity here between the adoption of makeup by women entering the public world in the 1920s in the west and the adoption of the veil by women entering the public world in some Muslim cultures in the 1980s/1990s. Research on the readoption of the veil by a new generation of women in Muslim countries suggests that women feel safer and freer to engage in occupations and movement in the public world through covering up (Abu-Odeh, 1995). It could be that the wearing of makeup signifies that women have no automatic right to venture out in public in the west on equal grounds with men. Makeup, like the veil, ensures that they are masked and not having the effrontery to show themselves as the real and equal citizens that they should be in theory. Makeup and the veil might show women's lack of entitlement.

Peiss acknowledges that big business, usually run by men, took over from the small locally owned salons which were producing their own products in the 1930s. The massive cosmetics corporations of today began to build their empires. The industry could no longer be defended as one that allowed women new opportunities of entrepreneurship, but Peiss remains upbeat. She says that the power of corporations, advertising and mass media in peddling makeup to women should be criticized but that the critics may have, "overlooked the web of intimate rituals, social relationships, and female institutions that gave form to American beauty culture" (Peiss, 1998, p. 7). Women created "intimacy", she argues, by sharing beauty secrets and experienced "pleasure, and community". This is another way in which the proponents of makeup have defended it against feminist criticism. Makeup, they say, gives women a shared and pleasurable women's culture. But there are other harmful practices in which women develop rituals, share secrets and create supportive networks. Female genital mutilation and Chinese footbinding have been said to offer similar satisfactions (Ping, 2000).

When male-run big business took over, promises were made to women which were clearly exploitative and duplicitous:

> In little more than a decade, an aesthetic of women's freedom and modernity had narrowed and turned in upon itself. *Vogue* could claim without irony that bright fingernails offered "a minor adventure" and a facial "doesn't stop at giving you a new face—it gives you a whole new point of view on life".
>
> (Peiss, 1998, p. 158)

By 1920, Peiss asserts, "the beauty industry had succeeded in delivering its message to women, that the fulfillment of individuality and femininity required the purchase of cosmetics" (1998, p. 167). In the interwar period the beauty industry became oppressive rather than liberatory apparently, and took the shape that we are familiar with in the present. By 1930 beauty contests had become normalized and were even being held in high schools, "employment tests appraised bodily appearance and guidance counsellors at Smith College routinely noted graduating students' 'attractiveness' in their records" (Peiss, 1998, p. 193). Commercial colleges and YWCAs began to offer "self-development" courses with instructions on skin care, makeup, manicuring, and hair styling to young women about to enter the workforce. Makeup had become a requirement that women could not escape instead of a sign of liberation. The message of advertising, Peiss explains, "was reinforced and refined in the workplace and in school, at home and at leisure, as women experienced growing pressure to adjust their looks to new norms of feminine appearance" (1998, p. 200).

Beauty Standards Constructed from White Dominance

The "choice" to wear makeup and engage in other grooming practices is not made in a political vacuum. There are very real material forces involved in constructing this "choice" for women. Peiss writes positively about the opportunities offered to black women in the interwar period to set up beauty salons and become entrepreneurs before big business took over the industry. By the 1960s it was clear that the beauty practices that black women were taught were aimed at emulating a white ideal. African-American women have written eloquently on the racism of beauty standards in the USA that not only have white women bleaching their faces and their hair, but create impossible goals of emulating whiteness for black women. This has led to an industry of hair straighteners, and face whiteners, and other products designed to enable black women to approximate to a white ideal. Since it is unlikely that black women are somehow naturally excluded from the province of essential beauty, it is clear that what is beautiful is constructed politically and incorporates race, class and sex prejudices. When black women are chosen for their "beauty" to be models, such as Iman from Somalia, or Waris Dirie, their faces and bodies are likely to conform to white ideals and not to resemble the commonest features of African-American women's faces (Young, 1999).

In the days of the black power movement of the 1960s black women rejected the requirement that they should use white beauty practices. They rejected the hair straightening that was virtually compulsory for black women in the 1950s and early 1960s in favour of a more "natural" look. Michelle Wallace explains that "Being feminine *meant* being white to us" (Walker, 2001, p. 256, emphasis in the original), and in protest she repudiated, "makeup, high heels, stocking, garter belts", and supportive underwear in favour of "T-shirts and dungarees, or loose African print dresses" (2001, p. 263). As part of this protest the Afro was born. But it was hard for black women to remain outside the dictates of fashion, the Afro itself became commoditized (p. 263).

Makeup and Male Dominance

Though the wearing of makeup is a pervasive aspect of the construction of femininity, there is surprisingly little research that fits makeup wearing into the political context of male domination. Quite comprehensive anthologies of research on "gender" do not mention makeup (Jackson and Scott, 2002). The one area of makeup use that has been studied is the workplace. Dellinger and Williams' (1997) study demonstrates very well that women are constrained to wear makeup in the workplace where it can be, quite simply, a job's worth issue. They carried out in-depth interviews with a diverse group of 20 women who worked in a variety of settings. They sought to "examine the appearance rules that women confront at work and how those rules reproduced assumptions about sexuality and gender" (1997, p. 151). Fourteen of the women wore makeup every day to work, two wore it some of the time, and four never or almost never. The women said that their workplaces did not have a formal dress code policy and that wearing makeup was their "personal choice". However many experienced, or perceived that they would experience, "negative consequences if their makeup is not properly applied" (Dellinger and Williams, 1997, p. 156). They felt that women who did not wear makeup did not appear to be "healthy", "heterosexual" or "credible". Women who usually wore makeup to work reported that on days that they did not they received comments about how they looked tired or did not look "good" and that such comments would affect how they felt at work that day. One woman specifically said that she wore makeup to avoid negative comments such as, "God, what's the matter with her? Is she sick or something?" (1997, p. 157).

On the other hand the wearing of makeup in the workplace was reinforced through positive comments. Many women said they wore makeup to feel confident about themselves or that it made them feel powerful. But at the same time they talked about feeling self-conscious without it, with one woman saying, "I don't like to look at myself in the mirror when I don't have it on" (Dellinger and Williams, 1997, p. 158). Some women were not comfortable in public places without makeup. A Taiwanese respondent said she wore makeup to give here a "wide-eyed" American look (p. 159). Women may well say makeup empowers them but the interesting question is, what disempowers them about being without their mask? The constraints imposed by sexism and racism and the political structures of male domination are likely to be responsible for women's discomfort about moving into the public world "barefaced".

Another pressure on women to wear makeup is the requirement that they should appear to be heterosexual. As Dellinger and Williams comment "makeup . . . marks women as heterosexual" (1997, p. 159). One heterosexual respondent commented that women who did not wear makeup in her workplace are thought to be "tomboys". The assumption of heterosexuality, the authors note, is "built into professionalism" and thus, "An implicit requirement for looking appropriately feminine is that women look 'pleasing' to men" (1997, p. 160). One heterosexual woman explained that men, "tend to work easier with someone who is easy to look at", thus the requirement of servicing men's sexual fantasies is translated into workplace appearance requirements for women and lesbians just don't really fit in (Dellinger and Williams, 1997, p. 160).

One lesbian respondent who did not wear makeup at home or at work said that when she started working as a social worker she got comments such as, "You need to wear a little bit of makeup", or "You need to get a perm", or "You need to get some better clothes" (Dellinger and Williams, 1997, p. 161). This lesbian passed for straight at work. Another lesbian "actively uses makeup at work as a way to smooth workplace interactions with men" (p. 163). She says she uses makeup to "mute her 'difference'" (p. 162). She is a tall woman and wearing makeup makes her male clients both less likely to think she is a lesbian and less likely to see her as a threat because of her size. Makeup, then, makes women look unthreatening. A heterosexual African-American woman says that she used makeup to "enhance her credibility in a racist society" (p. 166). She felt the need to emphasize how professional she was to lessen the effect of racism and makeup was a way to do this. This woman said she was prepared to "let the sexism" pass in favour of diluting racism.

The authors conclude that workplace pressures do construct women's choices to wear makeup and that such choices cannot be, "understood outside the context of these institutionalized workplace appearance norms" (Dellinger and Williams, 1997, p. 168). Interestingly the authors sought to address the recent suggestions in feminist scholarship that makeup wearing might not just be enforced but about "creativity and pursuit of bodily pleasure" for women and that women might even be able to use makeup in ways that resisted appearance norms. They clearly have little sympathy with these notions and their data do not support them. They consider the idea that makeup wearing is part of a women's culture that can be enjoyed by women in the workplace. Women's commenting on each other's use or absence of beauty practices could in theory be seen as a "topic of conversation that bonds women together. Women may be able to show their affection and concern for one another through compliments and advice" (1997, p. 169). But they point out that such comments can also be divisive and can, as one respondent expresses, make her feel inadequate. It does seem to be the case that harmful cultural practices are frequently carried out by and among women when the agency of men is not apparent. Women can seek to support each other through the ordeals of performing the practices, offer each other advice and shoulders to lean on. This would be a culture formed to survive oppression, however, and not unambiguously worthy of celebration.

This research does not support the idea that women can subvert the appearance norms associated with wearing makeup. The few examples that are given of such subversion are that some women said they only applied makeup once a day, or that they did not check and reapply, or that they wore the minimum they could get away with. These don't seem very revolutionary strategies. The authors reject the notion promoted by a school of queer post-structuralist theorists such as Judith Butler, who say that women can "perform" femininity and "play" with gender (Butler, 1990). They say that "resistance through bodily practices may be easier to find in studies that do not evaluate the actual constraints imposed on women by social institutions" (Dellinger and Williams, 1997, p. 169), in other words an attention to the forms of force and control in the workplace undermine the idea that makeup can be worn "playfully".

Dellinger and Williams conclude that the women in their study are not "cultural dopes" and, "act as knowledgeable agents within institutional constraints" (1997, p. 175). Thus they may be very aware of what they are doing and why but still feel it necessary to engage in the practice even if in a minimal form. The concluding paragraph conveys a point usually overlooked in writings about the joys of makeup wearing; that is, that this practice has implications for reproducing "inequality between men and women, and also between different groups of women" (1997, p. 175). Makeup wearing helps to construct inequality as well as being a reaction to it.

Sadly the 1990s witnessed a revival of the requirement of savagely differentiated dress codes for women in the workplace. As a *Vogue* article put it in 1991: "Women at work have reclaimed their sexuality . . . Dresses are back, makeup is in" (Hochswender, 1991, p. 234). The writer argues that many women executives see this as empowering them. The readoption of femininity results, she believes, from the fact that women have gained credibility in the workplace and can now use femininity to their advantage. It could represent the complete opposite, of course—the control of career women by forcing them into a feminine and nonthreatening mould. Indeed the *Vogue* article gives some useful examples of the sanctions that are employed against women who do not follow workplace femininity dress codes. In one case the accounting firm Price-Waterhouse denied a partnership to Ann Hopkins because she needed to, among other things, "walk more femininely, talk more femininely, dress more femininely, and wear makeup" (Hochswender, 1991, p. 230). She sued and won. While the tone of the article is upbeat about the delights of dressing in a feminine fashion in the workplace there are many examples that show that this is not about choice and pleasure. "Dressing for work", it states, "is a small act of daily courage" (Hochswender, 1991, p. 232). This does not sound playful and shows how women have every day to work out how to look sufficiently feminine and sexy but not too sexy and, of course, carry out their routine of beauty practices. Meanwhile, as she points out, it is not that way for men who "seem to have it a lot easier". Men can wear a uniform suit that "disguises their sexuality rather than enhances it". In other words they do not have to think how they can best dress to draw and entrance the eyes of their female workmates and, "Even the most extravagant men, the ones who wear custom clothes, can never be accused of looking like hookers" (Hochswender, 1991, p. 230). The woman has to agonize over how to look "tough but feminine, sexy but authoritative", which is a tough call.

Women's magazines may play a role in coercing women into makeup in the workplace. The magazine *Ebony* aimed at African-American women uses a hectoring tone in one article telling working women how they should dress. The opening sentence says ominously, "Wearing the proper attire for your work place—whether it is on an assembly line, at a typist's desk, in an executive suite or in a television studio—can make the difference in success or failure" (Townsel, 1996, p. 61). The article continues in a fashion likely to frighten women into compliance:

> In light of today's diverse fashion and cosmetic markets, working women have little excuse for derailing their otherwise promising careers, by committing flagrant dressing faux pas. In fact, even workers with limited time and finances can spruce up their professional image by paying close attention to their hair, nails and cosmetics, and by choosing sophisticated, business-appropriate attire for work.
>
> (Townsel, 1996, p. 61)

The *Ebony* article uses as an authority a woman who is a spokesperson for a cosmetics company. She says, not surprisingly, such things as, "Makeup is very important because your face is the first thing people see when you're in the workplace", and makeup provides the necessary, "clean, finished look" (1996, p. 62). As an example of how important appearance is in the workplace, the article features Teresa Fleming who works as a seat belt installer at a car assembly plant and, "makes deliberate efforts every day to maintain a feminine, clean-cut image in her workplace, which is typically hot and gritty" (Townsel, 1996, p. 64). She gets her hair cut and curled twice a week, applies eyeliner and lipstick daily and goes through extreme measures to maintain her long, manicured fingernails such as, "I've cut out room for two fingers in my work gloves, and I wrap my nails in tape before my shift . . . I haven't lost a nail in the last two years" (p. 64). Thus this woman is handicapped at work and has to engage in time-consuming and expensive practices. Compared with men this does seem an unfair disadvantage. The makeup company spokeswoman, probably employed in this article because her company is an important advertiser with the magazine, says that a woman's beauty regime should only take 7 minutes each morning. But the practices she recommends sound rather too complicated to be performed in such a short time. She does not allow for the thinking time involved when women adapt their makeup, as she says they should, to their day—for example, if they have any important meetings. She says women should use a toner to close pores and give a youthful appearance, a moisturizer and then, "your foundation, blush, mascara and a light lipstick—and you're out the door" (Townsel, 1996, p. 62). But, she says, nails must be clean and polished and they are not included in the 7 minutes and she does not even mention hair and clothing. All in all the beauty regimen is likely to take a long time out of the day.

There is very little research on the time that women sacrifice in beauty practices. A survey of 2,000 women by Marks and Spencer in the UK has found that the average woman takes the equivalent of 10 working days a year getting ready for work at 27 minutes per day, and 10 per cent take more than an hour per day. The majority of women spend 21 minutes getting ready for a shopping trip, 54 minutes for a night out with the girls and 59 minutes for "a romantic evening" (Hill, 2002). These are considerable amounts of time that men and the women who eschew such routines can spend on other activities.

It should be clear from these examples that makeup is not simply a matter of "choice" in the workplace but the result of a system of power relations that can require women to engage in this cultural practice. The idea that makeup is a "choice" is undermined by an examination of the tactics that cosmetics corporations employ to get children using makeup and wedded to their brands. Makeup manufacturers are targeting girls as young as 8. A market research study found that one-fourth of girls under 13 had experimented with makeup and the advertisers are keen to reach them (Cardona, 2000). Proctor and Gamble are seeking to market their Cover Girl cosmetics range to 8–10-year-old girls by making the use of makeup resemble play. Thus they have: "Peelers Polish 'peelable' nails, enamels and Pure magic Body Art, a package of body paint and stencils that comes in designs such as Halloween shapes" (Cardona, 2000, p. 15). They have kiosks in shopping malls to entice girl children in to surf their website, and display glitter and lip gloss in them rather than the more adult products in their range so that parents will not be alienated. A company called Kiss Products has licensed animated characters from Walt Disney Co. to promote their lip gloss and nail polish kits at Disney stores. The Cosrich Group has licensed Barbie to promote lip glosses and body glitter: "Disney's products for girls are packaged in boxes with pictures of Tinkerbell, Winnie-the-Pooh and other Disney characters, while Barbie makeup comes packaged with plastic charms and bracelets" (Cardona, 2000, p. 15). In the USA cosmetics industry estimates put sales to children at US$1 billion annually. One range of personal-care products is now targeting children as young as 6. The promotion of cosmetics as forms of play to children will create the "choices" of adult women. They will have been trained to understand makeup as a form of personal fulfilment and play at an age before they have had the opportunity to recognize any alternative.

Women cannot be said to make free "choices" to engage in beauty practices in a culture in which men have the power to enforce their requirements. A good example of the force of men's opinion in the creation of beauty practices lies in the way shaving is discussed on the The Carnal Knowledge Network website. The website, which is clearly run by and represents the views of men, asks the question, "Does it really matter if I'm too lazy to shave my legs?" The answer is, "The accepted norm in society today dictates that a woman shave her legs . . . Other women who do not experience these [medical] conditions SHOULD remove the hair from their legs. The facts are that the VAST majority of men prefer smooth shaven legs" (Carnal Knowledge Network, 2002). In response to the question, "Does this mean that women have to shave their legs just because most men seem to prefer this?", the response is:

> Obviously the answer is no, if you want to take the "high and mighty" attitude of it's my body and I'll do what I want to. You can grow shoulder length hair on your legs but YOU WILL be greatly limiting your chances of finding and keeping a mate by alienating yourself from the accepted norm. If you don't shave your legs and keep them clean and appealing, many guys will simply lose interest in you romantically (sorry, facts of life).
>
> (Carnal Knowledge Network, 2002)

The website's advice continues its haranguing tone. To women who might have the habit of not shaving their legs in winter when they are not wearing shorts the response is that such women will be labelled "that girl who doesn't shave her legs", and, "THIS IS WHAT WE TALK ABOUT WHEN YOU'RE NOT AROUND!!" It goes on: "most of us like a woman who takes the time to keep herself up; we're obsessed with it" (Carnal Knowledge Network, 2002).

The suggestion that women will not acquire male partners without shaving resembles the reasons given for the carrying out of harmful beauty practices in other cultures, such as female genital mutilation and the reconstructing of hymens; that is, girls have no chance of marrying without them. Though it might be expected that the pressures on young women to have male partners might be less in western cultures where they have more chance of a career that is not that of wife, they are still extreme. Feminine respectability in western culture requires attachment to a male partner.

The idea that women "choose" to engage in these practices is also undermined by an examination of just how painful and fraught they can be for the victims. The "Girl Talk" online discussion forum addresses shaving as well as other harmful beauty practices, and reveals a tortured and painful process in which young women seek to accommodate the pain and discomfort inherent in such practices. They communicate with each other in heartfelt messages about how to avoid the pain and deal with the problems that result. One problem that women who remove body hair encounter is ingrown hairs. One woman in the discussion forum describes the problem thus:

> I had a bikini wax a couple of months ago and ever since I have had horrible problems with in grown [sic] hairs. I have tried the lotions (tend skin etc.) and hot baths. I've even tried to get at them with tweezers, but that is just making the situation worse. Please let me know what else I can do!
>
> (Girl Talk, toria5, 9 July 2002)

Women respond to her with the names of other products she can use to help with the problem. Clearly cosmetics manufacturers make profits from selling both the cause of the problem and solutions for it, which is a nice little earner. Another problem that Masaki asks about is "red bumps on my legs from shaving" which prevent her from wearing shorts or skirts. She describes the problem as "terrible" (Girl Talk, masaki, 30 June 2002). Another woman writes of the problems she got from bleaching the hair on her arms. The bleaching led to "really gross, noticable roots [sic], even though I only did it a week ago", and she is considering waxing though she cannot afford it (Girl Talk, Victoria, 21 June 2002). Her questions are:

1. Does it look weird for your arms to be completely hairless?
2. In general, how fast does it grow back?
3. How can you conceal it while you're waiting for it to be long enough to wax?
4. In general, how long will it be from the time it starts to grow back until you can wax it again?
5. Approximately, how much does it cost? (Whole arm, not just forearm.)
6. Does the regrowth look or feel like stubble?

(Girl Talk, Victoria, 21 June 2002)

Another woman, Serenause, writes in about the problem of "underarm irritation" from shaving (Girl Talk, Serenause, 28 June 2002):

> I absolutely cannot shave my underarms without irritation—no matter what I do! I try to be really light and not press too hard with the razor, and I've tried to do it quickly and slowly. But I can never get a close shave, and furthermore, ALWAYS leaves red bumps . . . I've tried to put lotion there, including the . . . lotion that comes in the waxing kit for after hair removal. NOTHING works. The hair is to [sic] coarse to wax (and it's too painful!)—The result is unsightly for tanks/sleeveless shirts—what can I do? please help!

The young women engaging in these agonized exchanges could be said to be creating a women's culture around beauty practices, but it is a culture of survival designed to enable them to negotiate harmful cultural practices with slightly less pain. The exchanges suggest just how much of young women's attention, time, money and emotional energy are taken up with the practices that demonstrate their difference and enable them to play their part in the sexual corvée.

The exchanges resemble those carried out about much more damaging practices of self-mutilation on websites such as BME, Body Modification Ezine. On the BME website young women describe practices of cutting and burning their arms, breasts and other parts of their bodies (Jeffreys, 2000). They also write as if they feel compelled, but the practices are way beyond those that would be considered the ordinary requirements of beauty. On the BME site beauty practices have gone off the rails of social acceptability, but in their very obvious destruction of skin and flesh they may help us to understand the harm involved in such apparently respectable everyday practices as whole body depilation. An understanding of why young women continue with these practices requires an awareness of the very considerable force that has been required to create this result. Cynthia Enloe, in her work on international politics, *Bananas, Beaches and Bases* (1989), asks us to reflect on what forces have created situations that appear to those brought up in western culture as just facts of nature, such as treeless landscapes or all-women typing pools. These are not "natural" facts but the result of social and economic forces that favour a short-sighted destruction of natural resources or the containment and exploitation of women in cheap labour. Similarly when depilation is identified as a culturally constructed practice, rather than a fact of nature, it is possible to seek out the forces which create it.

Makeup and Mental Health

One of these forces is psychiatry. A useful example of the way in which male dominance enforces makeup use by women is the treatment of women in mental hospitals. Some hospital psychologists understand the maintenance of feminine beauty practices to signify "mental health" and enforce makeovers for women they consider recalcitrant. Resistance by women to these practices is seen as a symptom of ill health. Thus Michael Pertschuk says that the first thing medical students are taught is to observe the patient: "How is he dressed? Hair neat? Hands clean? If the patient is a woman, is she wearing makeup? How well is it applied? Has she attended to her hair and nails?" (Pertschuk, 1985, p. 217). The men are not required to wear makeup to show their mental health, but women are. "Attention to personal grooming", he says is, "a diagnostic tool" (1985, p. 218). Apparently depressives, "may not bother at all with cosmetics as the routine tasks of life become overwhelming" (p. 219). Pertschuk says that the most important thing for these depressed women to do is to accept their "female identity". Signs that they feel, "incapable of filling any aspect of this identity as they conceive it", are: "elimination of a figure through excess weight loss or gain, avoidance of cosmetics altogether and androgynous clothes selection" (1985, p. 219).

Pertschuk's big worry is that, "The woman who feels unable to meet the demands of a female identity and who grooms and dresses accordingly is indeed likely to be viewed as asexual by those around her" (1985, p. 221). The woman may desire precisely such freedom from men's gaze but Pertschuk will not allow it. He sees the solution for such women who refuse to service male sexuality as "appearance training". He explains how this cruel procedure was carried out on a 29-year-old woman with anorexia who, "In appearance . . . looked rather like a thin, frightened nine-year-old boy. She wore no makeup. Her hair was worn very short. She was dressed in nondescript slacks and a top.

She was extremely diffident in her manner" (1985, p. 222). He used what he calls a "flooding procedure" on her:

> We coaxed her into the situation she feared i.e. using cosmetics, and helped her work through her anxieties. Her initial response to the occupational therapist's extremely modest application of mascara, lipstick, and powder was to say that she now looked like a prostitute. However, after repeated application of cosmetics for a week, she became somewhat more accepting. The occupational therapist worked with Alice to teach her to apply makeup herself. The entire staff conscientiously attempted to reinforce her with compliments about her appearance. The next phase of training involved selection of clothes . . . The goal was for her to select a few items of more becoming apparel, specifically a dress. The patient had not worn a dress in nine years. Again with much coaxing, Alice was able to do this and was lavishly reinforced for her efforts.
>
> (Pertschuk, 1985, p. 222)

This attempt at something like dog obedience training did not, as Pertschuk says, "cure Alice", but he thinks it "did help" (1985, p. 223). She now wore dresses for appointments and was letting her hair grow so he was probably able to look on her with more satisfaction. She had a "sexual identity" for him.

In the same edited collection on the psychology of "cosmetic treatments" there are comments that reveal a remarkable prejudice against women who resist beauty practices. Douglas Johnson, writing on "Appearance and the Elderly" remarks that women, "at about age 50 . . . steadily decline into sexual oblivion" (Johnson, 1985, p. 153). Gerald Adams remarks that a study he conducted found, "that unattractive women are more likely to use an undesirable influence-style that includes demanding, interrupting, opinionated, submissive, and antagonistic behavior" (Adams, 1985, p. 139). It is alarming to think that some hospitalized women's mental health is in the hands of men whose attitudes would be likely to damage the self-esteem of even the most robust of women. The relationship between makeup and depression may be rather different from that espoused by the psychologists who do makeovers on hospitalized women. Researchers have found that, "Middle-aged females who get depressed tend to subscribe to a more traditional feminine role, and the degree of their depression is significantly related to their degree of acceptance of the feminine role" (Tinsley et al., 1984, p. 30). Emily Tinsley et al. say that their work supports the conclusion that, "women who adopt more androgynous and masculine sex roles tend to be more mentally healthy" (1984, p. 26). This completely contradicts the ideas of the makeover brigade.

Makeup Harmful to the Health of Women and Girls

Harmful cultural/traditional practices are identified in UN understandings, before all else, as those that are harmful to the health of women and girls. Makeup practices fit this criterion well because the substances that women apply to their hair, face and body in pursuit of beauty are directly dangerous to health. Hair dye, for instance, has been linked with bladder cancer. An American study of 3,000 women, half of whom had developed bladder cancer, found that, "Even after adjusting for cigarette smoking . . . women who use permanent hair dyes at least once a month for one year or longer have twice the risk of bladder cancer as non-users" (Robotham, 2001). Hairdressers exposed to dyes in the workplace are also at increased risk. The anti-bacterial agent triclosan which is used in cosmetics as well as tooth-pastes and other household products is under consideration for banning in Australia because a Swedish study has shown that the chemical accumulates in mothers' breast milk as well as in fish. It is likely that the chemical helps germs develop resistance to prescribed antibiotics (Strong, 2001). New prod-ucts that are increasingly being developed by the bio-tech industry are being marketed as beauty aids. These products, named "cosmeceuticals", might more properly be regulated as drugs because of the active effects they are supposed to have on the body. One, for instance, which contains antioxi-dants, will penetrate the skin and is supposed to scavenge for free radicals. Another is supposed to banish grey hair at the roots. But these products are not being regulated with the care usually applied to drugs (King, 2001).

In *Drop-Dead Gorgeous* (2002) Kim Erickson describes what is known about the toxic effects of the chemicals in conventional cosmetics from scientific re-search. She points out that women doing the daily beauty ritual expose them-selves to more than 200 synthetic chemicals before they have morning coffee. Many of them have been identified as toxic by the US Environmental Protection Agency. The US National Institute of Occupational Safety and Health has reported that 900 of the chemicals in cosmetics are toxic. One study, for instance, found that there were such high levels of lead in Grecian Formula and Lady Grecian Formula that researchers were unable to wash it off their hands after using the product. Another found that women who dyed their hair suffered greater chromosomal damage than women who did not use hair dyes. Allergic reactions to nail polish, which contains the most toxic array of chemi-cals, included lesions on the face, neck and hands of experimental subjects who were sensitive to toluene and formaldehyde (Erickson, 2002, p. 4).

Coal tar, Erickson explains, is a particularly dangerous ingredient. Coal tar colours can contain benzene, xylene, naphthalene, phenol and creosol and almost all such colours have been shown to cause cancer. This is impor-tant considering that two out of five women in the USA dye their hair. Another ingredient, formaldehyde, is found in nail polish, nail hardeners, soap, shampoos, and hair growth preparations. It is outlawed in Sweden and

Japan and the EEC allows its use only in low quantities. The lead in hair dyes is a known carcinogen and hormone disrupter. Propylene glycol is the most widely used delivery vehicle and solvent used in cosmetics in the place of glycerin. Its most well known use is in antifreeze and brake fluid. It is an acknowledged neurotoxin, has been linked to contact dermatitis, kidney damage, and liver abnormalities, and the inhibition of skin cell growth, but it is used in baby lotions and mascara. Erickson points out that talc, which is commonly used not just directly but in blushers, powders and eye colours, is chemically similar to asbestos and carcinogenic in animals. Women who regularly use talcum powder in the genital area increase their risk of ovarian cancer threefold. Toluene, found in nail polish, is subject to a warning from the Environmental Protection Agency because breathing in large amounts of the chemical can cause damage to the kidneys, the liver and the heart. There are estimated to be more than 200,000 visits yearly to the emergency room in the USA related to allergic reactions to cosmetics use.

There is no requirement for testing cosmetic products in the way that food or medicines are tested in the USA. The skin, however, is a highly-effective way of transmitting chemicals into the body, as in the use of skin patches for hormone replacement therapy. Thus the unregulated chemicals are absorbed into the bodies of the women who use conventional cosmetics products daily. The lack of regulation is maintained by the political influence of the immensely profitable cosmetics industry whose sales grew from $7 billion in 1970 to $28 billion in 1994 in the USA.

Apart from the damage to women's bodies directly, the chemicals used in cosmetics damage the environment in other ways. As Erickson puts it, "millions of gallons of synthetic chemicals are washed down the drain and into sewer systems every day" (2002, p. 9). The petrochemicals used in makeup pollute waterways and destroy marine life. The by-products of the chemicals as they degrade interfere with the functioning of hormones and thus sexual development. These hormone disrupters devastate wildlife. The cosmetics industry generates huge amounts of waste from product packaging, from which toxins can leach into soil and groundwater. As a form of collateral damage 10–15 million animals are tortured and killed every year in US laboratories that test the safety of cosmetic and household products.

Erickson does not, however, argue that makeup is unnecessary. Indeed she comments, apparently seriously, that "Lipstick is the finishing touch that makes your face come alive", unless the toxins kill you, of course (2002, p. 225). She accepts the inevitability of makeup use and recommends products made with natural ingredients or that women should, supposing they have a spare moment, make their own. Assuming that makeup could, as she suggests, be made from less physically harmful ingredients, this may help to alleviate one aspect of this harmful practice but would not affect others. Psychological harms may still be suffered in, for example, the everyday variety of body dysmorphic disorder, the sense of inadequacy, created by the makeup industry. Nor would it lessen the role of makeup in creating sexual difference.

A new product on the market called "Perfect Pout" in honour of its supposed effect, consists precisely of a toxic substance that causes skin irritation. It promises women luscious lips without collagen, "It gives you fuller looking lips in just 60 seconds" (Skin Doctors, 2002, p. 7). The product appears to be an irritant that causes the lips to swell. The text explains, "There isn't a man alive who doesn't get turned on by luscious, plump lips. They'll watch them moving as you speak. As you eat". The toxic substance lasts up to 5 hours but can be reapplied five times daily. In the advertisement Suzi of Newcastle is quoted as saying, "I feel so much sexier now I have a seductive pout—I see guys looking at my mouth and I know exactly what's going on in their heads."

Another health concern is the use of animal products in cosmetic production that could transmit Bovine Spongiform Encephalopathy (BSE) to humans. The British government's BSE Inquiry considered this problem and because little was known about how animal products were used an audit was conducted. There are four pages detailing the derivatives of the animal slaughter industry and the products they are used in. Cosmetics manufacture uses: brain, fat, placenta, spleen, thymus, bones in the form of tallow and gelatine, and skin/hide in the form of gelatine and collagen used in implants. As a result of concern about transmission the "Cosmetics Directive" of the European Union, which covered the materials that could be used in cosmetics manufacture, outlawed the use of certain animal derivatives such as tissues from, "the encephalon, the spinal cord and the eyes" and material from the skull, tonsils and spleens of "ovine and caprine" animals (i.e. sheep and goats) in amendments in 1997 and 1998 (Home Office, 2000). Tallow is still used despite the EU ban on other derivatives because there is, apparently, no suitable alternative. Since BSE is not confined to the EU, and the transmission is so inadequately understood, it is probably sensible for women in all countries to avoid cosmetics made with any animal parts. The use that the inquiry was particularly worried about was in anti-ageing creams where a break in the skin could facilitate transmission.

Everyday beauty practices take up women's time, energy, money and emotional space. The chemicals employed are a threat to women's health. Women can seek each other's support in the performance of these practices, particularly in finding out how to dull the pain and discomfort, but this does not form the basis of positive bonding networks between women so much as support networks of the oppressed. Though the supporters of makeup argue that it offers a realm for the exercise of women's creativity, this is rather limited. Women are not in a position to paint sunsets on their foreheads but are required to conform to strict rules in order to function in workplaces and escape criticism and discrimination. Men, and women who eschew makeup, clearly find other things to do with their time, money, creativity and emotional energies. Makeup steals years from women's lives and from the exercise of their talents in order to fulfil the requirements of the sexual corvée.

REFERENCES

Abu-Odeh, Lama (1995). Post-Colonial Feminism and the Veil: Considering the Differences. In Olsen, Frances E. (ed.) *Feminist Legal Theory.* Volume I. Aldershot: Dartmouth, pp. 523–534.

Adams, Gerald (1985). Attractiveness through the Ages: Implications of Facial Attractiveness Over the Life Cycle. In Graham, Jean Ann and Kligman, Albert M. (eds) *The Psychology of Cosmetic Treatments.* New York: Praeger, pp. 133–151.

Bartky, Sandra Lee (1990). *Femininity and Domination. Studies in the Phenomenology of Oppression.* New York: Routledge.

Benjamin, Harry and Masters, R.E.L. (1964). *Prostitution and Morality.* London: Souvenir Press.

Brownmiller, Susan (1984). *Femininity.* London: Paladin.

Butler, Judith (1990). *Gender Trouble: Feminism and the Subversion of Identity.* New York & London: Routledge.

Cardona, Mercedes M. (2000, 27 November). Young Girls Targeted by Makeup Companies; Marketers Must Walk Fine Line Not To Upset Parents. *Advertising Age,* 71: 15.

The Carnal Knowledge Network (n.d.). Personal Grooming. Removing Unpleasant Or Unsightly Hair! Retrieved 4 December 2002 from www.carnal.net/public/module/html

Daly, Mary (1979). *Gyn/Ecology: The Metaethics of Radical Feminism.* London: The Women's Press.

Davis, Kathy (1995). *Reshaping the Female Body: The Dilemma of Cosmetic Surgery.* New York: Routledge.

Dellinger, Kirsten and Williams, Christine L. (1997). Makeup at Work: Negotiating Appearance Rules in the Workforce. *Gender and Society,* April–May, 11, 2: 151–178.

Dworkin, Andrea (1974). *Woman Hating.* New York: E.P. Dutton.

Enloe, Cynthia (1989). *Bananas, Beaches and Bases: Making Feminist Sense of International Politics.* London: Pandora.

Erickson, Kim (2002). *Drop-Dead Gorgeous. Protecting Yourself from the Hidden Dangers of Cosmetics.* Chicago, IL: Contemporary Books.

Fallon, Patricia, Katzman, Melanie A. and Wooley, Susan C. (eds) (1994). *Feminist Perspectives on Eating Disorders.* New York: Guilford Press.

Farrow, Kevin (2002). *Skin Deep. A Guide to Safe, Chemical-Free Skincare and Cleaning Products.* Melbourne, Australia: Lothian Books.

Frost, Liz (1999). "Doing Looks": Women, Appearance and Mental Health. In Arthurs, Jane and Grimshaw, Jean (eds) *Women's Bodies: Discipline and Transgression.* London and New York: Cassell, pp. 117–136.

Girl Talk (2002). Online Discussion Board. Retrieved 10 July 2002 from http://boards.substance.com/messages/get/sbcell17/57.html

Hill, Amelia (2002, 21 April). I'll Be Ready in 21 Minutes, Dear. *The Observer.*

Hochswender, Woody (1991, October). Appearance at Work. Is a Fashionable Image Empowering—or Does It Undermine Authority? *Vogue,* pp. 230–238.

Home Office (2000). *The BSE Inquiry: The Report.* London: Home Office. Online at http://www.bseinquiry.gov.uk/index.htm

Jackson, Stevi and Scott, Sue (2002). *Gender. A Sociological Reader.* London: Routledge.

Jeffreys, Sheila (1997b). *The Idea of Prostitution.* Melbourne: Spinifex Press.

Jeffreys, Sheila (2000). Body Art and Social Status: Piercing, Cutting and Tattooing from a Feminist Perspective. *Feminism and Psychology,* November: 409–430.

Johnson, Douglas F. (1985). Appearance and the Elderly. In Graham, Jean Ann and Kligman, Albert M. (eds) *The Psychology of Cosmetic Treatments.* New York: Praeger, pp. 152–160.

King, Elizabeth (2001, 28 November). The New Frontier. *The Age*. Melbourne, Australia: John Fairfax Publications.

Lehrman, Karen (1997). *The Lipstick Proviso*. New York: Anchor Books.

Peiss, Kathy (1998). *Hope in a Jar. The Making of America's Beauty Culture*. New York: Metropolitan Books, Henry Holt and Company.

Peiss, Kathy (2001). On Beauty . . . and the History of Business. In Philip Scranton (ed.) *Beauty and Business. Commerce, Gender, and Culture in Modern America*. New York: Routledge, pp. 7–23.

Pertschuk, Michael J. (1985). Appearance in Psychiatric Disorder. In Graham, Jean Ann and Kligman, Albert M. (eds) *The Psychology of Cosmetic Treatments*. New York: Praeger, pp. 217–226.

Phillips, Katharine A. (1998). *The Broken Mirror. Understanding and Treating Body Dysmorphic Disorder*. Oxford: Oxford University Press.

Ping, Wang (2000). *Aching for Beauty. Footbinding in China*. Minneapolis: University of Minnesota Press.

Robotham, Julie (2001, 27 June). Hair Dye Linked to Cancer. *The Age*. Melbourne, Australia: John Fairfax Publications.

Skin Doctors Dermaceuticals (2002, 13 October). Kiss Your Thin Lips Goodbye Today! Advertisement. *The Sunday Age. Television Magazine*. Melbourne, Australia: John Fairfax Publications, p. 7.

Strong, Geoff (2001, 26 December). Ban on Cosmetic Chemical Mooted. *The Age*. Melbourne, Australia: John Fairfax Publications.

Tinsley, Emily G., Sullivan-Guest, S. and McGuire, John (1984). Feminine Sex Role and Depression in Middle-Aged Women. *Sex Roles*, 11, 1/2: 25–32.

Townsel, Lisa Jones (1996, September). Working Women: Dressing for Success. *Ebony*, pp. 60–65.

Walker, Susannah (2001). Black is Profitable. The Commodification of the Afro, 1960–1975. In Philip Scranton (ed.) *Beauty and Business. Commerce, Gender, and Culture in Modern America*. New York: Routledge, pp. 254–277.

Walkowitz, Judith (1992). *City of Dreadful Night: Narratives of Sexual Danger in Late-Victorian London*. London: Virago.

Walter, Natasha (1999). *The New Feminism*. London: Virago.

Young, Lola (1999). Racializing Femininity. In Arthurs, Jane and Grimshaw, Jean *Women's Bodies: Discipline and Transgression*. London and New York: Cassell, pp. 67–89.

18

"A WAY OUTA NO WAY"
Eating Problems among African-American, Latina, and White Women

BECKY W. THOMPSON

Becky W. Thompson is the author, with Randall Horton and M. L. Hunter, of *Fingernails across the Chalkboard: Poetry and Prose on HIV/AIDS* (2007). Thompson is also the author of *A Hunger So Wide and So Deep: A Multiracial View of Women's Eating Problems* (1994); *A Promise and a Way of Life: White Anti-Racist Activism* (2001); and *Mothering Without a Compass: White Mother's Love, Black Son's Courage* (2000). She coedited, with Sangeeta Tyagi, *Names We Call Home: Autobiography on Racial Identity* (1996) and *Beyond a Dream Deferred: Multicultural Education and the Politics of Excellence* (1993). She is an associate professor of sociology at Simmons College where she teaches courses in African American studies, women's studies, and sociology.

Bulimia, anorexia, binging, and extensive dieting are among the many health issues women have been confronting in the last 20 years. Until recently, however, there has been almost no research about eating problems among African-American, Latina, Asian-American, or Native American women; working-class women; or lesbians.[1] In fact, according to the normative epidemiological portrait, eating problems are largely a white, middle- and upper-class heterosexual phenomenon. Further, while feminist research has documented how eating problems are fueled by sexism, there has been almost no attention to how other systems of oppression may also be implicated in the development of eating problems.

In this article, I reevaluate the portrayal of eating problems as issues of appearance based in the "culture of thinness." I propose that eating problems begin as ways women cope with various traumas including sexual abuse, racism, classism, sexism, heterosexism, and poverty. Showing the interface between these traumas and the onset of eating problems explains why women may use eating to numb pain and cope with violations to their bodies.

This theoretical shift also permits an understanding of the economic, political, social, educational, and cultural resources that women need to change their relationship to food and their bodies.

Existing Research on Eating Problems

There are three theoretical models used to explain the epidemiology, etiology, and treatment of eating problems. The biomedical model offers important scientific research about possible physiological causes of eating problems and the physiological dangers of purging and starvation (Copeland 1985; Spack 1985). However, this model adopts medical treatment strategies that may disempower and traumatize women (Garner 1985; Orbach 1985). In addition, this model ignores many social, historical, and cultural factors that influence women's eating patterns. The psychological model identifies eating problems as "multidimensional disorders" that are influenced by biological, psychological, and cultural factors (Garfinkel and Garner 1982). While useful in its exploration of effective therapeutic treatments, this model, like the biomedical one, tends to neglect women of color, lesbians, and working-class women.

The third model, offered by feminists, asserts that eating problems are gendered. This model explains why the vast majority of people with eating problems are women, how gender socialization and sexism may relate to eating problems, and how masculine models of psychological development have shaped theoretical interpretations. Feminists offer the culture of thinness model as a key reason why eating problems predominate among women. According to this model, thinness is a culturally, socially, and economically enforced requirement for female beauty. This imperative makes women vulnerable to cycles of dieting, weight loss, and subsequent weight gain, which may lead to anorexia and bulimia (Chernin 1981; Orbach 1978, 1985; Smead 1984).

Feminists have rescued eating problems from the realm of individual psychopathology by showing how the difficulties are rooted in systematic and pervasive attempts to control women's body sizes and appetites. However, researchers have yet to give significant attention to how race, class, and sexuality influence women's understanding of their bodies and appetites. The handful of epidemiological studies that include African-American women and Latinas casts doubt on the accuracy of the normative epidemiological portrait. The studies suggest that this portrait reflects which particular populations of women have been studied rather than actual prevalence (Andersen and Hay 1985; Gray, Ford, and Kelly 1987; Hsu 1987; Nevo 1985; Silber 1986).

More important, this research shows that bias in research has consequences for women of color. Tomas Silber (1986) asserts that many well-trained professionals have either misdiagnosed or delayed their diagnoses of eating problems among African-American and Latina women due to stereotypical thinking that these problems are restricted to white women. As a consequence, when African-American women or Latinas are diagnosed, their eating problems tend to be more severe due to extended processes of starvation prior to intervention. In her autobiographical account of her eating problems, Retha Powers (1989), an African-American woman, describes being told not to worry about her eating problems since "fat is more acceptable in the Black community" (p. 78). Stereotypical perceptions held by her peers and teachers of the "maternal Black woman" and the "persistent mammy-brickhouse Black woman image" (p. 134) made it difficult for Powers to find people who took her problems with food seriously.

Recent work by African-American women reveals that eating problems often relate to women's struggles against a "simultaneity of oppression" (Clarke 1982; Naylor 1985; White 1991). Byllye Avery (1990), the founder of the National Black Women's Health Project, links the origins of eating problems among African-American women to the daily stress of being undervalued and overburdened at home and at work. In Evelyn C. White's (1990) anthology, *The Black Woman's Health Book: Speaking for Ourselves*, Georgiana Arnold (1990) links her eating problems partly to racism and racial isolation during childhood.

Recent feminist research also identifies factors that are related to eating problems among lesbians (Brown 1987; Dworkin 1989; Iazzetto 1989; Schoenfielder and Wieser 1983). In her clinical work, Brown (1987) found that lesbians who have internalized a high degree of homophobia are more likely to accept negative attitudes about fat than are lesbians who have examined their internalized homophobia. Autobiographical accounts by lesbians have also indicated that secrecy about eating problems among lesbians partly reflects their fear of being associated with a stigmatized illness ("What's Important" 1988).

Attention to African-American women, Latinas, and lesbians paves the way for further research that explores the possible interface between facing multiple oppressions and the development of eating problems. In this way, this study is part of a larger feminist and sociological research agenda that seeks to understand how race, class, gender, nationality, and sexuality inform women's experiences and influence theory production.

Methodology

I conducted 18 life history interviews and administered lengthy questionnaires to explore eating problems among African-American, Latina, and white women. I employed a snowball sample, a method in which potential respondents often first learn about the study from people who have already participated. This method was well suited for the study since it enabled women to get information about me and the interview process from people they already knew. Typically, I had much contact with the respondents prior to the interview. This was particularly important given the secrecy associated with this topic (Russell 1986; Silberstein, Striegel-Moore, and Rodin 1987), the necessity of women of color and lesbians to be discriminating about how their lives are studied, and the fact that I was conducting across-race research.

To create analytical notes and conceptual categories from the data, I adopted Glaser and Strauss's (1967) technique of theoretical sampling, which directs the researcher to collect, analyze, and test hypotheses during the sampling process (rather than imposing theoretical categories onto the data). After completing each interview transcription, I gave a copy to each woman who wanted one. After reading their interviews, some of the women clarified or made additions to the interview text.

Demographics of the Women in the Study

The 18 women I interviewed included 5 African-American women, 5 Latinas, and 8 white women. Of these women, 12 are lesbian and 6 are heterosexual. Five women are Jewish, 8 are Catholic, and 5 are Protestant. Three women grew up outside of the United States. The women represented a range of class backgrounds (both in terms of origin and current class status) and ranged in age from 19 to 46 years old (with a median age of 33.5 years).

The majority of the women reported having had a combination of eating problems (at least two of the following: bulimia, compulsive eating, anorexia, and/or extensive dieting). In addition, the particular types of eating problems often changed during a woman's life span. (For example, a woman might have been bulimic during adolescence and anorexic as an adult.) Among the women, 28 percent had been bulimic, 17 percent had been bulimic and anorexic, and 5 percent had been anorexic. All of the women who had been anorexic or bulimic also had a history of compulsive eating and extensive dieting. Of the women, 50 percent were compulsive eaters and dieters (39 percent) or compulsive eaters (11 percent) but had not been bulimic or anorexic.

Two-thirds of the women have had eating problems for more than half of their lives, a finding that contradicts the stereotype of eating problems as transitory. The weight fluctuation among the women varied from 16 to 160 pounds, with an average fluctuation of 74 pounds. This drastic weight change illustrates the degree to which the women adjusted to major changes in body size at least once during their lives as they lost, gained, and lost weight again. The average age of onset was 11 years old, meaning that most of the women developed eating problems prior to puberty. Almost all of the women (88 percent) consider themselves as still having a problem with eating, although the majority believe they are well on the way to recovery.

The Interface of Trauma and Eating Problems

One of the most striking findings in this study was the range of traumas the women associated with the origins of their eating problems, including racism, sexual abuse, poverty, sexism, emotional or physical abuse, heterosexism, class injuries, and acculturation.[2] The particular constellation of eating problems among the women did not vary with race, class, sexuality, or nationality. Women from various race and class backgrounds attributed the origins of their eating problems to sexual abuse, sexism, and emotional and/or physical abuse. Among some of the African-American and Latina women, eating problems were also associated with poverty, racism, and class injuries. Heterosexism was a key factor in the onset of bulimia, compulsive eating, and extensive dieting among some of the lesbians. These oppressions are not the same nor are the injuries caused by them. And certainly, there are a variety of potentially harmful ways that women respond to oppression (such as using drugs, becoming a workaholic, or committing suicide). However, for all these women, eating was a way of coping with trauma.

Sexual Abuse

Sexual abuse was the most common trauma that the women related to the origins of their eating problems. Until recently, there has been virtually no research exploring the possible relationship between these two phenomena. Since the mid-1980s, however, researchers have begun identifying connections between the two, a task that is part of a larger feminist critique of traditional psychoanalytic symptomatology (DeSalvo 1989; Herman 1981; Masson 1984). Results of a number of incidence studies indicate that between one-third and two-thirds of women who have eating problems have been abused (Oppenheimer et al. 1985; Root and Fallon 1988). In addition, a growing number of therapists and researchers have offered interpretations of the meaning and impact of eating problems for survivors of sexual abuse (Bass and Davis 1988; Goldfarb 1987; Iazzetto 1989; Swink and Leveille 1986). Kearney-Cooke (1988) identifies dieting and binging as common ways in which women cope with frequent psychological consequences of sexual abuse (such as body image disturbances, distrust of people and one's own experiences, and confusion about one's feelings). Root and Fallon (1989) specify ways that victimized women cope with assaults by binging and purging: bulimia serves many functions, including anesthetizing the negative feelings associated with victimization. Iazzetto's innovative study (1989), based on in-depth interviews and art therapy sessions, examines how a woman's relationship to her body changes as a consequence of sexual abuse. Iazzetto discovered that the process of leaving the body (through progressive phases of numbing, dissociating, and denying) that often occurs during sexual abuse parallels the process of leaving the body made possible through binging.

Among the women I interviewed, 61 percent were survivors of sexual abuse (11 of the 18 women), most of whom made connections between sexual abuse and the beginning of their eating problems. Binging was the most common method of coping identified by the survivors. Binging helped women "numb out" or anesthetize their feelings. Eating sedated, alleviated anxiety, and combated loneliness. Food was something that they could trust and was accessible whenever they needed it. Antonia (a pseudonym) is an Italian-American woman who was first sexually abused by a male relative when she was four years old. Retrospectively, she knows that binging was a way she coped with the abuse. When the abuse began, and for many years subsequently, Antonia often woke up during the middle of the night with anxiety attacks or nightmares and would go straight to the kitchen cupboards to get food. Binging helped her block painful feelings because it put her back to sleep.

Like other women in the study who began binging when they were very young, Antonia was not always fully conscious as she binged. She described eating during the night as "sleep walking. It was mostly desperate—like I had to have it." Describing why she ate after waking up with nightmares, Antonia said, "What else do you do? If you don't have any coping mechanisms, you eat." She said that binging made her "disappear," which made her feel protected. Like Antonia, most of the women were sexually abused before puberty, four of them before they were five years old. Given their youth, food was the most accessible and socially acceptable drug available to them. Because all of the women endured the psychological consequences alone, it is logical that they coped with tactics they could do alone as well.

One reason Antonia binged (rather than dieted) to cope with sexual abuse is that she saw little reason to try to be the small size girls were supposed to be. Growing up as one of the only Italian Americans in what she described as a "very WASP town," Antonia felt that everything from her weight and size to having dark hair on her upper lip were physical characteristics she was supposed to hide. From a young age she knew she "never embodied the essence of the good girl. I don't like her. I have never acted like her. I can't be her. I sort of gave up." For Antonia, her body was the physical entity that signified her outsider status. When the sexual abuse occurred, Antonia felt she had lost her body. In her mind, the body she lived in after the abuse was not really hers. By the time Antonia was 11, her mother put her on diet pills. Antonia began to eat behind closed doors as she continued to cope with the psychological consequences of sexual abuse and feeling like a cultural outsider.

Extensive dieting and bulimia were also ways in which women responded to sexual abuse. Some women thought that the men had abused them because of their weight. They believed that if they were smaller, they might not have been abused. For example when Elsa, an Argentine woman, was sexually abused at the age of 11, she thought her chubby size was the reason the man was abusing her. Elsa said, "I had this notion that these old perverts liked these plump girls. You heard adults say this too. Sex and flesh being associated." Looking back on her childhood, Elsa believes she made fat the enemy partly due to the shame and guilt she felt about the incest. Her belief that fat was the source of her problems was also supported by her socialization. Raised by strict German governesses in an upper-class family, Elsa was taught that a woman's weight was a primary criterion for judging her worth. Her mother "was socially conscious of walking into places with a fat daughter and maybe people staring at her." Her father often referred to Elsa's body as "shot to hell." When asked to describe how she felt about her body when growing up, Elsa described being completely alienated from her body. She explained,

> Remember in school when they talk about the difference between body and soul? I always felt like my soul was skinny. My soul was free. My soul sort of flew. I was tied down by this big bag of rocks that was my body. I had to drag it around. It did pretty much what it wanted and I had a lot of trouble controlling it. It kept me from doing all the things that I dreamed of.

As is true for many women who have been abused, the split that Elsa described between her body and soul was an attempt to protect herself from the pain she believed her body caused her. In her mind, her fat body was what had "bashed in her dreams." Dieting became her solution, but, as is true for many women in the study, this strategy soon led to cycles of binging and weight fluctuation.

Ruthie, a Puerto Rican woman who was sexually abused from 12 until 16 years of age, described bulimia as a way she responded to sexual abuse. As a child, Ruthie liked her body. Like many Puerto Rican women of her generation, Ruthie's mother did not want skinny children, interpreting that as a sign that they were sick or being fed improperly. Despite her mother's attempts to make her gain weight, Ruthie remained thin through puberty. When a male relative began sexually abusing her, Ruthie's sense of her body changed dramatically. Although she weighed only 100 pounds, she began to feel fat and thought her size was causing the abuse. She had seen a movie on television about Romans who made themselves throw up and so she began doing it, in hopes that she could look like the "little kid" she was before the abuse began. Her symbolic attempt to protect herself by purging stands in stark contrast to the psychoanalytic explanation of eating problems as an "abnormal" repudiation of sexuality. In fact, her actions and those of many other survivors indicate a girl's logical attempt to protect herself (including her sexuality) by being a size and shape that does not seem as vulnerable to sexual assault.

These women's experiences suggest many reasons why women develop eating problems as a consequence of sexual abuse. Most of the survivors "forgot" the sexual abuse after its onset and were unable to retrieve the abuse memories until many years later. With these gaps in memory, frequently they did not know why they felt ashamed, fearful, or depressed. When sexual abuse memories resurfaced in dreams, they often woke feeling upset but could not remember what they had dreamed. These free-floating, unexplained feelings left the women feeling out of control and confused. Binging or focusing on maintaining a new diet were ways women distracted or appeased themselves, in turn, helping them regain a sense of control. As they grew older, they became more conscious of the consequences of these actions. Becoming angry at themselves for binging or promising themselves they would not purge again was a way to direct feelings of shame and self-hate that often accompanied the trauma.

Integral to this occurrence was a transference process in which the women displaced onto their bodies painful feelings and memories that actually derived from or were directed toward the persons who caused the abuse. Dieting became a method of trying to change the parts of their bodies they hated, a strategy that at least initially brought success as they lost weight. Purging was a way women tried to reject the body size they thought was responsible for the abuse. Throwing up in order to lose the weight they thought was making them vulnerable to the abuse was a way to try to find the body they had lost when the abuse began.

Poverty

Like sexual abuse, poverty is another injury that may make women vulnerable to eating problems. One woman I interviewed attributed her eating problems directly to the stress caused by poverty. Yolanda is a Black Cape Verdean mother who began eating compulsively when she was 27 years old. After leaving an abusive husband in her early 20s, Yolanda was forced to go on welfare. As a single mother with small children and few financial resources, she tried to support herself and her children on $539 a month. Yolanda began binging in the evenings after putting her children to bed. Eating was something she could do alone. It would calm her, help her deal with loneliness, and make her feel safe. Food was an accessible commodity that was cheap. She ate three boxes of macaroni and cheese when nothing else was available. As a single mother with little money, Yolanda felt as if her body was the only thing she had left. As she described it,

> I am here, [in my body] 'cause there is no where else for me to go,
> Where am I going to go? This is all I got . . . that probably
> contributes to putting on so much weight cause staying in your
> body, in your home, in yourself, you don't go out. You aren't
> around other people . . . . You hide and as long as you hide you
> don't have to face . . . nobody can see you eat. You are safe.

When she was eating, Yolanda felt a momentary reprieve from her worries. Binging not only became a logical solution because it was cheap and easy but also because she had grown up amid positive messages about eating. In her family, eating was a celebrated and joyful act. However, in adulthood, eating became a double-edged sword. While comforting her, binging also led to weight gain. During the three years Yolanda was on welfare, she gained seventy pounds.

Yolanda's story captures how poverty can be a precipitating factor in eating problems and highlights the value of understanding how class inequalities may shape women's eating problems. As a single mother, her financial constraints mirrored those of most female heads of households. The dual hazards of a race- and sex-stratified labor market further limited her options (Higginbotham 1986). In an article about Black women's health, Byllye Avery (1990) quotes a Black woman's explanation about why she eats compulsively. The woman told Avery,

> I work for General Electric making batteries, and, I know it's killing me. My old man is an alcoholic. My kid's got babies. Things are not well with me. And one thing I know I can do when I come home is cook me a pot of food and sit down in front of the TV and eat it. And you can't take that away from me until you're ready to give me something in its place. (p. 7)

Like Yolanda, this woman identifies eating compulsively as a quick, accessible, and immediately satisfying way of coping with the daily stress caused by conditions she could not control. Connections between poverty and eating problems also show the limits of portraying eating problems as maladies of upper-class adolescent women.

The fact that many women use food to anesthetize themselves, rather than other drugs (even when they gained access to alcohol, marijuana, and other illegal drugs), is partly a function of gender socialization and the competing demands that women face. One of the physiological consequences of binge eating is a numbed state similar to that experienced by drinking. Troubles and tensions are covered over as a consequence of the body's defensive response to massive food intake. When food is eaten in that way, it effectively works like a drug with immediate and predictable effects. Yolanda said she binged late at night rather than getting drunk because she could still get up in the morning, get her children ready for school, and be clearheaded for the college classes she attended. By binging, she avoided the hangover or sickness that results from alcohol or illegal drugs. In this way, food was her drug of choice since it was possible for her to eat while she continued to care for her children, drive, cook, and study. Binging is also less expensive than drinking, a factor that is especially significant for poor women. Another woman I interviewed said that when her compulsive eating was at its height, she ate breakfast after rising in the morning, stopped for a snack on her way to work, ate lunch at three different cafeterias, and snacked at her desk throughout the afternoon. Yet even when her eating had become constant, she was still able to remain employed. While her patterns of eating no doubt slowed her productivity, being drunk may have slowed her to a dead stop.

Heterosexism

The life history interviews also uncovered new connections between hetero
sexism and eating problems. One of the most important recent feminist contributions has been identifying compulsory heterosexuality as an institution
which truncates opportunities for heterosexual and lesbian women (Rich
1986). All of the women interviewed for this study, both lesbian and heterosexual, were taught that heterosexuality was compulsory, although the
versions of this enforcement were shaped by race and class. Expectations
about heterosexuality were partly taught through messages that girls
learned about eating and their bodies. In some homes, boys were given more
food than girls, especially as teenagers, based on the rationale that girls need
to be thin to attract boys. As the girls approached puberty, many were told to
stop being athletic, begin wearing dresses, and watch their weight. For the
women who weighed more than was considered acceptable, threats about
their need to diet were laced with admonitions that being fat would ensure
becoming an "old maid."

While compulsory heterosexuality influenced all of the women's emerging sense of their bodies and eating patterns, the women who linked heterosexism directly to the beginning of their eating problems were those who
knew they were lesbians when very young and actively resisted heterosexual
norms. One working-class Jewish woman, Martha, began compulsively eating when she was 11 years old, the same year she started getting clues of her
lesbian identity. In junior high school, as many of her female peers began dating boys, Martha began fantasizing about girls, which made her feel utterly
alone. Confused and ashamed about her fantasies, Martha came home every
day from school and binged. Binging was a way she drugged herself so that
being alone was tolerable. Describing binging, she said, "It was the only
thing I knew. I was looking for a comfort." Like many women, Martha
binged because it softened painful feelings. Binging sedated her, lessened her
anxiety, and induced sleep.

Martha's story also reveals ways that trauma can influence women's
experience of their bodies. Like many other women, Martha had no sense of
herself as connected to her body. When I asked Martha whether she saw herself as fat when she was growing up she said, "I didn't see myself as fat.
I didn't see myself. I wasn't there. I get so sad about that because I missed so
much." In the literature on eating problems, *body image* is the term that is typically used to describe a woman's experience of her body. This term connotes
the act of imagining one's physical appearance. Typically, women with eating problems are assumed to have difficulties with their body image.
However, the term *body image* does not adequately capture the complexity
and range of bodily responses to trauma experienced by the women.
Exposure to trauma did much more than distort the women's visual image of
themselves. These traumas often jeopardized their capacity to consider
themselves as having bodies at all.

Given the limited connotations of the term *body image,* I use the term *body consciousness* as a more useful way to understand the range of bodily responses to trauma.[3] By body consciousness I mean the ability to reside comfortably in one's body (to see oneself as embodied) and to consider one's body as connected to oneself. The disruptions to their body consciousness that the women described included leaving their bodies, making a split between their body and mind, experiencing being "in" their bodies as painful, feeling unable to control what went in and out of their bodies, hiding in one part of their bodies, or simply not seeing themselves as having bodies. Binging, dieting, or purging were common ways women responded to disruptions to their body consciousness.

Racism and Class Injuries

For some of the Latinas and African-American women, racism coupled with the stress resulting from class mobility related to the onset of their eating problems. Joselyn, an African-American woman, remembered her white grandmother telling her she would never be as pretty as her cousins because they were lighter skinned. Her grandmother often humiliated Joselyn in front of others, as she made fun of Joselyn's body while she was naked and told her she was fat. As a young child, Joselyn began to think that although she could not change her skin color, she could at least try to be thin. When Joselyn was young, her grandmother was the only family member who objected to Joselyn's weight. However, her father also began encouraging his wife and daughter to be thin as the family's class standing began to change. When the family was working class, serving big meals, having chubby children, and keeping plenty of food in the house was a sign the family was doing well. But, as the family became mobile, Joselyn's father began insisting that Joselyn be thin. She remembered, "When my father's business began to bloom and my father was interacting more with white businessmen and seeing how they did business, suddenly thin became important. If you were a truly well-to-do family, then your family was slim and elegant."

As Joselyn's grandmother used Joselyn's body as territory for enforcing her own racism and prejudice about size, Joselyn's father used her body as the territory through which he channeled the demands he faced in the white-dominated business world. However, as Joselyn was pressured to diet, her father still served her large portions and bought treats for her and the neighborhood children. These contradictory messages made her feel confused about her body. As was true for many women in this study, Joselyn was told she was fat beginning when she was very young even though she was not overweight. And, like most of the women, Joselyn was put on diet pills and diets before even reaching puberty, beginning the cycles of dieting, compulsive eating, and bulimia.

The confusion about body size expectations that Joselyn associated with changes in class paralleled one Puerto Rican woman's association between her eating problems and the stress of assimilation as her family's class standing moved from poverty to working class. When Vera was very young, she was so thin that her mother took her to a doctor, who prescribed appetite stimulants. However, by the time Vera was eight years old, her mother began trying to shame Vera into dieting. Looking back on it, Vera attributed her mother's change of heart to competition among extended family members that centered on "being white, being successful, being middle class, . . . and it was always, 'Ay Bendito. She is so fat. What happened?'"

The fact that some of the African-American and Latina women associated the ambivalent messages about food and eating to their family's class mobility and/or the demands of assimilation while none of the eight white women expressed this (including those whose class was stable and changing) suggests that the added dimension of racism was connected to the imperative to be thin. In fact, the class expectations that their parents experienced exacerbated standards about weight that they inflicted on their daughters.

Eating Problems as Survival Strategies

Feminist Theoretical Shifts

My research permits a reevaluation of many assumptions about eating problems. First, this work challenges the theoretical reliance on the culture-of-thinness model. Although all of the women I interviewed were manipulated and hurt by this imperative at some point in their lives, it is not the primary source of their problems. Even in the instances in which a culture of thinness was a precipitating factor in anorexia, bulimia, or binging, this influence occurred in concert with other oppressions.

Attributing the etiology of eating problems primarily to a woman's striving to attain a certain beauty ideal is also problematic because it labels a common way that women cope with pain as essentially appearance-based disorders. One blatant example of sexism is the notion that women's foremost worry is about their appearance. By focusing on the emphasis on slenderness, the eating problems literature falls into the same trap of assuming that the problems reflect women's "obsession" with appearance. Some women were raised in families and communities in which thinness was not considered a criterion for beauty. Yet, they still developed eating problems. Other women were taught that women should be thin, but their eating problems were not primarily in reaction to this imperative. Their eating strategies began as logical solutions to problems rather than problems themselves as they tried to cope with a variety of traumas.

Establishing links between eating problems and a range of oppressions invites a rethinking of both the groups of women who have been excluded from research and those whose lives have been the basis of theory formation. The construction of bulimia and anorexia as appearance-based disorders is rooted in a notion of femininity in which white middle- and upper-class women are portrayed as frivolous, obsessed with their bodies, and overly accepting of narrow gender roles. This portrayal fuels women's tremendous shame and guilt about eating problems—as signs of self-centered vanity. This construction of white middle- and upper-class women is intimately linked to the portrayal of working-class white women and women of color as their opposite: as somehow exempt from accepting the dominant standards of beauty or as one step away from being hungry and therefore not suscepti- ble to eating problems. Identifying that women may binge to cope with poverty contrasts with the notion that eating problems are class bound. Attending to the intricacies of race, class, sexuality, and gender pushes us to rethink the demeaning construction of middle-class femininity and estab- lishes bulimia and anorexia as serious responses to injustices.

Understanding the link between eating problems and trauma also suggests much about treatment and prevention. Ultimately, their prevention depends not simply on individual healing but also on changing the social conditions that underlie their etiology. As Bernice Johnson Reagon sings in Sweet Honey in the Rock's song "Oughta Be a Woman," "A way outa no way is too much to ask/too much of a task for any one woman" (Reagon 1980).[4] Making it possible for women to have healthy relationships with their bod- ies and eating is a comprehensive task. Beginning steps in this direction include ensuring that (1) girls can grow up without being sexually abused, (2) parents have adequate resources to raise their children, (3) children of color grow up free of racism, and (4) young lesbians have the chance to see their reflection in their teachers and community leaders. Ultimately, the prevention of eating problems depends on women's access to economic, cultural, racial, political, social, and sexual justice.

NOTES

Author's Note: The research for this study was partially supported by an American Association of University Women Fellowship in Women's Studies. An earlier version of this article was presented at the New England Women's Studies Association Meeting in 1990 in Kingston, Rhode Island. I am grateful to Margaret Andersen, Liz Bennett, Lynn Davidman, Mary Gilfus, Evelynn Hammonds, and two anonymous re- viewers for their comprehensive and perceptive comments on earlier versions of this article. Reprint requests: Becky Wangsgaard Thompson, Dept. of Sociology, Simmons College, 300 The Fenway, Boston, MA 02115.

1. I use the term *eating problems* as an umbrella term for one or more of the follow- ing: anorexia, bulimia, extensive dieting, or binging. I avoid using the term *eating disorder* because it categorizes the problems as individual pathologies, which de- flects attention away from the social inequalities underlying them (Brown 1985). However, by using the term *problem* I do not wish to imply blame. In fact, throughout, I argue that the eating strategies that women develop begin as logical solutions to problems, not problems themselves.

2. By trauma I mean a violating experience that has long-term emotional, physical, and/or spiritual consequences that may have immediate or delayed effects. One reason the term *trauma* is useful conceptually is its association with the diagnostic label Post Traumatic Stress Disorder (PTSD) (American Psychological Association 1987). PTSD is one of the few clinical diagnostic categories that recognizes social problems (such as war or the Holocaust) as responsible for the symptoms identified (Trimble 1985). This concept adapts well to the feminist assertion that a woman's symptoms cannot be understood as solely individual, considered outside of her social context, or prevented without significant changes in social conditions.

3. One reason the term *consciousness* is applicable is its intellectual history as an entity that is shaped by social context and social structures (Delphy 1984; Marx 1964). This link aptly applies to how the women described their bodies because their perceptions of themselves as embodied (or not embodied) directly relate to their material conditions (living situations, financial resources, and access to social and political power).

4. Copyright © 1980. Used by permission of Songtalk Publishing.

REFERENCES

American Psychological Association. 1987. *Diagnostic and statistical manual of mental disorders.* 3rd ed. rev. Washington, DC: American Psychological Association.

Andersen, Arnold, and Andy Hay. 1985. Racial and socioeconomic influences in anorexia nervosa and bulimia. *International Journal of Eating Disorders* 4:479–87.

Arnold, Georgiana. 1990. Coming home: One Black woman's journey to health and fitness. In *The Black women's health book: Speaking for ourselves,* edited by Evelyn C. White. Seattle, WA: Seal Press.

Avery, Byllye Y. 1990. Breathing life into ourselves: The evolution of the National Black Women's Health Project. In *The Black women's health book: Speaking for ourselves,* edited by Evelyn C. White. Seattle, WA: Seal Press.

Bass, Ellen, and Laura Davis. 1988. *The courage to heal: A guide for women survivors of child sexual abuse.* New York: Harper & Row.

Brown, Laura S. 1985. Women, weight and power: Feminist theoretical and therapeutic issues. *Women and Therapy* 4:61–71.

———. 1987. Lesbians, weight and eating: New analyses and perspectives. In *Lesbian psychologies,* edited by the Boston Lesbian Psychologies Collective. Champaign: University of Illinois Press.

Chernin, Kim. 1981. *The obsession: Reflections on the tyranny of slenderness.* New York: Harper & Row.

Clarke, Cheryl. 1982. *Narratives.* New Brunswick, NJ: Sister Books.

Copeland, Paul M. 1985. Neuroendocrine aspects of eating disorders. In *Theory and treatment of anorexia nervosa and bulimia: Biomedical, sociocultural and psychological perspectives,* edited by Steven Wiley Emmett. New York: Brunner/Mazel.

Delphy, Christine. 1984. *Close to home: A materialist analysis of women's oppression.* Amherst: University of Massachusetts Press.

DeSalvo, Louise. 1989. *Virginia Woolf: The impact of childhood sexual abuse on her life and work.* Boston, MA: Beacon.

Dworkin, Sari H. 1989. Not in man's image: Lesbians and the cultural oppression of body image. In *Loving boldly: Issues facing lesbians,* edited by Ester D. Rothblum and Ellen Cole. New York: Harrington Park Press.

Garfinkel, Paul E., and David M. Garner. 1982. *Anorexia nervosa: A multidimensional perspective.* New York: Brunner/Mazel.

Garner, David. 1985. Iatrogenesis in anorexia nervosa and bulimia nervosa. *International Journal of Eating Disorders* 4:701–26.

Glaser, Barney G., and Anselm L. Strauss. 1967. *The discovery of grounded theory: Strategies for qualitative research.* New York: Aldine DeGruyter.

Goldfarb, Lori. 1987. Sexual abuse antecedent to anorexia nervosa, bulimia and compulsive overeating: Three case reports. *International Journal of Eating Disorders* 6:675–80.

Gray, James, Kathryn Ford, and Lily M. Kelly. 1987. The prevalence of bulimia in a Black college population. *International Journal of Eating Disorders* 6:733–40.

Herman, Judith. 1981. *Father-daughter incest.* Cambridge, MA: Harvard University Press.

Higginbotham, Elizabeth. 1986. We were never on a pedestal: Women of color continue to struggle with poverty, racism and sexism. In *For crying out loud,* edited by Rochelle Lefkowitz and Ann Withorn. Boston, MA: Pilgrim Press.

Hsu, George. 1987. Are eating disorders becoming more common in Blacks? *International Journal of Eating Disorders* 6:113–24.

Iazzetto, Demetria. 1989. When the body is not an easy place to be: Women's sexual abuse and eating problems. Ph.D. diss., Union for Experimenting Colleges and Universities, Cincinnati, Ohio.

Kearney-Cooke, Ann. 1988. Group treatment of sexual abuse among women with eating disorders. *Women and Therapy* 7:5–21.

Marx, Karl. 1964. *The economic and philosophic manuscripts of 1844.* New York: International.

Masson, Jeffrey. 1984. *The assault on the truth: Freud's suppression of the seduction theory.* New York: Farrar, Strauss & Giroux.

Naylor, Gloria. 1985. *Linden Hills.* New York: Ticknor & Fields.

Nevo, Shoshana. 1985. Bulimic symptoms: Prevalence and ethnic differences among college women. *International Journal of Eating Disorders* 4:151–68.

Oppenheimer, R., K. Howells, R. L. Palmer, and D. A. Chaloner. 1985. Adverse sexual experience in childhood and clinical eating disorders: A preliminary description. *Journal of Psychiatric Research* 19:357–61.

Orbach, Susie. 1978. *Fat is a feminist issue.* New York: Paddington.

———. 1985. Accepting the symptom: A feminist psychoanalytic treatment of anorexia nervosa. In *Handbook of psychotherapy for anorexia nervosa and bulimia,* edited by David M. Garner and Paul E. Garfinkel. New York: Guilford.

Powers, Retha. 1989. Fat is a Black women's issue. *Essence,* Oct., 75, 78, 134, 136.

Reagon, Bernice Johnson. 1980. Oughta be a woman. On Sweet Honey in the Rock's album, *Good News.* Music by Bernice Johnson Reagon; lyrics by June Jordan. Washington, DC: Songtalk.

Rich, Adrienne. 1986. Compulsory heterosexuality and lesbian existence. In *Blood, bread and poetry.* New York: Norton.

Root, Maria P. P., and Patricia Fallon. 1988. The incidence of victimization experiences in a bulimic sample. *Journal of Interpersonal Violence* 3:161–73.

———. 1989. Treating the victimized bulimic: The functions of binge-purge behavior. *Journal of Interpersonal Violence* 4:90–100.

Russell, Diana E. 1986. *The secret trauma: Incest in the lives of girls and women.* New York: Basic Books.

Schoenfielder, Lisa, and Barbara Wieser, eds. 1983. *Shadow on a tightrope: Writings by women about fat liberation.* Iowa City, IA: Aunt Lute Book Co.

Silber, Tomas. 1986. Anorexia nervosa in Blacks and Hispanics. *International Journal of Eating Disorders* 5:121–28.

Silberstein, Lisa, Ruth Striegel-Moore, and Judith Rodin. 1987. Feeling fat: A woman's shame. In *The role of shame in symptom formation,* edited by Helen Block Lewis. Hillsdale, NJ: Lawrence Erlbaum.

Smead, Valerie. 1984. Eating behaviors which may lead to and perpetuate anorexia nervosa, bulimarexia, and bulimia. *Women and Therapy* 3:37–49.

Spack, Norman. 1985. Medical complications of anorexia nervosa and bulimia. In *Theory and treatment of anorexia nervosa and bulimia: Biomedical, sociocultural and psychological perspectives,* edited by Steven Wiley Emmett. New York: Brunner/Mazel.

Swink, Kathy, and Antoinette E. Leveille. 1986. From victim to survivor: A new look at the issues and recovery process for adult incest survivors. *Women and Therapy* 5:119–43.

Trimble, Michael. 1985. Post-traumatic stress disorder: History of a concept. In *Trauma and its wake: The study and treatment of post-traumatic stress disorder,* edited by C. R. Figley. New York: Brunner/Mazel.

What's important is what you look like. 1988. *Gay Community News,* July, 24–30.

White, Evelyn C., ed. 1990. *The Black women's health book: Speaking for ourselves.* Seattle, WA: Seal Press.

———. 1991. Unhealthy appetites. *Essence,* Sept., 28, 30.

19

YELLOW WOMAN AND A BEAUTY OF THE SPIRIT

LESLIE MARMON SILKO

Leslie Marmon Silko, a former professor of English and fiction writing, is the author of novels, short stories, essays, poetry, articles, and filmscripts. She has won prizes, fellowships, and grants from such sources as the National Endowment for the Arts and *The Boston Globe.* She was the youngest writer to be included in *The Norton Anthology of Women's Literature,* for her short story "Lullaby." Ms. Silko lives in Tucson, Arizona.

My great-grandmother was dark and handsome. Her expression in photographs is one of confidence and strength. I do not know if white people then or now would consider her beautiful. I do not know if the old-time Laguna Pueblo people considered her beautiful or if the old-time people even thought in those terms. To the Pueblo way of thinking, the act of comparing one living being with another was silly, because each being or thing is unique and therefore incomparably valuable because it is the only one of its kind. The old-time people thought it was crazy to attach such importance to a person's appearance. I understood very early that there were two distinct ways of interpreting the world. There was the white people's way and there was the Laguna way. In the Laguna way, it was bad manners to make comparisons that might hurt another person's feelings.

In everyday Pueblo life, not much attention was paid to one's physical appearance or clothing. Ceremonial clothing was quite elaborate but was used only for the sacred dances. The traditional Pueblo societies were communal and strictly egalitarian, which means that no matter how well or how poorly one might have dressed, there was no social ladder to fall from. All food and other resources were strictly shared so that no one person or group had more than another. I mention social status because it seems to me that most of the definitions of beauty in contemporary Western culture are really codes for determining social status. People no longer hide their face-lifts and they discuss their liposuctions because the point of the procedures isn't just cosmetic, it is social. It says to the world, "I have enough spare cash that I can afford surgery for cosmetic purposes."

In the old-time Pueblo world, beauty was manifested in behavior and in one's relationships with other living beings. Beauty was as much a feeling of harmony as it was a visual, aural, or sensual effect. The whole person had to be beautiful, not just the face or the body; faces and bodies could not be separated from hearts and souls. Health was foremost in achieving this sense of well-being and harmony; in the old-time Pueblo world, a person who did not look healthy inspired feelings of worry and anxiety, not feelings of well-being. A healthy person, of course, is in harmony with the world around her; she is at peace with herself too. Thus an unhappy person or spiteful person would not be considered beautiful.

In the old days, strong, sturdy women were most admired. One of my most vivid preschool memories is of the crew of Laguna women, in their forties and fifties, who came to cover our house with adobe plaster. They handled the ladders with great ease, and while two women ground the adobe mud on stones and added straw, another woman loaded the hod with mud and passed it up to the two women on ladders, who were smoothing the plaster on the wall with their hands. Since women owned the houses, they did the plastering. At Laguna, men did the basket making and the weaving of fine textiles; men helped a great deal with the child care too. Because the Creator is female, there is no stigma on being female; gender is not used to control behavior. No job was a man's job or a woman's job; the most able person did the work.

My Grandma Lily had been a Ford Model A mechanic when she was a teenager. I remember when I was young, she was always fixing broken lamps and appliances. She was small and wiry, but she could lift her weight in rolled roofing or boxes of nails. When she was seventy-five, she was still repairing washing machines in my uncle's coin-operated laundry.

The old-time people paid no attention to birthdays. When a person was ready to do something, she did it. When she no longer was able, she stopped.

Thus the traditional Pueblo people did not worry about aging or about looking old because there were no social boundaries drawn by the passage of years. It was not remarkable for young men to marry women as old as their mothers. I never heard anyone talk about "women's work" until after I left Laguna for college. Work was there to be done by any able-bodied person who wanted to do it. At the same time, in the old-time Pueblo world, identity was acknowledged to be always in a flux; in the old stories, one minute Spider Woman is a little spider under a yucca plant, and the next instant she is a sprightly grandmother walking down the road.

When I was growing up, there was a young man from a nearby village who wore nail polish and women's blouses and permed his hair. People paid little attention to his appearance; he was always part of a group of other young men from his village. No one ever made fun of him. Pueblo communities were and still are very interdependent, but they also have to be tolerant of individual eccentricities because survival of the group means every one has to cooperate.

In the old Pueblo world, differences were celebrated as signs of the Mother Creator's grace. Persons born with exceptional physical or sexual differences were highly respected and honored because their physical differences gave them special positions as mediators between this world and the spirit world. The great Navajo medicine man of the 1920s, the Crawler, had a hunchback and could not walk upright, but he was able to heal even the most difficult cases.

Before the arrival of Christian missionaries, a man could dress as a woman and work with the women and even marry a man without any fanfare. Likewise, a woman was free to dress like a man, to hunt and go to war with the men, and to marry a woman. In the old Pueblo worldview, we are all a mixture of male and female, and this sexual identity is changing constantly. Sexual inhibition did not begin until the Christian missionaries arrived. For the old-time people, marriage was about teamwork and social relationships, not about sexual excitement. In the days before the Puritans came, marriage did not mean an end to sex with people other than your spouse. Women were just as likely as men to have a *si'ash,* or lover.

New life was so precious that pregnancy was always appropriate, and pregnancy before marriage was celebrated as a good sign. Since the children belonged to the mother and her clan, and women owned and bequeathed the houses and farmland, the exact determination of paternity wasn't critical. Although fertility was prized, infertility was no problem because mothers with unplanned pregnancies gave their babies to childless couples within the clan in open adoption arrangements. Children called their mother's sisters "mother" as well, and a child became attached to a number of parent figures.

In the sacred kiva ceremonies, men mask and dress as women to pay homage and to be possessed by the female energies of the spirit beings. Because differences in physical appearance were so highly valued, surgery to change one's face and body to resemble a model's face and body would be unimaginable. To be different, to be unique was blessed and was best of all.

20

JUST WALK ON BY
A Black Man Ponders His Power
to Alter Public Space

BRENT STAPLES

Brent Staples is assistant metropolitan editor of the *New York Times*.

My first victim was a woman—white, well dressed, probably in her early twenties. I came upon her late one evening on a deserted street in Hyde Park, a relatively affluent neighborhood in an otherwise mean, impoverished section of Chicago. As I swung onto the avenue behind her, there seemed to be a discreet, uninflammatory distance between us. Not so. She cast back a worried glance. To her, the youngish black man—a broad six feet two inches with a beard and billowing hair, both hands shoved into the pockets of a bulky military jacket—seemed menacingly close. After a few more quick glimpses, she picked up her pace and was soon running in earnest. Within seconds she disappeared into a cross street.

That was more than a decade ago. I was 22 years old, a graduate student newly arrived at the University of Chicago. It was in the echo of that terrified woman's footfalls that I first began to know the unwieldy inheritance I'd come into—the ability to alter public space in ugly ways. It was clear that she thought herself the quarry of a mugger, a rapist, or worse. Suffering a bout of insomnia, however, I was stalking sleep, not defenseless wayfarers. As a softy who is scarcely able to take a knife to a raw chicken—let alone hold it to a person's throat—I was surprised, embarrassed, and dismayed all at once. Her flight made me feel like an accomplice in tyranny. It also made it clear that I was indistinguishable from the muggers who occasionally seeped into the area from the surrounding ghetto. That first encounter, and those that followed, signified that a vast, unnerving gulf lay between nighttime pedestrians—particularly women—and me. And I soon gathered that being perceived as dangerous is a hazard in itself. I only needed to turn a corner into a dicey situation, or crowd some frightened, armed person in a foyer somewhere, or make an errant move after being pulled over by a policeman. Where fear and weapons meet—and they often do in urban America—there is always the possibility of death.

In that first year, my first away from my hometown, I was to become thoroughly familiar with the language of fear. At dark, shadowy intersections in Chicago, I could cross in front of a car stopped at a traffic light and elicit the *thunk, thunk, thunk, thunk* of the driver—black, white, male, female—hammering down the door locks. On less-traveled streets after dark, I grew accustomed to but never comfortable with people who crossed to the other side of the street rather than pass me. Then there were the standard unpleasantries with police, doormen, bouncers, cab drivers, and others whose business it is to screen out troublesome individuals *before* there is any nastiness.

I moved to New York nearly two years ago and I have remained an avid night walker. In central Manhattan, the near-constant crowd cover minimizes tense one-on-one street encounters. Elsewhere—visiting friends in SoHo, where sidewalks are narrow and tightly spaced buildings shut out the sky—things can get very taut indeed.

Black men have a firm place in New York mugging literature. Norman Podhoretz in his famed (or infamous) 1963 essay, "My Negro Problem—And Ours," recalls growing up in terror of black males; they "were tougher than we were, more ruthless," he writes—and as an adult on the Upper West Side of Manhattan, he continues, he cannot constrain his nervousness when he meets black men on certain streets. Similarly, a decade later, the essayist and novelist Edward Hoagland extols a New York where once "Negro bitterness bore down mainly on other Negroes." Where some see mere panhandlers, Hoagland sees "a mugger who is clearly screwing up his nerve to do more than just *ask* for money." But Hoagland has "the New Yorker's quick-hunch posture for broken-field maneuvering," and the bad guy swerves away.

I often witness that "hunch posture," from women after dark on the warrenlike streets of Brooklyn where I live. They seem to set their faces on neutral and, with their purse straps strung across their chests bandolier style, they forge ahead as though bracing themselves against being tackled. I understand, of course, that the danger they perceive is not a hallucination. Women are particularly vulnerable to street violence, and young black males are drastically overrepresented among the perpetrators of that violence. Yet these truths are no solace against the kind of alienation that comes of being ever the suspect, against being set apart, a fearsome entity with whom pedestrians avoid making eye contact.

It is not altogether clear to me how I reached the ripe old age of 22 without being conscious of the lethality nighttime pedestrians attributed to me. Perhaps it was because in Chester, Pennsylvania, the small, angry industrial town where I came of age in the 1960s, I was scarcely noticeable against a backdrop of gang warfare, street knifings, and murders. I grew up one of the good boys, had perhaps a half-dozen fist fights. In retrospect, my shyness of combat has clear sources.

Many things go into the making of a young thug. One of those things is the consummation of the male romance with the power to intimidate. An infant discovers that random flailings send the baby bottle flying out of the crib and crashing to the floor. Delighted, the joyful babe repeats those motions again and again, seeking to duplicate the feat. Just so, I recall the points at which some of my boyhood friends were finally seduced by the perception of themselves as tough guys. When a mark cowered and surrendered his money without resistance, myth and reality merged—and paid off. It is, after all, only manly to embrace the power to frighten and intimidate. We, as men, are not supposed to give an inch of our lane on the highway; we are to seize the fighter's edge in work and in play and even in love; we are to be valiant in the face of hostile forces.

Unfortunately, poor and powerless young men seem to take all this nonsense literally. As a boy, I saw countless tough guys locked away; I have since buried several, too. They were babies, really—a teenage cousin, a brother of 22, a childhood friend in his mid-twenties—all gone down in episodes of bravado played out in the streets. I came to doubt the virtues of intimidation early on. I chose, perhaps even unconsciously, to remain a shadow—timid, but a survivor.

The fearsomeness mistakenly attributed to me in public places often has a perilous flavor. The most frightening of these confusions occurred in the late 1970s and early 1980s when I worked as a journalist in Chicago. One day, rushing into the office of a magazine I was writing for with a deadline story in hand, I was mistaken for a burglar. The office manager called security and, with an ad hoc posse, pursued me through the labyrinthine halls, nearly to my editor's door. I had no way of proving who I was. I could only move briskly toward the company of someone who knew me.

Another time I was on assignment for a local paper and killing time before an interview. I entered a jewelry store on the city's affluent Near North Side. The proprietor excused herself and returned with an enormous red Doberman pinscher straining at the end of a leash. She stood, the dog extended toward me, silent to my questions, her eyes bulging nearly out of her head. I took a cursory look around, nodded, and bade her good night. Relatively speaking, however, I never fared as badly as another black male journalist. He went to nearby Waukegan, Illinois, a couple of summers ago to work on a story about a murderer who was born there. Mistaking the reporter for the killer, police hauled him from his car at gunpoint and but for his press credentials would have tried to book him. Such episodes are not uncommon. Black men trade tales like this all the time.

In "My Negro Problem—And Ours," Podhoretz writes that the hatred he feels for blacks makes itself known to him through a variety of avenues—one being his discomfort with that "special brand of paranoid touchiness" to which he says blacks are prone. No doubt he is speaking here of black men. In time, I learned to smother the rage I felt at so often being taken for a criminal. Not to do so would surely have led to madness—via that special "paranoid touchiness" that so annoyed Podhoretz at the time he wrote the essay.

I began to take precautions to make myself less threatening. I move about with care, particularly late in the evening. I give a wide berth to nervous people on the subway platforms during the wee hours, particularly when I have exchanged business clothes for jeans. If I happen to be entering a building behind some people who appear skittish, I may walk by, letting them clear the lobby before I return, so as not to seem to be following them. I have been calm and extremely congenial on those rare occasions when I've been pulled over by the police.

And on late-evening constitutionals along streets less traveled by, I employ what has proved to be an excellent tension-reducing measure: I whistle melodies from Beethoven and Vivaldi and the more popular classical composers. Even steely New Yorkers hunching toward nighttime destinations seem to relax, and occasionally they even join in the tune. Virtually everybody seems to sense that a mugger wouldn't be warbling bright, sunny selections from Vivaldi's *Four Seasons*. It is my equivalent of the cowbell that hikers wear when they know they are in bear country.

21

TAKING IT

LEONARD KRIEGEL

Leonard Kriegel, author of the novel *Quitting Time* and of the collection of essays *Falling*, is a professor of English and director of the Center for Worker Education at the City University of New York.

I n 1944, at the age of eleven, I had polio. I spent the next two years of my life in an orthopedic hospital, appropriately called a reconstruction home. By 1946, when I returned to my native Bronx, polio had reconstructed me to the point that I walked very haltingly on steel braces and crutches.

But polio also taught me that, if I were to survive, I would have to become a man—and become a man quickly. "Be a man!" my immigrant father urged, by which he meant "become an American." For, in 1946, this country had very specific expectations about how a man faced adversity.

Endurance, courage, determination, stoicism—these might right the balance with fate.

"I couldn't take it, and I took it," says the wheelchair-doomed poolroom entrepreneur William Einhorn in Saul Bellow's *The Adventures of Augie March*. "And I *can't* take it, yet I do take it." In 1953, when I first read these words, I knew that Einhorn spoke for me—as he spoke for scores of other men who had confronted the legacy of a maiming disease by risking whatever they possessed of substance in a country that believed that such risks were a man's wagers against his fate.

How one faced adversity was, like most of American life, in part a question of gender. Simply put, a woman endured, but a man fought back. You were better off struggling against the effects of polio as a man than as a woman, for polio was a disease that one confronted by being tough, aggressive, decisive, by assuming that all limitations could be overcome, beaten, conquered. In short, by being "a man." Even the vocabulary of rehabilitation was masculine. One "beat" polio by outmuscling the disease. At the age of eighteen, I felt that I was "a better man" than my friends because I had "overcome a handicap." And I had, in the process, showed that I could "take it." In the world of American men, to take it was a sign that you were among the elect—an assumption my "normal" friends shared. "You're lucky," my closest friend said to me during an intensely painful crisis in his own life. "You had polio." He meant it. We both believed it.

Obviously, I wasn't lucky. By nineteen, I was already beginning to understand—slowly, painfully, but inexorably—that disease is never "conquered" or "overcome." Still, I looked upon resistance to polio as the essence of my manhood. As an American, I was self-reliant. I could create my own possibilities from life. And so I walked mile after mile on braces and crutches. I did hundreds of push-ups every day to build my arms, chest, and shoulders. I lifted weights to the point that I would collapse, exhausted but strengthened, on the floor. And through it all, my desire to create a "normal" life for myself was transformed into a desire to become the man my disease had decreed I should be.

I took my heroes where I found them—a strange, disparate company of men: Hemingway, whom I would write of years later as "my nurse"; Peter Reiser, whom I dreamed of replacing in Ebbets Field's pastures and whose penchant for crashing into outfield walls fused in my mind with my own war against the virus; Franklin Delano Roosevelt, who had scornfully faced polio with aristocratic disdain and patrician distance (a historian acquaintance recently disabused me of that myth, a myth perpetrated, let me add, by almost all of Roosevelt's biographers); Henry Fonda and Gary Cooper, in whose resolute Anglo-Saxon faces Hollywood blended the simplicity, strength and courage a man needed if he was going to survive as a man; any number of boxers in whom heart, discipline and training combined to stave off defeats the boy's limitations made inevitable. These were the "manly" images I conjured up as I walked those miles of Bronx streets, as I did those relentless push-ups, as I moved up and down one subway staircase after another by turning each concrete step into a personal insult. And they were still the images when, fifteen years later, married, the father of two sons of my own, a Fulbright professor in the Netherlands, I would grab hold of vertical poles in a train in The Hague and swing my brace-bound body across the dead space between platform and carriage, filled with self-congratulatory vanity as amazement spread over the features of the Dutch conductor.

It is easy to dismiss such images as adolescent. Undoubtedly they were. But they helped remind me, time and time again, of how men handled their diseases and their pain. Of course, I realized even then that it was not the idea of manhood alone that had helped me fashion a life out of polio. I might write of Hemingway as "my nurse," but it was an immigrant Jewish mother—already transformed into a cliché by scores of male Jewish writers—who serviced my crippled body's needs and who fed me love, patience and care even as I fed her the rhetoric of my rage.

But it was the need to prove myself an American man—tough, resilient, independent, able to take it—that pulled me through the war with the virus. I have, of course, been reminded again and again of the price extracted for such ideas about manhood. And I am willing to admit that my sons may be better off in a country in which "manhood" will mean little more than, say, the name for an after-shave lotion. It is forty years since my war with the virus began. At fifty-one, even an American man knows that mortality is the only legacy and defeat the only guarantee. At fifty-one, my legs still encased in braces and crutches still beneath my shoulders, my elbows are increasingly arthritic from all those streets walked and weights lifted and stairs climbed. At fifty-one, my shoulders burn with pain from all those push-ups done so relentlessly. And at fifty-one, pain merely bores—and hurts.

Still, I remain an American man. If I know where I'm going, I know, too, where I have been. Best of all, I know the price I have paid. A man endures his diseases until he recognizes in them his vanity. He can't take it, but he takes it. Once, I relished my ability to take it. Now I find myself wishing that taking it were easier. In such quiet surrenders do we American men call it quits with our diseases.

22

I'M NOT FAT, I'M LATINA

CHRISTY HAUBEGGER

Christy Haubegger, a Mexican American native of Houston, is an attorney and the founder and publisher of *Latina* magazine, the first bilingual publication targeted to Hispanic women in the United States.

I recently read a newspaper article that reported that nearly 40 percent of Hispanic and African-American women are overweight. At least I'm in good company. Because according to even the most generous height and weight charts at the doctor's office, I'm a good 25 pounds overweight. And I'm still looking for the panty-hose chart that has me on it (according to Hanes, I don't exist). But I'm happy to report that in the Latino community, my community, I fit right in.

Latinas in this country live in two worlds. People who don't know us may think we're fat. At home, we're called *bien cuidadas* (well cared for).

I love to go dancing at Cesar's Latin Palace here in the Mission District of San Francisco. At this hot all-night salsa club, it's the curvier bodies like mine that turn heads. I'm the one on the dance floor all night while some of my thinner friends spend more time waiting along the walls. Come to think of it, I wouldn't trade my body for any of theirs.

But I didn't always feel this way. I remember being in high school and noticing that none of the magazines showed models in bathing suits with bodies like mine. Handsome movie heroes were never hoping to find a chubby damsel in distress. The fact that I had plenty of attention from Latino boys wasn't enough. Real self-esteem cannot come from male attention alone.

My turning point came a few years later. When I was in college, I made a trip to Mexico, and I brought back much more than sterling-silver bargains and colorful blankets.

I remember hiking through the awesome ruins of the Maya and the Aztecs, civilizations that created pyramids as large as the ones in Egypt. I loved walking through temple doorways whose clearance was only two inches above my head, and I realized that I must be a direct descendant of those ancient priestesses for whom those doorways had originally been built.

Christy Haubegger, "I'm Not Fat, I'm Latina" from *Essence* (December 1994), p. 50. Reprinted with the permission of the author.

For the first time in my life, I was in a place where people like me were the beautiful ones. And I began to accept, and even like, the body that I have.

I know that medical experts say that Latinas are twice as likely as the rest of the population to be overweight. And yes, I know about the health problems that often accompany severe weight problems. But most of us are not in the danger zone; we're just *bien cuidadas*. Even the researchers who found that nearly 40 percent of us are overweight noted that there is a greater "cultural acceptance" of being overweight within Hispanic communities. But the article also commented on the cultural-acceptance factor as if it were something unfortunate, because it keeps Hispanic women from becoming healthier. I'm not so convinced that we're the ones with the problem.

If the medical experts were to try and get to the root of this so-called problem, they would probably find that it's part genetics, part enchiladas. Whether we're Cuban-American, Mexican-American, Puerto Rican or Dominican, food is a central part of Hispanic culture. While our food varies from fried plaintains to tamales, what doesn't change is its role in our lives. You feed people you care for, and so if you're well cared for, *bien cuidada,* you have been fed well.

I remember when I used to be envious of a Latina friend of mine who had always been on the skinny side. When I confided this to her a while ago, she laughed. It turns out that when she was growing up, she had always wanted to look more like me. She had trouble getting dates with Latinos in high school, the same boys that I dated. When she was little, the other kids in the neighborhood had even given her a cruel nickname: la seca, "the dry one." I'm glad I never had any of those problems.

Our community has always been accepting of us well-cared-for women. So why don't we feel beautiful? You only have to flip through a magazine or watch a movie to realize that beautiful for most of this country still means tall, blond and underfed. But now we know it's the magazines that are wrong. I, for one, am going to do what I can to make sure that *mis hijas,* my daughters, won't feel the way I did.

23

THE TYRANNY OF THE ESTHETIC
Surgery's Most Intimate Violation

MARTHA COVENTRY

Martha Coventry, when asked by a photographer what culture she came from that would clitoridectomize its daughters, laughed and answered, "WASP culture." A middle-aged midwestern mother of two daughters, Coventry writes and speaks about intersexuality in order to change a world that treats different bodies as wrong bodies.

Big clitorises aren't allowed in America. By big, I mean over three-eighths of an inch for newborns, about the size of a pencil eraser. Tiny penises, under one inch, aren't allowed either.[1] A big clitoris is considered too capable of becoming alarmingly erect, and a tiny penis is not quite capable enough. Such genitals are confounding to the strictly maintained and comforting social order in America today, which has everyone believing that bodies come in only two ways: perfectly female and perfectly male. But genitals are surprisingly ambiguous. At least one out of every 2,000 babies is born with genitals that don't elicit the automatic "It's a girl!" or "It's a boy!"[2] Many more have genitals that are perceived as "masculinized" or "feminized," although the child's sex is not in doubt.

The American Academy of Pediatrics recommends surgically altering these children between the ages of six weeks and 15 months to fashion their bodies into something closer to perfection.[3] Everyone can then breathe easier, except for the child, who may well spend the rest of her or his life trying to let the breath flow easy and full through the fear and shame created by such devastating surgery.

On a November night in 1958, I was playing in the bathtub in the cheery, country home of my childhood. I was six years old. My mother came in and sat on the edge of the tub, her kind face looking worried. I glanced up at her, wondering, "Time to get out so soon?" She told me that I had to go to the hospital the next day for an operation. I knew this was about something between my legs. My chest felt tight and there was a rushing sound in my ears. I begged not to go. Please. But my mother told me only that I must. Not a

Martha Coventry, "The Tyranny of the Esthetic: Surgery's Most Intimate Violation" from *On the Issues* (Summer 1998), pp. 16–23, 60–61. Reprinted with the permission of the author.

word was said about what was going to happen or why. The next day, it took the surgeon 30 minutes to make a U-shaped incision around my half-inch clitoris, remove it, and put it in a specimen dish to send to the lab. He then closed the wound and stitched the skin up over the stump.

Take no comfort in the fact that this took place 40 years ago. Today, most parents and doctors in this country are still unable to see that a child has a right to her or his own sexual body, even if that body is deemed "abnormal" by their standards. If a parent is uncomfortable, a doctor can be found who will be willing to make irreversible changes in the child's body, in order to ease that discomfort. My gynecologist told me about a case in which he had been involved the year before: A woman brought her five-year-old daughter to his office in Minneapolis; the mother felt that the child's clitoris was too big. He examined the girl and assured the mother that her daughter would grow into her clitoris, which was no longer than the end of his little finger. The mother left. A few weeks later, he was called into an operating room to help another doctor who had run into trouble during a surgical procedure. On the table, he found the same little girl he had seen earlier. She was hemorrhaging from a clitorectomy attempted by the second doctor, from instructions he had read in a medical text. My physician stopped the bleeding, and managed to keep the girl's clitoris mostly intact.

It is not new in our culture to remove or alter the clitoris. Not so long ago, such surgery was commonly practiced to prevent masturbation and "unnatural sexual appetites." Although such justifications still lurk in the minds of parents and doctors ("Won't she become a lesbian?" is a concern of many mothers whose daughters have big clitorises), clitorectomies gained new status toward the end of the 1950s, as a "legitimate" way to make a child with atypical genitals feel and appear more normal. Surgical techniques learned during World War II led to advances in the field of cosmetic genital surgery; at about the same time, a new medical discipline—endocrinology, the study of the hormonal system—was established at Johns Hopkins University Medical School. A child's body could now be successfully altered by surgery and hormones to look just about any way you wanted it to look. And the controversial research into sex and gender roles by Johns Hopkins' John Money, Ph.D., led doctors to believe that by changing that body, you could make the child into a "normal" male or female, both physically and psychologically. Children could be made "right" if they were born "wrong." And American medicine, and our society at large, sees "imperfect" genitals as wrong.

That view is challenged by farsighted pediatric urologist Justine Schober, M.D., of Erie, Penn.: "Why should we say that, because this is a variation, that it is a wrong variation? If all their faculties work, their sexual sensitivities work, why should we presume that their body is wrong?"[4] But by seeing a child's body as wrong and by labeling such a child "intersexed," we turn a simple variation on a theme into a problem that can and should be fixed. And fixed it usually is, by surgery that sacrifices healthy erotic tissue for cosmetic reasons some five times a day in the U.S. The rules of the game are still the same as they were 40 years ago: Erase any sign of difference, tidy things up, and don't say another word.

After I had my clitorectomy, my innocent life became filled with fear and guilt. The secrecy surrounding my surgery began to undermine my entire sense of identity. I knew I had something between my legs cut off, and I could imagine only that it was a penis. Girls were Barbie-doll smooth, so there wasn't anything on a girl to cut off. Was I really a boy? Or perhaps the horrible thing I had somehow known about forever: hermaphrodite? The study of my father, a physician, was full of medical books, but I flipped through them quickly, drawn to the pictures of children with their eyes blacked out, knowing there was something we shared, yet terrified to find out what kind of freak I really was. Then, one night when I was 11 or 12, I found my parents, as they sat around the dining room table, looking at studio pictures of my sisters and me. My mother held up my photo and I heard her say the word "boy." My gut heaved. I was a boy. It was true. I blurted out, "What was that operation I had?" My father turned to me and said, "Don't be so self-examining." I never had the heart to tell this man who loved me so dearly that, by keeping the truth from me that night, by trying to protect me from my own wondering mind and wandering hands, he had sentenced me to a life of almost crippling fear in relation to my sexuality, even to a profound doubt of my right to be alive.

It would be 25 years before I could begin to start asking questions again. When I finally pressed my dying father as gently as I could for a reason why he and my mother wanted my clitoris removed, he said, "We didn't want you to be mistaken for a hermaphrodite." My father was a surgeon. No doctor had patronizingly spun to him tales of "improperly formed gonads," or lied to him about my medical condition, or told him I would become a lesbian if I had a big clitoris, or pretended that no other children like me existed. Just having a child with an abnormal body in Rochester, Minn., was bad enough for my parents. But doctors do lie—to parents and to children, in a gross insult to their intelligence and their right to the truth. Lying to children is a rule strictly adhered to, and enforced, by all but the most enlightened doctors. First, the surgery steals your body from you, then lies confirm that there is so little respect for you as a human being that you don't even deserve the truth.

X Marks the . . . .

Angela Moreno was a happy child growing up in the late seventies in Peoria, Ill. She was fairly sexually precocious with herself, and became very familiar with her clitoris: "I loved it, but had no name for it. I remember being amazed that there was a part of my body that was so intensely pleasurable. It felt wonderful under my hand. There was no fantasy, just pleasure—just me and my body." Life in the pleasure garden came to an abrupt end for

Angela when, at age 12, her mother noticed her protruding clitoris while Angela was toweling off after a bath. After being examined by the family doctor, she was sent to an endocrinologist. The endocrinologist revealed to her parents that, instead of the two X chromosomes that characterize the female genotype, Angela had an X and a Y. She was "genetically male." She had the external genitalia of a female because the receptors for the "male" hormone testosterone did not function; that is, her body was unable to respond to the androgenizing or masculinizing hormones it produced. Her parents were assured that if surgeons removed Angela's internal testes, and shortened her clitoris, she would be a "very normal little girl," albeit one born without ovaries or a uterus. This was lie number one.

Just because your body may look "normal" is no guarantee that you will feel that way. The truth is that the very thing surgery claims to save us from—a sense of differentness and abnormality—it quite unequivocally creates.

Doctors then told Angela's parents that if she didn't have surgery she might kill herself when she found out that she was different from other girls. It had happened to another patient, the physicians said, and it could happen to Angela. Although such speculation is not a lie, it is also not the whole truth. In my talks with scores of people with atypical genitals, it is those who have been surgically altered as children and left alone with their trauma who most often become suicidal. The isolation from others who have experienced what we are going through, the loneliness, is what kills us. Angela's parents were justifiably frightened and agreed to the surgery.

The final lie was to Angela herself, with her distraught parents' complicity. She was told, at her physician's suggestion, that her nonexistent ovaries could become cancerous and that she would have to go into the hospital and have them removed.

In 1985, at a leading children's hospital in Chicago, doctors removed the testes from Angela's abdomen. The clitoris that had brought her so much joy was not merely shortened, it was all but destroyed. She woke up and discovered the extent of her deceit: "I put my hand down there and felt something like the crusty top of some horrible casserole, like dried caked blood where my clitoris was. I wondered why no one told me and I just figured it was the kind of thing decent people don't talk about."

Angela became depressed and severely bulimic. "I blamed my body. My body had betrayed me. Made me someone worthy of that kind of treatment. I just studied and puked." She was a straight-A student in high school, but otherwise, her adolescence was a nightmare. She avoided becoming close to other girls her age, afraid she would be asked questions about the menstrual period she knew she would never have. The uncomplicated sexuality she had reveled in before the clitorectomy was gone, and she was desolated by the loss of erotic sensation. In an attempt to find out the truth, she returned to her original endocrinologist, who told her that her gonads had not formed properly, and her clitoris had grown because of an abnormal level of hormones. She did not tell Angela about her XY status or her testes. Angela fell deeper into darkness, sensing that she had not been given the whole story. Finally, at 20, weakened by chronic and near-lethal bingeing and purging, and suicidal, she checked herself into a psychiatric unit.

After her release, she began seeing a therapist who finally hit on the connection between her bulimia and the control she lost over her body at the time of surgery. Angela knew she had to find out the mystery of her body in order to get well. By now she was 23 and could legally obtain her medical records, yet it took a year for her to find the courage to write for them. When she received them and read the truth about herself, she could begin at last to save her own life. "Although the doctors had claimed that knowing the truth would make me self-destructive, it was *not* knowing what had been done to me—and why—that made me want to die."

In my case, I have XX chromosomes, and my outsized clitoris was the only part of my body that was not like that of most other girls.

Do these facts make you want to differentiate me from Angela? To say, "Wait a minute. You were simply a girl born with a big clitoris, but Angela had a real pathological condition." But the doctors removed Angela's clitoris for exactly the same reason they removed mine—they thought it offensively large. Her chromosomes and her abdominal testes had no bearing on the decision.

If you rush to see Angela as fundamentally different from me, if you see her as a real intersexual and me as just a normal woman, you do two very damaging things: You may see it as justified to perform cosmetic surgery on her and not on me because she really is "abnormal," and you separate us from each other and deny our right to find solace and strength in the sameness of our experience.

The doctor who was kind enough to help me begin to explore my early surgery did just that to me. I found the Intersex Society of North America on my own several months after my initial visit with him, and told him later how healing it had been to find others who knew intimately what my life had been like.[5] He had known about ISNA all along, he said, but didn't pass the information on to me because I was not intersexed. I was a real woman. He had tried to save me from a pathologizing label, but ended up enforcing my isolation instead.

New and Improved?

When a baby is born today with genitals that are ambiguous, a team of surgeons, pediatric endocrinologists, and social workers scramble to relieve what is called a "psychosocial emergency." Tests are done and orifices explored to determine as nearly as possible the baby's "true sex." Then, in almost all cases, doctors perform surgery to make the child look more like a girl, because, they say, the surgery required is easier to perform than trying to make the child look like a boy.

The form this feminizing surgery most often takes is the dissection and removal of healthy clitoral tissue—a clitorectomy, also known as "clitoral recession," "clitoral reduction," and "clitoroplasty." Sensitive, erectile tissue is stripped away from the shaft of the clitoris, and the glans is tucked away so expertly that all you see is the cute little love button that is the idealized clitoris. But the pleasure is almost gone, or gone completely, for the owner of that dainty new clit. If orgasms are possible, and they aren't for many women subjected to clitoral surgery, the intensity is greatly diminished. One woman whose clitoris was "recessed" writes: "If orgasms before the recession were a deep purple, now they are a pale, watery pink."[6]

Doctors maintain that modern surgery retains more clitoral sensation than the older forms of surgery, but they base their assurance on nerve impulses measured by machines—supposedly accurate and unbiased information—and not the real experience of thousands and thousands of women in this country. This is because no long-term post-surgical studies have been done. I, who had the old-style surgery, have clitoral sensation and orgasmic function, while those subjected to more modern surgeries often have neither. How much do doctors truly care about a child's sexual future if they decimate the one organ in the body designed solely for pleasure?

In 1965, Annie Green, then three years old, took a car trip with her father from the small town in Idaho where she lived to Spokane, Wash. She sat in the back seat with her stuffed animal, unaware that she was on her way to the hospital. The next day doctors removed her inch-long clitoris. She was never given any explanation of her surgery. As she got older, her attempts to find pleasure in masturbation failed, and she began to suspect she was very different from other girls. Then, during a visit to her sister's house as a teenager, she found the book *Our Bodies, Ourselves:* "I studied the female anatomy and read about sex from that book. That was when I learned I didn't have a clitoris. I remember looking at the diagram, feeling myself, and reading what a clitoris was over and over. My God, I couldn't figure out why I didn't have one. I couldn't fathom anyone removing it if it was that important. I was stunned, and I held it all in. I was only 14. I became depressed. I was disgusted with my body, and I thought there was no hope that I would ever be loved by anyone. I became a little teenage alcoholic. I drank heavily every weekend. I really blew it because I had been a really good athlete and an honor student."

Clitoral surgery on children is brutal and illogical, and no matter what name you give it, it is a mutilation. When I use the word mutilation, I can hear doors slamming shut in the minds of doctors all over this country. John Gearhart, a pediatric urologist at Johns Hopkins, has said, "To compare genital mutilation of young girls in Africa to reconstructive surgery of a young baby is a giant, giant leap of misrepresentation."[7] But neither Dr. Gearhart, nor anyone else, has ever bothered to ask those of us subjected to clitoral surgery as children if being taken to the hospital without explanation, having your healthy genitals cut and scarred, then left alone with the results feels like mutilation or "reconstructive surgery." Gearhart's mistake is to judge surgery only by the surgeon's intent and not by the effect on the child. I spoke with a woman recently who is young enough to be my daughter. With great effort, she told me of her clitoral surgery as a child. She implored me, "Why do they have to cut so deep, Martha? Why do they do that?"

Of the notable feminist voices raised long and loud in outrage over traditional genital surgeries practiced in parts of Africa, which are now denounced as "female genital mutilation" (FGM), not a single woman has said a word about the equally mutilating practice of surgically destroying the healthy genitals of children in their own country. Like Gearhart, they shrink when we describe our surgeries as mutilation. But do they believe that African mothers, any more than American surgeons, cut their children out of malicious intent? Could their silence be because they don't know what is happening in American hospitals? It's possible, but the issue has received media coverage in the past year, and many of them have had the facts explained to them in person or in writing.

I could speculate that these women don't want to take on a foe as formidable and familiar as the medical profession, and that it is simpler to point fingers at more barbaric countries. They may not want to dilute their cause with the sticky subjects of sex and gender that surround the issue of ambiguous genitalia. Or perhaps they don't want to be aligned with children they can only see as freaks of nature. Even the liberal-thinking Joycelyn Elders, the former Surgeon General, refers to children who blur gender lines in a less-than-humane way. When Elders, a professor of pediatric endocrinology who continues to promote "reconstructive surgery" for girls with big clitorises, was asked about the wisdom of genital surgery on such children, she responded with, "Well, you just can't have an *it!*"[8]

Each woman has her own reasons for turning away from this issue. But I challenge them to pay attention to the fact that in hospitals just down the street in any big American city, five children a day are losing healthy, erotic parts of their bodies to satisfy a social demand for "normalcy." There is no federal ban to save them. The surgery is left out of the law against FGM because it is deemed "necessary to the health of the child on whom it is performed."[9] But as social psychologist Suzanne Kessler at the State University of New York at Purchase points out, "Genital ambiguity is corrected not because it is threatening to the infant's life, but because it is threatening to the infant's culture."[10]

————

Doctors and parents believe society will reject a child with atypical genitals, and the child is made to pay with her or his body for the shortcoming of our culture. What is happening in American hospitals to healthy children is just as mutilating to the bodies—no matter how exquisite the surgical craftsmanship—and violating to the souls of these children as FGM. And frequently, the surgical craftsmanship falls far short of exquisite.

The strict sexual agenda for bodies in America extends to little boys as well. To grow up to be a real man, a boy will have to be able to do two things—pee standing up and penetrate a vagina with his penis. If a little boy has to sit like a girl to urinate because his urethra exits somewhere along the shaft of his penis rather than the tip (a condition that can occur in as many as 8 out of 1,000),[11] he may be subjected to many disheartening surgeries over the course of his childhood to correct this "defect," and be left with a lifetime of chronic infections and emotional trauma. And if the baby is born with a "too-small" penis that doctors decide will never be big enough to "successfully" penetrate a woman, physicians will probably make him into a "girl" through surgery and hormone treatments, because, in the words of one surgeon, "It's easier to poke a hole than to build a pole."

In the 40 years since surgical intervention to "correct" genitals that are viewed as abnormal was first prescribed, treatment protocols have been rarely questioned. After all, it is much more comfortable for doctors to assume all is well than to start digging around to find out if it's really true. Until recently, all discussions of what is done to people's sexual bodies have been hidden safely away in the pages of medical texts, where real lives are only "interesting cases," and pictures of genitals are disembodied curiosities or teaching tools. Many doctors would like to keep things that way. For example, Dr. Kenneth Glassberg, a pediatric urologist associated with the American Academy of Pediatrics (AAP), insists that people who speak up and tell their stories are doing a disservice by "scaring patients away."[12]

In a blatant disregard for patient feedback not seen in any other medical field, the AAP still advocates early surgery and insists that the "management" of children with atypical genitals has improved over the past several decades. Their refusal to consider the reality of the lives of people who have been treated by this protocol can be likened to an astronomer gazing at Mars through his telescope while ignoring the real live Martian tugging at his sleeve. The messy truth of what happens to children treated with surgery and hormones is simply ignored by the AAP, as they stubbornly cling to a treatment paradigm that has never been anything but experimental.

Cosmetic genital surgery on children is out of control. As the practice has careened along unexamined for decades, illustrious careers and reputations have been made, consciences have been swallowed, and terrific damage has been done. For a doctor even to hesitate before operating takes tremendous effort and self-reflection. The need for babies to have genitals that look typical has been perceived as so unquestionable that surgeons travel all over the world to perform surgery on children free of charge as a "humanitarian gesture."

Dr. Justine Schober challenges her fellow surgeons to realize that "when you do [this kind of] surgery on someone, you are responsible for them for the rest of their lives."[13] In less than two hours in a sterile operating room, a child's personal and sexual destiny can be changed forever. The stakes are excruciatingly high for the sake of appearances. Angela's story, Annie's story, and my own tell only the smallest fraction of the terrible fallout from these surgeries. No one is naive enough to say that life in a body seen as abnormal is a ticket to bliss. But it is not the bodies of these children that are wrong, it is the way people see them. And if these children grow up and want to change their bodies one day, that will be their right. Nobody, but nobody, no matter how loving, no matter how well intentioned, should have the power to steal precious parts of a body from a child before she or he even gets started in life.

NOTES

1. Suzanne J. Kessler, "Meanings of Genital Variability," a paper presented as part of a plenary symposium titled "Genitals, Identity, and Gender." The Society for the Scientific Study of Sexuality, November 1995, San Francisco. Further reference: Barbara C. McGillivray, "The Newborn with Ambiguous Genitalia," *Seminars in Perinatology* 16, no. 6 (1992): 365–68.

2. Melanie Blackless, Anthony Charuvastra, Amanda Derryck, Anne Fausto-Sterling, Karl Lauzanne, Ellen Lee, "How sexually dimorphic are we? Review and synthesis." *American Journal of Human Biology* Vol. 12, Issue 2, Date: March/April 2000, pp. 151–166.

3. News release from the American Academy of Pediatrics (American Academy of Pediatrics, 141 Northwest Point Blvd., Elk Grove, IL 60009-0927) distributed to the press on October 26, 1996.

4. Justine Schober, personal communication, March 1998.

5. Intersex Society of North America, PO Box 31791, San Francisco, CA, 415/575-3885 (email:info@isna.org, web:www.isna.org). ISNA is a peer-support and advocacy group operated by and for individuals born with anatomy or physiology that differs from cultural ideals of female and male.

6. Cheryl Chase, "Winged Labia: Deformity or Gift?" *Hermaphrodites with Attitude,* a publication of the Intersex Society of North America, 1, no. 1 (Winter 1994): 3–4.

7. Monika Bauerlein, "The Unkindest Cut," *Utne Reader* (September/October 1996): 16.

8. Joycelyn Elders, personal communication, September 1997.

9. Federal Prohibition of Female Genital Mutilation Act of 1995.

10. Suzanne J. Kessler, "The Medical Construction of Gender: Case Management of Intersexual Infants," *Signs: Journal of Women in Culture and Society* 16, no. 1 (1990): 3–26.

11. Justine Schober, personal communication, March 1998.

12. Geoffrey Cowley, "Gender Limbo," *Newsweek* (May 19, 1997): 64–66.

13. Justine Shober, personal communication, March 1998.

PART IV
Communication

Individuals, groups, institutions, systems, governments, world organizations, and the mass media all engage in communication, sometimes face to face and often in other ways—via phone, text messages, TV, in print, and via the Internet, for example. At the interpersonal level, telling the truth about one's experience is one task of communicating with others. The other task, frequently more challenging than the first, is listening carefully, empathizing, and trying to understand other people without being defensive or interrupting. Most people have a sense of how difficult this can be. A growing literature, especially related to counseling and psychotherapy, focuses on basic communication skills, such as listening, and on multicultural communication skills, which include acknowledging how the various intersections of gender, race, class, ethnicity, disability, sexual orientation, and age affect communication. The task of becoming multiculturally competent takes time and effort, and it is necessary for anyone who wants to communicate across cultures because most people are intimately familiar with only their own cultures.[1]

Communication patterns reflect power relationships. Those who have more power tend to control what is communicated including what gets media attention; they especially control the extent to which people with less power are listened to and seen for who they are without prejudice. In an examination of African American and Latina women in film, for example, Elizabeth Hadley Freydberg concludes that despite active protest from these two communities, the film industry continues to portray Latinas and African American women in stereotyped, insulting roles.[2]

The recent outrage and subsequent firing of Don Imus over the racist and sexist language he used to describe women basketball players illustrates both that racism and sexism are alive and well, and that when enough people express outrage, at least something might be done to suggest that this language is not acceptable. Imus's defense that he used words that are common in hip-hop did not cut it. Following this incident, rap producer Russell Simmons recommended the elimination of the "n," "b" and "h" words in popular music. Others have also made statements against the racism, sexism, violence, homophobia, and hyper-masculinity in hip-hop, including filmmaker Byron Hurt in his award-winning film "Hip Hop: beyond Beats and Rhymes." (To see parts of this film via YouTube, check out http://www.bhurt.com/beyondBeatsAndRhymes.php.) Professor Aminah Pilgrim at the University of Massachusetts Boston founded the Hip Hop Initiative in order to "guide hip hop and its listeners in a more positive direction." To this end, the Hip Hop Initiative has assembled a listening list of positive hip-hop and a list of helpful Web sites (contact hiphopforchange@yahoo.com).[3]

A couple of indications of diminishing stereotypes in the media have occurred lately. One is the hiring of an Asian anchor man for a news channel in Champaign, IL in April 2006. Kent Ninomiya is one of very few Asian men to ever receive an anchor appointment. Have you ever seen an Asian anchorman on TV?[4] More recently the soap opera *All My Children* included an episode in which real transgendered people spoke about their experiences in a "support group" for a male-to-female transgendered character in the show.[5]

Theories of the limited images of women in the media examine, among other things, the absence of women in positions of power in the communications industries, as well as the capitalist system that sells products and avoids offending potential consumers with more realistic images.[6] If we add race, sexual orientation, class, disability, and age to what is missing in the centers of power, this absence of many underrepresented groups serves to eliminate accurate images of many groups of people in the media.[7]

The dream that the Internet might create a more level communication playing field, where demographic traits mattered less, has not yet become a reality. Access to the Internet is still tied to social class, race and ethnicity, and education, and women's roles in cyber-related activities and industries are not equal to those of men. High-level computer science jobs are male-dominated, and gender differences in interaction in chat rooms seems to parallel gender differences in other realms of communication. Women are responding to this by establishing technology programs and Internet resources for girls and women generally, for people with disabilities, for low-income people, and for people of color, in order to increase access and to develop Web sites and e-mail lists and bulletins that are designed to be empowering.[8] Although men's use of cyberspace to enhance their access to pornography, sex tours, and sex with children has incensed some feminists who had hoped for better things from the Internet,[9] feminists are finding ways to use this resource creatively.[10]

Two other media trends have been sharply criticized recently. Boston University journalism professor Caryl Rivers, in a book entitled *Selling Anxiety: How the News Media Scare Women* (2007), argues that when professional women are presented in the media, they are typically presented as miserable career people who are facing dilemmas such as limited marriage prospects or poor sex or major childcare hassles. Her examination of social science research data related to women's lives does not support these images of women and she calls upon the media to pay more attention to evidence rather than create unsupported stereotypes. The other theme is outrage at what is marketed to girls. Professors Sharon Lamb and Lyn Mikel Brown argue in their book *Packaging Girlhood* (2006) that girls are being taught to be "pretty pink dolls," "cute little shoppers," and "hot teens" (p. 9). They hope that the book will help parents and girls dissect and analyze the media in order to frame new empowered pathways beyond those of shopper and hyper-feminine sex object.[11]

Literature from men's studies addresses the challenge of men's connections with each other, identifying various aspects of male-male communication that facilitate or impede close friendships. Sociologist Clyde Franklin, for example, identified ways in which upward mobility interrupts Black men's friendships.[12] Michael Messner, in a study of athletes, concluded that male athletes' "covert intimacy"—an intimacy based on doing things together rather than by intimate talk about personal issues—inhibits their ability to develop egalitarian relationships with either men or women.[13] Even when differences such as race and class are not present and power between the people involved is relatively equal, difficulty sharing feelings, intense competition for success, and fear of admitting dependency or vulnerability combine with homophobia to keep men apart in many circumstances in U.S. society.[14]

Communication is difficult because the array of prejudices we learn in childhood frequently follows us into adulthood, often unconsciously. As children, we learn attitudes in situations in which we have little or no control, and we frequently live in families in which communication is far from ideal.[15] Until schools and communities routinely work to help people appreciate diversity, acknowledge differences of power and privilege, listen to each other, and learn peaceful methods of dispute resolution, we are on our own as individuals to improve communication across differences.

This part of the book includes discussions of communication within relationships (Pat Parker, Phil Petrie, and Rosalind Barnett and Caryl Rivers), a discussion of media pressures on mothers (Susan Douglas and Meredith Michaels), a look at a Black woman's ambivalent relationship to hip hop (Ayana Byrd), and a look at whose voices are present in TV commentary on contemporary issues (Laura Zimmerman).

As you read the selections in this part, you might want to think about your own interpersonal relationships as they compare to or contrast with the relationship challenges described by Parker, Barnett and Caryl Rivers, and Petrie. Do you subscribe to the Mars/Venus "difference" approach or does the "similarities" approach that Barnett and Rivers present ring more true? How do your experiences communicating across differences compare with those described by Parker? Have you observed what Douglas and Michaels call the "new momism"? Where do you stand on the ways in which women and men are presented in mainstream hip-hop? Finally, have you noticed the absence of feminist commentators on TV or in major newspapers, as observed by Laura Zimmerman?

NOTES

1. See, for example, Joseph G. Ponterotto et al., eds. *Handbook of Multicultural Counseling* (Thousand Oaks, CA: Sage, 1995); Larry A. Samovar and Richard E. Porter, eds., *Intercultural Communication: A Reader* (Belmont, CA: Wadsworth, 1991). For a report of how different ethnic groups in the United States see each other, including the stereotypes their members hold about each other, see *Taking*

America's Pulse: Summary Report of the National Conference Survey on Inter-Group Relations (New York: National Conference of Christians and Jews, 1994).

2. Elizabeth Hadley Freydberg, "Sapphires, Spitfires, Sluts, and Superbitches: African Americans and Latinas in Contemporary American Film," in Kim Marie Vaz, ed., *Black Women in America* (Thousand Oaks, CA: Sage, 1995), pp. 222–43.

3. Bryan "Breezy" Sullivan, "The Hip Hop Initiative: A Redefinition of Values and Journey into Personal Transformation," *Lux: UMass Boston Student Magazine* 1, no. 2, Spring 2007: 12–13.

4. Kathryn S. Wenner, "Breaking Through," *American Journalism Review*, 25, no. 2 (June–July 2003): 8. http://www.wicd15.com/news/bios/ninomiya.shtml. For a discussion of why there are so few Asian anchormen, see Ben Fong-Torres, "Why Are There No Male Asian Anchormen on TV?" *San Francisco Chronicle*, "Datebook," 13 July 1986, pp. 51–55.

5. Ethan Jacobs, "Trans People Tell Their Stories on *All My Children*," *Bay Windows* 25, no. 12 (March 15–21, 2007): 1ff.

6. For a summary of these theoretical perspectives, see Margaret L. Andersen, *Thinking about Women: Sociological Perspectives on Sex and Gender*, 3rd ed. (New York: Macmillan, 1993), pp. 54–62.

7. For an examination of these issues, see Gail Dines and Jean M. Humez, eds., *Gender, Race, and Class in Media: A Text-Reader* (Thousand Oaks, CA: Sage, 2003).

8. Joyce Slaton, "Mind the Gap: Three Women Working to Close the Digital Divide in Their Own Communities," *Ms.*, April–May 2001, pp. 42–44.

9. Donna Hughes, "The Internet and the Global Prostitution Industry," in Susan Hawthorne and Renate Klein, eds., *Cyberfeminism: Connectivity, Critique, and Creativity* (North Melbourne, Victoria, Australia: Spinifex, 1999).

10. Susan Hawthorne and Renate Klein, eds., *Cyberfeminism: Connectivity, Critique, and Creativity* (North Melbourne, Victoria, Australia: Spinifex, 1999).

11. New Note: Rivers's book was published in 2007 by University Press of New England, Lebanon, NH; Lamb and Brown's was published in 2006 by St. Martin's Press, New York.

12. Clyde Franklin, "'Hey, Home—Yo, Bro': Friendship among Black Men," in Peter Nardi, ed., *Men's Friendships* (Thousand Oaks, CA: Sage, 1992), pp. 201–214.

13. Michael A. Messner, "Like Family: Power, Intimacy, and Sexuality in Male Athletes' Friendships," in Peter Nardi, ed., *Men's Friendships* (Thousand Oaks, CA: Sage, 1992), pp. 215–237.

14. Michael S. Kimmel and Michael A. Messner, eds., *Men's Lives*, 3rd ed. (Boston: Allyn & Bacon, 1995), p. 323; Gregory K. Lehne, "Homophobia among Men: Supporting and Defining the Male Role," in Kimmel and Messner, *Men's Lives*, pp. 325–336.

15. In my years as a teacher and psychotherapist, I have met only a small proportion of people who would like to continue using the communication patterns of the adults in the households in which they grew up; more frequently, they experienced successful communication with siblings—enjoying the relative equality of power that allowed for more open communication.

24

FOR THE WHITE PERSON WHO WANTS TO KNOW HOW TO BE MY FRIEND

PAT PARKER

Pat Parker, Black lesbian poet, feminist medical administrator, mother of two daughters, lover of women, softball devotee, and general progressive troublemaker, died of breast cancer on June 17, 1989, at the age of 45. Her 1978 work, *Movement in Black*, has recently been republished by Firebrand Books.

The first thing you do is to forget that i'm black.
Second, you must never forget that i'm black.

You should be able to dig Aretha,
but don't play her every time i come over.
And if you decide to play Beethoven—don't tell me
his life story. They make us take music appreciation too.

Eat soul food if you like it, but don't expect me
to locate your restaurants
or cook it for you.

And if some Black person insults you,
mugs you, rapes your sister, rapes you,
rips your house or is just being an ass—
please, do not apologize to me
for wanting to do them bodily harm.
It makes me wonder if you're foolish.

And even if you really believe Blacks are better lovers than
Whites—don't tell me. I start thinking of charging stud fees.

In other words—if you really want to be my friend—*don't*
make a labor of it. I'm lazy. Remember.

25

MEN AND WOMEN ARE FROM EARTH

ROSALIND BARNETT • CARYL RIVERS

Rosalind Barnett is a senior scientist at Brandeis University and director of its Community, Families, and Work Program.

Caryl Rivers is a professor of journalism at Boston University and is a nationally known columnist, author, journalist and media critic. Barnett and Rivers coauthored *She Works/He Works: How Two-Income Families Are Happier, Healthier, and Better-Off* (2007). They are also the authors of *Same Difference: How Gender Myths Are Hurting Our Relationships, Our Children, and Our Jobs* (2005).

D o men and women come from two separate "communication cultures" that make it difficult for them to hear one another? Are they doomed to moan, eternally, "You just don't understand?" Are women the caring, sharing, open sex, while men are hardwired to be strong, silent, self-absorbed, and uncomfortable with emotions? This portrait of the sexes has become conventional wisdom, promoted in best sellers such as John Gray's *Men Are From Mars, Women Are From Venus* and Deborah Tannen's *You Just Don't Understand*. The idea has also leached into the academic and therapy arenas.

The textbook *Language and Social Identity*, by Daniel N. Maltz and Ruth A. Borker, states flatly, "American men and women come from different sociolinguistic subcultures, having learned to do different things with words in a conversation." In this scenario, women are the relationship experts, holding marriages and friendships together by putting others first, avoiding conflict at the cost of their own wishes, and not putting burdens on men by demanding intimacy or understanding. Women speak "in a different voice," as feminist psychologist Carol Gilligan put it, because they are so tuned in to others.

Men, in contrast, lack empathy with others. If a friend or coworker approaches them to talk about problems, they change the subject or make a joke. In personal relationships men don't have a clue, and as parents, they are the inferior sex. They lack the inherent communication abilities necessary for parenting that nature confers on women.

Rosalind Barnett and Caryl Rivers, "Men and Women Are from Earth," from *The Women's Review of Books* 23, no. 2 (March–April 2006): 15–16. Reprinted with permission.

Is this dismal picture accurate? Do the best sellers, some textbooks, and the media's pop psychologists have it right? Are men and women so hamstrung by their communication styles that they are perpetually destined to misunderstand each other—ships eternally passing in the night?

As poetic and familiar as this idea seems, it is more fantasy than fact. New research tears this conventional wisdom to shreds. Women and men are far more alike than different in how they listen to people, the ways they react to others who are in trouble, and their ability to be open and honest in communication. As University of Wisconsin psychologists Kathryn Dindia and Mike Allen say, "It is time to stop perpetuating the myth that there are large sex differences in men's and women's self disclosure."

Women, Deborah Tannen says, use their unique conversational style to show involvement, connection, and participation, while men use speech to indicate independence and position in a hierarchy. Women seek connection and want to be liked, while men just want to press their own agenda. Tannen also states as fact that men always interrupt women.

Is this really how men and women behave? Sometimes yes, sometimes no. Tannen's problem is that she often sees gender as the main driver of communication, ignoring a whole host of other important factors—such as power, individual personalities, and the situation you're in when you are about to speak.

Do men always interrupt women? In fact, the sex differences here are trivial, conclude researchers Kristen Anderson and Campbell Leaper of the University of California at Santa Cruz, based on their meta-analyses of 43 studies. (A meta-analysis summarizes the findings of many studies.) The key to understanding interruptions is the situation—or, as the researchers put it, "The What, When, Where and How." Power is often the key.

Psychologist Elizabeth Aries of Amherst College found that men often interrupt women in conversation. But, when traditional power relationships are reversed—such as in many contemporary couples where the woman is the higher earner, or when male subordinates interact with female superiors—speech patterns also undergo a reversal. The person with less power interrupts less and works harder to keep the conversation going, whether that person is female or male. Those with more power, male or female, are likely to take control of the conversation. Do we really believe that Secretary of State Condoleezza Rice is often interrupted by her male aides? Or that a male law clerk would break into the sentences of Justice Ruth Bader Ginsberg? It's impossible to see the true communication dynamic if we are blinded by the notion that something buried deep in women's psyches chains them to the speech styles of the powerless.

As for men, are they in fact handcuffed by deep-seated inabilities to engage in conversations about emotion? According to essentialist theorists, who believe differences between men and women are innate rather than socially constructed, men are uncomfortable with any kind of communication that has to do with personal conflicts. They avoid talking about their problems. They avoid responding too deeply to other people's problems, instead giving advice, changing the subject, making a joke, or giving no response. Unlike women, they don't react to "troubles talk" by empathizing with others and expressing sympathy. These ideas are often cited in textbooks and in popular manuals, like those written by John Gray, of Mars and Venus fame.

After Gray nabs us with his attention-grabbing titles, he tells us that men are naturally programmed to go into their "caves" and not communicate with other people. Women must never try to talk to men when they withdraw, but must honor their behavior. A woman must not offer help to a man, because it makes him feel weak and incompetent. A woman must never criticize a man or try to change his behavior. She should never show anger. If she feels angry, she must wait until she is "more loving and centered" to talk to him. Only when she is loving and forgiving can she share her feelings. If a man pulls away from her, "He is just fulfilling a valid need to take care of himself for a while."

Gray cites the case of "Bill," who asks his wife, "Mary," to make a phone call for him while he is sitting on the couch watching TV. Mary reacts with a frustrated and helpless tone of voice. She says, "I can't right now, I already have too much to do, I have to change the baby's diaper, I have to clean up this mess, balance the checkbook, finish the wash, and tonight we are going out to a movie. I have too much to do. I just can't do it all!"

Bill goes back to watching TV and disconnects from her feelings. Bill, says Gray, is angry at Mary for making him feel like a failure. He retreats to his cave, "just taking care of himself." If Mary realized this, Gray suggests, she would smile at his request to do still one more chore and say sweetly that she's running behind. As for Bill, all he has to do, Gray suggests, is to say admiringly to Mary, "I just don't know how you do it!"

That line might just get Bill a damp diaper in the face. Gray does not suggest that Bill might a) change the baby's diaper; b) help clean up the house; c) balance the checkbook; or d) help with the wash.

Who has the power in this marriage—and isn't this really the issue? Gray's scenario puts women in a tight bind, while requiring little from men. Gray's prescription for heterosexual relationships is for the woman to leave the man alone while she supervises the kids' homework, cooks dinner, and cleans up. That's advice that gets couples into trouble, not out of it. A woman who takes Gray's advice at face value may be at serious risk for high stress. Unable to express her anger openly and to ask for what she really needs, always on edge because she must sense a man's every whim and need, she is likely to turn her anger inward.

This situation makes her communication inauthentic. She feels anger, but can't communicate it, and as a result she feels worse and worse about herself and her marriage. She is living a lie—and how good can anyone feel about that? On top of that, her husband has no idea of what she's feeling. There's no way he could be the helpful person he may actually want to be.

In fact, if women expected men to be unable to relate to other people's problems, they would never bother talking to men about such things.

Systematic research does not support those ideas. Erina L. MacGeorge, of Purdue University, and her colleagues at the University of Pennsylvania find no support for the idea that women and men constitute different "communication cultures." Based on three studies that used questionnaires and interviews to sample 738 people—417 women and 321 men—they conclude that: "Both men and women view the provision of support as a central element of close personal relationships; both value the supportive communication skills of their friends, lovers, and family members; both make similar judgments about what counts as sensitive, helpful support; and both respond quite similarly to various support efforts." When someone comes to men with a problem, they don't joke, tell the person to cheer up, change the topic, or run away as Gray and Tannen suggest they do. Both sexes are instead likely to offer sympathy and advice.

If men are having a problem, and someone offers a sympathetic response, they don't get angry, minimize, or push the other person away. Like women, they are comforted when people are concerned about them. There are no differences in how men and women handle emotional issues—theirs or others'. Kristen Neff of the University of Texas at Austin and Susan Harter of the University of Denver uncovered a similar lack of difference in men's and women's styles of conflict resolution. They found that 62 percent of men and 61 percent of women reported that they typically resolved conflicts in their relationships by compromising with their partners. This is a far cry from the idea that women always retreat, and men always insist on getting their way.

Similar doubts have also been raised about the "fact" that men can't share their feelings, and that they always retreat to their caves or take refuge in silence. A huge meta-analysis of 24,000 subjects in 205 peer-reviewed studies found that women disclose slightly more that men—but the effect was trivial. Practically speaking, there were no differences between the sexes.

Because therapists (and others) contend that the ability to self-disclose is crucial to success in therapy, they often believe that men's chances of being helped are relatively poor. But this is not so, according these research findings.

Even more importantly, the idea that women can't expect men to share, to lend a sympathetic ear, to compromise in settling issues, or to be good listeners can have disastrous consequences. Women who cling to such stereotypes will miss out on close relationships with their male partners and of course men will be further pigeonholed as distant, remote, and unavailable creatures. If that's how they are treated, maybe that's what they will turn into. And if men assume that women are too emotional to discuss problems rationally, they will simply clam up and miss the help and support they really need. Either way, rigid sex stereotypes promote self-fulfilling prophecies.

Unfortunately, the essentialist perspective has so colored the dialogue about the sexes that there is scant room for any narrative other than difference. As we've seen, the difference rhetoric can harm both men and women. Given how little empirical support exists for essentialist ideas, it's high time to broaden the dialogue. We believe that men and women are far more similar than different, a provocative idea that is backed by considerable research. We challenge the conventional wisdom, and we encourage others to do the same.

26

REAL MEN DON'T CRY . . . AND OTHER "UNCOOL" MYTHS

PHIL W. PETRIE

Phil W. Petrie is a freelance writer in New Jersey.

Things were not going well. Do they ever for young couples struggling to understand each other, raise a family, pay the mortgage and at least keep the Joneses in sight? I had wanted to comfort my pregnant wife, soothe her with words that would temper the harshness of our reality. The baby was due in two months and my employer had just informed me that I didn't have hospitalization coverage for childbirth. I was frustrated and wanted to scream, lay my head in my wife's lap and cry. I needed to be soothed as well as she. She wanted to talk about our predicament, needed to talk it out. So did I, but I couldn't. I felt that I had failed her. Guilt stood at my side. But how could she know any of that, since all I did was to turn on the stereo system—my electronic security blanket—and listen to Miles Davis. I was cool. Her words shot through the space of "All Blues." "You're a cold SOB," she hissed.

She's being emotional again, I thought, *Just like a woman.* I, on the other hand, was controlling the situation because I was cool— which in reality was only a few degrees away from being cold.

Phil W. Petrie, "Real Men Don't Cry . . . and Other 'Uncool' Myths" from *Essence* (November 1982), p. 73ff. Reprinted with the permission of the author.

Wasn't that what she really wanted from me as head of the household—control? Wasn't Freud correct when he proclaimed that our anatomy was our destiny (that is, our genitals determine our behavior)? In spite of her protestations that we had to talk, there was nothing in my upbringing that negated for me the power of coolness. I knew by the example of my elders that men controlled themselves and women did not.

In Mt. Olive, the Baptist church of my youth, it was expected that the "sisters" would "carry on" at church services. And they did. Moved by something that the preacher had said or by the mystery of a song, they would leap from their seats, run, scream, hurtle down the aisles. Transformed. Private feeling was suddenly public spectacle. Ushers came. White-gloved hands brushed away the tears. The men of the church, the elders, sat glued to their seats. I watched, instructed by this example of male control. I watched in silence but wished that I could know the electric transformation that moved those souls to dance.

"The larger culture creates expectations for males," says Dr. Walter Tardy, a psychiatrist in New York City. "In spite of the Women's Liberation Movement, men still live in a very macho culture and role play. Women tend to display their feelings more."

One of the roles men play is that of the rational being devoid of strong emotions. Profound feelings, it is thought, will interfere with the male task, whether that means making it at the nine-to-five or making it at war. Objective decisions must be made without distracting emotions, which women are thought to be prone to—even by some other women. For many persons, "being a man" is synonymous with being emotionless—cool.

One need not be told this. Like air, it seems to be a pervasive part of the male atmosphere. If one missed it at church (as I did not), one might pick it up at the barbershop or the playground—places where the elements of the culture are passed on without the benefit of critical examination.

Didn't Wimpy Sheppard tell me at Tom Simon's Barbershop that only babies, women and sissies cried? A man, he said, ain't supposed to cry. That's why my father, at the death of his mother, slipped out to the backyard away from his family to sit among the chickens and wail. How could I explain to my wife—to myself— that I couldn't rest my head in her lap and weep? I had to protect my masculinity. Asking me to cry, to drop my cool, was asking me to redefine my life.

Says Margo Williams, a widow residing in San Diego, California, with her two children, "If you can't let down to your mate, friend or what have you, then you have to ask yourself what the relationship is all about—is it worth being involved with? For me, it's not about my man being strong and hard. I want him to be a human being—warm, sensitive and willing to share his life with me."

What if he balks? Williams is asked. "If the relationship is a serious one, I would urge him to let us try to work through the problems," she says. "I would want to establish a relationship wherein we could express to each other our needs and wants—even express our dislikes. We have to establish an honest relationship."

Dr. Tardy cautions that "there are degrees of honesty. Do you tell the truth all of the time, or is a white lie something appropriate? One can only be just so honest. The truth may set you free, but some truths should be withheld because they can hurt more than they help. But even if you don't tell it all, you must tell *something*. Communication is the key."

Therein lies the danger of being cool and playing roles. In doing this, one reveals a persona rather than a person, plays a part rather than being part of the relationship. Communication, by its root definition, means "sharing, making something common between people." It is this fear of sharing—giving up something—that drives some men into being noncommunicative except in the area of sex.

Robert Staples, a sociologist, states in his book *Black Masculinity* (Black Scholar Press) that when Black men "have been unable to achieve status in the workplace, they have exercised the privilege of their manliness and attempted to achieve it [power] in the bedroom. Feeling a constant need to affirm their masculinity, tenderness and compassion are eschewed as signs of weakness, which leaves them vulnerable to the ever-feared possibility of female domination."

It could be argued that in today's climate of women's liberation, all men are on the defensive because of the developing assertiveness of women. No doubt some men—if not many—use sex as a controlling force. "But," says Wilbur Suesberry, a pediatrician practicing in Compton, California, "I don't believe that sex is racially restrictive. Black sexuality is a myth started and supported by whites and perpetuated by Blacks. Men find it difficult to express their inner feelings but they must find a way to do it. If you have things pent up inside of you and they do not come out in a healthy way, then they exit in an unhealthy way. Sex as an outlet for your emotions is not good. To communicate you can't sulk or take to the bed, you must talk." Talk? Yes, talk is a more precise method of communicating than sex, intuition or an "understanding."

> "The birth is due in two months," she persisted. "What are we going to do?" Annoyed, not at her but at the apparent futility of the situation, I turned up the record player and went deeper into myself. Didn't she *understand* me well enough to know that I would do something? Hadn't I always? Couldn't she look at me and see that I was worried too? Didn't she *trust* me well enough to know that I would do something? All of those questions might have been eliminated with my telling her simply and directly what my feelings really were. How could she really know them unless she

were a mind reader, just as I didn't know what she felt? Screaming
and crying isn't quite the same thing as communicating effectively.
I pulled her to me, caressed her.

Hugging and kissing are not substitutes for words, for language. Talking
to each other allows us to bring order to the disruption and confusion engen-
dered by silence. *Talk to me,* Little Willie John used to sing, *talk to me in your
own sweet gentle way.*

This simple verbal act is made all the more difficult for men (and women,
for that matter) if we don't know (or won't admit) what our feelings really are.
We can't talk about things if we can't conceptualize them. Communication is
more than mouthing words or rapping. I see it as defining an aspect of one's
life by framing that aspect into words and then sharing it with someone. It
is not only a problem for lovers; it also bedevils fathers and sons, mothers and
daughters. It is problematic because it drives you within. The first act of
communication is with your self—"the private self," Dr. Tardy calls it. This
journey within involves both introspection and openness.

Yet what I face within myself—if indeed I face it—may never be completely shared with anyone. An insistence that I communicate *all* of my feelings is asking too much. We men are now being urged not only to redefine
our roles and relationships with our mates and society but also to become
vulnerable by revealing our private selves to another public, although it may
be a public of only one. The degree to which I can do this—express *some* of
my feelings—is determined by the self-awareness I have of myself and the
trust I have for my spouse.

I closet my feelings out of self-protection and fear of the unknown.
Women in their newfound drive for liberation have the example of men to direct them. It seems that all women are asking for are some of the prerogatives
once claimed by men only. But what is to be the model for me? White men? I
think not. Granted they are the movers and shakers within this society, but
the madness of the world that they have created does not make them legitimate role models. Yet for many Black women the term *man* is synonymous
with *white man.* I resent being asked to pattern myself after a man whose
reality—full of avarice and destruction—is so antithetical to mine. I hold on
to my cool.

For Black men, being cool is not just an attitude; it becomes a political
stance, a metaphor for power. To give that up is, in effect, to render oneself
powerless—to lose control. For Black men, who control so little, to lose this cool
is to lose a weapon in their arsenal for survival. Do Black women know that?

> "Maybe you could call somebody [white?] who can help," she
> suggested, determined to get a word out of me. And if I can't find
> someone white to help us with my problems, I thought, then I can
> fold up and cry to you. Ugh. Is this what you ask of me: to imitate
> white men or act like women (that is, take control or cry)? What
> brave new world are you asking me to enter into by dropping my

cool, discarding my role as leader, drowning my strength with tears? It is a scenario that no other group of men in history has ever played. Yet you ask me, the most politically weak person within the society, to lead the way to this new world. How can you ask me that, baby? And if I go, will you cast me aside as being weak? You scream about a man who is strong enough to cry, strong enough to admit weaknesses, and at the same time you want a "take-charge" person, a man who won't let anyone run over him. Caught between such confusion, I turn to the ball game, to the television, to the silence within myself. Love is withheld. Restrained. Tentative.

"I think that our generation is too tentative," says Lee Atkins, a publishing-company sales representative living in Chicago. "Those of us born in the 1940's and before were given too many caveats. Black men or boys were told not to do this and not to do that. Avoid the police. Stay out of trouble. All of this was done to protect us in an extremely racist and hostile society. In effect, we were being told: behave or you will be destroyed." That made us cautious and we are now paying the price for all that caution. As men we find that we are too careful, too private, not open and not willing to explore. We find it difficult to open up even to those we care about the most.

"Those kids born in the 1950's and 1960's," Atkins continues, "were born into a world where the expectations for the Black male were more positive. A whole set of new possibilities was suddenly available. Sexually, things were more permissive, and in the do-your-own-thing attitude of the 1960's and 1970's Black men were actually encouraged to be more unconventional, to open up."

This has led to young Black men who are more candid about their feelings, more carefree in their attitudes. "I would be surprised," says Dr. Tardy, "if these young adults weren't more open in their dealings with each other. The drawback may be that they don't want to establish the permanent relations that were expected in the past. I can imagine that many young women will say that the young men today aren't 'serious' or are too much into themselves. That's the legacy of hanging loose."

Whether we are young or old, one thing is certain: we men cannot expect to go through a lifetime in silence, repressing our feelings, denying our emotions, without being run down by frustrations, failed opportunities and unfulfilled promises. And why would we do this? Is it because of the protrusion dangling between our legs? Is it because we hold on to a fixed role in a changing world? Or is it because of our fear of losing an imagined power? Perhaps the answer is all of the above. If so, we must rush to get rid of these contrived ghosts. In the real world our women are calling to us. How long will they keep it up before they give up? Or as writer Amiri Baraka asks, "How long till the logic of our lives runs us down?"

She stood before me pleading, belly swollen with my seed. She wasn't asking for much, just that I talk to her. She was richly human and was demanding that I be nothing less, saying that I couldn't be a man until I showed that I was human—warm, tender, compassionate, feeling, and able to express that feeling. It was difficult, but with a guide so dedicated to my good health I began the journey from within to without that day. We found the money for the hospital. But more important, I found that I could talk to her about me, could share my life in trust with her. I write this as a souvenir of remembrance—a gift for her.

27

THE NEW MOMISM

SUSAN J. DOUGLAS • MEREDITH W. MICHAELS

Susan J. Douglas is the Catherine Neafie Kellogg Professor of Communication Studies at the University of Michigan. She is author of *Listening In: Radio and the American Imagination* (2004), *Where the Girls Are: Growing Up Female with the Mass Media* (1995), and *Inventing American Broadcasting, 1899–1922 (1989).*

Meredith W. Michaels teaches philosophy at Smith College and writes about ethics and ideologies of reproduction and parenthood.

It's 5:22 P.M. You're in the grocery checkout line. Your three-year-old is writhing on the floor, screaming, because you have refused to buy her a Teletubby pinwheel. Your six-year-old is whining, repeatedly, in a voice that could saw through cement, "But mommy, puleeze, puleeze" because you have not bought him the latest "Lunchables," which features, as the four food groups, Cheetos, a Snickers, Cheez Whiz, and Twizzlers. Your teenager, who has not spoken a single word in the past four days except, "You've ruined my life," followed by "Everyone else has one," is out in the car, sulking, with the new rap-metal band Piss on the Parentals blasting through the headphones of a Discman.

To distract yourself, and to avoid the glares of other shoppers who have already deemed you the worst mother in America, you leaf through *People* magazine. Inside, Uma Thurman gushes "Motherhood Is Sexy."[1] Moving on to *Good Housekeeping,* Vanna White says of her child, "When I hear his cry at six-thirty in the morning, I have a smile on my face, and I'm not an early riser."[2] Another unexpected source of earth-mother wisdom, the newly maternal Pamela Lee, also confides to *People,* "I just love getting up with him in the middle of the night to feed him or soothe him."[3] Brought back to reality by stereophonic whining, you indeed feel as sexy as Rush Limbaugh in a thong.

You drag your sorry ass home. Now, if you were a "good" mom, you'd joyfully empty the shopping bags and transform the process of putting the groceries away into a fun game your kids love to play (upbeat Raffi songs would provide a lilting soundtrack). Then, while you steamed the broccoli and poached the chicken breasts in Vouvray and Evian water, you and the kids would also be doing jigsaw puzzles in the shape of the United Arab Emirates so they learned some geography. Your cheerful teenager would say, "Gee, Mom, you gave me the best advice on that last homework assignment." When your husband arrives, he is so overcome with admiration for how well you do it all that he looks lovingly into your eyes, kisses you, and presents you with a diamond anniversary bracelet. He then announces that he has gone on flex time for the next two years so that he can split childcare duties with you fifty-fifty. The children, chattering away happily, help set the table, and then eat their broccoli. After dinner, you all go out and stencil the driveway with autumn leaves.

But maybe this sounds slightly more familiar. "I won't unpack the groceries! You can't make me," bellows your child as he runs to his room, knocking down a lamp on the way. "Eewee—gross out!" he yells and you discover that the cat has barfed on his bed. You have fifteen minutes to make dinner because there's a school play in half an hour. While the children fight over whether to watch *Hot Couples* or people eating larvae on *Fear Factor,* you zap some Prego spaghetti sauce in the microwave and boil some pasta. *You* set the table. "Mommy, Mommy, Sam losted my hamster," your daughter wails. Your ex-husband calls to say he won't be taking the kids this weekend after all because his new wife, Buffy, twenty-three, has to go on a modeling shoot in Virgin Gorda for the *Sports Illustrated* swimsuit issue, and "she really needs me with her." You go to the TV room to discover the kids watching transvestites punching each other out on *Jerry Springer.* The pasta boils over and scalds the hamster, now lying prostrate on the floor with its legs twitching in the air. "Get your butts in here this instant or I'll murder you immediately," you shriek, by way of inviting your children to dinner. "I hate this pasta—I only like the kind shaped like wagon wheels!" "Mommy, you killded my hamster!"

If you're like us—mothers with an attitude problem—you may be getting increasingly irritable about this chasm between the ridiculous, honey-hued ideals of perfect motherhood in the mass media and the reality of mothers' everyday lives. And you may also be worn down by media images that suggest that however much you do for and love your kids, it is never enough. The love we feel for our kids, the joyful times we have with them, are repackaged into unattainable images of infinite patience and constant adoration so that we fear, as Kristin van Ogtrop put it movingly in *The Bitch in the House,* "I will love my children, but my love for them will always be imperfect."[4]

From the moment we get up until the moment we collapse in bed at night, the media are out there, calling to us, yelling, "Hey you! Yeah, you! Are you *really* raising your kids right?" Whether it's the cover of *Redbook* or *Parents* demanding "Are You a Sensitive Mother?" "Is Your Child Eating Enough?" "Is Your Baby Normal?" (and exhorting us to enter its pages and have great sex at 25, 35, or 85), the nightly news warning us about missing children, a movie trailer hyping a film about a cross-dressing dad who's way more fun than his stinky, careerist wife (*Mrs. Doubtfire*), or Dr. Laura telling some poor mother who works four hours a week that she's neglectful, the siren song blending seduction and accusation is there all the time. Mothers are subjected to an onslaught of beatific imagery, romantic fantasies, self-righteous sermons, psychological warnings, terrifying movies about losing their children, even more terrifying news stories about abducted and abused children, and totally unrealistic advice about how to be the most perfect and revered mom in the neighborhood, maybe even in the whole country. (Even *Working Mother*—which should have known better—had a "Working Mother of the Year Contest." When Jill Kirschenbaum became the editor in 2001, one of the first things she did was dump this feature, noting that motherhood should not be a "competitive sport.") We are urged to be fun-loving, spontaneous, and relaxed, yet, at the same time, scared out of our minds that our kids could be killed at any moment. No wonder 81 percent of women in a recent poll said it's harder to be a mother now than it was twenty or thirty years ago, and 56 percent felt mothers were doing a worse job today than mothers back then.[5] Even mothers who deliberately avoid TV and magazines, or who pride themselves on seeing through them, have trouble escaping the standards of perfection, and the sense of threat, that the media ceaselessly atomize into the air we breathe.

We are both mothers, and we adore our kids—for example, neither one of us has ever locked them up in dog crates in the basement (although we have, of course, been tempted). The smell of a new baby's head, tucking a child in at night, receiving homemade, hand-scrawled birthday cards, heart-to-hearts with a teenager after a date, seeing *them* become parents—these are joys parents treasure. But like increasing numbers of women, we are fed up with the myth—shamelessly hawked by the media—that motherhood is eternally fulfilling and rewarding, that it is *always* the best and most important thing you do, that there is only a narrowly prescribed way to do it right, and that if you don't love each and every second of it there's something really wrong with you. At the same time, the two of us still have been complete suckers, buying those black-and-white mobiles that allegedly turn your baby into Einstein Jr., feeling guilty for sending in store-bought cookies to the class bake sale instead of homemade like the "good" moms, staying up until 2:30 A.M. making our kids' Halloween costumes, driving to the Multiplex 18 at midnight to pick up teenagers so they won't miss the latest outing with their friends. We know that building a scale model of Versailles out of mashed potatoes may not be quite as crucial to good mothering as *Martha Stewart Living* suggests. Yet here we are, cowed by that most tyrannical of our cultural icons, Perfect Mom. So, like millions of women, we buy into these absurd ideals at the same time that we resent them and think they are utterly ridiculous and oppressive. After all, our parents—the group Tom Brokaw has labeled "the greatest generation"—had parents who whooped them on the behind, screamed stuff at them like "I'll tear you limb from limb," told them babies came from cabbage patches, never drove them four hours to a soccer match, and yet they seemed to have nonetheless saved the western world.

This book is about the rise in the media of what we are calling the "new momism": the insistence that no woman is truly complete or fulfilled unless she has kids, that women remain the best primary caretakers of children, and that to be a remotely decent mother, a woman has to devote her entire physical, psychological, emotional, and intellectual being, 24/7, to her children. The new momism is a highly romanticized and yet demanding view of motherhood in which the standards for success are impossible to meet. The term "momism" was initially coined by the journalist Philip Wylie in his highly influential 1942 bestseller *Generation of Vipers,* and it was a very derogatory term. Drawing from Freud (who else?), Wylie attacked the mothers of America as being so smothering, overprotective, and invested in their kids, especially their sons, that they turned them into dysfunctional, sniveling weaklings, maternal slaves chained to the apron strings, unable to fight for their country or even stand on their own two feet.[6] We seek to reclaim this term, rip it from its misogynistic origins, and apply it to an ideology that has snowballed since the 1980s and seeks to return women to the Stone Age.

The "new momism" is a set of ideals, norms, and practices, most frequently and powerfully represented in the media, that seem on the surface to celebrate motherhood, but which in reality promulgate standards of perfection that are beyond your reach. The new momism is the direct descendant and latest version of what Betty Friedan famously labeled the "feminine mystique" back in the 1960s. The new momism *seems* to be much more hip and progressive than the feminine mystique, because now, of course, mothers can and do work outside the home, have their own ambitions and money, raise kids on their own, or freely choose to stay at home with their kids rather than being forced to. And unlike the feminine mystique, the notion that women should be subservient to men is not an accepted tenet of the new momism. Central to the new momism, in fact, is the feminist insistence that women have choices, that they are active agents in control of their own destiny, that they have autonomy. But here's where the distortion of feminism occurs. The only truly enlightened choice to make as a woman, the one that proves, first, that you are a "real" woman, and second, that you are a decent, worthy one, is to become a "mom" and to bring to child rearing a combination of selflessness and professionalism that would involve the cross cloning of Mother Teresa with Donna Shalala. Thus the new momism is deeply contradictory: It both draws from and repudiates feminism.

The fulcrum of the new momism is the rise of a really pernicious ideal in the late twentieth century that the sociologist Sharon Hays has perfectly labeled "intensive mothering."[7] It is no longer okay, as it was even during the heyday of June Cleaver, to let (or make) your kids walk to school, tell them to stop bugging you and go outside and play, or, God forbid, serve them something like Tang, once the preferred beverage of the astronauts, for breakfast. Of course many of our mothers baked us cookies, served as Brownie troop leaders, and chaperoned class trips to Elf Land. But today, the standards of good motherhood are really over the top. And they've gone through the roof at the same time that there has been a real decline in leisure time for most Americans.[8] The yuppie work ethic of the 1980s, which insisted that even when you were off the job you should be working—on your abs, your connections, your portfolio, whatever—absolutely conquered motherhood. As the actress Patricia Heaton jokes in *Motherhood & Hollywood,* now mothers are supposed to "sneak echinacea" into the "freshly squeezed, organically grown orange juice" we've made for our kids and teach them to "download research for their kindergarten report on 'My Family Tree—The Early Roman Years.'"[9]

Intensive mothering insists that mothers acquire professional-level skills such as those of a therapist, pediatrician ("Dr. Mom"), consumer products safety inspector, and teacher, and that they lavish every ounce of physical vitality they have, the monetary equivalent of the gross domestic product of Australia, and, most of all, every single bit of their emotional, mental, and psychic energy on their kids. We must learn to put on the masquerade of the doting, self-sacrificing mother and wear it at all times. With intensive mothering, everyone watches us, we watch ourselves and other mothers, and we watch ourselves watching ourselves. How many of you know someone who swatted her child on the behind in a supermarket because he was, say, opening a pack of razor blades in the toiletries aisle, only to be accosted by someone she never met who threatened to put her up on child-abuse charges? In 1997, one mother was arrested for child neglect because she left a ten-year-old and a four-year-old home for an hour and a half while she went to the supermarket.[10] Motherhood has become a psychological police state.

Intensive mothering is the ultimate female Olympics: We are all in powerful competition with each other, in constant danger of being trumped by the mom down the street, or in the magazine we're reading. The competition isn't just over who's a good mother—it's over who's the best. We compete with each other; we compete with ourselves. The best mothers always put their kids' needs before their own, period. The best mothers are the main caregivers. For the best mothers, their kids are the center of the universe. The best mothers always smile. They always understand. They are never tired. They never lose their temper. They never say, "Go to the neighbor's house and play while Mommy has a beer." Their love for their children is boundless, unflagging, flawless, total. Mothers today cannot just respond to their kids' needs, they must predict them—and with the telepathic accuracy of Houdini. They must memorize verbatim the books of all the child-care experts and know which approaches are developmentally appropriate at different ages. They are supposed to treat their two-year-olds with "respect." If mothers screw up and fail to do this on any given day, they should apologize to their kids, because any misstep leads to permanent psychological and/or physical damage. Anyone who questions whether this is *the* best and *the* necessary way to raise kids is an insensitive, ignorant brute. This is just common sense, right?[11]

The new momism has become unavoidable, unless you raise your kids in a yurt on the tundra, for one basic reason: Motherhood became one of the biggest media obsessions of the last three decades, exploding especially in the mid-1980s and continuing unabated to the present. Women have been deluged by an ever-thickening mudslide of maternal media advice, programming, and marketing that powerfully shapes how we mothers feel about our relationships with our own kids and, indeed, how we feel about ourselves. These media representations have changed over time, cutting mothers some real slack in the 1970s, and then increasingly closing the vise in the late 1980s and after, despite important rebellions by Roseanne and others. People don't usually notice that motherhood has been such a major media fixation, revolted or hooked as they've been over the years by other media excesses like the O. J. Simpson trials, the Lewinsky-Clinton imbroglio, the Elian Gonzalez carnival, *Survivor,* or the 2002 Washington-area sniper killings in which "profilers" who knew as much as SpongeBob SquarePants nonetheless got on TV to tell us what the killer was thinking.

But make no mistake about it—mothers and motherhood came under unprecedented media surveillance in the 1980s and beyond. And since the media traffic in extremes, in anomalies—the rich, the deviant, the exemplary, the criminal, the gorgeous—they emphasize fear and dread on the one hand and promote impossible ideals on the other. In the process, *Good Housekeeping, People,* E!, Lifetime, *Entertainment Tonight,* and *NBC Nightly News* built an interlocking, cumulative image of the dedicated, doting "mom" versus the delinquent, bad "mother." There have been, since the early 1980s, several overlapping media frameworks that have fueled the new momism. First, the media warned mothers about the external threats to their kids from abductors and the like. Then the "family values" crowd made it clear that supporting the family was not part of the government's responsibility. By the late 1980s, stories about welfare and crack mothers emphasized the internal threats to children from mothers themselves. And finally, the media brouhaha over the "Mommy Track" reaffirmed that businesses could not or would not budge much to accommodate the care of children. Together, and over time, these frameworks produced a prevailing common sense that only you, the individual mother, are responsible for your child's welfare: The buck stops with you, period, and you'd better be a superstar.

Of course there has been a revolution in fatherhood over the past thirty years, and millions of men today tend to the details of child rearing in ways their own fathers rarely did. Feminism prompted women to insist that men change diapers and pack school lunches, but it also gave men permission to become more involved with their kids in ways they have found to be deeply satisfying. And between images of cuddly, New Age dads with babies asleep on their chests (think old Folger's ads), movies about hunky men and a baby (or clueless ones who shrink the kids), and sensational news stories about "deadbeat dads" and men who beat up their sons' hockey coaches, fathers too have been subject to a media "dad patrol." But it pales in comparison to the new momism. After all, a dad who knows the name of his kids' pediatrician and reads them stories at night is still regarded as a saint; a mother who doesn't is a sinner.

Once you identify it, you see the new momism everywhere. The recent spate of magazines for "parents" (i.e., mothers) bombard the anxiety-induced mothers of America with reassurances that they can (after a $100,000 raise and a personality transplant) produce bright, motivated, focused, fun-loving, sensitive, cooperative, confident, contented kids just like the clean, obedient ones on the cover. The frenzied hypernatalism of the women's magazines alone (and that includes *People, Us,* and *InStyle*), with their endless parade of perfect, "sexy" celebrity moms who've had babies, adopted babies, been to sperm banks, frozen their eggs for future use, hatched the frozen eggs, had more babies, or adopted a small Tibetan village, all to satisfy their "baby lust," is enough to make you want to get your tubes tied. (These profiles always insist that celebs all love being "moms" much, much more than they do their work, let alone being rich and famous, and that they'd spend every second with their kids if they didn't have that pesky blockbuster movie to finish.) Women without children, wherever they look, are besieged by ridiculously romantic images that insist that having children is the most joyous, fulfilling experience in the galaxy, and if they don't have a small drooling creature who likes to stick forks in electrical outlets, they are leading bankrupt, empty lives. Images of ideal moms and their miracle babies are everywhere, like leeches in the Amazon, impossible to dislodge and sucking us dry.

There is also the ceaseless outpouring of books on toilet training, separating one sibling's fist from another sibling's eye socket, expressing breast milk while reading a legal brief, helping preschoolers to "own" their feelings, getting Joshua to do his homework, and raising teenage boys so they become Sensitive New Age Guys instead of rooftop snipers or Chippendale dancers. Over eight hundred books on motherhood were published between 1970 and 2000; only twenty-seven of these came out between 1970 and 1980, so the real avalanche happened in the past twenty years.[12] We've learned about the perils of "the hurried child" and "hyperparenting," in which we schedule our kids with so many enriching activities that they make the secretary of state look like a couch spud. But the unhurried child probably plays too much Nintendo and is out in the garage building pipe bombs, so you can't underschedule them either.

Then there's the Martha Stewartization of America, in which we are meant to sculpt the carrots we put in our kids' lunches into the shape of peonies and build funhouses for them in the backyard; this has raised the bar to even more ridiculous levels than during the June Cleaver era. Most women know that there was a massive public relations campaign during World War II to get women into the workforce, and then one right after the war to get them to go back to the kitchen. But we haven't fully focused on the fact that another, more subtle, sometimes unintentional, more long-term propaganda campaign began in the 1980s to redomesticate the women of America through motherhood.[13] Why aren't all the mothers of America leaning out their windows yelling "I'm mad as hell and I'm not going to take it anymore"?

So the real question is how did the new momism—especially in the wake of the women's movement—become part of our national common sense? Why have mothers—who have entered the workforce in droves at exactly the same time that intensive mothering conquered notions of parenting—bought into it? Are there millions of us who conform to the ideals of the new momism on the outside, while also harboring powerful desires for rebellion that simply can't be satisfied by a ten-minute aromatherapy soak in the bathtub?

There are several reasons why the new momism—talk about the wrong idea for the wrong time—triumphed when it did. Baby boom women who, in the 1970s, sought to enter schools and jobs previously reserved for men knew they couldn't be just as good as the guys—they had to be better, in part to dispel the myths that women were too stupid, irrational, hysterical, weak, flighty, or unpredictable during "that time of the month" to manage a business, report the news, wear a stethoscope, or sell real estate. Being an overachiever simply went with the terrain of breaking down barriers, so it wouldn't be surprising to find these women bringing that same determination to motherhood. And some of us did get smacked around as kids, or had parents who crushed our confidence, and we did want to do a better job than that. One brick in the wall of the new momism.

Many women, who had started working in the 1970s and postponed having children, decided in the 1980s to have kids. Thus, this was a totally excellent time for the federal government to insist that it was way too expensive to support any programs for families and children (like maternity leave or subsidized, high-quality day care or even decent public schools) because then the U.S. couldn't afford that $320 billion appropriation to the Pentagon, which included money for those $1600 coffee makers and $600 toilet seats the military needed so badly in 1984.[14] (Imagine where we'd be today if the government had launched the equivalent of the G.I. bill for mothers in the 1980s!) Parents of baby boomers had seen money flow into America's schools because of the Sputnik scare that the Russkies were way ahead of the U.S. in science and technology; thus the sudden need to reacquaint American kids with a slide rule. Parents in the 1980s saw public schools hemorrhaging money. So the very institutions our mothers had been able to count on now needed massive CPR, while the prospect of any new ones was, we were told, out of the question. Guess who had to take up the slack? Another brick in the wall of the new momism.

The right wing of the Republican party—which controlled the White House from 1980 to 1992, crucial years in the evolution of motherhood—hated the women's movement and believed all women, with the possible exception of Phyllis Schlafly, should remain in the kitchen on their knees polishing their husband's shoes and golf clubs while teaching their kids that Darwin was a very bad man. (Unless the mothers were poor and black—those moms had to get back to work ASAP, because by staying home they were wrecking the country. . . .) We saw, in the 1980s and beyond, the rise of what the historian Ruth Feldstein has called "mother-blaming," attacks on mothers for failing to raise physically and psychologically fit future citizens.[15] See, no one, not even Ronald Reagan, said explicitly to us, "The future and the destiny of the nation are in your hands, oh mothers of America. And you are screwing up." But that's what he meant. Because not only are mothers supposed to reproduce the nation biologically, we're also supposed to regenerate it culturally and morally. Even after the women's movement, mothers were still expected to be the primary socializers of children.[16] Not only were our individual kids' well-being our responsibility, but also the entire fate of the nation supposedly rested on our padded and milk-splotched shoulders. So women's own desires to be good parents, their realization that they now had to make up for collapsing institutions, and all that guilt-tripping about "family values" added many more bricks to the wall.

But we are especially interested in the role that the mass media played, often inadvertently, and often, mind you, in the name of *helping* mothers—in making the new momism a taken-for-granted, natural standard of how women should imagine their lives, conceive of fulfillment, arrange their priorities, and raise their kids. After all, the media have been and are the major dispenser of the ideals and norms surrounding motherhood: Millions of us have gone to the media for nuts-and-bolts child-rearing advice. Many of us, in fact, preferred media advice to the advice our mothers gave us. We didn't want to be like our mothers and many of us didn't want to raise our kids the way they raised us (although it turns out they did a pretty good job in the end).

Thus, beginning in the mid-1970s, working mothers became the most important thing you can become in the United States: a market. And they became a market just as niche marketing was exploding—the rise of cable channels, magazines like *Working Mother, Family Life, Child,* and *Twins,* all supported by advertisements geared specifically to the new, modern mother. Increased emphasis on child safety, from car seats to bicycle helmets, increased concerns about Johnny not being able to read, the recognition that mothers bought cars, watched the news, and maybe didn't want to tune into one TV show after the next about male detectives with a cockatoo or some other dumbass mascot saving hapless women—all contributed to new shows, ad campaigns, magazines, and TV news stories geared to mothers, especially affluent, upscale ones. Because of this sheer increase in output and target marketing, mothers were bombarded as never before by media constructions of the good mother. The good mother bought all this stuff to stimulate, protect, educate, and indulge her kids. She had to assemble it, install it, use it with her child, and protect her child from some of its features. As all this media fare sought to advise mothers, flatter them, warn them and, above all, sell to them, they collaborated in constructing, magnifying, and reinforcing the new momism.

Here's the rub about the new momism. It began to conquer our psyches just as mothers entered the workforce in record numbers, so those of us who work (and those of us who don't) are pulled between two rather powerful and contradictory cultural riptides: Be more doting and self-sacrificing at home than Bambi's mother, yet more achievement-oriented at work than Madeleine Albright.[17] The other set of values that took hold beginning in the 1980s was "free-market ideology": the notion that competition in "the marketplace" (which supposedly had the foresight and wisdom of Buddha) provided the best solutions to all social, political, and economic problems. So on the job we were—and are—supposed to be highly efficient, calculating, tough, judgmental and skeptical, competitive, and willing to do what it takes to promote ourselves, our organization, and beat out the other guys. Many work environments in the 1980s and '90s emphasized increased productivity and piled on more work, kids or no kids, because that's what "the market" demanded. Television shows offered us role models of the kind of tough broads who succeeded in this environment, from the unsmiling, take-no-prisoners DA Joyce Davenport on *Hill Street Blues* to Judge Judy and the no-nonsense police lieutenant Anita Van Buren on *Law & Order.* So the competitive go-getter at work had to walk through the door at the end of the day and, poof, turn into Carol Brady: selfless doormat at home. No wonder some of us feel like Sybil when we get home: We have to move between these riptides on a daily basis. And, in fact, many of us want to be both women: successful at work, successful as mothers.

Now, here's the real beauty of this contorting contradiction. Both working mothers *and* stay-at-home mothers get to be failures. The ethos of intensive mothering has lower status in our culture ("stay-at-home mothers are boring"), but occupies a higher moral ground ("working mothers are neglectful").[18] So, welcome to the latest media catfight: the supposed war between working mothers and stay-at-home mothers. Why analyze all the ways in which our country has failed to support families while inflating the work ethic to the size of the *Hindenburg* when you can, instead, project this paradox onto what the media have come to call, incessantly, "the mommy wars." The "mommy wars" puts mothers into two, mutually exclusive categories—working mother versus stay-at-home mother, and never the twain shall meet. It goes without saying that they allegedly hate each other's guts. In real life, millions of mothers move between these two categories, have been one and then the other at various different times, creating a mosaic of work and child-rearing practices that bears no resemblance to the supposed ironclad roles suggested by the "mommy wars."[19] Not only does this media catfight pit mother against mother, but it suggests that all women be reduced to their one role—mother—or get cut out of the picture entirely.

At the same time that the new momism conquered the media outlets of America, we also saw mothers who talked back. *Maude,* Ann Romano on *One Day at a Time,* Erma Bombeck, Peg Bundy, *Roseanne,* Brett Butler, Marge Simpson, and the mothers in *Malcolm in the Middle* and *Everybody Loves Raymond* have all given the new momism a big Bronx cheer. They have represented rebellious mothering: the notion that you can still love your kids and be a good mother without teaching them Origami, explaining factor analysis to them during bath time, playing softball with them at six A.M., or making sure they have a funny, loving note in their lunch box each and every day. Since 1970, because of money and politics, the new momism has conquered much of the media, and thus our own self-esteem. But it has not done so uncontested. The same media that sell and profit from the new momism have also given us permission—even encouraged us—to resist it. However, it is important to note that much of this rebellion has occurred in TV sitcoms which, with a few exceptions, offer primarily short-term catharsis, a brief respite from the norms in dramatic programming, the news, and advice columns that bully us so effectively.

• • •

Because the media always serve up heroes and villains, there had to be the terrible mothers, the anti-Madonnas, the hideous counterexamples good mothers were meant to revile. We regret to report that nearly all of these women were African American and were disproportionately featured as failed mothers in news stories about "crack babies," single, teen mothers, and welfare mothers. One of the worst things about the new momism is that it is like a club, where women without kids, or women deemed "bad" mothers, like poor women and welfare mothers, don't belong. It is—with a few exceptions, like Clair Huxtable on *The Cosby Show*—a segregated club.

At the very same time that we witnessed the explosion of white celebrity moms, and the outpouring of advice to and surveillance of middle-class mothers, the welfare mother, trapped in a "cycle of dependency," became ubiquitous in our media landscape, and she came to represent everything wrong with America. She appeared not in the glossy pages of the women's magazines but rather as the subject of news stories about the "crisis" in the American family and the newly declared "war" on welfare mothers. Whatever ailed America—drugs, crime, loss of productivity—was supposedly her fault. She was portrayed as thumbing her nose at intensive mothering. Even worse, she was depicted as bringing her kids into the realm of market values, as putting a price on their heads, by allegedly calculating how much each additional child was worth and then getting pregnant to cash in on them. For middle-class white women in the media, by contrast, their kids were priceless.[20] These media depictions reinforced the divisions between "us" (minivan moms) and "them" (welfare mothers, working-class mothers, teenage mothers), and did so especially along the lines of race.

For example, one of the most common sentences used to characterize the welfare mother was, "Tanya, who has _____ children by _____ different men" (you fill in the blanks). Like zoo animals, their lives were reduced to the numbers of successful impregnations by multiple partners. So it's interesting to note that someone like Christie Brinkley, who has exactly the same reproductive MO, was never described this way. Just imagine reading a comparable sentence in *Redbook*. "Christie B., who has three children by three different men." But she does, you know.

At the same time that middle- and upper-middle-class mothers were urged to pipe Mozart into their wombs when they're pregnant so their kids would come out perfectly tuned, the government told poor mothers to get the hell out of the house and get to work—no more children's aid for them. Mothers like us—with health care, laptops, and Cuisinarts—are supposed to replicate the immaculate bedrooms we see in Pottery Barn Kids catalogs, with their designer sheets and quilts, one toy and one stuffed animal atop a gleaming white dresser, and a white rug on the floor that has never been exposed to the shavings from hamster cages, Magic Markers accidentally dropped with their caps off, or Welch's grape juice. At the same time, we've been encouraged to turn our backs on other mothers who pick their kids' clothes out of other people's trash and sometimes can't buy a can of beans to feed them. How has it come to seem perfectly reasonable—even justified— that one class of mother is supposed to sew her baby's diapers out of Egyptian cotton from that portion of the Nile blessed by the god Osiris while another class of mother can't afford a single baby aspirin?

NOTES

1. *People*, September 21, 1998.
2. *Good Housekeeping*, January 1995.
3. *People*, July 8, 1996.
4. Kristin van Ogtrop, "Attila the Honey I'm Home," *The Bitch in the House* (New York: William Morrow, 2002), p. 169.
5. "Motherhood Today—A Tougher Job, Less Ably Done," The Pew Research Center for the People & the Press, March 1997.

6. Philip Wylie, *Generation of Vipers* (New York: Holt, Rinehart and Winston, 1942). See also Ruth Feldstein's excellent discussion of momism in *Motherhood in Black and White: Race and Sex in American Liberalism, 1930–1965* (Ithaca: Cornell University Press, 2000), especially chapter 2.

7. Hays's book is must reading for all mothers, and we are indebted to her analysis of intensive mothering, from which this discussion draws. Sharon Hays, *The Cultural Contradictions of Motherhood* (New Haven: Yale University Press, 1996), p. 4.

8. For an account of the decline in leisure time see Juliet B. Schorr, *The Overworked American* (New York: Basic Books, 1992).

9. Patricia Heaton, *Motherhood & Hollywood* (New York: Villard Books, 2002), pp. 48–49.

10. See Katha Pollitt's terrific piece "Killer Moms, Working Nannies" in *The Nation,* November 24, 1997, p. 9.

11. Hays, pp. 4–9.

12. Based on an On-line Computer Library Center, Inc., search under the word *motherhood,* from 1970–2000.

13. Susan Faludi, in her instant classic *Backlash* (New York: Crown Publishers, 1991), made this point, too, but the book focused on the various and multiple forms of backlash, and we will be focusing only on the use of motherhood here.

14. Robert Lekachman, *Visions and Nightmares: America after Reagan* (New York: Collier Books, 1988), pp. 118–121.

15. For a superb analysis of the role of mother-blaming in American politics, see Ruth Feldstein, *Motherhood in Black and White* (Ithaca: Cornell University Press, 2000), especially pp. 7–9.

16. V. Spike Peterson, "Gendered Nationalism: Reproducing 'Us' versus 'Them,'" in A Lois Ann Lorentzen and Jennifer Turpin, eds., *The Women and War Reader* (New York: New York University Press, 1998).

17. This contradiction is central to Hays's argument.

18. Hays, p. 9.

19. Ibid.

20. Hays, p. 8.

28

CLAIMING JEZEBEL:
Black Female Subjectivity and Sexual
Expression in Hip-Hop

AYANA BYRD

Ayana Byrd is a writer and editor living in Brooklyn, New York. She is an entertainment journalist whose work has appeared in *Vibe, Rolling Stone, Honey, TV Guide*, and *Paper* magazines. She is the coauthor of *Hair Story: Untangling the Roots of Black Hair in America* (2001).

All it used to take was one "bitch" reference in a song, one gratuitous ass shake in a video and I was on a roll, criticizing the sexism of black men, denouncing the misogynistic societal structures set up by white men who supported it from their music industry corner offices, lamenting the misrepresented ways that black female bodies were on display. It didn't take much to get me back on my soapbox. But that, apparently, was a long time ago. Because today, allowed a receptive audience and the opportunity to wax passionately and even philosophically about the state of women in hip-hop—the art form that I once believed most defined me—I draw a big blank, barely able to muster up a half-hearted "You won't believe what I just heard . . ."

What happened since my rankled ire over Snoop Doggy Dogg's 1993 *Doggystyle* album cover of a black female behind wiggling, naked, out of a doghouse? Things haven't gotten any better. The "feminist rapper" Queen Latifah now uses the once taboo B word in her lyrics. Alongside Chaka Khan, who sings the hook for "It's All Good," the onetime "conscious" group De La Soul had a video complete with a Jacuzzi overflowing with near-naked women. Since the debut of rap videos, outfits in videos are skimpier, the sexual references lewder, and the complicity by women in their own exploitation more widespread. Yet all I generally feel is an apathy.

I can now listen to a song with the hook "Hoes/I've got hoes/in different area codes" and instead of cringing at thoughts of debasement, chuckle at the artist Ludacris's witty delivery. Maybe it's that I've defined my own sexuality and know for sure what I only suspected in the past—that these men aren't talking about me. The problem is, *they* don't know they're not talking about me. Further, a lot of women, particularly girls and young adults, aren't sure that they don't want to be talked about in this way. These songs, and the videos that illustrate them, offer the most broadly distributed examples of seemingly independent black women that many young and sexually pubescent girls see. And unfortunately few girls transitioning into womanhood understand that the representation of female bodies in rap videos is not an empowering power-of-the-pussy but a fleeting one.

Because I grew up in the 1970s and '80s, I find it easy to list all the people who looked like me that were on television. There was Penny on *Good Times,* Tootie from *The Facts of Life,* and the occasional appearance of Charlene on *Diff'rent Strokes.* In the mid-eighties, there were as well the wholesome Huxtable daughters of *The Cosby Show.* Those of us who came of age then had a near void of images upon which to draw for representations of black women our age, negative or positive. It was a decade devoted both to saving and to condemning the "Endangered Black Male." But teen pregnancy was skyrocketing, and often the predominant young black female faces on television were in public service spots against babies having babies. Yet there were few policies or social organizations that were addressing their need to be saved or uplifted.

As the eighties progressed, things didn't get much better. In film as well as television, portrayals of black women were at either extreme of the sexual spectrum. In Spike Lee's *She's Gotta Have It,* which has been raked over the coals by feminists since its release, the lead, Nola Darling, was, among other atrocities, raped by one of her lovers (the supposed nice one) and got back together with him for a short time. On *The Cosby Show,* the television program that perhaps came closest to engaging and entertaining an entire generation of black kids, the female characters were completely desexed. On one episode we learn that Denise, the "wild child" of the family, was a virgin until her wedding night. Though their cousin Pam and her friend Charmaine both flirt with the idea of "giving it up" to their boyfriends, they seem less interested in actually having sex than in keeping their mates happy.

As popular culture weighed in on young black female sexuality, there were also deeply embedded societal stereotypes with which to contend. The lingering effects of the Moynihan Report, the controversial paper by Daniel Patrick Moynihan, who would later become a U.S. Senator, were still being felt. It asserted that black social immobility was caused by a crisis in the black family, and that Black Superwomen had emasculated black men, causing a fissure in the normal family setting.[1] President Reagan had effectively constructed the idea of the Welfare Mother: a black woman who refused to get a job and be a normal contributor to society but instead sat at home all day (most likely in the projects), maybe hitting the crack pipe, having babies by a host of men, living off welfare checks that came out of the pockets of decent, hardworking (white)

Americans. Outside of academic conferences, few observers pointed out that the majority of women in the country on welfare were white, and that most women stayed on public assistance for two years or less.

By the early nineties there were other messages in which black women were made into villains. While the media highlighted the Tawana Brawley case, in which the fifteen-year-old black girl alleged a racist attack by white police officers but was found by a grand jury to be lying,[2] they virtually ignored the 1990 case of five white student athletes who were charged with sodomy and sexual abuse for repeatedly sexually assaulting a Jamaican woman in a fraternity house at St. John's University. In the latter case, there was more than enough evidence to convict, but according to one juror, the acquittal was based on the jury's desire to save the boys' lives from "ruin." Together the cases colluded in delegitimizing claims of rape by black women. There was also Mike Tyson's 1991 conviction for raping Desiree Washington. As vehemently as the white press sought to turn Tyson into a beast, many blacks cried foul to the champ's imprisonment. "What was she doing in his room anyway?" "That bitch set him up!" "How was she laughing and smiling at the show if just the night before he had raped her?" There was often more talk about how he had been framed than about the fact that Tyson had a history of physical abuse toward women. Around the same time, Clarence Thomas's self-declared "high-tech lynching" was played out on television screens across the nation, although it was women—Anita Hill and black women in particular—who were left feeling like the ones hanging from the tree of political, if not necessarily public, opinion.

So what does any of this have to do with hip-hop? It is telling that the women—whether they're the rappers topping the charts or the dancers in the videos—formed their own identities at a time when black female sexuality in the cultural marketplace was not at all positive. The way black women experience and interpret the world has indeed been determined by our having to wage constant battles in order to determine our subjectivity—to say that we are not whores à la Desiree Washington, tricksters and liars à la Tawana Brawley, or disgruntled spinsters à la Anita Hill. In *Black Looks* the cultural theorist bell hooks writes, "The extent in which Black women feel devalued, objectified, dehumanized in this society determines the scope and texture of their looking relations. Those Black women whose identities were constructed in resistance, by practices that oppose the dominant order, were most inclined to develop an oppositional gaze."[3] Yet those women whose identities were instead constructed in compliance with the status quo were most inclined to absorb these images and make these representations and stereotypes of heterosexual black female sexuality their own.

Today, through the music video, there are so many black female bodies on view on any given day of watching television that it is impossible to list them. In many ways that is probably the point. Through the constant barrage of hypersexualized images, the young, black female has ceased to be an anomaly in the marketplace and is now back in the slave era position of anonymous chattel. Hooks sums it up in *Black Looks* when she writes, "Just as nineteenth-century representations of *Black female* bodies were constructed to emphasize that these bodies were expendable, contemporary images (even those created in black cultural production) give a similar message."[4] The hip-hop video has taken rap music to a level never imagined during its roots in the house parties of the 1970s Bronx. Early rap videos were overwhelmingly low-budget affairs. But in the late 1980s, *Video Music Box*—now the longest-running hip-hop video show in New York City—debuted from Miami and collided with the national explosion of that same city's 2 Live Crew, forever changing hip-hop video.

Before Luther Campbell and his 2 Live Crew, there were countless images of scantily clad women in music videos. Bands like Van Halen and Mötley Crüe had perfected the art of the gratuitous bikini shot long before rappers. The difference was that these women were white. And they were not being depicted in a genre proclaiming itself to be politically charged and revolutionary. As the rap historian Tricia Rose explains in her seminal work *Black Noise,* "Rap music is a black cultural expression that prioritizes black voices from the margins of urban America."[5] During the Reagan and Bush administrations, as prisons went up as rapidly as homelessness and drug use, and police brutality spread across the country, hip-hop became the medium for the disenfranchised citizens of the inner city to state their rage, vent their concerns, educate themselves about political issues, and fight back against government propaganda. Public Enemy, whose lyrics advised the disenfranchised to "fight the power," or spoke to controversial urban realities ("I don't wanna be called yo nigga"), were by far the most visible political rappers, but they were hardly the only ones.

By the time of the "Me So Horny"s and "Baby Got Back"s of the rap world, there were legions of hip-hop tunes that were not deep or meaningful in their lyrical content. But the accompanying videos, with images of women with DD cups washing soapy car windows with their breasts, were ground-breaking. "The visualization of music has far-reaching effects on musical culture and popular culture generally, not the least of which is the increase in visual interpretations of sexist power relationships,"[6] Rose wrote. In short, it became as easy as the click of the cable remote to see images of black women as so sexually licentious, so insatiably horny that Van Halen's "Hot for Teacher" looked almost tame.

In the early days of the booty video, the depiction of women in the music was overwhelmingly cut-and-dried. With a few notable exceptions, they were portrayed as gold-digging vixens. Hip-hop music extended the idea with videos that showed women dressed in G-strings, bikinis, and strip-per outfits, oftentimes in situations that had nothing to do with the beach or a strip club. It was a time when many feminists and other interested onlook-ers noted that, as misconstrued and narrow as the representation of black women in rap music was, it would most likely be balanced once more women became viable, popular rappers. The idea was that, given the space to define themselves, female rappers would construct an image of black womanhood which encompassed a more realistic scope of sexuality, not to mention give voice to the day-to-day struggles of women living in the urban arenas that were typically the focus of hip-hop music.

The meteoric rise of Lil' Kim's career was the likely starting point for the muddying of the waters that has taken place for me and many others who once felt that there were only two sides in the sexual war of hip-hop. She is arguably the female rapper closest to achieving iconic status. And although she has attracted many fans based on interest in her music, Kim's real infamy stems from the public way she has lived her life. Nothing has been deemed too private for the diminutive rapper from Brooklyn. She's admitted that she never had her dad's acceptance and that as a teen she used sex and her body to survive. After the Notorious B.I.G., the man who had been her mentor as well as her married lover, died, she told *People* magazine how she kissed his urn each morning. On her sophomore album, *Notorious KIM,* she revealed how she aborted a pregnancy from her rap Svengali. We have watched Kim publicly wrestle with weight, undergo two breast enlargements, a nose job, blond hair, and blue contact lenses.

In 1995 Kim and her then-friend Foxy Brown opened the door for the public's acceptance of sexual female rappers. Before them, those relatively few women who were sexually brazen in hip-hop—groups like Hoes with Attitudes and Bytches Wit Problems are good examples—were often dismissed by cultural critics and feminists as willing participants in their own dehumanization. Instead, there was a perceived transgressiveness in Kim's and Foxy's acts of asserting desire and sexual wants in a culture where female sexuality is not typically linked with the pursuit of pleasure.

Yet while these two performers challenged notions of what it meant to be a woman in hip-hop, it could be argued that they were simultaneously supporting an image of black female sexuality that the white patriarchy had been trying to sell us since slavery. During the whole of the nineteenth century, for example, depictions of black female bodies were often sexualized in ways that white women's never were.[7] The black female was a licentious counterpart to the white woman's virtue, in fact making that virtue possible. The supposed sexuality of black women was the thing that white women could set themselves against. One of the most emblematic (and bizarre) representations of black female sexuality was the Hottentot Venus, whose "grossly overdeveloped labia," "enlarged clitoris," and large buttocks were seen as evidence of the "primitive sexuality of African women."[8] Like the African Hottentot, the black female body not only had a divergent sexual physiology made up of more pronounced sexual organs but a divergent sexual psychology that dictated uncontrollable "primitive" sexual desire. Although the Hottentot Venus was a medical myth, it was presented to the public as pure fact. Such fictions, whether they pertain to the hypersexual Hottentot or her diametrical opposite, the sexless archmother mammy, are all too powerful images. Contemporary black women are forced to negotiate the traces left by these contaminated constructions of black female sexuality.

Many black women who have always felt a need to strive for respectability in a culture that hypersexualizes them almost from birth see in Lil' Kim the freedom of "acting out" their sexuality. She not only refuses to shy away from the male gaze by desexing herself but openly preens for the male gaze while returning it. As bell hooks would say, she looks back. Some like to assert that rappers like Kim are intimidating men, shaking the very foundations of male sexuality by demanding that female sexual urgency and female pleasure be taken into account. Yet alongside demanding that they be sexually pleased, many female rappers convey a parallel overriding message in their lyrics: that the men who sexually satisfy them should also provide money, cash, and clothes.

By comparing the majority of female rappers in the entertainment marketplace with the undisputed queen of commercialized female sexual agency, Madonna, it becomes clearer how precariously drawn the line is between self-determination and coconspiring in one's own exploitation. "Madonna provides a perfect example of the postmodern, feminist heroine, selling the virtues of political indeterminacy in her insistent play with sexual expression," wrote Roseann M. Mandzuik in her essay "Feminist Politics and Postmodern Seductions." "Yet in her discourse as a postmodern icon, [there is] something [very] familiar in her transformation of politics into pleasure: Madonna sounds the same old cultural message that a woman's place is to be sensual, stylish and self-involved."[9] Underscoring this point and bringing it back to female rappers is Lil' Kim's video "How Many Licks," in which she turns herself into a doll with replaceable parts, a move so infused with self-objectification that it seems almost laughable in its obviousness. The question must be asked: What kind of transgressiveness is Kim enacting when she performs a femininity that mimics misogynistic patriarchal desires? In another song, she denounces her previous fear of fellatio: "Now I throw lips to the shit / Handle it like a real bitch." Can sexual empowerment be articulated by making oneself a powerful agent in the familiar pornographic images of sexual acts?

It would be easy to state that had these women, had all of us, been privy to more realistic images of black women in popular culture as we were growing up, things would be different today. But it's not that simple. There is a market impetus behind these images. "The artistry takes a backseat to the image," said Faith Newman, vice president of A&R at Jive Records, in the hip-hop publication *Blaze*. "Men control [these] women's careers, and it seems like if [the women] aren't looking like sluts or some hardcore dykes—excuse the expression—they aren't going to get the necessary push."[10] The commodification of blackness in the entertainment industry rewards black women much more readily for reactionary or regressive thinking about gender and sexuality. Both Foxy Brown and Lil' Kim, who were molded by older, already popular male rappers, have stated repeatedly that in the beginning of their careers they were pretty much told what their image would be and how they needed to play it up to sell records, whether this was how they chose to be depicted or not. "At sixteen I was just so happy to have a nice car and a nice home that I didn't complain about [my image]," Foxy said in

Essence magazine. "I had all the influences around me, and I wasn't always strong enough to come back like, 'No. I don't want to do that.'"[11]

Back in 1999, when my soapbox preaching had harshly turned on female rappers as the real problem, I wrote a review of Foxy Brown's second album, *Chyna Doll*. I declared that if we were supposed to believe Foxy was any kind of doll at all, it was of the blow-up variety, willing and ready at all times to be the receptacle for a man's sexual pleasures. While it was hardly a nuanced, subtle statement, it seemed, at the time, fitting to explain what appeared to be going on. Rappers like Trina, Hurricane G, and Charli Baltimore (another mistress of the Notorious B.I.G.), alongside Foxy and Kim, were reveling in the narrow confines of this Pussy Free-For-All. Because while, yes, these assertions of female sexual agency were a direct challenge to the notion that black male sexuality within hip-hop exists as a conquering force over women, it was, to put it in blunt vernacular, getting tired. While these female rappers were perhaps providing a voice for those who had been silent sexual objects in male hip-hop, the rules had not been overturned in how they were being read by the rest of the society. So though it may at first be shocking or new to assert that you, a woman, want sex *and* oral sex *and* a man who can last for a long time, after a few similarly themed songs, the shock has worn off and what is left is confirmation of something that many men of all races and quite a few non-black women had always suspected: black women are whores.

The near-total lack of media images depicting the real lives of working class, inner city black girls in the 1980s left a void, and that space was filled with male-centered constructs of the licentious black female. What will be the effect on a young black girl today as she is bombarded with images of black female asses, breasts, and dirty talk? A group of teen black girls at the mall dressed as if they had just finished taping a video could arguably be not much different from white girls in the eighties donning see-through lace getups and scaring their parents with recitations of "Like a Virgin." But it could also be said that more is at stake: the very grim realities of sexually transmitted diseases, AIDS, teen pregnancy, and sexual assault and abuse. Just as important, mainstream American culture interprets black cultural articulations of misogyny, sexism, and unbridled female sexuality differently from their white counterparts. In the 1990s, during the fiercest criticisms of teen pop star Britney Spears for sporting bare midriffs and see-through pants, she professed to be a virgin. When Foxy Brown came onto the scene, at age fifteen, she was featured on a song called "Ain't No Nigga," rhyming, "Ain't no nigga like the one I got/sleeps around but he gives me a lot," and very few people expressed disgust, or even shock, at her age. And with white suburban youth being one of the biggest consumer bases for rap music, it is safe to say that while some of the kids buying the CDs may have never met a black woman, they've all seen at least one (probably quite a few) wrap her legs around a pole and dance to a hip-hop tune during an afternoon spent watching BET, MTV, or the Box.

Of course, black women aren't the only ones being sexualized in the new millennium. Magazines like *Maxim* and *Rolling Stone* enjoy massive sales due in large part to the soft porn shots of white celebrities that grace their covers. Within all levels and substrata of society, women are dabbling with a hyper-sexual, yet decidedly pro-woman persona, epitomized by the characters on the popular HBO show *Sex and the City*. (Incidentally, the show's stylist, Patricia Fields, has admitted that Lil' Kim is a major influence for the wardrobe of Carrie, the Upper East Side, fashion-fabulous protagonist.)

And, of course, not all women rappers are playing out triple X-rated fantasies, just as not every video contains a bevy of near-naked ladies. Lauryn Hill has earned fans, respect, critical acclaim and awards with her mix of earthy sensuality and political and social awareness. Her themes run the gamut from love, motherhood, and simple reminiscing to the current state of gender relations. In "Lost Ones," Hill rhymes, "Don't be a hardrock when you really are a gem/Baby girl, respect is just the minimum," as she encourages women to seek their true selves and demand respect at the very least. The rapper Eve does not hesitate to admit that for a short time before her rap career she was a stripper. Yet it is told not as a way to entice but simply as a fact, and Eve seems to be very much in control of her current image, which is part pop star sass, part round-the-way-girl tough, and part sexy plaything.

So now, as I find myself humming along to a catchy "ho" anthem, I'm curious about what happened to my once-rankled ire. A few months ago, when I began thinking about this essay, I would probably have argued that my apathy was proof that while sexism and self-objectification still existed, there was a balance that allowed me to breathe easier. That maybe it was because women rappers have come into the industry, and while it's not the utopia of sexual equality I had hoped for, at the very least we are there, pushing the envelope, being recognized. Or that there's a likely chance the next song on the radio could be, if not redeeming, at least inoffensive to women. That for every thug love ode like the one by Bonnie Shyne, there's a "my beautiful queen" song by a "conscious" rapper like Common.

But now I can say that it's nothing like that. More likely I have calmed down because the powers that be—the programming executives, the music industry bigwigs, the video casting agents—have achieved a major goal. Through a saturation of the market with tramplike black women, I, too, have fallen victim to the normalizing effects of visual and lyrical hoochie overkill.

In order to see if that was the case, I took time off from being a pop culture consumer—I turned off the cable television and never listened to the radio unless I needed a weather update. I wanted to test whether I'd climb back up on the soapbox, newly charged with disgust and anger once I'd stopped being so used to all the ass. During my hiatus, Puffy became P. Diddy and made a public statement of apology to any Asian women he may have unintentionally offended with one line from his song "Diddy," yet offered nothing to the black women he's been insulting throughout his career. *Vibe* magazine printed an article on the current state of hip-hop for its 2001 year-end issue, and a full-page photo accompanying the piece was of a black woman's behind, even though the story never made any reference to it.

Two nights ago I found myself at a party for the rapper Jay Z's clothing line, Rocawear, where my time-out officially came to an end. The models, mostly men, were positioned inside cases meant to look like store window displays. And each black woman who was featured was wearing too-small shorts that let a portion of butt cheek peek out as she danced around a pole in front of excessively dressed men (coats, baggy pants, boots, hats) who offered her dollars. I looked around at the crowd and saw that few looked irritated or even seemed to question the ludicrousness of the setup. At the very least I hoped that some would find it passé. Just as I began searching for my car keys, more than aware that it was time for me to leave, the deejay put on the song that started all of this: "I've got hoes/I've got hoes/in different area codes." I didn't sing along, nor did I applaud Ludacris's linguistic wit. Instead I walked through the dancing bodies and headed out the door, wishing for a space in hip-hop where sex could be sexy and not insulting and women could be Smart and Interesting as well as Sexy. On that cold February night, it seemed like a goal that would be a long time coming.

NOTES

1. Officially titled "The Negro Family: The Case for National Action" and written in 1965.
2. In 1987 Tawana Brawley was found in upstate New York covered with racial slurs and charcoal. She alleged that a gang of six white police officers had "abducted and held her for four days in the woods, raping her repeatedly, writing KKK and NIG-GER on her belly, smearing her with dog feces and leaving her in a plastic garbage bag outside an apartment complex where her family had once lived," but a grand jury found her story to lack credibility. See http://www. time.com/time /magazine/1998/dom/980727/file.stories_sacred_lies18.html.
3. bell hooks, *Black Looks: Race and Representation* (Boston: South End Press, 1992), 127.
4. Ibid., 64.
5. Tricia Rose, *Black Noise: Rap Music and Black Culture in Contemporary America* (Middletown, Conn.: Wesleyan University Press, 1994), 2.
6. Ibid., 9.
7. The stereotypical depiction of the black female body as licentious during the nineteenth century was one of two primary stereotypes.
8. Jan Nederveen Pieterse, *White on Black: Images of Africa and Blacks in Western Popular Culture* (New Haven: Yale University Press, 1992), 181.
9. Roseann M. Mandzuik, "Feminist Politics and Postmodern Seductions: Madonna and the Struggle," in *The Madonna Connection: Representational Politics, Subcultural Identities, and Cultural Theory,* ed. Cathy Schwichtenberg (Boulder, Colo.: Westview Press, 1993), 183–84.
10. Quoted in Charisse Nikole, "Invisible Women," *Blaze,* April 1999, 68.
11. Michelle Buford and Christopher John Farley, "Foxy's Dilemma," *Essence,* August 1999, 72.

29

WHERE ARE THE WOMEN?
The Strange Case of the Missing Feminists.
When Was the Last Time You Saw One on TV?

LAURA ZIMMERMAN

Laura Zimmerman is cofounder and codirector of the Center for New Words (formerly New Worlds Bookstore in Cambridge, MA), a nonprofit organization promoting women's voices and ideas.

"The neutral voice in America is the white male," the *Nation* columnist Katha Pollitt recently told me when I asked her about political opinion-making in the US since 9/11. "Everyone else is providing color commentary. A woman's opinion about Iraq or the budget is seen as a woman's opinion. The same for a black person. And white men just don't have the idea that they are affected by the fact that they are white men."

For decades, this spurious claim to "neutrality" has justified a white male monopoly of the air waves and the printed page. In today's media-driven culture, these "experts" deliver the opinions that shape our lives and the country's political system. Frequently, it's the op-ed pages, elite opinion journals, and Sunday morning news programs that explicate, promote, and even guide national decisions. When women are excluded from these venues, we're excised from the public policy-making loop. At the same time, our exclusion confirms our apparent lack of authority to speak about critical political issues. Consciously or not, audiences become habituated to male voices and bylines and dependent on white male gravitas to explain what's happening in the world. As we witnessed at the time of 9/11 and later during the wars in Afghanistan and Iraq, national emergencies push women even further to the sidelines. "To feel voiceless in a democracy in so difficult a time," prize-winning journalist Geneva Overholser said on National Public Radio in November 2001, "is very close to feeling disenfranchised."

Many women have felt a renewed sense of second-class citizenry in the past two years. By muting women's voices, the media has belittled our authority and leadership and removed us from the public conversation. We have also been robbed of the platform to assert political opinions that specifically affect women. "News agencies do not gather the facts about issues of concern to women," Rita Henley Jensen, editor in chief of Women's eNews, an Internet news service for e-mail subscribers and major media outlets, told me. "They do not hear women's voices, literally. And by not having access to the media, women's organizations and advocates cannot build their communities of interest." Jensen has all-too-often witnessed male editors' unlikely concepts of "women's issues." In the late 1990s, at a public talk given by a top decision maker at *The Los Angeles Times,* Jensen asked how the paper was reaching out to women readers. He replied, "We have a brand-new lifestyle and home decorating section."

In the months following 9/11, women wrote only 8 percent of the op-ed articles in *The Washington Post, The New York Times,* and *USA Today.* During the wars in Afghanistan and Iraq, biased editorial choices persisted. "It hasn't been this bad for women scholars and journalists wanting to influence the national public agenda since the pre-women's movement days when women were completely invisible," Caryl Rivers, author and journalism professor at Boston University, wrote in an April 2003 commentary published by Women's eNews. More recently, Rivers confirmed that these conditions are still at an all-time low. "We're being systematically overlooked," she said. "I'm not talking about fringe people. People who have enjoyed access to the media are feeling very much frozen out. In the best of times women face a high barrier. Now they may be less inclined to keep hurling themselves against the barricades."

Indeed, as Rivers mentions in her article, even Pulitzer Prize winner and syndicated columnist Ellen Goodman "complained . . . about getting bumped too often" at *The Washington Post.* Jill Nelson, best-selling author and the first black woman on *The Washington Post Magazine's* staff, says she lost $10,000 in freelance work after 9/11. "It was an immediate post 9/11 paradigm shift," Nelson said. "If you weren't on the government-sponsored white male reaction page, you were not going to be heard." Previously contacted for commentary by CNN or other outlets every six weeks or so, Nelson went an entire year with only an occasional call—and those were to cover insignificant events such as OJ's most recent arrest.

At best, many editors are afflicted with a "one-woman-only" mentality. Currently, for example, the op-ed page of *The New York Times* carries Maureen Dowd. Before her, it had Anna Quindlen and before that, Flora Lewis. Before Lewis, it had no women columnists at all. "This is true in many newspapers and magazines," said Pollitt. "There's one star woman columnist. Editors don't have the 50/50 picture at all. They have the picture: men plus one woman, or maybe two." After an editor for a weekly or monthly magazine commissions one long piece by a woman, he or she has done the affirmative action for that issue. This unacknowledged quota system caps the number of accomplished women writers in major venues and all but eliminates the up and coming. Additionally, male editors tend to look for someone to father and mentor. Typically, it's another man who closely resembles them.

And then there's television. In December 2001, the White House Project, a national group advocating women's political leadership, announced that the frequency of women guests on Sunday morning talk shows dropped in the month following 9/11 from only 10.7 percent of guests to an even worse 9.4 percent. Among repeat appearances—the true measure of authoritative presence—women were a mere seven percent. The study showed that we were also afforded less airtime, placed in later segments, and underrepresented in every professional category. Nightly newscasts were equally imbalanced: A 2002 Fairness and Accuracy in Reporting (FAIR) study showed that in 2001, US sources interviewed on the three major networks were 92 percent white and 85 percent male. Women constituted only 15 percent of all sources, and in the categories of professional and political sources (think of all the qualified feminists you know who could have filled those seats!) a mere nine percent.

Television producers, like print editors, dislike risk-taking. As a rule, they seek sources who have been used previously, either on the air or in print—a perfect method to keep the circle of opinion-makers small and closed, making it an old-boy's network. Perhaps this stems as much from lack of imagination as from deliberate exclusion. No doubt the motives are varied and complex. But the result is clear: Television and print media suppress the views of women commentators on critical subjects like the effect of war and peace on women's lives, sexual violence and trafficking of women, how globalization affects women's lives, or what low wage earning women endure. Women commentators discussing subjects like these would cast a critical eye on the news and shake up the standard male-chosen topics.

Media leaders perpetuate sameness, exclude outsiders, and enforce unspoken quotas. Add to these norms a corporate structure that all but eliminates women from the top of the decision-making pyramid, and we're looking at a structure that nearly guarantees exclusion of feminist commentators. Especially in today's hyper-masculine, conservative culture, when progressive voices in general have been marginalized, feminists are barred from view. "I'm worried that elite journals like *The Atlantic* are looking for women to say provocative things," said Rivers. "That means you smash other women, dump on feminism, or say that the real victims are men. And you can't find a feminist with a show of her own on cable television and very few on talk radio."

What you can find, of course, are right-wing commentators like Laura Ingraham and Ann Coulter filling women's allotted air time and print space. Chances are, they will be mocking Hillary Clinton, attacking feminist "misfits," or asserting outrageous opinions, such as Coulter's that McCarthyism wasn't so bad after all. Recent articles in *The New York Times Magazine* and *The Nation* have analyzed the conservative machine that grooms and sponsors journalists (especially on college campuses), endows media think tanks, and operates a highly organized, long-term campaign to control and manipulate the media. "Our side has nothing like it," Pollitt said. "It doesn't spend the money. And when it does, it's much mushier. There's a deficiency of sharki-ness." Jensen also spoke about the vast sums conservatives have poured into the media, adding that women's organizations have moved in the opposite direction by diverting their resources into direct service. The result, Jensen believes, is the stifling of women's chances to affect the political workings of the country.

By themselves, these cultural and political forces present huge hurdles to progressive women. Add to these the personal ones. Many women distrust what is required of political commentators. We are not inclined to be thunder-ous and simplistic. In our eagerness to be fair-minded, we obsessively research subjects and worry too much about how we are received. Of course, we can also be bombastic, smart-alecky, and combative. But that's not our typ-ical tone. "Commentary, punditry, op-ed writing, and also the web lend them-selves to being brash and quick," media activist, journalist, and broadcaster Laura Flanders told me. "Historically, women have not been given to practice this. It's more acceptable for a man than a woman to be outrageous—but this seems to be changing on the right, not on the left."

Even people who write letters to the editor tend to be overwhelmingly male—and women also make fewer contacts with media ombudspersons. "It's not because women aren't reading the papers," said Overholser. "If you compare the percentage of women who read the paper with the percent of letter-writers, the numbers are very skewed." Other journalists, mentioning that women also submit fewer unsolicited manuscripts to magazine slush piles, speculated that we too quickly shy away from being told no, or dislike pestering people in charge—or that our lives have become so overwhelm-ingly busy we don't have time even to write a note. Perhaps we're not well-enough endowed with a trait that Katha Pollitt calls undiscourageability. Men are definitely not better writers, Pollitt says, and their perseverance does not necessarily win friends. But undaunted by dozens of rejections, they do increase their odds of getting published.

Then there's the problem that even those few women who have success-fully entered the arena of mainstream commentary often conceal their femi-nist leanings. "If a female journalist does begin to advocate for women or to promote a related story, she loses credibility in the newsroom," said Jensen. "It's the same experience that African Americans and Latinas have. No one asks white men to give up their interest in sports or the military. But if a woman were to advocate running a story every day on the front page of a major newspaper about defunding rape crisis centers, she might likely be asked, 'Do you have a hang-up about this?' Her credibility would definitely be challenged." As a result, with a few well-known exceptions, feminist spokespersons mostly publish or broadcast in independent media, such as alternative websites, community radio, *The Village Voice, The Progressive,* and others.

There was a time when US feminists viewed the media as too abstract and elitist to claim top priority. Pained and outraged by institutions that thwarted women's lives—racism, domestic violence, the law, medicine, theology, politics, academia—we directed our attention to these. At the same time, we helped build an environmental movement, a gay rights movement, and a human rights movement. We were not slackers. We simply had enough to do.

But the days of letting the media off the hook are over. Increasingly, a vast industry run by a handful of corporate executives saturates our public and personal lives with narrow, biased ideas and opinions. And in times of crisis, like 9/11 and the war in Iraq, it goes berserk with the sound of its own voice and the sight of its own face.

For decades, a number of prescient feminists have been warning us that a state of emergency for women and people of color exists in the media industry. "A serious effort to match the right's media assault with comparable vigor is crucial," wrote Laura Flanders years before most of us were thinking about this problem, "if only to respond to those newspaper editors and TV anchors who claim they don't hear from feminists as they do from their opponents."

How to win access to both the mainstream and alternative media, how to use it to advance equality, how to exert influence—these are the big questions. But backing away from their magnitude would be a mistake. So would assuming simple answers. Nothing should stop us from talking among ourselves, making a public clamor, or joining with media activists already in gear. "What's holding us back is access," Flanders writes in the concluding pages of her book. "But so what else is new? . . . The right to communicate is like any right. And like any right, it will not be given. It must be won."

PART V
Sexuality

The social construction of gender greatly affects how sexuality emerges in humans. Without the constraints put upon sexuality by gender, expressions of human sexuality would probably look very different than they currently do. In spite of these constraints, however, human sexuality encompasses a wide range of behaviors and identities. The expectation in mainstream U.S. society that feminine, heterosexual women and masculine, heterosexual men will have sex only with each other and by mutual agreement is challenged by many people who do not conform to the dominant norms. It is also challenged by the rates of abusive sexual exploitation perpetrated by the more powerful on the less powerful, most frequently by men against women, children, and less powerful men.

The combinations and permutations of biological sex, gender, and sexual orientation are many. A person could be, for example, genetically and biologically female, actively heterosexual, and "masculine" in appearance, identity, or behavior (whatever masculine means in her social and cultural context). The American Psychiatric Association (APA) took on this issue when it reversed its designation of gay men and lesbians as mentally ill. Deciding that homosexuality was not, in itself, pathological, it did define as mentally ill those children who preferred to behave like people of the other gender. Reinforcing the assumption that sex and gender should match, "gender identity disorder" became the pathological label for feminine boys and masculine girls. Thus, Tommi Avicolli and Linnea Due (Part II) would probably have been labeled sick—Avicolli for his preference for jump rope and his manner of walking and Due for her too-masculine presentation and her wish to marry a woman. There is no suggestion by the APA that the boys who teased and ostracized Avicolli or the teachers who ignored them or the scout leader who rejected Due because of her "masculinity" might, in fact, be the sick ones. Partly in response to this labeling, some gay men take on very masculine identities in adulthood, effectively distancing themselves from the "sissy" boys now considered pathological by the APA.[1] When high school football player Corey Johnson courageously came out as gay to his team, he was accepted and defended in an unusual example of community support; his masculinity seems to have bought him some privilege that Avicolli could not enjoy.[2] People in the transgender liberation movement are lobbying against the diagnosis of gender identity disorder, arguing that all gender expression should be supported and not pathologized.

When we acknowledge that one's genetic makeup is the only aspect of sexuality that is immutable, and that sexual behavior, sexual orientation, and gender do not necessarily line up in a predictable pattern, the options for the expression of gender and sexuality are many. Psychologist Carla Golden, in a study of undergraduates at an elite women's college in the Northeast, found that students' sexual identities did not necessarily match their sexual behavior. For example, some women who identified themselves as heterosexual were exclusively involved sexually with women; some who had never had a same-sex sexual experience nevertheless identified themselves as bisexual because they perceived in themselves the potential for same-sex attraction and sexual activity. Golden also interviewed women who identified themselves as "political lesbians" whose sexual behavior was exclusively heterosexual. Golden concludes that the congruence among sexual feelings, behavior, and identity is often lacking, and she urges people to acknowledge the complex expressions of sexuality and sexual identity that result.[3] It is also true that some people's sexual identity changes over time, something often not acknowledged. Do you happen to know anyone who at one point identified as gay or lesbian and later got involved in a relationship that would be defined as straight? Or vice versa? If so, how did the parties involved identify themselves?

Apart from examining the complex ways in which people define and express their sexuality, passionate debates and interesting topics abound in the field of sexuality. The origins of sexual orientations have been the subject of much research, as scholars explore the extent to which genetic predispositions or cultural influences might cause people to become heterosexual, gay, lesbian, or bisexual or to change sexual orientation.[4] Current research documenting the pervasive presence of pornography raises questions related to the extent to which human sexuality is dictated by the messages communicated in pornography.[5] Debate continues about whether pornography that is violent and degrading should continue to be legal in the United States.[6] Others argue for or against butch-femme roles in lesbian and gay communities.[7] Still others debate the pros and cons of sadomasochistic sexual practices.[8]

The debate about sex education in schools has created conflict in school districts in many parts of the United States (Should it exist? If so, with what content and starting at what age?).[9] Federal funding for sex education is currently limited to abstinence-only sex education. This program is designed to advocate for the psychological and physical benefits of abstinence and to present sex within heterosexual marriage as the only acceptable sexual expression. The American Civil Liberties Union has argued that this is a breach of freedom of speech, puts young people at risk for sexually transmitted diseases because nearly two-thirds are not abstinent during high school years, and discriminates against gay and lesbian youth. Schools that provide comprehensive sex education cannot qualify for federal funds. A survey of adults in 2004 suggests that only 15 percent think that abstinence only is the way to go. Surveys of parents and teachers find that a large majority want sex education for their children that covers such topics as contraception, abortion, and sexual orientation. This is particularly important, given that the United States has one of the highest teen pregnancy rates in the world.[10] A recent assessment of 11 abstinence-only programs concluded: "Abstinence-only programs show little evidence of sustained (long-term) impact on attitudes and intentions. Worse, they show some negative impacts on youth's willingness to use contraception, including condoms, to prevent negative sexual health outcomes related to sexual intercourse. Importantly, only in one state did any program demonstrate short-term success in delaying the initiation of sex; none of these programs demonstrates evidence of long-term success in delaying sexual initiation among youth exposed to the programs or any evidence of success in reducing other sexual risk-taking behaviors among participants."[11]

The emergence of Viagra has provoked interest in women's sexuality, as researchers explore whether it or a similar drug could increase women's sexual responses as well.[12] It has also provoked debate among pharmaceutical companies and feminist health advocates as the definition of "sexual dysfunction" is addressed. It is unclear to what extent women's sexual dysfunction even exists; whether, if it exists, it is similar to erectile dysfunction; and whether doctors and pharmaceutical companies are truly concerned about women's sexual well-being or simply concerned with profits. Feminist critics are worried that emphasis on sexual physiology and performance could obscure the complex psychosocial aspects of sexuality, and they question the alleged "equal opportunity" in the attempt to develop a female arousal drug.[13] A recent attempt by Procter & Gamble to market Intrinsa, a testosterone patch for women billed as a female Viagra, was unanimously rejected by a U.S. Food and Drug Administration advisory panel in December 2004. The drug had been tested for only six months on a limited group of women—those who had experienced surgical menopause and had low sexual drive. The lessons learned from the failure to do long-term studies on hormone replacement therapy before marketing it to millions of women seem to have had an effect: experts called for longer-term research with a diverse group of women before allowing the drug to be marketed.[14] The emergence of Viagra has also raised questions about insurance coverage of this male-specific, voluntary drug, especially in light of the fact that some health plans do not cover the costs of contraception.[15]

Recently the reproductive technology that makes it possible for postmenopausal women to give birth has raised questions about the double standard related to women bearing children after their typical childbearing years. A sixty-three-year-old woman who gave birth in California was criticized for doing so, while men who become fathers at sixty-three are more likely to be cheered on.[16]

The sexual use and abuse of women, children, and disempowered men (especially in prison, see Terry Kupers, Part IX) is a major issue in the study of sexuality. Human beings' potential for healthy, nonexploitive, enjoyable sexual expression with others is heavily influenced by the level of decision-making power we have over our own bodily expressions and the kind of caring (or lack thereof) that surrounds us as children.[17] The high rates of childhood sexual abuse (estimated at one in four girls, one in seven boys), followed by the rates of rape over a lifetime (estimated at one in three women and one in six men)[18] suggests that sexual pleasure will be severely curtailed for a large proportion of the U.S. population. Boys seem to have an especially difficult time dealing with sexual abuse, in part because of homophobia. Many worry that they will be called gay if the perpetrator was male (and the perpetrator usually is male) or that they will be called unmanly if they didn't automatically enjoy forced sex with a woman, since many men and boys are socialized to accept and like heterosexual activity whatever the circumstance. If, in fact, boy children are gendered female by male perpetrators, a boy is apt to feel like a "girl" and have a difficult time admitting what happened.[19]

The widespread abuse of women in prostitution, trafficking, pornography, and interpersonal relationships leaves millions of women worldwide in a state of long-term sexual victimization. For that population, the choices related to sexual orientation and identity, freedom of sexual expression, and gender bending become largely irrelevant against a backdrop of the need to survive.[20] We have recently seen increased attention to "comfort women" who were forced into prostitution by the Japanese army during World War II, as these now-elderly women find their voices and tell the truth about what they experienced.[21] The use of prostitutes, including child prostitutes by the U.S. military abroad, has led to an effort to end soldiers' use of child prostitutes.[22] Publicity about international sex trafficking is bringing this issue to more readers in the United States, as illustrated by a report of female sex slaves from China in Chicago and by new books on this grim subject.[23] Pedophiles have used the Internet to their advantage, sharing strategies for gaining access to children and selling child pornography. Lately, with many child pornography Web sites shut down, new child "model" Web sites have emerged that feature children in sexualized poses wearing little clothing.[24]

HIV and AIDS have curtailed the sexual activity and, literally, the lives of a large segment of the world's population, leaving millions of people infected or dead. Young men ages 20–24 in the United States are currently at highest risk for sexually transmitted infections (STIs), tied, in part, to their commitment to the risk-taking aspects of masculinity.[25] According to the Centers for Disease Control, in 2005, "The rate of AIDS diagnoses for black women was nearly 23 times the rate for white women. The rate of AIDS diagnoses for black men was 8 times the rate for white men."[26] An estimated one in four people in the United States will contract a sexually transmitted infection, some of which are without symptoms and can cause infertility and cancer.[27] (See the introduction to Part X of this text for a brief discussion of the new vaccine for prevention of the potentially cancer-causing human papillomavirus [HPV].) AIDS and STIs have forced many people to communicate about sex in ways they didn't need to before, and their presence has stimulated changed sexual practices for a large proportion of the U.S. population, although some people are still in denial about the importance of condom use, even when they have access to condoms.[28] Even the Catholic Church is considering easing up on its policy against condom use, as the reality of the transmission of AIDS takes on a life of its own. A new perspective on condoms defines them as disease control rather then birth control, especially in developing countries with high rates of AIDS. It remains to be seen to what extent permission or recommendation for condom use will become church policy, especially in places where AIDS is not devastating the population.[29] Silvana Paternostro, a journalist who grew up in Colombia, reports that AIDS in Latin America is often spread by heterosexually identified men who have unprotected sex with other men and infect their unsuspecting female partners; their lack of identification as gay and their consequent denial of the risks of same-sex unprotected sexual activity leave them at high risk both for the illness itself and to become agents of its transmission.[30]

All the preceding sexual issues are obviously embedded in cultural, racial, and class contexts. Sociologist Patricia Hill Collins provides another example, examining pornography, prostitution, and rape in the context of race, class, and gender oppression. She provides data about, and analysis of, the long-term sexual exploitation of African American women.[31]

In oppressed communities, there is sometimes pressure to not break rank with one's cultural group. Thus, sometimes women of color or women in small white ethnic communities are pressured not to address sexism within those communities. For similar reasons, gays, lesbians, bisexuals, and transgendered people sometimes feel pressured not to address homophobia or transphobia. The larger, mostly white, movements that are fighting for LGBT rights and women's rights have a history of racism that renders those movements uncomfortable, unsafe, or unacceptable for many people of color. Gays and lesbians of color, then, frequently deal with two communities that fail to acknowledge their whole selves: an LGBT community that fails to address racism and a racial/ethnic community that fails to address heterosexism.[32]

In an interesting and moving account of what it's like to be the only Black person in a group of white lesbians, writer Paula Ross reports:

> There is rarely a time when I can attend to my self as lesbian apart from my self as black, a diasporic offspring, one of the millions of Africa's daughters dispersed by imperialism, greed, and an overweening appetite for colonization. I stand around this campfire with fifteen other lesbians. We are all erotically and sexually connected to other women. My lover's butch and my femme identities are not questioned for an instant. But even here, I cannot forget about race. They can forget—perhaps at their own peril, but they do have the option.[33]

Homophobia thrives in many contexts. In a well-publicized trial in Egypt that was denounced by various human rights groups, twenty-three men were jailed for one to five years for homosexual activity.[34] In fact, in response to the homophobic atmosphere that exists in most places, many gays and lesbians wish they were straight. The ex-gay movement in the United States has attempted to assist with conversions to heterosexuality, with mixed success.

Recently, some active spokespersons for the ex-gay movement have resumed their lives as gays, creating an ex-ex-gay movement.[35]

This part of this book addresses sexuality from a range of perspectives, including one white man's use of pornography (Robert Jensen); male athletes' approaches to sexuality (Don Sabo); a look at the experience of a disabled lesbian in an intimate relationship with a gay man (Domenika Bednarska); and the difficulties faced by bisexual people from various racial and ethnic groups (Paula Rust). These authors would like to see a world that is free of sexual exploitation and that welcomes a flexible definition of sexual identity.

As you explore these readings, you might want to think about your own sexuality. How closely is it tied to your gender? How does your ethnic/cultural context affect your understanding of and your experience with your sexuality? Do the men you know have anything in common with Sabo and his teammates in the locker room? Have you thought much about people with disabilities and sexuality? Do you know people who identify as gay or lesbian but who have sex with the "opposite" gender? How do you react to bisexuality?

NOTES

1. For an interesting discussion of the process by which the American Psychiatric Association removed homosexuality from the pathology list and simultaneously added "gender identity disorder of childhood," see Eve Kosofsky Sedgwick, "How to Bring Your Kids Up Gay," in *Tendencies* (Durham, NC: Duke University Press, 1993), pp. 154–164.

2. Rick Reilly, "The Biggest Play of His Life," *Sports Illustrated* 92, 19, p. 114.

3. Carla Golden, "Diversity and Variability in Women's Sexual Identities," in the Boston Lesbian Psychologies Collective, eds., *Boston Lesbian Psychologies Collective, Lesbian Psychologies: Exploration and Challenges* (Chicago: University of Illinois Press, 1987), pp. 19–34.

4. For discussions of causes of sexual orientation and the development of sexual identity, see Alan P. Bell and Martin S. Weinberg, *Homosexualities: A Study of Human Diversity* (South Melbourne, Australia: Macmillan, 1978); Jan Clausen, *Beyond Gay or Straight: Understanding Sexual Orientation* (New York: Chelsea House, 1997); Ronald C. Fox, "Bisexuality in Perspective: A Review of Theory and Research" in Beth A. Firestein, ed., *Bisexuality: The Psychology and Politics of an Invisible Minority* (Thousand Oaks, CA: Sage, 1996), pp. 3–50; Martin S. Weinberg, *Dual Attraction: Understanding Bisexuality* (New York: Oxford University Press, 1994).

5. Robert Jensen, *Getting Off: Pornography and the End of Masculinity* (Cambridge, MA: South End Press, 2007); Pamela Paul, *Pornified: How Pornography Is Damaging Our Lives, Our Relationships, and Our Families* (New York: Henry Holt Owl Books, 2005).

6. For a discussion of class and pornography, see Laura Kipnis, "(Male) Desire and (Female) Disgust: Reading Hustler," in Lawrence Grossberg, Cary Nelson, and Paula Treichler, eds., *Cultural Studies* (New York: Routledge, 1992), pp. 373–391. For a presentation of the antipornography position in the feminist pornography debate, see Dorchen Leidholdt and Janice G. Raymond, eds., *The Sexual Liberals and the Attack on Feminism* (New York: Pergamon Press, 1990); Laura Lederer and Richard Delgado, eds., *The Price We Pay: The Case against*

Racist Speech, Hate Propaganda, and Pornography (New York: Hill and Wang, 1995). For a discussion of the feminist position in support of pornography, see Lisa Duggan and Nan D. Hunter, eds., *Sex Wars: Sexual Dissent and Political Culture* (New York: Routledge, 1995). For a recent attempt to bridge these two positions, see Gail Dines, Robert Jensen, and Ann Russo, *Pornography: The Production and Consumption of Inequality* (New York: Routledge, 1998). For an example from queer studies of the role of racism in gay pornographic videos, see Richard Fung, "Looking for My Penis: The Eroticized Asian in Gay Video Porn," in Bad Object-Choices, ed., *How Do I Look? Queer Film and Video* (Seattle, WA: Bay Press, 1991).

7. For a discussion of butch-femme roles in the lesbian community, see Joan Nestle, "Butch-Femme Relationships: Sexual Courage in the 1950s," in *A Restricted Country* (Ithaca, NY: Firebrand, 1987), pp. 100–109.

8. For a discussion of sadomasochism, see Robin Ruth Linden et al., eds., *Against Sadomasochism: A Radical Feminist Analysis* (San Francisco: Frog in the Well, 1982); Pat Califia, *Sapphistry: The Book of Lesbian Sexuality* (Tallahassee, FL: Naiad Press, 1980).

9. See Pepper Schwartz and Virginia Rutter, *The Gender of Sexuality* (Thousand Oaks, CA: Pine Forge, 1998), pp. 20–21.

10. American Civil Liberties Union, 22 August 2007, "Abstinence-Only-Until-Marriage Programs Censor Vital Health Care." http://www.aclu.org/reproductiverights/sexed/12670res20070822.html; The Alan Guttmacher Institute, 2002, "Teenagers' Sexual and Reproductive Health: Developed Countries." http://www.guttmacher.org/pubs/fb_teens.pdf.

11. Debra Hauser, MPH, Vice President, Advocates for Youth, "Five Years of Abstinence-Only-Until-Marriage Education: Assessing the Impact." June 11, 2007: http://www.advocatesforyouth.org/publications/stateevaluations/index.htm.; Alison Bowen and Nouhad Moawad, "Dems Rebuf Abstinence Funding," Women's eNews, May 25, 2007: http://www.womensenews.org/article.cfm? aid=3175.

12. Jennifer Babson, "At BU, a Fresh Look at Viagra—for Women," *Boston Sunday Globe,* 12 July 1998, pp. A1, A20.

13. Meika Loe, "Female Sexual Dysfuction: For Women or For Sale?" *The Network News* (January–February 2000), pp. 1, 6 (published by the National Women's Health Network).

14. Kathleen Phalen Tomaselli, "Intrinsa stalled by concerns about safety," *American Medical News,* January 17, 2005, http://www.ama-assn.org/amednews/2005/01/17/hlsc0117.htm.

15. The Alan Guttmacher Institute, 16 June 2004, "Contraceptive Insurance Coverage Has Improved Dramatically: State Laws Prove Effective but There Is More to Be Done." http://www.plannedparenthood.org/news-articles-press/politics-policy-issues/contraceptive-insurance-12701.htm.

16. Pepper Schwartz and Virginia Rutter, *The Gender of Sexuality* (Thousand Oaks, CA: Pine Forge Press, 1998), p. xiv.

17. Aline P. Zoldbrod, *Sex Smart: How Your Childhood Shaped Your Sexual Life and What to Do About It* (Oakland, CA: New Harbinger, 1998).

18. Bradley H. White and Sharon E. Robinson Kurpius (2002) "Effects of Victim Sex and Sexual Orientation on Perceptions of Rape," *Sex Roles: A Journal of Research,* March 2002, pp. 191–200.

19. I would like to acknowledge sociologist Gail Dines of Wheelock College for the idea that boy children can be gendered female by abusers.

20. Kathleen Barry, *The Prostitution of Sexuality: The Global Exploitation of Women* (New York: New York University Press, 1995).

21. Cynthia Enloe, *Manueuvers: The International Politics of Militarizing Women's Lives* (Berkeley: University of California Press, 2000); Maria Rosa Henson, *Comfort Woman: A Filipina's Story of Prostitution and Slavery under the Japanese Military* (Lanham, MD: Rowman & Littlefield, 1999).

22. Cynthia Enloe, *Manueuvers: The International Politics of Militarizing Women's Lives* (Berkeley: University of California Press, 2000); Sheila Jeffreys, "Double Jeopardy: Women, the US Military, and the War in Iraq," *Women's Studies International Forum* 30, no. 1 (January–February 2007): 16–25.

23. Charity Crouse, "Slaves of Chicago: International Sex Trafficking Is Becoming Big Business," *In These Times* 25, no. 3 (January 8, 2001): 7–8; Jesse Sage and Liora Kasten, *Enslaved: True Stories of Modern Slavery* (New York: Palgrave MacMillan, 2006); Kathryn Farr, *Sex Trafficking: The Global Market in Women and Children* (New York: Worth, 2004).

24. Kurt Eichenwald, "From Their Own Online World, Pedophiles Extend Their Reach," *The New York Times*, 21 August 2006; Kurt Eichenwald, "With Child Sex Sites on the Run, Nearly Nude Photos Hit the Web," *The New York Times*, 20 August 2006. For an example of one such Web page see: http://sparkle.artmodelingstudios.com/preview.html.

25. John Stoltenberg, "Of Microbes and Men," *Ms.*, August–September 2000, pp. 60–62.

26. Centers for Disease Control, June 2007, "Fact Sheet: HIV/AIDS among African Americans." http://www.cdc.gov/hiv/topics/aa/resources/factsheets/aa.htm.

27. Angela Bonavoglia, "Making Love in the Dark," *Ms.*, August–September 2000, pp. 54–59.

28. Jill Lewis, "'So How Did Your Condom Use Go Last Night, Daddy?' Sex Talk and Daily Life," in Lynne Segal, ed., *New Sexual Agendas* (New York: New York University Press, 1997), pp. 238–252; Carla Willig, "Trust as Risky Practice," in Lynne Segal, ed., *New Sexual Agendas* (New York: New York University Press, 1997), pp. 125–153.

29. Raphael Lewis, "Cleric Calls Condom Use 'Lesser Evil' in HIV Fight," *The Boston Globe*, 16 September 2000, p. A1ff; Elizabeth Dwoskin, "Cardinal Shifts on Condoms," Women's eNews, May 5, 2006: http://www.womensenews.org/article.cfm?aid=2721.

30. Silvana Paternostro, *In the Land of God and Man: A Latin Woman's Journey* (New York: Penguin Putnam, 1998).

31. Patricia Hill Collins, *Black Feminist Thought,* 2nd ed. (New York: Routledge, 2000).

32. Connie S. Chan, "Issues of Identity Development among Asian-American Lesbians and Gay Men," *Journal of Counseling and Development* 68, no. 1 (September–October 1989): 16–20; Surina Kahn, "The All-American Queer Pakistani Girl," in Gwen Kirk and Margo Okazawa-Rey, eds., *Women's Lives: Multicultural Perspectives,* 2nd ed. (Mountain View, CA: Mayfield, 2001).

33. Paula Ross, "What's Race Got to Do with It?" in Karla Jay, ed., *Dyke Life* (New York: Basic Books, 1995), p. 142.

34. Sarah El Deeb, "23 Jailed after Trial for Gay Sex," *The Boston Globe,* 15 November 2001, p. A8.

35. Tatsha Robertson, "Gays Return to the Fold: Many Cite Flaws of 'Conversion,'" *The Boston Globe,* 9 September 2000, pp. B1, B4.

30

A PORNOGRAPHIC WORLD
[What Is Normal?]

ROBERT JENSEN

Robert Jensen is the author of *The Heart of Whiteness: Confronting Race, Racism and White Privilege* (2005) and *Citizens of the Empire: The Struggle to Claim Our Humanity* (2004). He is an associate professor in the School of Journalism at the University of Texas at Austin.

My Story

I am a normal guy in a world in which no guy is really normal. I was raised in a conventional household (two parents, three siblings, one dog) in a part of the United States not known for radical thinking or countercultural lifestyles (Fargo, North Dakota). There I was exposed to the standard US ideology of male dominance, white supremacy, the inherent superiority of capitalism, and America's role as the moral exemplar of the world. I was raised to be a nice white guy who took his place in the world, worked hard, and didn't complain too much.

At the same time, there are aspects of my biography that are not so normal, such as experiences of abuse early in my life. But it turns out, when you start talking to guys, such things happened to lots of us. My sexual profile also might, at first glance, seem outside the norm; I have had sexual relationships with men and women, though most of my life has been lived as a heterosexual. But it turns out that such sexual ambiguity isn't so unusual for lots of men either.

As a child growing up, until my late teens, I typically was the shortest boy in my class and painfully thin. As a small, "faggy" kid, I knew I was an easy target. So, I spent a lot of energy trying not to appear to be homosexual. And it turns out that a lot of the men of my generation whom I have talked to over the years—no matter how macho they appeared on the surface—worried at some point about being tagged as gay when they were young.

Even with my lack of physical ability, I managed to be minimally competent in sports and played on baseball and basketball teams through junior high. Emotionally, I was what's typically called a "sensitive child," but I managed to fake my way through the routine interactions with other boys without getting beaten up. Other boys were not so lucky. I remember one in particular in junior high who endured endless cruelty for being a gangly, socially awkward kid. When other boys teased and attacked him, I stepped aside. I didn't actively participate in that abuse, but I never defended the boy; my fear of being similarly targeted kept me silent. As I write this, 35 years later, I can recall how deeply I empathized with his suffering, and how terrified I was of those boys turning on me.

I have never felt like a "real man," but it turns out that almost no man I know feels much confidence in that realm; even those who fit the specifications more closely rarely feel like they are fulfilling their masculine obligations. So, I wasn't normal, and at the same time I was well within the norm. Most important, I was raised to be normal. I was socialized to be a man, even if I lacked some of the physical or emotional attributes to fill the role very well. And part of that socialization involved the use of pornography.

Pornography Use

I was born in 1958, in the post-*Playboy* world. My first recollection of viewing sexual material is from early grade school, when one of the boys in my school got his hands on a biker magazine that had pictures of women with exposed breasts. I have no recollection of the specific images but do retain a clear memory of gathering in the backyard of a neighborhood boy's house to look at the magazine, which we had hidden under a leaf pile. It was at about the same time I began "playing doctor," exploring bodies with other boys and girls in the neighborhood. So, as I was consciously becoming aware of sexuality, my first recognizable cultural lesson on the subject came in a male-bonding ritual around men's use of an objectified woman, who existed only to provide sexual excitement for us.

[A footnote: This memory is so powerful that every time I see a poster called "Celebrate the Whole Boy" I am reminded of it. The picture on the poster is of five grade-school boys after football practice in the park as they listen to one of the boys playing the violin. In the picture it is fall, with leaves on the ground. Three of the boys are kneeling around the violin case, with the other two standing. The obvious irony is that a poster with a healthy message—that the culture's narrow conception of masculinity limits boys' development and that we should think of all the ways to nurture them—reminds me of the patriarchal training it is critiquing.]

That grade-school experience is the first recollection I have of what Sheila Jeffreys calls "the idea of prostitution," the notion that men can buy women's sexuality in various forms. Rather than seeing men's control and use of women for sex as natural and stemming from a biological imperative, Jeffreys argues that such behavior is socially constructed. "The idea of prostitution has to exist in a man's head first if he is to consider using a woman that way," she writes. "A necessary component of this idea is that it will be sexually exciting to so use a woman."[1]

So, let's mark my introduction into the idea of prostitution at age seven, gathered around the leaf pile, one of a group of boys experiencing our emerging sexuality in an act of male dominance, the ideological assertion of dominance made into a material reality in a picture. That magazine would decay by winter but, in those few months of fall, it taught us something about what it meant to be a man.

The story goes downhill from there.

In the 1960s and 70s, as I went through public school, the main medium for pornography was the magazine, and in my circle of friends there was a reasonably steady supply of them, tucked away under beds, shoved in the back of closets, and carefully hidden under piles of leaves. Some were pilfered from relatives—we all knew where dads and big brothers hid their stash. Others were retrieved from dumpsters; we knew when stores that sold pornography threw away out-of-date stock. Sometimes we looked at them in groups, sometimes alone.

At the end of junior high school and my first year of high school, I was hanging out with a group of guys who had learned the art of sneaking into movie theaters without paying. One of our targets was the Broadway Theater in Fargo, my hometown's only "dirty movie theater," where I saw parts of several hardcore pornographic films as a teenager. At the time I had no sexual experience beyond a few sessions of sexual experimentation with other kids (boys and girls) in grade school, and I really didn't understand much of what was happening on the screen, though I was transfixed by the intensity of my sexual reaction. At a conventional movie theater we sneaked in to see *Last Tango in Paris,* to which I had the same reaction and of which I understood even less.

[Another footnote: In one of those episodes at the Broadway, three of us approached the rear door in the alley with the intention of sneaking in. At the last minute, one of the other boys backed out, claiming to be nervous. But he encouraged us to go ahead, which we did. Once in the theater, we were extremely nervous, desperately afraid of being caught. A few minutes into the film, my companion thought he heard an usher coming toward us and decided to bolt for the exit, with me a few steps behind. He hit the exit door at full speed and met some resistance, but pushed it open and tumbled into the alley, falling over garbage cans. The friend who had stayed behind had dragged the cans in front of the door, assuming that when we tried to exit, we would find it blocked and get scared. Although we were angry at him in the moment, it never occurred to me that such a prank was quite a strange thing to do to a friend. Such cruelty was simply part of growing up male.]

In college, after becoming legally able to enter adult bookstores and theaters, I made occasional visits. Because there was only one such bookstore in Fargo and we risked being seen by friends or relatives while entering or leaving (not to mention while inside), most of those forays took place during trips to Minneapolis, again sometimes with friends and sometimes alone. While in college I also saw a few X-rated movies with friends (both all-male and mixed-gender groups), who treated the outings as campy fun, and I went to a couple of those movies on my own.

[One last footnote: One of my friends from college with whom I made a couple of those trips was a man with whom I had a sexual experience after we had graduated. He was among the most militantly heterosexual men I have ever known and, to the best of my knowledge, did not have a secret gay life. That experience is a reminder that the way most men present themselves to the world in sexual terms does not reflect the complexity of our lives, and we rarely have places to talk openly about that experience. It's one of the most obvious ways in which heterosexism/homophobia limits all men.]

In my 20s, as a working professional, I had a complex relationship to pornography. I typically did not purchase pornography to use at home, although through the years I occasionally bought magazines such as *Playboy* and *Penthouse*. I never showed pornography to women with whom I was involved, with the exception of one trip to an adult theater with a woman in college. I have never made homemade pornography or recorded sexual activity.

Throughout my 20s I would sometimes visit the stores or theaters, though I was increasingly uncomfortable using the material, I had no political critique at that point, nor did I have moral qualms about it; I was then, and remain today, a secular person and had no theological conflicts about the subject. My hesitations were emotional—it just felt wrong. I fell into what I later learned was a common pattern: I would feel intense sexual excitement, masturbate, and immediately feel a sense of shame. That experience would typically lead to a decision to stop using pornography, which would last for some weeks or months. But eventually I would find myself back in a bookstore or theater.

Pornographic Fallout

That pattern continued until I was about 30 years old, when I started graduate school and began studying the feminist critique of pornography. Since then, I have used pornography only in the course of four research projects on the content of video and internet pornography.

When people ask me the last time I used pornography—not as a researcher but as a consumer—my answer is "yesterday." By that, I don't mean that I watched a pornographic film yesterday, but that for those of us with a history of "normal" pornography use as children and young adults, quitting pornography doesn't necessarily mean we are pornography-free. My sexual imagination was in part shaped by the use of pornography. I still have in my head vivid recollections of specific scenes in pornographic films

I saw 25 years ago. To the degree possible, I try to eliminate those images when I am engaging in sexual activity today (whether alone or with my partner), and I think I'm pretty successful at it. The longer I'm away from pornography, the easier it gets. But the key term is "to the degree possible."

Even with the advances in neuroscience, we really don't know all that much about human memory, consciousness, and behavior. What is pretty clear is that what goes on in our heads and bodies is far more complex than we can ever fully understand. It would not be surprising if the images and ideas that we encounter during the act of achieving orgasm—especially early in our development—would have a powerful influence on us, one that might last in various ways throughout our lives.

What goes on in my body sexually is the result of not just what I think and feel in the moment, but a lifetime of training and experience. I wish I could neatly segregate and eliminate not only the effects of my past pornography use but the effects of all the ugly sexist training I have received in my life about sexuality. I wish I could wall myself off from the sexist messages and images that are all around me today. I wish I could find a way to create a space untouched by those forces in which I could live.

But if I am to be honest, I have to admit something that is painful to face: I still struggle against those forces. I have to work to bracket out of my mind—to the degree possible—those images. I have to work to remember that I can deepen my own experience of intimacy and sexuality only when I let go of those years of training in how to dominate.

It's hard to be honest about these things, because so much of what lives within us is rooted in that domination/subordination dynamic. But it's a good rule of thumb that the things that are difficult are the most important to confront. That's easy to say but hard to practice.

The Culture's Story

When I was born in 1958, the cultural conversation on pornography took place largely within a framework of moral assertions. The obscenity law that regulated sexual material was typically defended as necessary because such uses of sex were immoral, while defenders of pornography argued that individuals should be free to use such material because there was no harm to others and the state should not make moral decisions for people. The anti-pornography view was articulated mostly by conservative and religious people; liberals and secular people dominated the defense of pornography.

Beginning in the late 1970s, feminist anti-violence activists began to focus on the connections between men's violence against women and mass media, especially pornography. The framework for that critique was political; feminists were not arguing that any particular expression of sexuality was immoral. Instead, they focused on the political—on differences in power and men's subordination of women, and the concrete harms that followed.

By the mid-1990s, the feminist critique of pornography mostly had been pushed out of the public discussion and a new economic framework emerged. Journalists began writing routinely about pornography as an ordinary business that raised no particular moral or political concerns. These stories sometimes mentioned opposition to the industry, but simply as one aspect of doing business that pornographers had to cope with. Neither the conservative/ religious objections to pornography[2] nor the feminist critique[3] has disappeared, but the shift in the framework—the predominant way in which the culture engages pornography—is revealing. Opposition to pornography in the United States, rooted either in conservative religious faith or feminist politics, must articulate that position in a society that largely takes pornography as an uncontroversial part of contemporary culture. This is the normalization or mainstreaming of pornography.

I had been observing that normalization trend for two decades when I went for the first time, in January 2005, to the Adult Entertainment Expo sponsored by *Adult Video News,* the preeminent trade magazine of the pornography industry. Although I had been studying the industry for years, I had always avoided going to the AVN convention, which is held in Las Vegas. When I went in 2005 as part of the crew for a documentary on the industry, I finally understood why I had always instinctively stayed away.

Las Vegas

My job at the AEE was to move around on the convention floor with the film's director, Miguel Picker, and talk to the pornography producers, performers, and fans about why they make, distribute, and consume sexually explicit media. As we roamed the huge Sands Expo and Convention Center, which accommodated about 300 booths and thousands of people a day, rock music pulsated from multiple directions. There were photos of naked women everywhere, video screens running porn loops scattered throughout the hall, display tables of dildos and sex dolls. And around every corner were performers in various states of undress, signing posters and posing for pictures. Flashes popped constantly as fans photographed their favorite stars.

At the end of the first day of shooting, Miguel and I were tired. We had spent the day surrounded by images of women being presented and penetrated for the sexual pleasure of men. I had listened to young men tell me that pornography had taught them a lot about what women really want sexually. I had listened to a pornography producer tell me that he thinks anal sex is popular in pornography because men like to think about fucking their wives and girlfriends in the ass to pay them back for being bitchy. And I interviewed the producer who takes great pride that his Gag Factor series was the first to feature exclusively aggressive "throat fucking."

We walked silently from the convention center to the hotel, until I finally said, "I need a drink."

I don't want to feign naïveté. I wasn't particularly shocked by anything I saw that day. There was no one thing I learned on the convention floor that surprised me, nothing anyone said that was really that new to me. I had been working on the issue for more than 15 years at that point; it would have been hard for me to find anything at AEE shocking.

We stopped at the nearest hotel bar (which didn't take long, given how many bars there are in a Las Vegas hotel). I sat down with a glass of wine, and Miguel and I started to talk, searching for some way to articulate what we had just experienced, what we felt. I struggled to hold back tears, and then finally stopped struggling.

I hadn't had some sort of epiphany about the meaning of pornography. It's just that in that moment, the reality of the industry—of the products the industry creates and the way in which they are used—all came crashing down on me. My defenses were inadequate to combat a simple fact: The pornographers had won. The feminist arguments about justice and the harms of pornography had lost. The pornographers not only are thriving, but are more mainstream and normalized than ever. They can fill up a Las Vegas convention center, with the dominant culture paying no more notice than it would to the annual boat show.

My tears at that moment were for myself, because I realized in a more visceral way than ever that the pornographers had won and are helping to construct a world that is not only dangerous for women and children, but also one in which I have fewer and fewer places to turn as a man. Fewer places to walk and talk and breathe that haven't been colonized and pornographized. As I sat there, all I could say to Miguel was, "I don't want to live in this world."

I think Miguel didn't quite know what to make of my reaction. He was nice to me, but he must have thought I was going a bit over the top. I don't blame him; I was a bit over the top. After all, we were there to make a documentary film about the industry, not live out a melodrama about my angst in a Las Vegas hotel bar. The next day Miguel and I hit the convention floor again. At the end of that day, as we walked away, I made the same request. We sat at the same bar. I had another glass of wine and cried again. I think Miguel was glad it was the last day. So was I.

Two days after we left Las Vegas, Miguel called me from New York. This time he was the one crying. He told me that he had just come to his editing studio and had put on some music that he finds particularly beautiful, and then the floodgates opened. "I understand what you meant in the bar," he said, speaking through his own tears.

I tell this story not to highlight the sensitivity of two new-age men. Miguel actually is a sensitive person, though not very new age. I'm not new age, and I don't feel particularly sensitive these days. I often feel harsh and angry. Instead, I tell the story to remind myself that I am alive, that I haven't given up, that I still feel.

I tell the story to remind myself that I'm not alone in that struggle. In a world that trains men to struggle with each other for dominance and keep their emotional distance from each other, Miguel and I could connect. He's a musician and artist from Chile; I'm a journalist and professor from North Dakota. On the surface, we don't have much in common, except our humanity.

I have to remind myself of those things because in the short term, things are grim. The feminist critique that could help this culture transcend its current crisis—on every level, from the intimate to the global—has been attacked and marginalized, and the feminists with the courage to take the critique to the public have been demonized and insulted. That's the short term. In the long term, I believe human society will move out of patriarchy and into some other organizing principle that will emerge through struggle. The problem is, as the economist John Maynard Keynes put it, in the long run we're all dead.

Hope in the long run is rational only when we are willing to face difficult analyses and action in the short term.

NOTES

1. Sheila Jeffreys, *The Idea of Prostitution* (North Melbourne, Australia: Spinifex, 1997), 3.
2. See Morality in Media, http://www.moralityinmedia.org/.
3. See National Feminist Antipornography Movement, http://feministantipornographymovement.org/.

31

THE MYTH OF THE SEXUAL ATHLETE

DON SABO

Don Sabo, Ph.D., is professor of sociology at D'Youville College in Buffalo, New York. His latest books include *Prison Masculinities* (2001) (with Michael Messner), *Sex, Violence & Power in Sports* (1994), and (with Dave Gordon) *Men's Health & Illness: Gender, Power, & the Body* (1995). He coauthored the 1997 President's Council on Physical Fitness and Sport report *Physical Activity and Sport in the Lives of Girls*. He directed the nationwide Women's Sports Foundation study *Sport and Teen Pregnancy* (1998).

The phrase "sexual athlete" commonly refers to male heterosexual virtuosity in the bedroom. Images of potency, agility, technical expertise, and an ability to attract and satisfy women come to mind. In contrast, the few former athletes who have seriously written on the subject, like Dave Meggyesy and Jim Bouton, and films such as *Raging Bull* and *North Dallas Forty,* depict the male athlete as sexually uptight, fixated on early adolescent sexual antics and exploitative of women. The former image of athletic virility, however, remains fixed within the popular imagination. Partly for this reason, little has been said about the *real* connections between sports and male sexuality.

Locker-Room Sex Talk

Organized sports were as much a part of my growing up as Cheerios, television, and homework. My sexuality unfolded within the all-male social world of sports where sex was always a major focus. I remember, for example, when as prepubertal boys I and my friends pretended to be shopping for baseball cards so we could sneak peeks at *Playboy* and *Swank* magazines at the newsstand. After practices, we would talk endlessly about "boobs" and what it must feel like to kiss and neck. Later, in junior high, we teased one another in the locker room about "jerking off" or being virgins, and there were endless interrogations about "how far" everybody was getting with their girlfriends.

Eventually, boyish anticipation spilled into *real* sexual relationships with girls, which, to my delight and confusion, turned out to be a lot more complex than I ever imagined. While sex (kissing, necking, and petting) got more exciting, it also got more difficult to figure out and talk about. Inside, all the boys, like myself, needed to love and be loved. We were awkwardly reaching out for intimacy. Yet we were telling one another to "catch feels," be cool, connect with girls but don't allow yourself to depend on them. When I was a high-school junior, the gang in the weight room once accused me of being wrapped around my girlfriend's finger. Nothing could be further from the truth, I assured them, and to prove it I broke up with her. I felt miserable about this at the time, and I still feel bad about it.

Within the college jock subculture, men's public protests against intimacy sometimes became exaggerated and ugly. I remember two teammates, drunk and rowdy, ripping girls' blouses off at a party and crawling on their bellies across the dance floor to look up skirts. Then there were the late Sunday morning breakfasts in the dorm. We jocks would usually all sit at one table listening to one braggart or another describe his sexual exploits of the night before. Though a lot of us were turned off by such boasting, ego-boosting tactics, we never openly criticized it. Stories of raunchy, or even abusive sex, real or fabricated, were also assumed to "win points." A junior fullback claimed to have defecated on a girl's chest after she passed out during intercourse. There were also some laughing reports of "gang-bangs."

When sexual relationships were "serious," that is, tempered by love and commitment, the unspoken rule was silence. Rarely did we young men share our feeling about women, our uncertainty about sexual performance, or our disdain for the crudeness and insensitivity of some of our teammates. I now see the tragic irony in this: we could talk about casual sex and about using, trivializing, or debasing women, but frank discussions about sexuality that unfolded within a loving relationship were taboo. Within the locker-room subculture, sex and love were seldom allowed to mix. There was a terrible split between our inner needs and outer appearances, between our desire for love from women and our feigned indifference toward them.

Sex as a Sport

Organized sports provide a social setting in which gender (i.e., masculinity and femininity) learning melds with sexual learning. Our sense of "femaleness" or "maleness" influences the ways we see ourselves as sexual beings. Indeed, as we develop, sexual identity emerges as an extension of an already formed gender identity, and sexual behavior tends to conform to cultural norms. To be manly in sports, traditionally, means to be competitive, successful, dominating, aggressive, stoical, goal-directed, and physically strong. Many athletes accept this definition of masculinity and apply it in their relationships with women. Dating becomes a sport in itself, and "scoring," or having sex with little or no emotional involvement, is a mark of masculine achievement. Sexual relationships are games in which women are seen as opponents, and his scoring means her defeat. Too often, women are pawns in men's quests for status within the male pecking order. For many of us jocks, sexual relationships are about man as a hunter and woman as prey.

Why is this? What transforms us from boys who depend on women to men who misunderstand, alienate ourselves from, and sometimes mistreat women? One part of the problem is the expectation that we are supposed to act as though we want to be alone, like the cowboy who always rides off into the sunset alone. In sports, there is only one "most valuable player" on the team.

Too often this prevents male athletes from understanding women and their life experiences. Though women's voices may reach men's ears from the sidelines and grandstands, they remain distant and garbled by the clamor of male competition. In sports, communication gaps between the sexes are due in part to women's historical exclusion, from refusal to allow girls to play along with boys, and coaching practices which quarantine boys from the "feminizing" taint of female influence. One result of this isolation is that sexual myths flourish. Boys end up learning about girls and female sexuality from other males, and the information that gets transmitted within the male network is often inaccurate and downright sexist. As boys, we lacked a vocabulary of intimacy, which would have enabled us to better share sexual experiences with others. The locker-room language that filled our adolescent heads did not exactly foster insights into the true nature of women's sexuality—or our own, for that matter.

Performance and Patriarchy

Traditional gender learning and locker-room sexual myths can also shape men's lovemaking behavior. Taught to be "achievement machines," many athletes organize their energies and perceptions around a performance ethic that influences sexual relations. Men apply their goal-directedness and preoccupation with performance to their lovemaking. In the movie *Joe,* a sexually liberated woman tells her hard-hat lover that "making love isn't like running a fifty-yard dash."

Making intercourse the chief goal of sex limits men's ability to enjoy other aspects of sexual experience. It also creates problems for both men and their partners. Since coitus requires an erection, men pressure themselves to get and maintain erections. If erections do not occur, or men ejaculate too quickly, their self-esteem as lovers and men can be impaired. In fact, sex therapists tell us that men's preoccupation and anxieties about erectile potency and performance can cause the very sexual dysfunctions they fear.

It is important to emphasize that not only jocks swallow this limiting model of male sexuality. Sports are not the only social setting that promotes androcentrism and eroticism without emotional intimacy. Consider how male sexuality is developed in fraternities, motorcycle gangs, the armed forces, urban gangs, pornography, corporate advertising, MTV, magazines like *Playboy* or *Penthouse,* and the movies—to name but a few examples. These are not random and unrelated sources of traditional masculine values. They all originate in patriarchy.

Sexual relations between men and women in Western societies have been conducted under the panoply of patriarchal power. The sexual values that derive from patriarchy emphasize male dominance and the purely physical dimensions of the sex act while reducing women to delectable but expendable objects. An alternative conception of human sexuality, however, is also gaining ascendancy within the culture. Flowing out of women's experiences and based on egalitarian values, it seeks to integrate eroticism with love and commitment. It is deeply critical of the social forces that reduce women (and men) to sex objects, depersonalize relationships, and turn human sexuality into an advertising gimmick or commodity to be purchased. This is the sexual ethos proffered by the women's movement.

Today's young athletes don't seem as hooked as their predecessors on the hypermasculine image traditional sports have provided. Perhaps this is because alternative forms of masculinity and sexuality have begun to enter the locker-room subculture. More girls are playing sports than ever before, and coeducational athletic experiences are more common. As more women enter the traditionally male settings of sports, business, factories, and government, men are finding it more difficult to perceive women in only one dimension. Perhaps we are becoming better able to see them as fellow human beings and, in the process, we are beginning to search for alternative modes of being men.

What Do Men Really Want (or Need)?

Most of us do not really know what it is we want from our sexual lives. Men seem torn between yearning for excitement and longing for love and intimacy. On one side, we feel titillated by the glitter of corporate advertising. Eroticism jolts our minds and bodies. We're sporadically attracted by the simple hedonism of the so-called sexual revolution and the sometimes slick, sometimes sleazy veil of pornography, soft and hard. Many of us fantasize about pursuing eroticism without commitment; some actually live the fantasy. Yet more men are recently becoming aware of genuine needs for intimate relationships. We are beginning to recognize that being independent, always on the make and emotionally controlled, is not meeting our needs. Furthermore, traditional masculine behavior is certainly not meeting women's expectations or satisfying their emotional needs. More and more men are starting to wonder if sexuality can be a vehicle for expressing and experiencing love.

In our culture many men are suffering from sexual schizophrenia. Their minds lead them toward eroticism while their hearts pull them toward emotional intimacy. What they think they want rarely coincides with what they need. Perhaps the uneasiness and the ambivalence that permeate male sexuality are due to this root fact: the traditional certainties that men have used to define their manhood and sexuality no longer fit the realities of their lives. Until equality between the sexes becomes more of a social reality, no new model of a more humane sexuality will take hold.

As for me, I am still exploring and redefining my sexuality. Although I don't have all the answers yet, I do have direction. I am listening more closely to women's voices, turning my head away from the sexist legacy of the locker room, and pursuing a profeminist vision of sexuality. I feel good to have stopped pretending that I enjoy being alone. I never did like feeling alone.

32

PASSING LAST SUMMER

DOMINIKA BEDNARSKA

Dominika Bednarska is a doctoral student in English and disability studies at the University of California, Berkeley. She has been published in *Ghosting Atoms: Poems and Reflections Sixty Years After the Bomb, Medicinal Purposes,* and *What I Want from You: Voices of East Bay Lesbian Poets* (2006).

I want to write about last summer and passing but I don't know where to begin. It's tempting to begin at the dyke march, rolling through in my scooter (read: a type of electric wheelchair) with a painful hickey on my neck, procured the night before from N, a gay man I hardly knew. I let that butch dyke marching next to me think the hickey came from another woman.

I won't pretend that this decision had nothing to do with the disdain so many lesbians feel toward queer women who express any kind of desire for men. But the decision was more about not wanting to enter into a complicated discussion about queerness and identification with a total stranger, while marching. My experience the night before had been my only sexual encounter with a man since I began to identify as a lesbian. I couldn't imagine it erasing that identity, but there was a small part of me that felt fraudulent.

Yet in order to talk about passing and sexuality, first I must talk about being a crip.

I've started to say crip to nondisabled people now, the way I call them AB without offering an explanation. AB means able-bodied, and is used interchangeably in this essay with nondisabled. Some people use crip as short for cripple. I used to use the word crip only to mean a disabled person willing to claim that identity, but now I also say cripple to refer transgressively to other disabled people who are wheelchair users. I have always been both a crip and a cripple.

Disabled all my life, I distinctly remember threatening to sue a restaurant owner for demanding I sit in the back of an empty restaurant. I was seven. It was three years before the Americans with Disabilities Act, thirteen years after the Vocational Rehabilitation Act of 1973, which did the same thing as the ADA but was never enforced. I didn't have this context then. I had no idea there was actually a law that protected my civil rights; I was talking out of my ass, but we got reseated. It seems weird that I want to talk about disability and passing, because I use canes and an electric scooter for mobility. This equipment makes it obvious that I have some difficulty walking. For me to pass for AB, you would need to see me sitting at my desk or hear me on the phone, and even then the illusion would be short-lived. Eventually I would need to get up or roll away and you would know that I was disabled. Though once at a Halloween party, some guy asked me, "You don't really need those, do you?" I was dressed as a cat, but I guess my youth and skimpy clothes cast my canes as suspect.

I remember a conversation with a friend of mine who talked about the difficulty and stigma of outing oneself as disabled. I am rarely in situations where I get that choice. Unlike with my friend, people assume that I have some sort of disability. They stare or avoid eye contact. They challenge my own assessment of what I can do. They condescend. They become defensive when I raise the issue of wheelchair accessibility. They force me to accept help I don't need by manipulating my body, picking me up, or grabbing my arm. They sometimes refer to me as simply "the wheelchair."

Occasionally, people anticipate my need for a ramp or a curb cut because of my scooter. This, however, is rarely the case. Usually I need to remind them. I think about what a friend of mine, with an invisible disability, describes as "coming out": the difficulty of explaining exactly how her disability affects her and what her needs are in relation to the other person. But I have to do that as well.

I recognize that my claims of disability are met with less skepticism than hers because I use equipment and she doesn't, but I am forced to out myself because the scooter and canes don't express the exact specifics of my mobility. Can I walk? How far? Up stairs? My hands look fine, but I have bad tendonitis. Then there are the spasms, pain, and fatigue, all of which vary from day to day, hour to hour. The barrage of questions I am met with on a regular basis regarding my abilities is staggering—ranging from what my disability is to whether I take medication, drive a car, date, or have sex. These questions show how little is actually explained by the visibility of my scooter or canes. If outing has anything to do with understanding something about someone, explaining one's disability the way my friend described, I am always outing myself. Unfortunately, the stigma I experience as a result of moving through the world chiefly while sitting down does little to help others to understand my needs and abilities. I am not spared the talks about the parameters of my body, my functionality, or my mobility. Visible disability does not avoid these conversations. It means that first I have to erase what so-and-so thought she knew because her aunt's friend had MS or MD (which I don't have, and even if I did, what information would that give her about my body?).

Last summer, the same body began dealing with bad tendonitis along-side cerebral palsy, which impacted not only my ability to type and write, but also to walk, stand, and dance on my feet. I was instructed by my doctor to avoid these activities because I might lose function, strength, and even sensation in my hands. To an observer, it didn't look like anything was wrong, and I could still do these things myself, but putting weight on my hands through my canes caused my hands and arms to hurt, tingle, burn, and go numb. Still, I felt like a fraud—with attendants in my room helping me to transfer in and out of bed, tie my shoes, and take a shower. I had worked for years in physical therapy to learn to do these things independently. Sometimes I would cheat by doing them myself anyway, because it was faster, cheaper, and easier. Or by masturbating (very hand-intensive stuff). But particularly by having sex with N.

The night I went home with N, we chatted for a few hours, there being a kind of foreplay in his complaint that lesbians always hit on him at the local gay bar. I made the same complaint about gay men, particularly one guy who just wouldn't leave me alone. He kept dancing with me by wrapping his arm so that my throat was in the crook of his elbow, our height differential such that he was choking me. I kept pulling him off of me, and he kept replacing his arm. I went to sit down, but I got back up because I wanted to continue dancing. It was my whole reason for going out that night. Eventually this guy collapsed on top of me. The force of his fall knocked off my shoes. I had a bruise for several weeks, but I wasn't upset about that; I was upset about the fact that all of this happened in public, that more people would apologize as they simply brushed past me, and I would be treated as fragile for the rest of the night, even though I was not necessarily any less capable of staying on my feet than the guy who fell on top of me.

Another time, a man began dancing with me and grabbed my canes, lifting the ends up into the air and moving them back and forth as though they were arms. I had five seconds to prepare. I thought about tucking my head and pushing all of my weight forward to minimize the chance of cracking my head open on the dance floor. It worked pretty well. I fell in something of a cannonball position. In both of these cases, the men were thrown out of the club. In both cases, I remember being more upset about how I was being perceived than about the actual event itself, but I still felt attacked both times. I can't remember whether I told N these stories. They certainly came to mind when I made that comment about gay men coming on to me.

I remember explaining that my attraction to men ranged from sporadic to nonexistent and was not something I acted upon because I had no desire to be in relationships with men. Most of my emotional and intimate connections were with women. N said he felt the same way about women as I did about men. Looking back, I can see that we were negotiating our unexpected attraction. At the time, it felt like little more than small talk. But I guess the real proposition came with N's "I'm gay, you're gay; wanna make out?"

During sex, I could not avoid using my hands. Or maybe I could have, but it didn't make me feel sexy to ask for help I didn't "need," especially in bed. There are certain orgasms that would not have happened without me using my hands—many of which were rightfully mine. Or were they? It is strange to talk about entitlement to sexual satisfaction as a lesbian involved with a gay man.

A gay male friend of mine kept trying to understand this unprecedented turn of events by putting us into different boxes. He described me as an experimenting lesbian and N as a bisexual or N as experimenting and me as frustrated or confused. Perhaps, my friend said, we were both bisexual, but my friend just didn't see me that way because I am so interested in women. I think of myself as a lesbian and I feel I have no right to put someone in a different box than the one that they claim, even if the boxes seem to make a logical contradiction. My friend accepted this contradiction, but he did feel it was unfair that, of the two of us, I was the one sleeping with a gay man. I told him that if he ever wanted to sleep with a lesbian, I would fully support him. We both laughed, but I reminded him that sleeping with a woman who's queer allows for mutable gender possibilities that he may not have considered, at which point my comment seemed less funny and more like food for thought. Several of my lesbian-identified friends expressed shock that I had started seeing a man, but when I added that he was queer they seemed relieved. Some added, "Oh, well, I would sleep with a gay man."

It seemed rather arbitrary to choose this one relationship, which was primarily sexual, as transformative of my identity. I am very attracted to masculinity—butch, trans, and sometimes, rarely, even the most cliché of all: actual scrotum-toters. I draw the line somewhere, though: I have never had intercourse. I have nothing against it. There are just so many things that are more interesting to me sexually. Does this prove I'm a dyke? Does it minimize the importance of my relationships (all two) with men? Or would you call me bisexual? I felt like I was passing as bi when I talked about N. One friend invited me to her bi women's group. N began to refer to himself as bisexual and would get angry when I didn't follow his lead, though eventually he gave up. Did he chalk it up to semantic differences or denial?

I am aware, as I tell this story, that it is easier to talk about the ill-fitting nature of categories in relation to my own sexuality than it is to talk about disability in relation to sex. It is one thing to talk about parallels between the two identities and another to talk about how one identity affects the other. I don't know what it says that I have waited this long to reveal that N, like me, is disabled. He also uses a wheelchair and does not walk at all. Have I waited this long because I anticipate some sort of misunderstanding, a sense of "Oh, I see" from my imagined reader, as if our unlikely coupling is explained by the fact that we are both disabled?

Did I wait because of the stereotype that all disabled men are impotent or in some way lack the ability to satisfy sexually? This stereotype is so pervasive that it frequently becomes the only burning question with regard to disability and sexuality. In MTV's recent *Murderball,* a movie about two wheelchair rugby teams training for the Paralympics, an entire segment had to be devoted to how disabled men have sex, and specifically whether or not they can get it up. In fact, in a workshop I attended for queer women on sexuality, after a "discussion" of disability and sexuality that basically consisted of me talking about the ways in which disability informs sexuality, the only question I received was, "Can my wife's brother, with a spinal cord injury, still have sex?" Of course this woman ignored everything I'd just said, and despite being lesbian-identified, had reduced sex to an act that centered around erection and ejaculation. But even if she had asked the more specific question behind her question, there was only one person who would have been able to answer it. Perhaps I fear that the reader will ask the same question about N. Or assume that I chose him as a partner because I was less interested in traditional penetrative sex.

Perhaps I've waited because I fear that when people see me with a disabled partner they think that disability is the reason we are together. Perhaps I've waited because, in some sense, I fear that this is true. Not in the sense that I date people because of their disabilities, but in the sense that my scholarship, my writing, and my activism have often focused on disability issues. N and I met at a discussion on sex and disability. We had more flexibility about going home together because we both lived in accessible apartments. We both used accessible transportation. It made certain things easier.

But what did N and I really have in common? There were significant differences in our politics. N was interested in working within the establishment; my political beliefs are more socialist than capitalist. I had already tried the establishment route and had found it stifling. Unlike N, who expressed implicitly and explicitly that he did not want to be poor, I had been poor. I was raised by first-generation immigrants who managed—with racial privilege, luck, and hard work—to make a relatively clean departure to the middle class. I did worry about money from time to time, but I wasn't anxious about maintaining a particular class status. I deliberately chose a career that did not make people wealthy in order to effectively work on disability issues. I imagined N's family was more in line with the educated, well-off, white student body that I went to college with, but always felt slightly outside of and different from.

I distinctly remember N informing me that he tried to spend only a third of his social time with disabled people. I was disturbed by this proclamation, and we had a long conversation about it. N clarified that what he meant was that most of his social time was spent doing some kind of political organizing and he didn't want to be pigeonholed as someone who dealt only with disability issues. He also explained that when he first moved to the Bay Area he'd spent a lot of his time with disabled people and had felt he was losing his ability to relate to the nondisabled.

The ability to relate to the nondisabled was something I had to consciously develop, after attending a "special" (read ability- or crip-segregated) school until seventh grade (unlike N, who had always been mainstreamed). When I switched schools, I had to anticipate stigma and stereotype to a far greater degree. I was no longer allowed to walk in the halls without an adult; rumors were spread that my grades were high because teachers felt sorry for me; when the elevator broke, I was almost forced to leave. I wanted to be mainstreamed primarily because I was bored in all my classes (I was being forced to do work way below my grade level, and quickly losing any chance at getting into an academically challenging university, or a university at all). But another reason was that we didn't live in a world that was as segregated as my old school. I had to learn how to deal with increased prejudice and stigma. I had to learn how to live in an able-bodied world.

N is younger than me, and when I was his age I distinctly remember feeling resistance to other people with disabilities, especially in terms of dating. There was a point where dating an able-bodied person felt like the ultimate sign of normalcy and acceptance. I couldn't get past my own internalized sense of lack with regard to disability, at least in my most intimate relationships, even though this did not stop me from being vocal about ableist oppression, having disabled friends, and advocating disability pride. I remember feeling that same need to distance myself from people with disabilities, afraid that it would consume my identity, and further restrict me even more than ableism already had. Although, of course, this was a restriction I was imposing on myself as a result of ableism. I feel embarrassed to admit that I felt this way. Even now I occasionally worry that my widespread interest in disability makes me come across as a one-trick pony, not only in terms of the academy, but in terms of relating to people who have no interest in disability. Yet despite this residual internal resistance, I have had several relationships with disabled partners. The longest was with someone who had the same disability as N. Is it significant that both the women who N had been sexual with before me were disabled? Did he feel more comfortable with these women because of their disabilities? Or did they feel more comfortable with him because of his disability?

After all, disability can impact sex. In my case it requires more careful logistical negotiation in terms of positioning, due to my spasticity and lack of balance. If both partners are disabled in ways that limit their physicality, it makes certain positions nearly impossible. Hence, when someone asked me recently how my disability affected me, I replied, "Well, it sure does make me wish I paid more attention in high school physics to things like vectors and leverage." Having sex with someone who's both disabled and queer makes me feel freer, both from expectations around the body and around gender norms. My disabled queer lovers and I understand that the genitals are not the be-all and end-all of sexual pleasure. Sex is not centered around performing a prescribed set of acts, but around finding pleasure.

I'm fully aware that my desires around the kind of sex I want could change over time, depending on the partner and the possibilities and the mutability of our own desires. So many women I know who self-identify as lesbians express a desire or openness to having sex with men, but no desire for emotionally intimate relationships with them. I'm not sure what kinds of boxes it's most convenient to put these women into, or if acknowledging that desire confuses or misleads. Is it useful to use the term bisexual? And to what extent can we really know our desires, if what we want changes over time, and when sometimes we don't know what we want until we are presented with it?

I cringe as I write these words because I'm fearful of their misinterpretation. Have I just given ammunition to every sleazy, disrespectful man who trolls online posing as a lesbian, or goes to lesbian clubs and harasses women, attempting to get them to go home with him? I don't want to do us all that kind of disservice, but I want to acknowledge that one's feelings may change over time, and that feelings are not always possible to anticipate.

Similarly, I can't anticipate how my body will function, look, move, and feel with complete accuracy today. It may improve or get worse. Activities that didn't bother me today may begin to bother me tomorrow. I may experience sensations that take on new meaning. For instance, I used to just take the prickly numb feeling in my fingers as my hands falling asleep. Now, it means blood is not reaching my nerve endings properly and if I don't change position, if my circulation doesn't come back soon, I may very well be doing permanent nerve damage to my hand. It is impossible for me to know whether I will always have tendonitis in the way I experience it now, or even at all. Much in the same way, it is impossible to know what sorts of partnering and sexual activity I will choose in the future based solely on what has happened in the past. All I can do is speak from what appears to be true, from my experiences so far, with an understanding that they may not be indicative of the future.

33
———

THE IMPACT OF MULTIPLE
MARGINALIZATION

PAULA C. RUST

Paula C. Rust, Ph.D., is a sociologist. She is the author of *Bisexuality and the Challenge to Lesbian Politics: Sex, Loyalty and Revolution* (1995) and editor of *Bisexuality in the United States: A Social Science Reader* (1999).

One's sexuality is affected not only by the sexual norms of one's culture of origin but also by the position of one's culture of origin vis-à-vis the dominant culture of the United States. For individuals who belong to marginalized racial-ethnic, religious, or socioeconomic groups, the effects are numerous. Marginalized groups sometimes adopt the attitudes of the mainstream; other times, they reject these attitudes as foreign or inapplicable. McKeon (1992) notes that both processes shape the sexual attitudes of the white working class. On the one hand, the working class absorbs the homophobic attitudes promoted by the middle- and upper-class controlled media. At the same time, working-class individuals are rarely exposed to "liberal concepts of tolerance" taught in institutions of higher education which help moderate overclass heterosexism. On the other hand, working-class sexual norms are less centered around the middle-class notion of "propriety"—a value that working-class individuals cannot as readily afford. The result is a set of sexual norms that differs in complex ways from those facing middle- and upper-class bisexuals.

In marginalized racial and ethnic groups, racism interacts with cultural monosexism and heterosexism in many ways. In general, the fact of racism strengthens ethnic communities' desires to preserve ethnic values and traditions, because ethnicity is embodied and demonstrated via the preservation of these values and traditions. Tremble, Schneider, and Appathurai (1989) wrote, "After all, one can abandon traditional values in Portugal and still be Portuguese. If they are abandoned in the New World, the result is assimilation" (p. 225). Thus, ethnic minorities might cling even more tenaciously to traditional cultures than Euro-Americans do, because any cultural change reflects not a change in ethnic culture but a loss of ethnic culture. To the extent that ethnic values and traditions restrict sexual expression to heterosexuality, ethnic minority bisexuals will be under particular pressure to deny same-sex feelings in demonstration of ethnic loyalty and pride. Attempts to challenge these values and traditions by coming out as bisexual will be interpreted as a challenge to ethnic culture and identity in general.

Because homosexuality represents assimilation, it is stigmatized as a "white disease" or, at least, a "white phenomenon." Individuals who claim a bisexual, lesbian, or gay identity are accused of buying into white culture and thereby becoming traitors to their own racial or ethnic group. Previous researchers have found the attitude that lesbian or gay identity is a white thing among African Americans and Hispanics and the attitude that homosexuality is a "Western" behavior among Asian Americans (Chan, 1989; Espin, 1987; H., 1989; Icard, 1986; Matteson, 1994; Morales, 1989). In the current study, the association of gayness with whiteness was reported most often by African American respondents. One African American woman wrote that "when I came out, it was made clear to me that my being queer was in some sense a betrayal of my 'blackness.' Black women just didn't do 'these' kinds of things. I spent a lot of years thinking that I could not be me and be 'really' black too." Morales (1990) found that Hispanic men choose to identify as bisexual even if they are exclusively homosexual, because they see gay identity as representing "a white gay political movement rather than a sexual orientation or lifestyle" (p. 215). A Mexican woman in the current study wrote that she has "felt like . . . a traitor to my race when I acknowledge my love of women. I have felt like I've bought into the White 'disease' of lesbianism." A Puerto Rican woman reported that in Puerto Rico homosexuality is considered an import from the continental States. Chan (1989) found that Asian Americans tend to deny the existence of gays within the Asian American community, Wooden et al. (1983) reported this attitude among Japanese Americans, and Carrier et al. (1992) found denial of the existence of homosexuality among Vietnamese Americans who considered homosexuality the result of seduction by Anglo-Americans. Tremble et al. (1989) suggested that viewing homosexuality as a white phenomenon might permit ethnic minority families to accept their LesBiGay members, while transferring guilt from themselves to the dominant society.

Ironically, whereas racism can strengthen commitment to ethnic values and traditions, it can also pressure ethnic minorities to conform to mainstream values in an effort to gain acceptance from culturally dominant groups. Because members of ethnic minorities are often perceived by Euro-Americans as representatives of their entire ethnic group, the nonconformist behavior of one individual reflects negatively on the whole ethnic group. For example, African American respondents reported that homosexuality is considered shameful for the African American community because it reflects badly on the whole African American community in the eyes of Euro-Americans. A similar phenomenon exists among lesbians and gays, some of whom chastise their more flamboyant members with "How can you expect heterosexual society to accept us when you act like *that!?*" As one Black bisexual woman put it, "Homosexuality is frowned upon in the black community more than in the white community. It's as if I'm shaming the community that is trying so hard to be accepted by the white community."

The fact of ethnic oppression also interacts with particular elements of ethnic minority culture in ways that affect bisexuals. Specifically, the emphasis on the family found in many ethnic minority cultures is magnified by ethnic oppression in two ways. First, oppression reinforces the prescription to marry and have children among minorities which, for historical reasons, fear racial genocide (Greene, 1994; Icard, 1986). Second, the fact of racism makes the support of one's family even more important for ethnic minority individuals. As Morales (1989) put it, the "nuclear and extended family plays a key role and constitutes a symbol of their ethnic roots and the focal point of their ethnic identity" (p. 225). Ethnic minority individuals learn techniques for coping with racism and maintaining a positive ethnic identity from their families and ethnic communities; to lose the support of this family and community would mean losing an important source of strength in the face of the ethnic hostility of mainstream society (Almaguer, 1993; Chan, 1992; Icard, 1986). Thus, ethnic minority bisexuals have more to lose if they are rejected by their families than do Euro-American bisexuals. At the same time, they have less to gain because of the racism of the predominantly Euro-American LesBiGay community. Whereas Euro-American bisexuals who lose the support of their families can count on receiving support from the LesBiGay community instead (albeit limited by the monosexism of that community), ethnic minority bisexuals cannot be assured of this alternative source of support.

Because of fear of rejection within their own racial, ethnic, or class communities, many bisexuals—like lesbians and gay men—remain in the closet among people who share their racial, ethnic, and class backgrounds. For example, an African American–Chicana "decided to stay in the closet instead of risk isolation and alienation from my communities." Sometimes, individuals who remain closeted in their own racial-ethnic or class communities participate in the mainstream lesbian, gay, and bisexual community, which is primarily a Euro-American middle-class lesbian and gay community. Such individuals have to juggle two lives in two different communities, each of which is a valuable source of support for one aspect of their identity, but neither of which accepts them completely. Among people of their own racial, ethnic, or class background, they are not accepted and often not known as bisexuals, and among Euro-American lesbians and gays, they encounter both monosexism and class and racial prejudice or, at the least, a lack of support and understanding for the particular issues that arise for them because of their race, ethnicity, or class. Simultaneously, like other members of their racial, ethnic, or class community, they have to be familiar enough with mainstream Euro-American heterosexual culture to navigate daily life as a racial or ethnic minority; so they are, in effect, tricultural (Lukes & Land,

1990; Matteson, 1994; Morales, 1989). This situation leads not only to a complex social life but might also promote a fractured sense of self, in which one separates one's sexual identity from one's racial identity from one's American identity and experiences these identities as being in conflict with each other, just as are the communities that support each identity. Some individuals attempt to resolve this dilemma by prioritizing allegiances to these communities (Espin, 1987; Johnson, 1982; Morales, 1989), a response that Morales (1989, 1992) sees as a developmental stage preceding full integration of one's ethnic and sexual identities. More detailed descriptions of the antagonism between ethnic and gay communities and its effect on sexual minority individuals can be found in Gutiérrez and Dworkin (1992), Icard (1986), and Morales (1989, 1992).

Other bisexuals respond to the conflict between their racial/ethnic, class, and sexual communities by leaving their communities of origin in favor of mainstream LesBiGay communities. For most ethnic minority bisexuals, however, this does not solve the problem. For example, an Orthodox Jew who grieves her lost connection to the Jewish community wrote, "I still do not feel that my Jewish life and my queer life are fully integrated and am somewhat at a loss." This is true despite the large numbers of Jewish bisexuals, gays, and lesbians she has met, because "most Jewish people in the queer community are highly assimilated and are no help to me." The identities available for ethnic minorities in the LesBiGay community sometimes consist of racialized sexual stereotypes. Icard (1986), for example, describes the "Super Stud" and "Miss Thing" identities available for African American men in the gay male community. Such stereotypical identities limit and distort the potential for integrated identity development among ethnic minority bisexuals.

Finally, some people from cultures that stigmatize homosexuality choose neither to closet themselves nor to leave their cultures and communities of origin but to remain within their communities as "out" bisexuals, lesbians, or gays to challenge homophobic and biphobic attitudes. In fact, some react positively to their own stigmatization with increased pride. A Korean American immigrant woman explained that the "Asian shun of homosexuality/ bisexuality . . . makes me even more defensive yet proud of my orientation." The African American–Chicana mentioned earlier eventually decided to come out within the Latin and African American communities and now uses her "'outness' within [her] communities as a testimony to . . . diversity and to the strength [she has] developed from being raised Latina and African American."

A positive integration of one's racial, ethnic, or class identity with one's sexual identity is greatly facilitated by support from others who share an individual's particular constellation of identities. For some, finding kindred spirits is made difficult by demographic and cultural realities. But as more and more people come out, there are inevitably more "out" members of racial and ethnic minorities and among these, more bisexuals. Many respondents described the leap forward in the development of their sexual identities that became possible when they finally discovered a community of bisexuals, lesbians, or gays with a similar racial or ethnic background. A Jewish Chicana reported that she is "finding more people of my ethnic backgrounds going through the same thing. This is affirming." Similarly, a Chicano is "just now starting to integrate my sexuality and my culture by getting to know other gays/bis of color." An African American woman reported that "it wasn't until I lived in Washington, D.C., for a number of years and met large numbers of Black lesbians that I was able to resolve this conflict for myself." Many Jewish respondents commented on the fact that there are many Jewish bisexuals, lesbians, and gays, and noted that receiving support from these peers was important in the development and maintenance of their positive sexual identities. One man, when asked to describe the effect of his racial or ethnic cultural heritage on his sexuality, said simply, "I'm a Jewish Agnostic Male-oriented Bisexual. There are lots of us." Some Jewish respondents also commented that being racially white facilitated their acceptance in the mainstream LesBiGay community and permitted them to receive support from this community that was not as available to individuals of other racial and ethnic backgrounds. Of course, it is this same assimilationist attitude that caused the Orthodox Jewish woman quoted earlier to find a lack of support among Jewish LesBiGays.

For individuals who belong to racial or ethnic minorities, the discovery that one is bisexual is a discovery that one is a double or triple minority. It is even more the case for bisexuals than for lesbians and gays, because bisexuals are a political and social minority within the lesbian and gay community. Many racial and ethnic minority individuals experience their coming out as a process of further marginalization from the mainstream, that is, as an exacerbation of an already undesirable position. An African American woman described being bi as "just one other negative thing I have to deal with. My race is one and my gender another." This can inhibit coming out for individuals who are reluctant to take on yet another stigmatized identity. For example, Morales (1990) reported that some Hispanic men limit their coming out, because they do not want to risk experiencing double discrimination in their careers and personal lives. A Black woman in the current study said that she is "unwilling to come too far 'out' as I already have so many strikes against me."

Many respondents found, however, that their experiences as racial or ethnic minorities facilitated their recognition and acceptance of their sexuality. This was most common among Jewish respondents, many of whom explained that their history as an oppressed people sensitized them to other issues of oppression. One man wrote, "The Jewish sense of being an outsider or underdog has spurred my rebelliousness; the emphasis on learning and questioning has helped to open my mind." A woman wrote, "My Jewish ethnicity taught me about oppression and the need to fight it. It gave me the tools to be able to assert that the homophobes (like the anti-Semites) are wrong." Some non-Jewish respondents also found that their experiences as ethnic minorities facilitated their coming out as bisexual. For example, a woman of Mexican, Dutch, and Norwegian descent wrote that her cultural background "has made me less afraid to be different." She was already ethnically different, so she was better prepared to recognize and accept her sexual difference. Similarly, an Irish Tsalagi Indian man found being outside the mainstream to be a liberating position; he wrote, "I have always felt alienated from the cultural norm, so I'm only affected in the sense that this alienation has allowed me the freedom to visualize myself on my own terms."

   Many bisexuals of mixed race or ethnicity feel a comfortable resonance between their mixed heritage and their bisexuality. In a society where both racial-ethnic and sexual categories are highly elaborated, individuals of mixed heritage or who are bisexual find themselves straddling categories that are socially constructed as distinct from one another. The paradox presented by this position was described by a bisexual woman of Native American, Jewish, and Celtic heritage who wrote, "Because I am of mixed ethnicity, I rotate between feeling 'left out' of every group and feeling 'secretly' qualified for several racial/cultural identities. I notice the same feeling regarding my sexual identity." Other respondents of mixed racial and ethnic backgrounds also saw connections between their ethnic heritage and their bisexuality. For example, an Asian European woman wrote,

> Being multiracial, multicultural has always made me aware of nonbipolar thinking. I have always been outside people's categories, and so it wasn't such a big leap to come out as bi, after spending years explaining my [racial and cultural] identity rather than attaching a single label [to it].

A Puerto Rican who grew up alternately in Puerto Rico and a northeastern state explained,

> The duality of my cultural upbringing goes hand in hand with the duality of my sexuality. Having the best of both worlds (ethnically speaking—I look white but am Spanish) in my everyday life might have influenced me to seek the best of both worlds in my sexual life—relationships with both a man and a woman.

A Black Lithuanian Irish Scottish woman with light skin, freckles, red curly hair, and a "Black political identity," who is only recognized as Black by other Blacks, wrote, "As with my race, my sex is not to be defined by others or absoluted by myself. It is a spectrum."

   However, individuals whose mixed heritages have produced unresolved cultural difficulties sometimes transfer these difficulties to their bisexuality. A "Latino-Anglo" who was raised to be a "regular, middle-class, all-American," and who later became acculturated to Latin culture, wrote,

> Since I am ethnically confused and pass as different from what I am, as I do in sexual orientation also, I spend a lot of time

underground. . . . I think it has definitely been a major factor in the breakup of two very promising long-term relations.

Similarly, a transgendered bisexual respondent of mixed European, Native American, and North African heritage believes that the pressures she feels as a transgenderist and a bisexual are closely related to the fact that her parents "felt it necessary to hide a large part of their ethnic and racial heritage," although she did not elaborate on the nature of these pressures.

In contrast to bisexuals from marginalized racial-ethnic, religious, or class backgrounds, middle- or upper-class Protestant Euro-Americans experience relatively few difficulties integrating their sexual identities with their cultural backgrounds and other identities. Euro-American bisexuals might have difficulty developing a positive bisexual identity in a monosexist culture, but unlike Bisexuals of Color, they have no particular problems integrating their sexual identity with their racial identity, because these identities are already integrated in the LesBiGay community. Being Euro-American gives them the luxury of not dealing with racial identity. Not surprisingly, when asked how their racial-ethnic background had affected their sexuality, most Euro-Americans did not mention their race at all. Instead, Euro-Americans tended to attribute their sexual upbringing to the peculiarities of their parents, their religion, their class, or their geographic location within the United States. One woman explained,

> I do not associate my racial-ethnic cultural background and my sexuality. Undoubtedly I would think and feel differently if I were of a different background but I'm not able to identify the effect of my background on my sexuality.

REFERENCES

Almaguer, T. (1993). Chicano men: A cartography of homosexual identity and behavior. In H. Abelove, M. A. Barale, & D. M. Halperin (Eds.), *The lesbian and gay studies reader.* New York: Routledge.

Carrier, J., Nguyen, B., & Su, S. (1992). Vietnamese American sexual behaviors and HIV infection. *Journal of Sex Research, 29*(4), 547–560.

Chan, C. S. (1989). Issues of identity development among Asian American lesbians and gay men. *Journal of Counseling and Development, 68*(1), 16–21.

Chan, C. S. (1992). Cultural considerations in counseling Asian American lesbians and gay men. In S. H. Dworkin & F. Gutiérrez (Eds.), *Counseling gay men and lesbians* (pp. 115–124). Alexandria, VA: American Association for Counseling and Development.

Espin, O. (1987). Issues of identity in the psychology of Latina lesbians. In Boston Lesbian Psychologies Collective (Eds.), *Lesbian psychologies: Explorations and challenges* (pp. 35–51). Urbana: University of Illinois Press.

Greene, B. (1994). Ethnic-minority lesbians and gay men: Mental health and treatment issues. *Journal of Consulting and Clinical Psychology, 62*(2), 243–251.

Gutiérrez, F. J., & Dworkin, S. H. (1992). Gay, lesbian, and African American: Managing the integration of identities. In Dworkin & Gutiérrez (Eds.), *Counseling gay men and lesbians* (pp. 141–155).

H., P. (1989). Asian American lesbians: An emerging voice in the Asian American community. In Asian Women United of California (Eds.), *Making waves: An anthology of writings by and about Asian American women* (pp. 282–290). Boston: Beacon.

Icard, L. (1986). Black gay men and conflicting social identities: Sexual orientation versus racial identity. *Journal of Social Work and Human Sexuality, 4*(1/2), 83–92.

Johnson, J. (1982). *The influence of assimilation on the psychosocial adjustment of Black homosexual men.* Unpublished dissertation, California School of Professional Psychology, Berkeley.

Lukes, C. A., & Land, H. (1990, March). Biculturality and homosexuality. *Social Work,* 155–161.

Matteson, D. R. (1994). *Bisexual behavior and AIDS risk among some Asian American men.* Unpublished manuscript.

McKeon, E. (1992). To be bisexual and underclass. In E. R. Weise (Ed.), *Closer to home: Bisexuality & feminism* (pp. 27–34). Seattle, WA: Seal.

Morales, E. S. (1989). Ethnic minority families and minority gays and lesbians. *Marriage and Family Review, 14*(3/4), 217–239.

Morales, E. S. (1990). HIV infection and Hispanic gay and bisexual men. *Hispanic Journal of Behavioral Sciences, 12*(2), 212–222.

Morales, E. S. (1992). Counseling Latino gays and Latina lesbians. In Dworkin, S. H. and Gutiérrez, F. (Eds.), *Counseling gay men and lesbians: Journey to the end of the rainbow* (pp. 125–139).

Tremble, B., Schneider, M., & Appathurai, C. (1989). Growing up gay or lesbian in a multicultural context. *Journal of Homosexuality, 17*(1–4), 253–267.

Wooden, W. S., Kawasaki, H., & Mayeda, R. (1983). Lifestyles and identity maintenance among gay Japanese American males. *Alternative Lifestyles, 5*(4), 236–243.

PART VI
◆ Families

The structures of families reflect gender expectations within particular cultures, and cultures themselves are shaped by surrounding or embedded social forces such as sexism, poverty, and homophobia. For example, the wish to have male offspring who are expected to support parents in old age affects whether or not girls even get born in some cultures. In China and in parts of India, sex-selective abortion has changed the gender ratio in favor of boys. An estimated 50 to 80 million more girls and women might be alive today in India and China if discrimination against girls and women had not occurred. One-child policies in China have especially encouraged sex-selective abortions. Sex selection occurs in India even though sex tests on fetuses and sex-selective abortions are illegal there.[1]

Attention to changing gender expectations within families is on many people's minds, especially in the United States. People in the U.S. women's and men's movements have been talking about this issue for decades, but today people from all walks of life are addressing it. Even the National Conference of Catholic Bishops has urged married couples to move beyond gender stereotypes and develop more equality in marriages through shared decision making, shared household duties when both spouses are employed, fathers who are actively engaged in their children's lives, and the expression of feeling by both spouses.[2] Explicit attention to fathers has increased as more fathers—both single and coupled—enjoy and embrace their roles (or don't),[3] as divorced fathers fight for custody,[4] as young fathers join mentoring programs to help them learn parenting skills,[5] and as putative fathers face the legal challenge of registering as potential fathers to protect their rights, especially when the women they impregnate want to place the children for adoption.[6]

In 1998, 59.5 percent of married women were in the labor force. The task of balancing paid work and family work now affects women across the economic spectrum; it is no longer a challenge only for poor and working-class women, who have always been in the paid workforce. In 1998, for example, 66.5 percent of women college graduates with a child under one year of age were in the labor force. At the end of the twentieth century, the husband worked outside the home and the wife did unpaid work at home in only 19 percent of families.[7] However, women who work outside the home are most likely to be responsible for arranging child care, and they continue to do most of the housework, working what sociologist Arlie Hochschild called the "second shift."[8]

Family life requires complex negotiations and compromises that are often hidden from view. For example, in a family studied by Arlie Hochschild and Anne Machung, the wife gave up her ideal of a marriage in which household tasks and child care would be shared; she redefined what her husband was willing to do as acceptable to keep the marriage together. He was unwilling to take on much responsibility at home and would have preferred that she work part time so she could handle the work at home with less conflict. Committed to her career, she did not want to work part time. The image of the happy professional mother, her child in one hand and a briefcase in the other, is seldom what it appears to be, even for professional women with enough money to hire people to serve as nannies or house-keepers at home.[9] The reality of the effects of having children on women's wages has finally hit home, leading researcher Ann Crittenden (Part VIII) to refer to mothers as "society's involuntary philanthropists."[10] The ideology of what sociologist Sharon Hays calls "intensive mothering" reinforces the gender divide because this ideology advises women to spend a lot of time, energy, and money on their children. This frequently results in conflicts with employers because the ideology of the workplace is at odds with the ideology of intensive mothering.[11] (See Susan Douglas and Meredith Michaels, Part IV.)

Sociologist Scott Coltrane, after taking a careful look at the changing division of labor in families, concludes that gradually men have begun to share more equally in family life, especially in the area of child care, and he predicts that this trend toward equality in family life will continue, though perhaps gradually and with resistance on both sides.[12] An intergenerational study of Mexican men's roles in the early 1990s by anthropologist Matthew Gutmann found that younger Mexican men were participating more in housework and childrearing as a result of women working outside the home and were not needing to have a lot of children to prove their masculinity.[13] The data in this field are being debated, however, related to changes in men's contributions to housework. Sociologists Julie Press and Eleanor Townsley found that a careful look at two large surveys that have informed the litera-ture on housework participation (not childcare) revealed overreporting of time spent on housework by both husbands and wives. They conclude, also, that "the overreport we document is large enough to cast doubt on the conclusion that husbands have increased their supply of domestic labor to the household in the past 25 years."[14] Related to this, in a survey of men mar-ried to women, writer Neil Chethik found that those who believed that their wives thought household tasks were pretty fairly divided were more satis-fied with their marital sex lives. He concluded that it is important for couples to work out the conflicts over household chores.[15]

The stress and turmoil that poverty imposes on families is well docu-mented.[16] Sociologist Anne R. Roschelle, in an analysis of families of color in the 1987–88 National Survey of Families and Households, argues that one powerful effect of poverty on communities of color has been to weaken support networks, calling into question the assumption that cuts in welfare support will simply force people to lean on their support networks. Those networks, previously documented in the social science literature (see also Patricia Hill Collins, this part), appear to have weakened to some extent.[17]

The risk of becoming homeless is a pernicious presence for poor families. Many families that escape homelessness function at the margins of the social order, living in crowded conditions and working, at times, in the informal economy—outside the realm of W-2 forms, benefits, and any protection from exploitation by employers.[18] Recent data on mortgage foreclosures underscore a real or potential crisis facing many families. Subprime loans are offered at higher interest rates to people whose credit history or income defines them as "unqualified" for lower interest rates. Poor people, especially Latinos and African Americans, frequently end up with subprime loans, although they are not necessarily less qualified than some whites who receive prime rate loans. An estimated 20 percent of subprime mortgage loans granted in 2005 and 2006 are expected to end in foreclosures. In New Orleans, an area that needs serious economic investment to revitalize following hurricane Katrina, 49 percent of the loans granted to African Americans have been subprime, adding elevated risk of foreclosure in an already highly stressed context.[19]

In response to the conditions of poor families, especially single mothers with children, professor of education Valerie Polakow asks, "Where are our commitments to the existential futures of children as we approach the twenty-first century?" Clearly, the structure of the economy is wreaking havoc in many families, although, as Pokalow argues, homelessness and poverty are often pathologized, causing victims of poverty to be labeled and blamed for their conditions. Rather, she argues, society should focus on the economic structure as the source of blame and potential solutions.[20] Political scientist Shirley M. Geiger, examining the public perceptions and public policies concerning African American single mothers argues that their poverty is a result of both conscious action and inaction that is damaging to all poor families, 40 percent of which are headed by white men.[21] Frank F. Furstenberg comes to a similar conclusion regarding poor single fathers, arguing that unless the social order provides adequate incomes for young fathers, most will continue to stay disengaged from their children.[22]

Education and the availability of decent jobs can be effective in helping people get themselves and their families out of poverty.[23] Yet the Personal Responsibility and Work Opportunity Reconciliation Act (PRWORA) of 1996—otherwise known as the welfare reform act—cut back options for education, required people to work in low-wage jobs, and added funding for questionable marriage promotion programs. The assumption that marriage will lift a woman and her children out of poverty is questionable, and marriage promotion programs have yet to be carefully evaluated regarding both the escape-from-poverty point of view and the values that they communicate when offered via faith-based agencies. Domestic violence, substance abuse, and incarceration are frequent causes of relationship break-ups or of fathers' limited involvement with their children, suggesting that in many cases women are better off without their children's fathers.[24] In their book, *Promises I Can Keep: Why Poor Women Put Motherhood before*

Marriage (2005) sociologists Kathryn Edin and Maria Kefalas document the lives of poor single mothers who are much more committed to their children than they are to their children's fathers when those fathers are not viable partners. Authors of a study of fathers' risk factors (addiction, domestic violence, and incarceration) conclude, "We suggest that policies to promote marriage and responsible fatherhood be mindful that some fathers they are targeting have characteristics that may not be conducive to increased involvement while other fathers face personal and institutional barriers to involvement."[25]

Many people in the United States and in Europe are marrying later, simply building families without marriage, or not marrying at all. Recent headlines like "51% of Women are Now Living Without Spouse" and "Facing Middle Age With No Degree, and No Wife" (in reference to men who do not attend college) suggest this trend.[26] Single motherhood, stereotypically associated with poor women of color, is not necessarily linked to poverty. A study of middle-class single mothers who chose parenthood suggests that alternative support systems in the context of adequate finances can offer what a single mother needs to raise a child. And public attitudes support single parenthood in ways they did not 30 years ago.[27] In a study of single women, some of whom were single mothers, the presence of a good friendship network was one of several factors that characterized single women who coped well without husbands.[28]

The movement to establish the right of gay men and lesbians to marry or at least establish civil unions provides an example of changing attitudes and changing family arrangements in various countries and U.S. states (see the Introduction to this book and readings in this part by E. J. Graff and by Pat Gozemba and Karen Kahn). Even some traditionally Catholic countries have decided to allow marriage (Spain) or civil unions (Italy). Although many gay and lesbian couples might choose not to marry even where allowed, their support of the right to do so is strong.[29] The struggle for the right of same-sex couples to marry continues in all U.S. states except Massachusetts. Many same-sex couples in Massachusetts and elsewhere also see the limitations of same-sex marriage. On the one hand, they celebrate the new state-level rights and benefits now available and applaud the decision from the perspectives of civil rights and family legitimization. On the other, the structure of marriage with its many benefits rankles fair-minded people who believe that all family structures—single parents, unmarried couples of any kind, older siblings or close friends living together, other household compositions— deserve and need the supports that marriage often brings, such as access to a partner's health insurance coverage, hospital visitation rights, tax benefits, inheritance rights, etc.[30] Although some legal protections for unmarried same-sex couples—such as joint adoptions or domestic partner insurance coverage—are available in many states,[31] many other benefits are lacking. The Defense of Marriage Act (DOMA), which defines marriage as between one man and one woman and prohibits recognition of marriages from other jurisdictions, has been passed by 38 states. In recent cases in Michigan and Ohio, courts ruled that state-funded domestic partner benefits or services for same-sex couples are illegal under the DOMA laws.[32] Sociologist Dalton Conley suggests that each person have the right to designate recipients of the 1,000+ legal rights and obligations granted to married couples as she or he saw fit, regardless of their relationship (perhaps grant health care proxy and visitation to one person, health care coverage to another person, share property tax-free with another, etc.); such designation could change when desired.[33]

Fertility is an issue for many couples, with both partners seen as potentially responsible as data are emerging about the role of toxic environments in male reproduction along with information about lower sperm counts with advancing age. (See Cynthia Daniels, Part VIII, regarding the former.) In January 2006 a male fertility test was marketed in the United Kingdom for at-home use that assesses the quantity of viably active sperm; it is now available in the United States.[34] The pressure to have and rear children, especially on women, has led to a lucrative fertility services industry.

Finally, the wars in Iraq and Afghanistan are putting a lot of pressure on families as soldiers are separated from their families for long periods of time and often come home with PTSD, injuries, and compromised educations or jobs. Child custody issues are beginning to emerge for veterans as well because the caretaking spouse is in a better position to take charge of the children in cases of divorce, separation, or marital conflict.[35]

The readings in this part address a range of family issues, including challenges to Black women's reproductive rights and family cohesion (Jeanne Flavin); various family and child-care arrangements in African American communities that attempt to address the crises that Black families currently face (Patricia Hill Collins); men's experiences as involved fathers (Kathleen Gerson); the challenges of raising an African American son in a lesbian family (Audre Lorde); the challenge of breaking away from a father whose definition of "manhood" is unacceptable (Raul Ybarra); a defense of same-sex marriage (E. J. Graff); and a glimpse of the joyful atmosphere in Massachusetts when same-sex couples were finally allowed to marry (Pat Gozemba and Karen Kahn). The authors in this chapter give voice to many of the challenging aspects of family life today. Embedded in their stories and research are implications for changes in personal relationships and policy, including addressing racism in the context of poverty, facing the realities confronted by incarcerated mothers, support for fathers' caring involvement in family life, the development of jobs that pay enough to keep families going, and the legitimization of same-sex marriage.

As you read these essays, you might want to think about the family contexts in which you were raised. To what extent do the various authors speak to your experience or contradict it? What alternatives do you think would make sense for incarcerated mothers and their children? Where do you stand on same-sex marriage?

NOTES

1. Celia W. Dugger, "Modern Asia's Anomoly: The Girls Who Don't Get Born," *The New York Times,* 6 May 2001, p. 4 (WK); Agence France-Presse, "India Cracks Down on Sex Tests for Fetuses," *The New York Times,* 6 May 2001, p. 14 (NE).

2. National Conference of Catholic Bishops, *Follow the Way of Love* (Washington, DC: United States Catholic Conference, 1994), pp. 20–21.

3. Obie Clayton, Ronald B. Mincy, and David Blankenhorn, eds. *Black Fathers in Contemporary American Society* (New York: Russell Sage Foundation, 2003); Doris Sue Wong, "Single Fathers Embrace Role, Fight Stereotype," *The Boston Globe,* 5 July 1999, p. A1; See Gerson, this Part.

4. Kate Zernike, "Divorced Dads Emerge as a Political Force," *The Boston Globe,* 19 May 1998, p. A1.

5. Erica Thesing, "Mentoring Programs Focusing on Fatherhood," *The Boston Globe,* 17 June 2000, p. B4.

6. See: http://laws.adoption.com/statutes/putative-fathers-2.html.

7. All data in this paragraph are from Barbara Reskin and Irene Padavic, *Women and Men at Work*, 2nd ed. (Thousand Oaks, CA: Pine Forge Press, 2002), pp. 149–50.

8. Ibid., pp. 149–53. See also Arlie Russell Hochschild with Anne Machung, *The Second Shift: Working Parents and the Revolution at Home* (New York: Avon Books, 1990).

9. Hochschild and Machung, *The Second Shift.*

10. Ann Crittenden, *The Price of Motherhood: Why the Most Important Job in the World Is Still the Least Valued* (New York: Henry Holt, 2001), p. 9.

11. Sharon Hays, *The Cultural Contradictions of Motherhood* (New Haven, CT: Yale University Press, 1996).

12. Scott Coltrane, "The Future of Fatherhood: Social, Demographic, and Economic Influences on Men's Family Involvements," in William Marsiglio, ed., *Fatherhood: Contemporary Theory, Research, and Social Policy* (Thousand Oaks, CA: Sage, 1995), pp. 255–74.

13. Matthew C. Gutmann, "The Meaning of Macho," in Louise Lamphere, Heléna Ragoné, and Patricia Zavella, eds., *Situated Lives: Gender and Culture in Everyday Life* (New York: Routledge, 1997), pp. 223–34.

14. Julie E. Press and Eleanor Townsley, "Wives' and Husbands' Housework Reporting: Gender, Class, and Social Desirability," *Gender & Society* 12, no. 2 (April 1998): p. 214.

15. Neil Chethik, *VoiceMale: What Husbands Really Think about Marriages, Their Wives, Sex, Housework, and Commitment* (New York: Simon & Schuster, 2006), p. 119.

16. Elliot Liebow, *Tell Them Who I Am: The Lives of Homeless Women* (New York: Penguin, 1993); Valerie Polakow, *Lives on the Edge: Single Mothers and Their Children in the Other America* (Chicago: University of Chicago Press, 1994); Doug A. Timmer, Stanley D. Eitzen, and Kathryn D. Talley, *Paths to Homelessness: Extreme Poverty and the Urban Housing Crisis* (Boulder, CO: Westview Press, 1994).

17. Anne R. Roschelle, *No More Kin: Exploring Race, Class, and Gender in Family Networks* (Thousand Oaks, CA: Sage, 1997), pp. 199–202.

18. See, for example, "Patchworking: Households in the Economy," in Nazli Kibria, *Family Tightrope: The Changing Lives of Vietnamese Americans* (Princeton, NJ: Princeton University Press, 1993), pp. 73–107.

19. See the Center for Responsible Lending: http://www.responsiblelending.org/issues/mortgage/reports/page.jsp?itemID=31217189; United for a Fair Economy,

"New Report Highlights Lending Disparities and High-Cost Loans in New Orleans Metro Area," 18 May 2007: http://www.faireconomy.org/press/2007/new_orleans_lending.html.

20. Polakow, *Lives on the Edge*, p. 3.

21. Shirley M. Geiger, "African-American Single Mothers: Public Perceptions and Public Policies," in Kim Marie Vaz, ed., *Black Women in America* (Thousand Oaks, CA: Sage, 1995), pp. 244–57.

22. Frank F. Furstenburg, Jr., "Fathering in the Inner City: Paternal Participation and Public Policy," in William Marsiglio, ed., *Fatherhood: Contemporary Theory, Research, and Social Policy* (Thousand Oaks, CA: Sage, 1995), pp. 119–47.

23. Valeria Polakow, Sandra S. Butler, Luisa Stormer Deprez, and Peggy Kahn, eds., *Shut Out: Low Income Mothers and Higher Education in Post-Welfare America* (Albany: State University of New York Press, 2004).

24. Beth Skilken and Julie E. Artis, "Critiquing the Case for Marriage Promotion," *Violence Against Women* 10, no. 11 (November 2004): 1226–44; Jean Hardisty, "Promoting Marriage to Cure Poverty?" *Peacework* 34, no. 374 (April 2007): 14–15 (http://www.peaceworkmagazine.org/node/535).

25. Maureen R. Waller and Raymond Swisher, "Fathers' Risk Factors in Fragile Families: Implications for "Healthy" Relationships and Father Involvement," *Social Problems* 53, no. 3 (August 2006): 392–420.

26. Sam Roberts, "51% of women . . ." *The New York Times*, 16 January 2007, http://nytimes.com/2007/01/16/us/l6census.html?th=&emc=th&pagewanted=print; Eduardo Porter and Michelle O'Donnel, "Facing Middle Age . . ." *The New York Times*, 6 August 2006, http://nytimes.com/2006/08/06/us/06marry.html?ei=5070&en=e5a5b8b0400da47e&ex=1155; Molly Moore, "Among French, Little Love Is Lost for Traditional Trips to the Altar," *The Boston Globe*, 24 November 2006, p. A26.

27. Rosanna Hertz, *Single by Chance, Mothers by Choice: How Women Are Choosing Parenthood without Marriage and Creating the New American Family* (New York: Oxford University Press, 2006). See Kathryn Edin and Maria Kefalas, *Promises I Can Keep: Why Poor Women Put Motherhood Before Marriage* (Berkeley: University of California, 2005), p. 200 for a discussion about attitudes toward childbirth outside marriage.

28. E. Kay Trimberger, *The New Single Woman* (Boston: Beacon Press, 2005).

29. Gretchen A. Stiers, *From This Day Forward: Commitment, Marriage, and Family in Lesbian and Gay Relationships* (New York: St. Martin's Griffin, 1999).

30. Kay Whitlock, "The Perfect Storm: Why Progressives Must Reframe the Narrow Terms of Marriage Politics," *Peacework* 34, no. 374 (April 2007): 4–6 (http://www.peaceworkmagazine.org/node/529).

31. Associated Press, "N.J. Gay Parents Exchange Vows," *The Boston Globe*, 22 June 1998, p. A4.

32. Whitlock, "The Perfect Storm," p. 5.

33. Dalton Conley, "Spread the Wealth of Spousal Rights," *The New York Times*, 20 May 2007, http://nytimes.com/2007/05/20/opinion/20conley.html?ei=50707en=3859bf629bdcc.

34. NPR, New Home Fertility Test Kits for Men, Women, 4 June 2007: http://www.npr.org/templates/story/story.php?storyId=10712488.

35. AP, "Deployed troops fight for lost custody of kids," 5 May 2007: http://www.msnbc.msn.com/id/18506417/.

34

CONTEMPORARY CHALLENGES TO BLACK WOMEN'S REPRODUCTIVE RIGHTS

JEANNE FLAVIN

Jeanne Flavin is associate professor of sociology at Fordham University. She is coauthor of the book *Class, Race, Gender, and Crime: Social Realities of Justice in America* (2006). Her publications reflect her interest in promoting more humane responses to people (including pregnant women) who use drugs and people infected with HIV.

Although contemporary society by and large condemns slavery, we are much less willing to recognize that similarly oppressive patterns continue to be exercised today. As during slavery, contemporary efforts to regulate black women's reproductive capacities encompass all aspects of reproduction from conception through child-raising. Although scholars of punishment have paid substantial attention to how incarcerated women's lives are controlled and regulated (see Britton 2003; McCorkel 2003; Roth 2004a) less attention has been given to the ways in which other institutions regulate women's lives, e.g., the welfare system and the child protective system. The control exercised by these systems is exercised with the full support of large sectors of the voting public, politicians, the media, policymakers, social service agencies, and the courts. Operating interdependently, these structures construct low-income black women as "irresponsible" individuals who should be prevented from conceiving, and, in some cases, from raising a child.

Complicating matters, contemporary discussions tend to steer clear of any direct mention of race, and instead insist that the problem of poverty and single-parent families is "color-blind" or "race-blind." But declaring something to be the case does not make it so. One cannot discuss poverty without describing a reality that is not only disproportionately experienced by black women, but also is conceptualized in racialized (and racist) ways. Consequently, any discussion of poor women's reproduction is essentially—though not exclusively—a discussion of poor black women. In turn, these discussions, declarations of race-blindness notwithstanding, are colored by historic patterns of control over poor black women getting pregnant, having children, and raising them. Although the policies described below affect many women who are not black, the roots of these policies are entrenched in concerns about black women's reproductive capacity.

While, during slavery, black women's fecundity was encouraged, contemporary efforts seek to limit it. Once slavery was abolished and black women's capacity to bear children lost its economic value to dominant-class whites, black women's childbearing was devalued and discouraged by European Americans (Neubeck and Cazenave 2001, 152). Public and private incentives designed to pressure women to use long-term contraceptives, and welfare reform measures such as "family caps" provide evidence that economic interests and deeply seated biases continue to reign, over humanity and recognition of black women's bodily and personal integrity.

The eugenics movements of the twentieth century advocated the systematic and involuntary sterilization of "undesirables" for official reasons ranging from mental impairment to promiscuity to poverty. Between the early 1900s and the 1970s, at least 60,000 Americans (and perhaps as many as 100,000 to 150,000) in more than thirty states were sterilized against their will (Sinderbrand 2003; May 1995; see also Calavita, this volume). These efforts often targeted black women and other women of color. During the first half of the twentieth century, compulsory sterilization was aimed at "feeble-minded" and "genetically inferior" women. Many eugenic theorists equated racial inferiority with sexual degeneracy. At the time, many women were incarcerated in prisons or other institutions for engaging in nonmarital sexual behavior. As Elaine Tyler May notes, "Nonmarital sexual activity was a code for class and a marker for hereditary inferiority. There is no evidence that middle-class or affluent women were ever labeled feebleminded or sterilized against their will" (May 1995, 203). After World War II, institutional sterilizations declined, but the practice continued outside of institutions. Sterilizations were disproportionately performed on Native American, black, and Hispanic women, and justified by claims that this would save taxpayers' money by lowering welfare costs.

Evidence of the consequences of nativist fears is also found in more recent history. In 1990, Norplant received FDA approval. Within two years, over a dozen state legislatures proposed measures such as implanting women on welfare and those convicted of drug or child abuse with Norplant (Roberts 1997). All states and the District of Columbia made Norplant available through Medicaid. Many clinic staff emphasized the benefits of Norplant, while downplaying side effects such as depression, weight gain, and prolonged and heavy bleeding. Disadvantaged women's requests to have Norplant removed were met with opposition from clinic staff. Medicaid policy in some states authorized doctors' removal of Norplant only in cases of medical necessity. Norplant was eventually removed from the market in 2002.

In the wake of successful court challenges and wider public awareness of the medical complications associated with Norplant, overt federal and state efforts to sterilize poor women have become less popular. At least one private effort, however, continues to gain strength. Since 1997, Project Prevention has reinforced the racialized economic divide in our responses to women's reproduction by paying over one thousand drug-using women (and a few dozen men) two hundred dollars each for getting sterilized or using long-term birth control, such as Depo-Provera, Norplant, or IUDs. Project Prevention is funded largely by wealthy conservatives such as talk-show host Dr. Laura Schlessinger (Yeoman 2001). The program was originally named Children Requiring a Caring Kommunity or C.R.A.C.K., reflecting the founder's focus on crack cocaine rather than on substances like alcohol and tobacco that also pose a threat to fetal health but are more commonly used by white and middle-class women. Although C.R.A.C.K. was pitched as a sincere effort to improve the quality of women's and children's lives, evidence suggests otherwise. The program used to give clients more money if they were permanently sterilized than if they undertook a form of temporary sterilization such as Norplant. Further, the outreach strategies of Project Prevention/C.R.A.C.K. reveal the race-based roots of the program. Outreach efforts target communities of color, while ignoring drug and alcohol use in white communities. In Oakland, California, for example, billboards were placed in African American neighborhoods (Allina 2002). In 1998, founder Barbara Harris was quoted as saying: "We don't allow dogs to breed. We spay them. We neuter them. We try to keep them from having unwanted puppies, and yet these women are literally having litters of children" (Vega 2003). Project Prevention's website (www.projectprevention.org) reports that the organization relies heavily on referrals from probation offices, jails, drug treatment programs, methadone clinics and law enforcement agencies; staff receive fifty dollars for referring people to Project Prevention. This arrangement is troubling for a variety of reasons, not the least of which is that it supplies a financial incentive for state agents to encourage women to forgo their reproductive rights.

Although the popularity of privately-funded efforts such as Project Prevention has not been accompanied by similar government efforts in recent years, abuses of power by the state still occur. In July 2003, a Michigan judge ordered a woman to submit to a medically "verifiable" method of birth control (such as Norplant, Depo-Provera, or an IUD) in an abuse and neglect proceeding regarding her two children *(Family Independence Center v. Renee Gamez* 2003).[1] The Family Court alleged that Renee Gamez had physically neglected her children due to drug use. The judge argued that, because Gamez's drug use made it likely that she would bear a child with special needs, the state had a compelling interest in ordering her to be placed on birth control as part of the parent/agency reunification agreement.

In a friend of the court brief, the Michigan branch of the American Civil Liberties Union (ACLU) outlined some of the problems inherent in court-mandated contraceptive use. First, the Constitution protects a woman's right to make reproductive decisions free from unwarranted government intrusion. Just as the court cannot force a woman to have an abortion against her will, it cannot make her submit to a contraceptive method. Second, other, less intrusive, and more directly relevant means exist to protect children and rehabilitate troubled parents, such as counseling and supervised parenting times. Third, arguing—as the judge did in *Gamez*—that a prohibition on having an additional child is justified if any risk exists that the child might have "special needs," raises the question of whether the state may limit the procreation of parents who have a family history of genetic disorders, or of mothers who are on prescription medicine (e.g., for seizures) that may have adverse effects on a fetus.

Other actions assume different, and arguably more insidious, forms. In *Welfare Racism*, for example, sociologists Kenneth J. Neubeck and Noel A. Cazenave (2001) suggest that the authors of the Personal Responsibility and Work Opportunity Reconciliation Act of 1996 (PRWORA) aimed not only to force indolent black mothers receiving welfare to take jobs (or gain "work opportunities"), but also to discourage poor people of color from reproducing.[2]

Around half of all states have enacted "family caps" or "child exclusion" policies. Normally, states set the amount of public assistance payments based on factors such as the number of family members and the sources and amount of income. In states that have family cap laws, however, a woman who has another child while she is already receiving public assistance does not receive an increased payment. Forcing some women to raise an additional child without extra income, the argument goes, will deter other women on welfare from having more children. Basically, family caps aim to promote birth control through the prospect of increased impoverishment (Neubeck and Cazenave 2001, 159). No evidence exists to indicate that women have children in order to make money (Children's Defense Fund 2004). It is not surprising, then, that the General Accounting Office (GAO) reported that "[W]e cannot conclude that family cap policies reduce the incidence of out-of-wedlock births" (GAO 2001, 3). In fact, the same GAO report cited anecdotal evidence that family cap laws may unintentionally harm children above and beyond requiring they live in more impoverished families. All states with family cap policies have procedures to enroll eligible children in Medicaid and food stamps programs even when their families' benefits have been capped. Some women are not aware of this. They may be less likely to report the birth of children subject to the family cap to a caseworker; thus making it less likely that these children will be enrolled in or receive public benefits to which they are entitled.

At the same time that federal and state governments have endeavored to discourage low-income women from getting pregnant and having children, they have limited poor women's ability to terminate an unwanted or unplanned pregnancy. Medicaid offers comprehensive reproductive health care, including family planning, prenatal care, and services related to childbirth. Yet, since 1976, the Hyde Amendment has prevented low-income women (who are disproportionately women of color) from receiving an abortion federally funded through Medicaid (except in a few cases such as rape or incest).[3] All but seventeen states also restrict public funding for abortion.

By selectively withholding benefits to a woman who needs to end her pregnancy but not to one who elects to carry her pregnancy to term, politicians are able to impose their own choices on poor women (ACLU 2003). Consequently, many women who seek abortions are not able to obtain them. The situation is particularly bleak for women being charged or held in jails and prisons across the country. In many jail systems, women must first secure a court order in order to secure an abortion, a process which can take weeks or potentially months and may require the payment of lawyer's fees. Further, even with a court order, many counties will not transport pregnant inmates to abortion facilities or cover the cost of the abortion.

Rachel Roth (2004a) surveyed forty-four states and the District of Columbia and conducted a LexisNexis search of relevant state statutes, administrative regulations, and attorney general opinions to find out the status of abortion policies in prisons and jails. State policies vary widely, even within the same federal circuit. New Jersey, for example, has clearly articulated and readily available policies. New Jersey not only provides abortions for prisoners who are up to eighteen weeks of pregnancy, but also makes all arrangements. By contrast, in Delaware, not only must women pay for abortions, but they are charged $100 for transportation and security, which is provided by "moonlighting" correctional officers on Saturdays. At least one-third of all states have no official written policy governing incarcerated women's access to abortion. Another study found that over one in four pregnant women who used cocaine (and around one in sixteen other women) who gave birth in Washington, DC, hospitals considered abortion when they discovered they were pregnant, but could not afford it (Flavin 2002).

Once a low-income black woman becomes pregnant, states have sought to control her behavior during pregnancy, as illustrated by the response to pregnant women who use illegal drugs. Since the 1980s, over two hundred women in more than thirty states have been arrested and charged for their alleged drug use or other actions during pregnancy (Center for Reproductive Law and Policy 2000). In some of these cases, charges were dropped before trial, but, in many others, women have been pressured into pleading guilty or accepting plea bargains, some of which have resulted in incarceration. Upon appeal, most courts have found that prosecutions of women for their conduct during pregnancy are without legal basis or unconstitutional. In at least one case, however, the state supreme court involved upheld a woman's criminal child neglect conviction and eight-year prison sentence for drug use during pregnancy, even though the woman, Cornelia Whitner, had asked the criminal court to place her in drug treatment and ultimately gave birth to a healthy child (*Whitner v. South Carolina* 1998).[4]

Proponents of prosecution, court intervention, increased medical surveillance, and other measures designed to recognize "fetal rights" claim that such measures are necessary to protect the fetus from harm. Even a cursory examination of this claim, however, reveals the flawed assumptions upon which it is based. For example, although maternal cocaine use does add risk of poor fetal outcomes to pregnancy, cocaine exposure does not automatically result in poor fetal health. In contrast to the devastating impact predicted by sensationalist media accounts, meta-analyses (i.e., studies of many other studies) examining the effects of prenatal cocaine exposure have found *small or no effects* on physical growth, cognition, language skills, motor skills, behavior, attention, affect, and neurophysiology (Frank et al. 2001; Lester, LaGasse, and Seifer 1998). Children exposed to cocaine in utero "are not hopelessly damaged and destined to become a burden to society" (Lester, LaGasse, and Seifer 1998, 634). In fact, research suggests that poverty, environment, and their correlates, such as poor nutrition and tobacco use, influence children's development as much or more than prenatal exposure to drugs (Frank et al. 2001). Unfortunately, such medical information is lost on people like the South Carolina state court judge who, after reviewing the prosecution of a woman who had used cocaine while pregnant, observed "Now this little baby's born with crack. When he is seven years old . . . they can't run. They just run around in class like a little rat. Not just black ones. White ones too" (quoted in Paltrow 2001, 247).

On a strictly pragmatic level, it is not clear how arresting a woman *after* she gives birth can be expected to have a retroactive impact on the previous nine months of her pregnancy. Similarly, "protecting the fetus" by incarcerating pregnant women wrongly assumes that jails and prisons offer high-quality prenatal care programs, nutritional diets, and violence- and drug-free environments. As for any possible deterrent effect caused by fear of prosecution and imprisonment, the nature of addiction (and the corresponding lack of effective drug treatment on demand) makes it more likely that a woman will be deterred from seeking prenatal care and drug treatment, for fear of being punished, than be deterred from using drugs.

In light of the flawed logic and limitations of punitive policies, many states have moved away from prosecution and punishment. Instead, they encourage reporting maternal drug use to child protective services. The federal government's Administration for Children and Families (ACF) recognizes that drug use does not automatically render someone an unfit parent, and that parental substance abuse in and of itself should not be equated with child maltreatment. Consequently, ACF stipulates that parental substance abuse should not be reported to child protective services as a form of child maltreatment unless there is reason to believe that the parent's alcohol or other drug abuse is so severe that the child has been or is likely to be harmed due to such substance abuse, *or* unless other specific state legislation exists (NCCANI 2003). Therein lies part of the problem. Such legislation *does* exist in many states, although the conditions that trigger mandatory reporting laws vary widely. Some states require only a positive toxicology screen at birth or physical signs of addiction or dependence, while other states require an assessment of the newborn's imminent risk of harm or need for protection.

Although in some respects an improvement over use of the criminal justice system to enforce expectations of how pregnant women should act, use of the child welfare system (and the welfare system's use of family caps) changes the site of reproductive control, but not the impact. Poverty and institutional racism continue to collude and seriously undermine low-income black women's ability to raise their own children. In particular, the increased use of foster care and the involuntary termination of parental rights undermine black women's attempts to raise their children, often with long-lasting and detrimental effects.

In 2003, around 906,000 children were found to be victims of child maltreatment, mostly neglect. Only one in four child victims of maltreatment are black, yet black children comprise nearly 35 percent of the 523,000 children in foster care (DHHS 2005a, 2005b).[5] In *Shattered Bonds: The Color of Child Welfare* (2002), Northwestern University law professor Dorothy Roberts asks why black children are disproportionately likely to be removed from their parents and placed under state supervision. Why is the child welfare system focused, not on assisting parents to take care of their children, but on punishing parents for their failures by threatening to take their children away? Why does our system focus on "protecting" children by blaming their parents, rather than truly promoting children's welfare? Roberts concludes that America has tolerated the destructiveness of separating parents from their children *because* of the color of America's child welfare system. "This protective function falls heaviest on African American parents," Robert asserts, "because they are most likely to suffer from poverty and institutional discrimination and to be blamed for the effects on their children" (Roberts 2002, 74).

Studies suggest that many women are poor, not because they have children, are lazy and make bad choices, but rather because dropping wages have made it increasingly difficult for female-headed households to escape poverty. Contrary to popular belief, the average family on welfare is no larger than the average nonrecipient's family and people do not get rich on welfare. Over 70 percent of the families receiving TANF in 2001 had only one or two children.[6] The maximum TANF benefit for a family of three in a typical state was only $362/month, with a possible food stamp benefit of an additional $288/month. This provides a combined annual income of $7,800, far below the federal poverty guideline of around $14,000 for a family of three. Nor do welfare programs drain government budgets; they constitute only about 1 percent and 2 percent of federal and state budgets, respectively (Armas 2003; Children's Defense Fund 2004; APA 2003). Misconceptions about poor women persist in large part because they contribute to an ideology that "has helped to create and to maintain invidious distinctions between welfare recipients and other workers, thereby supporting seriously constrained policy. . . . The fact that [the stereotype associated with 'typical welfare recipient'] is both so strong and so far from the reality of the lives of most welfare recipients is a key to understanding the increasingly punitive nature of welfare policy since the early 1980s" (Rose 2000, 144).

Welfare reform's work requirements and family cap laws make it extremely difficult for the poorest welfare recipients to take care of their children. Children are removed because of inadequacy of income more than for any other factor (Lindsey 1994). Poverty makes it more likely that a child will be exposed to poor nutrition, health problems, unsafe housing, and other threats to her physical well-being. Inadequate housing or lack of housing also causes children to remain in foster care longer.

In addition to ideology, political trends contribute to the long-term or permanent separation of children from their parents (Roberts 2002). Specifically, state and federal child welfare systems' original focus on family preservation has shifted to a focus on "freeing" children in foster care for adoption, by accelerating the termination of parental rights. The mass incarceration of black adults also has contributed to the long-term or permanent separation of children from their parents.

In the past quarter-century, the government has responded to the deficiencies of an overburdened child welfare system, and the harm it can cause to children and their families, in two distinct ways. In 1980, the Adoption Assistance and Child Welfare Act (AACWA) focused on keeping children safely in their families and safely reuniting children in foster care with their biological families. In 1997, AACWA was amended by the Adoption and Safe Families Act (ASFA). Instead of trying to reduce the number of children languishing in foster care by safely keeping families together, ASFA promoted adoption and the speedier termination of parental rights.[7] ASFA orders state governments to begin termination proceedings if efforts to reunite the family do not work within fifteen months. In other words, ASFA encourages judges to enforce statutory deadlines related mainly to the length of time a children has spent out of parents' custody, not to child abuse. This is all the more troubling when one considers that victims of severe abuse are only a tiny minority of children in foster care; most children in foster care are removed from their homes because of poverty-related neglect (GAO 1999). Moreover, most children want to remain with their biological parents, regardless of the circumstances; involuntary separation can cause deep psychological harm (see Roberts 2002).

Although federal law still requires states to make reasonable efforts to reunify children with their families, it also urges states to make concurrent efforts to prepare them for adoption. It is one thing to remove barriers to the adoption of children who are already available to be adopted, and quite another to treat the legal relationship between children in foster care and their parents as a barrier to adoption (Roberts 2002, 113). Researchers at Chapin Hall Center for Children at the University of Chicago predict that the number of children adopted from foster care in Illinois, Michigan, Missouri, New Jersey, and New York will exceed the foster care caseloads in those states some time between 2004 and 2006 (Anonymous 2002). At present, far more children in foster care are eligible for adoption than are successfully placed. According to the Urban Institute, in 1999, only around one in three of the half million foster care children available for adoption were successfully placed. Younger, white, or Hispanic females were more likely to be adopted than other children. Agencies' efforts to recruit black families may not be fruitful since black parents already adopt foster children at a rate double their proportion in the population (Green 2003).

The erosion of the black family through the extensive use of foster care is exacerbated by the disproportionately high rates of incarceration of black women and men. In 1999, 1.4 million children had a father in a state or federal prison, another 126,000 children had a mother in prison. Most mothers are incarcerated for nonviolent drug or property offenses. Two-thirds of women lived with their children prior to being incarcerated; one-third of all mothers lived alone with their children prior to arrest (Mumola 2000). While most children of incarcerated fathers live with their mothers, most children of incarcerated women live not with their father but with a grandparent or other relative, often a grandmother (Snell and Morton 1994; Mumola 2000).

Under TANF, a grandmother (or other relative) can only receive assistance for sixty months in her lifetime. If she has exhausted this limit while raising her own children, she can no longer receive TANF to care for, say, her incarcerated daughter's child. One possible solution is formally to place the children of incarcerated parents in foster care with the grandmother. After all, states are already directed to place children with relatives whenever possible, and the average foster care payment is typically greater than the average monthly payment under TANF. To receive foster care assistance, however, the children must be in state custody. Thus a grandmother needing financial assistance and supportive services to care for her grandchild may have to allege the child's mother neglected, abused, or abandoned the child, which may later contribute to the termination of the incarcerated mother's parental rights.

The courts may consider incarceration to be an aspect of abandonment and thus a justification to terminate parental rights. ASFA permits exceptions to the fifteen-month termination rule if a child is living with a relative or if other "compelling reasons" exist. But even if children do reside in a relative's home, caseworkers are unlikely to invoke these exceptions unless the child has a close and sustained relationship with the incarcerated parent, *and* the caseworker is aware of it. Further, around 10 percent of incarcerated mothers' children are in foster homes and do not qualify for such an exemption (Mumola 2000; Crary 2003). Once the mother of a child in foster care has been incarcerated at least fifteen months, state governments are mandated to start termination proceedings (NCCANI 2002).

Many obstacles exist that interfere with incarcerated women's ability to maintain contact with their children and the caseworkers, including limited access to telephones, restriction to making collect calls, lack of message-taking services for inmates, mothers' relocation to another facility, children's move to another foster home, imprisonment in geographically remote areas (making it difficult to transport children for visits), lack of adequate space and staff to permit child-parent visits, corrections' failure to produce parents for Family Court hearings even when the termination of parental rights is at stake. Women's lack of legal assistance to help guide them through the complex process also limits their ability to be effective advocates for themselves. Martha L. Raimon of the Women's Prison Association observes that, without adequate information about the incarcerated women's circumstances and their relationships with their children, "foster care agencies make vital decisions about the children's future simply based on the number of months spent in foster care and without a meaningful inquiry into what is best for the children. Stated differently, permanency is sacrificed in the name of expediency" (Raimon 2000, 425). Although incarcerated mothers can seek exemptions from termination, child-protection agencies in many states do not routinely encourage such efforts. "Instead of looking closely at the circumstances, agencies push the button for termination," Raimon notes. "It's faster, it's cleaner, it doesn't take as much work. I'm afraid we're sucking large numbers of children and parents down a black hole who otherwise could have maintained their family ties" (quoted in Crary 2003).

The criminal justice system, welfare system, and child welfare systems have become inextricably intertwined. Incarceration and poverty do not have a "ripple effect" on black families, so much as a tsunami effect. Congressional testimony and sensationalist media coverage of a few (admittedly horrific) cases contribute to the perception that low-income black women—not just those who are incarcerated—are unfit mothers. At the same time, foster and adoptive parents, who often have better incomes and less chaotic lives, are idealized. ASFA and the policies described earlier depend upon and perpetuate a belief in a false dichotomy that pits parents' rights against children's rights. No evidence exists to suggest that ASFA and other measures provide any overall social benefit for children. Moreover, seeing the situation as a dichotomy precludes serious consideration of how material and social assistance to mothers stands to benefit children as well (Stein 2000, 590).

What drives child welfare and other reproductive policies appears not to be a genuine and deep-seated concern about the physical and emotional well-being of children so much as the expression of a thinly veiled attempt to dictate what constitutes a "good mother," particularly when the mother in question is poor and black. Although prenatal exposure to alcohol is a leading cause of mental retardation, only four states currently require that fetal alcohol syndrome be reported (NCCANI 2003). Some states specifically mention prenatal drug exposure in their statutes defining child abuse and neglect but limit the definition of "drug exposure" to illegal substances. Around thirty-four states make exemptions for parents who choose not to seek medical care for their children because of their religious beliefs, but only around one-third of states' definitions of neglect grant exemptions for poverty. That is, in a minority of states, if a family living in poverty was not providing adequate food for their children, it would only be considered neglect if the parents were aware of food assistance programs but did not use them (NCCANI 2002). In sum, flawed and prejudiced assumptions equating drug use or poverty with parental unfitness underlie many official policies related to reporting to child protective services and foster care, often with devastating consequences.

The Legacy: Stereotyping and Paternalism

Examining the negative and unfounded stereotypes associated with being a black woman can help us understand the increasingly punitive and controlling nature of welfare and criminal justice policy. Under slavery, stereotypes about black women abounded. Believing enslaved women to be deceptive and crafty, slave owners denied them privacy and subjected their reproductive lives to close surveillance. Believing that slave women possessed superhuman strength and a high tolerance for pain made it easier to justify subjecting pregnant women and new mothers to arduous physical labor on the plantations and denying them adequate food and rest. Believing they were not as emotionally attached to their children helped justify separating mothers from their children.

Contemporary stereotypes portray black women as careless, promiscuous welfare queens who breed children to get more money (Collins 1990; Roberts 2002). Those who use drugs will "do anything" and are completely indifferent to any harm they may cause to themselves or others (Humphries 1999). Such stereotypes go hand-in-hand with paternalistic efforts to control black women's reproduction. To the uninformed ear, paternalism may sound like a good thing (or at least not like a bad thing). It remains, however, a dehumanizing structural arrangement. By stigmatizing and controlling the behaviors of a subordinate group, paternalistic practices help maintain systems of social, cultural, and economic oppression. Paternalism not only makes it easier to justify punishment, it directs us to punish women "for their own good." Moreover, demonizing women makes it easier to justify separating mothers from their children through incarceration.

Now, as during slavery, black and low-income women "are dealt with as if they are incapable of understanding their own best interests or functioning autonomously without guidance by their social superiors" (Neubeck and Cazenave 2001, 135–136). Legislators' attempts to blame black women for a range of social ills, and their attempts to control black women's fecundity, pregnancies, and child-raising are two sides of the same coin.

Today, public discourse overtly linking race and reproduction is rare (Neubeck and Cazenave 2001). Yet, the peculiar view, originating in slavery, that the government and other official actors have a paternalistic right to control black women's reproduction continues to shape our current policies. Many of our policies are developed by people who by and large do not appreciate the reality of poverty. They reflect middle-class Horatio Alger-like assumptions that all women can pull themselves up by their bootstraps if sufficiently motivated by, for example, financial incentives to not have children, or threats of having their children taken away. Even liberal policies that recognize that poor black families are victims of societal injustice "[use this] victimization as an excuse to intervene in their families instead of a reason to work toward social change" (Roberts 2002, 256).

Paternalistic policies and practices such as family caps, birth control incentives, foster care, and termination of parental rights purport to be race-neutral but in reality are anything but. At one end of the spectrum, low-income black women are viewed as self-centered individuals who can and should carry full responsibility for their actions; at the other end, they are defined as victims of social circumstance who cannot be trusted to make good decisions for themselves. Both positions stereotype poor black women as unable or unwilling to exert some positive influence over their reproductive capacities. Whether inspiring policies of increased surveillance, punishment, mandatory treatment, or termination of parental rights, for the "mother's own good" or in the interest of children, neither position seriously considers that low-income black women may exert some positive influence over their lives and bodies (cf. Flavin 2002).

If we aim to promote the health and well-being of women and children, our purposes would be better served by recognizing all women as allies—not adversaries or incompetents—who share a goal of freely chosen pregnancies that result in healthy women and children. Low-income women should play a greater role in setting the agenda. Advocacy and grassroots organizations should be sought as active allies—not only informing policies, but serving as a bridge between formal agencies of social control and the women and children they purport to serve.

Admittedly, the trust needed for effective alliances may not be readily forthcoming after more than a century of trying to control the most intimate aspects of black women's lives and bodies. Our willingness to blame women even in the face of staggering evidence of structural inequality highlights our refusal to recognize and address institutionalized racism. Unless we acknowledge the racist roots of our current laws and policies, however, we will be condemned to reproduce them.

NOTES

1. In May 2004, a New York family court judge, Marilyn O'Connor, barred a couple from procreating until they could prove they could take care of their offspring. She repeated her actions in December 2004 with a second woman (Dobbin 2005).
2. PRWORA's emphasis on heterosexual marriage as a means of ending women's dependence on governmental assistance raises its own set of troubling issues (see Abramowitz 1996; Mink 1998; and Quadagno 1994).

3. Similar restrictions not only affect poor women on Medicaid, but also deny federally funded abortion to Native Americans, federal employees and their dependents, Peace Corps volunteers, low-income residents of Washington, DC, federal prisoners, military personnel and their dependents, and disabled women who rely on Medicare.

4. On March 21, 2001, the Supreme Court ruled in the South Carolina case of *Ferguson v. City of Charleston* that, contrary to past practice, a public hospital cannot test pregnant women for drug use without their consent and turn the results over to police. Nurses and physicians at a public hospital in Charleston instituted a policy whereby pregnant women were tested for cocaine. Those who tested positive were arrested by the police at the hospital on charges of child abuse (Daniels 2000). Over five years, the Medical University of South Carolina arrested thirty women on these grounds. All but one of the women arrested was black; the exception gave birth to a mixed-race baby. Some were taken to jail during their eighth month of pregnancy; others were arrested in their hospital gowns, still bleeding from childbirth (Paltrow 2001; Flavin 2002).

5. Around one in five victims of child maltreatment were physically abused and one in ten were sexually abused. Around half of all victims of child maltreatment were white, one-quarter (25 percent) were African American, and one-tenth were Hispanic (DHHS 2005a). Of the estimated 523,000 children in foster care in 2003, 35 percent were black/Non-Hispanic, 39 percent were white/Non-Hispanic, and 17 percent were Hispanic (DHHS 2005b).

6. The Personal Responsibility and Work Opportunity Reconciliation Act of 1996 replaced the Aid to Families with Dependent Children (AFDC) program with the Temporary Assistance to Needy Families (TANF) program. When people talk about "welfare," they are referring to TANF.

7. Termination of parental rights severs legal and physical ties between parent and child. As the Legal Services of New Jersey termination of parental rights handbook explains, "If your parental rights to your child are terminated, you will no longer have the right to visit with the child, speak to him or her on the telephone, communicate with the child by mail, or be told where the child is or what is happening to him or her. Your legal right to your relationship and your family's legal right to its relationship with your child will be permanently and completely ended. You will only be able to have contact with your child if the adoptive parents give you permission" (Shear 2002, no pagination).

REFERENCES

Allina, Amy. 2002. Cash for birth control: Discriminatory, unethical, ineffective, and bad public policy. *Network News* 27: 5–6.

American Civil Liberties Union (ACLU). 2003. *Public funding for abortion: promoting reproductive freedom for low-income women.* Fact sheet. Available at: http://www.aclu.org/ReproductiveRights/ReproductiveRights.cfm?ID=9039&c=1.

American Psychological Association (APA). 2003. *Making welfare to work really work.* Available at: http://www.apa.org/pi/wpo/welfaretowork.html. Retrieved October 4, 2005.

Anonymous. 2002. More adoptions out of foster care. *State Legislatures* 28: 7.

Armas, Genaro C. 2003. Poverty climbs, incomes slide: Census releases numbers on household finances. Washington, DC: Associated Press, September 26.

Britton, Dana M. 2003. *At work in the iron cage.* New York: New York University Press.

Calavita, Kitty. 2007. Immigration, social control, and punishment in the industrial era. In *Race, gender, and punishment: From colonialism to the war on terror,* eds. Mary Bosworth and Jeanne Flavin, 117–133. New Brunswick, NJ: Rutgers University Press.

Center for Reproductive Law and Policy (CRLP). 2000. *Punishing women for their behavior during pregnancy.* New York: CRLP, September. Available at: http://www.crlp.org/pub_bp_punwom.html. Retrieved October 1, 2003.

Children's Defense Fund. 2004. *Basic facts on welfare.* Available at: http://www.childrensdefense.org/familyincome/welfare/basicfacts.aspx. Retrieved July 7, 2005.

Collins, Patricia Hill. 1990. *Black feminist thought: Knowledge, consciousness, and the politics of empowerment.* New York: Routledge, Chapman & Hall.

Crary, David. 2003. Love locked away: A civil rights group is helping imprisoned mothers keep custody of their children. *Washington Post,* March 23.

Flavin, Jeanne. 2002. A glass half full? Harm reduction among pregnant women who use cocaine. *Journal of Drug Issues* 32: 973–998.

Frank, Deborah, Marilyn Augustyn, Wanda Knight, Tripler Pell, and Barry Zuckerman. 2001. Growth, development, and behavior in early childhood following prenatal cocaine exposure. *Journal of the American Medical Association* 285: 1613–1625.

General Accounting Office (GAO). 1999. *Foster care: States' early experiences implementing the Adoption and Safe Families Act.* Washington, DC: GAO.

———. 2001. *Welfare reform: More research needed on TANF family caps and other policies for reducing out-of-wedlock births.* Washington, DC: GAO.

Green, Rob. 2003. Who will adopt the foster-care children left behind? Fact sheet. Washington, DC: Urban Institute. Available at: http://www.urban.org/url.cfm?ID=310809.

Humphries, Drew. 1999. *Crack mothers: Pregnancy, drugs, and the media.* Columbus: Ohio University Press.

Lester, Barry, Linda LaGasse, and Ronald Seifer. 1998. Cocaine exposure and children: The meaning of subtle effects. *Science* 282: 633–634.

Lindsey, Duncan. 1994. *The welfare of children.* New York: Oxford University Press.

May, Elaine Tyler. 1995. *Barren in the promised land.* Cambridge, MA: Harvard University Press.

McCorkel, Jill A. 2003. Embodied surveillance and the gendering of punishment. *Journal of Contemporary Ethnography* 32, 1: 41–75.

Mumola, Christopher. 2000. *Incarcerated parents and their children.* Washington, DC: Bureau of Justice Statistics.

National Clearinghouse on Child Abuse and Neglect Information (NCCANI). 2002. Current trends in child maltreatment reporting laws. Child Abuse and Neglect State Statutes Series. Washington, DC: NCCANI.

———. 2003. *Reporting child maltreatment in cases involving parental substance abuse.* Washington, DC: NCCANI. Available at: http://www.calib.com/nccanch/pubs/usermanuals/subabuse/report.cfm. Retrieved October 1, 2003.

Neubeck, Kenneth, and Noel Cazenave. 2001. *Welfare racism: Playing the race card against America's poor.* New York: Routledge.

Paltrow, Lynn. 2001. The War on Drugs and the war on abortion. *Southern Law Review* 28: 201–252.

Raimon, Martha. 2000. Barriers to achieving justice for incarcerated parents. *Fordham Law Journal* 70: 421–426.

Roberts, Dorothy. 1997. *Killing the black body: Race, reproduction, and the meaning of liberty.* New York: Vintage Books.

———. 2002. *Shattered bonds: The color of child welfare.* New York: Basic Civitas Books.

Rose, Nancy. 2000. Scapegoating poor women: An analysis of welfare reform. *Journal of Economic Issues* 34: 143–157.

Roth, Rachel. 2004a. Do prisoners have abortion rights. *Feminist Studies* 30, 2: 353–381.

Sinderbrand, Rebecca. 2003. Eugenics: Clearing the collective conscience. *Newsweek,* June 2, 12.

Snell, Tracy, and Danielle Morton. 1994. *Women in prison.* Washington, DC: Bureau of Justice Statistics.

Stein, Theodore. 2000. The Adoption and Safe Families Act: Creating a false dichotomy between parents' and childrens' rights. *Families in Society* 81: 586–592.

U. S. Department of Health and Human Services (DHHS) Administration on Children, Youth, and Families. 2005a. *Child Maltreatment 2003*. Washington, DC: U.S. Government Printing Office.

————. 2005b. *The AFCARS report: Preliminary FY 2003 estimates as of April 2005* (10). Available at: http://www.acf.hhs.gov/programs/cb/stats_research/afcars/tar/report10.htm. Last accessed March 29, 2006.

Vega, Cecilia. 2003. Sterilization offer to addicts reopens ethics issue. *New York Times,* January 6.

Yeoman, Barry. 2001. Surgical Strike. *Mother Jones* 26, 21–22.

35

BLOODMOTHERS, OTHERMOTHERS, AND WOMEN-CENTERED NETWORKS

PATRICIA HILL COLLINS

Patricia Hill Collins is professor of sociology at the University of Maryland, College Park and author of *Black Feminist Thought: Knowledge, Consciousness, and the Politics of Empowerment* (2002), *Black Sexual Politics: African Americans, Gender, and the New Racism* (2004), and *From Black Power to Hip Hop: Racism, Nationalism, and Feminism* (2006).

In many African-American communities, fluid and changing boundaries often distinguish biological mothers from other women who care for children. Biological mothers, or bloodmothers, are expected to care for their children. But African and African-American communities have also recognized that vesting one person with full responsibility for mothering a child may not be wise or possible. As a result, othermothers—women who assist bloodmothers by sharing mothering responsibilities—traditionally have been central to the institution of Black motherhood (Troester 1984).

The centrality of women in African-American extended families reflects both a continuation of African-derived cultural sensibilities and functional adaptations to intersecting oppressions of race, gender, class, and nation

(Tanner 1974; Stack 1974; Martin and Martin 1978; Sudarkasa 1981b; Reagon 1987). Women's centrality is characterized less by the *absence* of husbands and fathers than by the significance of women. Though men may be physically present or have well-defined and culturally significant roles in the extended family, the kin unit tends to be woman-centered. Bebe Moore Campbell's (1989) parents separated when she was small. Even though she spent the school year in the North Philadelphia household maintained by her grandmother and mother, Campbell's father assumed an important role in her life. "My father took care of me," Campbell remembers. "Our separation didn't stunt me or condemn me to a lesser humanity. His absence never made me a fatherless child. I'm not fatherless now" (p. 271). In woman-centered kin units such as Campbell's—whether a mother-child household unit, a married couple household, or a larger unit extending over several households—the centrality of mothers is not predicated on male powerlessness (Tanner 1974, 133).

Organized, resilient, women-centered networks of bloodmothers and othermothers are key in understanding this centrality. Grandmothers, sisters, aunts, or cousins act as othermothers by taking on child-care responsibilities for one another's children. Historically, when needed, temporary child-care arrangements often turned into long-term care or informal adoption (Stack 1974; Gutman 1976). These practices continue in the face of changing social pressures. Andrea Hunter's (1997) research on Black grandmothers explores how Black parents rely on grandmothers for parenting support. This traditional source of support became even more needed in the 1980s and 1990s, when increasing numbers of Black mothers saw their teenage children fall victim to drugs and the crime associated with it. Many witnessed their sons killed or incarcerated, while their daughters became addicts. In many cases, these young men and women left behind children, who often ended up in foster care. Other children did not, primarily because their grandmothers took responsibility for raising them, often under less than optimal conditions.

In many African-American communities these women-centered networks of community-based child care have extended beyond the boundaries of biologically related individuals to include "fictive kin" (Stack 1974). Civil rights activist Ella Baker describes how informal adoption by othermothers functioned in the rural Southern community of her childhood:

> My aunt who had thirteen children of her own raised three more. She had become a midwife, and a child was born who was covered with sores. Nobody was particularly wanting the child, so she took the child and raised him . . . and another mother decided she didn't want to be bothered with two children. So my aunt took one and raised him . . . they were part of the family. (Cantarow 1980, 59)

Stanlie James recounts how othermother traditions work with notions of fictive kin within her own extended family. James notes that the death of her grandmother in 1988 reunited her family, described as a host of biological and fictive kin. James's rendition of how one female family member helped James's nine-year-old daughter deal with the loss of her great-grandmother illustrates the interactions among women-centered extended kin networks, fictive kin, and othermother traditions. The woman who helped James's daughter was not a blood relative but had been "othermothered" by James's grandmother and was a full member of the extended family. James's grandmother believed that because all children must be fed, clothed, and educated, if their biological parents could not discharge these obligations, then some other member of the community should accept that responsibility. As James points out, "This fictive kin who stepped in to counsel my daughter was upholding a family tradition that had been modeled by my grandmother some fifty years before" (James 1993, 44).

Even when relationships are not between kin or fictive kin, African-American community norms traditionally were such that neighbors cared for one another's children. Sara Brooks, a Southern domestic worker, describes the importance that the community-based child care a neighbor offered her daughter had for her: "She kept Vivian and she didn't charge me nothin either. You see, people used to look after each other, but now its not that way. I reckon its because we all was poor, and I guess they put theirself in the place of the person that they was helpin'" (Simonsen 1986, 181). Brooks's experiences demonstrate how the African-American cultural value placed on cooperative child care traditionally found institutional support in the adverse conditions under which so many Black women mothered.

Othermothers can be key not only in supporting children but also in helping bloodmothers who, for whatever reason, lack the preparation or desire for motherhood. In confronting racial oppression, maintaining community-based child care and respecting othermothers who assume child-care responsibilities can serve a critical function in African-American communities. Children orphaned by sale or death of their parents under slavery, children conceived through rape, children of young mothers, children born into extreme poverty or to alcoholic or drug-addicted mothers, or children who for other reasons cannot remain with their bloodmothers have all been supported by othermothers, who, like Ella Baker's aunt, take in additional children even when they have enough of their own.

Young women are often carefully groomed at an early age to become othermothers. As a 10-year-old, Ella Baker learned to be an othermother by caring for the children of a widowed neighbor: "Mama would say, 'You must take the clothes to Mr. Powell's house, and give so-and-so a bath.' The children were running wild. . . . The kids . . . would take off across the field. We'd chase them down, and bring them back, and put 'em in the tub, and wash 'em off, and change clothes, and carry the dirty ones home, and wash them. Those kind of things were routine" (Cantarow 1980, 59).

Many Black men also value community-based child care but historically have exercised these values to a lesser extent. During slavery, for example, Black children under age 10 experienced little division of labor. They were dressed alike and performed similar tasks. If the activities of work and play are any indication of the degree of gender role differentiation that existed among slave children, "then young girls probably grew up minimizing the difference between the sexes while learning far more about the differences between the races" (White 1985, 94). Because they are often left in charge of younger siblings, many young Black men learn how to care for children. Geoffrey Canada (1995) recounts how he had to learn how to fight in his urban neighborhood. The climate of violence that he and his two brothers encountered mandated developing caretaking skills, especially since his single mother had to work and could not offer them the protection that they needed. Thus, differences among Black men and women in behaviors concerning children may have more to do with male labor force patterns and similar factors. As Ella Baker observes, "My father took care of people too, but . . . my father had to work" (Cantarow 1980, 60).

Historically, within Black diasporic societies, community-based child care and the relationships among bloodmothers and othermothers in women-centered networks have taken diverse institutional forms. In some polygynous West African societies, the children of the same father but different mothers referred to one another as brothers and sisters. While a strong bond existed between the biological mother and her child—one so strong that, among the Ashanti for example, "to show disrespect toward one's mother is tantamount to sacrilege" (Fortes 1950, 263)—children could be disciplined by any of their "mothers." Cross-culturally, the high status given to othermothers and the cooperative nature of child-care arrangements among bloodmothers and othermothers in Caribbean and other Black diasporic societies gives credence to the importance that people of African descent place on mothering (Sudarkasa 1981a).

Although the political economy of slavery brought profound changes to Africans enslaved in the United States, beliefs in the importance of motherhood and the value of cooperative approaches to child care continued. During slavery, while older women served as nurses and midwives, their most common occupation was caring for the children of parents who worked (White 1985). Informal adoption of orphaned children reinforced the importance of social motherhood in African-American communities (Gutman 1976). The relationship between bloodmothers and othermothers also survived the transition from a slave economy to post-emancipation Southern rural agriculture. Children in Southern rural communities were not solely the responsibility of their biological mothers. Aunts, grandmothers, and others who had time to supervise children served as othermothers (Dougherty 1978). The significant status that women enjoyed in family networks and in African-American communities continued to be linked to their bloodmother and othermother activities.

In the 1980s, the entire community structure of bloodmothers and othermothers came under assault. Racial desegregation as well as the emergence of class-stratified Black neighborhoods greatly altered the fabric of Black civil society. African-Americans of diverse social classes found themselves in new residential, school, and work settings that tested this enduring theme of bloodmothers, othermothers, and woman-centered networks. In many inner-city, working-class neighborhoods, the very fabric of African-American community life eroded when crack cocaine flooded the streets. African-American children and youth often formed the casualties of this expanding market for drugs, from the increasing number of Black children in foster care (Nightingale 1993), to children threatened by violence (Canada 1995), to those killed. Residents of Central Harlem interviewed by anthropologist Leith Mullings repeatedly expressed concern about losing the community's children, leading Mullings to observe, "The depth of worry about children growing up in these conditions is difficult to convey" (Mullings 1997, 93). Given this situation, it is remarkable that even in the most troubled communities, remnants of the othermother tradition endure. Bebe Moore Campbell's 1950s North Philadelphia neighborhood underwent startling changes in the 1980s. Increases in child abuse and parental neglect left many children without care. But some residents, such as Miss Nee, continued the othermother tradition. After raising her younger brothers and sisters and five children of her own, Miss Nee cared for three additional children whose families fell apart. Moreover, on any given night Miss Nee's house may have been filled by up to a dozen children because she had a reputation for never turning away a needy child ("Children of the Underclass" 1989).

Black middle-class women and their families found challenges from another direction. In some fundamental ways, moving into the middle class means adopting the values and lifestyles of White middle-class families. While the traditional family ideal is not the norm, the relative isolation of such families from others is noteworthy. U.S. middle-class family life is based on privatization—buying a big house so that one need not cooperate with one's neighbors, or even see them. American middle-class families participate in the privatization of everything, from schools and health care, to for-fee health clubs and private automobiles. Working-class African-Americans who experience social mobility thus may encounter a distinctly different value system. Not only are woman-centered networks of bloodmothers and othermothers much more difficult to sustain structurally—class-stratified residential and employment patterns mean that middle-class Black women often see working-class and poor Black women only as their employees or clients—such ideas are often anathema to the ethos of achievement. From the security firms that find ways to monitor nannies, to the gated-communities of suburbia, purchasing services appears to be the hallmark of American middle-class existence. In this context, stopping to help others to whom one is not related and doing it for free can be seen as rejecting the basic values of the capitalist market economy.

In this context, these relationships among bloodmothers and othermothers and the persistence of woman-centered networks may have greater theoretical importance than currently recognized. The traditional family ideal assigns mothers full responsibility for children and evaluates their performance based on their ability to procure the benefits of a nuclear family household. Within this capitalist marketplace model, those women who "catch" legal husbands, who live in single-family homes, who can afford private school and music lessons for their children, are deemed better mothers than those who do not. In this context, those African-American women who continue community-based child care challenge one fundamental assumption underlying the capitalist system itself: that children are "private property" and can be disposed of as such. Under the property model that accompanies the traditional family ideal, parents may not literally assert that their children are pieces of property, but their parenting may reflect assumptions analogous to those they make in connection with property. For example, the exclusive parental "right" to discipline children as parents see fit, even if discipline borders on abuse, parallels the widespread assumption that property owners may dispose of their property without consulting members of the larger community.

By seeing the larger *community* as responsible for children and by giving othermothers and other nonparents "rights" in child rearing, those African-Americans who endorse these values challenge prevailing capitalist property relations. In Harlem, for example, Black women are increasingly the breadwinners in their families, and rates of households maintained by single mothers remain high. These families are clearly under stress, yet to see the household formation itself as an indication of decline in Black family organization misreads a more complex situation. Leith Mullings suggests that many of these households participate in fluid, familylike networks that have different purposes. Women activate some networks for socialization, reproduction, and consumption, and others for emotional support, economic cooperation, and sexuality. The networks may overlap, but they are not coterminous (Mullings 1997, 74).

The resiliency of women-centered family networks and their willingness to take responsibility for Black children illustrates how African-influenced understandings of family have been continually reworked to help African-Americans as a collectivity cope with and resist oppression. Moreover, these understandings of woman-centered kin networks become critical in understanding broader African-American understandings of community. At the same time, the erosion of such networks in the face of the changing institutional fabric of Black civil society points to the need either to refashion these networks or develop some other way of supporting Black children. For far too many African-American children, assuming that a grandmother or "fictive kin" will care for them is no longer a reality.

REFERENCES

Campbell, Bebe Moore. 1989. *Sweet Summer: Growing Up with and without My Dad.* New York: Putnam.

Canada, Geoffrey. 1995. *First Stick Knife Gun: A Personal History of Violence in America.* Boston: Beacon.

Cantarow, Ellen. 1980. *Moving the Mountain: Women Working for Social Change.* Old Westbury, NY: Feminist Press.

"Children of the Underclass." 1989. *Newsweek.* September 11, 16–27.

Dougherty, Molly C. 1978. *Becoming a Woman in Rural Black Culture.* New York: Holt, Rinehart and Winston.

Fortes, Meyer. 1950. "Kinship and Marriage among the Ashanti." In *African Systems of Kinship and Marriage,* ed. A. R. Radcliffe-Brown and Daryll Forde, 252–84. New York: Oxford University Press.

Gutman, Herbert, 1976. *The Black Family in Slavery and Freedom,* 1750–1925. New York: Random House.

Hunter, Andrea. 1997. "Counting on Grandmothers: Black Mothers' and Fathers' Reliance on Grandmothers for Parenting Support." *Journal of Family Issues* 18 (3): 251–69.

James, Stanlie. 1993. "Mothering: A Possible Black Feminist Link to Social Transformation?" In *Theorizing Black Feminisms: The Visionary Pragmatism of Black Women,* ed. Stanlie James and Abena Busia, 44–54. New York: Routledge.

Martin, Elmer, and Joanne Mitchell Martin. 1978. *The Black Extended Family.* Chicago: University of Chicago Press.

Mullings, Leith. 1997. *On Our Own Terms: Race, Class, and Gender in the Lives of African American Women.* New York: Routledge.

Nightingale, Carl Husemoller. 1993. *On the Edge: A History of Poor Black Children and Their American Dreams.* New York: Basic Books.

Reagon, Bernice Johnson. 1987. "African Diaspora Women: The Making of Cultural Workers." In *Women in Africa and the African Diaspora,* ed. Rosalyn Terborg-Penn, Sharon Harley, and Andrea Benton Rushing, 167–80. Washington, D.C.: Howard University Press.

Simonsen, Thordis, ed. 1986. *You May Plow Here: The Narrative of Sara Brooks.* New York: Touchstone.

Stack, Carol D. 1974. *All Our Kin: Strategies for Survival in a Black Community.* New York: Harper and Row.

Sudarkasa, Niara. 1981a. "Female Employment and Family Organization in West Africa." In *The Black Woman Cross-Culturally,* ed. Filomina Chioma Steady, 49–64. Cambridge, MA: Schenkman.

————.1981b. "Interpreting the African Heritage in Afro-American Family Organization." In *Black Families,* ed. Harriette Pipes McAdoo, 37–53. Beverly Hills, CA: Sage.

Tanner, Nancy. 1974. "Matrifocality in Indonesia and Africa and among Black Americans." In *Woman, Culture, and Society,* ed. Michelle Z. Rosaldo and Louise Lamphere, 129–56. Stanford, CA: Stanford University Press.

Troester, Rosalie Riegle. 1984. "Turbulence and Tenderness: Mothers, Daughters, and 'Othermothers' in Paule Marshall's *Brown Girl, Brownstones.*" *Sage: A Scholarly Journal on Black Women* 1 (2): 13–16.

White, Deborah Gray. 1985. *Ar'n't I a Woman? Female Slaves in the Plantation South.* New York: W. W. Norton.

36

DILEMMAS OF INVOLVED FATHERHOOD

KATHLEEN GERSON

Kathleen Gerson is professor of sociology at New York University and the author of several books, including *No Man's Land: Men's Changing Commitments to Family and Work* (1993), *Hard Choices: How Women Decide about Work, Career, and Motherhood* (1985), and *The Time Divide: Work, Family, and Gender Inequality* (with Jerry A. Jacobs), (2004).

> *Work's a necessity, but the things that really matter are spending time with my family. If I didn't have a family, I don't know what I would have turned to. That's why I say you're rich in a lot of ways other than money. I look at my daughter and think, "My family is everything."*
>
> —CARL, *A THIRTY-FOUR-YEAR-OLD UTILITIES WORKER*

Social disapproval and economic inequality put full-time domesticity out of reach for almost all men. Yet most also found that economic necessity and employer intransigence made anything less than full-time work an equally distant possibility. Few employers offered the option of part-time work, especially in male-dominated fields. Arthur, a married sanitation worker planning for fatherhood, complained:

> If it was feasible, I would love to spend more time with my child. That would be more important to me than working. I'd love to be able to work twenty-five hours a week or four days a week and have three days off to spend with the family, but most jobs aren't going to accommodate you that way.

Yet, even if part-time work were available, involved fathers still needed the earnings that only full-time and overtime work could offer. Lou, the sewage worker who worked the night shift in order to spend days with his young daughter, could not accept lower wages or fewer benefits:

> If I knew that financially everything would be set, I'd stay home. I'd like to stay more with my daughter. It's a lot of fun to be with a

very nice three-year-old girl. But if I work less, I would equate it to less money and then I wouldn't be taking care of my family. If it meant less work and the same or more money, I'd say, "Sure!" I'd be dumb if I didn't.

Dean, the driver for a city department of parks, agreed that his economic obligations could not take a backseat to his nurturing ones:

It always comes down to the same thing: I would like to have more time to spend with my children, but if I didn't have money, what's the sense of having time off? If I could work part-time and make enough money, that would be fine and dandy.

Since involved fathers tried to nurture as well as support their children, they made an especially hard choice between money and time. Like many mothers, they had to add caretaking onto full-time workplace responsibilities, but employers are generally reluctant to recognize male (or female) parental responsibility as a legitimate right or need.[1] Worse yet, paternal leaves are rarely considered a legitimate option for men even if they formally exist. Involved fathers wished to take time off for parenting, but like most men they were reluctant to do so for fear of imperiling their careers.[2] And even though most employers allow health-related leaves with impunity, they have not been so flexible when it comes to the job of parenting. Workers receive the message that illness is unavoidable, but parenting is voluntary—an indication of a lack of job commitment. Our current corporate culture thus makes parenting hazardous to anyone's career, and choosing a "daddy track" can be just as dangerous as the much-publicized "mommy track." Juan, a financial analyst, knew he could not pull back from his job for more than a few days or a week without jeopardizing his job security. To parental leave,

I'd say yes, but realistically no. It would be a problem because it's very difficult for me to tell my boss that I have to leave at such a time. I have deadlines to meet. If I leave the office for two or three months, my job is in jeopardy.

Because employers did not offer flexible options for structuring work on a daily basis or over the course of a career, some involved fathers looked to self-employment or home-based work for more flexibility and control. Craig, the ex-dancer currently working in an office, hoped he would be able to integrate work and parenting by working at home:

I would like to find myself in the situation where I'm not locked into a nine-to-five schedule. Ultimately, I hope I'm doing consulting on my own at home, which means time close to the family. So that in the middle of my own workday, at the house, I'm available. I can just put my work aside and play Daddy.

Most could not even entertain this option. They had to fit parenting in around the edges of their work lives.[3]

Domestic arrangements also impede full equality. Child rearing remains an undervalued, isolating, and largely invisible accomplishment for *all* parents. This has fueled women's flight from domesticity and also dampened men's motivation to choose it. Russell, the legal-aid attorney and father of two, recognized that child rearing was less valued than employment:

> I think I would feel somewhat meaningless to not be engaged in any form of productive work—although certainly raising children is productive work. But I couldn't be responsible for that on a full-time basis. While I love my guys, I don't think I could be around them all the time.

Child rearing can be invisible as well as undervalued. Unlike the size of a paycheck or the title one holds at work, there are few socially recognized rewards for the time a parent devotes to raising a child or the results it produces. This made only the most dedicated, like Hank, willing to consider full-time parenting:

> Nobody will know the time and the effort I put in the family. They will look down on it. I would devote time, hours, and nobody will be happy with it except me because I'll know what I was trying for.

The forces pulling women out of the home are stronger than the forces pulling men into it. Since the social value of public pursuits outstrips the power and prestige of private ones, men are likely to resist full-time domesticity even as women move toward full-time employment. This process is similar to the one pulling women into male-dominated occupations while leaving men less inclined to enter female-dominated ones. In addition, just as women in male-dominated occupations face prejudice and discrimination, fathers who become equal or primary parents are stigmatized—treated as "tokens" in a female-dominated world.[4] Roger shied away from the pervasive questioning about his life as a custodial parent:

> I think I've become somewhat more introverted than I used to be—because I get tired of explaining my situation at home. . . . The thing that blows all the kids' minds—they're all living with Mommy and my kids are living with Daddy.

In the face of such disincentives, most involved fathers rejected staying home for the same reasons many women do and more. Female breadwinning and male homemaking did not seem acceptable even when they made economic sense. Robin, a stockbroker, rejected domesticity precisely because his poor work prospects left him in no state to bear the additional stigma of becoming a househusband. Although he was making a lot less money than his wife was, he felt too "demoralized" to consider staying home. "I'm not secure enough, I guess, to stay home and be a househusband."

Of course, involved fathers actively resisted the discrimination they encountered. They asserted their nurturing competence and insisted on being taken as seriously as female parents are. The prevailing skepticism about men's parental abilities, however, made this an uphill battle. Ernie complained:

> I believe I have as much right in raising the child as she does, but I found a lot of reverse discrimination—people assuming that the mother takes care of the child. It's a lot of stereotyping, a lot that's taken for granted. Like pediatricians: they speak to my wife; they won't speak to me. I say, "Hey, I take care of her, too." They look at me like I'm invisible. The same thing with the nursery school. I went out on all the interviews. They looked at me like, "What're *you* doing here?"

Economic, social, and ideological arrangements thus made involved fatherhood difficult. The lack of workplace and domestic supports diluted and suppressed the potential for involvement even among the most motivated men. In the absence of these hurdles, fathers who wished to be involved might have participated far more than they actually did. They might, in fact, have made choices that now remain open to a rapidly diminishing number of women. Ernie wished he had options that only full-time mothers enjoy:

> I'm not the type that has career aspirations and is very goal-oriented. If I didn't have to work, I wouldn't. But I would volunteer. I would work in a nursery school. I would do a lot more volunteer work with my daughter's school. I would love to go on trips like the mothers who don't work, be more active in the P.T.A. I would love that. But I can't.

As the supports for homemaking mothers erode, supports for equal and primary fathers have not emerged to offset the growing imbalance between children's needs and families' resources. Fathers have had to depend on paid help, relatives, and already overburdened wives even when they did not wish to do so.

These obstacles not only left mothers giving up more. They also made involved fathers appear heroic about *whatever* they did. Comparisons with other men could be used to ward off complaints and resist further change. Ernie maintained:

> Sometimes she didn't think I did enough. I couldn't stand that because I thought I was doing too much. I really felt I was doing more than I should, whatever that means. I told her to go talk to some of her friends and see what their husbands are doing.

Nurturing fathers faced deeply rooted barriers to full equality in parenting. Social arrangements at work and in the home dampened even willing men's ability to share equally. The truncated range of choices open to most of these men limited the options of their wives, ex-wives, and partners as well. We can only guess how many mothers' helpers would become equal parents if these obstacles did not exist or, better yet, were replaced by positive supports for involved fatherhood.

Benefiting from the Loss of Privilege:
Incentives for Change

If full equality remained beyond the reach of most involved fathers, they nevertheless moved a notable distance toward it. They were not simply forced to make concessions; nor were they just being altruistic. They also perceived offsetting, if unheralded, benefits. After all, parenting can be its own reward—offering intrinsic pleasures and a powerful sense of accomplishment. Rick explained:

> I have an extremely close relationship with my kids, and that makes me feel good. The fact that they're both doing very well in school—I know that at least a little bit of that comes from having been with them when they were young. So there's all those interactions in seeing them on their way to being healthy and vibrant kids.

These feelings took on added significance when other avenues for building self-esteem were blocked. Todd, the aspiring actor who became a construction worker, hoped his talents could be channeled toward his daughter instead of his job:

> If there's any Creator at all up there, She or It or They're going to ask for some sort of accounting at the end. They're going to be pleased if they gave you a certain amount of gifts and you were able to do something with them. I'd still like to be a part of something more meaningful than putting in a new fire hydrant—I guess through my influence on this little one's life.

If children offered a source of pride for those whose workplace aspirations had not been met, this was not just a concern for passing on genes or the family name. Contributions of time and emotions counted more. Carl, who chose utility repair work so that he could care for his daughter after school, saw his "investment" reflected in her talents and achievements:

> I've had a lot of compliments on her, and I take them as a compliment also. It's something that became part of you—teaching them different things, helping them grow up. They'll do something, and it's like seeing a reflection of you.

As work opportunities stall in an age of stagnant economic growth, parenting offers men another avenue for developing self-esteem. But economically successful fathers also reaped benefits from involvement because it balanced lives that would otherwise have been more narrowly focused on paid work. For Charles, the attorney with a young son, caretaking provided a legitimate reason for limiting the demands of work: "I'm working a little less hard, taking on fewer responsibilities. . . . But I think it's great. I don't need all the other shit."

Children also provided the hope of permanence in an age of divorce. Even happily married fathers came to see their children as the bedrock of stability in a shaky world, the one bond that could not be severed or assailed. Having been reared by a single mother, Juan viewed his children rather than his wife as the best chance for enduring emotional ties: "What if one day my wife and I get sick of each other after so many years? So I would like to have children."

Involved fatherhood also provided emotional supports by creating a bond between husbands and wives. Married men were less likely to feel rejected by their wives and excluded from the new relationships that form with the birth of a child. Timothy, the worker at a city dump, could not understand why less-involved fathers complained of being rejected when a new baby arrived:

> They have these books about how fathers are supposed to go
> through blues because the wife is giving her attention to the child.
> Is this some kind of maniac that wrote this? I take care of him just
> as much as she does.

Sharing the load of caring for a newborn also seemed to decrease the chances that a mother would feel overwhelmed and alone during a critical, and trying, turning point in a marriage.[5] Carlos hoped that sharing the caretaking would help him avoid the hostility that he felt unequal arrangements would generate:

> I think it's a great burden to have one parent do all the caretaking.
> It would burn out that person, and they're not going to be able to
> respond to you. Then I would start feeling resentment towards her
> and possibly the child. So the only way I could see avoiding that is
> by sharing the responsibility.

Since involved fathers believed that a satisfying relationship depended on both partners being able to meet their needs, thwarting a partner's dreams by refusing to participate seemed to be a Pyrrhic victory. The costs of not sharing appeared greater than the costs of sharing. Carl was pleased to escape his parents' pattern:

> My parents are the old school. He never really touched a dish. I like
> what I'm doing better. The older way, I feel the woman will think,
> "I never really had an opportunity to do things." She will become
> resentful later on. Where my wife can't say nothing because she's
> had her freedom, she's worked, she's not stayed in the kitchen
> barefoot and pregnant, and I did what I had to do. I feel in the long
> run it pays off. The other way, maybe she would have left.

Involved fatherhood thus offered two ways of coping with the risks of marriage in an era of divorce. It provided another source of emotional sustenance in the event that the marital bond did not survive. And it offered a way to build less rancorous relationships by reducing wives' resentment. Indeed, there is growing evidence that egalitarian relationships do provide benefits to husbands and wives. In one report, wives whose husbands participate in domestic duties showed lower rates of depression than those with husbands who don't, while another found that the more housework a husband does, the lower are the chances that his wife has considered divorce.[6]

Emotional gratification and marital peace were not the only payoffs. In agreeing to share the domestic load, men can also share the economic load. Their wives' income lessens the pressure to work long hours and take on second jobs. Wesley was pleased to exchange extra hours at work for domestic sharing:

> If Cindy wants to be home, she can stay home. But that would probably mean I would have to either get myself another job or work overtime on the job I have. I would do it. She knows that. But she doesn't want me to. We spend more time with each other this way.

Involved fathers also believed their children would benefit in both the short and long runs—perceptions that research on both married and divorced fathers supports.[7] Larry observed:

> Having spent a lot of time with both of us, she's not really dependent on either one of us. Mommy's like daddy; daddy's like mommy. At times I am her mother. It's good to switch roles. She don't run to mommy or run to daddy. She runs to both of us.

They hoped their example would help their daughters and sons develop a flexible approach to building their own lives. Ernie decided his involvement created a better domestic environment for his daughter:

> The sharing—it's a good role model for her. She sees me cook. I'm trying to teach her baking, and I think it's nice my daughter is learning baking from her father. So I'm hoping she sees that it's split and not that just the wife does this and the man does that.

He also hoped his participation would give his daughter a sense of self-reliance, agreeing with a growing group of psychologists who argue that girls no less than boys need their fathers. Both sexes identify in varying degrees with both parents, and girls look to fathers as well as mothers to provide models for living:[8]

> Raising my child, that is my priority—seeing that she's raised well in the sense of preparing her to face the world, trying to get her exposed as much as possible, so she may find out what she likes to pursue. I hope she has a career. I hope she finds something she really likes and works for it.

These men concluded that their domestic arrangements would also benefit their sons, echoing recent research showing that sons of involved fathers are likely to show a more developed capacity for empathy.[9] Wesley thus concluded that his two sons "feel close to the two of us. Maybe when they get married, they'll share in the house."

Just as these fathers created families that differed from the households in which they were reared, so their children will take the lessons of their childhood into unknown futures. Involved fathers' belief in the advantages of domestic sharing cannot guarantee a similar response in their children, but it can and did strengthen their own resolve to create a more egalitarian household. As more fathers become involved, their growing numbers should prompt wider social acceptance of egalitarian households, bolstering the option to make such choices.

Ultimately, however, men's movement toward domestic equality will depend on their ability to overcome the obstacles to change and their desire to resist the social pressures to conform. Equal fathers were willing and able to defy social expectations, to overcome social constraints, and to reject the pathways of the past. There is good reason to believe that their outlooks and choices reflect a simmering mood among many American men, who long for more work flexibility and fewer work demands. There is even reason to believe many would be willing to relinquish some earnings in exchange for spending more time with their families. A *Time* survey found that 56 percent of a random sample of men said they would forfeit up to one-fourth of their salaries "to have more family and personal time," and 45 percent "said they would probably refuse a promotion that involved sacrificing hours with their families."[10] Carl reflects this mood:

> It's amazing how many people don't understand the way I feel.
> I would prefer to be home than work overtime, where they would
> kill to get it. They say, "What are you, rich?" No, but you only need
> a certain amount of money to live. God forbid you walk down the
> street and get struck by a car, or whatever, and it's over. I don't
> want to say, "Why didn't I spend more time with my family?" It's
> not going to happen to me. You can control it.

By focusing on the advantages and discounting the drawbacks of their choices, men are able to overcome some of the social and ideological barriers to equal parenting. In adding up the sacrifices and the gains, Larry spoke for the group: "I've given some things up, sure, but the changes in my lifestyle are eighty or ninety percent in the positive."

Though few in number, equal fathers demonstrate that men can discover or acquire nurturing skills and find pleasure in using them. Those men who did find support for being an equal father made contingent choices just like those who did not. In both instances, different circumstances could easily have produced different outcomes. It is not surprising that Rick found his rare and unexpected path to be a matter of chance:

> I have very conservative attitudes in many respects. The fact that
> we got married and had children was very conservative. The fact

that within those parameters, we shared, co-shared, work and family—that was not conservative. We've never discussed it, but I feel that the outcome is built much more on chance. I may not have always felt that way, but my own experiences confirmed it.

Chance, however, is just another way of saying that his choice was based on unusual and unexpected opportunities. Given how rare are the supports for involved fathering and how pervasive the obstacles, its rise is even more significant than its limited nature. For the potential of the many men who wish to be more involved to be realized, however, the unusual circumstances that now prompt only a small fraction of men to become equal parents must become real for a much larger group.

NOTES

1. See Lawson, Carol. 1991. "Baby Beckons: Why Is Daddy at Work?" *New York Times* (May 16); C1, C8. The Family Leave Act that finally became law in 1993 is an important first step, but much more will be needed for men to feel able to choose equal parenting.
2. Joseph H. Pleck. 1983. "Husbands' Paid Work and Family Roles: Current Research Trends," *Research in the Interweave of Social Roles: Jobs and Families* 3: 251–333.
3. Barbara J. Risman and Maxine P. Atkinson. 1990. "Gender in Intimate Relationships: Toward a Dialectical Structural Theory." Paper presented at the National Council on Family Relations Theory, Construction, and Research Methodology Workshop (November), Seattle, Washington. According to Risman and Atkinson: "No matter how involved 'new feminist' fathers become in child-care, they . . . are expected to work harder and are constrained from leaving less than optimal jobs because of their economic responsibilities. When they do care for their children after work, they are praised highly by friends, family members, and wives as wonderful, modern, 'involved' fathers" (pp. 15–16).
4. Hal Strauss. 1989. "Freaks of Nature." *American Health* (January–February): 70–71; Rosabeth M. Kanter. 1977. *Men and Women of the Corporation*. New York: Basic Books; Bryan E. Robinson. 1986. "Men Caring for the Young: A Profile." In *Men's Changing Roles in the Family*, pp. 151–61. Edited by Robert A. Lewis and Marvin B. Sussman. New York: Haworth Press, 1986. Men who become primary parents face barriers similar to those faced by the first female managers, who had to cope with being "tokens." Strauss discusses the stigmatization and social isolation of househusbands. Kanter analyzes how the first female managers were tokens in the corporation. Robinson, 1986, reports that male caregivers who work in nursery schools and day-care programs also faced discrimination and stigma from employers, co-workers, and even parents.
5. See Alice A. Rossi. 1960. "Transition to Parenthood." *Journal of Marriage and the Family* 30: 26–39.
6. Joan Huber and Glenna Spitze. 1983. *Sex Stratification: Children, Housework, and Jobs*. New York: Academic Press; Catherine E. Ross, John Mirowsky, and Joan Huber. 1983. "Dividing Work, Sharing Work, and In-Between: Marriage Patterns and Depression." *American Sociological Review* 48 (6) (December): 809–23; See also Michael E. Lamb, Joseph H. Pleck, and James A. Levine. 1987. "Effects of Increased Paternal Involvement on Fathers and Mothers." In *Reassessing Fatherhood: New Observations on Fathers and the Modern Family*, pp. 103–25. Edited

by Charlie Lewis and Margaret O'Brien. Newberry Park, CA: Sage Publications; Arlie R. Hochschild with Anne Machung. 1989. *The Second Shift: Working Parents and the Revolution at Home.* New York: Viking.

7. See Frank F. Furstenberg, Jr., S. Phillip Morgan, and Paul D. Allison. 1987. "Paternal Participation and Children's Well-Being After Marital Dissolution." *American Sociological Review* 52(5):695–701; Shirley M. H. Hanson. 1986. "Father/Child Relationships: Beyond *Kramer vs. Kramer.*" In *Men's Changing Roles in the Family,* pp. 135–50. Edited by Robert A. Lewis and Marvin B. Sussman. New York: Haworth Press, 1986; Michael E. Lamb, ed. 1976. *The Role of the Father in Child Development.* New York: Wiley; J. W. Santrock and R. A. Warshak. 1979. "Father Custody and Social Development in Boys and Girls." *Journal of Social Issues* 32: 112–25; J. W. Santrock, R. A. Warshak, and G. L. Elliot. 1982. "Social Development and Parent-Child Interaction in Father-Custody and Stepmother Families." In *Nontraditional Families: Parenting and Child Development,* pp. 289–314. Edited by Michael E. Lamb. Hillside, NJ: Lawrence Erlbaum.

8. Victoria Secunda. 1992. *Women and Their Fathers: The Sexual and Romantic Impact of the First Man in Your Life.* New York: Delacorte Press.

9. Daniel Goleman. 1990. "Surprising Findings about the Development of Empathy in Children." *New York Times* (July 10): C1.

10. Reported in Judith Stacey. 1991. "Backwards toward the Post-Modern Family." In *America at Century's End,* pp. 17–34. Edited by Alan Wolfe. Berkeley and Los Angeles: University of California Press. See also Phyllis Moen and Donna I. Dempster-McClain. 1987. "Employed Parents: Role Strain, Work Time, and Preferences for Working Less." *Journal of Marriage and the Family* 49 (3): 579–90; Eli Chinoy. 1955. *Automobile Workers and the American Dream.* New York: Random House. If Chinoy found that automobile workers in the 1950s dreamed about retiring, inheriting wealth, or opening their own businesses as an alternative to dead-end factory jobs, then the decline of well-paying, secure manufacturing jobs over the last decade has given this dream of independence through self-employment new life.

37

MAN CHILD
A Black Lesbian Feminist's Response

AUDRE LORDE

Audre Lorde, who passed away in 1992, grew up in the West Indian community of Harlem in the 1930s, the daughter of immigrants from Grenada. She attended Hunter College (later becoming professor of English there), ventured to the American expatriate community in Mexico, and participated in the Greenwich Village scene of the early 1950s. She is a major figure in the lesbian and feminist movements. Among her works are *Sister Outsider* (1984), *Zami: A New Spelling of My Name* (1982), *Uses of the Erotic* (1978), *Chosen Poems Old and New* (1982), *The Black Unicorn* (1978), and *From a Land Where Other People Live* (1973).

This article is not a theoretical discussion of Lesbian Mothers and their Sons, nor a how-to article. It is an attempt to scrutinize and share some pieces of that common history belonging to my son and to me. I have two children: a fifteen-and-a-half-year-old daughter Beth, and a fourteen-year-old son Jonathan. This is the way it was/is with me and Jonathan, and I leave the theory to another time and person. This is one woman's telling.

I have no golden message about the raising of sons for other lesbian mothers, no secret to transpose your questions into certain light. I have my own ways of rewording those same questions, hoping we will all come to speak those questions and pieces of our lives we need to share. We are women making contact within ourselves and with each other across the restrictions of a printed page, bent upon the use of our own/one another's knowledges.

The truest direction comes from inside. I give the most strength to my children by being willing to look within myself, and by being honest with them about what I find there, without expecting a response beyond their years. In this way they begin to learn to look beyond their own fears.

All our children are outriders for a queendom not yet assured.

My adolescent son's growing sexuality is a conscious dynamic between Jonathan and me. It would be presumptuous of me to discuss Jonathan's sexuality here, except to state my belief that whomever he chooses to explore this area with, his choices will be nonoppressive, joyful, and deeply felt from within, places of growth.

Audre Lorde, "Man Child: A Black Lesbian Feminist's Response" from *Sister Outsider: Essays and Speeches*. Reprinted with the permission of The Crossing Press, a division of Ten Speed Press, Berkeley, CA, www.tenspeed.com.

One of the difficulties in writing this piece has been temporal; this is the summer when Jonathan is becoming a man, physically. And our sons must become men—such men as we hope our daughters, born and unborn, will be pleased to live among. Our sons will not grow into women. Their way is more difficult than that of our daughters, for they must move away from us, without us. Hopefully, our sons have what they have learned from us, and a howness to forge it into their own image.

Our daughters have us, for measure or rebellion or outline or dream; but the sons of lesbians have to make their own definitions of self as men. This is both power and vulnerability. The sons of lesbians have the advantage of our blueprints for survival, but they must take what we know and transpose it into their own maleness. May the goddess be kind to my son, Jonathan.

Recently I have met young Black men about whom I am pleased to say that their future and their visions, as well as their concerns within the present, intersect more closely with Jonathan's than do my own. I have shared vision with these men as well as temporal strategies for our survivals and I appreciate the spaces in which we could sit down together. Some of these men I met at the First Annual Conference of Third World Lesbians and Gays held in Washington, D.C., in October, 1979. I have met others in different places and do not know how they identify themselves sexually. Some of these men are raising families alone. Some have adopted sons. They are Black men who dream and who act and who own their feelings, questioning. It is heartening to know our sons do not step out alone.

When Jonathan makes me angriest, I always say he is bringing out the testosterone in me. What I mean is that he is representing some piece of myself as a woman that I am reluctant to acknowledge or explore. For instance, what does "acting like a man" mean? For me, what I reject? For Jonathan, what he is trying to redefine?

Raising Black children—female and male—in the mouth of a racist, sexist, suicidal dragon is perilous and chancy. If they cannot love and resist at the same time, they will probably not survive. And in order to survive they must let go. This is what mothers teach—love, survival—that is, self-definition and letting go. For each of these, the ability to feel strongly and to recognize those feelings is central: how to feel love, how to neither discount fear nor be overwhelmed by it, how to enjoy feeling deeply.

I wish to raise a Black man who will not be destroyed by, nor settle for, those corruptions called *power* by the white fathers who mean his destruction as surely as they mean mine. I wish to raise a Black man who will recognize that the legitimate objects of his hostility are not women, but the particulars of a structure that programs him to fear and despise women as well as his own Black self.

For me, this task begins with teaching my son that I do not exist to do his feeling for him.

Men who are afraid to feel must keep women around to do their feeling for them while dismissing us for the same supposedly "inferior" capacity to feel deeply. But in this way also, men deny themselves their own essential humanity, becoming trapped in dependency and fear.

As a Black woman committed to a liveable future, and as a mother loving and raising a boy who will become a man, I must examine all my possibilities of being within such a destructive system.

Jonathan was three and one half when Frances, my lover, and I met; he was seven when we all began to live together permanently. From the start, Frances' and my insistence that there be no secrets in our household about the fact that we were lesbians has been the source of problems and strengths for both children. In the beginning, this insistence grew out of the knowledge, on both parts, that whatever was hidden out of fear could always be used either against the children or ourselves—one imperfect but useful argument for honesty. The knowledge of fear can help make us free.

> for the embattled
> there is no place
> that cannot be
> home
> nor is.[1]

For survival, Black children in America must be raised to be warriors. For survival, they must also be raised to recognize the enemy's many faces. Black children of lesbian couples have an advantage because they learn, very early, that oppression comes in many different forms, none of which have anything to do with their own worth.

To help give me perspective, I remember that for years, in the name-calling at school, boys shouted at Jonathan not—"your mother's a lesbian"—but rather—"your mother's a nigger."

When Jonathan was eight years old and in the third grade, we moved, and he went to a new school where his life was hellish as a new boy on the block. He did not like to play rough games. He did not like to fight. He did not like to stone dogs. And all this marked him early on as an easy target.

When he came in crying one afternoon, I heard from Beth how the corner bullies were making Jonathan wipe their shoes on the way home whenever Beth wasn't there to fight them off. And when I heard that the ringleader was a little boy in Jonathan's class his own size, an interesting and very disturbing thing happened to me.

My fury at my own long-ago impotence, and my present pain at his suffering, made me start to forget all that I knew about violence and fear, and blaming the victim, I started to hiss at the weeping child. "The next time you come in here crying . . . ," and I suddenly caught myself in horror.

This is the way we allow the destruction of our sons to begin—in the name of protection and to ease our own pain. *My* son get beaten up? I was about to demand that he buy that first lesson in the corruption of power, that might makes right. I could hear myself beginning to perpetuate the age-old distortions about what strength and bravery really are.

And no, Jonathan didn't have to fight if he didn't want to, but somehow he did have to feel better about not fighting. An old horror rolled over me of being the fat kid who ran away, terrified of getting her glasses broken.

About that time a very wise woman said to me, "Have you ever told Jonathan that once you used to be afraid, too?"

The idea seemed far-out to me at the time, but the next time he came in crying and sweaty from having run away again, I could see that he felt shamed at having failed me, or some image he and I had created in his head of mother/woman. This image of woman being able to handle it all was bolstered by the fact that he lived in a household with three strong women, his lesbian parents and his forthright older sister. At home, for Jonathan, power was clearly female.

And because our society teaches us to think in an either/or mode—kill or be killed, dominate or be dominated—this meant that he must either surpass or be lacking. I could see the implications of this line of thought. Consider the two western classic myth/models of mother/son relationships: Jocasta/Oedipus, the son who fucks his mother, and Clytemnestra/Orestes, the son who kills his mother.

It all felt connected to me.

I sat down on the hallway steps and took Jonathan on my lap and wiped his tears. "Did I ever tell you about how I used to be afraid when I was your age?"

I will never forget the look on that little boy's face as I told him the tale of my glasses and my after-school fights. It was a look of relief and total disbelief, all rolled into one.

It is as hard for our children to believe that we are not omnipotent as it is for us to know it, as parents. But that knowledge is necessary as the first step in the reassessment of power as something other than might, age, privilege, or the lack of fear. It is an important step for a boy, whose societal destruction begins when he is forced to believe that he can only be strong if he doesn't feel, or if he wins.

I thought about all this one year later when Beth and Jonathan, ten and nine, were asked by an interviewer how they thought they had been affected by being children of a feminist.

Jonathan said that he didn't think there was too much in feminism for boys, although it certainly was good to be able to cry if he felt like it and not to have to play football if he didn't want to. I think of this sometimes now when I see him practicing for his Brown Belt in Tae Kwon Do.

The strongest lesson I can teach my son is the same lesson I teach my daughter: how to be who he wishes to be for himself. And the best way I can do this is to be who I am and hope that he will learn from this not how to be me, which is not possible, but how to be himself. And this means how to move to that voice from within himself, rather than to those raucous, persuasive, or threatening voices from outside, pressuring him to be what the world wants him to be.

And that is hard enough.

Jonathan is learning to find within himself some of the different faces of courage and strength, whatever he chooses to call them. Two years ago, when Jonathan was twelve and in the seventh grade, one of his friends at school who had been to the house persisted in calling Frances "the maid." When Jonathan corrected him, the boy then referred to her as "the cleaning woman." Finally Jonathan said, simply, "Frances is not the cleaning woman, she's my mother's lover." Interestingly enough, it is the teachers at this school who still have not recovered from his openness.

Frances and I were considering attending a Lesbian/Feminist conference this summer, when we were notified that no boys over ten were allowed. This presented logistic as well as philosophical problems for us, and we sent the following letter:

> Sisters:
>
> Ten years as an interracial lesbian couple has taught us both the dangers of an oversimplified approach to the nature and solutions of any oppression, as well as the danger inherent in an incomplete vision.
>
> Our thirteen-year-old son represents as much hope for our future world as does our fifteen-year-old daughter, and we are not willing to abandon him to the killing streets of New York City while we journey west to help form a Lesbian-Feminist vision of the future world in which we can all survive and flourish. I hope we can continue this dialogue in the near future, as I feel it is important to our vision and our survival.

The question of separatism is by no means simple. I am thankful that one of my children is male, since that helps to keep me honest. Every line I write shrieks there are no easy solutions.

I grew up in largely female environments, and I know how crucial that has been to my own development. I feel the want and need often for the society of women, exclusively. I recognize that our own spaces are essential for developing and recharging.

As a Black woman, I find it necessary to withdraw into all-Black groups at times for exactly the same reasons—differences in stages of development and differences in levels of interaction. Frequently, when speaking with men and white women, I am reminded of how difficult and time-consuming it is to have to reinvent the pencil every time you want to send a message.

But this does not mean that my responsibility for my son's education stops at age ten, any more than it does for my daughter's. However, for each of them, that responsibility does grow less and less as they become more woman and man.

Both Beth and Jonathan need to know what they can share and what they cannot, how they are joined and how they are not. And Frances and I, as grown women and lesbians coming more and more into our power, need to relearn the experience that difference does not have to be threatening.

When I envision the future, I think of the world I crave for my daughters and my sons. It is thinking for survival of the species—thinking for life.

Most likely there will always be women who move with women, women who live with men, men who choose men. I work for a time when women with women, women with men, men with men, all share the work of a world that does not barter bread or self for obedience, nor beauty, nor love. And in that world we will raise our children free to choose how best to fulfill themselves. For we are jointly responsible for the care and raising of the young, since *that* they be raised is a function, ultimately, of the species.

Within that tripartite pattern of relating/existence, the raising of the young will be the joint responsibility of all adults who choose to be associated with children. Obviously, the children raised within each of these three relationships will be different, lending a special savor to that eternal inquiry into how best can we live our lives.

Jonathan was three and a half when Frances and I met. He is now fourteen years old. I feel the living perspective that having lesbian parents has brought to Jonathan is a valuable addition to his human sensitivity.

Jonathan has had the advantage of growing up within a nonsexist relationship, one in which this society's pseudo-natural assumptions of ruler/ruled are being challenged. And this is not only because Frances and I are lesbians, for unfortunately there are some lesbians who are still locked into patriarchal patterns of unequal power relationships.

These assumptions of power relationships are being questioned because Frances and I, often painfully and with varying degrees of success, attempt to evaluate and measure over and over again our feelings concerning power, our own and others'. And we explore with care those areas concerning how it is used and expressed between us and between us and the children, openly and otherwise. A good part of our biweekly family meetings are devoted to this exploration.

As parents, Frances and I have given Jonathan our love, our openness, and our dreams to help form his visions. Most importantly, as the son of lesbians, he has had an invaluable model—not only of a relationship—but of relating.

Jonathan is fourteen now. In talking over this paper with him and asking his permission to share some pieces of his life, I asked Jonathan what he felt were the strongest negative and the strongest positive aspects for him in having grown up with lesbian parents.

He said the strongest benefit he felt he had gained was that he knew a lot more about people than most other kids his age that he knew, and that he did not have a lot of the hang-ups that some other boys did about men and women.

And the most negative aspect he felt, Jonathan said, was the ridicule he got from some kids with straight parents.

"You mean, from your peers?" I said.

"Oh no," he answered promptly. "My peers know better. I mean other kids."

NOTE

1. From "School Note" in *The Black Unicorn* (W. W. Norton and Company, New York, 1978), p. 55. Copyright © 1978 by Audre Lorde. Reprinted with the permission of W. W. Norton & Company, Inc.

38

I AM A MAN

RAUL E. YBARRA

Raul E. Ybarra, Ph.D. says about himself: Somehow I managed to receive my bachelors in Plant Science and masters in English Composition from California State University Fresno. I then graduated with my doctorate from the University of Illinois at Chicago, specializing in language, literacy and rhetoric. I am currently an associate professor at the College of Public and Community Service at the University of Massachusetts Boston. This excerpt is from a much larger piece entitled *I Am a Man* in which I chronicle my struggles to get my formal education. I often come to school early on my teaching days at the University of Massachusetts Boston. I go to the Wits End Cafe, buy a cup of black coffee and sit alone trying to prepare mentally for the day's events. This is also the time when I most often think about home, about how I managed to end up 3,000 miles from home. I think about what I've done, what I have accomplished.

Even though it was difficult, I continued working as a janitor at night and went to school during the day. On weekends I worked out in the fields doing anything from planting the crops to irrigating, to harvesting, and anything in between. I was not able to keep any of the money, however. My father took most of it. "For room and board," he'd say. Then he'd give me about forty dollars back. Then he'd tell me to give half of the forty to my brothers. My younger brothers did not have to work; all they needed to do was go to school. In addition, I had to go looking for my younger brothers when they were off at football or basketball games, dances, or whatever.

Whenever my father saw that I was the only one in my room, he asked me where my brothers were. "I don't know," was my usual answer. "Ve a buscarlos. And don't come back until you find them," was his usual command.

I'd get in his little, light blue Chevy Luv and go into town. Most of the time I didn't have any idea where to look for them, so I'd drive around until I got tired or ran low on gas. Then I'd stop at the local 7–11 store for a Diet Pepsi and play video games.

As soon as I stepped inside the store, the sales clerk, who was usually a high school student, would jokingly say "No, they're not here," and laugh.

I'd laugh along with him even though I didn't like it. But I knew that there was nothing I could do. Most of the students knew who I was and what I was doing. So I'd put a burrito in the microwave and eat it while I played games.

"Eating frozen burritos again?" the boy behind the counter joked. "Why don't you tell your mother to make you some? Be a man about it."

I'd just ignore him and continue playing Pac Man or Star Blaster. All the time I was there, I knew I was the butt of many jokes about looking for my brothers and eating food made by a machine. Sometimes I did know where my brothers were, but I still didn't look for them, even though I knew I was going to get in trouble for not finding them.

"¡Estúpido!" my father called me as soon as he saw me get out of the pickup alone. I knew what would follow before he even said it. "Did you look for them? Why couldn't you find them? You go to school, and you can't do anything right!"

All the time he yelled at me, I didn't say anything back. I just stared at him, at his feet. They were swollen with a couple of toenails missing, and their color was more yellow than the rest of his skin.

"Tu no sabes hacer nada," he continued yelling. "You're useless. Go to bed."

Then I'd slowly walk to my bedroom, angry—angry at my brothers for getting me into trouble, angry at my father for making me do his work, angry at myself for being too scared to say anything back. I'd just lie in my bed listening to my breathing as I slowly calmed down. Later I'd hear my brothers come home giggling and laughing, and I'd pretend to be asleep. The noise, however, usually woke my father up. "Raul, why can't you keep them quiet?" he'd yell. That was enough most of the time to calm my brothers down, so I didn't have to say anything. But one night I answered back, "Because they're not my sons."

The entire house suddenly became quiet. My brothers' breathing became very loud as they pretended to be asleep. The floor creaked louder and louder as my father walked toward our bedroom. When the door opened, it seemed to whine. The color of my father's skin made it difficult for me to see him clearly, but I made out his outline standing in the doorway. He was in his white underwear with a belt in his hand.

"¿Que dijites?" he asked.

"Nada," I answered, also shaking my head.

"Levantate."

I slowly pulled the blanket off of me and stood.

"¡Mentiroso!" he said as he swung his belt across my face. "I don't want lies." Then he left the room.

Tears poured down my face, stinging the mark on my cheek, as I stood clenching my teeth and gripping the bedpost. "Hombres no lloran," I remembered my father saying. I wanted to prove I was a man. I didn't want to cry, so I closed my eyes, but that only made the tears come faster. I got back in bed without turning, pulled the blanket over me and stared at the bunk above, forcing myself not to think of anything.

Back then I wondered why my younger brothers didn't have to work, why I started working at ten years of age and they didn't. I had no idea. Now I do. Albert and I were the older ones. We had to support our younger brothers. But Albert wasn't there; I was. I was quiet, didn't complain, kept my grades up. My brothers did none of these. I wanted to leave, to do what Albert and my sisters did, but I didn't. And I knew the reason. My father was a big man to me still. I was scared.

A month later, I graduated from high school and, according to my father, it was time to go and work like a man. I started the summer like the summers before: weeds in June, sweet potatoes in July, and grapes in August. In late August, I wanted to start college, but my father took me with him to knock almonds. He began by banging the trees with a rubber mallet, and I followed with a twenty-foot bamboo pole in my hands, knocking the almonds that clung to the tree. We worked fifteen hours a day that week. We started at eight to give the sun time to dissipate the moisture and worked until eleven at night, using spotlights after dark. At the end of the day, we went home tired, sweaty, and covered with dust. I just wanted to clean myself up and go to bed.

On Saturday, after we had gotten off work, I sat down in a chair, thankful that the next day was Sunday. I didn't have to get up. I started taking off my shoes when my father whistled. I thought about pretending I didn't hear, but I realized that would just get him angry. I got up slowly and dragged myself over to him.

"Tráigame una cerveza," he said.

I was tired, tired of working long hours, tired of following his orders. I wanted to say, "No. Go get it yourself," but I went to the kitchen, grabbed a beer, and started taking it to him.

I was almost to him when he yelled, "¡Andale pronto!"

All I could think about was how my father treated me. I realized I wasn't a man to him. He never wanted me to be a man, only a slave like my mother. I was there to bring him his beer, bring him his shoes, work for him. Now I saw why my brother and sisters had left. They too didn't like the way they were treated, and they too were scared of him. But they left anyway. I realized now why Anna let herself get pregnant, why Margaret went to live with a man, why Albert just left without saying anything to anybody, why he never bothered to tell anybody where he went. Fear. I knew why I was still there, still being his slave. . . . I didn't say anything; I didn't go anywhere; I followed orders. Gripping the beer can tightly, I gave it to him. He didn't even look at me. Instead, he reached down and patted Tico.

I was angry, angry at the dog. He was better treated, petted when he did something right. I never got that attention.

I don't remember everything that happened next. I do remember white foam splashing from the can that hit the floor. I remember Jose coming between us pushing me away as I went for my father.

"Pinche Perro. Hijo de perra," my father kept yelling at me over and over.

Jose and Richard held me back, while I yelled, "Fuck you! Fuck you!" at the same time struggling to break loose. "I ain't your fucking slave no more." Then I saw my mother crying, holding onto my father's arm, trying to calm him down.

My brothers were holding me back, telling me, "Calm down, man. Calm down. Man, what's you trying to do?"

"Let go," I yelled, trying to free myself from their grip. But they just held tighter, too afraid to let go for fear I'd attack my father. My mother walked over, stopped in front of me, and slapped my face.

I looked at her. I saw the dog jumping wildly, barking. I looked at my father. He was the same height as I was, his skin a dull brown, his hair now more grey than black. He didn't look proud or menacing with his belly sticking out and his shoulders slouched. I realized then that this was my father, the man I had patterned myself after, the man I had wanted to be.

After they saw I was calm enough, my brothers let me go. I turned to leave, and one of them gave me a helping push. I quickly shoved the arm away and glared at them.

I heard my mother say "ya no Raul." I walked out the door and down the street, kicking and hitting anything in my way. I ended up at a house of a friend, Don Mier, one of the few instructors who had helped me through high school.

By the time I got there, my right hand was swollen to where I couldn't close it, but I was calm enough to start worrying about where I was going to stay. Don wasn't at home, so I sat on his patio table to think about what I was going to do next. When I woke, it was already daylight, and Don still wasn't home, so I broke into his house, washed up, ate, and was gone before he came. The next night I did the same thing, slept on the patio table, but he saw me in the morning. He never asked any questions. He just told me I could stay there as long as I wanted, but I would have to pay rent when I could afford it.

"I only need a couple of days," I remember telling him, "to figure out what I'm going to do."

39

WHAT IS MARRIAGE FOR?

E. J. GRAFF

E. J. Graff is contributing editor to *The American Prospect* and *Out* magazines, and a visiting scholar at the Brandeis Women's Studies Research Center. Her work has appeared in such publications as *The Boston Globe, The New York Times Magazine, Ms., The Nation, The Village Voice, The Women's Review of Books,* and more than a dozen anthologies. This address is based on her book entitled *What Is Marriage For: The Strange Social History of Our Most Intimate Institution* (Beacon Press, 1999).

Back in the 1970s, when I first fell in love, I knew I would never get married. As did most of my friends during the 1980s, I expected we would live together without the intrusion of law. And besides, who ever imagined two women marrying?

But today my marriage—or rather, the possibility of its legal recognition—is being debated around the world. Three countries—the Netherlands, Belgium, and Canada—now offer same-sex couples full civil marriage rights. The Massachusetts Supreme Judicial Court has said that full marriage rights must be made available to our state's same-sex couples beginning May 17, 2004. Other countries—including all six Scandinavian countries, Germany, and South Africa—offer lesbian and gay couples just about everything about marriage except the word. Many more countries, provinces, and states give us roughly half of full marriage's legal obligations, recognitions, rights, and responsibilities: Australia, New Zealand, Hungary, Israel, Portugal, France, eleven out of seventeen provinces in Spain, and two provinces in Argentina. And more countries and states are on their way in the next two or three years. Taiwan has said it will pass a same-sex marriage law. South Africa, Sweden, Spain, and New Jersey are all strong contenders for full marriage rights. Switzerland, England, and Scotland will soon add "all-but-marriage" systems that offer just about everything but the word. California is expanding its domestic partnership registry to be essentially the equal of Vermont's civil unions, and I expect more Argentinian and Brazilian states and provinces to follow suit.

My job here is to give some historical background to all this discussion. How is it that for the first time in western history, the world is debating

E. J. Graff, "What Is Marriage For?" from *New England Law Review* 38 (2004). Copyright © 2004 by E. J. Graff. Reprinted with the permission of the author.

whether to recognize a life commitment between two women or two men? And, second, why do same-sex couples—or different-sex couples, for that matter—need or want marriage?

To answer the first question, I want to examine the idea that marriage is some solid, immovable pillar of society; that what we see in 1950s sitcom reruns is exactly what marriage has always been. False. Here is the first key point of my talk, and of my book: Marriage has always been a social battleground, its rules constantly shifting to fit each culture and class, each era and economy. Let me give you some examples. Did you know that Abraham and Sarah, that founding couple in the Torah or Bible, were half-siblings, sharing a father? That only the upper-class third of Romans had the right to marry legally—everyone else lived together outside the law? That a Jewish man whose wife did not give birth within the first ten years of marriage was, in some parts of the world, required by Jewish law to marry again, with or without divorcing his first wife? That Christianity for its first five hundred to a thousand years ignored marriage, considering it tainted and secular, and did not declare it a sacrament until 1215?

There is a lot more "Ripley's Believe It Or Not" to marriage's history, but for the rest, you will have to read my book.

The point is this: Marriage has not been one revered, immutable, monogamous thing for 6000 years. Rather, marriage has always been hot political territory, constantly redefined to fit every time societies change. Nevertheless, a big historical shift did have to take place for us to stop thinking marriage meant boy plus girl equals baby and to start talking about girl plus girl equals love.

That change really exploded in the mid-nineteenth century. The phrase "traditional marriage," which is thrown around so easily on editorial pages, really should be used only to mean marriage for money. Traditionally, the engagement feast was the moment that the two families finished negotiations and finally signed, witnessed, and notarized the marriage contract (and maybe the two started living together). The marriage ceremony was when property actually changed hands, a ceremony that was often overseen by a notary, rather than a priest. If your family had property, they found another family with whom you exchanged it. And if you worked—if your ancestors, like mine, came from the class of butchers, bakers, and candlestick makers—marriage was your complete plan of labor. The farmer required a farmwife; the fisherman required a fishwife to get his goods to market. The German guilds would not let a man move up from journeyman to master until he had a wife, the business partner who would feed the apprentices, keep the books, and oversee the cleaning of the shop. As one historian wrote, "for many centuries marriage for love was the dubious privilege of those without property"—that bottom quintile who were near starvation, who did not even have two dresses and a cookpot to bring to the marriage as dowry.

Of course the pair cared for each other, unless they irritated each other to death—do you not care for, or hate, your coworkers? But everyone expected you to talk about the important money matters first, and assumed that afterwards, you could work out such details as affection, sex, and maybe even love.

But a funny thing happened to marriage on the way to the twentieth century. Marriage stopped being the way you exchanged those limited resources, land or labor. Today we are expected to make a living by making individual decisions about which talents or inclinations to trust. And—here is a key point—once you can make your own living, you can also make your own bed. Capitalism pushed marriage through the looking glass: Now we expect people to talk about love first, and money last—maybe very last, when they are getting a divorce.

That change led to some ferocious nineteenth and twentieth century battles over marriage's rules, battles that all lead directly to same-sex marriage. For instance, after a very nasty battle, and despite almost seventy-five years of ferocious opposition by the Catholic Church and the mainline Protestant hierarchy, and some ugly federal laws, contraception is now legal—which tells us that our society believes marriage is justified by making intimacy, not just by making babies. And if marriage isn't for making babies, then why can't same-sex couples marry?

After an even nastier battle, divorce is legal for other causes than the traditional Protestant causes of adultery and attempted murder—because society now believes that the heart is what makes and unmakes a marriage. We no longer see marriage as a labor contract but as a love commitment. When you love, you are married . . . when you can no longer love, you are no longer married—a very new idea in history. And if our society believes that a couple marries for love, why can't same-sex couples marry?

After equally nasty battles, our societies consider men and women to be formally equal—a woman can vote and own property, a man can raise children. Sometimes that equality is very theoretical in individual marriages, but it is absolutely true in law. Except for the entrance requirement, we no longer have gender requirements within marriage. And if the sexes are equal—if marriage doesn't automatically turn one partner into lord and master and the other partner into Laura Petrie—why can't same-sex couples marry?

All of these changes were revolutionary in their time. And here is the point: lesbians and gay men are following, not leading, the massive changes that were made between 1850 and 1950 in our public marriage philosophy. Sex for intimacy; marriage for love; gender equality; me and my gal.

Let me make that point a little more strongly. It is no more radical for a girl to fall in love with mathematics or basketball than to fall in love with another girl. If she can commit herself to any career she wants, why can she not commit herself to any spouse she wants? The battle against same-sex marriage is a battle against basic feminism—and even more, a battle against the choices opened to us by our highly mobile capitalism. But today's economy, like today's marriages, cannot live by feudal rules. In our world, we believe that the talents and hopes and inclinations that we find inside ourselves count—whether in work or in love.

Which brings us to another question: Why should same-sex couples want to marry, and why should society care? Not every same-sex couple wants to marry. Some want to remain outside the institution, just as some different-sex couples decide never to visit a justice of the peace. The question is whether people should be free to make their own choices about whether or not to register their bonds publicly, and not have that choice ruled out by the government.

But same-sex couples want and need marriage, when we do, for the same reasons that different-sex couples do. When we talk about this, it is important to remember that marriage is an incredibly overstuffed suitcase of a word, meaning four overlapping but separate things. Today we are not talking about the inner bond, the commitment, freely entered into by two people, which I have. We are not talking about the wedding, the ceremony, which celebrates the bond between two people and their communities, and which I have already had. We are not . . . debating changes to religious marriage, which each religion defines vastly differently. Just imagine locking a Catholic, an Orthodox Jew, and a Southern Baptist in a room and refusing to let them out until they agree on the rules of divorce. Ha! That is a bloody fantasy, which would reprise the history of Western Europe, which gave us the concept of a strict separation between church beliefs and civil law.

Today we are talking about the governmental, legal recognition of the bond made between two people. And for that—for civil marriage—the most important purpose is justice. Civil marriage, legal marriage, is the way society adjudicates an incredible array of disputes over who counts to whom. If I am hit by a car when traveling in Utah, would a Salt Lake City hospital let the woman I consider my spouse oversee my care, or would it force me to go through that alone? If I had been killed on September 11, would the woman I consider my spouse, and who relies on and makes it possible for me to earn my income, be eligible for governmental aid or my social security benefits? When I die, who gets to decide whether to donate my organs? If I win the Massachusetts lottery, who can I will it to? As a later panel will tell you, civil unions or domestic partnership will not cut it; in American law, only the M-word covers it all.

Obviously, some of these are incredibly petty, and some very large. That is the point. The rules of marriage have accumulated over centuries to cover an astonishing array of contingencies. As a result, civil marriage is an unbelievably comprehensive shorthand, a shared legal mailbox that lets the state, employers, courts, pension programs, life insurers, health insurers, car rental companies, frequent flyer programs, jails, hospitals, food stamp programs, banks, cemeteries—and more—decide which relationships to take seriously.

Our medieval ancestors did not need civil marriage. Most of them lived in small villages where everyone knew who was married—with or without a ceremony—and who was not. We need civil marriage. We live in a highly complex world, in which each of us regularly bumps into dozens of institutional strangers. For today's couples to fulfill the vows that make wedding guests weep—to care for each other in sickness and in health, for richer or for poorer, and even after the moment of crisis that is death—their bond must be marked and recognizable for the institutions around them.

And the watermark of marriage really does matter. I know far too many heartbreaking stories that have happened to couples who did not have that state stamp. Let me tell you just two. In October 2000, Bobby Daniel and William Flanigan were visiting Bobby's family back east when Bobby, who had AIDS, got ill and was sent to the Maryland Shock Trauma Center in Baltimore. There, as Bobby spent six hours sliding into a coma before he died, the hospital refused to allow William into his beloved's room—until Bobby's sister showed up and insisted that William could go in. The two men were both 34 years old, were registered as domestic partners in California, and carried with them the power of attorney that said William should oversee Bobby's healthcare. By the time William got into Bobby's room, it was too late. He never regained consciousness; they never got to say goodbye. Bobby's mother put it this way: "My son Bobby not only suffered in his final hours, but he suffered alone."

In Pennsylvania a few years ago, Sherry Barone and Cynthia Friedman had been together 13 years when Friedman got cancer. They signed as many legal documents as they could to ensure Barone would be in charge: wills; powers of attorney; health proxies; written instructions giving rights to the survivor to carry out any wishes. But after Friedman died, the cemetery refused to follow Barone's instructions to inscribe the epitaph Friedman had requested. The widowed Barone had to go to court for a year of legal wrangling before she could honor her dead spouse's wishes. Imagine doing that while you are grieving.

As we have just seen in the Terri Schiavo right-to-die case in Florida, when there is a crisis, a spouse can be overridden by the government. But only a spouse has standing in the debate. Had Terri Schiavo's spouse instead been female, she would have had no legal voice, no standing in court.

Unfortunately, the history of humanity is the history of disagreement. Lesbian and gay couples and our families are neither better nor worse than others: We too squabble over inheritances, epitaphs, hospital decisions, breakups. The purpose of the civil institution of marriage, in Western law, is to apply a just consensus to private disputes. Given that all human beings occasionally need such Solomonic intervention, same-sex couples belong.

And to close again with our main point: Marriage has been a kind of Jerusalem, an archaeological site on which the present is constantly building over the past, so that history's many layers twist and tilt into today's walls and floors. Many people believe theirs is the one true claim to this holy ground. But marriage has always been a battleground, owned and defined first by one group and then another. While marriage may retain its ancient name, very little else in this city has remained the same—not its boundaries, boulevards, or daily habits—except the fact that it is inhabited by human beings like me.

40

FREE TO MARRY, AT LAST—MAY 17, 2004

PATRICIA A. GOZEMBA • KAREN KAHN

Patricia A. Gozemba—professor, feminist, environmental activist—is the author of *Pockets of Hope: How Teachers and Students Change the World* (Eileen de los Reyes, coauthor).

Karen Kahn, former editor of *Sojourner: The Women's Forum* is editor of *Frontline Feminism 1975–1995: Essays from Sojourner's First 20 Years* (with Robin Morgan).

Susan Shepherd and Marcia Hams, a couple for twenty-seven years, proved to the world that wanting to have the first legal same-sex marriage license in the country meant that you'd do the extraordinary. Cambridge, a city well known for its progressive politics, would be the first municipality to open for business, at 12:01 a.m. on Monday, May 17. Susan secured the first place in line at Cambridge City Hall, and on Saturday, May 15, the longtime Cambridge residents tucked into sleeping bags under their big tarp close to the front door. The couple, along with their twenty-four-year-old son, Peter, is wild about sports, and so this made sense to Marcia: "If people can do this for Red Sox tickets, we certainly can do this for our lives."

On Sunday, more couples arrived to get in line. A family festival took shape on the sloping lawn of City Hall. Dogs and kids cavorted. Frisbees flew. Handstands and somersaults wowed the gathering crowds. Kids and adults played catch. Couples held hands and shared their wedding plans. Every once in a while people would pinch themselves, wondering if the bliss

Patricia A. Gozemba and Karen Kahn, "Free to Marry, at Last—May 17, 2004" from *Courting Equality: A Documentary History of America's First Legal Same-Sex Marriages* (Beacon Press, 2007). www.courtingequality.com. Reprinted with the permission of the authors.

would last, if they'd really get marriage licenses, if there would really be a wedding for them.

At 10:30 p.m. on Sunday night, when Mayor Michael Sullivan invited couples into City Hall for music, speeches, and a champagne and cake reception, the crowd of supporters outside had swelled; by midnight, the media estimated the crowd had reached ten thousand. TV crews lit up the scene. The excitement built. Kids waved glow sticks. Everyone sensed history in the making. Inside, the Boston Women's Rainbow Chorus belted out "Going to the Chapel" and the Cambridge Chorus wowed the couples with the Beatles' hit "Can't Buy Me Love." When Mayor Sullivan said, "It is a day to celebrate the immense commitment that couples make to each other. . . . It is a day to recognize the commitment . . . of oneself to something greater than oneself," the couples cheered him on appreciatively.

The countdown to the first second of May 17 began inside and outside the building, and the city block rocked with cheers at 12:01 a.m. Within the hour, the first couples emerged, waving their completed white application cards to the wild applause of thousands. Reporters and TV crews pressed in. Well-wishers handed the couples roses, threw confetti and rice, and kept up spirited rounds of "Going to the Chapel," "God Bless America," and "America the Beautiful."

Shepherd, clutching the first fully legal U.S. marriage license application for a gay couple, told a reporter, "This is like winning the World Series and the Stanley Cup on the same day. I'm trying not to lose it. We just really feel awesome. It's awesome." Her partner, Hams, thinking of their son, Peter, an NCAA hockey star, looked into a TV camera and said, "There's a kid somewhere that's watching this. It's going to change his whole life."

While Shepherd and Hams had planned to be at Cambridge City Hall, Ralph Hodgdon and Paul McMahon, who had been together for almost forty-nine years, did not have marriage at the top of their agenda. That all changed, though, on Sunday, May 16, just after 11 p.m. As they watched the eleven-o'clock news they saw the huge crowds and exuberant party building at Cambridge City Hall. That was it. They rushed out and took the subway to the festivities, just to be supportive. Once at City Hall, they got swept up in the spirit. McMahon recalls, "We got there and the excitement was so wonderful, it was so positive and people were so supportive, the next thing you know we're in line."

When they emerged at five-thirty in the morning with their completed application, a crew from *Good Morning America* pounced on them. McMahon and Hodgdon became two of the new faces of commitment and love—and, soon, marriage. On May 29, 2004, looking very handsome in their tuxedoes, they celebrated their forty-ninth anniversary by getting married by a justice of the peace in the Boston Public Garden.

By the close of business on May 17, Cambridge topped the state in marriage applications, taking in 268, and then issuing licenses to couples who obtained court waivers on the usual three-day waiting period. Few failed to notice the incredible generosity of city workers, ranging from the superintendent of schools to the chief public health officer to the city clerk's staff, who volunteered to stay up all night ushering in this historic era of marriage equality.

Cambridge was also the site of the first marriage when, shortly after 9 a.m., city clerk Margaret Drury married a couple that had been together for eighteen years. Tanya McCloskey and Marcia Kadish promised each other "my friendship, my support, my love." Media from around the world captured the moment. The two women, who up until then had led largely private lives, found themselves coming out to an international audience as a married couple. McCloskey, lost for words, choked out, "I'm so happy right now. This is a dream come true. To stand in front of all these people makes us nervous but proud." Kadish agreed: "I'm glowing from the inside. Happy is an understatement."

PART VII
Education

There is substantial agreement in the United States that equal opportunity is something worth providing to our citizens and that the education system is the central institution that should prepare people for equal opportunity.[1] Many changes in the U.S. education system during the past several decades have been implemented with the goal of eliminating the education gap between white students and students of color, between poor children and wealthier ones, and between boys and girls and men and women. Sociologist Roslyn Mickelson and political scientist Stephen Smith have taken a close look at the effects of some of these changes. Programs designed to increase the education level of poor children have helped to equalize levels of education. For example, compensatory education (such as Head Start), and various other initiatives, have helped to create a situation where Black and white women and men, on average, achieve similar levels of education (about 13 years), in spite of the fact that a majority of children in the United States still attend schools segregated by race, ethnicity, and class. A look at income, however, reveals continuing disparity, with whites earning more than Blacks and men earning more than women.[2]

Mickelson and Smith consider three issues related to inequality: equality, equality of educational opportunity, and equality of educational outcomes. They conclude that the United States has no interest in equality and has failed to establish equality of educational outcomes. Thus, as a country we support equal educational opportunity but have not designed an economy that would guarantee a living wage for everyone who achieves a certain level of education.

Research demonstrates that race, class, and gender continue to affect students' experiences in spite of efforts to the contrary. Jonathan Kozol, for example, described in 1991 how race and poverty intersected in brutally impoverished schools in several U.S. cities, severely limiting learning. Looking at the situation of children in schools years later, he observed little progress and a disheartening level of resegregation.[3] Jorge Noriega looks at the history of American Indian education in the United States and concludes that it has been, and continues to be (with minor exceptions), a cultural disaster, designed primarily for indoctrination to the white majority culture and limiting career options to vocational ones.[4] In a recent assessment of the implementation of the mandates of the No Child Left Behind Act (NCLB) in Texas, the authors, all involved in education reform in Texas and supportive of the goals of NCLB, underscore the issues that go beyond what happens in schools: "Educators, while not abdicating their responsibility to educate each child to high standards regardless of their background, must help policy makers and the public understand that, when American schoolchildren have adequate housing and health care; are provided appropriate preschool, after-school, and summer programs; and have parents who earn a living wage, schools will work better, students will flourish as learners and as leaders, and the promise of comprehensive accountability will be fulfilled."[5] In an experiment to both encourage success in school and to offer cash incentives to poor families, New York City families and children will receive cash for attending parent-teacher conferences, for scoring high on standardized tests, and for high attendance rates.[6]

Reports on gender and education reveal troublesome results for students of both genders. A report entitled "How Schools Shortchange Girls," commissioned by the American Association of University Women Educational Foundation, documents how gender, race, and class all affect educational achievement. Some of the data suggest that class is the most important of these three variables.[7] Bernice Sandler, director of the Project on the Status and Education of Women at the Association of American Colleges and Universities, discovered that men in college were given both overt and subtle support, whereas women were undermined in both overt and subtle ways. Studying interaction in classrooms, Sandler found frequent cases of disparaging remarks about women, such as sexist jokes made by male professors and also found subtle differences in the treatment of male and female students, such as men being called on more frequently than women, by faculty of both genders.[8]

Educators David and Myra Sadker, concluding overall that girls experience discrimination in schools, nevertheless observed that although boys receive more attention than girls at both the elementary and secondary levels, that attention does not necessarily lead to success. They reported that boys are more likely to receive lower grades, to suffer from learning disabilities, to be assigned to special education classes, to be suspended, and to drop out than are girls.[9] Similar findings have been reported by other researchers working on the situations of boys.[10] Some of these writers and educators are exploring ways to allow boys to express their traditionally high energy without pathologizing it. Some recommend all-boy environments to support and nurture boys, a suggestion that troubles others who have fought for coeducation at all levels. Recent federal guidelines on single-sex education allow the development of single-sex schools as long as comparable course work and facilities are available for both sexes.[11] Educators David Sadker and Karen Zittleman express caution concerning this option, noting failures of single-sex schools and threats to Title IX, the federal law preventing sex discrimination in education. Calling attention to such things as bullying and sexual harassment, they point out that gender is a major missing element in NCLB.[12] Providing a supportive school environment for transgendered children in single-sex environments could be even more challenging than it already is in mixed-sex environments—to which school would a transgendered child wish to go or be allowed to go? What these data on boys obscure, however, is the reality that boys generally achieve higher grades on standardized tests, especially in math, and are more economically successful into adulthood, in spite of the difficult time that some of them have in school. Clearly, some boys need more help than others. In short, all children need more effective educations in contexts that promote equality related to gender, class, race, ability, and culture (see Myra Sadker and David Sadker and Michael Kimmel, this part).

Although women outnumber men as college students, this gender discrepancy is most pronounced at lower-status institutions. Men tend to major in more lucrative fields such as engineering, computer science, business, and physics, and the five occupations most likely to be held by women include secretary, receptionist, bookkeeper, nurse, and hairdresser/cosmetologist.[13] The choice of which fields women and men pursue is obviously a crucial aspect of education as it relates to occupational outcomes. Thus, some scholars have attempted to analyze the effects of race and gender on educational outcomes while others have looked at the experience of women and people of color in various careers.[14] Programs designed to encourage the study of math and science by boys and girls of color and white girls have also emerged with the goal of addressing the under-representation of white women and women and men of color in mathematical and scientific careers.[15] Programs designed to support white female graduate students and graduate students of color in math and science have also emerged in recent years, along with advice to college administrators on how to support and keep faculty of color.[16]

A recent issue of *The Journal of Men's Studies* focuses on African American men in academia. Among the range of issues addressed, one article focuses on the importance of preparing African American boys for academic track careers via a project aimed at younger men entitled Gentlemen on the Move.[17] Another article looks at African American men studying engineering. The authors found that an essential aspect of persistence in the engineering program was a commitment to prove critics wrong by working extra hard.[18] In short, in spite of illusions to the contrary, there is much work to do in overcoming the effects of racism when people of color enter fields of study and work that have been predominantly white.

Educators have documented ways in which subtle and overt stereotypes are reinforced in the curriculum, and many have worked toward eliminating them. Substantial attention has been given to gendered images in children's books, and now attention is focusing on the intersections of gender with other factors such as race and class.[19] Other scholars are examining the success or failure of the testing system for various groups. For example, in a finding that helps explain why bright Black students do not perform as well as expected on tests, Claude Steele, a social psychologist at Stanford University, identified what he calls "stereotype vulnerability"—the tendency for group members to perform badly when they think their performance is a reflection of their group. Concerned that even highly qualified Black students tended to earn increasingly lower grades as they progressed through college, Steele set out to identify the cause. He found that when Black

Stanford University undergraduates were given a difficult verbal test, those who were told that it was a "genuine test of your verbal abilities and limitations" received lower scores than the white students also being tested. But when another group of Black students taking the same test was told that it was designed to study "psychological factors involved in solving verbal problems," they performed as well as the white students. Steele repeated this experiment in various places and formats, documenting that stereotype vulnerability also affected women when they were told that a given math test showed "gender differences." It even affected white men who were told that Asians tended to outperform whites on a difficult math test.[20]

The context of test taking is just one aspect of higher education's hidden curriculum—the myriad messages, subtle and obvious, that affect students' attitudes and performance, apart from course content. Classroom interaction has been the subject of much research, as educators attempt to establish more gender-equal classrooms.[21] Other scholars observe the social environment on campuses. In an ethnographic study of Black and white women on two college campuses, anthropologists Dorothy Holland and Margaret Eisenhart found that peer culture eroded career plans for many women in both groups as romance became more important than their studies.[22] Yet even if without career plans, women generally perform better than men in college, earning higher GPAs and consequently more honors degrees.[23]

Pressure to conform in K–12 classrooms puts pressure on many kinds of young people, from girls who are "too masculine," to Black girls who are "too loud," to boys who are "too feminine." Students who fail to conform to white heterosexist hegemonic expectations, for whatever reasons, are defined as "other" and often pay a high price. Anthropologist Signithia Fordham argues that educators need to accept a range of behavior in students and not expect conformity to narrow standards; after intensive research in an urban school in Washington, DC, she was especially concerned about Black children who were expected to conform to white expectations ("acting white"), rather than be supported to develop their own ways of expressing themselves within the context of a challenging academic program.[24]

Pressure for gender conformity can also be very difficult. In a study of schooling in England, educator Máirtín Mac an Ghaill recounts an incident in a schoolyard that shook the gender rules: a male student, happy over passing his exams, brought flowers to Mac an Ghaill. Mac an Ghaill was scolded for the incident.[25] In two illustrative cases in the United States, boys who were acting "too effeminate" were the subject of ridicule in schools. The Center for Constitutional Rights helped a grandmother intervene in a situation in which her grandson had been referred to as a girl and called "girlish" by his teacher and his peers. The intervention succeeded in convincing the teacher to apologize and in convincing the school to institute seminars on sexual harassment and gender-based name calling for fifth and sixth graders.[26] According to the U.S. Supreme Court, schools receiving federal funds are responsible for student-on-student harassment if they know about it and do not intervene and if it is severe enough to interfere with the victim's education.[27] As a result, schools are becoming more proactive in preventing harassment, including harassment of gay and lesbian young people.[28] In the second case, a Massachusetts child who is physically male and transgendered challenged a school's decision to disallow female dress. Many months later, the city finally agreed to allow her to come to school in female attire.[29] Transgendered teachers are an issue as well, as schools and parents grapple with whether or not to support the hiring or continued employment of transgendered teachers, and as states debate whether transgender rights deserve protection.[30] As of 2006, four states plus the District of Columbia had laws protecting the rights of transgender students; educators, psychologists, and others are beginning to see gender variance as naturally occurring rather than as a disorder.[31]

Frequently, prejudice against LGBTQ teenagers is so strong that they drop out of school. The Hetrick-Martin Institute in New York City (http://www.hmi.org/) was founded to serve LGBTQ youth, offering an alternative high school and many other services and activities for those who cannot tolerate mainstream schooling. Many of the young people they serve are among the estimated 100,000–200,000 LGBTQ youth who run away or are kicked out of their homes each year.[32] In Massachusetts, state law has mandated support for gay and lesbian students in high schools to create a climate that will be more welcoming, especially given the high suicide rate of gay teens. K–12 schools, it seems, have become a primary battleground for gay, lesbian, and transgender rights.[33] In Lexington, Massachusetts, two sets of heterosexual parents whose children attend a public school filed a lawsuit objecting to the assignment of a book on diverse families that included some families with same-sex parents, as well as a book in which a prince married a prince. Apparently, the fact that same-sex marriage is legal in Massachusetts did not adequately justify the presence of same-sex relationships in the curriculum.[34] Battles continue over abstinence-only versus comprehensive sex education, which is also related, at least in part, to LGBTQ issues.[35]

College campuses serve as a battleground for gender equality as well. The September 2000 issue of *Men's Health* ranked colleges based on how male-friendly they were; issues such as the presence of a large women's studies department were cause for a low ranking.[36] A woman who wanted to play football at Duke University was awarded $2 million in damages when she was cut from the team by a coach who had suggested that she participate in beauty pageants instead of football.[37] Sexual harassment and date rape are constant issues on college campuses.[38] (See Jackson Katz, this Part.)

Affirmative action, which requires employers and educational institutions to "actively seek inclusion of qualified minorities among their pool of applicants,"[39] is another issue affecting higher education. Ironically, once the state of Texas eliminated affirmative action in college admissions, the state legislature passed a law mandating that all students in the top 10 percent of their high school class be granted automatic admission to institutions of higher education in Texas. Because of the high level of school segregation in Texas, the effect of the legislation has been to increase the level of diversity in undergraduate colleges in Texas. In states with more integrated schools, this sort of alternative to affirmative action would not succeed in diversifying the student body. Some colleges are changing admissions procedures to include examining a range of factors such as SAT scores, class rank, race/ethnicity, and experience such as overcoming adversity. The goal of such policies is to have a diverse student body for educational purposes (supporting a university's mission), rather than to right past discrimination.[40] An ironic result of the presence of more women in higher education is a move by some campuses to give preference to male applicants to achieve gender balance when preferences for legacies and athletes still do not produce enough men.[41]

The Texas alternative did not affect graduate schools. With the elimination of affirmative action, applications to the University of Texas School of Law immediately dropped among Blacks, Mexican Americans, Asian Americans, and whites, with the largest decline occurring among Blacks—66 percent. Admissions of Black and Latino students to law school in both Texas and California—the two states that had eliminated affirmative action at the time of the study—dropped considerably at that time. This provoked attorney Robert J. Grey, chair of the House of Delegates of the American Bar Association, to express concern over the decline in minority lawyers that will result if fewer people of color continue to apply to law school.[42] In the midst of fluctuations in applications by students of color, the legality of taking race into account as a factor in admission was in the courts, related to two lawsuits against the University of Michigan. The U.S. Supreme Court ultimately decided that the use of race as *a factor* in admissions was acceptable in the University of Michigan Law School but that the University of Michigan undergraduate system of awarding points for race was not constitutional.[43] Other colleges are now revising their affirmative action procedures to align their admissions policies with the Court's decisions.

The readings in this part of the book address issues in both K–12 and higher education, including interaction (and lack thereof) of boys and girls in elementary schools (Myra and David Sadker), the debate about the situation of boys in schools (Michael Kimmel), conflicts and discrimination in research universities (Ben Barres and bell hooks), and an antiviolence program implemented on many campuses using student athletes as leaders (Jackson Katz). The messages in this section echo many that have been heard throughout this book so far: people need validation of their varied experiences, knowledge is incomplete without a broad range of voices and perspectives, and discrimination greatly interferes with people's abilities to move freely in the world and achieve their goals. Barres's experience as both female and male sheds interesting light on gender discrimination in science.

As you read these essays, you might want to consider how your own school experience reflects, or doesn't, that described by the authors. For example, if you have been in gender-mixed classrooms, do women and men/girls and boys speak in proportion to their numbers in the class? Are teachers less likely to call on girls? Have boys seemed more at risk for not doing well or dropping out? Who among your friends had higher SAT scores? In college, have you observed any of the dynamics reported by hooks or Barres? Do you know anyone who has changed gender? If so, what has their experience been like? What do you know about violence and sexual harassment on campus? Do you think the Mentors in Violence Program would be helpful on your campus? Would you participate if it were offered? Would you support relaxed college admission standards for men to achieve gender balance on campuses? Would you hold the same opinion related to, say, racial or social class balance?

NOTES

1. Roslyn Mickelson and Stephen Smith, "Education and the Struggle against Race, Class, and Gender Inequality," in Berch Berberoglu, ed., *Critical Perspectives in Sociology: A Reader* (Dubuque, IA: Kendall-Hunt, 1991).

2. Mickelson and Smith, "Education and the Struggle."

3. Jonathan Kozol, *Savage Inequalities* (New York: Crown, 1991); *The Shame of the Nation* (New York: Crown, 2005).

4. Jorge Noriega, "American Indian Education in the United States: Indoctrination for Subordination to Colonialism," in M. Annette Jaimes, ed., *The State of Native America* (Boston: South End Press, 1992), pp. 371–402.

5. Sarah W. Nelson, Marla W. McGhee, Lionel R. Meno, and Charles L. Slater, "Fulfilling the Promise of Educational Accountability," *Phi Delta Kappan*, 88, no. 9 (May 2007): 702–709.

6. Jennifer Medina, "Schools Plan to Pay Cash for Marks," *The New York Times*, 19 June 2007, p. B1.

7. American Association of University Women Educational Foundation, *How Schools Shortchange Girls* (New York: Marlowe & Co., 1995).

8. Bernice Resnick Sandler, "The Classroom Climate: Still a Chilly One for Women," in Carol Lasser, ed., *Educating Men and Women Together: Coeducation in a Changing World* (Urbana: University of Illinois Press in conjunction with Oberlin College, 1987). Reprinted in Karin Bergstrom Costello, *Gendered Voices: Readings from the American Experience* (New York: Harcourt Brace, 1996), pp. 359–68. Sandler does not discuss the intersections of gender with other factors.

9. Myra Sadker and David Sadker, *Failing at Fairness: How Our Schools Cheat Girls* (New York: Simon & Schuster, 1994).

10. Carey Goldberg, "After Girls Get Attention, Focus Shifts to Boys' Woes," *The New York Times*, 22 April 1998, p. A1; Christina Hoff Sommers, *The War against Boys: How Misguided Feminism Is Harming Our Young Men* (New York: Simon & Schuster, 2000).

11. Greg Toppo, "US to Boost Single-Sex Schools: Education Dept. Offers Rules to Encourage Growth," *The Boston Globe*, 9 May 2002, p. A4.

12. David Sadker and Karen Zittleman, "Gender Bias Lives, for Both Sexes," *Principal*, 84 (March/April 2005), pp. 18–22.

13. David Sadker, "Gender Games," *The Washington Post*, 31 July 2000, p. A19.

14. Lisa M. Frehill, "Subtle Sexism in Engineering," in Nijole V. Benokraitis, ed., *Subtle Sexism: Current Practices and Prospects for Change* (Thousand Oaks, CA: Sage, 1997), pp. 117–35.

15. David Johnson, ed., *Minorities and Girls in School: Effects on Achievement and Performance* (Thousand Oaks, CA: Sage, 1997).

16. For a description of one such program, contact the New England Board of Higher Education, 45 Temple Place, Boston, MA 02111. JoAnn Moody, *Faculty Diversity: Problems and Solutions* (New York: RoutledgeFalmer, 2004).

17. Daryl Bailey, "Preparing African-American Males for Postsecondary Options." *The Journal of Men's Studies* 12, no. 1 (Fall 2003): 15–24.

18. James L. Moore III, Octavia Madison-Colmore, and Dionne M. Smith, "The Prove-Them-Wrong Syndrome: Voices from Unheard African-American Males in Engineering Disciplines," *The Journal of Men's Studies* 12, no. 1 (Fall 2003): pp. 61–73.

19. For a recent look at gendered images in children's books and references to prior work in this area, see Roger Clark, Rachel Lennon, and Leanna Morris, "Of Caldecotts and Kings: Gendered Images in Recent American Children's Books by Black and Non-Black Illustrators," *Gender & Society* 7, no. 2 (June 1993): 227–45.

20. See Claude Steele and Joshua Aronson, "Stereotype Threat and the Intellectual Test Performance of African Americans," *Journal of Personality and Social Psychology* 69, no. 5 (Fall 1995): pp. 797–811. For a discussion of bias, especially gender bias, in standardized college entrance tests (PSAT and SAT), see Myra Sadker and David Sadker, "Test Drive," in Sadker and Sadker, eds., *Failing at Fairness*.

21. Magda Lewis, "Interrupting Patriarchy: Politics, Resistance, and Transformation in the Feminist Classroom," *Harvard Educational Review* 60, no. 4 (November 1990): 467–88; Sara N. Davis, Mary Crawford, and Jadwiga Sebrechts, eds., *Coming into Her Own: Educational Success in Girls and Women* (San Francisco: Jossey-Bass, 1999); Berenice Malka Fisher, *No Angel in the Classroom* (Lanham, MD: Rowman & Littlefield, 2001); Sharon Bernstein, "Feminist Intentions: Race, Gender and Power in a High School Classroom," *NWSA Journal* 7, no. 2 (1995): 18–34.

22. Dorothy C. Holland and Margaret A. Eisenhart, *Educated in Romance: Women, Achievement, and College Culture* (Chicago: University of Chicago Press, 1990).

23. Tamar Lewin, "At Colleges, Women Are Leaving Men in the Dust," *The New York Times Magazine*, 9 July 2006, pp. A1ff.

24. Signithia Fordham, *Blacked Out: Dilemmas of Race, Identity and Success at Capital High* (Chicago: University of Chicago Press, 1996).

25. For an extended discussion of this, see Máirtín Mac an Ghaill, *The Making of Men: Masculinities, Sexualities and Schooling* (Buckingham, United Kingdom: Open University Press, 1994).

26. Margaret Carey, "In re Minor Child," *Center for Constitutional Rights Docket* (New York: Center for Constitutional Rights, 1998), p. 76.

27. Mary Leonard, "Schools Can Be Liable if Pupils Harass," *The Boston Globe*, 25 May 1999, p. A1.

28. Anna Gorman, "Educators Taking Steps to Protect Homosexual Pupils," *The Boston Globe*, 15 September 2000, p. A29.

29. Rick Klein, "Brockton Boy Still at Home: Talks Continue on Class Return," *The Boston Globe*, 18 October 2000, p. B2; "Student Allowed to Wear Female Clothing," *The Boston Globe*, 17 May 2001, p. B2.

30. Stephanie Simon, "Transgender Protection Debated in Minn.," *The Boston Globe*, 10 April 1999, p. A9.

31. Patricia Leigh Brown, "Supporting Boys and Girls When the Line Isn't Clear," *The New York Times*, 2 December 2006, p. A1ff.

32. David Crary, AP, "More Help Urged for Homeless Gay Youth," January 30, 2007; Ian Urbina, "Gay Youths Find Place to Call Home in Specialty Shelters," *The New York Times*, 17 May 2007, p. 18.

33. Eric Rofes, "Gay Issues, Schools, and the Right-Wing Backlash," *Resist* 8, no. 5 (June 1999): 1–3.

34. American Civil Liberties Union of Massachusetts, "Court Dismisses Suit against Books on Diverse Families," *The Docket* 37, no. 1 (April 2007): 8. At the time of this writing, the plaintiffs had lost but were considering an appeal.

35. Kristin Luker, *When Sex Goes to School: Warring Views on Sex—and Sex Education—Since the Sixties* (New York: W.W. Norton).

36. Lawrence Roy Stains, "The Best and Worst Colleges for Men," *Men's Health*, April 2000, p. 120.

37. "Title IX Victory," *Outlook* 95, no. 1 (2001): 9.

38. Ruth Sidel, *Battling Bias: The Struggle for Identity and Community on College Campuses* (New York: Viking Penguin, 1994).

39. A. E. Sadler, ed., *Affirmative Action* (San Diego, CA: Greenhaven Press, 1996), p. 6.

40. Arthur L. Coleman, "'Affirmative Action' through a Different Looking Glass," *Diversity Digest* 5, no. 3 (Spring 2001): 1ff.

41. Tamar Lewin, "At College."

42. Evelyn Apgar, "Impact of California, Texas Decisions," *The New Jersey Lawyer*, 7 September 1998, p. 1.

43. CNN, "Narrow Use of Affirmative Action Preserved in College Admissions," 25 December 2003. www.cnn.com/2003/LAW/06/23/scotus.affirmative.action/.

41

MISSING IN INTERACTION

MYRA SADKER • DAVID SADKER

David Sadker is a professor at American University (Washington, DC) and, along with his late wife *Myra Pollack Sadker* (1943–1995) gained a national reputation for work in confronting gender bias and sexual harassment. He has directed more than a dozen federal education grants and has authored 5 books and more than 75 articles. His research and writing document sex bias from the classroom to the boardroom. Dr. Myra Pollack Sadker pioneered much of the research documenting gender bias in America's schools.

As the snapshots continue, the underlying gender messages become clear. The classroom consists of two worlds: one of boys in action, the other of girls' inaction. Male students control classroom conversation. They ask and answer more questions. They receive more praise for the intellectual quality of their ideas. They get criticized. They get help when they are confused. They are the heart and center of interaction. Watch how boys dominate the discussion in this upper elementary class about presidents.

The fifth-grade class is almost out of control. "Just a minute," the teacher admonishes. "There are too many of us here to all shout out at once. I want you to raise your hands, and then I'll call on you. If you shout out, I'll pick somebody else."

Order is restored. Then Stephen, enthusiastic to make his point, calls out.

Stephen: I think Lincoln was the best president. He held the country together during the war.
Teacher: A lot of historians would agree with you.
Mike: (seeing that nothing happened to Stephen, calls out): I don't. Lincoln was okay, but my Dad liked Reagan. He always said Reagan was a great president.
David: (calling out): Reagan? Are you kidding?
Teacher: Who do you think our best president was, Dave?
David: FDR. He saved us from the depression.

Max: (calling out): I don't think it's right to pick one best presi-
                 dent. There were a lot of good ones.
Teacher: That's interesting.
Kimberly: (calling out): I don't think the presidents today are as good
                 as the ones we used to have.
Teacher: Okay, Kimberly. But you forgot the rule. You're supposed to
                 raise your hand.

The classroom is the only place in society where so many different, young, and restless individuals are crowded into close quarters for an extended period of time day after day. Teachers sense the undertow of raw energy and restlessness that threatens to engulf the classroom. To preserve order, most teachers use established classroom conventions such as raising your hand if you want to talk.

Intellectually, teachers know they should apply this rule consistently, but when the discussion becomes fast-paced and furious, the rule is often swept aside. When this happens and shouting out begins, it is an open invitation for male dominance. Our research shows that boys call out significantly more often than girls. Sometimes what they say has little or nothing to do with the teacher's questions. Whether male comments are insightful or irrelevant, teachers respond to them. However, when girls call out, there is a fascinating occurrence. Suddenly the teacher remembers the rule about raising your hand before you talk. And then the girl, who is usually not as assertive as the male students, is deftly and swiftly put back in her place.

Not being allowed to call out like her male classmates during the brief conversation about presidents will not psychologically scar Kimberly; however, the system of silencing operates covertly and repeatedly. It occurs several times a day during each school week for twelve years, and even longer if Kimberly goes to college, and, most insidious of all, it happens subliminally. This micro-inequity eventually has a powerful cumulative impact.

On the surface, girls appear to be doing well. They get better grades and receive fewer punishments than boys. Quieter and more conforming, they are the elementary school's ideal students. "If it ain't broke, don't fix it" is the school's operating principle as girls' good behavior frees the teacher to work with the more difficult-to-manage boys. The result is that girls receive less time, less help, and fewer challenges. Reinforced for passivity, their independence and self-esteem suffer. As victims of benign neglect, girls are penalized for doing what they should and lose ground as they go through school. In contrast, boys get reinforced for breaking the rules; they are rewarded for grabbing more than their fair share of the teacher's time and attention.

Even when teachers remember to apply the rules consistently, boys are still the ones who get noticed. When girls raise their hands, it is often at a right angle, arm bent at the elbow, a cautious, tentative, almost insecure gesture. At other times they raise their arms straight and high, but they signal silently. In contrast, when boys raise their hands, they fling them wildly in the air, up and down, up and down, again and again. Sometimes these hand signals are accompanied by strange noises, "Ooh! Ooh! Me! Me! Ooooh!" Occasionally they even stand beside or on top of their seats and wave one or both arms to get attention. "Ooh! Me! Mrs. Smith, call on me." In the social studies class about presidents, we saw boys as a group grabbing attention while girls as a group were left out of the action.

When we videotape classrooms and play back the tapes, most teachers are stunned to see themselves teaching subtle gender lessons along with math and spelling. The teacher in the social studies class about presidents was completely unaware that she gave male students more attention. Only after several viewings of the videotape did she notice how she let boys call out answers but reprimanded girls for similar behavior. Low-achieving boys also get plenty of attention, but more often it's negative. No surprise there. In general, girls receive less attention, but there's another surprise: Unlike the smart boy who flourishes in the classroom, the smart girl is the student who is least likely to be recognized.

When we analyzed the computer printouts for information about gender and race, an intriguing trend emerged. The students most likely to receive teacher attention were white males; the second most likely were . . . males [of color]; the third, white females; and the least likely, . . . females [of color]. In elementary school, receiving attention from the teacher is enormously important for a student's achievement and self-esteem. Later in life, in the working world, the salary received is important, and the salary levels parallel the classroom: white males at the top and . . . females [of color] at the bottom. In her classroom interaction studies, Jacqueline Jordan Irvine found that black girls were active, assertive, and salient in the primary grades, but as they moved up through elementary school, they became the most invisible members of classrooms.

In our research in more than one hundred classrooms, . . . boys were more likely to be praised, corrected, helped, and criticized—all reactions that foster student achievement. Girls received the more superficial "Okay" reaction, one that packs far less educational punch. In her research, Jacqueline Jordan Irvine found that black females were least likely to receive clear academic feedback.

At first teachers are surprised to see videotapes where girls are "Okay'd" and boys gain clear feedback. Then it begins to make sense, "I don't like to tell a girl anything is wrong because I don't want to upset her," many say. This vision of females as fragile is held most often by male teachers." What if she cries? I wouldn't know how to handle it."

The "Okay" response is well meaning, but it kills with kindness. If girls don't know when they are wrong, if they don't learn strategies to get it right, then they never will correct their mistakes. And if they rarely receive negative feedback in school, they will be shocked when they are confronted by it in the workplace.

• • •

Ashley Reiter, National Winner of the 1991 Westinghouse Talent Competition for her sophisticated project on math modeling, remembers winning her first math contest. It happened at the same time that she first wore her contact lenses. Triumphant, Ashley showed up at school the next day without glasses and with a new medal. "Everybody talked about how pretty I looked," Ashley remembers. "Nobody said a word about the math competition."

The one area where girls are recognized more than boys is appearance. Teachers compliment their outfits and hairstyles. We hear it over and over again—not during large academic discussions but in more private moments, in small groups, when a student comes up to the teacher's desk, at recess, in hallways, at lunchtime, when children enter and exit the classroom: "Is that a new dress?" "You look so pretty today." "I love your new haircut. It's so cute." While these comments are most prevalent in the early grades, they continue through professional education: "That's a great outfit." "You look terrific today."

When teachers talk with boys about appearance, the exchanges are brief—quick recognition and then on to something else. Or teachers use appearance incidents to move on to a physical skill or academic topic. In one exchange, a little boy showed the teacher his shiny new belt buckle. Her response: "Cowboys wore buckles like that. They were rough and tough and they rode horses. Did you know that?"

• • •

Boy Bastions—Girl Ghettos

Raphaela Best spent four years as an observer in an elementary school in one of Maryland's most affluent counties. She helped the children with school-work, ate lunch with them, and played games with them in class and at re-cess. As an anthropologist, she also took copious notes. After more than one thousand hours of living with the children, she concluded that elementary school consists of separate and unequal worlds. She watched segregation in action firsthand. Adult women remember it well.

A college student recalled, "When I was in elementary school, boys were able to play basketball and kick ball. They had the side of the playground with the basketball hoops." Another college woman remembers more formal segregation: "I went to a very small grammar school. At recess and gym the boys played football and the girls jumped rope. All except one girl and one boy—they did the opposite. One day they were pulled aside. I'm not exactly sure what they were told, but the next day the schoolyard was divided in two. The boys got the middle and the girls got the edge, and neither sex was allowed on the other's part."

A third grader described it this way: "Usually we separate ourselves, but my teacher begins recess by handing a jump rope to the girls and a ball to the boys." Like the wave of a magic wand, this gesture creates strict gender lines.

"The boys always pick the biggest areas for their games," she says. "We have what's left over, what they don't want."

Every morning at recess in schoolyards across the country, boys fan out over the prime territory to play kick ball, football, or basketball. Sometimes girls join them, but more often it's an all-male ball game. In the typical schoolyard, the boys' area is ten times bigger than the girls'. Boys never ask if it is their right to take over the territory, and it is rarely questioned. Girls huddle along the sidelines, on the fringe, as if in a separate female annex. Recess becomes a spectator sport.

Teachers seldom intervene to divide space and equipment more evenly, and seldom attempt to connect the segregated worlds—not even when they are asked directly by the girls.

"The boys won't let us play," a third grader said, tugging at the arm of the teacher on recess duty. "They have an all-boys club and they won't let any girls play."

"Don't you worry, honey," the teacher said, patting the little girl's hair. "When you get bigger, those boys will pay you all the attention you want. Don't you bother about them now."

As we observed that exchange, we couldn't help but wonder how the teacher would have reacted if the recess group had announced "No Catholics" or if white children had blatantly refused to play with Asians.

Barrie Thorne, a participant observer in elementary schools in California and Michigan whose students are mainly from working-class families, captured the tiny incidents that transform integrated classes into gender-divided worlds: Second-grade girls and boys eat lunch together around a long rectangular table. A popular boy walks by and looks the scene over. "Oooh, too many girls," he says, and takes a place at another table. All the boys immediately pick up their trays and abandon the table with girls, which has now become taboo.

Although sex segregation becomes more pervasive as children get older, contact points remain. School life has its own gender rhythm as girls and boys separate, come together, and separate again. But the points of contact, the together games that girls and boys play, often serve to heighten and solidify the walls of their separate worlds.

"You can't get me!" "Slobber Monster!" With these challenges thrown out, the game begins. It may be called "Girls Chase the Boys" or "Boys Chase the Girls," or "Chase and Kiss." It usually starts out one on one, but then the individual boy and girl enlist same-sex peers. "C'mon, let's get that boy." "Help, a girl's gonna get me!"

Pollution rituals are an important part of these chases. Children treat one another as if they were germ carriers. "You've got cooties" is the cry. (Substitute other terms for different cultures or different parts of the country.) Elaborate systems are developed around the concept of cooties. Transfer occurs when one child touches another. Prepared for such attack, some protect themselves by writing C. V. (cooties vaccination) on their arms.

Sometimes boys give cooties to girls, but far more frequently girls are the polluting gender. Boys fling taunts such as "girl stain" or "girl touch" or "cootie girl." The least-liked girls, the ones who are considered fat or ugly or poor, become "cootie queens," the real untouchables of the class, the most contaminating females of all.

Chasing, polluting, and invasions, where one gender attacks the play area of the other, all function as gender intensifiers, heightening perceived differences between female and male to an extreme degree. The world of children and the world of adults is composed of *different* races, but each gender is socially constructed as so different, so alien that we use the phrase "the *opposite* sex."

It is boys who work hardest at raising the walls of sex segregation and intensifying the difference between genders. They distance themselves, sending the message that girls are not good enough to play with them. Watch which boys sit next to the girls in informally sex-segregated classrooms and lunchrooms; they are the ones most likely to be rejected by male classmates. Sometimes they are even called "girls." A student at The American University remembers his school lunchroom in Brooklyn:

> At lunch our class all sat together at one long table. All the girls sat on one side, and the boys sat on the other. This was our system. Unfortunately, there were two more boys in my class than seats on the boys' side. There was no greater social embarrassment for a boy in the very hierarchical system we had set up in our class than to have to sit on the girls' side at lunch. It happened to me once, before I moved up the class social ladder. Boys climbed the rungs of that ladder by beating on each other during recess. To this day, twenty years later, I remember that lunch. It was horrible.

Other men speak, also with horror, of school situations when they became "one of the girls." The father of a nine-year-old daughter remembered girls in elementary school as "worse than just different. We considered them a subspecies." Many teachers who were victims of sexist schooling themselves understand this system and collaborate with it; they warn noisy boys of a humiliating punishment: "If you don't behave, I'm going to make you sit with the girls."

Most little girls—five, six, seven, or eight—are much too young to truly understand and challenge their assignment as the lower-caste gender. But without challenge over the course of years, this hidden curriculum in second-class citizenship sinks in. Schools and children need help—intervention by adults who can equalize the playing field.

We have found that sex segregation in the lunchroom and schoolyard spills over into the classroom. In our three-year, multi-state study of one hundred classrooms, our raters drew "gender geography" maps of each class they visited. They found that more than half of the classes were segregated by gender. There is more communication across race than across gender in elementary schools.

We have seen how sex segregation occurs when children form self-selected groups. Sometimes the division is even clearer, and so is the impact on instruction.

> The students are seated formally in rows. There are even spaces between the rows, except down the middle of the room where the students have created an aisle large enough for two people standing side by side to walk down. On one side of the aisle, the students are all female; on the other side, all male. Black, white, Hispanic, and Asian students sit all around the room, but no student has broken the gender barrier.
>
> The teacher in the room is conducting a math game, with the right team (boys) against the left team (girls). The problems have been put on the board, and members of each team race to the front of the room to see who can write the answer first. Competition is intense, but eventually the girls fall behind. The teacher keeps score on the board, with two columns headed "Good Girls" and "Brilliant Boys."

The gender segregation was so formal in this class that we asked if the teacher had set it up. "Of course not." She looked offended. "I wouldn't think of doing such a thing. The students do it themselves." It never occurred to the well-meaning teacher to raise the issue or change the seats.

In our research we have found that gender segregation is a major contributor to female invisibility. In sex-segregated classes, teachers are pulled to the more talkative, more disruptive male sections of the classroom or pool. There they stay, teaching boys more actively and directly while the girls fade into the background.

42

"WHAT ABOUT THE BOYS?"
What the Current Debates Tell Us—
and Don't Tell Us—about Boys in School

MICHAEL S. KIMMEL

Michael S. Kimmel is professor of sociology at SUNY at Stony Brook. His many books include, among others: *Manhood in America* (2005, 2nd edition), *The Gendered Society* (2004), and, coedited with Michael A. Messner, *Men's Lives* (2005, 7th edition).

I've placed the question contained in my title—"what about the boys?"—in quotation marks. In that way, I can pose two different questions to frame the discussion of boys in school. First, the question within the quotation marks is the empirical one: What *about* the boys? What's going on with them? The second question, expressed by the question *and* the quotation marks, is cultural and political: Why is the question "what about the boys?" such a pressing question on the cultural agenda? Why is the question popping up increasingly in the cultural conversation about gender? Why has it become one of the litany of questions that compose the backlash against feminism?

I believe that the answers to both questions are linked. But first let's look at each separately.

What about the Boys?

Are boys in trouble in school? At first glance, the statistics would suggest that they are. Boys drop out of school, are diagnosed as emotionally disturbed, and commit suicide four times more often than girls; they get into fights twice as often; they murder ten times more frequently and are 15 times more likely to be the victims of a violent crime. Boys are six times more likely to be diagnosed with Attention Deficit Disorder (see, for example, Knickerbocker).

If they can manage to sit still and not get themselves killed, the argument seems to go, boys get lower grades on standardized tests of reading and writing, and have lower class rank and fewer honors than girls (Kleinfeld).

Michael S. Kimmel, "'What about the Boys?' What the Current Debates Tell Us (and Don't Tell Us) about Boys in School" from *Michigan Feminist Studies* 14 (1999): 1–28. Copyright © 1999 by Michael S. Kimmel. Reprinted with permission.

Finally, if they succeed in dodging the Scylla of elementary and high school, they're likely to dash themselves against the Charybdis of collegiate male bashing. We read that women now constitute the majority of students on college campuses, passing men in 1982, so that in eight years women will earn 58 percent of bachelor's degrees in U.S. colleges. One reporter tells us that if present trends continue, "the graduation line in 2068 will be all females." (That's like saying that if the enrollment of black students at Ol' Miss was 1 in 1964, 24 in 1968 and 400 in 1988, that by 1994 there should have been no more white students there.) Doomsayers lament that women now outnumber men in the social and behavioral sciences by about three to one, and that they've invaded such traditionally male bastions as engineering, where they now make up about 20 percent of all students, and biology and business, where the genders are virtually on par (see Lewin; Koerner).

So, the data might seem to suggest that there are fewer and fewer boys, getting poorer grades, with increasing numbers of behavioral problems. Three phenomena—numbers, achievement and behavior—compose the current empirical discussion about where the boys are and what they are doing.

"What about the Boys?"

These three themes—numbers, grades, behavior—frame the political debate about boys as well. (Now I'm going to include the quotation marks.) Given these gender differences, it's not surprising that we're having a national debate. After all, boys seem not only to be doing badly, but they are also doing worse than girls. What may be surprising, though, is the way the debate is being framed.

To hear some tell it, there's a virtual war against boys in America. Bestsellers' subtitles counsel us to "protect" boys, to "rescue" them. Inside these books, we read how boys are failing at school, where their behavior is increasingly seen as a problem. We read that boys are depressed, suicidal, emotionally shut down. Therapists advise anguished parents about boys' fragility, their hidden despondence and depression, and issue stern warnings about the dire consequences if we don't watch our collective cultural step.

But if there is a "war against boys" who has declared it? What are the sides of the conflict? Who is to blame for boys' failures? What appears to be a concern about the plight of boys actually masks a deeper agenda—a critique of feminism. And I believe that in the current climate, boys need defending against precisely those who claim to defend them; they need rescuing from precisely those who would rescue them.

The arguments of these jeremiads go something like this: First, we hear, feminism has already succeeded in developing programs for girls, enabling and encouraging girls to go into the sciences, to continue education, to imagine careers outside the home. But, in so doing, feminists have over-emphasized the problems of girls, and distorted the facts. Particularly objectionable are the findings of the American Association of Unversity Women (AAUW) reports on the "chilly classroom climate." According to these critics, the salutary effects of paying attention to girls have been offset by the increasing problematization of boys. It was feminists, we hear, who pitted girls against boys, and in their efforts to help girls, they've "pathologized" boyhood.

Elementary schools, we hear, are "anti-boy," emphasizing reading and restricting the movements of young boys. They "feminize" boys, forcing active, healthy and naturally rambunctious boys to conform to a regime of obedience, "pathologizing what is simply normal for boys," as psychologist Michael Gurian put it (qtd. in Zachary 1). In *The Wonder of Boys*, Gurian argues that with testosterone surging through their little limbs, we demand that they sit still, raise their hands, and take naps. We're giving them the message, he says, that "boyhood is defective" (qtd. in Zachary, 1). . . .

Today, women teachers are still to blame for boys' feminization. "It's teachers' job to create a classroom environment that accommodates both male and female energy, not just mainly female energy," explains the energetic therapist Michael Gurian (qtd. in Knickerbocker, 2). Since women also may run those boy scout troops and may actually run circles around the boys on the soccer field, men may be feeling a tad defensive these days. Not to worry—we can always retreat into our den to watch "The Man Show" and read *Men's Health* magazine.

In this way, the problem of boys is a problem caused entirely by women who both feminize the boys and pathologize them in their rush to help girls succeed. I'll return to these issues later, but for now, let me turn to what I see are the chief problems with the current "what about the boys?" debate.

What's Wrong with the "What about the Boys?" Debate

First, it creates a false opposition between girls and boys, pretending that the educational reforms undertaken to enable girls to perform better actually hindered boys' educational development. But these reforms—new initiatives, classroom configurations, teacher training, increased attentiveness to students' processes and individual learning styles—actually enable larger numbers of boys to get a better education.

And since, as Susan McGee Bailey and Patricia Campbell point out in their comment on "The Gender Wars in Education" in the January, 2000 issue of the *WCW Research Report*, "gender stereotypes, particularly those related to education, hurt both girls and boys," the challenging of those stereotypes, decreased tolerance for school violence and bullying, and increased attention to violence at home actually enables *both* girls *and* boys to feel safer at school (13).

Second, the critics all seem to be driven to distraction by numbers—the increasing percentages of women in high education and the growing gender gap in test scores. But here's a number they don't seem to factor in: zero—as in zero dollars of *any* new public funding for school programs for the past twenty years, the utter dearth of school bond issues that have passed, money from which might have developed remedial programs, intervention strategies, and teacher training. Money that might have prevented cutting school sports programs and after-school extra-curricular activities. Money that might have enabled teachers and administrators to do more than "store" problem students in separate classes.

Nor do the critics mention managed care health insurance, which virtually demands that school psychologists diagnose problem behavior as a treatable medical condition so that drugs may be substituted for costly, "unnecessary" therapy. These numbers—numbers of dollars—don't seem to enter the discussion about boys, and yet they provide the foundation for everything else. But even the numbers they *do* discuss—numbers and test scores—don't add up. For one thing, more *people* are going to college than ever before. In 1960, 54 percent of boys and 38 percent of girls went directly to college; today the numbers are 64 percent of boys and 70 percent of girls (Mortenson).

And while some college presidents fret that to increase male enrollments they'll be forced to lower standards (which is, incidentally, exactly the opposite of what they worried about 25 years ago when they all went coeducational) no one seems to find gender disparities going the other way all that upsetting. Of the top colleges and universities in the nation, only Stanford sports a 50–50 gender balance. Harvard and Amherst enroll 56 percent men, Princeton and Chicago 54 percent men, Duke and Berkeley 52 percent and Yale 51 percent. And that doesn't even begin to approach the gender disparities at Cal Tech (65 percent male, 35 percent female) or MIT (62 percent male, 38 percent female) (Gose "Liberal Arts Colleges Ask"). Nor does anyone seem driven to distraction about the gender disparities in nursing, social work, or education. Did somebody say "what about the girls?" Should we lower standards to make sure they're gender balanced?

In fact, much of the great gender difference we hear touted in actually what sociologist Cynthia Fuchs Epstein calls a "deceptive distinction," a difference that appears to be about gender but is actually about something else—in this case, class or race (see Epstein *Deceptive Distinctions*). Girls' vocational opportunities are far more restricted than boys' are. Their opportunities are from the service sector, with limited openings in manufacturing or construction. A college-educated woman earns about the same as a high-school educated man, $35,000 to $31,000 (Gose "Colleges Look for Ways").

The shortage of male college students is also actually a shortage of *nonwhite* males. The gender gap between college-age white males and white females is rather small, 51 percent women to 49 percent men. But only 37 percent of black college students are male, and 63 percent female, and 45 percent of Hispanic students are male, compared with 55 percent female (Lewin). (If this is a problem largely of class and race, why do the books that warn of this growing crisis have cute little white boys on their covers?)

These differences among boys—by race, or class, for example—do not typically fall within the radar of the cultural critics who would rescue boys. These differences are incidental because, in their eyes, all boys are the same: aggressive, competitive, rambunctious little devils. And this is perhaps the central problem and contradiction in the work of those who would save boys. They argue that it's testosterone that makes boys into boys, and a society that paid attention to boys would have to acknowledge testosterone. We're making it impossible for boys to be boys. . . .

Feminist emphases on gender discrimination, sexual harassment, or date rape only humiliate boys and distract us from intervening constructively. These misdiagnoses lead to some rather chilling remedies. Gurian suggests reviving corporal punishment, both at home and at school—but only when administered privately with cool indifference and never in the heat of adult anger. He calls it "spanking responsibly" (*A Fine Young Man* 175), though school boards and child welfare agencies might call it child abuse. . . .

What's Missing from the Debate about Boys

I believe that it is *masculinity* that is missing in the discussions of both fathers and sons. Though we hear an awful lot about *males*, we hear very little about *masculinity,* about the cultural meanings of the biological fact of maleness. Raising the issue of masculinity, I believe, will enable us to resolve many of these debates.

When I say that masculinity is invisible in the discussion, what could I possibly mean? How is masculinity invisible? Well, let me ask you this: when I say the word "gender," what gender do you think of? In our courses and our discourses, we act as if women alone "had" gender. This is political; this is central. . . .

Let me give you two . . . illustrations of this. . . . In a recent article about the brutal homophobic murder of Mathew Shepard, the reporter for the *New York Times* writes that "[y]oung men account for 80 percent to 90 percent of people arrested for 'gay bashing' crimes, says Valerie Jenness, a sociology professor who teaches a course on hate crimes" at U.C. Irvine. Then the reporter quotes Professor Jenness directly: "'This youth variable tells us they are working out identity issues, making the transition away from home into adulthood" (Brooke, A16). Did you hear it disappear? The *Times* reporter says "young men" account for . . . ," the sociologist, the expert, is quoted as saying, "this youth variable." That is what invisibility looks like.[1]

. . . Here's one more illustration of the invisibility of masculinity in the discussion of young boys, and how that invisibility almost always plays out as a critique of feminism. Asked to comment on the school shootings at Columbine and other high schools, House Majority Leader Tom DeLay said that guns "have little or nothing to do with juvenile violence" but rather, that the causes were daycare, the teaching of evolution, and "working mothers who take birth control pills" (qtd. in *The Nation* 5).

Some of the recent boy books do get it; they get that masculinity—not feminism, not testosterone, not fatherlessness, and not the teaching of evolution—is the key to understanding boyhood and its current crisis. For example, in *Raising Cain,* Dan Kindlon and Michael Thompson write that male peers present a young boy with a "culture of cruelty" in which they force him to deny emotional neediness, "routinely disguise his feelings," and end up feeling emotionally isolated (89). And in *Real Boys,* therapist William Pollack calls it the "boy code" and the "mask of masculinity"—a kind of swaggering posture that boys embrace to hide their fears, suppress dependency and vulnerability, and present a stoic, impervious front.

What exactly is that "boy code?" Twenty-five years ago, psychologist Robert Brannon described the four basic rules of manhood.

1. "No Sissy Stuff"—one can never do anything that even remotely hints of femininity; masculinity is the relentless repudiation of the feminine.
2. "Be a Big Wheel"—Wealth, power, status are markers of masculinity. We measure masculinity by the size of one's pay-check. In the words of that felicitous Reagan-era phrase, "He who has the most toys when he dies, wins."
3. "Be a Sturdy Oak"—what makes a man a man is that he is reliable in a crisis, and what makes a man reliable in a crisis is that he resembles an inanimate object. Rocks, pillars, trees are curious masculine icons.
4. "Give em Hell!"—exude an aura of daring and aggression. Live life on the edge. Take risks (Brannon and David).

Of course, these four rules are elaborated by different groups of men and boys in different circumstances. There are as sizable differences among different groups of men as there are differences between women and men. Greater in fact. Just because we make masculinity visible doesn't mean that we make other categories of experience—race, class, ethnicity, sexuality, age—invisible. What it means to be a 71-year-old, black, gay man in Cleveland is probably radically different from what it means to a 19-year-old, white, heterosexual farm boy in Iowa.

. . . [W]e can't forget that all masculinities are not created equal. All American men must also contend with a singular vision of masculinity, a particular definition that is held up as the model against which we all measure ourselves. We thus come to know what it means to be a man in our culture by setting our definitions in opposition to a set of "others"—racial minorities, sexual minorities, and, above all, women. As the sociologist Erving Goffman once wrote:

> In an important sense there is only one complete unblushing male
> in America: a young, married, white, urban, northern, heterosexual,

Protestant, father, of college education, fully employed, of good complexion, weight, and height, and a recent record in sports. . . . Any male who fails to qualify in any one of these ways is likely to view himself—during moments at least—as unworthy, incomplete, and inferior. (128)

I think it's crucial to listen carefully to those last few words. When men feel that they do not measure up, Goffman argues, they are likely to feel "unworthy, incomplete and inferior." It is, I believe, from this place of unworthiness, incompleteness and inferiority that boys begin their efforts to prove themselves as men. And the ways they do it—based on misinformation and disinformation—is what is causing the problems for girls and boys in school.

How Does the Perspective on Masculinity Transform the Debate?

Introducing masculinities into the discussion alleviates several of the problems with the "what about the boys?" debate. It enables us to explore the ways in which class and race complicate the picture of boys' achievement and behaviors, for one thing. For another, it reveals that boys and girls are on the same side in this struggle, not pitted against each other.

For example, when Kindlon and Thompson describe the things that *boys* need, they are really describing what *children* need. Adolescent boys, Kindlon and Thompson inform us, want to be loved, get sex, and not be hurt (195–6). And girls don't? Parents are counseled to: allow boys to have their emotions (241); accept a high level of activity (245); speak their language and treat them with respect (247); teach that empathy is courage (249); use discipline to guide and build (253); model manhood as emotionally attached (255); and teach the many ways a boy can be a man (256). Aside from the obvious tautologies, what they advocate is exactly what feminist women have been advocating for girls for some time.

Secondly, a focus on masculinity explains what is happening to those boys in school. Consider again the parallel for girls. Carol Gilligan's astonishing and often moving work on adolescent girls describes how these assertive, confident and proud young girls "lose their voices" when they hit adolescence (see, for example, Brown and Gilligan). At the same moment, William Pollack notes, boys become *more* confident, even beyond their abilities. You might even say that boys *find* their voices, but it is the inauthentic voice of bravado, of constant posturing, of foolish risk-taking and gratuitous violence. The "boy code" teaches them that they are supposed to be in power, and thus begin to act like it. . . .

What's the cause of all this posturing and posing? It's not testosterone, but privilege. In adolescence, both boys and girls get their first real dose of gender inequality: girls suppress ambition, boys inflate it.

Recent research on the gender gap in school achievement bears this out. Girls are more likely to undervalue their abilities, especially in the more traditionally "masculine" educational arenas such as math and science. Only the most able and most secure girls take such courses. Thus, their numbers tend to be few, and their grades high. Boys, however, possessed of this false voice of bravado (and many facing strong family pressure) are likely to *overvalue* their abilities, to remain in programs though they are less qualified and capable of succeeding. This difference, and not some putative discrimination against boys, is the reason that girls' mean test scores in math and science are now, on average, approaching that of boys. Too many boys who over-value their abilities remain in difficult math and science courses longer than they should; they pull the boys' mean scores down. By contrast, few girls, whose abilties and self-esteem are sufficient to enable them to "trespass" into a male domain, skew female data upwards.

A parallel process is at work in the humanities and social sciences. Girls' mean test scores in English and foreign languages, for example, also outpace boys. But this is not the result of "reverse discrimination"; rather, it is because the boys bump up against the norms of masculinity. Boys regard English as a "feminine" subject. Pioneering research in Australia by Wayne Martino found that boys are uninterested in English because of what it might say about their (inauthentic) masculine pose (see, for example, Martino "Gendered Learning Practices," "'Cool Boys'"; see also Yates "Gender Equity," "The 'What about the Boys' Debate"; Lesko). "Reading is lame, sitting down and looking at words is pathetic," commented one boy. "Most guys who like English are faggots" (Martino "Gendered Learning Practices" 132). The traditional liberal arts curriculum is seen as feminizing: as Catharine Stimpson recently put it sarcastically, "real men don't speak French" (qtd. in Lewin A26).

Boys tend to hate English and foreign languages for the same reasons that girls love it. In English, they observe, there are no hard and fast rules, but rather one expresses one's opinion about the topic and everyone's opinion is equally valued. "The answer can be a variety of things, you're never really wrong," observed one boy. "It's not like math and science where there is one set answer to everything." Another boy noted:

> I find English hard. It's because there are no set rules for reading
> texts . . . English isn't like math where you have rules on how to do
> things and where there are right and wrong answers. In English
> you have to write down how you feel and that's what I don't like.
> (Martino "Gendered Learning Practices" 133)

Compare this to the comments of girls in the same study:

> I feel motivated to study English because . . . you have freedom in
> English—unlike subjects such as math and science—and your view
> isn't necessarily wrong. There is no definite right or wrong answer

and you have the freedom to say what you feel is right without it being rejected as a wrong answer. (Martino "Gendered Learning Practices" 134)

It is not the school experience that "feminizes" boys, but rather the ideology of traditional masculinity that keeps boys from wanting to succeed. "The work you do here is girls' work," one boy commented to a researcher. "It's not real work" (Mac an Ghaill 59; for additional research on this, see Lesko). . . .

The Real Boy Crisis Is a Crisis of Masculinity

Making masculinity visible enables us to understand what I regard as the *real* boy crisis in America. The real boy crisis usually goes by another name. We call it "teen violence," "youth violence," "gang violence," "suburban violence," "violence in the schools." Just who do we think are doing it—girls?

Imagine if all the killers in the schools in Littleton, Pearl, Paducah, Springfield, and Jonesboro were all black girls from poor families who lived instead in New Haven, Newark, or Providence. We'd be having a national debate about inner-city, poor, black girls. The entire focus would be on race, class, and gender. The media would invent a new term for their behavior, as with "wilding" a decade ago. We'd hear about the culture of poverty, about how living in the city breeds crime and violence, about some putative natural tendency among blacks towards violence. Someone would even blame feminism for causing girls to become violent in a vain imitation of boys. Yet the obvious fact that these school killers were all middle-class, white boys seems to have escaped everyone's notice.

Let's face facts: Men and boys are responsible for 95 percent of all violent crimes in this country. Every day 12 boys and young men commit suicide—seven times the number of girls. Every day 18 boys and young men die from homicide—ten times the number of girls (see Kimmel *The Gendered Society*). From an early age, boys learn that violence is not only an acceptable form of conflict resolution, but one that is admired. Four times more teenage boys than teenage girls think fighting is appropriate when someone cuts into the front of a line. Half of all teenage boys get into a physical fight each year.

And it's been that way for many years. No other culture developed such a violent "boy culture," as historian E. Anthony Rotundo calls it in his book, *American Manhood*. Where else did young boys, as late as the 1940s, actually carry little chips of wood on their shoulders daring others to knock it off so that they might have a fight? It may be astonishing to readers that "carrying a chip on your shoulder" is literally true—a test of manhood for adolescent boys.

In what other culture did some of the reigning experts of the day actually *prescribe* fighting for young boys' healthy masculine development? The celebrated psychologist, G. Stanley Hall, who invented the term "adolescence," believed that a non-fighting boy was a "nonentity," and that it was "better even an occasional nose dented by a fist . . . than stagnation, general cynicism and censoriousness, bodily and psychic cowardice" (154).

And his disciples vigorously took up the cause. Here, for example is J. Adams Puffer in 1912, from his successful parental advice book, *The Boy and His Gang:*

> There are times when every boy must defend his own rights if he is not to become a coward, and lose the road to independence and true manhood. . . . The strong willed boy needs no inspiration to combat, but often a good deal of guidance and restraint. If he fights more than, let us say, a half-dozen times a week—except of course, during his first week at a new school—he is probably over-quarrelsome and needs to curb. (91)

Boys are to fight an average of once a day, except during the first week at a new school, during which, presumably they would have to fight more often!

From the turn of the century to the present day, violence has been part of the meaning of manhood, part of the way men have traditionally tested, demonstrated and proved their manhood. Without another cultural mechanism by which young boys can come to think of themselves as men, they've eagerly embraced violence as a way to become men.

I remember one little childhood game called "Flinch" that we played in the school yard. One boy would come up to another and pretend to throw a punch at his face. If the second boy flinched—as any *reasonable* person would have done—the first boy shouted "you flinched" and proceeded to punch him hard on the arm. It was his right; after all, the other boy had failed the test of masculinity. Being a man meant never flinching.

In the recent study of youthful violent offenders, psychologist James Garbarino locates the origins of men's violence in the ways boys swallow anger and hurt. Among the youthful offenders he studied, "[d]eadly petulance usually hides some deep emotional wounds, a way of compensating through an exaggerated sense of grandeur for an inner sense of violation, victimization, and injustice" (128). In other words, as that famous Reagan-era bumper-sticker put it, "I don't just get mad, I get even." Or, as one prisoner said, "I'd rather be wanted for murder than not wanted at all" (132).

James Gilligan is even more specific. In his book *Violence,* one of the most insightful studies of violence I've ever read, he argues that violence has its origins in "the fear of shame and ridicule, and the overbearing need to prevent others from laughing at oneself by making them weep instead" (77).

Recall those words by Goffman again—"unworthy, incomplete, inferior." Now listen to these voices: First, here is Evan Todd, a 255-pound defensive lineman on the Columbine football team, an exemplar of the jock culture that Dylan Klebold and Eric Harris—the gunmen at Columbine High School—found to be such an interminable torment: "Columbine is a clean, good place, except for those rejects," Todd says. "Sure we teased them. But what do you expect with kids who come to school with weird hairdos and horns on their hats? It's not just jocks; the whole school's disgusted with them. They're a bunch of homos, grabbing each others' private parts. If you want to get rid of someone, usually you tease 'em. So the whole school would call them homos" (qtd. in Gibbs and Roche 50–51). Harris says people constantly made fun of "my face, my hair, my shirts" (44). Klebold adds, "I'm going to kill you all. You've been giving us s__ for years" (44).

Our Challenge

If we really want to rescue boys, protect boys, promote boyhood, then our task must be to find ways to reveal and challenge this ideology of masculinity, to disrupt the facile "boys will be boys" model, and to erode boys' sense of entitlement. Because the reality is that it is this ideology of masculinity that is the problem for *both* girls *and* boys. And seen this way, our strongest ally, it seems to me, is the women's movement.

To be sure, feminism opened the doors of opportunity to women and girls. And it's changed the rules of conduct: in the workplace, where sexual harassment is no longer business as usual; on dates, where attempted date rape is no longer "dating etiquette"; and in schools, where both subtle and overt forms of discrimination against girls—from being shuffled off to Home Economics when they want to take physics, excluded from military schools and gym classes, to anatomy lectures using pornographic slides—have been successfully challenged. And let's not forget the legal cases that have confronted bullying, and sexual harassment by teachers and peers.

More than that, feminism has offered a blueprint for a new boyhood and masculinity based on a passion for justice, a love of equality, and expression of a fuller emotional palette. So naturally, feminists will be blamed for male bashing—feminists imagine that men (and boys) can do better (see, for example, Miedzian; Silverstein and Rashbaum).

And to think feminists are accused of male bashing! Actually, I think the anti-feminist right wing are the real male bashers. Underneath the anti-feminism may be perhaps the most insulting image of masculinity around. Males, you see, are savage, predatory, sexually omnivorous, violent creatures, who will rape, murder and pillage unless women perform their civilizing mission and act to constrain us. "Every society must be wary of the unattached male, for he is universally the cause of numerous social ills," writes David Popenoe (12). When they say that boys will be boys, they mean boys will be uncaged, uncivilized animals. Young males, conservative critic Charles Murray wrote recently, are "essentially barbarians for whom marriage . . . is an indispensible civilizing force" (23). And what of evolutionary psychologist Robert Wright, who recently "explained" that women and men are hard-wired by evolutionary imperatives to be so different as to come from different planets. "Human males," he wrote, "are by nature oppressive, possessive, flesh-obsessed pigs" (22). Had any radical feminist said these words, anti-feminist critics would howl with derision about how feminists hated men!

And here's that doyenne of talk radio, Dr. Laura Schlesinger: "Men would not do half of what they do if women didn't let them," she told an interviewer for *Modern Maturity* magazine recently. "That a man is going to do bad things is a fact. That you keep a man who does bad things in your life is your fault" (qtd. in Goodman 68).

Now it seems to me that the only rational response to these insulting images of an unchangeable, hard-wired, violent manhood is, of course, to assume they're true. Typically when we say that boys will be boys, we assume that propensity for violence is innate, the inevitable fruition of that prenatal testosterone cocktail. So what? That only begs the question. We still must decide whether to organize society so as to maximize boys' "natural" predisposition toward violence, or to minimize it. Biology alone cannot answer that question, and claiming that boys will be boys, helplessly shrugging our national shoulders, abandons our political responsibility.

Besides, one wants to ask, which biology are we talking about? Therapist Michael Gurian demands that we accept boy's "hard wiring." This "hard wiring," he informs us, is competitive and aggressive. "Aggression and physical risk taking are hard wired into a boy," he writes. Gurian claims that he likes the kind of feminism that "is not anti-male, accepts that boys are who they are, and chooses to love them rather than change their hard wiring" (*A Fine Young Man* 53–4).

That's too impoverished a view of feminism—and of boys—for my taste. I think it asks far too little of us, to simply accept boys and this highly selective definition of their hard-wiring. Feminism asks more of us—that we *not* accept those behaviors that are hurtful to boys, girls, and their environment—because we can do better than what this *part* of our hard wiring might dictate. We are also, after all, hard-wired towards compassion, nurturing and love, aren't we?

Surely we wouldn't insult men the way the right-wing insults men, by arguing that only women are hard-wired for love, care-giving, and nurturing, would we? (I am sure that those legions of men's rights types, demanding custody wouldn't dare do so!) I'm reminded of a line from Kate Millett's path-breaking book, *Sexual Politics,* more than thirty years ago:

> Perhaps nothing is so depressing an index of the inhumanity of the male supremacist mentality as the fact that the more genial human traits are assigned to the underclass: affection, response to sympathy, kindness, cheerfulness. (324–6)

The question, to my mind, is not whether or not we're hard wired, but rather which hard wiring elements we choose to honor and which we choose to challenge.

I remember one pithy definition that feminism was the radical idea that women are people. Feminists also seem to believe the outrageous proposition that, if given enough love, compassion and support, boys—as well as men—can also be people. That's a vision of boyhood I believe is worth fighting for.

NOTES

This paper began as the keynote address at the 6th annual K–12 Gender Equity in Schools Conference, Wellesley College Center for Research on Women, Wellesley College, January, 2000. A revised version was also presented at The Graduate School of Education, Harvard University, May, 2000. Although modified and revised, I have tried to retain the language and feeling of the original oral presentation. I am grateful to Susan McGee Bailey and Carol Gilligan for inviting me, and to Amy Aronson, Peggy McIntosh, Martin Mills, and Nan Stein, for their comments and support, and to the editors at *Michigan Feminist Studies,* and especially Laura Citrin, for their patience and editorial precision.

1. In fairness to Professor Jenness, whose work on gay bashing crimes I admire, it is possible that her quotation was only part of what she said, and that it was the newspaper, not the expert, who again rendered masculinity invisible.

REFERENCES

American Association of University Women. *How Schools Shortchange Girls: The AAUW Report, A Study of Major Findings on Girls and Education.* Washington, DC: American Association of University Women Educational Foundation, 1992.

Bailey, Susan McGee, and Patricia B. Campbell, "The Gender Wars in Education." *WCW Research Report.* Wellesley, MA: Wellesley Center for Research on Women, 1999/2000.

Brannon, Robert, and Deborah David. "Introduction" to *The Forty-Nine Per Cent Majority.* Reading, MA: Addison, Wesley, 1976.

Brooke, James. "Men Held in Beating Lived on the Fringes." *The New York Times,* 16 October 1998: A16.

Brown, Lyn Mikel, and Carol Gilligan. *Meeting at the Cross-roads.* New York: Ballantine, 1992.

Epstein, Cynthia Fuchs. *Deceptive Distinctions.* New Haven: Yale UP, 1988.

Garbarino, James. *Lost Boys: Why Our Sons Turn Violent and How We Can Save Them.* New York: The Free Press, 1999.

Gibbs, Nancy, and Timothy Roche. "The Columbine Tapes." *Time* 154 (25), 20 December 1999: 40–51.

Gilligan, Carol. *In a Different Voice.* Cambridge: Harvard UP, 1982.

Gilligan, James. *Violence.* New York: Vintage, 1997.

Goffman, Erving. *Stigma: Notes on the Management of Spoiled Identity.* Englewood Cliffs, NJ: Prentice-Hall, 1963.

Goodman, Susan. "Dr. No." *Modern Maturity,* September–October, 1999.

Gose, Ben. "Liberal Arts Colleges Ask: Where Have the Men Gone?" *Chronicle of Higher Education,* 6 June 1997: A35–6.

———. "Colleges Look for Ways to Reverse a Decline in Enrollment of Men." *Chronicle of Higher Education,* 26 November 1999: A73.

Gurian, Michael. *A Fine Young Man: What Parents, Mentors, and Educators Can Do to Shape Adolescent Boys into Exceptional Men.* New York: Jeremy P. Tarcher/Putnam, 1998.

────. *The Wonder of Boys: What Parents, Mentors, and Educators Can Do to Shape Boys into Exceptional Men.* New York: Jeremy P. Tarcher/Putnam, 1996.

Hall, G. Stanley. "The Awkward Age." *Appleton's Magazine,* August 1900.

Kimmel, Michael. *The Gendered Society.* New York: Oxford UP, 2000.

Kindlon, Dan, and Michael Thompson. *Raising Cain: Protecting the Emotional Life of Boys.* New York: Ballantine, 1999.

Kleinfeld, Judith. "Student Performance: Males Versus Females." *The Public Interest,* Winter 1999.

Knickerbocker, Brad. "Young and Male in America: It's Hard Being a Boy." *Christian Science Monitor,* 29 April 1999.

Koerner, Brendan. "Where the Boys Aren't." *U.S. News and World Report,* 8 February 1999.

Lesko, Nancy, ed. *Masculinities and Schools.* Newbury Park, CA: Sage Publications, 2000.

Lewin, Tamar. "American Colleges Begin to Ask, Where Have All the Men Gone?" *The New York Times,* 6 December 1998.

Mac an Ghaill, Mairtin. *The Making of Men: Masculinities, Sexualities and Schooling.* London: Open UP, 1994.

────. "'What about the Boys?': Schooling, Class and Crisis Masculinity." *Sociological Review,* 44 (3), 1996.

Martino, Wayne. "Gendered Learning Practices: Exploring the Costs of Hegemonic Masculinity for Girls and Boys in Schools." *Gender Equity: A Framework for Australian Schools,* Canberra: np, 1997.

────. "'Cool Boys,' 'Party Animals', 'Squids,' and 'Poofters': Interrogating the Dynamics and Politics of Adolescent Masculinities in School." *British Journal of Sociology of Education,* 20 (2), 1999.

Miedzian, Myriam. *Boys will be Boys: Breaking the Link between Masculinity and Violence.* New York: Doubleday, 1991.

Millett, Kate. *Sexual Politics.* New York: Random House, 1969.

Mills, Martin. "Disrupting the 'What about the Boys?' Discourse: Stories from Australia" paper presented at the Men's Studies Conference, SUNY at Stony Brook, 6 August 1998.

Mortenson, Thomas. "Where Are the Boys? The Growing Gender Gap in Higher Education." *The College Board Review,* 188, August 1999.

Murray, Charles. "The Emerging British Underclass." London: IEA Health and Welfare Unit, 1990.

The Nation. "News of the Week in Review." 15 November 1999.

Pollack, William. *Real Boys: Rescuing Our Sons from the Myths of Boyhood.* New York: Henry Holt, 1998.

Popenoe, David. *Life Without Father.* New York: The Free Press, 1996.

Priest, R., A. Vitters, and H. Prince. "Coeducation at West Point." *Armed Forces and Society,* 4 (4), 1978.

Puffer, J. Adams. *The Boy and His Gang.* Boston: Houghton, Mifflin, 1912.

Rotundo, E. Anthony. *American Manhood: Transformations of Masculinity from the Revolution to the Present Era.* New York: BasicBooks, 1993.

Silverstein, Olga, and Beth Rashbaum. *The Courage to Raise Good Men.* New York: Penguin, 1995.

Wright, Robert. "The Dissent of Woman: What Feminists Can Learn from Darwinism." *Matters of Life and Death: Demos Quarterly,* 10, 1996.

Yates, Lyn. "Gender Equity and the Boys Debate: What Sort of Challenge Is It?" *British Journal of Sociology of Education,* 18 (3), 1997.

────. "The 'What about the Boys?' Debate as a Public Policy Issue." Ed. Nancy Lesko. *Masculinities and Schools.* Newbury Park, CA: Sage Publications, 2000.

Zachary, G. Pascal. "Boys Used to Be Boys, But Do Some Now See Boyhood as a Malady?" *The Wall Street Journal,* 2 May 1997.

43
_____

DOES GENDER MATTER?

BEN A. BARRES

Ben A. Barres, M.D., Ph.D., is a professor of neurobiology at Stanford Medical School with over 40 authored or co-authored scientific publications.

"Few tragedies can be more extensive than the stunting of life, few injustices deeper than the denial of an opportunity to strive or even to hope, by a limit imposed from without, but falsely identified as lying within."

— STEPHEN JAY GOULD

When I was 14 years old, I had an unusually talented maths teacher. One day after school, I excitedly pointed him out to my mother. To my amazement, she looked at him with shock and said with disgust: "You never told me that he was black." I looked over at my teacher and, for the first time, realized that he was an African-American. I had somehow never noticed his skin color before, only his spectacular teaching ability. I would like to think that my parents' sincere efforts to teach me prejudice were unsuccessful. I don't know why this lesson takes for some and not for others. But now that I am 51, as a female-to-male transgendered person, I still wonder about it, particularly when I hear male gym teachers telling young boys "not to be like girls" in that same derogatory tone.

Hypothesis Testing

Last year, Harvard University president Larry Summers suggested that differences in innate aptitude rather than discrimination were more likely to be to blame for the failure of women to advance in scientific careers.[1] Harvard professor Steven Pinker then put forth a similar argument in an online debate,[2] and an almost identical view was elaborated in a 2006 essay by Peter Lawrence entitled "Men, Women and Ghosts in Science."[3] Whereas Summers prefaced his statements by saying he was trying to be provocative, Lawrence did not. Whereas Summers talked about "different availability of aptitude at the high end," Lawrence talked about average

Ben A. Barres, "Does Gender Matter?" from *Nature* (July 2006). Copyright © 2006. Reprinted with the permission of Macmillan Publishers, Ltd.

aptitudes differing. Lawrence argued that, even in a utopian world free of bias, women would still be under-represented in science because they are innately different from men.

Lawrence draws from the work of Simon Baron-Cohen[4] in arguing that males are "on average" biologically predisposed to systematize, to analyze and to be more forgetful of others, whereas females are "on average" innately designed to empathize, to communicate and to care for others. He further argues that men are innately better equipped to aggressively compete in the "vicious struggle to survive" in science. Similarly, Harvard professor Harvey Mansfield states in his new book, *Manliness,* that women don't like to compete, are risk adverse, less abstract and too emotional.[5]

I will refer to this view—that women are not advancing because of innate inability rather than because of bias or other factors—as the Larry Summers Hypothesis. It is a view that seems to have resonated widely with male, but not female, scientists. Here, I will argue that available scientific data do not provide credible support for the hypothesis but instead support an alternative one: that women are not advancing because of discrimination. You might call this the "Stephen Jay Gould Hypothesis." I have no desire to make men into villains (as Henry Kissinger once said, "Nobody will ever win the battle of the sexes; there's just too much fraternizing with the enemy"). As to who the practitioners of this bias are, I will be pointing my finger at women as much as men. I am certain that all the proponents of the Larry Summers Hypothesis are well-meaning and fair-minded people, who agree that treatment of individuals should be based on merit rather than on race, gender or religion stereotypes.

The Sums Don't Add Up

Like many women and minorities, however, I am suspicious when those who are at an advantage proclaim that a disadvantaged group of people is innately less able. Historically, claims that disadvantaged groups are innately inferior have been based on junk science and intolerance.[6] Despite powerful social factors that discourage women from studying maths and science from a very young age,[7] there is little evidence that gender differences in math abilities exist, are innate or are even relevant to the lack of advancement of women in science.[8] A study of nearly 20,000 math scores of children aged 4 to 18, for instance, found little difference between the genders (Figure 1),[9] and, despite all the social forces that hold women back from an early age, one-third of the winners of the elite Putnam Math Competition last year were women. Moreover, differences in math-test results are not correlated with the gender divide between those who choose to leave science.[10] I will explain why I believe that the Larry Summers Hypothesis amounts to nothing more than blaming the victim, why it is so harmful to women, and what can and should be done to help women advance in science.

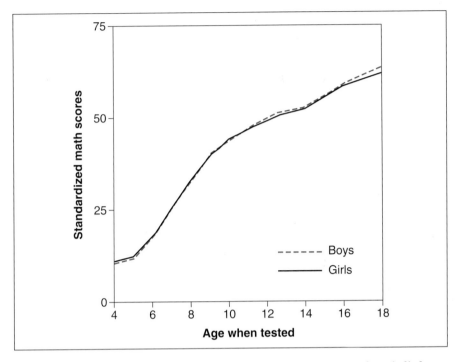

FIGURE 1 Math-test scores for ages 4 to 18. In the United States there is little to distinguish the math-test scores of boys and girls throughout school.

If innate intellectual abilities are not to blame for women's slow advance in science careers, then what is? The foremost factor, I believe, is the societal assumption that women are innately less able than men. Many studies, summarized in Virginia Valian's excellent book *Why So Slow?*,[11] have demonstrated a substantial degree of bias against women—more than is sufficient to block women's advancement in many professions. Here are a few examples of bias from my own life as a young woman. As an undergrad at the Massachusetts Institute of Technology (MIT), I was the only person in a large class of nearly all men to solve a hard math problem, only to be told by the professor that my boyfriend must have solved it for me. I was not given any credit. I am still disappointed about the prestigious fellowship competition I later lost to a male contemporary when I was a PhD student, even though the Harvard dean who had read both applications assured me that my application was much stronger (I had published six high-impact papers whereas my male competitor had published only one). Shortly after I changed sex, a faculty member was heard to say "Ben Barres gave a great seminar today, but then his work is much better than his sister's."

Anecdotes, however, are not data, which is why gender-blinding studies are so important.[11] These studies reveal that in many selection processes, the bar is unconsciously raised so high for women and minority candidates that

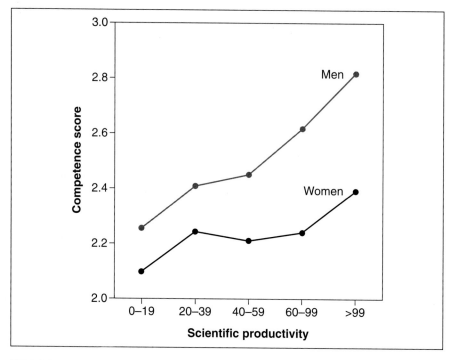

FIGURE 2   Competence scores awarded after peer review. Peer reviewers in Sweden award lower competence scores to female scientists than to similarly productive male scientists.

few emerge as winners. For instance, one study found that women applying for a research grant needed to be 2.5 times more productive than men in order to be considered equally competent (Figure 2).[12] Even for women lucky enough to obtain an academic job, gender biases can influence the relative resources allocated to faculty, as Nancy Hopkins discovered when she and a senior faculty committee studied this problem at MIT. The data were so convincing that MIT president Charles Vest publicly admitted that discrimination was responsible. For talented women, academia is all too often not a meritocracy.

In Denial

Despite these studies, very few men or women are willing to admit that discrimination is a serious problem in science. How is that possible? Valian suggests that we all have a strong desire to believe that the world is fair.[11] Remarkably, women are as likely as men to deny the existence of gender-based bias.[13]Accomplished women who manage to make it to the top may "pull up the ladder behind them," perversely believing that if other women are less successful, then one's own success seems even greater. Another explanation is a phenomenon known as "denial of *personal disadvantage,*" in which women compare their advancement with other women rather than with men.[14]

My own denial of the situation persisted until last year, when, at the age of 50, several events opened my eyes to the barriers that women and minorities still face in academia. In addition to the Summers speech the National Institutes of Health (NIH) began the most prestigious competition they have ever run, the Pioneer Award, but with a nomination process that favoured male applicants.[15] To their credit, in response to concerns that 60 of 64 judges and all 9 winners were men, the NIH has revamped their Pioneer Award selection process to make it fairer. I hope that the Howard Hughes Medical Institute (HHMI) will address similar problems with their investigator competitions. When it comes to bias, it seems that the desire to believe in a meritocracy is so powerful that until a person has experienced sufficient career-harming bias themselves they simply do not believe it exists.

My main purpose in writing this commentary is that I would like female students to feel that they will have equal opportunity in their scientific careers. Until intolerance is addressed, women will continue to advance only slowly. Of course, this feeling is also deeply personal to me (see "Personal experiences"). The comments of Summers, Mansfield, Pinker and Lawrence about women's lesser innate abilities are all wrongful and personal attacks on my character and capabilities, as well as on my colleagues' and students' abilities and self-esteem. I will certainly not sit around silently and endure them.

Mansfield and others claim that women are more emotional than men. There is absolutely no science to support this contention. On the contrary, it is men that commit the most violent crimes in anger—for example, 25 times more murders than women. The only hysteria that exceeded MIT professor Nancy Hopkins' (well-founded) outrage after Larry Summers' comments was the shockingly vicious news coverage by male reporters and commentators. Hopkins also received hundreds of hateful and even pornographic messages, nearly all from men, that were all highly emotional.

Taboo or Untrue?

There is no scientific support, either, for the contention that women are innately less competitive (although I believe powerful curiosity and the drive to create sustain most scientists far more than the love of competition). However, many girls are discouraged from sports for fear of being labelled tomboys. A 2002 study did find a gender gap in competitiveness in financial tournaments, but the authors suggested that this was due to differences in self confidence rather than ability.[16] Indeed, again and again, self confidence

---

Personal Experiences

As a transgendered person, no one understands more deeply than I do that there are innate differences between men and women. I suspect that my transgendered identity was caused by fetal exposure to high doses of a testosterone-like drug. But there is no evidence that sexually dimorphic brain wiring is at all relevant to the abilities needed to be successful in a chosen academic career. I underwent intensive cognitive testing before and after starting testosterone treatment about 10 years ago. This showed that my spatial abilities have increased as a consequence of taking testosterone. Alas, it has been to no avail; I still get lost all the time when driving (although I am no longer willing to ask for directions). There was one innate difference that I was surprised to learn is apparently under direct control of testosterone in adults—the ability to cry easily, which I largely lost upon starting hormone treatment. Likewise, male-to-female transgendered individuals gain the ability to cry more readily. By far, the main difference that I have noticed is that people who don't know I am transgendered treat me with much more respect: I can even complete a whole sentence without being interrupted by a man.

---

has been pointed to as a factor influencing why women "choose" to leave science and engineering programs. When women are repeatedly told they are less good, their self confidence falls and their ambitions dim.[17] This is why Valian has concluded that simply raising expectations for women in science may be the single most important factor in helping them make it to the top.[18]

Steven Pinker has responded to critics of the Larry Summers Hypothesis by suggesting that they are angry because they feel the idea that women are innately inferior is so dangerous that it is sinful even to think about it.[19] Harvard Law School professor Alan Dershowitz sympathizes so strongly with this view that he plans to teach a course next year called "Taboo." At Harvard we must have veritas; all ideas are fair game. I completely agree. I welcome any future studies that will provide a better understanding of why women and minorities are not advancing at the expected rate in science and so many other professions.

But it is not the idea alone that has sparked anger. Disadvantaged people are wondering why privileged people are brushing the truth under the carpet. If a famous scientist or a president of a prestigious university is going to pronounce in public that women are likely to be innately inferior, would it be too much to ask that they be aware of the relevant data? It would seem that just as the bar goes way up for women applicants in academic selection processes, it goes way down when men are evaluating the evidence for why women are not advancing in science. That is why women are angry. It is incumbent upon those proclaiming gender differences in abilities to rigorously address whether suspected differences are real before suggesting that a whole group of people is innately wired to fail.

What happens at Harvard and other universities serves as a model for many other institutions, so it would be good to get it right. To anyone who is upset at the thought that free speech is not fully protected on university campuses, I would like to ask, as did third-year Harvard Law student Tammy Pettinato: what is the difference between a faculty member calling their African-American students lazy and one pronouncing that women are innately inferior? Some have suggested that those who are angry at Larry Summers' comments should simply fight words with more words (hence this essay). In my view, when faculty tell their students that they are innately inferior based on race, religion, gender or sexual orientation, they are crossing a line that should not be crossed—the line that divides free speech from verbal violence—and it should not be tolerated at Harvard or anywhere else. In a culture where women's abilities are not respected, women cannot effectively learn, advance, lead or participate in society in a fulfilling way.

Take Action

Although I have argued that the Larry Summers Hypothesis is incorrect and harmful, the academic community is one of the most tolerant around. But, as tolerant as academics are, we are still human beings influenced by our culture. Comments by Summers and others have made it clear that discrimination remains an under-recognized problem that is far from solved. The progress of science increasingly depends on the global community, but only 10% of the world's population is male and caucasian. To paraphrase Martin Luther King, a first-class scientific enterprise cannot be built upon a foundation of second-class citizens. If women and minorities are to achieve their full potential, all of us need to be far more proactive. So what can be done?

First, enhance leadership diversity in academic and scientific institutions. Diversity provides a substantially broader point of view, with more sensitivity and respect for different perspectives, which is invaluable to any organization. More female leadership is vital in lessening the hostile working environment that young women scientists often encounter. In addition to women and under-represented minority groups, we must not forget Asians and lesbian, gay, bisexual and transgendered folks. There are enough outstanding scientific leaders in these racial and gender groups that anyone with a will to achieve a diverse leadership in their organization could easily attain it.

Speak Out

Second, the importance of diverse faculty role models cannot be overstated. There is much talk about equal opportunity, but, in practice, serious attention still needs to be directed at how to run fair job searches. Open searches often seem to be bypassed entirely for top leadership positions, just when it matters most—search committees should not always be chaired by men and the committee itself should be highly diverse.[20] Implementation of special hiring strategies and strong deans willing to push department chairs to recruit top women scientists are especially effective. It is crucial in the promotion process that merit be decided by the quality, not quantity, of papers published.

Women faculty, in particular, need help from their institutions in balancing career and family responsibilities. In an increasingly competitive environment, women with children must be able to compete for funding and thrive. Why can't young faculty have the option of using their tuition benefits, in which some universities pay part of the college tuition fees for the children of faculty, for day care instead? Tuition benefits will be of no help if female scientists don't make tenure. And institutions that have the financial capability, such as HHMI, could help by making more career-transition fellowships available for talented women scientists.

Third, there should be less silence in the face of discrimination. Academic leadership has a particular responsibility to speak out, but we all share this responsibility. It takes minimal effort to send a brief message to the relevant authority when you note a lack of diversity in an organization or an act of discrimination. I don't know why more women don't speak out about sexism at their institutions, but I do know that they are often reluctant, even when they have the security of a tenured faculty position. Nancy Hopkins is an admirable role model, and it is time that others share the burden. It doesn't only have to be women that support women. I was deeply touched by the eloquent words of Greg Petsko[21] following Summers' comments. And it has been 30 years since I was a medical student, but I still recall with gratitude the young male student who immediately complained to a professor who had shown a slide of a nude pin-up in his anatomy lecture.

Fourth, enhance fairness in competitive selection processes. Because of evaluation bias, women and minorities are at a profound disadvantage in such competitive selection unless the processes are properly designed.[22] As the revamped NIH Pioneer Award demonstrates, a few small changes can make a significant difference in outcome. By simply changing the procedure so that anyone can self-nominate and by ensuring a highly diverse selection committee, the number of women and minority winners went up to more than 50% from zero. This lesson can and should now be applied to other similar processes for scientific awards, grants and faculty positions. Alas, too many selection committees still show a striking lack of diversity—with typically greater than 90% white males. When selection processes are run fairly, reverse discrimination is not needed to attain a fair outcome.

Confidence Booster

Finally, we can teach young scientists how to survive in a prejudiced world. Self-confidence is crucial in advancing and enjoying a research career. From an early age, girls receive messages that they are not good enough to do science subjects or will be less liked if they are good at them. The messages come from many sources, including parents, friends, fellow students and, alas, teachers. When teachers have lower expectations of them, students do less well. But we are all at fault for sending these messages and for remaining silent when we encounter them. Teachers need to provide much more encouragement to young people, regardless of sex, at all stages of training. Occasional words of encouragement can have enormous effects.

All students, male and female, would benefit from training in how to be more skillful presenters, to exert a presence at meetings by asking questions, to make connections with faculty members who may help them to obtain grants and a job, and to have the leadership skills necessary to survive and advance in academia. Because women and minorities tend to be less confident in these areas, their mentors in particular need to encourage them to be more proactive. I vividly recall my PhD supervisor coming with me to the talks of famous scientists and forcing me to introduce myself and to ask them questions. There is a great deal of hallway mentoring that goes on for young men that I am not sure many women and minorities receive (I wish that someone had mentioned to me when I was younger that life, even in science, is a popularity contest—a message that Larry Summers might have found helpful as well). It is incumbent on all of us who are senior faculty to keep a look out for highly talented young people, including women and minority students, and help them in whatever way possible with their careers.

NOTES

1. Summers, L. *Letter to the Faculty Regarding NBER Remarks* www.president.harvard.edu/speeches/summers/2005/facletter.html (2005).
2. *The Science of Gender and Science. Pinker vs. Spelke: A Debate* www.edge.org/3rd_culture/debate05/debate05_index.html (2005).
3. Lawrence, P. A. *PLoS Biol.* 4, 13–15 (2006).
4. Baron-Cohen, S. *The Essential Difference: Men, Women, and the Extreme Male Brain* (Allen Lane, London, 2003).
5. Mansfield, H. *Manliness* (Yale Univ. Press, New Haven, 2006).
6. Gould, S. J. The *Mismeasure of Man* (W. W. Norton & Co, New York, 1996).
7. Steele, C. M. *Am. Psychol.* 52, 613–629 (1997).
8. Spelke, E. S. *Am. Psychol.* 60, 950–958 (2005).
9. Leahey, E. & Guo, G. *Soc. Forces* 80.2, 713–732 (2001).
10. Xie, Y. & Shauman, K. *Women in Science: Career Processes and Outcomes* (Harvard Univ. Press, Cambridge, 2003).
11. Valian, V. *Why So Slow?* (MIT Press, Cambridge, 1998).
12. Wennerås, C. & Wold, A. *Nature* 387, 341–343 (1997).

13. Rhode, D. L. *Speaking of Sex: The Denial of Gender Inequality* (Harvard Univ. Press, Cambridge, 1997).
14. Valian, *Why So Slow?*
15. Carnes, M. *et al. J Womens Health* 14, 684–691 (2005).
16. Gneezy, U., Niederle, M. & Rustichini, A. *Q. J. Econ.* **18**, 1049–1074 (2003).
17. Fels, A. *Necessary Dreams* (Pantheon Press, New York, 2004).
18. Valian, *Why So Slow?*
19. Pinker, S. *New Repub.* 15 (14 Feb, 2005).
20. Carnes, *J. Womens Health;* Moody, J. *Faculty Diversity: Problems and Solutions* (Taylor and Francis, New York, 2004).
21. Petsko, G. A. *Genome Biol.* 6, 1–3 (2005).
22. Valian, *Why So Slow?;* Wennerås & Wold, *Nature;* Carnes, *J. Womens Health;* Moody, *Faculty Diversity.*

44

BLACK AND FEMALE
Reflections on Graduate School

BELL HOOKS

bell hooks (nee Gloria Watkins) is Distinguished Professor of English at City College in New York. Although hooks is mainly known as a feminist thinker, her writings cover a broad range of topics on gender, race, teaching and the significance of media for contemporary culture. She is the author of many books, the most recent of which are *We Real Cool: Black Men and Masculinity* (2004) and *When Angels Speak of Love* (2007).

Searching for material to read in a class about women and race, I found an essay in *Heresies: Racism is the Issue* that fascinated me. I realized that it was one of the first written discussions of the struggles black English majors (and particularly black women) face when we study at predominantly white universities. The essay, "On Becoming A Feminist Writer," is by Carole Gregory. She begins by explaining that she has been raised in racially segregated neighborhoods but that no one had ever really explained "white

bell hooks, "Black and Female: Reflections on Graduate School" from *Talking Back: Thinking Feminist, Thinking Black.* Reprinted with the permission of South End Press and Between the Lines.

racism or white male sexism." Psychically, she was not prepared to confront head-on these aspects of social reality, yet they were made visible as soon as she registered for classes:

> Chewing on a brown pipe, a white professor said, "English departments do not hire Negroes or women!" Like a guillotine, his voice sought to take my head off. Racism in my hometown was an economic code of etiquette which stifled Negroes and women.
>
> "If you are supposed to explain these courses, that's all I want," I answered. Yet I wanted to kill this man. Only my conditioning as a female kept me from striking his volcanic red face. My murderous impulses were raging.

Her essay chronicles her struggles to pursue a discipline which interests her without allowing racism or sexism to defeat and destroy her intellectual curiosity, her desire to teach. The words of this white male American Literature professor echo in her mind years later when she finds employment difficult, when she confronts the reality that black university teachers of English are rare. Although she is writing in 1982, she concludes her essay with the comment:

> Many years ago, an American Literature professor had cursed the destiny of "Negroes and women." There was truth in his ugly words. Have you ever had a Black woman for an English teacher in the North? Few of us are able to earn a living. For the past few years, I have worked as an adjunct in English. Teaching brings me great satisfaction; starving does not. . . . I still remember the red color of the face which said, "English departments do not hire Negroes or women." Can women change this indictment? These are the fragments I add to my journal.

Reading Carole Gregory's essay, I recalled that in all my years of studying in English department classes, I had never been taught by a black woman. In my years of teaching, I have encountered students both in English classes and other disciplines who have never been taught by black women. Raised in segregated schools until my sophomore year of high school, I had wonderful black women teachers as role models. It never occurred to me that I would not find them in university classrooms. Yet I studied at four universities—Stanford, University of Wisconsin, University of Southern California, and the University of California, Santa Cruz—and I did not once have the opportunity to study with a black woman English professor. They were never members of the faculty. I considered myself lucky to study with one black male professor at Stanford who was visiting and another at the University of Southern California even though both were reluctant to support and encourage black female students. Despite their sexism and internalized racism, I appreciated them as teachers and felt they affirmed that black scholars could teach literature, could work in English departments. They offered a degree of support and affirmation, however relative, that countered the intense racism and sexism of many white professors.

Changing hiring practices have meant that there are increasingly more black professors in predominantly white universities, but their presence only mediates in a minor way the racism and sexism of white professors. During my graduate school years, I dreaded talking face-to-face with white professors, especially white males. I had not developed this dread as an undergraduate because there it was simply assumed that black students, and particularly black female students, were not bright enough to make it in graduate school. While these racist and sexist opinions were rarely directly stated, the message was conveyed through various humiliations that were aimed at shaming students, at breaking our spirit. We were terrorized. As an undergraduate, I carefully avoided those professors who made it clear that the presence of any black students in their classes was not desired. Unlike Carole Gregory's first encounter, they did not make direct racist statements. Instead, they communicated their message in subtle ways—forgetting to call your name when reading the roll, avoiding looking at you, pretending they do not hear you when you speak, and at times ignoring you altogether.

The first time this happened to me I was puzzled and frightened. It was clear to me and all the other white students that the professor, a white male, was directing aggressive mistreatment solely at me. These other students shared with me that it was not likely that I would pass the class no matter how good my work, that the professor would find something wrong with it. They never suggested that this treatment was informed by racism and sexism; it was just that the professor had for whatever "unapparent" reason decided to dislike me. Of course, there were rare occasions when taking a course meant so much to me that I tried to confront racism, to talk with the professor; and there were required courses. Whenever I tried to talk with professors about racism, they always denied any culpability. Often I was told, "I don't even notice that you are black."

In graduate school, it was especially hard to choose courses that would not be taught by professors who were quite racist. Even though one could resist by naming the problem and confronting the person, it was rarely possible to find anyone who could take such accusations seriously. Individual white professors were supported by white-supremacist institutions, by racist colleagues, by hierarchies that placed the word of the professor above that of the student. When I would tell the more supportive professors about racist comments that were said behind closed doors, during office hours, there would always be an expression of disbelief, surprise, and suspicion about the accuracy of what I was reporting. Mostly they listened because they felt it was their liberal duty to do so. Their disbelief, their refusal to take responsibility for white racism made it impossible for them to show authentic concern or help. One professor of 18th century literature by white writers invited me to his office to tell me that he would personally see to it that I would never receive a graduate degree. I, like many other students in the class, had written a paper in a style that he disapproved of, yet only I was given this response. It was often in the very areas of British and American literature where racism abounds in the texts studied that I would encounter racist individuals.

Gradually, I began to shift my interest in early American literature to more modern and contemporary works. This shift was influenced greatly by an encounter with a white male professor of American literature whose racism and sexism was unchecked. In his classes, I, as well as other students, was subjected to racist and sexist jokes. Any of us that he considered should not be in graduate school were the objects of particular scorn and ridicule. When we gave oral presentations, we were told our work was stupid, pathetic, and were not allowed to finish. If we resisted in any way, the situation worsened. When I went to speak with him about his attitude, I was told that I was not really graduate school material, that I should drop out. My anger surfaced and I began to shout, to cry. I remember yelling wildly, "Do you love me? And if you don't love me then how can you have any insight about my concerns and abilities? And who are you to make such suggestions on the basis of one class?" He of course was not making a suggestion. His was a course one had to pass to graduate. He was telling me that I could avoid the systematic abuse by simply dropping out. I would not drop out. I continued to work even though it was clear that I would not succeed, even as the persecution became more intense. And even though I constantly resisted.

In time, my spirits were more and more depressed. I began to dream of entering the professor's office with a loaded gun. There I would demand that he listen, that he experience the fear, the humiliation. In my dreams I could hear his pleading voice begging me not to shoot, to remain calm. As soon as I put the gun down he would become his old self again. Ultimately in the dream the only answer was to shoot, to shoot to kill. When this dream became so consistently a part of my waking fantasies, I knew that it was time for me to take a break from graduate school. Even so I felt as though his terrorism had succeeded, that he had indeed broken my spirit. It was this feeling that led me to return to graduate school, to his classes, because I felt I had given him too much power over me and I needed to regain that sense of self and personal integrity that I allowed him to diminish. Through much of my graduate school career, I was told that "I did not have the proper demeanor of a graduate student." In one graduate program, the black woman before me, who was also subjected to racist and sexist aggression, would tell me that they would say she was not as smart as me but she knew her place. I did not know my place. Young white radicals began to use the phrase "student as nigger" precisely to call attention to the way in which hierarchies within universities encouraged domination of the powerless by the powerful. At many universities the proper demeanor of a graduate student is exemplary when that student is obedient, when he or she does not challenge or resist authority.

During graduate school, white students would tell me that it was important not to question, challenge, or resist. Their tolerance level seemed much higher than my own or that of other black students. Critically reflecting on the differences between us, it was apparent that many of the white students were from privileged class backgrounds. Tolerating the humiliations and degradations we were subjected to in graduate school did not radically call into question their integrity, their sense of self-worth. Those of us who were coming from underprivileged class backgrounds, who were black, often were able to attend college only because we had consistently defied those who had attempted to make us believe we were smart but not "smart enough"; guidance counselors who refused to tell us about certain colleges because they already knew we would not be accepted; parents who were not necessarily supportive of graduate work, etc. White students were not living daily in a world outside campus life where they also had to resist degradation, humiliation. To them, tolerating forms of exploitation and domination in graduate school did not evoke images of a lifetime spent tolerating abuse. They would endure certain forms of domination and abuse, accepting it as an initiation process that would conclude when they became the person in power. In some ways they regarded graduate school and its many humiliations as a game, and they submitted to playing the role of subordinate. I and many other students, especially non-white students from non-privileged backgrounds, were unable to accept and play this "game." Often we were ambivalent about the rewards promised. Many of us were not seeking to be in a position of power over others. Though we wished to teach, we did not want to exert coercive authoritarian rule over others. Clearly those students who played the game best were usually white males and they did not face discrimination, exploitation, and abuse in many other areas of their lives.

Many black graduate students I knew were concerned about whether we were striving to participate in structures of domination and were uncertain about whether we could assume positions of authority. We could not envision assuming oppressive roles. For some of us, failure, failing, being failed began to look like a positive alternative, a way out, a solution. This was especially true for those students who felt they were suffering mentally, who felt that they would never be able to recover a sense of wholeness or well-being. In recent years, campus awareness of the absence of support for international students who have many conflicts and dilemmas in an environment that does not acknowledge their cultural codes has led to the development of support networks. Yet there has been little recognition that there are black students and other non-white students who suffer similar problems, who come from backgrounds where we learned different cultural codes. For example, we may learn that it is important not to accept coercive authoritarian rule from someone who is not a family elder—hence we may have difficulties accepting strangers assuming such a role.

Not long ago, I was at a small party with faculty from a major liberal California university, which until recently had no black professors in the English department who were permanent staff, though they were sometimes visiting scholars. One non-white faculty member and myself began to talk about the problems facing black graduate students studying in English departments. We joked about the racism within English departments, commenting that other disciplines were slightly more willing to accept study of the lives and works of non-white people, yet such work is rarely affirmed in English departments, where the study of literature usually consists of many works by white men and a few by white women. We talked about how some departments were struggling to change. Speaking about his department, he commented that they have only a few black graduate students, sometimes none, that at one time two black students, one male and one female, had been accepted and both had serious mental health problems. At departmental meetings, white faculty suggested that this indicated that black students just did not have the wherewithal to succeed in this graduate program. For a time, no black students were admitted. His story revealed that part of the burden these students may have felt, which many of us have felt, is that our performance will have future implications for all black students and this knowledge heightens one's performance anxiety from the very beginning. Unfortunately, racist biases often lead departments to see the behavior of one black student as an indication of the way all black students will perform academically. Certainly, if individual white students have difficulty adjusting or succeeding within a graduate program, it is not seen as an indication that all other white students will fail.

The combined forces of racism and sexism often make the black female graduate experience differ in kind from that of the black male experience. While he may be subjected to racial biases, his maleness may serve to mediate the extent to which he will be attacked, dominated, etc. Often it is assumed that black males are better able to succeed at graduate school in English than black females. While many white scholars may be aware of a black male intellectual tradition, they rarely know about black female intellectuals. African-American intellectual traditions, like those of white people, have been male-dominated. People who know the names of W.E.B. Du Bois or Martin Delaney may have never heard of Mary Church Terrell or Anna Cooper. The small numbers of black women in permanent positions in academic institutions do not constitute a significant presence, one strong enough to challenge racist and sexist biases. Often the only black woman white professors have encountered is a domestic worker in their home. Yet there are no sociological studies that I know of which examine whether a group who has been seen as not having intellectual capability will automatically be accorded respect and recognition if they enter positions that suggest they are representative scholars. Often black women are such an "invisible presence" on campuses that many students may not be aware that any black women teach at the universities they attend.

Given the reality of racism and sexism, being awarded advanced degrees does not mean that black women will achieve equity with black men or other groups in the profession. Full-time, non-white women comprise less than 3 percent of the total faculty on most campuses. Racism and sexism, particularly on the graduate level, shape and influence both the academic performance and employment of black female academics. During my years of graduate work in English, I was often faced with the hostility of white students who felt that because I was black and female I would have no trouble finding a job. This was usually the response from professors as well if I expressed fear of not finding employment. Ironically, no one ever acknowledged that we were never taught by any of these black women who were taking all the jobs. No one wanted to see that perhaps racism and sexism militate against the hiring of black women even though we are seen as a group that will be given priority, preferential status. Such assumptions, which are usually rooted in the logic of affirmative action hiring, do not include recognition of the ways most universities do not strive to attain diversity of faculty and that often diversity means hiring one non-white person, one black person. When I and other black women graduate students surveyed English departments in the United States, we did not see masses of black women and rightly felt concerned about our futures.

Moving around often, I attended several graduate schools but finally finished my work at the University of California, Santa Cruz, where I found support despite the prevalence of racism and sexism. Since I had much past experience, I was able to talk with white faculty members before entering the program about whether they would be receptive and supportive of my desire to focus on African-American writers. I was given positive reassurance that proved accurate. More and more, there are university settings where black female graduate students and black graduate students can study in supportive atmospheres. Racism and sexism are always present, yet they do not necessarily shape all areas of graduate experience. When I talk with black female graduate students working in English departments, I hear that many of the problems have not changed, that they experience the same intense isolation and loneliness that characterized my experience. This is why I think it is important that black women in higher education write and talk about our experiences, about survival strategies. When I was having a very difficult time, I read *Working It Out*. Despite the fact that the academics who described the way in which sexism had shaped their academic experience in graduate school were white women, I was encouraged by their resistance, by their perseverance, by their success. Reading their stories helped me to feel less alone. I wrote this essay because of the many conversations I have had with black female graduate students who despair, who are frustrated, who are fearful that the experiences they are having are unique. I want them to know that they are not alone, that the problems that arise, the obstacles created by racism and sexism are real—that they do exist—they do hurt but they are not insurmountable. Perhaps these words will give solace, will intensify their courage, and renew their spirit.

45

MENTORS IN VIOLENCE PREVENTION

JACKSON KATZ

Jackson Katz is internationally recognized for his groundbreaking work in gender violence prevention with men and boys, particularly in the sports culture and the military. He is cofounder of the multiracial, mixed-gender Mentors in Violence Prevention (MVP) program at Northeastern University's Center for the Study of Sport in Society. Katz also directs the first worldwide gender violence prevention program in the history of the United States Marine Corps. For more information, see www.jacksonkatz.com.

> *"There's nothing better than excelling at a game you love. There's nothing worse than thinking your accomplishments as a player outweigh your responsibilities as a person."*
>
> —DOUG FLUTIE[1]

> *"If a marine is a great warrior on the battlefield and he comes home and beats his wife, he is not a good marine."*
>
> —LT. GENERAL GEORGE CHRISTMAS,
> UNITED STATES MARINE CORPS (RET.)[2]

It was while in graduate school in the early 1990s that I developed the beginnings of MVP, a program to work with high school and college male student athletes on the issues of rape, battering, sexual harassment, and all forms of men's violence against women. I was not interested in working with "jocks" simply because of their particular problems. There is no question that men's violence against women is a serious problem in the male sports culture—at all levels. Anyone who has paid the slightest attention to the sports pages over the past couple of decades knows how sadly common it is to read about alleged assaults by male athletes. There is a widespread public perception that male college student athletes are disproportionately responsible for acts of sexual aggression against women, although to date no full-scale national studies have conclusively proven this point. But my

---

Jackson Katz, "Mentors in Violence Prevention" ["MVP: Athletes and Marines"], from *The Macho Paradox: Why Some Men Hurt Women and How All Men Can Help* (Naperville, IL: Sourcebooks, Inc., 2006). Reprinted by permission.

interest in the male sports culture had less to do with athlete perpetration and more to do with the leadership platform afforded male athletes. The rationale was simple. Male athletes, as exemplars of traditional masculine success, already have status with their fellow men. If they could be persuaded to speak out about sexual and domestic violence, they could have influence not only in the athletic subculture, but in the larger male culture that continues to look to athletics for definitions of what it means to be a "real man." In particular, leadership from men in athletics could make it safer for other men to "come out" against sexism. Eventually, this would result in a growing intolerance in male culture for some men's sexist violence.

Striking examples of this strategy can be found in politics. Political scientists and historians frequently observe that President Richard Nixon, a renowned anti-communist, was the first U.S. president to open relations to communist China. Because of his anti-communist credentials, no one could credibly accuse Nixon of being a weak-kneed liberal who was ready to sell out American interests to the Chinese. And surely it is more than historical coincidence that Lyndon Johnson, a white southerner from Texas who talked like a good ol' boy, was able to champion civil rights and was critical to the enactment of historic federal civil rights legislation.

Another interesting illustration of this leadership concept comes from the world of beer marketing. Consider this mini-history of Miller Lite beer: In 1972, Miller Brewing Company bought the rights to Meister Brau Light, a "diet" beer the small Chicago brewery had been attempting to market to women. Miller's market research had determined that men wanted a beer that would not fill them up, but they did not want to drink a "feminine" beer. So Miller had a problem, because in 1972 men made up approximately 85 percent of the beer market in the U.S. Miller's strategy was to run an advertising campaign that showed famous football players drinking Miller Lite beer. The most popular featured Dick Butkus, an iconic white linebacker for the Chicago Bears, and Bubba Smith, an iconic African American defensive lineman for the Baltimore Colts. They placed Butkus and Smith in a bar room scene surrounded by their friends, with a Miller Lite beer in their hands. The unspoken message of the campaign was: Dick Butkus and Bubba Smith can drink Lite beer and no one is going to accuse them of being wimps. You can, too. As a result, the Miller Lite campaign became one of the most successful advertising campaigns in TV history. It won Clio awards for advertising excellence in 1977 and 1978, and throughout the 1980s and 1990s Miller Lite was the official beer of the National Football League.

How did a beer travel the distance in just a few short years from being considered a "wimpy diet beer" to becoming the official beer of the NFL? First, a smart marketing person identified the problem. Millions of men are hypersensitive about appearing unmanly, so the challenge is to make it manly to buy the product. The best way is to create an association between the Lite beer and recognizably masculine figures. In other words, if Dick Butkus and Bubba Smith take a "risk" and publicly identify themselves with Lite beer, it is easier for men with less status in the masculine hierarchy to do likewise. The same principle applied in recent years when Mike Ditka, the tough-as-nails football coach, appeared on television commercials and exhorted men to take the "Levitra challenge" and use a male sexual-enhancement drug, or when Rafael Palmiero, the home-run-hitting major league baseball star, made a similar pitch for Viagra.[3]

Why not utilize this approach to get more men to speak out about gender violence? As we have seen, a set of unexamined beliefs in male-peer culture has historically kept men silent. It is wimpy to confront other men's sexism. It is wimpy to question men's enjoyment of women as sex objects. Men who treat women with dignity and respect cannot be real men. What could be more effective to counteract the silencing power of these beliefs than to enlist the support of recognizably masculine men? And where better to find them than the sports culture?

• • •

In 1992 I approached Dr. Richard Lapchick, the civil rights activist and director of Northeastern University's Center for the Study of Sport in Society, and proposed the idea of a program to train high school and college male student athletes to be leaders in gender-violence prevention. With initial funding from the U.S. Department of Education, I, Lapchick, and the center's associate director, Art Taylor, started the Mentors in Violence Prevention (MVP) program in 1993. The program was designed to train student athletes and other student leaders to use their status to speak out against rape, battering, sexual harassment, gay-bashing, and all forms of sexist abuse and violence. A female component was added in the second year with the complementary principle of training female student athletes and others to be leaders on these issues. Today, when MVP is implemented in the sports culture and other educational settings it is a mixed-gender initiative, although a key feature of the model is small-group, single-sex discussions of the issues.

MVP is the most widely utilized gender violence prevention model in college athletics—for both men and women. Numerous Division I athletic programs such as Kentucky, Wisconsin, Notre Dame, and the University of Florida regularly participate in MVP trainings conducted by members of the MVP staff, who are all former college and professional athletes. In 2005, the Southeastern Conference (SEC) became the first major college athletic conference to fund MVP training for schools conference-wide. The National Collegiate Athletic Association uses MVP materials in their Life Skills program. Since 1998, the 2002, 2004, and 2005 Super Bowl champion New England Patriots football club have held MVP trainings each year with the players in rookie camp, along with the coaching staff and front office personnel. The 2004 World Series champion Boston Red Sox implemented the program for the first time in spring training of 2005, along with other sports organizations such as the New York Jets and Major League Lacrosse.

MVP has also been implemented in the United States military. In fact, the MVP program is the first system-wide gender-violence prevention program in the history of the U.S. Marine Corps. MVP trainers have been working all over the world with marines since 1997. MVP trainings and workshops have also been held with officers and enlisted personnel from the army, navy, and air force, as well as personnel from the service academies.

Beyond Sports Culture

Although MVP began in the sports culture and is increasingly utilized there, the MVP model is equally effective with the general population of college and high school students, and in other institutional settings. When a high school implements MVP, for example, student athletes and coaches are typically part of the program, but so are band members, kids in the drama club, and student government leaders—as well as skater kids, smoker kids, and kids who have nothing to do with traditional student leadership groups. On college campuses, athletic programs can implement MVP, but so can the housing department, Greek affairs, health education, and new student orientation.[4]

The MVP model is one of the first educational initiatives to utilize the concept of "bystanders" in an approach to gender-violence and bullying prevention. It focuses on men not as perpetrators or potential perpetrators, but as empowered bystanders who can confront abusive peers—and support abused ones. It focuses on women not as victims or potential targets of harassment, rape, and abuse, but as empowered bystanders who can also take leadership roles. In this model, a "bystander" is defined as a family member, friend, classmate, teammate, coworker—anyone who is imbedded in a family, social, or professional relationship with someone who might be abusive, or experiencing abuse.

The heart of the MVP model is interactive discussion, with both single-sex and mixed-gender applications. One of its goals is better inter-gender dialogue about issues like sexual violence, relationship abuse, and sexual harassment. But single-sex sessions provide young men and women with a comfortable space within which to explore some of the more charged aspects of these difficult subjects. In all-male sessions, men will sometimes say things they simply would not say with women present (and vice versa).

As noted by one of the pioneers of sexual assault prevention education with men, the psychologist Alan Berkowitz, all-male workshops on rape and other forms of gender violence allow men "to speak openly without fear of judgment or criticism by women." This is by no means intended to disparage coeducational learning, or the contributions women make to men's education on this or any other issue. But I and many of my colleagues have cofacilitated countless single-sex discussions where men have said things we know they would not have said if women were present.

Sometimes I wish my female friends and colleagues could eavesdrop on these conversations, because they would be fascinated by the dialogue and impressed by the insightful—and sometimes courageous—comments men make.

For example, one night in the mid-1990s Byron Hurt* and I were conducting a workshop with an entire Division I college football team in the South. The group of a hundred was too big for an intimate conversation, and a lot of guys were joking and making snide remarks. Then a young man in the back rose and addressed his teammates. "You guys laughing and talking better listen to what these guys are saying. My mom went through something like this, and it wasn't pretty," he said. "This shit is serious." The mood in the room instantly changed, and the rest of the session was animated but respectful.

Other times I am thankful there are no women in the room, because some men's misogynistic attitudes and victim-blaming propensities can come pouring out in an all-male setting. In those settings, for example, I have heard more than a few high school boys and college men claim that it is okay to make aggressive sexual comments about girls' bodies to girls in school hallways, in malls, or out on the streets. "Girls like that," some of them will say. "Especially if they dress sexy." When someone points out that regardless of how they dress, girls do not appreciate this sort of male commentary, some guys are dismissive. "What's the big deal anyway? They should get over it." If a young man had the chutzpah to say that in a mixed-gender setting (in my experience, most do not), one of his female peers would more than likely confront him—sometimes angrily. I have seen this happen: A guy makes a victim-blaming comment like "She should have known what to expect," about a woman who was raped at a party. "I can't believe how ignorant some guys are!" one of his female classmates exclaims. "Do guys actually believe that girls like to be treated as if they're in a porn video? You guys are so immature." Her female friends nod or shout out their agreement. Meanwhile, the guy who made the controversial comment desperately tries to defend himself. His friends jump in to support him. The conversation then quickly turns into a "battle between the sexes" with everyone feeling pressured to take the side of their sex. The whole scene sends a strong message to other guys who either agree with the original speaker, have a more complex view of the issue at hand, or completely disagree with him. The message is to stay silent, because they could easily be accused by the girls of being insensitive or sexist, or attacked by the boys for not maintaining male solidarity. The result is that the dialogue is less productive than it could be if people were comfortable being honest.

Chances are a conversation about the same subject in an all-male setting would play out differently. MVP sessions are typically led by people who are slightly older than the target group.[5] They are not authority figures laying down the law, but more like older brothers and sisters there to provide guidance on difficult issues. In many settings, high school juniors and seniors work with incoming ninth graders, or with middle school students. In college, upperclassmen (and upperclasswomen) work with first-year students, etc. A male MVP trainer might respond to the victim-blaming comment by

---

* Editor's note: Byron Hurt is a documentary filmmaker whose most recent film is *Hip Hop: Beyond Beats and Rhymes* (www.bhurt.com).

saying, "Are you sure you want to say that? Doesn't a girl have the right to say no to sex whenever she wants? Wouldn't you want that right for yourself?" This gives the guy a chance to hear another young man's perspective, and while it might challenge his beliefs, it does so in a way that allows him to reconsider, rather than retreat into defensiveness and hostility.

Many all-male (or all-female) MVP sessions begin with an interactive exercise. The exercise is designed to highlight the role of the bystander by asking people to visualize a powerful and clear-cut bystander scenario. MVP trainers explain to participants that they will be asked to visualize a woman (or man) close to them who is being assaulted—physically or sexually—by a man. In most cases, this exercise takes place in single-sex groups, although it has been used in mixed-gender settings (it was originally designed for men only). In either case, MVP trainers are instructed to tell people not to participate if they feel uncomfortable in any way. As the exercise begins, participants are asked to close their eyes (unless they choose not to) and think about a woman (or man) close to them—such as a mother, sister, wife, girlfriend. Then they are asked to imagine that she/he is being assaulted by a man. After they let that sit for a moment, the MVP trainers ask the group to imagine there is another man in the room who is in a position to stop the assault, but he does not. He either stands there and watches, or gets up and leaves. Once people think about this for a few moments, they are asked to open their eyes. As you might expect, men often react strongly to this exercise. They are upset about the assault, and angry at the bystander who failed to act. They often say the bystander is "just as guilty" as the perpetrator. One marine said, "He gets the second bullet."

Then the MVP trainers ask the following questions: how did you feel when you imagined a woman (or man) close to you being assaulted, and how did you feel about the bystander? In answer to the first question, it sometimes takes a while for men to say they felt any emotions aside from the socially approved "masculine" ones of anger and rage. There is no doubt that many men experience a range of feelings, such as powerlessness and sadness. One goal of this exercise is to validate publicly in a roomful of men that it is okay and common for men to have such feelings. But the chief goal of the exercise, and the reason it was created, is to get people to contemplate the role and responsibility of the bystander. The imagined scenario is deliberately clear-cut, and people usually express anger at the bystander for failing to intervene. Anger at the perp, sadness, and helplessness about the victim are also common reactions. Many people—men and women—say they choose not to visualize the scenario because it is too painful or difficult to experience.

But here is the catch. When MVP sessions get into discussions about different real-life bystander scenarios, people often give all sorts of nuanced reasons why they or other bystanders do not or would not get involved. Real life quite often turns out to be a lot more complex than that exercise. By referring back to the clarity of people's perceptions and expectations of the imagined bystander, this comparison makes a powerful point about those nuances and complexities and how they can obscure the central moral question: what can a responsible person do when faced with the opportunity to prevent an act of violence?

MVP uses real-life situations that speak to the experiences of young men and women in college, high school, and other areas of social life. The chief curricular innovation of MVP is a training tool called the Playbook, which consists of a series of realistic scenarios depicting abusive male (and sometimes female) behavior.[6] The scenarios have names that are taken from sports. The Playbook—with separate versions for men and women—transports participants into scenarios as witnesses to actual or potential abuse, and then challenges them to consider a number of concrete options for intervention before, during, or after an incident. Consider the following scenario from the MVP Playbook for high school males, which goes by the name "Slapshot":

> You're in the hallway between classes. You see a couple you know arguing, then you see the guy push his girlfriend into her locker. The guy isn't a close friend of yours, and neither is the young woman, but you do hang around with the same group of people. Nobody else is doing anything.

Many people mistakenly believe that they have only two options in instances of actual or potential violence: intervene physically and possibly expose themselves to personal harm, or do nothing. As a result, in MVP sessions when we initially introduce the idea that bystanders have a responsibility to act, people often voice fears about their safety, and say that they would not want to get involved because the price of intervention is too high. However, physical force and passive acceptance are only two of countless possible options. There are numerous ways that bystanders can prevent, interrupt, or intervene in abusive behaviors, and the majority carry little or no risk of physical confrontation. Since this variety of possible interventions is not always self-evident, part of the process of working with men as bystanders is to introduce them to as many nonviolent, non-threatening options as possible. But first, the MVP model helps men to develop a train of thought about the costs and benefits of intervention:

> This is an ugly situation . . . This guy is being real rough with this girl . . . I wonder what's going on? Should I say something? But if nobody else is stepping in, why should I? If I say something, he might come after me. Am I ready to get into a fight, if it comes to that? What if he's got a weapon? Besides, if he treats her like that and she stays with him, who am I to get involved? Is it any of my business? But if I don't do something, I'm saying it's okay for a guy to abuse a young woman. What should I do in this situation?

Although they focus on specific cases of abuse, MVP scenarios are designed to stimulate wide-ranging discussions about the dynamics of male-peer culture, masculinity, sex, violence, abuses of power, and conformist behavior. In all-male sessions, boys and men discuss such questions as: Why do men hit women? Why do men sexually assault women? How do cultural definitions of manhood contribute to sexual and domestic violence and other sexist behaviors? Why do some men make it clear that they won't accept that sort of behavior from their peers, while others remain silent? How is the silence of peers understood by abusers? What message is conveyed to victims when the abuser's friends don't confront him? Why do some heterosexually identified men harass and beat up gay men? Does the accompanying silence on the part of some of their heterosexual peers legitimize the abuse? Why or why not?

After they read the "train of thought," the facilitators spark discussion with a series of questions designed to explore the role of the bystander:

- Why would a guy who is a bystander in this scenario not say something?
- What are the risks of saying or doing something to interrupt or confront the abusive behavior?
- What is the message to the victim when no one speaks up or acts on her behalf?
- What is the message to the perpetrator when no one confronts him or expresses disapproval of his abusive behavior?
- What, if anything, is the responsibility of the bystander to the victim?
- What, if anything, is the responsibility of the bystander to the perpetrator or potential perpetrator? (Note: in the scenario the bystander is usually positioned as a friend, teammate, or coworker of the boy or man who is being abusive.)

The answers typically reveal a great deal about the dynamics of male-peer cultures and the pressures on young men to conform. For example, many guys admit that they would not be happy to see a guy treat his girlfriend this way, but they would not say anything. The guy who is abusing his girlfriend might be older than him, or bigger. He might be more popular. People might think he is not "cool" if he tries to get involved. It is much easier to intervene in theory than it is when the pressure is on, your palms are sweaty and your heart is pounding.

Once the participants have had time to discuss these questions, the conversation shifts to the options:

1. Nothing. It's none of my business.
2. Attempt to distract the couple somehow, maybe by talking loudly, in order to defuse the situation.
3. Shout out something so that everyone in the hallway hears, like, "Hey, what are you doing? Leave her alone!" and stick around to make sure the situation has "cooled" down.
4. Talk to the girl at some point and let her know I saw what was going on and am willing to help her.

5. Don't do anything immediately. But as soon as possible, that day or later, I should make a point of talking to the guy and suggesting he get some counseling to deal with his abusive behavior.
6. Talk to a group of his friends, and/or talk to a group of her friends. Tell them what I saw and urge the group to make a decision about how to proceed.
7. Talk to my parents, a guidance counselor, the school social worker, a teacher, or the school nurse, and ask their advice on what to do.
8. Personal option.[7]

When he was a member of the original MVP program in the 1990s, the documentary filmmaker Byron Hurt used to recount an incident he witnessed in college. He was in the cafeteria at lunchtime with a group of men and women friends who were seated around a large table. Another male student whom they all knew came into the room, walked over to one of the women and leaned over to tell her something. She kissed him on the cheek. It all seemed innocent enough, until he abruptly reacted to the kiss with anger. He grabbed her by the shirt, lifted her out of her seat, and pushed her up against a concrete post next to the table. She started to cry. Everyone saw what happened, but no one said anything. Not even "hey, what do you think you're doing?" No one asked her if she was all right. Hurt sat there in shocked silence. At the time, he was the quarterback of his college Division I AA football team. He was well-known and well-respected. He was built more like a linebacker than a quarterback. Why didn't he speak up? "The dude was kind of cool," he said. "I was scared and paralyzed by the thought of what might happen if I said something." If the quarterback of the football team is intimidated into silence, imagine the pressure on average guys.

The overall goal of the MVP model is to stimulate dialogue and critical thinking about the ethical choices bystanders face when they witness abusive behaviors, and to help people think through the costs and benefits of action or inaction. It is also to reposition the bystander—the one who speaks out and confronts his abusive peer—as strong and courageous, not "weak," "uncool," or a "narc." It is not appropriate to tell people how they should act in every situation; there are too many unknown variables to be prescriptive. It is likewise not realistic to expect a group of guys to agree about the best course of action to consider in any given scenario, especially since there are no "right" or "wrong" answers. The idea is to provide people with a greater menu of options in the hope that if at some point they are in a position to act, they will have more good options to choose from. The only option discouraged in MVP is to "do nothing."

The following scenario from the college men's playbook, called "Illegal Motion," describes a disturbingly common event:

At a party, you see a friend trying to get an obviously drunk woman to leave with him. She's not just buzzed; she's stumbling over her own feet. You know the woman, and she seems reluctant.

This scenario always sparks lively dialogue, in part because it involves two of the central preoccupations of contemporary college social life: getting drunk and having sex. The MVP trainers ask the men if they would intervene in this situation, and if not, why not. Most college and high school men say they would not. It's not their business, they say. It happens all the time. How do you know it is going to end badly? Many of them have been in these situations—and not only as bystanders. The train of thought gives them more to think about:

> Men and women who are drinking hook up all the time . . . Then again, she looks really drunk. Maybe she's not in a position to make a good decision . . . I know a lot of "date rape" involves alcohol. Could this be one of those situations? . . . But what if I'm overreacting? Won't my friend be mad at me? Will he even listen to me? . . . But if I don't do something, I might be letting her down. What should I do?

After they read the "train of thought," the facilitators spark discussion with a series of questions:

- What, if anything, is the responsibility of the bystander to the drunk woman?
- Does it matter how well you know her, or if you know her at all? How would you feel if a woman you loved found herself in this situation, and no one intervened on her behalf?
- Does it matter how she ended up drunk? Is that relevant? What if you have seen her drunk before? Does that matter? What if someone slipped a roofie in her drink? Is it possible to tell?
- What, if anything, is the responsibility of the bystander to the guy who is trying to "hit it" with her? Does it matter how well you know him? What if he is your teammate or fraternity brother? Do you have a special responsibility to stop him from doing something that could get *him* in trouble?
- How many people here know the state law on the matter of sexual consent involving alcohol? Under the law in every state a person is considered unable to give consent if they are inebriated, which means that if a man sexually penetrates a drunk woman (or man) he can be prosecuted for rape.

I ask the men whom they feel they have a responsibility toward: the woman who is drunk, the man, or both. Their answers are sometimes encouraging, like when they say they care about both of them: her because she is vulnerable, and him because he might get in trouble. But on several occasions I have heard college-aged men state matter-of-factly that if the woman got herself in that predicament and she's eighteen or older, they are not responsible to her because "she knew what she was doing." Those coldly presented sentiments confirm what some feminists have maintained for decades: that in our sexist and increasingly pornographic culture, boys and men are socialized to objectify and dehumanize women—especially young sexually active women.

This is disturbing, but not as revealing as some of the responses by men who say they *would* do something. Some guys say they would "get their friend out of there," because he might do something stupid, or face a false accusation of rape the next day. In other words, help *him* before he puts himself in a compromising situation, be his friend by looking out for *his* interests—not the woman's—in a potential rape scenario. Just as often, guys assert that they would urge the drunk woman's friends to look out for *her* interests by getting her out of there. Many men want to avoid the possibility of a direct confrontation with their friend even when they know he might be trying to take sexual advantage of a drunk and vulnerable young woman. Perhaps they are anxious about the possibility of violence. They might realistically be concerned that the guy could get belligerent and take a swing at them. But their reticence is also undoubtedly rooted in social anxiety, their fear based on an unconscious awareness that if they come to the defense of a vulnerable woman they might be seen as soft or sensitive, and hence lose standing among their peers.

The "Illegal Motion" scenario also provides the context for a discussion about false accusations of rape. Many men in college—athletes, fraternity members, and others—believe they or their friends are at significant risk of being falsely accused of rape by a woman. This phenomenon is what Alan Berkowitz refers to as men's "false fear of false accusation." I do not immediately tell the men how I feel about this fear, but I do share with them the FBI statistic about the number of rapes that are *not* reported: between 80 and 90 percent. In other words, the vast majority of women (and men) who are raped never report it to the officials. I ask them why they think this is. With help they usually come up with many of the key reasons: the rape itself was traumatic, and they don't want to put themselves through the trauma of the legal process; doing a "rape kit" to collect evidence is painful, invasive, and can be highly embarrassing, as medical professionals need to extract pubic hairs and swabs from a woman's genitals or anus; the woman's sexual behavior and character are often attacked by people who take the side of the alleged rapist; perhaps the woman knows the man who raped her and is furious with him, but even so does not want to see him to go to prison. Once the men have gone through this list, I pose the question: if these disincentives are powerful enough to keep the vast majority of actual rape victims from reporting the crime, how realistic is it to believe that large numbers of women are falsely doing so? Why would they want to invite the heartache and social stigma? I always make sure to acknowledge that false reports of rape do occur—in anywhere from 2 to 8 percent of cases, depending on how one defines "false" and whose research they rely on.[8] There is no doubt that being falsely accused of rape is a horrendous and potentially traumatizing experience. It is also important to recognize that men of color have a slightly more justified fear of false accusation, even though it is, as Berkowitz says, primarily a "false fear."

The conversation in an MVP session—whether it is with a group of high school students or in a roomful of marines—really picks up when someone confesses that he would not say anything if he saw one of his boys in a situation like the "Illegal Motion" scenario because "I wouldn't want to be a blocker." A "cock-blocker," or "CB," is a widely used term in the hip-hop generation, but most people over thirty have never heard it, unless they work closely with kids or have kids of their own who speak openly with them. A "CB" refers to a man who gets in the way of another man's "game," or attempt to hook up with a woman. Needless to say it is not a term of endearment. If a guy develops a reputation as a cock-blocker, he risks a possible loss of status in the male hierarchy, which amazingly for many men is too high a price to pay for preventing a possible rape.

Once there is some discussion about these questions, the facilitators move to the options:

1. Do nothing. It's really none of my business.
2. Try to get my friend to leave her alone. Tell him he has to be real careful dealing sexually with a drunk woman.
3. Find some of her friends and try to convince them to get her home safely.
4. Approach the woman and ask her how she feels, and if she wants help getting home.
5. Try to find the person whose apartment or house it is, or someone who seems responsible, and ask them to assist me in defusing this situation.
6. Get a group of my friends together, male and female, and confront my friend, firmly telling him to stop pursuing this drunk woman.
7. Personal option.

. . . One of the enduring lessons of MVP is that when you approach men with the intent of enlisting them as allies in the fight against gender violence—rather than as potential perpetrators—many of them rise to the challenge. Men who have participated in MVP sessions often say the experience was nothing like what they expected. Whether from personal history or paranoia, a lot of men expect to be lectured at in a gender-violence prevention workshop. Many of them are impressed when they find out instead that it's not a lecture but a dialogue, and that rather than being blamed for men's violence against women they are being challenged to do something about it. Jeff O'Brien, who has directed MVP since 1999, tells this story about a session with a professional football team:

> The guys were predictably reluctant as we began our first of three trainings with the group. We had good discussions on the first day, and when we began day two, a big linebacker just bluntly stated

"You guys are some cool motherfuckers . . . when you first showed up I thought this was going to be bullshit, but y'all are keepin' it real." That's a compliment in "guy-speak," and the best way he could express his appreciation for the value of the discussions we were having and still be a "man."

On another occasion, when O'Brien and some colleagues finished a training with an elite college football team, they were given the "double-clap," a gesture reserved for their inner-team activities, and a sign of solidarity and respect. This is notable because MVP trainers do not pander to pampered male athletes—they confront sexist beliefs and victim-blaming statements when they arise and challenge the men to resist peer pressure and become leaders—*off* the field. One indication that the MVP approach resonates with a lot of men is that many of them stay after sessions to talk with the trainers. O'Brien, a former All-American college football player who has conducted hundreds of MVP trainings across the U.S. with high school, college, and professional athletes, explains it this way: "We do gender-violence prevention, but for us this means having honest conversations with guys about how we've all been socialized as men. I believe that most men are longing for male relationships that have some depth and genuineness. Outside of a ninety-minute training, we are complete strangers, yet guys ask us for advice on all sorts of life issues."

NOTES

1. This quote by college and professional football star Doug Flutie comes from the *Coaching Boys Into Men Playbook,* produced and distributed by the Family Violence Prevention Fund. Go to www.endabuse.org for more information about the Coaching Boys Into Men campaign.
2. One of the first things I did when I started working with the Marines in the mid-1990s was to attend a luncheon in the Washington D.C. area in honor of General Christmas's retirement. He said this in his speech.
3. Palmiero, whose reputation was severely damaged when he tested positive for steroids in 2005, made some revealing comments about being a pitchman for Viagra in a 2002 interview with the *Fort Worth Star-Telegram.* As Richard Sandomir reported in the *New York Times* on August 2, 2005, Palmiero said that being the athletic front man for the little blue pill was "not like doing a Nike commercial or something. I think it takes courage, and I think I've got what it takes to do this."
4. The first community to embrace MVP city-wide is Sioux City, Iowa. With visionary leadership from Judy Stafford and Cindy Waitt, and funding from the Waitt Family Foundation, MVP has been implemented in all of the public high schools in that heartland city. The principal of North High School, Alan Heisterkamp, has provided exemplary leadership in bringing in and sustaining MVP, and in developing structures to evaluate and measure outcomes.
5. MVP has been implemented in dozens of high schools and middle schools in eastern Massachusetts. One of the most successful institutionalizations of MVP has been in the Newton, Massachusetts, public schools. Over the past six years, hundreds of Newton high school students have been trained in MVP

and subsequently have given presentations to thousands of middle school students. A Newton public school teacher, Nancy Beardall has been the guiding force and tireless advocate who has nurtured MVP's growth there.

6. MVP playbooks are customized for target populations. For example, there are separate playbooks for high school boys, high school girls, college men, and college women. There are also trainer's guides that accompany each playbook. For information about how to order copies, see www.jacksonkatz.com/playbooks.html.

7. The scenarios in MVP playbooks include several options for bystander intervention before, during, or after an incident, but the list is by no means comprehensive. A "personal option" is included in each scenario to suggest the idea that individual creativity and resourcefulness are critical aspects of successful bystander intervention.

8. The question of how often rape is falsely reported is controversial. Many professionals and researchers in the sexual assault field believe the number to be extremely low. The reason why some studies—such as the Uniform Crime Reports—arrive at a higher number (8 percent) is that in spite of major advances in training in recent years, many law enforcement personnel unilaterally determine rape allegations to be "unfounded" if the alleged victim is drunk or on drugs, presents inconsistencies in her (or his) story, or otherwise does not meet the definition of a sympathetic victim. In some states, as recently as the 1980s rape victims were forced to take lie detector tests, which are not only highly unreliable but also serve to stigmatize victims and discourage them from coming forward.

PART VIII
Paid Work and Unemployment

As noted in the introduction to the readings on education, equality of educational opportunity cannot produce equality in society. Once people enter or attempt to enter the workforce, they face three major obstacles. First, the economic structure blocks many people from finding any type of work at all. Second, the economic structure fails to provide enough jobs that pay a decent wage. Third, discrimination in the workplace limits the progress of many, either by keeping people out or by blocking their upward mobility.

The economic system in the United States privileges a small proportion of the population with large amounts of wealth and leaves a huge proportion with varying degrees of economic difficulty, including brutal poverty. According to sociologist G. William Domhoff, a long-term analyst of power and powerlessness in the United States, in 2001, the top 1 percent of upper-class households owned 33.4 percent of the net worth in the country, while the bottom 80 percent of households held only 15.5 percent of net worth. Between 1990 and 2005, CEO salaries rose 298 percent (adjusted for inflation) while production workers' salaries went up just 4.3 percent.[1] The racial wealth gap is even wider: whites enjoy a median net worth 10 times that of Blacks ($106,400 compared to $10,700), while Latinos' net worth is even lower—$3,000; 26 percent of Native Americans and 13 percent of Asian Americans are poor compared to 8 percent of whites.[2] Many women on welfare struggle to provide basic needs for themselves and their children and face cutoffs when they reach the maximum time allowed on Temporary Assistance for Needy Families (TANF), the 1996 replacement for Aid to Families with Dependent Children (AFDC).

Progressive economists debate ways to redistribute U.S. wealth more fairly by creating a more socialistic economic structure, closing tax loopholes that benefit the rich, or redistributing some of the defense budget to social services and education. But politicians continue to support benefits for the rich and to cut social services. This situation has been exacerbated following September 11, 2001, as a larger proportion of federal and state budgets is now spent on defense and security. Other critics of the system call for tax reform, arguing that the current tax laws treat women unequally.[3]

Many people face the effects of discrimination in the workplace on the basis of gender, race, ability, sexual orientation, or other factors. This discrimination includes sexual and other harassment, blocked access to jobs or promotions, or wage gaps that privilege the earnings of certain groups over others. For example, occupations dominated by women or people of color generally have lower pay scales.[4] Discrimination and prejudice are sometimes confusingly subtle but often there nonetheless.[5] Disability or being gay, lesbian, or transgender can serve as the kiss of death in some work situations.[6] Some recent examples include women earning 76.5 percent of men's wages for the same full-time work in 1999,[7] the exclusion of women from roles as ministers in the Southern Baptist Convention in June 2000,[8] the persistently different experiences of Black and white women in the business world,[9] the persistent harassment of gays and lesbians in the military, leading to more discharges than before the "don't ask, don't tell" policy,[10] and the dismal record of hiring women in most fire departments (not to mention the harassment the few women firefighters typically receive).[11] Around the world, the use of computers has left women segregated at the bottom of the technology hierarchy, as they have become the "data and keyboard drones" of the information world.[12] As an illustration of the pace at which women's wages are catching up with men's, sociologists Irene Padavik and Barbara Reskin report "Since 1964 when Congress outlawed pay discrimination based on sex, women have been catching up with men's earnings at a little less than a half of a percent per year. If this rate of progress continues, the sexes will not earn equal pay until 2055."[13]

The assertion that the pay gap between women and men is caused by discrimination is argued convincingly in a study by economist and former Lieutenant Governor of Massachusetts Evelyn Murphy. Looking both at numbers and at individual women's experiences, she documents how failure to hire, tracking of women into lower-paid jobs, failure to promote, and sexual harassment all contribute to the wage gap.[14] In a recent setback to filing claims of wage discrimination, a May 2007 Supreme Court decision in the case of *Ledbetter v. Goodyear Tire & Rubber Co.* "dealt a near-fatal blow to our ability to use Title VII of the landmark Civil Rights Act of 1964 to remedy pay discrimination based on sex, race, national origin, and other protected grounds. . . . The Court ruled that a Title VII complaint must be filed within 180 days of the specific action that sets discriminatory pay, regardless of its ongoing and continuing discriminatory impact on the employee. As a result, many victims of pay discrimination will be left without an effective remedy, even though their rights have been violated."[15] Thus, if a woman realizes after the 180-day window that her male colleagues have been receiving more pay than she for similar work, she may not sue.

The dearth of high-paying jobs combined with systematic discrimination against many groups leaves large numbers of people in the United States either without work or without adequate income. Even middle-class people are struggling to hold their own, no longer able to assume that they will do as well as their parents. Although home ownership is up because of very low interest rates, many people cannot afford to buy houses like the ones they grew up in, and others cannot buy houses at all.[16] Others, as mentioned in Part VI, are lured by predatory lenders into subprime loans via initial low payments that later they cannot afford; many end up losing their homes.

Even in high-paying contexts, sex discrimination continues. For example, Morgan Stanley recently decided to settle a sex discrimination case, paying $54 million to a group of past and present female employees in one of its securities divisions. Although denying guilt, it chose not to go to trial. It also agreed to provide diversity training focused on enhancing women's success in the firm. Other large securities firms (Merrill Lynch and Smith Barney) have reportedly paid more than $200 million to settle discrimination suits to women who worked for them.[17] In a recent study of women working in Wall Street firms, sociologist Louise Marie Roth found that women earn 29 percent less than men. To remedy this she recommends a ban on gender-stereotyped socializing and clearer performance criteria.[18] Professional occupations can be especially stressful for upwardly mobile people of color. In a study of middle class African American women, Veronica Chambers addressed the conflicts of upward mobility among black heterosexual women. The women she interviewed experienced isolation—feeling not at home in either white or black communities—although some expressed satisfaction at overcoming obstacles.[19]

Sexual harassment in the workplace is a very common experience for women and affects some men as well. In a study of women physicians, 32 percent reported unwanted sexual attention, and 48 percent reported the use of sexist teaching materials during their training.[20] In a 1991 survey by the U.S. Navy, 44 percent of enlisted women and 33 percent of female officers reported sexual harassment within the year prior to responding to the survey. By comparison, 8 percent of enlisted men and 2 percent of male officers reported sexual harassment in the same time period.[21] Work contexts obviously vary in relation to this issue, ranging from a pervasive sexualized atmosphere aimed at many women (as in the case against Mitsubishi that settled for $34 million[22]), to isolated cases of harassment. In 1998, the U.S. Supreme Court decided for the first time that a male-male case of sexual harassment did qualify as sexual harassment under federal law, and other cases followed,[23] even though some people question the appropriateness of that definition of sexual harassment.[24]

Where people are situated in the workplace affects their perception and experience of how fair the workplace is. In the Navy survey just mentioned, men perceived the equal opportunity climate in the Navy to be more positive than did women; white male officers had the most positive perceptions with African American women holding the least positive perceptions; and women who had been sexually harassed had more negative perceptions of the climate than did those who had not been sexually harassed. In another study that compared Black and white women in professional and managerial positions, sociologists Lynn Weber and Elizabeth Higginbotham found that the vast majority of white women perceived no race discrimination in their various workplaces, whereas a large majority of Black women did.[25]

By contrast, some equality gains have been made: Israeli women in 2000 won the right to serve in any army position including combat units,[26] Japanese women won in 2000 a sex discrimination case related to promotion and pay that was filed in 1987,[27] boys have braved teasing and ridicule to become ballet dancers,[28] and Pride at Work, a national organization of gay, lesbian, bisexual, and transgendered labor activists, became an official constituency group of the AFL-CIO in August 1997.[29]

The conflict between work and family is a persistent and unresolved issue facing parents who work outside the home. Women's increased participation in the workforce has exacerbated this.[30] Some corporations are developing "family friendly" policies including such options as flex time, job sharing, child care, and paid family leave. But according to a recent study of one of the top 100 companies for working mothers identified by *Working Woman* magazine, policies that look good on paper are frequently not available to all workers; often this is a result of mothers being pressured not to use the policies.[31] Sociologist Arlie Hochschild, in her book *The Time Bind,* looks at the relationship between work and family and concludes that corporate culture, with its pressure to put in long hours at the office, is to blame for the bind most families are in. She argues for new social values that would encourage spending less time at work and more time with children, family, and community. In support of her position, she cites corporate experiments that have increased efficiency while saving time.[32]

Economist Sylvia Ann Hewlett acknowledges the lack of fit between what she calls "extreme jobs"—70-hour-per-week male competitive model jobs—and many women's needs to have a life outside of work especially as they care for young children and other loved ones. Although 37 percent of professional women stop out of work for a while—she calls this off-ramping—93 percent try to get back into the workforce after an average of just 2.2 years out. As cofounder of the Hidden Brain Drain Task Force (http://www.worklifepolicy.org/documents/initiatives-taskforce.pdf) with business woman Carolyn Buck Luce and professor Cornell West, Hewlett is working with corporations to develop ways to help women who step out of the workforce get back in (on-ramp), and to help business and industry use the deep talent pool that goes unused when professional women and men of color and white women are either kept out entirely or kept out of high positions. Hiring women to work part-time, even one day a week on specific projects, is becoming a viable strategy for some companies. Hewlett is optimistic about both challenging the demands of extreme jobs and finding a way for women to work the amount of time that they want to work. Currently a fourth of women with professional and graduate degrees are not in the work force; two-thirds would like to be working but cannot find jobs that are compatible with raising children. Hewlett thinks that demographics should boost the need for skilled professionals and open space for alternatives to the extreme job model as baby boomers retire, as the U.S. government issues fewer work visas to foreign workers, and as other countries with growing economies attract skilled workers who might otherwise have come here.[33]

The fate of Social Security is especially important to women. If President Bush succeeds in getting support to set up private investment accounts as alternatives to Social Security, women will end up proportionally worse off than men, according to the Institute for Women's Policy Research (IWPR). Among many reasons why the current system is better, IWPR points out that "women rely on Social Security for a larger part of their income in retirement than do men, because women are less likely to have income from pensions than men (30 percent vs. 47 percent) and their pension benefits are less than half of men's on average. Social Security provides more generous benefits to lower earnings for the amount of taxes paid, as compared with higher earnings. Because women have lower earnings on average than men, they benefit from this redistribution toward lower earners. Since women's life expectancy is nearly five years longer than men (80 vs. 75), women rely disproportionately on survivors' benefits, and on the cost of living adjustment in Social Security, which protects them from inflation as they age. Social Security provides benefits to living and surviving spouses. Despite their increasing employment and improved lifetime earnings, 34 percent of women still rely on the spouse benefits (based on their husbands' or ex-husbands' earnings records) for their retirement security." According to IWPR, the changes proposed by the Bush administration do not provide these same protections and are likely to greatly increase poverty levels among older women.[34]

The situation of women workers around the world varies depending on the social support offered by governments. Within Europe, for example, the number of women in paid work is highest in Scandinavia, apparently because of the availability of publicly funded child care. Women in Sweden and Finland had more children than in other European countries for the same reason.[35] On the other hand, some analysts observe that the presence of supportive family leave policies, which also exist in Scandinavia, can reinforce gender segregation in the workplace.[36]

Globalization has had a huge impact on workers worldwide. U.S. corporations have moved many factories to parts of the world where wages are lower. The plight of women who cannot earn a decent living in their home countries and who come to the United States as domestic workers is gaining attention, revealing situations in which the workers live isolated, lonely lives while someone else cares for their children far away in their home countries.[37] These immigrants share many of the experiences of invisibility and disempowerment experienced by Black domestic workers in the United States described by sociologist Judith Rollins.[38]

An estimated 50,000 undocumented workers are trafficked to the United States each year to work as prostitutes, agricultural workers, sweatshop laborers, or domestic workers. Many are enslaved by their employers, have few rights, and often fear for their lives. Only in the late 1990s was there a serious move to prosecute perpetrators of involuntary servitude, especially sexual slavery.[39] Many women work in sweatshop conditions in both the United States and abroad, particularly in the garment industry.[40] Immigration reform was being discussed as this book went to press. The future of an estimated 9.3 million undocumented workers (based on the 2002

Current Population Survey) was on the agenda as politicians weighed the pros and cons of granting paths to permanent residency or citizenship for current undocumented workers, allowing "guest workers" to have temporary work visas, and allowing next of kin to enter the country legally if undocumented people were to become documented.[41]

This part of this book looks at many work issues, including welfare reform in the context of immigration and the global economy (Alejandra Marchevsky and Jeanne Theoharis), the effects of motherhood on earnings (Ann Crittenden), the effect of globalization on women's work and lives worldwide (Barbara Ehrenreich and Arlie Russell Hochschild), the situation of enslaved domestic workers (Joy Zarembka), the global sneaker industry (Cynthia Enloe), and work hazards in three professions—homophobia in male professional team sports and in the military (Eric Anderson and Jeffrey McGowan) and health hazards faced by men serving in the military (Cynthia Daniels). Implied or stated in these pieces are suggestions for change at personal, organizational, and world policy levels.

As you consider these readings, think about the work issues that you and your family and friends have faced—economic and otherwise. Do you know people struggling with poverty? Do you know any undocumented workers or students in the United States? If so, what are their lives like? Have you observed a drop in income among parents who are primary caretakers for their children? Do you think about domestic workers and the risks some of them run to live and work in the United States? Do you ever think about who made your sneakers and what they got paid to do that? Can you imagine a member of the New England Patriots coming out gay? Do you know anyone who was exposed to Agent Orange or Gulf War toxicity? If so, how is their health? Do you know any gay or lesbian members of the military? If so, what was their experience like?

NOTES

1. G. William Domhoff, 2006, "Wealth, Income, Power." http://sociology.ucsc.edu/whorulesamerica/about.html.
2. Meizhu Lui, *Doubly Divided: The Racial Wealth Gap* (Boston: United for a Fair Economy, 2004). www.faireconomy.org.
3. Mimi Abramovitz and Sandra Morgan, *Taxes Are a Woman's Issue: Reframing the Debate* (New York: Feminist Press, 2006).
4. Irene Padavik and Barbara Reskin, *Women and Men at Work*, 2nd ed. (Thousand Oaks, CA: Pine Forge Press, 2002), pp. 108–112.
5. Yanick St. Jean and Joe R. Feagin, "Racial Masques: Black Women and Subtle Gendered Racism," in Nijole V. Benokraitis, ed., *Subtle Sexism: Current Practices and Prospects for Change* (Thousand Oaks, CA: Sage, 1997), pp. 179–200.
6. For a discussion of discrimination against gay men in the workforce, see Martin P. Levine, "The Status of Gay Men in the Workplace," in Michael S. Kimmel and Michael A. Messner, eds., *Men's Lives*, 3rd ed. (Boston: Allyn & Bacon, 1995), pp. 212–24. Michelle Fine and Adrienne Asch report that it is estimated that between 65 percent and 76 percent of women with disabilities

are unemployed: "Disabled Women: Sexism without the Pedestal," in Mary Jo Deegan and Nancy A. Brooks, eds., *Women and Disability: The Double Handicap* (New Brunswick, NJ: Transaction, 1985), pp. 6–22.

7. Associated Press, "Women Said to Earn 76.5% of Men's Wage," *The Boston Globe,* 27 May 2000, p. A10.

8. Brad Liston and Michael Paulson, "Southern Baptists Deliver a 'No' on Women as Pastors," *The Boston Globe,* 15 June 2000, p. A1.

9. Ella J. E. Bell and Stella M. Nkomo, *Our Separate Ways: Black and White Women and the Struggle for Professional Identity* (Boston: Harvard Business School Press, 2001).

10. Debbie Emery, "The Mother of All Witch Hunts," *Out* (June 1996), p. 176.

11. Joseph P. Kahn, "Under Fire," *The Boston Globe Magazine,* 7 December 1997, pp. 19ff; David Armstrong, "Brotherhood Under Fire: Big-City Departments Facing Reform of Closed Culture and Old-Boy Traditions," *The Boston Globe,* 9 January 2000, pp. A1ff.

12. Christa Wichterich, *The Globalized Woman: Reports from a Future of Inequality* (New York: Zed Books, 2000), p. 47.

13. Padavik and Reskin, *Women and Men at Work,* p. 146.

14. Evelyn Murphy with E.J. Graff, *Getting Even: Why Women Don't Get Paid like Men—and What to Do About It* (New York: Simon & Schuster, 2005).

15. Liz Gilchrist, "Supreme Court Moves Backward on Equal Pay," May 30, 2007, National Organization for Women Web site: http://www.now.org/issues/economic/070530equalpay.html.

16. Katherine S. Newman, *Declining Fortunes: The Withering of the American Dream* (New York: Basic Books, 1993).

17. Patrick McGeehan, "Morgan Stanley Settles Bias Suit with $54 Million," *New York Times,* 13 July 2004, p. A1.

18. Louise Marie Roth, *Selling Women Short: Gender and Money on Wall Street* (Princeton, NJ: Princeton University Press, 2006).

19. Veronica Chambers, *Having It All? Black Women and Success* (New York: Doubleday, 2003).

20. M. Catherine Vukovich, "The Prevalence of Sexual Harassment among Female Family Practice Residents in the United States," *Violence and Victims* 11, no. 2 (1996): 175–80.

21. Carol E. Newell, Paul Rosenfeld, and Amy L. Culbertson, "Sexual Harassment Experiences and Equal Opportunity Perceptions of Navy Women," *Sex Roles: A Journal of Research* 32, nos. 3–4 (February 1995): 159–68.

22. Harriet Brown, "After the Suit, How Do Women Fit in at Mitsubishi?" *Ms.,* September/October 1998, pp. 32–36.

23. Thomas M. Sipkins and Joseph G. Schmitt, "Same-Sex Harassers Get Equal Time; After 'Oncale,' Employers Should Consider Implementing Sexual Harassment Policies That Deal with Same-Sex Perpetrators," *The National Law Journal* 20, no. 41 (June 8, 1998): B7; Stephanie Ebbert, "Man Wins Same-Sex Lawsuit Judgment," *The Boston Globe,* 19 June 1998, p. D40.

24. Elizabeth Pryor Johnson and Michael A. Puchades, "Same-Gender Sexual Harassment: But Is It Discrimination Based on Sex?" *Florida Bar Journal,* December 1995, pp. 79–160.

25. Lynn Weber and Elizabeth Higginbotham, "Black and White Professional-Managerial Women's Perceptions of Racism and Sexism in the Workplace," in Elizabeth Higginbotham and Mary Romero, eds., *Women and Work: Exploring Race, Ethnicity, and Class* (Thousand Oaks, CA: Sage, 1997), pp. 153–75.

26. Associated Press, "Israeli Law Lifts Barriers for Women Soldiers," *The Boston Globe,* 5 January 2000, p. 14.

27. Yuri Kageyama, "Women Win Bias Case in Japan," *The Boston Globe,* 23 December 2000, p. A16.

28. Stephen Kiehl, "Difficult Journey of Dance: Braving Taunts, More Boys Turn to Art of Ballet," *The Boston Globe,* 2 August 1998, p. B1.

29. Carol Schachet, "Gay and Lesbian Labor Gains a Voice: Pride at Work Is Officially Recognized by the AFL-CIO," *Resist* 7, no. 5 (June 1998): 1–3.

30. For a history of women's participation in the paid labor force, see Elizabeth Higginbotham, "Introduction" in Elizabeth Higginbotham and Mary Romero, eds., *Women and Work,* pp. xv–xxxii.

31. Jane Kiser, "Behind the Scenes at a 'Family Friendly' Workplace," *Dollars and Sense,* no. 215 (January/February 1998), pp. 19–21.

32. Arlie Russell Hochschild, *The Time Bind: When Work Becomes Home and Home Becomes Work* (New York: Metropolitan Books, 1997).

33. Sylvia Ann Hewlett, *Off-Ramps and On-Ramps: Keeping Talented Women on the Road to Success* (Boston: Harvard Business School Press, 2007).

34. Institute for Women's Policy Research, "Women and Social Security," 2005. http://womenandsocialsecurity.org/Women%5FSocial%5Security.

35. Christa Wichterich, *The Globalized Woman,* p. 99.

36. Deborah Figart and Ellen Mutari, "It's About Time: Will Europe Solve the Work/Family Dilemma?" *Dollars and Sense,* no. 215 (January/February 1998), pp. 27–31.

37. Pierette Hondagneu-Sotelo, *Doméstica: Immigrant Workers Cleaning and Caring in the Shadows of Affluence* (Berkeley: University of California Press, 2001); Rhacel Salazar Parreñas, *Servants of Globalization: Women, Migration, and Domestic Work* (Stanford, CA: Stanford University Press, 2001); Grace Chang, *Disposable Domestics: Immigrant Women Workers in the Global Economy* (Boston: South End Press, 2000).

38. Judith Rollins, *Between Women: Domestics and Their Employers* (Philadelphia: Temple University Press, 1985).

39. Michelle Herrera Mulligan, "Fields of Shame," *Latina* (May 2000), pp. 110ff.

40. Miriam Ching Yoon Louie, *Sweatshop Warriors: Immigrant Women Workers Take on the Global Factory* (Boston: South End Press, 2001).

41. Jeffrey S. Passel, Randolph Capps, and Michael E. Fix. "Undocumented Workers: Facts and Figures," Urban Institute, January 12, 2004: http://www.urban.org/publications/1000587.html.

46

THE END OF WELFARE AS WE KNOW IT
An Overview of the PRWORA*

ALEJANDRA MARCHEVSKY • JEANNE THEOHARIS

Alejandra Marchevsky is associate professor of liberal studies at California State University, Los Angeles.

Jeanne Theoharis is associate professor of political science at Brooklyn College of CUNY. She is coeditor of *Groundwork: Local Black Freedom Movements* (2005) and *Freedom North: Black Freedom Struggles Outside the South, 1940–1980* (2005).

By the mid-1990s, the national debate over "personal responsibility" focused nearly exclusively on the black and immigrant welfare poor— this in spite of the federal government's own statistics showing that poor whites made up the majority of the nation's welfare recipients.[1] Although families on welfare were slightly smaller than the average U.S. family and less than 9 percent of immigrant households received cash public assistance,[2] most politicians and journalists continued to promote the idea that blacks were making careers of having babies just to collect a larger welfare check and Latino immigrants with their overly large families were crossing the border illegally to cash in on American entitlements. While the immigrant population that used public assistance was a diverse sampling of immigrants from Europe, Asia, and Latin America, public images centered on Mexicans and Puerto Ricans (although Puerto Ricans are citizens not immigrants).[3] Rather than describe a government program that kept women and children hovering at the poverty line, but had succeeded in combating widespread hunger in many communities, "welfare" had become a code word for race and the linchpin in a national debate over American culture and citizenship.

Media stories similarly highlighted the substandard work ethic among blacks and Latinos, who allegedly preferred waiting for their next welfare check instead of looking for a job. In reality, three-quarters of welfare recipients did not remain long on welfare but moved from welfare to underpaid work with great frequency.[4] In their comparative study of welfare recipients and single-mothers in low-wage jobs, sociologists Katherine Edin and Laura Lein found that the economic gap between working women and women on welfare (most of whom were also working) was insignificant. Based on their actual incomes and their labor market opportunities, work was not a route out of poverty for either group of women.[5] Edin and Lein's ethnographic findings were confirmed in national data that show that work in the 1990s often did not lift a family out of poverty. While a full-time, minimum-wage worker with two children in the 1970s lived above the poverty line, the same family made $8840 a year in 1995—far below the poverty line of $12,188.[6] For many parents in minimum-wage jobs, AFDC was a necessary means to supplement what they were denied in the private sector: an income they could survive on and health benefits for their family.

Rather than respond to the real demographics of poverty—an inadequate labor market, a lack of childcare and health benefits, urban divestment from social services and public education, and rising college costs—the authors of welfare reform drew upon two-dimensional caricatures of welfare recipients to shape a legislation that would slash welfare numbers and impose moral values on the poor.[7] Almost two-thirds of the 1996 welfare law involved a litany of rules and sanctions on family and sexual life. Already familiar with a punitive system that tracked their personal behavior, welfare recipients now had to navigate a more complicated system of eligibility standards and penalties: mothers under the age of eighteen must be living with an adult and enrolled in school or they lose all benefits; parents convicted of fraud or drug possession (no matter which drug or what quantity) face a lifetime ban on benefits; families who move to a higher benefit state are subject to the lower benefit levels of their home state; and parents who fail to immunize their children or send them to school will lose some or all of their cash benefits.

Alongside these "family values" provisions, the PRWORA established a maximum five-year lifetime limit on cash benefits and stipulated that at least 80 percent of each state's welfare recipients must be working a minimum number of hours within two years. Notably, federal work requirements operate from an "any job is better than welfare" philosophy. States were not required to provide basic education or skills development to their welfare clients or to track employment outcomes and wages through time. Welfare clients who cannot find a job were given a choice of losing all of their benefits or working in the public sector in exchange for a monthly welfare stipend (known as "workfare"). Under PRWORA, workfare participants were not protected under minimum wage provisions or national fair labor standards.

One of the most telling features of workfare has been the use of welfare recipients to replace unionized workers. Since workfare jobs did not have to be newly created jobs, workfare was often used to undermine the successes unions had been gaining in the service sector by replacing full-time salaried workers with part-time below-minimum-wage employees. In New York City, for example, Mayor Rudolph Giuliani fired 22,000 municipal workers and replaced them largely with workfare workers. Part-time workfare workers then constituted three-fourths of the laborforce in the Parks Department and one-third of the Sanitation Department. They also helped staff the city's welfare agency, housing authority, and public hospitals. The fiscal advantage to the city was clear: the average New York City clerical worker's hourly wage is $12.32 not including benefits but a workfare worker costs the city $1.80 an hour for a 20-hour work week and earns no benefits.[8]

This was not the outcome that the architects of the PRWORA put forth. The assumptions behind the work-first provisions of the PRWORA—like those of low-paid immigrant work more broadly—were that welfare recipients would take the jobs that no one else wanted. Reformers played on the racial antagonism of (imagined white) workers toward (imagined colored and free-loading) welfare recipients to distract workers from the economic ramifications of welfare reform and to prevent any alliances between recipients and workers.[9] Thus, workfare in practice not only ensured the public and private sectors of an available, cheap new workforce, but also threatened to drive down wages and force more Americans into poverty.

Welfare reform has also meant big profits for Wall Street. Under generous tax breaks implemented by the Clinton administration, private employers who hire former welfare recipients could deduct up to 50 percent of their employees' wages from their taxes.[10] Large corporations vied for more than $20 billion in federal and state grants to run welfare-to-work services. Maximus, the nation's largest company specializing in government-contracted welfare work, boasted an annual revenue of $127 million and over 1,600 employees nationwide who have taken over the duties of traditional caseworkers in the public sector.[11] Public support of the poor, then, had been replaced with a money trail for corporations.

The Anti-Immigrant Provisions of PRWORA

Alongside this attack on workers' rights, PRWORA also served as a covert means for immigration reform, as it created "new lines of stratification between citizens and noncitizens," making citizenship a requirement for most social entitlements in U.S. society.[12] Whereas in the past, permanent residents and citizens were by and large guaranteed equal access to public assistance, the 1996 law banned noncitizens from food stamp and old-age (SSI) assistance. Only certain refugees and asylees, veterans and their families, and legal immigrants who could provide proof of 40 quarters (or ten years) of work in the United States were exempt from the cut-offs.[13] On August 22, 1996, over one million legal immigrants became ineligible for food stamps, and half a million elderly and disabled immigrants became ineligible for SSI benefits. Although Congress partially restored noncitizen benefits in 1997, 1998, and 2002, the vast majority of legal immigrants remain ineligible for food stamp and old-age assistance.[14]

Along with citizenship status, PRWORA also established timing of arrival as a new criterion for public assistance. Legal immigrants who arrive after August 1996 became ineligible for all means-tested federal benefits (including cash assistance, food stamps, SSI, public health insurance, and public housing) for their first five years in the United States.[15] Even after they have met this five-year waiting requirement, immigrants now confront a system in which it is much riskier to apply, and harder to qualify, for assistance. New rules introduced in 1996 make immigrant sponsors legally responsible for their charges for up to five years, and also stipulate that when an immigrant applies for assistance, his or her income and resources be "deemed" to include the sponsor's income and resources.[16] In effect, federal law requires legal immigrants to demonstrate much higher levels of need than citizens in order to qualify for assistance.

A less-publicized feature of welfare reform was its frontal attack on illegal immigration. Under AFDC, undocumented immigrants were not eligible for public assistance, but their U.S.-born children were. While this distinction remains in place, all state agencies who receive federal funding are required "to furnish the INS with the name and address of, and any other identifying information about, any individual who the [agency] knows is unlawfully in the United States."[17] This reporting requirement was accompanied by a new system of information sharing between public service agencies and the INS. Previously prohibited by federal law, welfare caseworkers can now directly contact immigration agents for information about their clients. An undocumented mother who applies for public assistance for her U.S.-born child risks the threat, not only of deportation, but also of having to repay any public benefits that were improperly received (whether or not there is proven intent to deceive).[18] The implications of these new rules for undocumented immigrants move far beyond the sphere of the welfare system, transforming every public service agency into an arm of the INS.

The PRWORA's assault on immigrant rights was enhanced by two additional laws passed by Congress in the same year. The Illegal Immigration Reform and Immigrant Responsibility Act (IIRIRA), ratified in September 1996, allocated billions of dollars to border enforcement, opened up new interagency collaboration between the INS and local police authorities, and greatly expanded the power of the state to arrest and deport "criminal aliens." Its companion bill, the Antiterrorism and Effective Death Penalty Act, passed in April 1996, expedited procedures for the removal of "alien terrorists," including providing state and local authorities access to confidential immigration and naturalization files through court order. Together these three laws stripped noncitizens of the right to due process (a cornerstone of American civil liberties) and created a heightened anti-immigrant climate that would pave the way for the intensified offensive against immigrant rights in the wake of September 11th.[19] The labor market benefits of this legislation should not be underestimated. As Parenti argues in *Lockdown America,* secret detentions, expedited deportations, and stepped-up INS raids of immigrant workplaces and neighborhoods provide an invaluable service to American employers by intimidating immigrant workers from demanding better wages, organizing unions, and protesting inhumane working conditions. Moreover, immigration scholars Philip Kretsedemas and Ana Aparicio note that the devolution of federal authority to local government and service providers has placed job creation "in the hands of local labor markets" and enabled a fine-tuning of welfare-to-work policy to the specific needs of local employers. As they conclude, "This policy regime has increased the pressures that poor immigrants already face to take immediate available work opportunities, often in the informal and lowest-paying sectors of the economy."[20]

Welfare's Missing in Action: Assessing the Aftermath of the PRWORA

No sooner had President Clinton signed the PRWORA into law, than Republicans and Democrats were jostling for airtime, eager to take credit for ending a morally corrupt entitlement system. Celebrants of welfare reform, from members of Congress to state governors to the mainstream press, rushed to publish statistics and rosy human interest stories of dropping welfare numbers as evidence of the success of "ending welfare as we knew it."[21] Between 1993 and 1997 (though the PRWORA had just passed in 1996), Clinton's Council of Economic Advisors reported, almost three million recipients had fallen off the rolls, a 20 percent drop nationwide.[22] By the summer of 1999, Clinton would once again declare welfare reform a success, citing new evidence that 35 percent of all welfare recipients had moved into work or "work-related activities."[23] And in 2002, the Bush administration reported that the number of welfare recipients in the United States had dropped by 62 percent, or over nine million people, between 1993 and 2001.

As with much of the public debate that enshrouded welfare reform, these statistics were largely tautological. Poor families were leaving the welfare rolls because they were being pushed off of welfare.[24] As states rushed to secure federal block grants by reducing their welfare rolls, welfare review boards found that half of the cases they reviewed, where recipients had lost some or all of their benefits, were the result of erroneous state action.[25] By 2002, experts reported that at any given time about one-third of all recipients in the nation were under sanction for failing to comply with welfare regulations—a doubling of the sanction rate since 1996.[26] According to the Commission on Civil Rights, however, white recipients were less likely to be sanctioned: "There are disparities in access to and utilization of services, there is discrimination in the delivery of welfare benefits, whether intentional or not, and civil rights considerations are paramount."[27] Welfare politics in the United States had become a numbers game. Politicians could cite changes that happened before the 1996 passage as evidence of the success of welfare reform, and states could count multiple exits by the same family as proof that they are reducing their rolls, yet did not keep records of return applications or explain how applicants left the rolls or what happened to them once off public assistance.

The labor market effects of welfare reform have also been significant. Introducing a large body of low-wage workers into the labor market has driven up competition for low-wage jobs and driven down wages. A 1997 study of what kinds of jobs would be available to low-skilled welfare recipients in the Midwest, for example, found "twenty-two workers for each job that pays at least a poverty wage; sixty-four workers for every job that pays 150 percent of poverty ($18,417/year); and ninety-seven workers for each job at a living wage ($25,907/year for a family of three)."[28] Even in regions with significant job growth, rising employment rates have been accompanied by rising poverty rates and growing class polarization. Out of the 300,000 new jobs created in Los Angeles County between 1993 and 1999, for example, the vast majority pay less than $25,000 a year, and barely one in ten averages above $60,000. Los Angeles's transformation into a polarized economy is further evidenced by the fact the region's economic recovery has "yielded no net jobs in industries that pay solid middle-class salaries."[29] With the fastest growing job category into the twenty-first century, according to the Bureau of Labor Statistics, being cashiers, job creation in most U.S. cities is concentrated in industries that specialize in poverty wages and flexible labor arrangements.[30] Moreover, larger economic trends confirm welfare reform's benefits to employers. In countries with narrowing social assistance—United States, Great Britain, Canada, Japan, and Australia—the relative wages of low-skilled workers fell, but in European countries with higher benefits, despite rising unemployment, wages remained stable. Within the United States "reform" has depressed wages. One Salt Lake City official told the *New York Times* that "without the welfare people . . . we would have had to raise the wage . . . maybe 5 percent."[31] Thus, the "economic miracle" of the New Economy looked more like a crisis from the vantage point of low-income families.

One of the untold stories of TANF* (which has cost the federal government $4 billion more than AFDC) was the ways that states and private companies have gained financially since 1996. While framed within an anti-government discourse, welfare reform neither limited government spending nor government intervention in people's lives. Before the passage of PRWORA, states spent 80 percent of their welfare budgets on actual cash relief; by 2001, this dropped to 50 percent with the rest going to private companies, nonprofits, and the states themselves to administer programs and monitor poor women.[32] For instance, most of the money being collected from "deadbeat dads" is being kept by the state and not shared with the family—with the understanding that the state deserves child support collections because it has been "the Man" supporting

---

Editor's Note: Temporary Assistance to Needy Families and Aid to Families with Dependent Children.

these women. Maximus, Lockheed Martin IMS, Citigroup, Randstad, and Electronic Data Systems (Ross Perot's company), to name a few, all secured multihundred-million-dollar contracts and reaped significant profits in the PRWORA market. This despite evidence of fraud; accused of mismanagement and corruption in Los Angeles, New York, and Milwaukee, Maximus still received contracts to provide welfare services in all 50 states and every major city and county in the nation.

While private firms receiving millions in public contracts and employer tax breaks are subject to little oversight, people who continue to receive public assistance are required to negotiate an ever-more complicated maze of rules, regulations, and restrictions. Before a hungry family can apply for the food stamps they are entitled to under law, they must complete an application that averages 12 pages, eight pages longer than applications for a federal firearms permit or a school bus driver's license. Another study in Ohio concluded that a typical recipient would likely face "770 questions related to personal and financial circumstances" and regulations covered in 4,300 pages with another 2,000 pages of clarification.[33] Bureaucratic hurdles and stepped-up state surveillance of poor families have successfully produced a 33 percent decrease in food stamp applications—matched by what local charities and social service agencies report as a threefold increase in the demand for emergency food services. Such surveillance produces a climate of fear—by compromising poor women's access to privacy and due process, many recipients would "voluntarily" disenroll to escape this surveillance.

Equally alarming was the cynical shift in welfare discourse after 1996. Having created the much-maligned character of the welfare recipient, federal and state welfare agencies in partnership with private industry now needed to resuscitate the image of welfare recipients in order to get businesses to hire them. Across billboards and on the radio, these "welfare-to-work partnerships" launched advertising campaigns to promote welfare recipients as ideal employees by publicizing the same information that had been obscured in debates to reform welfare: welfare recipients want to work and have work experience, welfare recipients have on average two children and are conscientious about work and their children.[34] Yet, neither these portraits of welfare recipients as "ordinary Americans," nor the celebratory stories of former recipients as "heroic working mothers" that flooded newspapers and news magazines after 1996, tell the whole story of welfare reform. The same media sources that characterized welfare reform as a success also published separate findings showing that the number of families lacking health care was increasing precipitously, that food pantries and emergency shelters were reporting increased need, that childcare was a major problem for most families, and that children whose parents have workfare jobs (or have found other low-wage work) were watching more television, being supervised less, and not doing better in school. What is telling, then, is that this accumulation of data provided no significant momentum to undercut the fundamental consensus about the success of the legislation.

Conclusion: A Post-National, Post-Racial World?

Despite these alarming trends, American journalists as well as readers, politicians as well as voters, continue myopically to applaud the drop in welfare numbers by turning away from a broader analysis of the nature of work and poverty in the global economy. As recent studies of welfare reform show, job growth and rising employment rates are not reliable indicators of poverty reduction in this post-Fordist economy. Rather, poverty is today a product of work for those Americans at the bottom of the socioeconomic structure, as it is for the majority of workers around the world. The trends we see in the United States—the erosion of wages, benefits, and working conditions, the incorporation of greater numbers of women, racial minorities, and immigrants into the low-wage workforce, and widening class divisions—are magnified at the global level as multinationals migrate freely and continuously across national borders in search of bigger profits.

Welfare reform, like NAFTA, followed from the logic of global free trade: open the market, get rid of the artificial barriers and subsidies, and all will have the chance to prosper. Yet, neither PRWORA nor NAFTA dismantled the barriers to economic and racial equality so much as recast globalization through a mix of neoclassical economics and bootstrap individualism. Thus, while supporters of NAFTA proposed "to bridge the racial and cultural borders that divide the Americas," and to "empower" Mexican workers by granting them entry into a First World economy, NAFTA supporters tellingly never proposed opening the border or extending U.S. citizenship to Mexican migrants.[35] Similarly, proponents of the PRWORA celebrated American ideals of opportunity and responsibility, while chipping away at the labor protections that could provide former recipients with actual opportunity in the workplace.[36] The effect of these policies on both sides of the border is greater economic and social instability, as more than a million and a half Mexican workers lost their jobs through NAFTA, and as millions of recipients and their children in the United States race against the welfare clock in search of a sustainable livelihood.

Citing the expansive reach of multinational corporations and the increased mobility of people and commodities across national borders, critics across the political spectrum have charged that globalization has resulted in the decline of the power of the nation-state and meanings of American nationalism.[37] However, while framed through an anti-government discourse, neoliberal policies like welfare reform do not reduce government so much as reshape it. As the social state is "downsized" through the elimination and privatization of social services, schools, hospitals, and transportation, the positive public benefits that were once the hallmark of U.S. citizenship are increasingly accessible only to those who can afford them. At the same time, as states replace schools with prisons, cities rush to grow their police forces, and the Border Patrol doubles in size, the punitive arm of the state extends its surveillance over the nation's poor. The result is a federal government that actively facilitates the flexibility of capital by forcing millions of workers into a deregulated labor market, while it erects higher barriers to full citizenship in the national community. That contemporary efforts to circumscribe the benefits of citizenship continue to posit people of color, both immigrant and U.S.-born, as national outsiders further suggests that the symbolic power of white Americanism has not suffered under globalization.

In this newly privatized civil society, where U.S. citizens-qua-consumers are presumably "empowered" to choose their schools as well as their racial identities, those individuals who freely make the wrong choices are marked (workfare workers in NYC are required to wear a bright orange vest), punished, or "rehabilitated." Motivational counselors, job club programs, and individualized work plans all bombard welfare recipients with a post-feminist discourse of women's "self-sufficiency," and encourage them to associate their children's well-being with a minimum-wage paycheck. In this way, welfare recipients today report a decline in all indicators of family well-being—from income, to nutrition, to quality time with their children—and yet often still conclude that working has improved their self-esteem and made them better mothers. This individualization of free choice bolsters the ideology of meritocracy at the heart of post-1960s American politics by locating choice in the private, psychological terrain of the "self," thus obscuring the ways in which choices are themselves structured by political economy. The tautological nature of this ideology is evident in the equation of good and bad choices with class and racial position. In post–civil rights America, the nation can call upon welfare recipients to achieve "self-sufficiency" in a labor market that lacks adequate wages, safe childcare, decent medical coverage, and affordable housing, and, in the same breath, blame the continued marginalization of black and Latina workers on their self-defeating cultures and unfortunate lifestyle choices. The ideology of "choice" ultimately rests on racialized and gendered ideas about what kinds of work and remuneration different kinds of people deserve, while simultaneously ensuring that those on the losing end of the globalization equation are made responsible for their own failure and subjection.

NOTES

1. In fact, most welfare recipients were white, lived in the suburbs, were in their twenties and thirties, and had two kids. Michael Moore, *Downsize This* (New York, 1997), 69.
2. "Welfare: Facts and Fiction" in *Ms.* (May/June 1995), 93; U.S. Census, "Selected Characteristics of the Foreign-Born Population by Year of Entry and Selected Countries of Birth," 1990.
3. Comparing Mexican immigrants to Middle Eastern and Asian immigrants in California, William A. V. Clark found that Mexicans have the highest poverty rate and the lowest welfare dependency rate of all three groups. Clark, *California Cauldron*, 76. Similarly, after examining U.S. Census data from 1990 (ibid.), we found that Mexican immigrants received AFDC at a slightly higher rate than Russian immigrants (3.1 percent to 2.4 percent, respectively), but that

Russians received "other welfare" (SSI, food stamps, etc.) at a much higher rate than Mexicans (7.5 percent compared to less than 1 percent). Furthermore, the percentages are significantly higher for Vietnamese, Laotian, and Cambodian immigrants in part due to the connection between public assistance and refugee resettlement policy.

4. Numerous studies have shown that women on welfare want to work and do so when they can find jobs. "Over a two-year interval . . . the typical mother held 1.7 jobs during that period. Forty-four percent held two or more jobs." David Zucchino, *The Myth of the Welfare Queen* (New York, 1997), 64.

5. Kathryn Edin and Laura Lein, *Making Ends Meet: How Single Mothers Survive Welfare and Low-Wage Work* (New York, 1997).

6. "Welfare: Facts and Fiction," 93.

7. Such caricatures were so symbolically powerful that the new TANF system seemed to be designed with them in mind. For example, although faced with evidence that teenage mothers make up a small minority of all welfare recipients, welfare policymakers nonetheless concentrated their efforts on combating teen pregnancy.

8. Vanessa Tait, "'Workers Just Like Anyone Else': Organizing Workfare Unions in New York City," in *Still Lifting, Still Climbing: African American Women's Contemporary Activism,* ed. Kimberly Springer (New York, 1999), 304–305.

9. While most unions did not break with Clinton or Congress over the legislation, since its passage, new coalitions and organizing efforts have begun to form. A number of SEIU and AFSCME locals as well as community groups such as the Kensington Welfare Rights Union have begun the work of bringing together welfare recipients and union workers to see their common interests.

10. Tait, 314. Under the Work Opportunity Tax Credit, employers who hire a TANF recipient can claim up to 40 percent of that employee's first-year wages (not to exceed $2,400). Under the Welfare To Work Tax Credit, employers who hire an AFDC or TANF recipient who has received welfare for at least 18 consecutive months can claim 35 percent of that employee's first-year wages, and 50 percent of that employee's second-year wages.

11. Adam Cohen, "When Wall Street Runs Welfare," *Time Magazine* (March 23, 1998). Valerie Polakow cites a similar example of Lockheed Martin, the weapons industry giant and now private welfare administrator, in *A New Introduction to Poverty,* ed. Louis Kushnik and James Jennings (New York, 1999), 168.

12. Audrey Singer, "Welfare Reform and Immigrants: A Policy Review," in *Immigrants, Welfare Reform, and the Poverty of Policy,* 22–25. Singer notes that this new citizenship criterion departs from past U.S. policy and international standards; in most industrialized democracies, permanent residents are eligible for the same benefits as citizens.

13. While the work documentation requirement would be hard for any citizen to meet, it was nearly impossible for an immigrant population concentrated in informal and seasonal employment.

14. During the summer of 1997, due largely to the efforts of immigrant advocacy groups and, interestingly, agribusiness lobbyists (who sought to protect a steady supply of cheap immigrant farm labor), Congress passed the Balanced Budget Act. This legislation restored limited food stamp benefits to "pre 8/22" legal immigrant children, seniors, and disabled persons, Hmong Vietnam era veterans, and extended benefits to refugees and asylees from five to seven years. Congress also changed the PRWORA's provision that prohibits states from using federal funds to aid legal immigrants to allow states to *purchase* federal food stamps for legal immigrants. Numerous states with large immigrant populations provide limited food stamps to legal immigrants under this provision. California and New York, for

example, have used state funds to purchase federal food stamps for children, elderly, and disabled legal immigrants. Texas provides such benefits to elderly and disabled legal immigrants. See DeLaet, *U.S. Immigration Policy,* 108–109.

15. Immigrants who arrived in the United States after the passage of PRWORA were ineligible for food stamps and SSI until they became naturalized citizens. This changed under the Farm Security and Rural Investment Act of 2002, which established a five-year waiting period for "qualified immigrants," exempted children from the waiting period, and made "qualified immigrants" eligible for disability-related insurance, regardless of their date of entry.

16. California Immigrant Welfare Collaborative, *Immigrants and Welfare in California* (Spring 1998), Section B, 1–36. Even prior to the passage of the PRWORA, federal legislation moved toward restrictions on immigrant eligibility for public benefits. The 1990 Immigration Act required that sponsors sign an "Affidavit of Support" stating that they will support the immigrant at 125 percent of the poverty line until that immigrant becomes a U.S. citizen or works for 40 "qualifying quarters." Under such affidavits, sponsors also assume financial responsibility for any public costs incurred by the legal immigrant under their sponsorship.

17. Lynn H. Fujiwara, "Asian Immigrant Communities and Welfare Reform," in *Whose Welfare?* Gwendolyn Mink, ed. (Ithaca, NY, 1999), 125.

18. By December 1997, there were reports that INS officials were unlawfully stopping legal immigrants at the border and at airports and making repayment of legally obtained public benefits a condition for reentry into the United States. See, for example, December 17, 1997 letter from the U.S. Department of Health and Human Services to State TANF Directors regarding this matter. *Immigrants and Welfare in California,* Tab H.9.

19. The USA PATRIOT Act passed by Congress with little debate in October 2001 permits the detention of noncitizens for mere suspicion of "terrorist" involvement, expands terrorism laws to include "domestic terrorism," denies readmission to the United States of foreign nationals for engaging in free speech, and allows the indefinite detainment of noncitizens in six-month increments without meaningful judicial review. As legal scholar David Cole writes in *Enemy Aliens* (New York, 2003), "[F]or purposes of regulating immigration, "terrorist activity" is defined much more expansively, to include support of the otherwise lawful and nonviolent activities of virtually any group that has used violence, and any use of threat to use a weapon against person or property ("other than for mere personal monetary gain"). . . . With the stroke of the pen, President Bush denied foreign nationals basic rights of political association, political speech, due process, and privacy" (58).

20. Kretsedemas and Aparicio 9. Parenti advances a similar argument in chapter 7 of *Lockdown America.*

21. There has been much less coverage of the rising activism in the face of these devastating changes. From workfare organizing in New York City, to the Economic Human Rights campaign of the Kensington Welfare Rights Union, to community protests in the Mission Hill section of Boston, the activism of former welfare recipients and their allies has not fit with the prevailing celebration of welfare reform and thus received little media attention.

22. Lisa Dodson in *Don't Call Us Out of Name* (Boston, 1998) cautions, "When we find one of the many low-income mothers who has found a better place, more education, a decent job, a chance to develop, let us all recall history . . . the vast majority of families on welfare have always moved on, moved up through their own tenacious determination, with the help of their family and decent programs for real education and opportunity" (224).

23. James Gerstenzang, "Clinton Touts Welfare-To-Work Progress," *Los Angeles Times,* August 4, 1999, A-3.

24. Beginning in the mid-1980s, and culminating with the passage of the PRWORA, numerous states had been carving away at cash and food stamp assistance, making it easier for caseworkers to terminate clients' benefits and imposing strict work requirements and behavioral rules. Even before the federal overhaul in 1996, over half of the nation's recipients were covered by state welfare rules that, without the waiver program implemented by the Reagan administration in 1986, would have violated federal law.

25. Barbara Vobejda and Judith Haveman, "Sanctions Fuel Drop in Welfare Rolls," *Washington Post,* March 23, 1998, A01.

26. Sharon Hays, *Flat Broke with Children* (New York, 2003), 41.

27. U.S. Commission on Civil Rights, "A New Paradigm for Welfare Reform," 2002, 1.

28. Mark Weisbrot, "Welfare Reform: The Jobs Aren't There," http://www.rtk.net/preamble/welfjobs/fulltex.2.html. Cited in Mink, *Whose Welfare? 2.*

29. Don Lee, "L.A. County Jobs Surge Since '93, but Not Wages," *Los Angeles Times,* July 26, 1999, A-1.

30. John MacArthur, *The Selling of "Free Trade": NAFTA, Washington, and the Subversion of American Democracy* (New York, 2000), 19. See, for example, the Urban Institute's study of welfare reform's labor market effects on 20 metropolitan areas: Robert Lerman, Pamela Loprest, and Caroline Ratcliffe, "How Well Can Urban Labor Markets Absorb Welfare Recipients?" (New York: Urban Institute, 2000).

31. Frances Fox Piven, "Welfare and Work," in *Whose Welfare?,* 88.

32. Stephen Pimpare, *The New Victorians: Poverty, Politics, and Propaganda in Two Gilded Eras* (New York, 2004).

33. John Gilliom, *Overseers of the Poor: Surveillance, Resistance, and the Limits of Privacy* (Chicago, 2001), 103.

34. See, for example, the website of the Welfare-to-Work Partnership (www.welfaretowork.org), a nonprofit organization created and governed by the CEOs of corporations like United Airlines, Burger King, Sprint, Monsanto, and UPS.

35. This language describing NAFTA is drawn from a 1995 *Los Angeles Times* 16-article special section entitled "The Melding Americas." Claiming that the borders between the Americas are dissolving through free trade and the democratization of Latin America, most of the *Times* stories focused on the "The Cultural Ties [That] Mend Continental Divide." The transnationalism celebrated in this special section was one undergirded by a "universal" (American) consumer ethic, as article after article glowed over the success of U.S. performers (Gloria Estefan, Edward James Olmos, and Jean-Claude Van Damme) and other consumer commodities in the Latin American market. A similar blend of "global Americanism" was evident when President Clinton lauded NAFTA as an opportunity to export American ideals throughout the continent. *Los Angeles Times,* "Special Section: The Melding Americas," July 18, 1994, Section D.

36. On the day President Clinton signed the PRWORA, he extolled how the new law would restore "America's basic bargain of providing opportunity and demanding in return responsibility." *New York Times,* August 23, 1996, A1.

37. For varying renditions of this argument, see: Linda Basch, Nina Glick Schiller, and Cristina Szanton Blanc, *Nations Unbound: Transnational Projects, Postcolonial Predicaments, and Deterritorialized Nation-States* (Amsterdam, 1994); Brimelow, *Alien Nation;* Brubaker, *Immigration and the Politics of Citizenship in Europe and North America;* Geyer, *Americans No More;* and Peter Schuck and Rogers Smith, *Citizenship without Consent: Illegal Aliens in the American Polity* (New Haven, CT, 1985).

47

SIXTY CENTS TO A MAN'S DOLLAR

ANN CRITTENDEN

Ann Crittenden is the author of *Killing the Sacred Cows: Bold Ideas for a New Economy* (1993). A former reporter for *The New York Times* and a Pulitzer Prize nominee, she has also been a reporter for *Fortune,* a financial writer for *Newsweek,* a visiting lecturer at M.I.T. and Yale, and an economics commentator for CBS News. She lives with her husband and son in Washington, DC.

In the Bible, in Leviticus, God instructs Moses to tell the Israelites that women, for purposes of tithing, are worth thirty shekels while men are worth fifty—a ratio of 60 percent.[1] For fifty years, from about 1930 to 1980, the value of employed women eerily reflected that biblical ratio: The earnings of full-time working women were only 60 percent of men's earnings. In the 1980s, that ratio began to change. By 1993, women working full-time were earning an average of seventy-seven cents for every dollar men earned. (In 1997, the gap widened again, as the median weekly earnings of full-time working women fell to 75 percent of men's earnings.)

But lo and behold, when we look closer, we find the same old sixty cents to a man's dollar. The usual way to measure the gender wage gap is by comparing the hourly earnings of men and women who work full-time year-round. But this compares only the women who work like men with men—a method that neatly excludes most women. . . . [O]nly about half of the mothers of children under eighteen have full-time, year-round paying jobs.[2]

To find the real difference between men's and women's earnings, one would have to compare the earnings of *all* male and female workers, both full- and part-time. And guess what one discovers? The average earnings of all female workers in 1999 were 59 percent of men's earnings.[3] Women who work for pay are still stuck at the age-old biblical value put on their labor.

My research turned up other intriguing reflections of the 60 percent ratio: A survey of 1982 graduates of the Stanford Business School found that ten years after graduation, the median income of the full- and part-time employed female M.B.A.s amounted to $81,300, against the men's median income of $139,100. Again, the women's share is 58 percent. Another study, of 1974 graduates of the University of Michigan Law School, revealed that in the late 1980s the women's average earnings were 61 percent of the men's— despite the fact that 96 percent of the women were working, and that the men and women were virtually identical in terms of training. The authors of this study concluded that the women's family responsibilities were "certainly the most important single cause of sex differences in earnings."[4]

Conservatives frequently tout women's economic gains in order to charge that women's advocates who haven't folded their tents and gone home must be making up things to complain about. In a polemic titled *Who Stole Feminism?* Christina Hoff Sommers lambasts feminist activists for wearing a button stating that women earn fifty-nine cents to a man's dollar, which, she claims, is "highly misleading and now egregiously out of date."[5] Sommers is right if we skim over what she calls such "prosaic matters" as the fact that people who have primary responsibility for a child have different work patterns from people without caring responsibilities. But if we are interested in the real differences in the earnings of employed men and women, those buttons still tell the real story.

The Cost of Being a Mother

A small group of mostly female academic economists has added another twist to the story. Their research reveals that working mothers not only earn less than men, but also less per hour than childless women, even after such differences as education and experience are factored out. The pay gap between mothers and nonmothers under age thirty-five is now larger than the wage gap between young men and women.

The first comprehensive estimates of the cost of motherhood in terms of lost income were made in England by Heather Joshi of the City University in London and Hugh Davies of Birkbeck College of the University of London. The two economists estimated that a typical middle-class British mother of two forfeits almost *half* of her potential lifetime earnings.[6]

In the United States, similar work has been done by Jane Waldfogel at Columbia University. Waldfogel set out to assess the opportunity cost of motherhood by asking exactly how much of the dramatic wage gains made by women in the 1980s went to women without family responsibilities. How many of the female winners in the 1980s were people like Donna Shalala, Janet Reno, Elizabeth Dole, and Carole Bellamy, the director of UNICEF: childless women whose work patterns were indistinguishable from those of traditional males.

Back in the late 1970s, Waldfogel found, the difference between men's and women's pay was about the same for all women. Nonmothers earned only slightly higher wages. But over the next decade things changed.[7] By 1991, thirty-year-old American women without children were making

90 percent of men's wages, while comparable women with children were making only 70 percent. Even when Waldfogel factored out all the women's differences, the disparity in their incomes remained—something she dubbed the "family wage gap."[8]

———

Why do working mothers earn so much less than childless women? Academic researchers have worried over this question like a dog over a bone but haven't turned up a single, definitive answer.[9]

Waldfogel argues that the failure of employers to provide paid maternity leaves is one factor that leads to the family wage gap in the United States. This country is one of only six nations in the world that does not require a paid leave. (The others are Australia, New Zealand, Lesotho, Swaziland, and Papua New Guinea.)[10] With no right to a paid leave, many American mothers who want to stay at home with a new baby simply quit their jobs, and this interruption in employment costs them dearly in terms of lost income. Research in Europe reveals that when paid maternity leaves were mandated, the percentage of women remaining employed rose, and women's wages were higher, unless the leaves lasted more than a few months.[11]

In the United States as well, women who are able to take formal paid maternity leave do not suffer the same setback in their wages as comparably placed women who do not have a right to such leaves. This is a significant benefit to mothers in the five states, including California, New York, and New Jersey, that mandate temporary disability insurance coverage for pregnancy and childbirth.[12]

Paid leaves are so valuable because they don't seem to incur the same penalties that employers impose on even the briefest of unpaid career interruptions. A good example is the experience of the 1974 female graduates of the University of Michigan Law School. During their first fifteen years after law school, these women spent an average of only 3.3 months out of the workplace, compared with virtually no time out for their male classmates. More than one-quarter of the women had worked part-time, for an average of 10.1 months over the fifteen years, compared with virtually no part-time work among the men. While working full-time, the women put in only 10 percent fewer hours than full-time men, again not a dramatic difference.

But the penalties for these slight distinctions between the men's and women's work patterns were strikingly harsh. Fifteen years after graduation, the women's average earnings were not 10 percent lower, or even 20 percent lower, than the men's, but almost 40 percent lower. Fewer than one-fifth of the women in law firms who had worked part-time for more than six months had made partner in their firms, while more than four-fifths of the mothers with little or no part-time work had made partner.[13]

Another survey of almost 200 female M.B.A.s found that those who had taken an average of only 8.8 months out of the job market were less likely to reach upper-middle management and earned 17 percent less than comparable women who had never had a gap in their employment.[14]

Working-class women are also heavily penalized for job interruptions, although these are the very women who allegedly "choose" less demanding occupations that enable them to move in and out of the job market without undue wage penalties. The authors of one study concluded that the negative repercussions of taking a little time out of the labor force were still discernible after twenty years.[15] In blue-collar work, seniority decides who is eligible for better jobs, and who is "bumped" in the event of layoffs. Under current policies, many women lose their seniority forever if they interrupt their employment, as most mothers do. Training programs, required for advancement, often take place after work, excluding the many mothers who can't find child care.[16]

Mandatory overtime is another handicap placed on blue-collar mothers. Some 45 percent of American workers reported in a recent survey that they had to work overtime with little or no notice.[17] In 1994 factory workers put in the highest levels of overtime ever reported by the Bureau of Labor Statistics in its thirty-eight years of tracking the data. Where does that leave a woman who has to be home in time for dinner with the kids? Out of a promotion and maybe out of a job. Increasingly in today's driven workplace, whether she is blue- or white-collar, a woman who goes home when she is supposed to go home is going to endanger her economic well-being.

The fact that many mothers work part-time also explains some of the difference between mother's and comparable women's hourly pay. (About 65 percent of part-time workers are women, most of whom are mothers.)[18] Employers are not required to offer part-time employees equal pay and benefits for equal work. As a result, nonstandard workers earn on average about 40 percent less an hour than full-time workers, and about half of that wage gap persists even for similar workers in similar jobs.

Many bosses privately believe that mothers who work part-time have a "recreational" attitude toward work, as one Maryland businessman assured me. Presumably, this belief makes it easier to justify their exploitation. But the working conditions they face don't sound very much like recreation. A recent survey by Catalyst, a research organization focused on women in business, found that more than half of the people who had switched to part-time jobs and lower pay reported that their workload stayed the same. Ten percent reported an increase in workload after their income had been reduced. Most of these people were mothers.[19]

Another factor in the family wage gap is the disproportionate number of mothers who operate their own small businesses, a route often taken by women who need flexibility during the child-rearing years. Female-owned small businesses have increased twofold over small businesses owned by men in recent years.[20] In 1999, women owned 38 percent of all U.S. businesses, compared with only 5 percent in 1972, a remarkable increase that is frequently cited as evidence of women's economic success. One new mother noted that conversations at play groups "center as much on software and modems as they do on teething and ear infections."[21]

Less frequently mentioned is the fact that many of these women-owned businesses are little more than Mom-minus-Pop operations: one woman trying to earn some money on the side, or keep her career alive, during the years when her children have priority. Forty-five percent of women-owned businesses are home-based. And the more than one-third of businesses owned by women in 1996 generated only 16 percent of the sales of all U.S. businesses in that year.[22]

In 1997, although women were starting new businesses at twice the rate of men, they received only 2 percent of institutional venture capital, a principal source of financing for businesses with serious prospects for growth. Almost one-quarter of female business owners financed their operations the same way that they did their shopping: with their credit cards.[23]

Some researchers have suggested that mothers earn less than childless women because they are less productive. This may be true for some mothers who work at home and are subject to frequent interruptions, or for those who are exhausted from having to do most of the domestic chores, or distracted by creaky child-care arrangements. But the claim that mothers have lower productivity than other workers is controversial and unproven. It is easier to demonstrate that working mothers face the same old problem that has bedeviled women in the workplace for decades.

It's Discrimination, Stupid

It is revealing that those occupations requiring nurturing skills, such as child care, social work, and nursing, are the most systematically underpaid, relative to their educational and skill demands.[24] These are also, of course, the occupations with the highest percentage of females. But men who are primary caregivers also pay a heavy price: a "daddy tax," if you will. This suggests that at least part of the huge tax on mothers' earnings is due to work rules and practices and habits of mind that discriminate against anyone, of either sex, who cannot perform like an "unencumbered" worker. In other words, discrimination against all good parents, male or female.

Surveys have found that wives may adore husbands who share the parenting experience, but employers distinctly do not. A majority of managers believe that part-time schedules and even brief parental leaves are inappropriate for men.[25] When Houston Oiler David Williams missed one Sunday game to be with his wife after the birth of their first child, he was docked $111,111.

A survey of 348 male managers at twenty Fortune 500 companies found that fathers from dual-career families put in an average of *two* fewer hours per week—or about 4 percent less—than men whose wives were at home. That was the only difference between the two groups of men. But the fathers with working wives, who presumably had a few more domestic responsibilities, earned almost 20 percent less. There it is again: a 20 percent family wage gap.[26]

"Face time still matters as much or more than productivity in many companies," Charles Rodgers, a management consultant in Boston, said. Rodgers told me about a man in a high-tech company who regularly came to work two hours early so that he could occasionally leave early for Little League games with his son. He was given a poor performance rating.[27]

Such discrimination is hard to quantify, but it is potentially a powerful political issue. When the Clinton administration announced that it was banning employment discrimination against *parents* working in the federal government, there were so many calls to a White House staffer assigned to the case that her machine stopped taking messages.

Only eight states currently have laws prohibiting discrimination against parents in the workplace. Examples include taking a primary parent off a career track out of an assumption that the individual couldn't do the work; hiring someone without children over a more qualified person with children; forcing a primary parent to work overtime, or else; and refusing to hire a single parent, though the employer hires single, childless people. In the course of my reporting, I encountered numerous mothers who felt that their employer's refusal to arrange a shorter workweek, particularly after the birth of a second baby, amounted to career-destroying discrimination.

NOTES

1. Amity Shales, "What Does Woman Want?" *Women's Quarterly* (summer 1996): 10.
2. According to June O'Neill, an economist and former head of the Congressional Budget Office, "Full-time year-round workers are not likely to be representative of all workers. Women are less likely to be in this category than men." See June O'Neill and Solomon Polachek, "Why the Gender Gap in Wages Narrowed in the 1980s," *Journal of Labor Economics* 2, no. 1, pt. 1 (1993): 208–9.
3. U.S. Bureau of the Census, Current Population Reports, *Money Income in the U.S.: 1995,* Washington, D.C., March 2000, P60-209, pp. 46–49.
4. Robert G. Wood, Mary E. Corcoran, and Paul N. Courant, "Pay Differentials Among the Highly-Paid: The Male-Female Earnings Gap in Lawyers' Salaries," *Journal of Labor Economics* 11, no. 3 (1993): 417–41.
5. Christina Hoff Sommers, *Who Stole Feminism?* (New York: Simon & Schuster, 1994), p. 240.
6. The estimate of a 47 percent loss of lifetime earnings was presented by Hugh Davies at a session of the Allied Social Science Association in New York City on January 4, 1999. It is based on the British Household Poll Survey of 1994. Using earlier data, Davies and Joshi calculated that the mommy tax on a typical British secretary was the equivalent of $324,000—not counting lost pension benefits. See Heather Joshi, "Sex and Motherhood as Handicaps in the Labour Market," in *Women's Issues in Social Policy,* ed. Mavis Maclean and Dulcie Grove (London: Routledge, 1991), p. 180. See also Heather Joshi, "The Cost of Caring," in *Women and Poverty in Britain: The 1990's,* ed. Carol Glendenning and Jane Millar (New York: Harvester Wheatsheaf, 1992), p. 121. Also see Heather Joshi and Pierella Paci, *Unequal Pay for Men and Women* (Cambridge, Mass.: M.I.T. Press, 1998).
7. Jane Waldfogel, "Women Working for Less: Family Status and Women's Pay in the US and UK," Malcolm Wiener Center for Social Policy Working Paper D-94–1, Harvard University, 1994.

8. Jane Waldfogel, "Understanding the 'Family Gap' in Pay for Women with Children," *Journal of Economic Perspectives* 12, no. 1 (winter 1998): 137–56. See also Waldfogel, "The Family Gap for Young Women in the United States and Britain," *Journal of Labor Economics* 11 (1998): 505–19. Looking at two different cohorts of young women, one averaging age thirty in 1981 and the other about thirty in 1990, Waldfogel found that the nonmothers' wages rose from 72 percent to 90 percent of men's between 1981 and 1990. But the wages of mothers rose less, from 60 percent to only 70 percent of men the same age during the same period. The more children a woman had, the lower her earnings, even with all other factors being equal.

   Waldfogel also uncovered a wage gap of 20 percentage points for young women in the United Kingdom. Nonmothers at age thirty-three earn 84 percent of men's pay, while mothers earn only 64 percent. See Jane Waldfogel, "The Family Gap for Young Women in the US and UK: Can Maternity Leave Make a Difference?" Malcolm Wiener Center for Social Policy, Harvard University, October 1994, pp. 1, 20.

9. See Paula England and Michelle Budig, "The Effects of Motherhood on Wages in Recent Cohorts: Findings from the National Longitudinal Survey of Youth," unpublished paper, 1999.

10. Elizabeth Olson, "U.N. Surveys Paid Leave for Mothers," *New York Times*, February 16, 1998.

11. Christopher J. Ruhm, "The Economic Consequences of Parental Leave Mandates: Lessons from Europe," *Quarterly Journal of Economics* CXIII, no. 1 (1998): 285–317. Ruhm found that longer leaves (of nine months or more) were associated with a slight reduction in women's relative wages, but Waldfogel discovered that mothers in Britain who exercised their right to a ten-month paid maternity leave and returned to their original employer had wages no different from those of childless women.

   See also "Working Mothers Then and Now: A Cross-Cohort Analysis of the Effects of Maternity Leave on Women's Pay," in *Gender and Family Issues in the Workplace,* ed. Francine Blau and Ronald Ehrenberg (New York: Russell Sage Foundation, 1997).

12. Heidi Hartmann, Institute for Women's Policy Research, personal communication, January 8, 1995. Hartmann's research has shown that fully 11 percent of women who have no paid leave have to go on public assistance during their time with a new baby.

13. Wood, Corcoran, and Courant, "Pay Differentials," pp. 417–28.

14. This 1993 study was coauthored by Joy Schneer of Rider University's College of Business Administration and Frieda Reitman, professor emeritus at Pace University's Lubin School of Business.

15. Joyce Jacobsen and Arthur Levin, "The Effects of Intermittent Labor Force Attachment on Female Earnings," *Monthly Labor Review* 118, no. 9 (September 1995): 18.

16. For a good discussion of the obstacles to mothers' employment in relatively well-paying blue-collar work, see Joan Williams, *Unbending Gender: Why Family and Work Conflict and What to Do About It* (New York: Oxford University Press, 2000), pp. 76–81.

17. This survey of 1,000 workers was conducted by researchers at the University of Connecticut and Rutgers University, and was reported in the *Wall Street Journal,* May 18, 1999.

18. A survey of more than 2,000 people in four large corporations found that 75 percent of the professionals working part-time were women who were doing so

because of child-care obligations. Only 11 percent of the male managers surveyed expected to work part-time at some point in their careers, compared with 36 percent of women managers. *A New Approach to Flexibility: Managing the Work/Time Equation* (New York: Catalyst, 1997), pp. 25–26.

19. There is other evidence that many so-called part-timers are increasingly working what used to be considered full-time—thirty-five to forty hours a week—for lower hourly pay than regular full-timers. See Reed Abelson, "Part-time Work for Some Adds Up to Full-Time Job," *New York Times,* November 2, 1998.

20. In the five years from 1988 through 1992, the number of women-owned sole proprietorships, partnerships, and similar businesses soared 43 percent, compared with overall growth of 26 percent in such businesses. *Wall Street Journal,* January 29, 1996.

21. Tracy Thompson, "A War Inside Your Head," *Washington Post Magazine,* February 15, 1998, p. 29.

22. Information on women-owned businesses provided by the National Foundation for Women Business Owners in Washington, D.C., September 2000.

23. Noelle Knox, "Women Entrepreneurs Attract New Financing," *New York Times,* July 26, 1998.

24. For the relatively low value placed on the caring professions, see Paula England, George Farkas, Barbara Kilbourne, Kurt Beron, and Dorothea Weir, "Returns to Skill, Compensating Differentials, and Gender Bias: Effects of Occupational Characteristics on Wages of White Women and Men," *American Journal of Sociology* 100, no. 3 (November 1994): 689–719.

25. On corporate attitudes toward part-time work for men, see the study cited in note 17. Another study found that 63 percent of large employers thought it was inappropriate for a man to take *any* parental leave, and another 17 percent thought it unreasonable unless the leave was limited to two weeks or less. Martin H. Malin, "Fathers and Parental Leave," *Texas Law Review* 72 (1994): 1047, 1089; cited in Williams, *Unbending Gender,* p. 100.

26. This study, by Linda Stroh of Loyola University, was reported by Tamar Lewin, "Fathers Whose Wives Stay Home Earn More and Get Ahead, Studies Find," *New York Times,* October 12, 1994.

27. Charles Rodgers, personal communication, October 1993.

48

GLOBAL WOMAN

BARBARA EHRENREICH • ARLIE RUSSELL HOCHSCHILD

Barbara Ehrenreich is the author of *Bait and Switch: The (Futile) Pursuit of the American Dream* (2006), *Nickel and Dimed: On (Not) Getting by in America* (2002), *Blood Rites: Origins and History of the Passions of War* (1998), and numerous other works.

Arlie Russell Hochschild is the author of *The Second Shift* (2003), *The Time Bind* (2001), and *The Commercialization of Intimate Life and Other Essays* (2003). She teaches sociology at the University of California at Berkeley.

"Whose baby are you?" Josephine Perera, a nanny from Sri Lanka, asks Isadora, her pudgy two-year-old charge in Athens, Greece.

Thoughtful for a moment, the child glances toward the closed door of the next room, in which her mother is working, as if to say, "That's my mother in there."

"No, you're *my* baby," Josephine teases, tickling Isadora lightly. Then, to settle the issue, Isadora answers, "Together!" She has two mommies—her mother and Josephine. And surely a child loved by many adults is richly blessed.

In some ways, Josephine's story—which unfolds in an extraordinary documentary film, *When Mother Comes Home for Christmas,* directed by Nilita Vachani—describes an unparalleled success. Josephine has ventured around the world, achieving a degree of independence her mother could not have imagined, and amply supporting her three children with no help from her ex-husband, their father. Each month she mails a remittance check from Athens to Hatton, Sri Lanka, to pay the children's living expenses and school fees. On her Christmas visit home, she bears gifts of pots, pans, and dishes. While she makes payments on a new bus that Suresh, her oldest son, now drives for a living, she is also saving for a modest dowry for her daughter, Norma. She dreams of buying a new house in which the whole family can live. In the meantime, her work as a nanny enables Isadora's parents to devote themselves to their careers and avocations.

But Josephine's story is also one of wrenching global inequality. While Isadora enjoys the attention of three adults, Josephine's three children in Sri Lanka have been far less lucky. According to Vachani, Josephine's youngest child, Suminda, was two—Isadora's age—when his mother first left home to work in Saudi Arabia. Her middle child, Norma, was nine; her oldest son, Suresh, thirteen. From Saudi Arabia, Josephine found her way first to Kuwait, then to Greece. Except for one two-month trip home, she has lived apart from her children for ten years. She writes them weekly letters, seeking news of relatives, asking about school, and complaining that Norma doesn't write back.

Although Josephine left the children under her sister's supervision, the two youngest have shown signs of real distress. Norma has attempted suicide three times. Suminda, who was twelve when the film was made, boards in a grim, Dickensian orphanage that forbids talk during meals and showers. He visits his aunt on holidays. Although the oldest, Suresh, seems to be on good terms with his mother, Norma is tearful and sullen, and Suminda does poorly in school, picks quarrels, and otherwise seems withdrawn from the world. Still, at the end of the film, we see Josephine once again leave her three children in Sri Lanka to return to Isadora in Athens. For Josephine can either live with her children in desperate poverty or make money by living apart from them. Unlike her affluent First World employers, she cannot both live with her family and support it.

Thanks to the process we loosely call "globalization," women are on the move as never before in history. In images familiar to the West from television commercials for credit cards, cell phones, and airlines, female executives jet about the world, phoning home from luxury hotels and reuniting with eager children in airports. But we hear much less about a far more prodigious flow of female labor and energy: the increasing migration of millions of women from poor countries to rich ones, where they serve as nannies, maids, and sometimes sex workers. In the absence of help from male partners, many women have succeeded in tough "male world" careers only by turning over the care of their children, elderly parents, and homes to women from the Third World. This is the female underside of globalization, whereby millions of Josephines from poor countries in the south migrate to do the "women's work" of the north—work that affluent women are no longer able or willing to do. These migrant workers often leave their own children in the care of grandmothers, sisters, and sisters-in-law. Sometimes a young daughter is drawn out of school to care for her younger siblings.

This pattern of female migration reflects what could be called a world-wide gender revolution. In both rich and poor countries, fewer families can rely solely on a male breadwinner. In the United States, the earning power of most men has declined since 1970, and many women have gone out to "make up the difference." By one recent estimate, women were the sole, primary, or coequal earners in more than half of American families.[1] So the question arises: Who will take care of the children, the sick, the elderly? Who will make dinner and clean house?

While the European or American woman commutes to work an average twenty-eight minutes a day, many nannies from the Philippines, Sri Lanka, and India cross the globe to get to their jobs. Some female migrants from the Third World do find something like "liberation," or at least the chance to become independent breadwinners and to improve their children's material lives. Other, less fortunate migrant women end up in the control of criminal employers— their passports stolen, their mobility blocked, forced to work without pay in brothels or to provide sex along with cleaning and child-care services in affluent homes. But even in more typical cases, where benign employers pay wages on time, Third World migrant women achieve their success only by assuming the cast-off domestic roles of middle- and high-income women in the First World—roles that have been previously rejected, of course, by men. And their "commute" entails a cost we have yet to fully comprehend.

The migration of women from the Third World to do "women's work" in affluent countries has so far received little scholarly or media attention—for reasons that are easy enough to guess. First, many, though by no means all, of the new female migrant workers are women of color, and therefore subject to the racial "discounting" routinely experienced by, say, Algerians in France, Mexicans in the United States, and Asians in the United Kingdom. Add to racism the private "indoor" nature of so much of the new migrants' work. Unlike factory workers, who congregate in large numbers, or taxi drivers, who are visible on the street, nannies and maids are often hidden away, one or two at a time, behind closed doors in private homes. Because of the illegal nature of their work, most sex workers are even further concealed from public view.

At least in the case of nannies and maids, another factor contributes to the invisibility of migrant women and their work—one that, for their affluent employers, touches closer to home. The Western culture of individualism, which finds extreme expression in the United States, militates against acknowledging help or human interdependency of nearly any kind. Thus, in the time-pressed upper middle class, servants are no longer displayed as status symbols, decked out in white caps and aprons, but often remain in the background, or disappear when company comes. Furthermore, affluent careerwomen increasingly earn their status not through leisure, as they might have a century ago, but by apparently "doing it all"—producing a full-time career, thriving children, a contented spouse, and a well-managed home. In order to preserve this illusion, domestic workers and nannies make the house hotel-room perfect, feed and bathe the children, cook and clean up— and then magically fade from sight.

The lifestyles of the First World are made possible by a global transfer of the services associated with a wife's traditional role—child care, homemaking, and sex—from poor countries to rich ones. To generalize and perhaps oversimplify: in an earlier phase of imperialism, northern countries extracted natural resources and agricultural products—rubber, metals, and sugar, for example—from lands they conquered and colonized. Today, while still relying on Third World countries for agricultural and industrial labor, the wealthy countries also seek to extract something harder to measure and quantify, something that can look very much like love. Nannies like Josephine bring the distant families that employ them real maternal affection, no doubt enhanced by the heartbreaking absence of their own children in the poor countries they leave behind. Similarly, women who migrate from country to country to work as maids bring not only their muscle power but an attentiveness to detail and to the human relationships in the household that might otherwise have been invested in their own families. Sex workers offer the simulation of sexual and romantic love, or at least transient sexual companionship. It is as if the wealthy parts of the world are running short on precious emotional and sexual resources and have had to turn to poorer regions for fresh supplies.

There are plenty of historical precedents for this globalization of traditional female services. In the ancient Middle East, the women of populations defeated in war were routinely enslaved and hauled off to serve as household workers and concubines for the victors. Among the Africans brought to North America as slaves in the sixteenth through nineteenth centuries, about a third were women and children, and many of those women were pressed to be concubines, domestic servants, or both. Nineteenth-century Irishwomen—along with many rural Englishwomen—migrated to English towns and cities to work as domestics in the homes of the growing upper middle class. Services thought to be innately feminine—child care, housework, and sex—often win little recognition or pay. But they have always been sufficiently in demand to transport over long distances if necessary. What is new today is the sheer number of female migrants and the very long distances they travel. Immigration statistics show huge numbers of women in motion, typically from poor countries to rich. Although the gross statistics give little clue as to the jobs women eventually take, there are reasons to infer that much of their work is "caring work," performed either in private homes or in institutional settings such as hospitals, hospices, child-care centers, and nursing homes.

The statistics are, in many ways, frustrating. We have information on legal migrants but not on illegal migrants, who, experts tell us, travel in equal if not greater numbers. Furthermore, many Third World countries lack data for past years, which makes it hard to trace trends over time; or they use varying methods of gathering information, which makes it hard to compare one country with another. Nevertheless, the trend is clear enough for some scholars, including Stephen Castles, Mark Miller, and Janet Momsen, to speak of a "feminization of migration."[2] From 1950 to 1970, for example, men predominated in labor migration to northern Europe from Turkey, Greece, and North Africa. Since then, women have been replacing men. In 1946, women were fewer than 3 percent of the Algerians and Moroccans living in France; by 1990, they were more than 40 percent.[3]

Overall, half of the world's 120 million legal and illegal migrants are now believed to be women.

Patterns of international migration vary from region to region, but women migrants from a surprising number of sending countries actually out-number men, sometimes by a wide margin. For example, in the 1990s, women make up over half of Filipino migrants to all countries and 84 percent of Sri Lankan migrants to the Middle East.[4] Indeed, by 1993 statistics, Sri Lankan women such as Josephine vastly outnumbered Sri Lankan men as migrant workers who'd left for Saudi Arabia, Kuwait, Lebanon, Oman, Bahrain, Jordan, and Qatar, as well as to all countries of the Far East, Africa, and Asia.[5] About half of the migrants leaving Mexico, India, Korea, Malaysia, Cyprus, and Swaziland to work elsewhere are also women. Throughout the 1990s women outnumbered men among migrants to the United States, Canada, Sweden, the United Kingdom, Argentina, and Israel.[6]

Most women, like men, migrate from the south to the north and from poor countries to rich ones. Typically, migrants go to the nearest compara-tively rich country, preferably one whose language they speak or whose religion and culture they share. There are also local migratory flows: from northern to southern Thailand, for instance, or from East Germany to West. But of the regional or cross-regional flows, four stand out. One goes from Southeast Asia to the oil-rich Middle and Far East—from Bangladesh, Indonesia, the Philippines, and Sri Lanka to Bahrain, Oman, Kuwait, Saudi Arabia, Hong Kong, Malaysia, and Singapore. Another stream of migration goes from the former Soviet bloc to western Europe—from Russia, Romania, Bulgaria, and Albania to Scandinavia, Germany, France, Spain, Portugal, and England. A third goes from south to north in the Americas, including the stream from Mexico to the United States, which scholars say is the longest-running labor migration in the world. A fourth stream moves from Africa to various parts of Europe. France receives many female migrants from Morocco, Tunisia, and Algeria. Italy receives female workers from Ethiopia, Eritrea, and Cape Verde.

Female migrants overwhelmingly take up work as maids or domestics. As women have become an ever greater proportion of migrant workers, receiving countries reflect a dramatic influx of foreign-born domestics. In the United States, African-American women, who accounted for 60 percent of domestics in the 1940s, have been largely replaced by Latinas, many of them recent migrants from Mexico and Central America. In England, Asian migrant women have displaced the Irish and Portuguese domestics of the past. In French cities, North African women have replaced rural French girls. In western Germany, Turks and women from the former East Germany have replaced rural native-born women. Foreign females from countries outside the European Union made up only 6 percent of all domestic workers in 1984. By 1987, the percentage had jumped to 52, with most coming from the Philippines, Sri Lanka, Thailand, Argentina, Colombia, Brazil, El Salvador, and Peru.[7]

The governments of some sending countries actively encourage women to migrate in search of domestic jobs, reasoning that migrant women are more likely than their male counterparts to send their hard-earned wages to their families rather than spending the money on themselves. In general, women send home anywhere from half to nearly all of what they earn. These remittances have a significant impact on the lives of children, parents, siblings, and wider networks of kin—as well as on cash-strapped Third World governments. Thus, before Josephine left for Athens, a program sponsored by the Sri Lankan government taught her how to use a microwave oven, a vacuum cleaner, and an electric mixer.

Over the last thirty years, as the rich countries have grown much richer, the poor countries have become—in both absolute and relative terms—poorer. Global inequalities in wages are particularly striking. In Hong Kong, for instance, the wages of a Filipina domestic are about fifteen times the amount she could make as a schoolteacher back in the Philippines. In addition, poor countries turning to the IMF or World Bank for loans are often forced to undertake measures of so-called structural adjustment, with disastrous results for the poor and especially for poor women and children. To qualify for loans, governments are usually required to devalue their currencies, which turns the hard currencies of rich countries into gold and the soft currencies of poor countries into straw. Structural adjustment programs also call for cuts in support for "noncompetitive industries," and for the reduction of public services such as health care and food subsidies for the poor. Citizens of poor countries, women as well as men, thus have a strong incentive to seek work in more fortunate parts of the world.

But it would be a mistake to attribute the globalization of women's work to a simple synergy of needs among women—one group, in the affluent countries, needing help and the other, in poor countries, needing jobs. For one thing, this formulation fails to account for the marked failure of First World governments to meet the needs created by its women's entry into the workforce. The downsized American—and to a lesser degree, western European—welfare state has become a "deadbeat dad." Unlike the rest of the industrialized world, the United States does not offer public child care for working mothers, nor does it ensure paid family and medical leave. Moreover, a series of state tax revolts in the 1980s reduced the number of hours public libraries were open and slashed school-enrichment and after-school programs. Europe did not experience anything comparable. Still, tens of millions of western European women are in the workforce who were not before—and there has been no proportionate expansion in public services.

Secondly, any view of the globalization of domestic work as simply an arrangement among women completely omits the role of men. Numerous studies, including some of our own, have shown that as American women took on paid employment, the men in their families did little to increase their contribution to the work of the home. For example, only one out of every five men among the working couples whom Hochschild interviewed for *The*

Second Shift in the 1980s shared the work at home, and later studies suggest that while working mothers are doing somewhat less housework than their counterparts twenty years ago, most men are doing only a little more.[8] With divorce, men frequently abdicate their child-care responsibilities to their ex-wives. In most cultures of the First World outside the United States, powerful traditions even more firmly discourage husbands from doing "women's work." So, strictly speaking, the presence of immigrant nannies does not enable affluent women to enter the workforce; it enables affluent *men* to continue avoiding the second shift.

The men in wealthier countries are also, of course, directly responsible for the demand for immigrant sex workers—as well as for the sexual abuse of many migrant women who work as domestics. Why, we wondered, is there a particular demand for "imported" sexual partners? Part of the answer may lie in the fact that new immigrants often take up the least desirable work, and, thanks to the AIDS epidemic, prostitution has become a job that ever fewer women deliberately choose. But perhaps some of this demand, as we see in Denise Brennan's [work] on sex tourism, grows out of the erotic lure of the "exotic."[9] Immigrant women may seem desirable sexual partners for the same reason that First World employers believe them to be especially gifted as caregivers: they are thought to embody the traditional feminine qualities of nurturance, docility, and eagerness to please. Some men feel nostalgic for these qualities, which they associate with a bygone way of life. Even as many wage-earning Western women assimilate to the competitive culture of "male" work and ask respect for making it in a man's world, some men seek in the "exotic Orient" or "hot-blooded tropics" a woman from the imagined past.

Of course, not all sex workers migrate voluntarily. An alarming number of women and girls are trafficked by smugglers and sold into bondage. Because trafficking is illegal and secret, the numbers are hard to know with any certainty. Kevin Bales estimates that in Thailand alone, a country of 60 million, half a million to a million women are prostitutes, and one out of every twenty of these is enslaved. As Bales's chapter in [*Global Woman*] shows, many of these women are daughters whom northern hill-tribe families have sold to brothels in the cities of the south. Believing the promises of jobs and money, some begin the voyage willingly, only to discover days later that the "arrangers" are traffickers who steal their passports, define them as debtors, and enslave them as prostitutes. Other women and girls are kidnapped, or sold by their impoverished families, and then trafficked to brothels. Even worse fates befall women from neighboring Laos and Burma, who flee crushing poverty and repression at home only to fall into the hands of Thai slave traders.[10]

If the factors that pull migrant women workers to affluent countries are not as simple as they at first appear, neither are the factors that push them. Certainly relative poverty plays a major role, but, interestingly, migrant women often do not come from the poorest classes of their societies.[11] In fact, they are typically more affluent and better educated than male migrants. Many female migrants from the Philippines and Mexico, for example, have high school or college diplomas and have held middle-class—albeit low-paid—jobs back home. One study of Mexican migrants suggests that the trend is toward increasingly better-educated female migrants. Thirty years ago, most Mexican-born maids in the United States had been poorly educated maids in Mexico. Now a majority have high school degrees and have held clerical, retail, or professional jobs before leaving for the United States.[12] Such women are likely to be enterprising and adventurous enough to resist the social pressures to stay home and accept their lot in life.

Noneconomic factors—or at least factors that are not immediately and directly economic—also influence a woman's decision to emigrate. By migrating, a woman may escape the expectation that she care for elderly family members, relinquish her paycheck to a husband or father, or defer to an abusive husband. Migration may also be a practical response to a failed marriage and the need to provide for children without male help. In the Philippines, . . . Rhacel Salazar Parreñas tells us, migration is sometimes called a "Philippine divorce."[13] And there are forces at work that may be making the men of poor countries less desirable as husbands. Male unemployment runs high in the countries that supply female domestics to the First World. Unable to make a living, these men often grow demoralized and cease contributing to their families in other ways. Many female migrants, including those in Michele Gamburd's [work], tell of unemployed husbands who drink or gamble their remittances away.[14] Notes one study of Sri Lankan women working as maids in the Persian Gulf: "It is not unusual . . . for the women to find upon their return that their Gulf wages by and large have been squandered on alcohol, gambling and other dubious undertakings while they were away."[15]

To an extent then, the globalization of child care and housework brings the ambitious and independent women of the world together: the career-oriented upper-middle-class woman of an affluent nation and the striving woman from a crumbling Third World or postcommunist economy. Only it does not bring them together in the way that second-wave feminists in affluent countries once liked to imagine—as sisters and allies struggling to achieve common goals. Instead, they come together as mistress and maid, employer and employee, across a great divide of privilege and opportunity.

This trend toward global redivision of women's traditional work throws new light on the entire process of globalization. Conventionally, it is the poorer countries that are thought to be dependent on the richer ones—a dependency symbolized by the huge debt they owe to global financial institutions. What we explore . . . , however, is a dependency that works in the other direction, and it is a dependency of a particularly intimate kind. Increasingly often, as affluent and middle-class families in the First World come to depend on migrants from poorer regions to provide child care, homemaking, and sexual services, a global relationship arises that in some ways mirrors the traditional relationship between the sexes. The First World takes on a role like that of the old-fashioned male in the family—pampered, entitled, unable to cook, clean, or find his socks. Poor countries take on a role like that of the traditional woman within the family—patient, nurturing, and self-denying. A division of labor feminists critiqued when it was "local" has now, metaphorically speaking, gone global.

To press this metaphor a bit further, the resulting relationship is by no means a "marriage," in the sense of being openly acknowledged. In fact, it is striking how invisible the globalization of women's work remains, how little it is noted or discussed in the First World. Trend spotters have had almost nothing to say about the fact that increasing numbers of affluent First World children and elderly persons are tended by immigrant care workers or live in homes cleaned by immigrant maids. Even the political groups we might expect to be concerned about this trend—antiglobalization and feminist activists—often seem to have noticed only the most extravagant abuses, such as trafficking and female enslavement. So if a metaphorically gendered relationship has developed between rich and poor countries, it is less like a marriage and more like a secret affair.

But it is a "secret affair" conducted in plain view of the children. Little Isadora and the other children of the First World raised by "two mommies" may be learning more than their ABC's from a loving surrogate parent. In their own living rooms, they are learning a vast and tragic global politics.[16] Children see. But they also learn how to disregard what they see. They learn how adults make the visible invisible. That is their "early childhood education."

NOTES

1. See Ellen Galinsky and Dana Friedman, *Women: The New Providers,* Whirlpool Foundation Study, Part 1 (New York: Families and Work Institute, 1995), p. 37.
2. In addition to material directly cited, this introduction draws from the following works: Kathleen M. Adams and Sara Dickey, eds., *Home and Hegemony: Domestic Service and Identity Politics in South and Southeast Asia* (Ann Arbor: University of Michigan Press, 2000); Floya Anthias and Gabriella Lazaridis, eds., *Gender and Migration in Southern Europe: Women on the Move* (Oxford and New York: Berg, 2000); Stephen Castles and Mark J. Miller, *The Age of Migration: International Population Movements in the Modern World* (New York and London: The Guilford Press, 1998); Noeleen Heyzer, Geertje Lycklama à Nijehold, and Nedra Weerakoon, eds., *The Trade in Domestic Workers: Causes, Mechanisms, and Consequences of International Migration* (London: Zed Books, 1994); Eleanore Kofman, Annie Phizacklea, Parvati Raghuram, and Rosemary Sales, *Gender and International Migration in Europe: Employment, Welfare, and Politics* (New York and London: Routledge, 2000); Douglas S. Massey, Joaquin Arango, Graeme Hugo, Ali Kouaouci, Adela Pellegrino, and J. Edward Taylor, *Worlds in Motion: Understanding International Migration at the End of the Millennium* (Oxford: Clarendon Press, 1999); Janet Henshall Momsen, ed., *Gender, Migration, and Domestic Service* (London: Routledge, 1999); Katie Willis and Brenda Yeoh, eds., *Gender and Immigration* (London: Edward Elgar Publishers, 2000).

3. Illegal migrants are said to make up anywhere from 60 percent (as in Sri Lanka) to 87 percent (as in Indonesia) of all migrants. In Singapore in 1994, 95 percent of Filipino overseas contact workers lacked work permits from the Philippine government. The official figures based on legal migration therefore severely underestimate the number of migrants. See Momsen, 1999, p. 7.

4. Momsen, 1999, p. 9.

5. Sri Lanka Bureau of Foreign Employment, 1994, as cited in G. Gunatilleke, *The Economic, Demographic, Sociocultural and Political Setting for Emigration from Sri Lanka International Migration*, vol. 23 (3/4), 1995, pp. 667–98.

6. Anthias and Lazaridis, 2000; Heyzer, Nijehold, and Weerakoon, 1994, pp. 4–27; Momsen, 1999, p. 21; "Wistat: Women's Indicators and Statistics Database," version 3, CD-ROM (United Nations, Department for Economic and Social Information and Policy Analysis, Statistical Division, 1994).

7. Geovanna Campani, "Labor Markets and Family Networks: Filipino Women in Italy," in Hedwig Rudolph and Mirjana Morokvasic, eds., *Bridging States and Markets: International Migration in the Early 1990s* (Berlin: Edition Sigma, 1993), p. 206.

8. For information on male work at home during the 1990s, see Arlie Russell Hochschild and Anne Machung, *The Second Shift: Working Parents and the Revolution at Home* (New York: Avon, 1997), p. 277.

9. Dennis Brennan, "Selling Sex for Visas: Sex Tourism as a Stepping-Stone to International Migration," *Global Woman: Nannies, Maids and Sex Workers in the New Economy*, eds. Barbara Ehrenreich and Arlie Hochschild (New York: Henry Holt, 2002), 154–168.

10. Kevin Bales, *Disposable People: New Slavery in the Global Economy* (Berkeley: University of California Press, 1999), p. 43. Kevin Bales, "Because She Looks Like a Child," in *Global Woman: Nannies, Maids and Sex Workers in the New Economy*, eds. Barbara Ehrenreich and Arlie Hochschild (New York: Henry Holt, 2002), 207–229.

11. Andrea Tyree and Katharine M. Donato, "A Demographic Overview of the International Migration of Women," in *International Migration: The Female Experience*, ed. Rita Simon and Caroline Bretell (Totowa, NJ: Rowman & Allanheld, 1986), p. 29. Indeed, many immigrant maids and nannies are more educated than the people they work for. See Pei-Chia Lan's paper in this volume.

12. Momsen, 1999, pp. 10, 73.

13. Rhacel Salazar Parreñas, "The Care Crisis in the Philippines: Children and Transnational Families in the New Global Economy," in *Global Woman: Nannies, Maids and Sex Workers in the New Economy*, eds. Barbara Ehrenreich and Arlie Hochschild (New York: Henry Holt, 2002), 39–54.

14. Michele Gamburd, "Breadwinners No More," in *Global Woman: Nannies, Maids and Sex Workers in the New Economy*, eds. Barbara Ehrenreich and Arlie Hochschild (New York: Henry Holt, 2002), 190–206.

15. Grete Brochmann, *Middle East Avenue: Female Migration from Sri Lanka to the Gulf* (Boulder, Colo.: Westview Press, 1993), pp. 179, 215.

16. On this point, thanks to Raka Ray, Sociology Department at the University of California, Berkeley.

49

AMERICA'S DIRTY WORK
Migrant Maids and Modern-Day Slavery

JOY M. ZAREMBKA

Joy M. Zarembka, the daughter of a domestic worker from Kenya, is the director of Break the Chain Campaign. She is also the author *of The Pigment of Your Imagination: Mixed Race Families in Britain, Kenya, Zimbabwe and Jamaica* (2007) (www.ThePigment .com), which explores the various configurations of "race" in different countries.

Imagine you are locked away in a strange home. You do not speak your captor's language. On the rare occasions when you are escorted off the premises, you are forbidden to speak to anyone. You are often fed the leftover food of the children you are required to watch while completing your around-the-clock household duties. You have never been paid for your labors, and the woman of the house physically abuses you.

While this scenario seems to hark back to an earlier time in U.S. history, it describes Noreena Nesa's* recent working conditions in the Washington, D.C., area. Tucked behind the manicured lawns and closed doors of our wealthiest residents live some of the most vulnerable people in the United States: abused migrant domestic workers, who are sometimes the victims of slavery and human trafficking.

Marie Jose Perez, for example, left Bolivia in 1997, excited because she had always dreamed of flying on an airplane and hopeful that she would soon be able to support her family in Bolivia with her wages as a live-in maid. But once her plane landed in Washington, D.C., her employer, a human rights lawyer for the Organization of American States, confiscated her passport and forced her to work days more than twelve hours long, for less than one dollar per hour. She was not allowed to leave the house without her employer. When a friend of her employer's raped her, the human rights lawyer refused to take her to the hospital, claiming that medical care would be too expensive.

---

*Some names have been changed.

Ruth Gnizako, a fifty-two-year-old West African woman, says she was approached by a wealthy relative who worked for the World Bank. The relative promised her a house and a car if she would come serve as a housekeeper and nanny to his five children in suburban Maryland. When she arrived, she was required to sleep with a pair of one-year-old twins in her arms every night, essentially providing twenty-four-hour care with no days off. When the family went out, Ruth was forced to wait outside, in the hallway of the apartment building, until they returned. Both husband and wife repeatedly beat Ruth, and they igored her request to return to West Africa.

When neighbors heard Ruth screaming during the beatings, they called the Prince George's County Police Department. But the police were unable to understand her broken French, so they relied on her abusive employers for translation. Ruth attempted to reenact the beatings by gesturing physical blows to herself. Her employers, seeing an opportunity, told the police, "See, she's showing you how she beats herself. She's crazy." Ruth was taken to a local mental institution where she was forcibly sedated, her arms and legs tied to the bedposts. By the time the doctors contacted a French interpreter by phone, Ruth was feeling the effects of the psychoactive drugs, and, in her limited French, she could not manage to recount the traumatic events. Frustrated, the hospital staff called Ruth's employers and asked them to retrieve her.

When Ruth returned to the couple's home, they told her that if she upset them, they would call the police again and send her to the hospital permanently. They went on to claim that the security guard who patrolled the area was specifically sent to monitor her behavior and to make sure she did not harm their children. Intimidated by the barriers of language and culture, and still shaken from her terrifying experience at the mental institution, Ruth believed these threats. She suffered many more solitary months of beatings and servitude before the couple's neighbors finally managed to help her escape and contact the local authorities. In the end, Ruth found herself emotionally unable to participate in the U.S. Justice Department's criminal investigation of her former employers and returned home without collecting a dime.

Global Mothers

Noreena, Marie Jose, and Ruth are among a growing number of migrant women known to suffer under conditions that look very much like slavery after they legally enter the United States as domestic workers. The global economic changes that push women from developing nations to migrate for domestic work have also contributed to the recent rise of domestic worker abuse. Developed countries and international lending organizations such as the International Monetary Fund (IMF) and World Bank often prescribe preconditions for loans to developing countries that include cutting basic social services, devaluing local currencies, and imposing wage freezes. These structural adjustment programs create hardships that are borne most severely by those at the bottom of the economic ladder, a significant proportion of whom are women. The world's poor are often faced with few better options than to leave their home countries in search of work overseas, even if they do so with no assurances and at grave personal risk. Once they arrive in the United States, migrant women are sometimes forced into employment situations to which they did not agree and from which they have no escape.

Modern-day slavery, trafficking, and migrant domestic worker abuse result from the illegal manipulation and deception of hopeful migrants, most of whom believe they are going to the United States in order to better their situations. The new global economy permits transnational corporations and other actors in developed countries to transport capital, labor, goods, and services across state lines with relative ease. In the case of slavery and human trafficking, these goods, services, and labor become one: an unpaid or poorly paid person becomes a commodity that can be used again and again for accumulating profit. Traffickers tell migrants that they will earn many times more money abroad than they could at home. If they were employed by law-abiding people, these workers could indeed increase their earnings. Dora Mortey, an articulate Ghanaian schoolteacher, was one of those who believed the odds were on her side. Little did she know she would be worked around the clock as a nanny and housekeeper, and paid only around forty cents an hour.

Dora had signed an employment agreement with a World Bank official in Ghana. Nonetheless, when she got to the Washington area, she was handed a daily schedule that began at 5:45 A.M. and ended at 9:30 P.M., far exceeding the agreed-upon forty-hour workweek. After four months of working for only $100 a month, Dora asked that her contract be honored. The family decided to terminate her services and put her on the next plane to Ghana. She managed to escape from the moving car as her employer drove her to the airport; but the employer scratched an 'X' across her visa and promptly delivered her passport to the Immigration and Naturalization Service (INS), requesting her immediate arrest and deportation. Uncertain what to do, Dora took a cab from Washington to New Jersey to seek refuge with the one person she knew in the United States. Back at the airport, an astute INS official suspected foul play. Eventually, Dora was granted a stay of deportation while she pursued legal action against her former employers.

Each year, thousands of domestic workers like Dora enter the United States on special visas issued by the U.S. State Department. Foreign nationals, diplomats, officials of international agencies, and, in some cases, U.S. citizens with permanent residency abroad, are permitted to "import" domestic help on A-3, G-5, and B-1 visas. Nearly four thousand A-3 and G-5 visas are issued annually—A-3 visas for household employees of diplomats and G-5 visas for employees of international agencies such as the World Bank, IMF, and United Nations. The B-1 visa is a catch-all business category that, in part, allows other foreign nationals and American citizens with permanent residency abroad the option of bringing household employees with them when they visit the United States. Every year, 200,000 B-1 visas are issued, but the State Department does not keep records of B-1 domestic workers. As a result, their locations and working conditions remain particularly obscure. And the B-1 domestic workers may be at special risk for exploitation. All three visa types list the name of the worker's legal employer, but unlike the A-3 and G-5 visa holders, B-1 domestic workers have no option of legally transferring to another employer. They are left with few alternatives if they are enslaved or abused.

Even for A-3 and G-5 domestic workers, who are allowed to transfer to other diplomats or international officials, it is often difficult to find a suitable employer while suffering in an exploitative arrangement. Although the State Department, embassies, and international institutions involved (including the IMF, World Bank, and UN) keep records of the whereabouts of A-3 and G-5 domestic workers, this information is classified as confidential, for the privacy of the employer. Domestic violence and anti-incest advocates have challenged the privacy justification on the grounds that a lot of abuse occurs behind closed doors; other advocates have argued that in addition to being domiciles, these homes are also workplaces, subject to employment standards. Nonetheless, social service agencies remain uninformed of the whereabouts of domestic workers, which leaves them unable to prevent abuse or act on it before it is too late.

Patterns

Abuse and exploitation follow such uncannily predictable patterns that many in the social service world almost wonder if there is an "Abusers Manual" being circulated like samizdat. Typically, when the woman arrives in the United States, her employer illegally confiscates her passport and other travel documents. If the worker signed an official contract in a U.S. embassy abroad, that contract is often replaced with a new contract that stipulates longer hours and lower pay. Even the false contract is often subsequently ignored. Although U.S. labor law dictates that all workers be paid at least minimum wage, it is not uncommon to hear reports of women being paid fifty cents or a dollar an hour—in some cases, nothing at all. With yearly salaries at the World Bank and IMF averaging over $120,000 tax-free, the income disparity is striking, especially in situations where domestic workers are told that all or part of their meager wage is being withheld to offset their room and board.

Many women find themselves working nearly around the clock, seven days a week. The exploitative employer usually tells the worker that she may not leave the house unaccompanied, use the telephone, make friends, or even converse with others. The worker is often denied health insurance and social security, even if these benefits have been deducted from her pay. Some domestic workers are subjected to physical battery and sexual assault; others who have serious health conditions are denied medical treatment, which can result in long-term illness. Some domestic workers are given as gifts to the mistresses of diplomats, or traded and loaned out to American families who further exploit them. One Ghanaian woman reported that her employer's American wife referred to her not by name but rather as "the Creature." Yet another woman reported being called "the Slave." Others have been required to sleep on the floor, sometimes in the kitchen, laundry room, or unfurnished basement. An Ivy League professor, who paid her domestic worker $40 a month, slapped her for smoking outside. One domestic worker reported that she was made to kiss her employer's feet. A Malawian man recalls being forced to bathe in a bucket in the backyard rather than in the home of his American employer. A Filipina was forced to wear a dog collar and, at times, sleep outside with the family's dogs.

Typically, if an abused domestic worker complains, the employer threatens to send her home or turn her over to the police. The employer may also threaten to retaliate against her family if she speaks out; on several occasions, family members have been contacted and harassed after a domestic worker has escaped from an abusive situation. Legal issues in the United States also militate against leaving exploitative jobs: women who flee abusive employers are immediately considered "out of status," ineligible for other employment, and liable to be deported by the Immigration and Naturalization Service. As one neighbor who helped a Haitian domestic worker escape says, "When she ran away, she was out of a job, out of money, out of a home, out of status, and, quite frankly, out of her mind."

While some abusive employers use violence and the threat of violence to keep their domestic workers captive, others rely on psychological coercion. In one recent case, Hilda Rosa Dos Santos, a dark-skinned housekeeper from Brazil, was trapped for twenty years, with no pay and insufficient food, in the home of a Brazilian couple who convinced her that Americans disliked black people so intensely that she would likely be raped or killed if she went outside. Similarly, an Indonesian maid was informed by her Saudi Arabian bosses that Americans disliked Muslims so much that it was unsafe for her to leave the house. Abusive employers often point to violence on television to bolster claims about the dangers of American life. Unfamiliar with the English language or with American culture and laws, these women live as prisoners in the homes they clean.

Many women suffer in silence because they do not know their rights, nor do they have any idea where to go to seek help. Some may leave an abusive situation only to find themselves in even worse circumstances. Consider Tigris Bekele, who quickly found herself in jail on two felony counts of child abuse and grand larceny, all because she fled her job as a live-in maid after being exploited, sexually harassed, and threatened. Unfortunately, the day she decided to escape from her abusive employer, there was a bomb scare at the employer's children's school. The children were sent home at 10:00 A.M., a time when Tigris was not required to work as a nanny. But finding themselves alone, the children called the Virginia police. Tigris was arrested for leaving the children unattended.

The police record does not mention that Tigris was paid only $100 a week for around-the-clock chores because her Middle Eastern employer claimed that "that was enough money for a black person." Nowhere does it mention that the man of the house attempted to fondle and kiss her on various occasions. Nor does it mention that the woman of the house forced her to cut her hair and stop wearing makeup, threatening to kill Tigris if she had sex with her husband. Instead, the police record indicates that she is being held on $20,000 bail. It states that she allegedly stole a piece of jewelry, a claim that is often wielded against runaway domestic workers. Her employers had confiscated her passport and visa; when Tigris scoured the house to "steal" her belongings back, her employers accused her of stealing their personal effects.

Even though she came legally to the United States on a domestic worker visa program, if Tigris is convicted, she will be deported to her home country in East Africa, where she is fleeing political persecution. Tigris had been sending remittances to her father, and she has recently learned from relatives that she will be arrested if she returns because the government claims that the money is being used to launch political opposition. A felony conviction in the United States will automatically render it impossible for her to seek asylum here. While some domestic workers end up in court seeking judgments against their abusers, Tigris finds herself on the wrong side of the courtroom.

A Comparison

Some migrant workers who come to the United States to perform child care and light housework do so as participants in another, markedly different visa program. The congressionally sponsored au pair program—au pair means "an equal" in French—largely recruits young, middle-class women from Europe for "educational and cultural exchange" on J-1 visas. Ava Sudek, from the Czech Republic, experienced life in the United States both as a J-1 and as an A-3 visa holder. She thoroughly enjoyed her time as a J-1 au pair and thoroughly despised her time as an A-3 domestic worker. Ava's experience with the two visa programs highlights their striking dissimilarity.

When Ava arrived as an au pair, she was flown to a New York hotel for a week-long orientation session. There she was introduced to other nannies who would be living in the same region, so that they could form a network of friendships. Once she joined the employer's family, she attended another orientation program, where she received information on community resources and educational opportunities, as well as the contact numbers of other nannies in her local support network. Every month, she and her employers were required to check in with a counselor, who would help them resolve any disputes that arose or report any problems.

After completing a successful year with her au pair family, Ava decided to stay on an A-3 visa and work as a domestic worker for a French diplomat's family. There were no orientations, no information booklets, no contact numbers, no counselors, and no educational programs. In practice, for A-3 domestic workers, there is often no freedom. Ava felt like she was being held captive. She was not allowed to leave the house even during her off hours without a day's advance notice. Work hours and nonwork hours blurred together. When she asked for days off, her employers often refused to grant her request, telling her, "Perhaps another time." They did not pay her overtime. Within a month of obtaining her A-3 visa, Ava fled for the Czech Republic, where she dreamed of opening an au pair agency in her hometown. She did not bother to try to collect the overtime wages she was owed: her employer, as a high-level diplomat, was protected by diplomatic immunity.

Ava had the opportunity to hold both a J-1 and an A-3 visa, but few women of color from developing countries are so lucky. Most of them migrate on A-3, B-1, or G-5 visas, which do not come remotely close to offering the protections or the comforts J-1 visas provide European women. The different policies governing the temporary workers on these two visa programs are thick with racist and classist implications. Simply put, women of color in the domestic worker program deserve the same safety net and rigorous oversight granted to white women in the nanny program.

Solutions

Theoretically, the domestic worker visa program provides a window of opportunity for people from developing countries to enter the United States and earn a decent wage. What the program fails to do, however, is to ensure adequate protection for its visa holders. One simple improvement would be to establish independent monitoring and counseling like that which is provided to au pairs. Access to independent social workers, lawyers, and monitors would furnish live-in domestic workers with a system of safeguards to protect their legal rights and ensure employer compliance with contract conditions and labor laws.

By and large, migrant domestic workers belong to a hidden work force tucked away in private homes. Severe cases of domestic worker abuse differ from other cases of slavery and trafficking, such as those uncovered in brothels, farms, and sweatshops, because workers under the latter conditions have contact with one another. Each domestic worker, by contrast, is employed by an individual boss. Not only are the workers without peer support, but their cases involve no smuggling or trafficking rings for law enforcement to target for investigation. The result is that less attention is paid to these seemingly isolated incidents.

Far from their home countries, abused domestic workers are cut off from their families and their cultures, not to mention the protection that social networks and familiar institutions would provide. Many abusive employers incur the expense of hiring overseas precisely for this reason: they believe that they can increasingly control non-English speaking help. Such workers are less likely to run away in the United States. Lack of familiarity with the American legal system also works to the disadvantage of abused domestic workers.

So where do these workers turn for help? A loose network of churches, lawyers, social service agencies, and good Samaritans have formed a modern-day underground railroad for women attempting to escape abusive employers. Because some domestic workers are only allowed out of the house on Sundays, churches are frequently a first stop on the path to freedom. One Catholic sister has files on several hundred G-5 and A-3 workers she has assisted over the years, beginning in the 1970s. Other good Samaritans have just happened to take initiatives when they've encountered domestic workers in need. Street vendors, taxicab drivers, neighbors, and complete strangers have been known to assist domestic workers in distress. Social service organizations and pro bono lawyers then help domestic workers with housing, medical care, mental health needs, and legal assistance.

Policy on matters affecting domestic workers has improved, but there are still troubling gaps in the protections these workers receive. Congress passed trafficking legislation in 2000 that allows federal law enforcement to convict not only traffickers who control their victims by force but also those who coerce workers by means of threats, psychological abuse, fraud, or deception. Domestic workers who bring criminal claims (such as sexual and physical abuse, or psychological coercion) against their former employers are granted work authorization, while domestic workers with civil claims (back pay, overtime, and the like) remain out of status and are considered illegal. Although the INS often turns a blind eye to out-of-status G-5, A-3, and B-1 domestic workers with civil claims, the threat of deportation and the lack of work authorization makes it unappealing for these workers to seek legal redress. It is time-consuming and difficult to find a pro bono lawyer, and migrants who come to the United States as temporary workers often have families to feed in their home countries; they are not really at liberty to sit around waiting for lengthy and uncertain court proceedings. Moreover, domestic workers with civil cases are so vulnerable and have so little bargaining power that they are sometimes re-enslaved as they wait out the long court process without job or housing options. It is certainly disheartening to think that a migrant domestic worker in a potentially violent situation is legally better off staying and getting beaten because she will later be able to receive a work permit, social services, and legal status. If she leaves before violence erupts, she receives nothing.

No shelters currently exist in the United States for trafficked women, and this remains one of the biggest obstacles facing nongovernmental organizations (NGOs) that attempt to assist domestic workers. NGOs sometimes have to ask women who are not in grave physical danger to stay in their exploitative situations while advocates scramble to find culturally appropriate housing. The Justice Department faces a small housing crisis every time a new criminal case involving trafficking is filed. On one occasion, police dropped a domestic worker on the private doorstep of an NGO worker in the middle of the night, for lack of housing alternatives.

Because few housing options are available to abused domestic workers, NGOs often turn to ethnic communities for assistance with housing, clothing, medical care, and mental health needs. Most of these communities are small and tight-knit. This presents a safety risk for some domestic workers, who find temporary housing in their ethnic communities only to be easily located by their abusers, who sometimes hail from the same background and know those communities well. Most domestic violence shelters will not accommodate domestic workers because they were not beaten by romantic partners; most homeless shelters refuse to assist due to language barriers and lack of beds. Domestic workers often end up relying on compassionate strangers—everyday people who open their homes and hearts to individuals in need.

Fortunately, advocates and domestic workers have been organizing to find solutions to these problems at both the policy and the grassroots levels. Groups such as CASA de Maryland's Mujeres Unidas de Maryland (United Women of Maryland) are forming workplace cooperatives to advocate for improved conditions for all workers. Former and current domestic workers take to the streets, parks, buses, and churches looking for potentially abused domestic workers and educating them about their rights, using Spanish-language legal literature. When a volunteer encounters an exploited employee, she directs her to bilingual legal assistance. The increase in outreach has resulted in an increase in the number of reported cases of domestic worker abuse. Mujeres Unidas has developed self-esteem classes, in which formerly abused or exploited domestic workers extend their support to others suffering under similar circumstances. The group has now formed a twenty-four-member, democratically controlled cleaning cooperative whose goal is to provide dignified day jobs and equitable working conditions. Most impressive, 10 percent of all the cleaning service's proceeds are funneled to social justice organizations.

While most members of Mujeres Unidas are Latina, other ethnically based organizations in the Washington, D.C., area are also engaged in efforts to curb domestic worker abuse; among them are a Filipina organization, Shared Communities, and the Ethiopian Community Development Council. More than twenty-five Washington-based organizations have joined forces to create the Campaign for Migrant Domestic Workers Rights (now Break the Chain Campaign), a coalition whose aim is to change public policy and to strengthen the safety net available to G-5, A-3, and B-1 domestic workers. These efforts involve lawyers, feminists, labor activists, human rights activists, community-based organizations, and social service agencies.

Related campaigns have sprung up elsewhere in the country. In New York, groups such as Andolan, Worker's Awaaz, and the Committee Against Anti-Asian Violence's Women Workers Project are working together; and in California, the Coalition Against Slavery and Trafficking, and the Korean Immigrant Workers Advocates, address similar issues. Workers rights' clinics in Washington, Los Angeles, and New York often provide relief to individuals escaping slavelike conditions. A nationwide Freedom Network (USA) to Empower Enslaved and Trafficked Persons recently formed in response to incidents of trafficking and slavery uncovered among laborers and sex workers.

Noreena, Marie Jose, Ruth, Dora, Hilda, Tigris, and Ava were all able to seek assistance from concerned neighbors, lawyers, and advocates. But it remains unclear how many other women currently toil in isolation, unpaid and abused. In the 1970s, the battered women's movement established a network of advocacy groups and shelters for women who were abused by their spouses; the movement even managed, through arduous grassroots efforts, to change public policy and public consciousness about domestic violence. Its work is not done. But the groups that have committed their time and resources to assisting trafficked and enslaved domestic workers have only now embarked on a similar movement: they are building a new underground railroad, one stretch of track at a time.

50

THE GLOBETROTTING SNEAKER

CYNTHIA ENLOE

Cynthia Enloe is Research Professor of International Development and Women's Studies at Clark University. Her recent books include *Bananas, Beaches and Bases: Making Feminist Sense of International Politics* (2000), *Maneuvers: The International Politics of Militarizing Women's Lives* (2000), *The Curious Feminist: Searching for Women in A New Age of Empire* (2004), and *Globalization and Militarism: Feminists Make the Link* (2007).

Four years after the fall of the Berlin Wall marked the end of the Cold War, Reebok, one of the fastest-growing companies in United States history, decided that the time had come to make its mark in Russia. Thus it was with considerable fanfare that Reebok's executives opened their first store in downtown Moscow in July 1993. A week after the grand opening, store managers described sales as well above expectations.

Reebok's opening in Moscow was the perfect post-Cold War scenario: commercial rivalry replacing military posturing; consumerist tastes homogenizing heretofore hostile peoples; capital and managerial expertise flowing freely across newly porous state borders. Russians suddenly had the "freedom" to spend money on U.S. cultural icons like athletic footwear, items priced above and beyond daily subsistence: at the end of 1993, the average Russian earned the equivalent of $40 a month. Shoes on display were in the $100 range. Almost 60 percent of single parents, most of whom were women, were living in poverty. Yet in Moscow and Kiev, shoe promoters had begun targeting children, persuading them to pressure their mothers to spend money on stylish, Western sneakers. And as far as strategy goes, athletic shoe giants have, you might say, a good track record. In the U.S. many inner-city boys who see basketball as a "ticket out of the ghetto" have become convinced that certain brand-name shoes will give them an edge.

But no matter where sneakers are bought or sold, the potency of their advertising imagery has made it easy to ignore this mundane fact: Shaquille O'Neal's Reeboks are stitched by someone; Michael Jordan's Nikes are

Author's Note: This article draws from the work of South Korean scholars Hyun Sook Kim, Seung-kyung Kim, Katherine Moon, Seungsook Moon, and Jeong-Lim Nam.

stitched by someone; so are your roommate's, so are your grandmother's. Those someones are women, mostly Asian women who are supposed to believe that their "opportunity" to make sneakers for U.S. companies is a sign of their country's progress—just as a Russian woman's chance to spend two months' salary on a pair of shoes for her child allegedly symbolizes the new Russia.

As the global economy expands, sneaker executives are looking to pay women workers less and less, even though the shoes that they produce are capturing an ever-growing share of the footwear market. By the end of 1993, sales in the U.S. alone had reached $11.6 billion. Nike, the largest supplier of athletic footwear in the world, posted a record $298 million profit for 1993—earnings that had nearly tripled in five years. And sneaker companies continue to refine their strategies for "global competitiveness"—hiring supposedly docile women to make their shoes, changing designs as quickly as we fickle customers change our tastes, and shifting factories from country to country as trade barriers rise and fall.

The logic of it all is really quite simple; yet trade agreements such as the North American Free Trade Agreement (NAFTA) and the General Agreement of Tariffs and Trade (GATT) are, of course, talked about in a jargon that alienates us, as if they were technical matters fit only for economists and diplomats. The bottom line is that all companies operating overseas depend on trade agreements made between their own governments and the regimes ruling the countries in which they want to make or sell their products. Korean, Indonesian, and other women workers around the world know this better than anyone. They are tackling trade politics because they have learned from hard experience that the trade deals their governments sign do little to improve the lives of workers. Guarantees of fair, healthy labor practices, of the rights to speak freely and to organize independently, will usually be left out of trade pacts—and women will suffer. The recent passage of both NAFTA and GATT ensures that a growing number of private companies will now be competing across borders without restriction. The result? Big business will step up efforts to pit working women in industrialized countries against much lower-paid working women in "developing" countries, perpetuating the misleading notion that they are inevitable rivals in the global job market.

All the "New World Order" really means to corporate giants like athletic shoemakers is that they now have the green light to accelerate long-standing industry practices. In the early 1980s, the field marshals commanding Reebok and Nike, which are both U.S.-based, decided to manufacture most of their sneakers in South Korea and Taiwan, hiring local women. L.A. Gear, Adidas, Fila, and Asics quickly followed their lead. In short time, the coastal city of Pusan, South Korea, became the "sneaker capital of the world." Between 1982 and 1989 the U.S. lost 58,500 footwear jobs to cities like Pusan, which attracted sneaker executives because its location facilitated international transport. More to the point, South Korea's military government had an interest in suppressing labor organizing, and it had a comfortable military alliance with the U.S. Korean women also seemed accepting of Confucian philosophy, which measured a women's morality by her willingness to work hard for her family's well-being and to acquiesce to her father's and husband's dictates. With their sense of patriotic duty, Korean women seemed the ideal labor force for export-oriented factories.

U.S. and European sneaker company executives were also attracted by the ready supply of eager Korean male entrepreneurs with whom they could make profitable arrangements. This fact was central to Nike's strategy in particular. When they moved their production sites to Asia to lower labor costs, the executives of the Oregon-based company decided to reduce their corporate responsibilities further. Instead of owning factories outright, a more efficient strategy would be to subcontract the manufacturing to wholly foreign-owned—in this case, South Korean—companies. Let them be responsible for workers' health and safety. Let them negotiate with newly emergent unions. Nike would retain control over those parts of sneaker production that gave its officials the greatest professional satisfaction and the ultimate word on the product: design and marketing. Although Nike was following in the footsteps of garment and textile manufacturers, it set the trend for the rest of the athletic footwear industry.

But at the same time, women workers were developing their own strategies. As the South Korean pro-democracy movement grew throughout the 1980s, increasing numbers of women rejected traditional notions of feminine duty. Women began organizing in response to the dangerous working conditions, daily humiliations, and low pay built into their work. Such resistance was profoundly threatening to the government, given the fact that South Korea's emergence as an industrialized "tiger" had depended on women accepting their "role" in growing industries like sneaker manufacture. If women reimagined their lives as daughters, as wives, as workers, as citizens, it wouldn't just rattle their employers; it would shake the very foundations of the whole political system.

At the first sign of trouble, factory managers called in government riot police to break up employees' meetings. Troops sexually assaulted women workers, stripping, fondling, and raping them "as a control mechanism for suppressing women's engagement in the labor movement," reported Jeong-Lim Nam of Hyosung Women's University in Taegu. It didn't work. It didn't work because the feminist activists in groups like the Korean Women Workers Association (KWWA) helped women understand and deal with the assaults. The KWWA held consciousness-raising sessions in which notions of feminine duty and respectability were tackled along with wages and benefits. They organized independently of the male-led labor unions to ensure that their issues would be taken seriously, in labor negotiations and in the pro-democracy movement as a whole.

The result was that women were at meetings with management, making sure that in addition to issues like long hours and low pay, sexual assault at the hands of managers and health care were on the table. Their activism paid off: in addition to winning the right to organize women's unions, their earnings grew. In 1980, South Korean women in manufacturing jobs earned 45 percent of the wages of their male counterparts; by 1990, they were earning more than 50 percent. Modest though it was, the pay increase was concrete progress, given that the gap between women's and men's manufacturing wages in Japan, Singapore, and Sri Lanka actually widened during the 1980s. Last, but certainly not least, women's organizing was credited with playing a major role in toppling the country's military regime and forcing open elections in 1987.

Without that special kind of workplace control that only an authoritarian government could offer, sneaker executives knew that it was time to move. In Nike's case, its famous advertising slogan—"Just Do It"—proved truer to its corporate philosophy than its women's "empowerment" ad campaign, designed to rally women's athletic (and consumer) spirit. In response to South Korean women workers' newfound activist self-confidence, the sneaker company and its subcontractors began shutting down a number of their South Korean factories in the late 1980s and early 1990s. After bargaining with government officials in nearby China and Indonesia, many Nike subcontractors set up shop in those countries, while some went to Thailand. China's government remains nominally Communist; Indonesia's ruling generals are staunchly anti-Communist. But both are governed by authoritarian regimes who share the belief that if women can be kept hard at work, low paid, and unorganized, they can serve as a magnet for foreign investors.

Where does all this leave South Korean women—or any woman who is threatened with a factory closure if she demands decent working conditions and a fair wage? They face the dilemma confronted by thousands of women from dozens of countries. The risk of job loss is especially acute in relatively mobile industries; it's easier for a sneaker, garment, or electronics manufacturer to pick up and move than it is for an automaker or a steel producer. In the case of South Korea, poor women had moved from rural villages into the cities searching for jobs to support not only themselves, but parents and siblings. The exodus of manufacturing jobs has forced more women into the growing "entertainment" industry. The kinds of bars and massage parlors offering sexual services that had mushroomed around U.S. military bases during the Cold War have been opening up across the country.

But the reality is that women throughout Asia are organizing, knowing full well the risks involved. Theirs is a long-term view; they are taking direct aim at companies' nomadic advantage, by building links among workers in countries targeted for "development" by multinational corporations. Through sustained grassroots efforts, women are developing the skills and confidence that will make it increasingly difficult to keep their labor cheap. Many are looking to the United Nations conference on women in Beijing, China, this September [1995], as a rare opportunity to expand their cross-border strategizing.

The Beijing conference will also provide an important opportunity to call world attention to the hypocrisy of the governments and corporations doing business in China. Numerous athletic shoe companies followed Nike in setting up manufacturing sites throughout the country. This included Reebok—a company claiming its share of responsibility for ridding the world of "injustice, poverty, and other ills that gnaw away at the social fabric," according to a statement of corporate principles.

Since 1988, Reebok has been giving out annual human rights awards to dissidents from around the world. But it wasn't until 1992 that the company adopted its own "human rights production standards"—after labor advocates made it known that the quality of life in factories run by its subcontractors was just as dismal as that at most other athletic shoe suppliers in Asia. Reebok's code of conduct, for example, includes a pledge to "seek" those subcontractors who respect workers' rights to organize. The only problem is that independent trade unions are banned in China. Reebok has chosen to ignore that fact, even though Chinese dissidents have been the recipients of the company's own human rights award. As for working conditions, Reebok now says it sends its own inspectors to production sites a couple of times a year. But they have easily "missed" what subcontractors are trying to hide—like 400 young women workers locked at night into an overcrowded dormitory near a Reebok-contracted factory in the town of Zhuhai, as reported last August in the *Asian Wall Street Journal Weekly.*

————

Nike's cofounder and CEO Philip Knight has said that he would like the world to think of Nike as "a company with a soul that recognizes the value of human beings." Nike, like Reebok, says it sends in inspectors from time to time to check up on work conditions at its factories; in Indonesia, those factories are run largely by South Korean subcontractors. But according to Donald Katz in a recent book on the company, Nike spokesman Dave Taylor told an in-house newsletter that the factories are "[the subcontractors'] business to run." For the most part, the company relies on regular reports from subcontractors regarding its "Memorandum of Understanding," which managers must sign, promising to impose "local government standards" for wages, working conditions, treatment of workers, and benefits.

In April, the minimum wage in the Indonesian capital of Jakarta will be $1.89 *a day*—among the highest in a country where the minimum wage varies by region. And managers are required to pay only 75 percent of the wage directly; the remainder can be withheld for "benefits." By now, Nike has a well-honed response to growing criticisms of its low-cost labor strategy. Such wages should not be seen as exploitative, says Nike, but rather as the first rung on the ladder of economic opportunity that Nike has extended to workers with few options. Otherwise, they'd be out "harvesting coconut meat in the tropical sun," wrote Nike spokesman Dusty Kidd, in a letter to the *Utne Reader.* The all-is-relative response craftily shifts attention away from reality: Nike didn't move to Indonesia to help Indonesians; it moved to ensure that its profit margin continues to grow. And that is pretty much guaranteed in a country where "local standards" for wages rarely take a worker over the poverty line. A 1991 survey by the International Labor Organization (ILO) found that 88 percent of women working at the Jakarta minimum wage at the time—slightly less than a dollar a day—were malnourished.

A woman named Riyanti might have been among the workers surveyed by the ILO. Interviewed by the *Boston Globe* in 1991, she told the reporter who had asked about her long hours and low pay: "I'm happy working here. . . . I can make money and I can make friends." But in fact, the reporter discovered that Riyanti had already joined her coworkers in two strikes, the first to force one of Nike's Korean subcontractors to accept a new women's union and the second to compel managers to pay at least the minimum wage. That Riyanti appeared less than forthcoming about her activities isn't surprising. Many Indonesian factories have military men posted in their front offices who find no fault with managers who tape women's mouths shut to keep them from talking among themselves. They and their superiors have a political reach that extends far beyond the barracks. Indonesia has all the makings for a political explosion, especially since the gap between rich and poor is widening into a chasm. It is in this setting that the government has tried to crack down on any independent labor organizing—a policy that Nike has helped to implement. Referring to a recent strike in a Nike-contracted factory, Tony Nava, Nike representative in Indonesia, told the *Chicago Tribune* in November 1994 that the "troublemakers" had been fired. When asked about Nike policy on the issue, spokesman Keith Peters struck a conciliatory note: "If the government were to allow and encourage independent labor organizing, we would be happy to support it."

Indonesian workers' efforts to create unions independent of governmental control were a surprise to shoe companies. Although their moves from South Korea have been immensely profitable [see Figure 1], they do not have the sort of immunity from activism that they had expected. In May 1993, the murder of a female activist outside Surabaya set off a storm of local and international protest. Even the U.S. State Department was forced to take note in its 1993 worldwide human rights report, describing a system similar to that which generated South Korea's boom 20 years earlier: severely restricted union organizing, security forces used to break up strikes, low wages for men, lower wages for women—complete with government rhetoric celebrating women's contribution to national development.

Yet when President Clinton visited Indonesia last November, he made only a token effort to address the country's human rights problem. Instead, he touted the benefits of free trade, sounding indeed more enlightened, more in tune with the spirit of the post–Cold War era than do those defenders of protectionist trading policies who coat their rhetoric with "America first" chauvinism. But "free trade" as actually being practiced today is hardly *free*

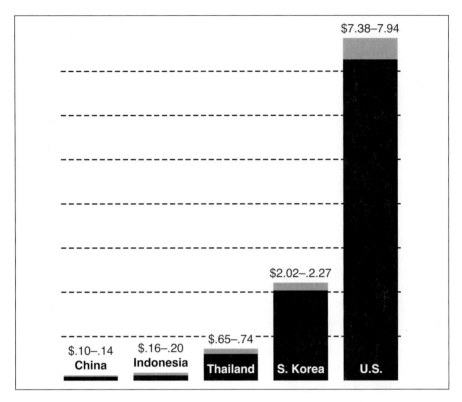

$7.38–7.94

$2.02–.2.27

$.65–.74

$.10–.14
China

$.16–.20
Indonesia

Thailand

S. Korea

U.S.

FIGURE 1   Hourly Wages in Athletic Footwear Factories

for any workers—in the U.S. or abroad—who have to accept the Indonesian, Chinese, or Korean workplace model as the price of keeping their jobs.

The not-so-new plot of the international trade story has been "divide and rule." If women workers and their government in one country can see that a sneaker company will pick up and leave if their labor demands prove more costly than those in a neighbor country, then women workers will tend to see their neighbors not as regional sisters, but as competitors who can steal their precarious livelihoods. Playing women off against each other is, of course, old hat. Yet it is as essential to international trade politics as is the fine print in GATT.

But women workers allied through the networks like the Hong Kong–based Committee for Asian Women are developing their own post–Cold War foreign policy, which means addressing women's needs: how to convince fathers and husbands that a woman going out to organizing meetings at night is not sexually promiscuous; how to develop workplace agendas that respond to family needs; how to work with male unionists who push women's demands to the bottom of their lists; how to build a global movement.

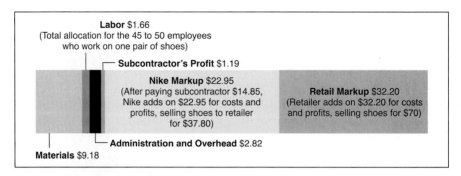

FIGURE 2   A $70 Pair of Nike Pegasus: Where the Money Goes

These women refuse to stand in awe of the corporate power of the Nike or Reebok or Adidas executive. Growing numbers of Asian women today have concluded that trade politics have to be understood by women on their own terms. They will be coming to Beijing this September [1995] ready to engage with women from other regions to link the politics of consumerism with the politics of manufacturing. If women in Russia and Eastern Europe can challenge Americanized consumerism, if Asian activists can solidify their alliances, and if U.S. women can join with them by taking on trade politics—the post–Cold War sneaker may be a less comfortable fit in the 1990s.

[See Figure 2 for an example of the price markup on shoes.]

51

THE CENTER OF
MASCULINE PRODUCTION
Gay Athletes in Professional Sports

ERIC ANDERSON

Eric Anderson is lecturer on sociology at Stony Brook University, State University of New York, and the author of *Trailblazing: The True Story of America's First Openly Gay Track Coach* (2000).

One Athlete's Story: Steven, Closeted NFL Player

The name Steven Thompson is an alias, but it represents a real, gay National Football League player who is currently playing and one whose front as a gladiator betrays his inner anxiety and fear.[1] "I'm not brave. I'm gutless really," he told sport writer Mike Freeman in his book *Bloody Sundays* (2003, 142). "I do feel alone, and sometimes like a coward. I get frustrated and angry, but I also know that now is not the time for me to call a team meeting and say, 'What's up everybody? I'm gay.' Now is not the time, and unfortunately that moment will not come in my lifetime" (151). Thompson fears that should he come out or if word leaks out or people simply figure out that he is gay, he will suffer public ridicule, be singled out for violence, or be driven out of the sport by a hostile workplace. Surprisingly, his psychologist agrees with him, reinforcing the hegemony of silence and telling him that it is okay to remain shackled by fear.

At one point, Thompson flirted with coming out. But as alcohol fueled hostility during a San Francisco dinner, the heterosexual teammate he thought would safely harbor his proclamation clamored, "Somebody should kill those fucking faggots," squashing Thompson's belief in his broadmindedness. Thompson recoiled even more when another teammate said, "We are in Fagville" (141).

Thompson had heard San Francisco referred to as Faggot City before, and he was certainly no stranger to homophobic discourse. He had heard his parents use the terms frequently when he was a kid, and frequently heard faggot as a name for one who doesn't play through pain in the NFL. Thompson, a

Eric Anderson, "The Center of Masculine Production: Gay Athletes in Professional Sports," from *In the Game: Gay Athletes and the Cult of Masculinity* (Albany, NY: State University of New York Press, 2005). Reprinted by permission.

better than average player, has inflicted pain and received a great deal of pain himself. He has, after all, played in the NFL for many years. But Thompson laments upon the emotional not the physical when it comes to coming out. "I know keeping this secret is eating me up inside." He says, "But right now, I don't care. I love this game so much I won't do anything to jeopardize it" (151).

One might question such devout love for a violent game; a game that, paradoxically, is positioned in ideological opposition to his hidden identity. One might ask why Thompson would choose to live in a social space predicated upon demonizing the identity he relates to. But perhaps, for all its homophobia, pain, and homonegative violence football somehow provides Thompson a shelter from something he fears more than marginalization. Indeed, his willingness to remain closeted indicates that whatever he fears about coming out, the consequences of doing so are judged as being worse than living the segmented life of a closeted superstar. Whatever the answers, he is not the only one in this position, he claims to know other closeted NFL players too, in what he calls, "an underground network of gay NFL players" (152). . . .

Professional-Sized Fear

Team sport athletes (gay and straight) often represent a paradox in masculinity. Whereas they are assumed to be fearless because they are associated with orthodox masculinity, whereas they are thought to possess emotional strength, independence, and courage, in actuality, they are also quite scared. They are neither emotionally strong, independent, nor courageous. Team sport athletes cowardly adhere to the strictest of gender roles, and if Michael Messner is right about professional sports being the center of masculine production, then professional athletes are the most likely to do what they are told.

Professional athletes may be afraid of deviating even slightly from the masculine ascription, because the terrain outside masculine boundaries is viewed as a contentious and stigmatized space. Essentially, team sport athletes exhibit toughness only on the outside. They are members of the cult of athleticism, tithing their agency and vowing complacency to team norms. They are not freethinking and free speaking; rather their ideologies are largely shaped by the cult, and they express uniformity in thought and action—benevolent to the ideology of orthodox masculinity.

In order to make salient this point, I frequently challenge the athletes in my courses to come to class wearing a dress. Generally saying, "We think that athletes are brave because they put up with physical brutality, and in that aspect they are. But when it comes to bravery of self-expression, or fearing stepping outside predetermined masculine boundaries, they are the most afraid. Let's see how much you truly don't care what other people think of you." I chide them, "Come to class in a dress." Highlighting my point Thompson says, "I love playing football more than I love myself and my sense of pride and well-being" (cited in Freeman 2003, 143).

In short, athletes who best represent hegemonic masculinity are often afraid to be anything but hypermasculine. Following masculine mandates has been shown to damage self-esteem, which in turn has been shown to make athletes more accepting of abuse from coaches and teammates (Coakley 2002). Perhaps the ultimate example of an athlete following masculine scripts and of doing what he is told comes to us from Billy Bean* who so adhered to the expectations of his teammates that he skipped the funeral of his lover in order to make a baseball game!

Billy Bean's sacrifice (missing his lover's funeral for a baseball game) might seem extreme to those from outside the institution of baseball. However, sacrifice is the hallmark of sport, and for those with enough talent and desire to emulate masculinity enough to make it to the elite levels of sport, the near-total institution requires them to sacrifice health, education, stability, security, friendship, family, and gender expression for the sake of athletic elitism and the social merit that accompanies it. Ironically, whereas athletes are willing to sacrifice all types of personal freedoms for athletic success, they are not willing to sacrifice athletic success for personal freedom.[2]

When it comes to sacrificing personal freedom for physical safety, gay team sport athletes find themselves in another paradox. Whereas athletes are commonly thought to be intimidating, closeted gay athletes fear that the level of violence, in an already violent sport, might intensify if it were known that they were gay. So even though they are not supposed to be capable of being intimidated, they are. And there might be some reason for this: openly gay athletes might genuinely be targeted for extra (illegitimate) violence by other athletes. Retired gay football player Esera Tuaolo said:

> The one thing I could never do was talk about it. Never. No one in the NFL wanted to hear it, and if anyone did hear it, that would be the end for me. I'd wind up cut or injured. I was sure that if a GM didn't get rid of me for the sake of team chemistry, another player would intentionally hurt me, to keep up the image. (cited in Freeman 2003, 155)

Furthermore, Thompson tells of a situation on his NFL team in which his coach described a player from another team who was suspected of being gay, by saying, "He's soft, real soft, and some of you guys know what I'm talking about. He gets hit, he folds up like a bitch. So smack him around and he will give up." The coach added, "Just don't bend over when you're near him" (cited in Freeman 2003).

There is no doubt that intentional violence occurs in these spaces. Minnesota Viking player (and Reverend) Reggie White said:

> Sometimes you have to hit somebody to get them out of the game cuz if you get them out of the game then it gives you a better opportunity

---

Editor's Note: A professional baseball player who came out after he retired.

to win. When you see Emmit Smith pull a hamstring a week before the game, you're thinking good this is my job and my job is to go out and do whatever I need to win. (cited in Kaufman 2003)

Similarly, Thompson said that when playing against this team he noticed the player in question was getting more than his fair share of late hits, cheap shots, spit on, and kicks to his stomach. After one play in which the player suspected of being gay was left on the ground, Thompson went to help him up. "Don't help that fag up!" a teammate exclaimed (Freeman 2003). Thompson didn't, and never helped him up again.

Professional Pressure

In addition to being afraid of breaking with the cult of masculinity and being victimized by violence, gay athletes might also be pressured to remain closeted by their fears of having their athletic performance decreased as a result of social pressures from coming out. In professional sports, careers are made and destroyed by a finite number of chances. Gay athletes who have come out after retiring and those who are still closeted both express that coming out would have a significant effect toward bringing unwanted pressure to their athletic experience. They suggest that the stress of coming out, combined with the already exacting pressures to perform at the world-class level, would make coming out highly distracting to a team that is "playing" for million-dollar contracts. Billy Bean told *Sports Illustrated*:

> It would be very difficult for a player to come out today. This guy has to play in stadiums with 40,000 people. What's he going to hear if he strikes out? Overnight this guy's career will have nothing to do with his athletic ability. It's not a safe time to do it. (cited in Menez 2001)

In the October 2002 issue of *Out* he added:

> To put your sexuality at the forefront of your life when you're a professional athlete, that's really hard. The sport has to be at the forefront. To sacrifice that, that's a huge thing. When you are at the top of your game you do realized how hard it was to get there, and you do know how short-lived that can be. And overnight you are changing the focus of your game. It doesn't take a long time to slide off that scale. (cited in Konigsberg 2002, 81)

But this attitude is just one side of the coin. They fail to account for the effect that the distraction, depression, anxiety, and fear of being outed against one's will might also have on a player; something which he articulates in his autobiography.

> My confusion was hard to shake, even at the ballpark, which always had been my sanctuary. I would stand in center field, my

every move scrutinized by 40,000 screaming fans, worrying about my parents' reaction to the inevitable tabloid headlines about the queer ballplayer when I should've been focusing on the location of the next pitch or on getting the best possible jump on a hit my way. Striding to the plate, I'd catch myself wondering about how my otherwise sturdy, dependable body could possibly harbor such desires. . . . I regressed to the stage of a rookie. (2003, 103)

He later says, "My emotional turmoil was obviously contributing to my inability to concentrate on the field. My self-confidence, the foundation of any player, was shot" (107).

Similarly, retired gay NFL player Esera Tuaolo said:

I would get a sack, force a fumble, stuff a play on the goal line. And hours later, in the middle of the night, I'd wake up sweating, clutching my chest and gasping for breath. Maybe someone who knows saw that, I'd think to myself. Maybe they'll call the coach, or the owner, or the papers. Sometimes I'd spend hours lying awake, praying for the anxiety attack to end, hoping my head would stop spinning on top of my banged-up body.[3]

The contradictory statements lead one to wonder just what the effect of stress is on an athlete, and whether the stress of remaining closeted is more deleterious to performance than the stress of dealing with pressures as an openly gay athlete. While I cannot sociologically assess the situation for professional athletes (because there are not enough to study), the insights I have gained from studying openly gay high school and college athletes might help illuminate the complexity of the situation.

Openly gay high school and college athletes tell me that they too faced crippling fears of being discovered. However, these same athletes unanimously expressed an empowerment as a result of coming out. They reported an intoxicating sense of agency in controlling one's social space. Similarly, Olympic gold medalist Mark Tewksbury even tells me that his performance dramatically improved after telling his coach that he was gay. "I dropped 1.3 seconds off my backstroke in just ten months because I freed so much of my energies after finally telling my coach that I was gay. I had been working for years to gain tenths of seconds, but after I told him I dropped 1.3!"[4] Other gay athletes have also expressed similar performance related gains after coming out. Bob dropped his 800-meter time from 1:56 to 1:51 shortly after coming out, a substantial improvement that he attributes to his feeling less socially restricted.* "I was just looser, more relaxed," he said. "Like a giant weight was removed from my back."

Editor's Note: Bob, one of the 30 openly gay athletes interviewed by Eric Anderson, was captain of his team when he came out.

Ultimately, it is the not knowing what *might* happen after coming out of the closet that cripples gay athletes. However, after coming out of the closet, their tactics change. General panic is replaced with strategic and empowered thinking. This sense is nearly universal among the athletes I interviewed. When they came out publicly it was almost always coupled with the desire to have come out sooner. Conversely, athletes who come out covertly report less empowerment from being out. Indeed, these athletes often maintain a general sense of anxiety about who knows and what they might think and they find themselves stuck in the second-class citizenship of don't ask, don't tell.

While remaining closeted, or managing a compartmentalized identity (choosing to be out in some arenas and not in others) is most certainly *stressful,* it does not necessarily mean that the stress will result in poorer performance. Terry (the professional football player) and Aaron (the professional hockey player) report stress from managing their identity in this manner, but they do not report that their choice to remain in the closet has had a deleterious effect on their performance. And although they cannot know this with certainty, because they have not tried coming out, I do not feel comfortable enough drawing broad conclusions about the effect of coming out in sport and performance with professional athletes.

NOTES

1. The quotes from Thompson are from the book *Bloody Sundays,* written by a respected *New York Times* sports columnist. Although I can have no guarantee that the interview he conducted with Thompson is true, I have no reason to doubt its authenticity either.

2. It should be noted that this statement is somewhat misleading because the athletes I've interviewed are those who have chosen to remain in sport. Athletes who have dropped out of sport are not represented by my study. Therefore, I can't really say what percentage of athletes are willing to sacrifice personal freedom for athletic success.

3. This quote was found in the November 11, 2002 issue of *ESPN: the Magazine,* http://espn.go.com/magazine/vol5no23tuaolo.html.

4. Mark Tewksbury tells me that he estimates that he gained six years of training improvement by coming out of the closet to his teammates and coach.

REFERENCES

Coakley, Jay. 2002. *Sport in society: Issues and controversies.* Boston: McGraw-Hill.

Freeman, Mike. 2003. *Bloody Sundays.* New York: William Morrow.

Kaufman, King. 2003, January 8. Football: America's favorite homoerotic sport. http://www.salon.com/news/sports/col/Kaufman/2003/01/08/homoerotic/.

Konigsberg, Bill. 2002, October. Billy Bean. *Out.*

Menez, Gene. 2001, May 22. The toughest out. http://sportsillustrated.cnn.com/features/scorecard/news/2001/05/22/sc.

Messner, Michael. 1987. The meaning of success: The athletic experience and the development of identity. In Harry Brod (Ed.), *The making of masculinities: The new men's studies.* Allen and Unwin.

———. 1992. *Power at play: Sports and the problem of masculinity.* Boston: Beacon Press.

52

MEN AT WAR
Vietnam and Agent Orange

CYNTHIA R. DANIELS

Cynthia R. Daniels is associate professor of political science at Rutgers University. She is the author of *At Women's Expense: State Power and the Politics of Fetal Rights* (1993).

> *"We have drafted the unborn and the unborn are now going to war with their fathers and mothers."*
>
> VIETNAM VETERAN ACTIVIST MICHAEL RYAN[1]

> *"Dioxin still kills Vets and their children."*
>
> NJ AGENT ORANGE COMMISSION WEB SITE,
> BANNER HEADLINE, 5/30/01

> *"The government ought to treat these children as if they had been shot in Vietnam."*
>
> REP. LANE EVANS, D-IL[2]

From 1962 to 1971, the U.S. military sprayed 19 million gallons of Agent Orange and other herbicides from Air Force planes over the forests in Vietnam. The herbicide killed the vegetation that provided cover for enemy troops.[3] Strange illnesses, birth defects, and cancers began to appear in the early 1960s among the Vietnamese farm families and mountain people who lived under the toxic rain. Suspicions that these were caused by Agent Orange were reinforced in 1969 by a U.S. study showing that exposure to dioxin, one ingredient in Agent Orange, produced cancer and birth defects in lab animals. By 1971, with concerns over health effects rising, the U.S. military halted the spraying.[4]

It was not until five years after the war's end, in 1978, that a Veterans Administration (VA) caseworker began to notice a similar pattern of illnesses among the Vietnam veterans she was seeing in Chicago.[5] She suspected that their strange symptoms—chronic rashes, nerve disorders, cancers, and problems with their children—were due to their toxic exposures in war, and she brought her concerns to the VA. The VA and military officials dismissed her concerns, arguing that any residue of dioxin sprayed from the air would have quickly dissipated in the sunlight, posing little risk to American troops. Almost 3 million troops had served in Vietnam, and no one knew how many had been exposed to Agent Orange.

Frustrated by the lack of response by the military, Vietnam vets turned to both Congress and the courts. Based on the early studies of dioxin, some of which had shown serious health effects on workers who produced it from the early 1950s, 15,000 vets filed suit against the seven companies that had manufactured Agent Orange. In addition, they demanded funding from Congress for further research. In 1979, Congress authorized $100 million for the Department of Veterans Affairs to conduct a study of the health effects of Agent Orange.

In the meantime, collaborations began between occupational health physicians Steven and Jeanne Stellman and a number of Vietnam veteran organizations.[6] A name familiar from the 1977 DBCP pesticide incident,* Jeanne Stellman had already been involved in studies on the impact of pesticide exposures on male reproductive health. The Stellmans helped a vets' organization, Citizen Soldier, conduct a survey of 500 Vietnam vets in 1980 and found that men who showed physical symptoms of toxic exposure to dioxin had twice the incidence rate of children with congenital anomalies than men without symptoms.[7] Too small for findings of any significance, the survey nevertheless suggested that something was going on that warranted more research. Jeanne Stellman approached the American Legion, then active in lobbying for better investigations into Agent Orange exposure, and the Legion commissioned the Stellmans to conduct more research.[8]

In 1982, the Air Force decided to begin its own study. It would compare the health of soldiers who had flown Agent Orange spraying missions over Vietnam—known as Ranch Hands—to the health of unexposed vets. Although limited in size to only 1,000 men, it was the only group of soldiers for whom exposure information could at that time be confirmed. The Air Force assigned Lieutenant General Murphy Chesney to head the study—the man who had been in charge of health and safety for Air Force personnel during the Vietnam War, including assessments of the safety of Agent Orange spraying.[9]

By 1983, the $100 million study Congress had ordered the VA to conduct in 1979 had not even been started. As one *Washington Post* reporter put it: "The VA foresaw to its horror a multibillion-dollar drain on its budget should medical care and/or compensation be granted."[10] Congress pulled

---

Editor's Note: DBCP is a pesticide that causes sterility in men. It was removed from the U.S. market in the late 1970s.

the project from the VA and turned it over to the Centers for Disease Control (CDC).[11] The first phase of the CDC study focused on birth defects, examining 4,800 babies born with birth defects in the Atlanta area from 1968 to 1980 and comparing them with a control group of 3,000 healthy children born in Atlanta. In 1984, the CDC released its findings: no positive associations were found between Agent Orange exposure and birth defects in general. But when controlling for possible levels of exposure, based on the places and times of service in Vietnam (information provided by the Army), the study found statistically significant associations between Agent Orange exposure and slightly increased rates of spina bifida, cleft palate, and certain tumors for children of Vietnam vets.[12] Few inferences could be drawn, the CDC argued, because the increases were so slight and the study so small. Of the nearly 8,000 babies in the study, only 696 had fathers who had served in Vietnam. Of these, perhaps a fourth had been exposed to Agent Orange. Unless exposure to Agent Orange produced astoundingly high rates of birth defects, finding statistical significance in these small numbers (given how seldom such birth defects occur) was difficult at best. The birth defect spina bifida, for instance, normally occurred in about 5 of 10,000 births.[13]

Growing scientific evidence linking dioxin exposure not only to birth defects but also to a range of cancers pushed the manufacturers of Agent Orange to seek a settlement in their case with the vets. In 1984, just hours before jury selection was to begin, the chemical companies decided to settle the vets' class action suit for $180 million. As part of the settlement agreement, the benefits were to be shared with all vets who were exposed to Agent Orange. By 1989, 250,000 vets had applied to be included in that settlement class.[14]

In 1987, after $50 million and five years of study, the CDC decided to end its Agent Orange study. Limited information about levels of exposures, the CDC argued, made it impossible to conduct reliable scientific research.

In the meantime, Vietnam vets with illnesses they suspected were caused by Agent Orange exposure continued to seek disability compensation through the Department of Veterans Affairs. For ten years after the war, they were turned away on the grounds that there was insufficient evidence of a causal association. The political irony was not lost on the vets. As one investigative reporter put it, "The shameful truth is the VA has gone to great lengths to make sure there would be no scientific evidence."[15] Or as Jeanne Stellman put it, "It was a studied, purposeful effort not to ask or answer any of the right questions."[16] In addition to delays at the VA, by the end of the 1980s, the Air Force had been accused of delaying and withholding "damaging" data from their study, particularly on reproductive effects, of political manipulation of the study design, and of failure to provide adequate representation of vets on the study's review board, as required by the study protocol.[17]

Turning again to the courts, the vets sued the VA over what they considered to be unreasonable denial of their claims. In 1989, a federal court in California ruled in their favor, agreeing that the VA's standard for assessing compensation claims had been too restrictive. The court ordered a reexamination of every Vietnam vet claim denied since 1985. Diseases with a proven "positive association" with a wartime exposure were to be compensated. "Positive association" was to be legally defined as when "the credible evidence for the association is equal to or outweighs the credible evidence against the association." Where evidence was mixed, vets were to be given the benefit of the doubt.[18]

By the late 1980s, the Vietnam vets were joined by a key political ally. Retired Navy Admiral Elmo Zumwalt had been chief of naval operations in Vietnam and had himself ordered Agent Orange spraying in the Mekong Delta. His son, Elmo Zumwalt Jr., had commanded a Navy boat in the same area. In 1988, his son died of cancer, and his grandson, Russell Zumwalt, was diagnosed with a "sensory integration dysfunction," the same communication disorder that exposed vets had complained of in their own children. Zumwalt was convinced that both were caused by his son's herbicide exposure during the war.[19] Zumwalt became an advocate for research and compensation for the vets.

In addition, a number of key Congressional actors, including Vietnam vet Senator John F. Kerry (D-MA), also joined the fight. Until 1990, the only disease for which the VA provided disability payments from Agent Orange exposure was chloracne, a severe skin disorder long known to be common among workers in plants that produced dioxin. Cosponsored by Senators Kerry and Alan Cranston (D-CA) and Rep. Lane Evans (D-IL), the Agent Orange bill would order the VA to extend benefits to Vietnam vets disabled by either of two forms of cancer: soft-tissue sarcoma and non-Hodgkin's lymphoma. In addition, it would mandate that the National Academy of Sciences review all scientific evidence on the possible health effects of exposure to Agent Orange, to be updated every two years, and that these reviews inform VA judgments about disability claims.[20] In an act whose irony would only later become apparent, the Senate passed the Agent Orange bill the same day U.S. Marines led the first major ground battle of the Persian Gulf War—January 30, 1991. Eager to appear supportive of veterans in the midst of the emerging military conflict in the Persian Gulf, President George H. W. Bush signed the Agent Orange bill into law.[21]

As mandated by the act, in 1993 the National Academy of Sciences (NAS) released its first review. It classified evidence of the health effects of dioxin exposure into five categories: "health outcomes with sufficient evidence of association," "limited/suggestive evidence of association," "inadequate/insufficient evidence of association," "limited/suggestive evidence of no association," or "sufficient evidence of no association."[22] The report confirmed "sufficient evidence" of an association between Agent Orange exposure and soft-tissue sarcoma, non-Hodgkin's lymphoma, Hodgkin's disease, chloracne, and the liver disease known as PCT. The NAS also found "limited/suggestive" evidence of associations between Agent Orange exposure and respiratory cancers, multiple myeloma, and prostate cancer. The

VA extended disability compensation to all these illnesses except prostate cancer.[23] All soldiers who served in Vietnam and who were disabled by any of these illnesses would be eligible for disability payments, regardless of their individual proof of exposure to Agent Orange. Depending on their level of disability, disability payments would range from $90 to $1,800 per month.

On reproductive effects, the review found only "inadequate evidence" of associations with reproductive disorders, including birth defects, spontaneous abortion, infertility, testicular cancer, childhood cancer, and female reproductive problems. There would be no compensation for the children of vets.

In March 1996, NAS released its second report, this time finding "limited/suggestive evidence" of a link between paternal exposure and spina bifida in the children of exposed men. It based this assessment on a reexamination of the portion of the Air Force's Ranch Hand study that appraised reproductive outcomes, as well as two additional nongovernmental studies. Although the Ranch Hand study had been conducted in 1984, the Air Force had delayed its release for eight years by claiming they needed to verify data from birth records and "perform additional data analyses."[24] Indeed, a Government Accounting Office examination of the Ranch Hand study (conducted in response to complaints of delays) found that the level of verification required in Ranch Hand was "highly unusual and virtually unprecedented for a study of its size."[25] Nevertheless, the evidence, now combined with two additional studies, was enough to justify bumping spina bifida up from the "insufficient" into the "limited/suggestive" category of association. Secretary of Veterans Affairs Jesse Brown reported that he was "deeply concerned" about the report.[26]

President Clinton found political opportunity in the 1996 NAS report. At the time the report was released, Clinton's legitimacy with the military was flagging. In the midst of one of many sexual harassment scandals, Clinton had attempted to shield himself against legal charges by appealing to a 1940 law that exempted "military personnel" from damage suits while in "military service." His attempt was met with derision by both the public and the military. Publicly embarrassed, on May 27 he withdrew his request for exemption.

Just one day later, May 28, Clinton called a press conference flanked by Retired Navy Admiral Elmo Zumwalt and dozens of Vietnam vets. In an apparent attempt to restore military favor, Clinton ordered the VA to extend disability coverage to Vietnam vets disabled by two additional diseases, prostate cancer and the nerve disorder peripheral neuropathy. In a remarkable move, he proposed legislation to extend benefits to the children of Vietnam vets for spina bifida. It would be the first time in U.S. history that the children of veterans would be compensated for illnesses traced to the exposures of their fathers. Extending veterans' benefits beyond vets themselves required the approval of Congress.[27]

In Congress, Senator John Kerry introduced, with Senators Jay Rockefeller (D-WV) and Thomas Daschle (D-SD), legislation to extend VA benefits to the approximately 3,000 children of vets with spina bifida.[28] The resistance to the "children-of-war" measure was substantial. Some estimated the cost to support children with spina bifida at $326 million in the first five years, and some argued the move was motivated more by politics than by science. As Veterans Affairs Committee Chairman Senator Alan Simpson (R-WY) put it, "Few words are more effective in evoking an emotional response from us all than the words 'veterans' or 'innocent children.' However, I sincerely believe that the creation of new and precedent-setting entitlements should be decided on the basis of sound medicine and sound science, rather than on the basis of emotion."[29] But such resistance couldn't outweigh the pressure from veterans' organizations representing the millions of men who had fought in war. By September the bill was signed into law.

By the year 2001, nine diseases were on the VA's list of compensated diseases, and diabetes would soon be added.[30] The 2001 NAS report had also suggested that childhood leukemia could also be traced to paternal Agent Orange exposure, and the secretary of veterans affairs had asked Congress for permission to extend benefits to the children who had survived the disease, though most had already died.[31] Of the 2.3 million surviving Vietnam vets, 8,600 veterans and 850 of their children have received disability benefits as a result of their Agent Orange exposure.[32]

More than thirty years after the end of the Vietnam War, plagued by problems and at an estimated total cost of $200 million, the Air Force's Ranch Hand study continues, scheduled to be completed in the year 2006.[33] With only 1,000 "exposed" men in the study, matched up against 1,300 "unexposed" soldiers, many believe the study's small size will seriously limit any of its conclusions.

In the meantime, the Stellmans, like other independent researchers, continued their research, developing databases of information tracking Agent Orange spraying in Vietnam, as well as data on troop locations and movements during the war. In the late 1980s, the judge in the vets' class action suit against the chemical producers of Agent Orange had asked the Stellmans to become "exposure consultants" in the case to help determine which soldiers were eligible to be part of the settlement class. The court had asked the White House to provide information about spraying and troop movements during the war, and the White House refused, informing all executive agencies not to cooperate with the inquiry.[34] The court then filed a freedom of information inquiry requesting access to the information. As Jeanne Stellman recalls, "Suddenly, one day, there appeared 42 reels of computer tape at our office." It was the record of troop and battalion movements in the most heavily sprayed areas of Vietnam. "We had the underlying data that in a million years, we didn't think we would ever see."[35] In 1989 they began processing the data in order to conduct their assessments for the class action suit.

The Stellmans have since supplemented that data with information from the National Archives. In 1996, they received a major grant from the NAS's Institute of Medicine to clean and process the data, providing the first major database specifying both spraying activities and troop placements during the war. When completed, the project will provide the first reliable database, now more than twenty-five years after the war's end. In the meantime, the Vietnam Veterans of America have initiated a joint research project on the effects of Agent Orange on the South Vietnamese soldiers and families who were—and continue to be—affected by residues of dioxin that remain in the land and water in Vietnam.[36]

Recognition of the harms done by Agent Orange exposure, both to soldiers and to their children, had taken nearly three decades. It came only with the fierce lobbying of organizations representing millions of vets, political alliances with members of Congress and prominent military officials, and the support of scientific researchers who had spent years piecing together information about exposures and veterans' health problems. Recognition of the male-mediated effects of dioxin on the children of vets had in part also been produced by political opportunism: first, in George H. W. Bush's efforts to win support for a new war in the Persian Gulf—a war that would itself produce similar claims of war-induced harms—and then in Bill Clinton's attempts to win favor with the military by offering benefits.

When Clinton extended benefits to spina bifida children, it was the first time the federal government had publicly recognized the possibility that the exposures of men could transmit harm to the children men fathered. The extension of benefits to children so harmed was implicit recognition that men's bodies were both vulnerable and deeply connected to the children they fathered. Consciousness of this vulnerability would not be lost on the soldiers who fought in the Persian Gulf War.

Gulf War Babies

It is 1993, and thirteen of the fifteen babies born to male Gulf War veterans in the small town of Waynesboro, Mississippi, have been born with unexplained health defects: rare blood disorders; underdeveloped lungs, fingers missing or fused together, club feet. In Fayetteville, North Carolina, ten children of vets have died of rare disorders: liver cancers, heart defects, children born with no spleen. In Yorba Linda, California, a child of a Gulf War soldier prepares for surgery after being born with a deformed heart on the wrong side of his chest.[37] Like the Vietnam veterans before them, the soldiers of the Persian Gulf War suspected that their wartime exposures to toxins might have damaged the health of the children they fathered.[38] It would seem a cruel irony if in fulfilling their role as soldiers they had lost their capacity to father healthy children.

Gulf War soldiers heading to war were exposed to a remarkable mix of toxins. Required to take a string of vaccines against plague, typhoid, anthrax, and cholera before leaving for war, they were also ordered to swallow tablets to protect against nerve gas attacks once they arrived in Kuwait. In their encampments, they might inhale diesel mist from fuel used to damp down blowing sand dust, smoke from the fuel oil used to burn human waste, or petroleum fumes from oil-well fires in the field. On the war field, they might be exposed to chemical or biological weapons used by Iraqis or uranium in the armor plating of their own tanks or the uranium-tipped ammunition they carried. At the end of the day, they might shower with water contaminated with fuel, climb into sleeping bags dried by the leaded exhaust of army vehicles, and then bunk in tents sprayed with pesticides to control sand flies and scorpions. This was truly a war saturated by the products of the petrochemical industry.

In 1994, the U.S. Government Accounting Office reported that Gulf War soldiers were potentially exposed to twenty-one toxins that have been identified by the U.S. government as reproductive hazards, including arsenic, benzene, cadmium, lead, mercury, nickel, toluene, xylene, and ethanol. No one knows how many soldiers were exposed to these hazards, the extent of their exposures, or the combinations of their exposures. No one knows what happens when one person is simultaneously exposed to viruses, pesticides, solvents, and heavy metals all at the same time. It was not until 1994, three years after the war ended, that the federal government began to fund the bulk of research on the health effects of the war. Of the earliest studies, most focused on stress or posttraumatic stress disorder as a cause of Gulf War veterans' health problems. Prior to 1996, only one study was funded to examine the effects of chemical warfare agents. The study of reproductive effects came late in the game. By 1997, only four of the ninety-one studies funded by the U.S. government on Gulf War illnesses examined the possible reproductive effects of Gulf War exposures.[39]

As a result of newspaper reports of birth defect clusters in Waynesboro, Mississippi, researchers from the federal government initiated a number of studies, focusing primarily on rates of congenital birth defects in children fathered by Gulf War soldiers. No definitive link could be found. There were substantial problems with all of the studies: Some included only veterans still on active duty, when by 1993, 44% of those who had served in the war were out of service. Others studied small groups of veterans, although birth defects, because they are so rare, require large studies. In addition, most studies examined only those birth defects classified as "structural congenital malformations" diagnosed in the first year after birth. Birth defects that might become apparent as a child grew older were not assessed. Studies on birth defects could not pick up increased rates of miscarriage or difficulties conceiving. In addition, given that soldiers tend to be in better health than the average American—the "healthy warrior" effect—one might expect rates of health problems in the veteran population to be lower than the average for the United States as a whole. Studies found that rates of birth defects for Gulf War soldiers were the same as the U.S. average. A more accurate measure would compare rates of birth defects for Gulf War veterans against the rate of birth defects for veterans as a whole.[40]

One significant area of research has focused on the effects of depleted uranium (DU) exposure on soldiers' health. DU is a low-level radioactive heavy metal that is a by-product of the process used to enrich uranium. Because of its extreme density, it is used on the cap or tip of armor-piercing munitions to better penetrate hard targets, like armored tanks. DU is also incorporated into U.S. tank armor to protect against penetration by enemy strikes. When DU munitions strike an object, it "breaks into fragments and fine particles that ignite easily, and it produces uranium dust particles that can be inhaled or ingested."[41] During the Gulf War, a number of these DU munitions were mistakenly used against U.S. tanks, exposing more than 100 U.S. soldiers on or within those tanks to depleted uranium, as well as those soldiers sent to rescue them. In addition, hundreds of soldiers may have been exposed as they "passed through and inhaled smoke from burning DU, handled spent DU munitions, or entered DU-contaminated vehicles on the battlefield or in salvage yards."[42] A study conducted by the Veterans Administration released in the year 2000 found that men with fragments of DU still embedded in their bodies continue, ten years later, to excrete elevated levels of uranium in their urine and that these elevated levels were related to "subtle perturbations" in the reproductive and central nervous systems.[43]

Studies on the possible reproductive effects of Gulf War exposures continue. Some of these focus on populations of veterans exposed to specific toxic substances during the war, like DU or sarin. Others examine medical records from civilian hospitals where the children of veterans who have left active duty have been born. Others expand the scope of reproductive problems examined, such as higher rates of miscarriage or subtler birth defects.[44] Scientists continue to study the reported clusters of "Gulf War babies" with high levels of skepticism after early studies could prove no link between birth defects and wartime exposures.

Like the problems faced by Vietnam vets, for both technical and political reasons, accurate information about Gulf War exposures has been nearly impossible to obtain. It was not until June 1996, after years of evasion and denial, that the Department of Defense acknowledged that some veterans may have been exposed to the nerve gas sarin after the demolition of an Iraqi ammunition facility during the war. Exposure information has been collected by researchers from veterans themselves, but the first of these studies was not initiated until six years after the war's end. Recall problems plague such studies, and of course it is impossible to collect information from soldiers who have died.[45]

By the year 2000, more than 100,000 of the 700,000 soldiers who served in the war had registered with the Department of Defense and Veterans Administration programs as having a range of health problems that they suspected resulted from their Gulf War service. About 90% of these 100,000 soldiers are symptomatic, suffering from a wide variety of health problems and disabilities.[46]

Scientific and political controversy continues over the very existence of Gulf War syndrome, let alone the causal connections between Gulf War service and birth defects or reproductive health problems. In assessing the state of knowledge about Gulf War syndrome in general, Howard Kipen and Nancy Fiedler, two leading researchers in the field, have observed:

> At least in the case of Gulf War symptoms, careful epidemiology has been done to show us that compared with soldiers who did not deploy to the Persian Gulf, those who deployed had two- to threefold increase in symptoms, without apparent medical explanation. What we still do not have agreement on is what lies beneath these symptoms. . . . There is a problem out there. We still do not know what it is.[47]

It had taken more than twenty-five years for Vietnam vets to gain recognition of their own and their children's illnesses. Gulf War vets face even more considerable barriers. So far, the Gulf War studies have been inconclusive. And compared with Vietnam, questions of epidemiology are far more complicated, given the multiple exposures soldiers experienced over a relatively short period of time. As Jeanne Stellman has observed, "Epidemiology is largely a statistical game and you have to be able to sort out normal background events from abnormal rates. I'm sorry to say, from an epidemiological point of view, the [Gulf] War wasn't big enough or long enough to be able to answer many of these questions. . . ."[48]

The Paradoxes of Reproductive Masculinity

Evidence that conflicts with norms of reproductive masculinity—evidence of men's vulnerabilities to harms, men's lack of virility, and men's central and critical connection to the health of their children—has been systematically met with skepticism at best and derision at worst from many scientists, policy makers, and even men themselves. Men do not want to be seen, nor do they want to see themselves, as the subjects of pain and suffering or, in this case, as those who are responsible for transmitting pain and suffering to their children.

By the turn of the twenty-first century, evidence of male-mediated fetal harm entered a public scene with masculinity already deep in crisis. Changing gender roles, the economic decline of traditionally male-dominated industries, and advances in reproductive technologies had all created a sense, whether real or imagined, that men's grip on reproductive power was slipping. Evidence that men were being rendered sterile by toxins at work or at war or, worse, were transmitting harm to their children added insult to the injury already done to American masculinity. In this sense, the skepticism with which such evidence was met—by scientists and policy makers alike—was not surprising.

Ideals of masculinity rest on presumptions of men's ability to *produce, sustain, and protect* their children. Evidence of male reproductive harm threatened to undermine each of these presumptions. Men damaged by environmental or workplace toxins might not be able to produce children at all. A workplace that threatened to undermine male reproductive health might also undermine the family work ethic that drove men into the workplace in the first place. And wartime toxins could throw into question the ability—and the willingness—of men to go to war to protect nation, hearth, and home.

In science, as in all areas of human inquiry, the pursuit of knowledge is linked and often constrained by the implications of that knowledge. As ethicists have long observed, the question is never just "What can I know?" but always also "With that knowledge, what ought I do?"[49] If we were to know that certain toxins—workplace, wartime, lifestyle, or medical—produced fetal harm through men, what would we do with that knowledge? The politics of reproductive risks has focused primarily on the health risks and often "bad behavior" of women. If industrial workplaces were "too dangerous" for women, women could simply be removed from the job. If wartime exposures posed a risk to fertile or pregnant women's health, then women could be banned from service. If women's drug, alcohol, or nicotine addiction proved a threat to their "unborn children," then the state could post public warnings in bars and restaurants, print warnings on alcohol or cigarette packs, launch public education campaigns against drinking or drug use in pregnancy, and criminally prosecute pregnant women who chose to ignore such warnings. Would we really be prepared to do the same to men?

At what cost would we mandate a workplace safe for the reproductive health of both men and women? If workplace toxins posed a reproductive threat to men, would we be prepared to allow only sterile men to work or shut down industry to make the workplace safe for men? Evidence that work harmed not only men but also men's ability to father healthy children might undermine the very incentives that drove men into toxic workplaces in the first place—the support of their wives and children. Indeed, the DBCP scandal galvanized workers, unions, researchers, and regulatory agencies in a way never before witnessed not because it threatened the health of men but because it suggested that work and manliness might be antithetical—that work might in fact undo manliness. The cultural prescription that had led to a profound neglect of men's health—the unwillingness to see male reproductive vulnerability—was the same cultural prescription that called for dramatic action once the damaging effects of DBCP became undeniable. The only way to reinstate the work ethic at the heart of masculinity was to virtually ban the chemical from production.

If wartime toxins proved a threat to the health of the future children of soldiers, would we ban such weapons of war or refuse to send men to the front lines? Evidence of male-mediated reproductive harm at war threatened the prescription that men rule and protect the nation. A state that had poisoned men on the battlefield and then masked its own complicity in the poisoning neither reflected the interests of its citizen-soldiers nor deserved their loyalty. Recognition of the reproductive vulnerability of men at war might throw into question not only the state's legitimacy in the eyes of soldiers but also the very willingness of soldiers to go to war. It was a recognition that also involved significant economic costs to both private producers of toxins and the public agencies that would be held responsible for the care of sick soldiers and their children. Only the political organizing of millions of Vietnam vets and the threatened loss of the state's legitimacy in the eyes of its citizen-soldiers generated action by the state. Recognition of male-mediated toxicity at work and at war posed the threat of structural change never posed in the same way by risks thought to be "contained" to pregnancy.

Evidence of male-mediated fetal harm from men's private behaviors threatened to throw into question men's reproductive self-sovereignty— their right to do whatever they pleased with their own bodies. If studies showed, as they already have, that older men had higher risks of fathering children with birth defects, would we be prepared to recommend that men over the age of fifty not father children? Evidence of the damage wrought by men's drinking, drug use, or smoking might require interventions that the state has typically been unwilling to make, at least for men. If and when such interventions do come, they will most likely target (as the state has done in the case of women) those men most marginal in the hierarchy of masculinity—low-income men who use or abuse illegal drugs, "crack dads." In the meantime, ideals of reproductive masculinity make it all the more difficult to believe that such signs of manhood as beer drinking or cigarette smoking could potentially threaten both male seed and the health of the children such men father.

More equitable approaches to questions of male-mediated harm would subject male and female research to equal levels of scientific scrutiny. It would involve better protecting men from the harms of work, war, and environmental toxins. It would require educating both men and women about the risks of drug, alcohol, and cigarette use both before conception and throughout pregnancy. Where the evidence suggested equivalent levels of susceptibility, it would mean instituting public policies that recognize men's and women's common human vulnerabilities. And where the evidence suggested harms particular to one sex or the other, it would require differential treatment of men and women, as appropriate. But it would not assume, as much of the science and public policy has so far, that men are less susceptible to the harms of the outside world or more distant from the problems of human reproduction, including the children they father.

Research on male-mediated harm has been met with deep political, cultural, and scientific skepticism not only because it threatens to undermine assumptions of masculine invulnerability but also because it threatens to disrupt . . . the assumption of men's distance from the children they father. This distance is predicated on the assumption of a biological and social reproductive division of labor that presumably distances men from both physical production of and social responsibility for children. Assumptions about the distance of men from fetal harm and the ultimate responsibility of women for the health of their children make the science of male-mediated toxicity simply more difficult to believe.

. . . The assumption that men are more distant from the children they father . . . has led to a profound skepticism of male-mediated harm. Yet the distance of men from the children they father appears to be produced as much by cultural belief as by the biology of reproduction. Despite the limitations of current research, studies of the father-fetal relationship have revealed deeper connections between men and their children. It has slowly extended the bridge from men to their babies from the moment of conception, across pregnancy, and now beyond birth. Such research first established men's contribution to couple infertility once thought to be primarily a "female" problem.[50] Research then demonstrated that problems in pregnancy—miscarriage, retarded fetal growth, developmental defects, and stillbirth loss—might also be attributable to men. And now research suggests connections between men and birth defects and childhood diseases. Men's contribution to procreation was no longer fleeting, no longer concluded by the fertilization of an egg.

Each extension of the bridge between men and their children has been met with increasing levels of resistance, not just because effects further from the point at which a sperm disappears into an egg are more difficult to prove but because such evidence places men closer and closer to culpability for the health problems of their children. As the avenues for male-mediated harm have multiplied, so, too, have men's responsibilities for fetal harm. Women would no longer bear the blame alone for the failure to conceive or for miscarriage, stillbirth, low birth weight, birth defects, or childhood diseases.

In the end, the failure to see the damage done to men and their children from reproductive toxins has more to do with what [medical scientist Gladys] Friedler [2001] termed a "reluctance to look" than with what the evidence gives us to see. This reluctance has both privileged and damaged men. It has privileged men by perpetuating assumptions of the superior strength and invulnerability of the male body. It has also protected men from culpability for the potential harm caused by their toxic exposures. But it is a privilege that has also come not just at men's expense—a price paid in the form of a profound neglect of the reproductive health of men—but at the expense of the men, women, and children whose health is increasingly placed at risk not just by the toxic work, wars, and drugs of the twenty-first century but by continuing myths of reproductive masculinity.

NOTES

1. As quoted by Gerald Nicosia, *Home to War* (New York: Crown, 2001), 590.
2. As quoted by Linda Kanamine, "Congress Considering Children-of-War Measure," *USA Today* (12 September 1996): 4A.
3. Earl Lane, "Study: Agent Orange Linked to Spina Bifida," *Houston Chronicle* (15 March 1996): 10.
4. Occupational health practitioners in the United States had also reported increased rates of a skin disease, chloracne, in the men who worked producing the chemical in New Jersey in 1962. Lane, "Study: Agent Orange," 10.
5. Jan Barry, "Troubling Questions about Dioxin," *New York Times* (11 September 1983): 26.
6. Mary McGrory, "Justice for Vietnam Veterans," *Washington Post* (9 May 1989): A2.
7. S. Stellman and J. Stellman, "Health Problems among 535 Vietnam Veterans Potentially Exposed to Herbicides," *American Journal of Epidemiology* 112 (1980): 444.
8. Stellman interview (12 June 2001).
9. Clark Brooks, "Fatal Flaws: How the Military Misled Vietnam Veterans and Their Families about the Health Risks of Agent Orange," *San Diego Union-Tribune* (1 November 1998): A1.
10. McGrory, "Justice for Vietnam Veterans," A2.
11. Barry, "Troubling Questions about Dioxin," 26.
12. J. D. Erickson, J. Mulinare, P. W. McClain, T. G. Fitch, L. M. James, A. B. McClearn, and M. J. Adams Jr., "Vietnam Veterans' Risks for Fathering Babies with Birth Defects," *Journal of the American Medical Association* 252 (August 1984): 903–912. Also see, for analysis of this and other related studies, Lowell E. Sever, Tye E. Arbuckle, and Anne Sweeney, "Reproductive and Developmental Effects of Occupational Pesticide Exposure: The Epidemiologic Evidence," *Occupational Medicine: State of the Art Reviews* 12 (April–June 1997).
13. Pete Earley, "Second Federal Study; Agent Orange Risk Doubted," *Washington Post* (17 August 1984): A1.
14. Earley, "Second Federal Study," A1; McGrory, "Justice for Vietnam Veterans," A2.
15. McGrory, "Justice for Vietnam Veterans," A2.
16. Stellman interview (21 March 2001).
17. A 1999 GAO investigatory report confirmed that in "1984 and 1985, Air Force management and the White House at the time tried to direct certain aspects of the Air Force scientists' research." See U.S. General Accounting Office. "Agent Orange: Actions Needed to Improve Communications of Air Force Ranch Hand Study Data and Results," in *Report to the Ranking Minority Member Committee on Veterans Affairs,* House of Representatives (December 1999): GAO/NSIAD–00–31.
18. *Nehmer v. U.S. Veterans' Administration,* 712 F. Supp. 1404 (N.D. Cal.1989); also see USGAO, "Agent Orange."
19. For an interesting account of political manipulation of the Air Force study and the role of Zumwalt, see Brooks, "Fatal Flaws," A1.
20. Institute of Medicine, National Academy of Sciences, *Veterans and Agent Orange: Health Effects of Herbicides Used in Vietnam* (Washington, DC: National Academy Press, 1994).
21. Brooks, "Fatal Flaws," A1.
22. USGAO, "Agent Orange," 4.
23. These included non-Hodgkin's lymphoma, soft-tissue sarcoma, Hodgkin's disease, porphyria cutanea tarda (a liver disease known as PCT), multiple myeloma,

and respiratory cancers of the lungs, bronchus, larynx, and trachea. Institute of Medicine, *Veterans and Agent Orange: Update 1996* (Washington, DC: National Academy Press, 1997).

24. USGAO, "Agent Orange," 5.

25. USGAO, "Agent Orange," 12.

26. Earl Lane, "Study: Agent Orange," 10.

27. See reports in Paul Richter, "Clinton Expands U.S. Benefits for Veterans Exposed to Agent Orange," *Los Angeles Times* (29 May 1996): 18; Ron Fournier, "Agent Orange Aid Expanded," *Chicago Sun-Times* (29 May 1996): 31; John F. Harris and Bill McAllister, "President Adds VA Benefits after AO Study; Prostate Cancer, Nervous Disorder Covered," *Washington Post* (29 May 1996): A01.

28. Spina bifida is a birth defect in which the backbone fails to close, allowing for possible herniation of the spinal cord.

29. As quoted by Kanamine, "Congress Considering Children-of-War Measure," *USA Today* (12 September 1996): 4A.

30. Philip Shenon, "Air Force Links Agent Orange to Diabetes," *New York Times* (29 March 2000): A23.

31. The specific form of leukemia is acute myelogenous leukemia (AML). David Brown, "Children's Leukemia Risk Tied to Agent Orange; Panel's Finding of Possible Causation Means Vietnam Vets' Offspring May Be Compensated," *Washington Post* (20 April 2001): A2.

32. Brown, "Children's Leukemia Risk," and Kathleen Sullivan, "Lawyers Badger VA to Help Vets Hurt by Dioxin," *San Francisco Chronicle* (11 March 2001): A17.

33. USGAO, "Agent Orange."

34. Stellman telephone interview (7 June 2001).

35. Stellman interview (21 March 2001).

36. Julie Schmit, "Countries Consider Joint Study of Agent Orange," *USA Today* (16 March 2000): 15A.

37. See J. R. Moehringer on Yorba: "Legacy of Worry," *Los Angeles Times* (22 October 1995): A3; Richard Serrano on Fayetteville: "Birth Defects in Gulf Vets' Babies Stir Fear, Debate," *Los Angeles Times* (14 November 1994): A1.1; Simon Tisdall on Mississippi: "Gulf Babies Maimed at Birth, *Guardian* (23 December 1993): Al.

38. For a more complete analysis of the science of paternally mediated fetal effects and social construction of paternal-fetal harm, see Cynthia R. Daniels, "Between Fathers and Fetuses: The Social Construction of Male Reproduction and the Politics of Fetal Harm," *Signs: Journal of Women in Culture and Society* 22 (1997): 579–616.

39. U.S. General Accounting Office, *Gulf War Illnesses*, 42, 43, and 46.

40. One study was conducted by the U.S. Department of Veteran Affairs, the Mississippi State Department of Health, and the Centers for Disease Control and Prevention. See Alan D. Penman, Russell S. Tarver, and Mary M. Currier, "No Evidence of Increase in Birth Defects and Health Problems among Children Born to Persian Gulf War Veterans in Mississippi," *Military Medicine* 161 (January 1996): 1–6. Also see David N. Cowan, Robert F. DeFraites, Gregory C. Gray, Mary B. Goldenbaum, and Samuel M. Wishik, "The Risk of Birth Defects among Children of Persian Gulf War Veterans," *New England Journal of Medicine* 336 (5 June 1997): 1650–1656.

41. U.S. General Accounting Office, *Depleted Uranium Health Effects*, U.S. GAO/NSIAD (2000), 6.

42. USGAO, *Depleted Uranium*, 7.

43. USGAO, *Depleted Uranium*, 9; and see M. A. McDiarmid, J. P. Keogh, F. J. Hooper, K. McPhaul, K. Squibb, R. Kane, R. DiPino, M. Kabat, B. Kaup, L. Anderson, D. Hoover, L. Brown, M. Hamilton, D. Jacobson-Kram, B. Burrows, and M. Walsh, "Health Effects of Depleted Uranium on Exposed Gulf War Veterans," *Environmental Research* 82 (February 2000): 168–180.
44. Studies also continue on the 51,000 British soldiers deployed to the war, as well as the 4,500 Canadian soldiers sent to the Gulf. CBC News Online, "Pentagon Looking at Possible Cause of Gulf War Syndrome" (19 October 1999); Jim Bronskill, "Health Woes Plague Gulf War Babies," *Ottawa Citizen* (29 June 1998).
45. USGAO, *Gulf War Illnesses,* 42.
46. USGAO, *Depleted Uranium,* 13.
47. Howard M. Kipen and Nancy Fiedler, "Invited Commentary: Sensitivities to Chemicals—Context and Implications," *American Journal of Epidemiology* 150 (1999): 13–16. Quote from p. 16.
48. Stellman interview (21 March 2001).
49. This is a paraphrase of the ethical questions posed by Immanuel Kant. This point was made in a keynote address by Charles Scriver at the second International Conference on Male-Mediated Developmental Toxicity, June 2001, Montreal, Canada.
50. "Women . . . generally bore the onus of a barren marriage," observe Margaret Marsh and Wanda Ronner, in their interesting history of infertility in the United States. See *The Empty Cradle: Infertility in America from Colonial Times to the Present* (Baltimore: Johns Hopkins University Press, 1996), 16.

REFERENCES

Friedler, Gladys, Telephone interview with C. Daniels (7 February 2001).
Stellman, Jeanne, Interview with C. Daniels (12 June 2001).
———. Telephone interview with C. Daniels (21 March 2001).
———. Telephone interview with C. Daniels (7 June 2001).
U.S. General Accounting Office, "Gulf War Illnesses: Improved Monitoring of Clinical Progress and Reexamination of Research Emphasis Are Needed," *Report to the Chairmen and Ranking Minority Members of the Senate Committee on Armed Services and the House Committee on National Security,* GAO/NSIAD–97–163, June 1997, www.gao.gov/archive/1997/ns97163.pdf.

53

FORT BRAGG: COMMAND

JEFFREY McGOWAN

Jeffrey McGowan joined the army in the late 1980s and served for ten years. Since leaving the service, McGowan has developed a successful sales career in the pharmaceutical industry. In February 2004, he and his partner, Billiam van Roestenberg, were the first same-sex couple to be married on the East Coast. They live in New Paltz, New York.

At the time of the conflict described in this excerpt, Jeffrey McGowan was an Army Captain and unit commander at Fort Bragg, North Carolina.

For the most part we rode back to the base in silence, Lopez and I. When he first got in he said to me, quietly, "I know I haven't done anything wrong, sir . . . nothing," and I turned my head toward him briefly and nodded to let him know I believed him. Of course, it wasn't what he'd done, it's what he *was* that they were having a problem with. If that isn't un-American, well, I don't know what is.

I felt bad for the guy. And the fact that I couldn't say anything about myself, the irony of that, was just incredibly depressing. Here I was, a gay man who was probably going to be asked to initiate the persecution of another gay man. Could things get any worse? How could I believe in *this* army? I tried to imagine what he must be going through. And the realization that it could just as easily be me, that it one day *might* be me, was sobering, to say the least. I feared for Sergeant Lopez and for what I might be asked to do. Was it possible to remain in the army as a gay man and still maintain one's integrity? I was beginning to see how impossible that was. I was beginning to see just how compromised I might up end up becoming.

The very next morning there was a message for me to meet Colonel Fazio at HQ. . . . I was supposed to have met him at his office at nine, but my office was on his way, so he figured he'd just drop by. I smiled as he lifted up a brown paper bag with another cup of coffee in it for me.

"Thank you, sir. This is a surprise, sir. I was just on my way to see you."

Fazio smiled. . . . He was a great guy, easy to talk to, with an excellent sense of humor, and I thought of him as my mentor.

"So, Jeff, you had quite the day yesterday," he said, blowing on his steaming coffee, then chuckling a little before taking a sip from the cup. Before I had the chance to answer he said, "Tell me, Jeff, what kind of soldier is your motor sergeant?"

"A good one, sir. He works hard. Never had a problem with him." I waited for his response. I figured if anyone knew the right way to handle this, Colonel Fazio would.

"Really?"

I looked up from my cup and noticed that the colonel was busying himself with clipping the end of a black Maduro cigar. He then lit it and casually blew out a thick column of smoke. I wasn't sure how to answer the question, so I said nothing.

"So how's his section doing?"

His eyes followed a particularly graceful ring of smoke up to the ceiling, then they slowly trailed down and landed squarely on me. I smiled somewhat guardedly, and just as I was about to speak he broke in again, "So, Jeff, what's up with this bust, anyway? What's going on? What'd they say they're looking for?" . . .

"They made multiple arrests, sir. Apparently there was pornography involved." I shrugged my shoulders.

"Seems that this mess has made its way up the chain of command to the corps commander; apparently one of these"—he considered his choice of words carefully—"little queers got an outside advocacy group involved, you know this Don't-Ask-Don't-Tell horse shit and all. There is the potential for some serious blowback behind it all." He laughed again and winked at me, adding, "No pun intended . . . so the process has been slowed down considerably."

"The process, sir?"

He raised his eyebrow at me, then blew another ring of smoke in my direction.

"The process of safeguarding the army. You don't think we'd allow them to stay in, do you?"

"Absolutely not, sir," I answered much too quickly. In all my life, I'd never felt more ashamed of myself than I did at that very moment.

"So tell me about his performance, Jeff."

"He's an excellent worker, sir, never had a problem with him, and the rest of the troops like him."

"Late?"

"No, sir."

"There is talk that the subjects who were outed—you know, the ones who weren't coconspirators—are not going to get sectioned out. We're not supposed to ask, and this guy certainly didn't tell. Needless to say we're going to have to . . . deal with the situation."

Suddenly the whole thing became clear to me. The colonel expected me to develop a pattern of offenses against Sergeant Lopez, to find fault wherever I could and create a paper trail. This trumped-up paper trail, created by me, would eventually carry enough weight to bring him down. It was a crushing blow to hear this coming from the man whom I'd admired for so long and who'd come to represent for me all that I thought was good in the army.

I thought maybe I could appeal to his reason. "I don't want to sound like I'm not a team player, sir," I said, "but I'm just not getting it."

Colonel Fazio didn't like repeating anything twice, particularly to a hand-picked subordinate. He turned deadly serious and leaned into me. "They do not serve in the U.S. Army, McGowan. We find them, we get rid of them. No questions asked. It's been happening since the beginning of time."

"I know the old policy, sir, but I'm aware of the new policy as well, and he never really came forward and said he was . . . gay. So we can't really do anything. It's not fair." I knew I was asking for it big-time.

He lurched forward on the edge of the couch and poked the cigar at me.

"Fair? We are not working in a democracy, Captain. There *is* no fair here. I do not even want to consider the possibility that you don't understand your responsibilities here. Now . . . in *fairness,* I am going to ask you this one last time, is there anything I need to know?"

I dropped my head. I needed to think this out clearly. It was now not only Sergeant Lopez's career on the line but my own as well. Finally, I looked at him and said, firmly, "Sir, I understand your view. But with all due respect, I have to say I am extremely uncomfortable with what it is you're asking me to do."

An eerie calm came over him. He sat back into the couch and relit his cigar. I knew this wasn't a good sign. It was worse than yelling, this silence, because I knew he'd moved to the next level. The colonel was a brilliant tactician. He didn't get to wear those oak leaves for nothing. If he wanted, he could have me demoted to base cesspool cleaner for the duration of my career.

There was no getting around it now. Lopez was fucked, and I was fucked for trying to save him.

"Jeff, where do you see yourself going from here?" he said, refusing to look at me, looking down the ash of the cigar instead. "Increased responsibility requires a broad understanding of army values and an ability to protect the institution." He stood up slowly.

I started to rise, but he pushed the palm of his hand at me. "Remain seated," he said, and walked briskly out of my office.

I just stood there, staring at the closed door, feeling numb at first, then frightened, then very, very angry, and then finally just terribly sad. Most of all I was disappointed in Colonel Fazio. We had talked at great length about his pride in the army's diversity. We had talked about his children at barbecues. He was a terrific husband and father, and not only did I enjoy his company, I liked his family as well.

The truth was I was taking this very personally. It felt as if all the things he'd said about Lopez were aimed at me, too, and that hurt like hell.

Now, I had been on the wrong end of his anger before. And I'd learned that if it turned out he was wrong he'd usually come around and try to make good. This time, though, I didn't care whether or not he came around.

Don't get me wrong. I was as much a careerist in the army as he was. And I knew he could squeeze me out as easily as he intended to squeeze out Sergeant Lopez. What bothered me the most wasn't his hatred (or fear, or both, depending on your point of view) of homosexuals. He was a product of his environment, after all. He'd been in the army his entire adult life, and the army provides little incentive (you could probably argue it provides disincentives) to develop your own thoughts on the issue of gays in the military. Why distinguish yourself from everyone else? What would he have to gain? I can't pretend that I was shocked by his intolerance.

No, what bothered me more than anything was just how personally he'd taken the whole thing, as if Lopez's mere existence (and mine, by extension) in his unit was a personal affront to his character and command. In fact, it had nothing at all to do with him personally. But, of course, he couldn't see that, at least not right away. I spent the next few days expecting a phone call informing me that I was being relieved of my command, but the call never came. When the weekend finally arrived, I tried to relax and put the whole thing out of my mind. On Friday night there was a "hail and farewell," a function we had regularly to welcome new officers to the base and say good-bye to those who were leaving. I sat gloomily at the bar, convinced that any "greeting" on my part would be a waste of time since my days were numbered. Just when I thought I'd head home, I was approached by one of the most beautiful women I've ever known. It was Maggie Fazio, the colonel's wife. . . . She smiled as she sat next to me at the bar.

"You on the lam from the New York authorities, old boy?"

I smiled. "Apparently I'm wanted in all fifty, I'm told."

"Don't be so hard on yourself, Jeff. . . . Things have a way of coming round." Her presence was always like a gift. I breathed easy for the first time in days. Maybe the death blow was not so close after all. "Has he told you anything, Maggie?"

"Oh, hells bells, Jeff, you know how he is. When someone is twisting them on him, all he does is talk about them but not really about the issue at hand. You, of course, have been the topic of conversation for a number of dinners and breakfasts. I have never seen the man quite so angry; now why not tell me your side of the story?"

I told Maggie Fazio the whole story. . . . It felt good to get it all out and to have such a sympathetic ear. I ended up with this:

"To go after this man was no different than going after someone because they're black or a woman. I believe in fairness. Soldiers have to know that if they follow the rules they will be treated fairly. Lopez did nothing wrong. It was a witch hunt at best, and as much as I like your husband—you know how much I like the colonel, right? [Maggie Fazio nodded her head]—I just couldn't let myself be a part of it. Whether he was gay or not never really entered into the grand scope of things. If he was, the policy states that we shouldn't ask, so technically he deserved a reprieve. But they still want him out—by any means available. It just isn't right."

I finished off my third whiskey and was about to say good-bye to her when she tilted her head at me and smiled.

"He is a handful, Jeff, isn't he?" she asked, rolling her eyes and laughing softly. "You can't blame him for doing something he thought was right by the old guard, yes?"

I nodded. And I couldn't blame him, really.

"But, Jeff, I get it. I get it," she repeated, patting my hand, "and I know for a fact that eventually he'll get it, too."

With that she stood up, gently kissed my cheek, and disappeared into the crowd. . . . I didn't know what to feel now. Maybe she was right. Maybe the colonel would come around. But even if he did, it wouldn't be soon enough to save me. I was doomed. I hunkered down and ordered another whiskey.

That Monday I went into the office earlier than usual. I'd planned actually to start going through my desk, so convinced I was that Colonel Fazio was going to give me the ax. When I walked into the room, the first thing I noticed was an envelope lying on the floor, a few feet from the door, as if someone had slipped it underneath. I opened it. Inside was a card with a picture of a gorilla on it. The card read, "It takes a big man to know he was wrong." Below that, in the undeniably strong handwriting I'd come to recognize instantly, was the signature, Colonel Joseph Fazio.

Sergeant Lopez survived without any adverse action taken against him, but when it came time to reenlist he refused to consider the possibility. He could read the writing on the wall: there was no future for him in the military.

It was really the final nail in the coffin for me, I knew that I was no different from Lopez, and I was smart enough to know that I might not have a godfather to save me in a similar situation. I knew that when my command ended, I would leave the army. It was a bittersweet decision, but I had achieved many of the goals that I had dreamed of as a boy, and I felt that I wanted to live a complete life without the artificial restraints of this hermetically sealed culture.

PART IX
Violence at Home and Abroad

Violence and abuse pervade U.S. society and put millions of people at risk for direct or indirect attack. When we consider the numbers of people who have been victims of violence with those whose loved ones have been victims and those who fear victimization, nearly everyone in this society is touched by violence. Add to that the attacks on the United States on September 11, 2001, and the U.S.-initiated wars in the Middle East and we have a society infused with real or potential terror. However, as with the other issues addressed in this book, people's position in the matrix of domination and privilege affects their experiences.

Domestic violence is a case in point. A recent survey in Asian American communities suggests that domestic abuse is a major problem, with 69 percent of respondents reporting being hit by their parents while growing up; many people believe that divorce is not an option even in violent marriages and a code of silence seems to prevail about the violence.[1] Another study found that among poor and working-class white women 92 percent had experiences with childhood and/or adult abuse and most told no one, again controlled by a code of silence. In that same study, 68 percent of African American women reported domestic violence but were much more likely to have taken action in response to it by telling someone, finding alternate shelter, or getting the abuser out of the home.[2]

Although some people attempted to deny the reality of violence in the United States prior to September 11, 2001, it had become increasingly difficult to do so in the face of the many mass shootings in schools by white boys; whatever sense of safety that existed in suburban and rural areas had already been shaken. The recent killings at Virginia Tech suggest that violence can occur anywhere. In all communities, many children are terrorized by adults, often by their parents or other family members, sometimes by pedophiles and kidnappers outside their families. Women are physically and sexually attacked and terrorized in many social contexts, especially in their own homes, primarily by men. Boys and men are frequently attacked and terrorized by each other, starting with school-yard fights, and continuing in violent sports, military training, street violence, gangs, war, and physically dangerous jobs. People and communities of color, Jewish communities, gay men, lesbians, bisexuals, and transgendered people are often victims of hate crimes.[3] Institutions and the people within them are increasingly becoming victims of terrorism, as evidenced by attacks on abortion clinics (including years of anthrax threats), on doctors who perform abortions, and on government institutions such as in the case of the 1995 Oklahoma City bombing.[4] Worldwide, women's low status correlates with high rates of rape, abuse, discrimination, death in childbirth, sexual slavery, sexually transmitted diseases, infanticide, and genital mutilation, all in a context of inadequate legal protection.[5] An estimated two out of five women in the United States will be physically or sexually assaulted in their lifetimes.[6] The crucial role of judges in granting restraining orders and helping to protect battered women is being examined, with the goal of making the judicial process more accountable to battered women.[7]

The daily crime reports in all urban areas and many suburban and rural ones suggest a country at war with itself. Many urban children are growing up in war zones, caught in the emotional and literal crossfire between warring teenagers and adults; many will, unfortunately, be pressed into gangs as their only option for a sense of meaning in life and into violence as their only means of self-defense.[8] Ironically, while gender socialization teaches women to fear violence and be vulnerable and teaches men to not fear it and be strong, men are at higher risk for every type of violence except sexual assault. Simultaneously, women are taught to fear attacks by strangers but, in fact, are much more likely to be attacked by people they know.[9] Children, too, taught to fear strangers, are most likely to be sexually assaulted by a relative or an acquaintance such as a teacher.[10] Recent outrage at the extent to which the Boston Archdiocese protected pedophile priests at children's expense may actually lead to some constructive changes as Massachusetts considers requiring clergy to become mandatory reporters of child abuse and as the Catholic Church is pressed to play a proactive role in sexual abuse prevention within its ranks.[11]

Although the rate of violent crime has gone down to some extent or stayed stable in recent years,[12] the rate of prison construction and imprisonment has gone up significantly, leading to what is now referred to as the prison-industrial complex in the United States. The United States now has the highest incarceration rate in the world.[13] Critics of this system focus especially on the physical, emotional, and sexual abuse that inmates, both men and women, experience and on the reality that prison is more apt to punish than "correct" in spite of the alleged philosophy of many departments of correction. Some critics also raise questions about why so many prisons are being built, suggesting that there are economic rather than correctional reasons behind the prison boom (e.g., creation of jobs and profit for the corporations that build and run prisons).[14] The fact that community-based programs for male batterers are more effective than criminal justice interventions suggests that an increase in alternative programs would make more sense than construction of new prisons.[15] A recent study of women of color and law enforcement finds that the growth of law enforcement (including activity of the Immigration and Naturalization Service) has disproportionately affected women of color, leading to increased incarceration and detainment, abuse within these settings, and denial of reproductive and sexual autonomy. According to the study, between 1985 and 1996 the number of women of color imprisoned tripled and that of women detained by the INS doubled. The two fastest growing inmate populations are U.S.-born women of color and immigrants of color.[16]

A movement toward a new system of justice, called restorative justice, is gaining ground as people in the judicial system along with community activists attempt to move toward community solutions to crime rather than punitive ones. With the goals of holding offenders accountable and also integrating them into the community rather than sending them to prison, meetings occur between offenders and their victims in an effort to educate offenders and provide an opportunity for them to "make things right" with the support of community members. The needs of people on both sides of the offense are addressed.[17]

The study of trauma has shed much light on violence and its effects on victims. Focusing on victims of war, torture, rape, incest, domestic violence, and other horrors, psychiatrist Judith Lewis Herman describes the dynamics of abuse and identifies symptoms experienced by survivors including post-traumatic stress, addictions, suicidal feelings, suicide attempts, and general life upheaval.[18] The rates of violence are even more upsetting when we consider the devastating pain, loss of time, and loss of quality of life that results from such violence. Most women who have been raped, for example, take at least a few months or, more frequently, several years to recover.[19] Thousands of veterans of the Vietnam and now the Iraq and Afghanistan wars have not been able to get their lives together since their war experiences. When I think about the profound waste of human potential and life due to violence, I often wonder how different the world would be without it. And it is not just the victims who suffer; their families and friends, as well as the families of the perpetrators of violence, are forced to turn their attention to violence rather than to more productive concerns. An estimated 325,000 children in the United States are sexually abused each year, and hundreds of thousands are involved as sex workers worldwide. These children are usually left with permanent scars.[20] Concern about trafficking in children emerged after the 2004 tsunami as fear that some of the thousands of children whose parents were lost in the disaster would be sold into slavery under the guise of "adoption."[21]

Many institutions and norms are blamed for violence against women. They include the system of gender inequality that creates an image of women as inferior objects worthy of disrespect; pornography, which sexualizes women's inferior status and presents women as fair game for sexual abuse; privacy, since it encourages a lot of violence to remain behind closed doors; women's unemployment and poverty, which keeps women from leaving abusive men; and men's participation in sports.[22] The latter is a growing problem, according to writer Jeff Benedict, former director of research for the Center for the Study of Sport in Society at Northeastern University. In his study of both publicized and unpublicized cases of violence against women by college and professional athletes, he concludes that athletes commit more violence against women than their numbers would predict and expresses dismay at the fact that so many athlete role models are setting a poor example for boys and young men.[23] As a result of this, the Mentors in Violence Prevention program was founded, described by

Jackson Katz in Part VII. Given that nearly two-thirds of college women polled in 2005 reported being sexually harassed during their college years, these programs are especially important.[24]

The case of the gang rape of a retarded girl by a group of high school athletes in Glen Ridge, New Jersey, led the late writer Bernard Lefkowitz to conclude that the rape might only have been prevented if the community had taken a close look at what it was modeling for its children:

> Adults might have forstalled the unfolding tragedy in their town if they had questioned their own values, if they had challenged the assumptions of the culture that defined how people treated one another in Glen Ridge. . . . What happened to Leslie Faber is impor-tant because it reveals the extreme outcome of the behavior of young men who are made to feel omnipotent. If a culture is mea-sured by how it treats its weakest members, the Glen Ridge case, first to last, revealed American culture at its basest.[25]

Another important theme to mention here is the high rate of civilian vio-lence that men perpetrate against each other, particularly in prisons, in street warfare—such as gangs—and in other masculine institutions that involve initiations and hazing such as fraternities and sports. Violence against gay men and transgendered people by (presumably heterosexual) men, as in the recent murders of Matthew Shepard and Navajo gay/two-spirit teen Fred C. Martinez, is another aspect of men's violence against men, representing extreme and tragic examples of sociologist Michael Kimmel's hypothesis that masculinity is essentially about homophobia—about defining oneself as not a "sissy" and not a female.[26]

There is a growing literature on women's and girls' roles as perpetrators of violence, surrounded by much debate over many aspects of this issue.[27] Researchers and activists are concerned with how to compute valid rates of female violence, how to understand the causes of violence, how to measure its effects in terms of harm and death, and the need to examine the purpose of the violence (for example, women tend to use violence to stop or attempt to stop a violent event or relationship, whereas men tend to use violence as a means of control). Included in such discussions is the tendency for women to be more likely than men to admit to having used force against another per-son, therefore skewing the data.[28]

Prevention of violence is a central aspect of studies of violence at all levels (interpersonal, intergroup, and international). A "culture of peace" perspective on violence explores new ways of approaching violence preven-tion, and an examination of causes of male violence is a central aspect of this work.[29] Attention to men and boys as victims of violence, as mentioned in the introduction to this text, has received increasing attention, including within the culture of peace framework. Thus, in a Norwegian study that attempted to explain men's violence against women, Øystein Gullvåg Holter found that the predictors of male violence against women related not so much to their relationships with women or to masculine identity but to their relationships to men. They were more likely to be aggressive toward women if they had been bullied, especially in childhood or youth by boys or men or if they had experienced violence in the family of origin, particularly from their fathers. Holter also found that when men engage in care work such as child care, they are more likely to have a positive attitude toward it and to be less violent. Men in Norway have the option of a month of paid paternity leave and most take it.[30]

The education and nurturance of boys and young men is a primary approach to violence and sexual harassment prevention. The goals include helping boys to recognize their needs, to learn alternatives to violence, and to develop caring relationships with people of both sexes. The Oakland Men's Project in California has run antiviolence workshops for boys around the United States. Other groups of men are getting together to tap the energy of the 25 percent of men who say they are willing to work toward stopping violence against women. Rather than simply treating batterers, they are working on prevention. For example, on Father's Day every year since 2003, the Founding Fathers Campaign (www.endabuse.org) has taken out a full-page ad in the Sunday *New York Times*, signed by many celebrities. Their "Coaching Boys into Men" program (http://www.coaches-corner.org/) is aimed at educating men and boys about prevention of violence against women by changing attitudes and encouraging healthy, violence-free relationships. The Canadian White Ribbon Campaign to end violence against women has sponsored workshops in schools, corporations, and trade unions across Canada.[31]

Women in many parts of the world have been involved in efforts to end and/or prevent violence and to promote peace. Some have been involved in local efforts to stop violence and bring perpetrators to justice, such as in the case of the estimated 350 unsolved murders of women in Ciudad Juarez, Mexico, since 1993.[32] Others have attempted to end war in such places as Bosnia, Northern Ireland, and Israel/Palestine. In these particular peace efforts, women from different sides of the conflicts have come together to work toward peace (see Gila Svirsky, Part XI).[33]

This part of this book addresses violence in a range of contexts including the U.S. war in the Middle East. The readings begin with a discussion of self-defense for women in the context of interpersonal violence (Melanie Kaye/Kantrowitz), followed by an analysis of Eminem's misogyny (Jackson Katz). Then we hear about experiences of men who have been abused and how they react to those kinds of experiences (Richard Hoffman and Terry A. Kupers). We also learn about abuse of girls and how their aggressive defenses to abuse often land them in detention (Schaffner). This is followed by a look at trafficking in women (Jan Goodwin). Following these essays are three pieces related to the attacks on September 11 (Desiree Taylor), the Abu Ghraib prison scandal in Iraq (Cynthia Enloe), and women's experiences in the U.S. military (Helen Benedict).

As you read these essays, think about your connections to them. Has violence or sexual harassment touched your life? Do you know any women or men who have been in prison? Do you know any veterans? If so, how do their experiences match, or not, those described in these readings? To what extent does Taylor's discussion of safety make sense to you? Have you ever analyzed the "climate" of an institution that you are involved in as Enloe does in her discussion of the military? Have you faced the kinds of sexual assault and sexualized atmosphere described by Benedict and Katz? If so, how do you handle those kinds of situations? What do you think of the idea of women-only train cars that allow women to get away from being harassed in public? Some such train cars exist in Brazil, Tokyo, Mexico City, Mumbai, and Cairo.[34]

NOTES

1. "Asian Family Violence Report Calls for Action," *New Moon: The Newsletter of the Asian Task Force against Domestic Violence* 11, no. 2 (2000): 1, 3–5; "Asian Family Violence Report," www.atask.org.

2. Michelle Fine and Lois Weis, "Disappearing Acts: The State and Violence against Women in the Twentieth Century," *Signs* 25, no. 4 (Summer 2000): 1139–46.

3. "Bias Incidents Reported During 1994," *Klanwatch Intelligence Report* 77 (March 1995), pp. 14ff.

4. For articles on clinic violence and the ongoing commitment to providing abortion to women who want one, see *Ms.,* May/June 1995, pp. 42–66; and (no author), "Welcome to My World," an interview with Merle Hoffman, founder and president of Choices Women's Medical Center in Queens, NY, *Women's Review of Books* XIX, no. 3 (December 2000): pp. 8–9; and Ruth Rosan, "Blind, Unpredictable Terror," *San Francisco Chronicle,* 29 October 2001. For a discussion of recent militia activity that threatens public officials, see "Extremists Pose Increasing Threat of Violence to Police, Other Public Officials," *Klanwatch Intelligence Report* 80 (October 1995), pp. 1ff.

5. Lyndsay Griffiths, "Hardships Plague Women Worldwide, UN Report Says," *The Boston Globe,* 21 September 2000, p. A14; Beth Gardiner, "Torture of Women Said to Be 'Global,'" *The Boston Globe,* 21 March 2001, p. A12; *Miami Herald*, "Man Pleads Guilty to Sex-Slave Operation," 16 January 1999, p. 5B.

6. Associated Press, "2 of 5 Women Encounter Sexual or Physical Abuse, Study Finds," *The Boston Globe,* 6 May 1999, p. A25.

7. James Ptacek, *Battered Women in the Courtroom: The Power of Judicial Responses* (Boston: Northeastern University Press, 1999).

8. For a moving autobiography of gang life, see Luis Rodríguez, *Always Running* (New York: Simon & Schuster, 1993).

9. Jocelyn A. Hollander, "Vulnerability and Dangerousness: The Construction of Gender through Conversation about Violence," *Gender & Society* 15, no. 1 (February 2001): 83–109; Jordana Hart, "Statistics Say Abuse Hits Close to Home: Most Young Victims Know Their Molester," *The Boston Globe,* 30 May 2000, pp. B1, B8.

10. Raymond Hernandez, "Children's Sexual Exploitation Underestimated, Study Finds," *New York Times on the Web,* September 10, 2001, www.nytimes.com/2001/01/10/national/10CHIL.html?todaysheadlines=&pagewanted=print9/10/01; Lee H. Bowker, "The Coaching Abuse of Teenage Girls," in Lee H. Bowker, ed., *Masculinities and Violence* (Thousand Oaks, CA: Sage, 1998).

11. Walter V. Robinson, "Scores of Priests Involved in Sex Abuse Cases: Settlements Kept Scope of Issue Out of Public Eye," *The Boston Globe,* 31 January 2002, pp. A1ff; Stephen Kurkjian and Farah Stockman, "DA Sees Lack of Priest Controls: Archdiocese Had No Rule on Abuse," *The Boston Globe,* 1 February 2002, pp. B1ff.

12. Eric Lichtblau, "Attacks between Partners Fall: Justice Dept. Data Seen as Encouraging," *The Boston Globe,* 18 May 2000, p. A3.

13. Silja J. A. Talvi, "The Craze of Incarceration," *The Progressive* (May 2001), pp. 40–44.

14. For a disturbing look at treatment of male inmates in a maximum security prison, see Mara Taub, "Super-Max Punishment in Prison," *Resist Newsletter* 9, no. 1 (2000): 1–2. See also John Raymond Cook, *Asphalt Justice: A Critique of the Criminal Justice System in America* (Westport, CT: Praeger, 2001); Joseph T. Hallinan, *Going Up the River: Travels in a Prison Nation* (New York: Random House, 2001); Sue Pleming, "Abuse of Women Inmates Seen Rampant: Misconduct Found in All but One State, Amnesty USA Says," *The Boston Globe,* 7 March 2001, p. A7; and Don Sabo, Terry A. Kupers, and Willie London, eds., *Prison Masculinities* (Philadelphia: Temple University Press, 2001).

15. R. Emerson Dobash, Russell P. Dobash, Kate Cavanagh, and Ruth Lewis, *Changing Violent Men* (Thousand Oaks, CA: Sage, 2000).

16. Anannya Bhattacharjee, *Whose Safety? Women of Color and the Violence of Law Enforcement* (Philadelphia: American Friends Service Committee, Committee on Women, Population, and the Environment, 2001). Available full-text online at www.afsc.org/JusticeVisions.htm.

17. Kay Pranis, "Peacemaking Circles: Restorative Justice in Practice Allows Victims and Offenders to Begin Repairing the Harm," *Corrections Today* 59, no. 7 (December 1997): 72ff; Howard Zehr, "A Restorative Lens" in *Changing Lenses* (Waterloo, Ontario: Herald Press, 1990), pp. 177–214.

18. Judith Lewis Herman, *Trauma and Recovery* (New York: Basic Books, 1992).

19. Herman cites several studies of rape victims in *Trauma and Recovery,* pp. 47–48. See also Catherine Cameron, *Resolving Childhood Trauma: A Long-Term Study of Abuse Survivors* (Thousand Oaks, CA: Sage, 2000).

20. Raymond Hernandez, "Children's Sexual Exploitation Underestimated, Study Finds," *New York Times on the Web,* September 10, 2001, www.nytimes.com/2001/01/10/national/10CHIL.html?todaysheadlines=&pagewanted=print9/10/01; Grant Peck, "Sex Trade Lures More Children, UN Says," *The Boston Globe,* 8 December 2001, p. A5; Marian Uhlman, "Sex Trade Targeting the Young Is Called Hidden Epidemic," *The Boston Globe,* 11 September 2001, p. A6.

21. Natasha Bita, "Sadly, the human scum also rises: Tsunamis swamp Asia," *The Weekend Australian,* January 8, 2005, Section: Features, Weekend Inquirer, p. 20.

22. For a look at debates about these alleged causes of violence, see Karin L. Swisher, Carol Wekesser, and William Barbour, eds., *Violence against Women* (San Diego, CA: Greenhaven Press, 1994).

23. Jeff Benedict, *Public Heroes, Private Felons: Athletes and Crimes against Women* (Boston: Northeastern University Press, 1997).

24. American Association of University Women, "Drawing the Line: Sexual Harassment on Campus," 2006: http://www.aauw.org/research/dtl.cfm.

25. Bernard Lefkowitz, *Our Guys* (New York: Vintage Books, 1997), pp. 493–94.

26. Michael S. Kimmel, "Masculinity as Homophobia" (1994). For a range of essays on men and violence against women, children, and men, see Lee H. Bowker, ed., *Masculinities and Violence* (Thousand Oaks, CA: Sage, 1998).

27. James Garbarino, *See Jane Hit: Why Girls Are Growing More Violent and What We Can Do About It* (New York: Penguin, 2006); Lyn Mikel Brown, *Girlfighting: Betrayal and Rejection among Girls* (New York: New York University Press, 2003); Juanita Díaz-Cotto, *Chicana Lives and Criminal Justice: Voices from El Barrio* (Austin: University of Texas Press, 2006).

28. For a discussion of these issues, see Walter D. Keseredy and Martin D. Schwartz, *Women Abuse on Campus: Results of the Canadian National Survey* (Thousand Oaks, CA: Sage, 1998); Nancy Worcester, "What Is the Battered Women's Movement Saying about Women Who Use Force?" *Wisconsin Coalition against Domestic Violence Newsletter* 20, no. 1 (Spring 2001): 2–5, 16–17.

29. Ingeborg Breines, Robert Connell, and Ingrid Eide, eds., *Male Roles, Masculinities and Violence: A Culture of Peace Perspective* (Paris: United Nations Educational, Scientific and Cultural Organization, 2000).

30. Øystein Gullvåg Holter, "Masculinities in Context: On Peace Issues and Patriarchal Orders," in Ingeborg Breines, Robert Connell, and Ingrid Eide, eds., *Male Roles, Masculinities and Violence: A Culture of Peace Perspective* (Paris: United Nations Educational, Scientific and Cultural Organization, 2000), pp. 61–83.

31. Paul Kivel, *Boys Will Be Men: Raising our Sons for Courage, Caring and Community* (Gabriola Island, BC, Canada: New Society Publishers, 1999); Michael Kaufman, "Working with Men and Boys to Challenge Sexism and End Men's Violence," in Breines, Connell, and Eide, eds., *Male Roles, Masculinities and Violence*, pp. 213–22.

32. Chris Kraul, "Frustration Grows over Killings: In Juarez, Victims' Families Complain That Despite Special Prosecutor's Work, Answers Are Few and More Women Are Dying," *Los Angeles Times,* 1 February 2005, part A, p. 3.

33. Cynthia Cockburn, *The Space between Us: Negotiating Gender and National Identities in Conflict* (New York: Zed Books, 1998).

34. Anna Sussman, "In Rio Rush Hour, Women Relax in Single Sex Trains," *Women's eNews*, 23 May 2006. http://www.womensenews.org/article.cfm?aid=2750.

54

WOMEN, VIOLENCE, AND RESISTANCE[1]

MELANIE KAYE/KANTROWITZ

Melanie Kaye/Kantrowitz was born in 1945 in Brooklyn, New York, and has worked in social change movements since the sixties. A graduate of the City College of New York, she earned her Ph.D. in Comparative Literature at the University of California at Berkeley. A writer, activist, and teacher, she lives in New York City. She is author of *The Colors of Jews: Racial Politics and Radical Diaspora* (2002), *My Jewish Face & Other Stories* (1990), coeditor of *The Tribe of Dina: A Jewish Woman's Anthology* (1989), and former editor and publisher of *Sinister Wisdom,* a lesbian/feminist journal.

Blocks to Resistance

Imagination: To Consider Violence

A woman raped by a landlord showing her an apartment remarks, "The only degrading thing I can recall about it is simply not being able to hit the guy. I just really wanted to sock him in the teeth."[2]

> Another woman, awakened and raped with a knife at her throat: . . . You never forget it and you're never the same. . . . It hits you where you're most vulnerable. . . . About six months to a year later some of the vulnerability disappeared. It was replaced by rage. Oh, I wish now I had hit him. Or killed him.[3]

Listen to women cheer at karate demonstrations simulating attack when the woman playing "victim" strikes back. Think about women's reaction to *Thelma & Louise*.[4] In response to violence, it's natural to consider violence.

Yet as a movement, we don't.

If a woman is abused and strikes back, we often work for her defense. We respond to her risk. But we do not ourselves shoulder it, even as a movement. Nor do we encourage women to avail ourselves of violence as a serious, perhaps effective option.

Why?

Obvious response #1: *Violence is wrong.*
Obvious response #2: *Violence won't work.*

Melanie Kaye/Kantrowitz, excerpt from "Women, Violence and Resistance" from *The Issue Is Power: Essays on Women, Jews, Violence and Resistance.* Reprinted with the permission of Aunt Lute Books.

What do we mean, *wrong?* What do we mean, *work?* When women are prepared to use violence, they are less likely to get raped, abused, and murdered.

Listen.

> . . . all of a sudden he got this crazy look in his eye and he said to me, "Now I'm going to kill you." Then I started saying my prayers. I knew there was nothing I could do. He started to hit me—I still wasn't sure if he wanted to rape me at this point—or just to kill me. He was hurting me, but hadn't yet gotten me into a strangle-hold because he was still drunk and off balance. Somehow we pushed into the kitchen where I kept looking at this big knife. But I didn't pick it up. Somehow no matter how much I hated him at that moment, I still couldn't imagine putting the knife in his flesh, and then I was afraid he would grab it and stick it into me. . . .[5]

I couldn't imagine.
I was afraid.

I couldn't imagine corresponds to *it's wrong.* Sticking the knife into his flesh is unimaginable, too horrible.

This horror, this failure of imagination might have cost her life. Her life against his, and she chooses his.

I was afraid corresponds to *it won't work.* Using the knife might make it worse. But how much worse could it get? He's already threatened to kill her.

Is this in women's interest?

If we avoid the question of using violence because it makes us uncomfortable, many men have no such compunctions. They continue to rape, mutilate, beat and kill us. So we are not avoiding violence, only the guilt we associate with using it. Something about innocence is dangerous here. We are innocent because helpless. As long as we insist on maintaining our innocence, we lock ourselves into helplessness. In this way we become complicit with our oppression.

A few feminists have touched on the question. Phyllis Chesler, M. F. Beal, Karen Haglund conclude similarly; in Chesler's words:

> Women, like men, must be capable of violence or self-defense before their refusal to use violence constitutes a free and moral choice rather than "making the best of a bad bargain."[6]

But how do we become capable? What if we are already capable? And what if we don't refuse?

Let us begin to imagine putting the knife in his flesh. If we choose not to, let the reason *not* be that we couldn't imagine doing it. The women who wrote the excellent *Women's Gun Pamphlet* have an answer to the *violence is wrong* voice:

> The only way I've figured out to try and eliminate the all-nurturing masochist in each of us is to remember that the man or men who

attack, rape, mutilate, and try to kill you, have done and will do the same to as many women as they can. While you defend yourself, bear in your mind all the women you love that you are fighting for, especially those you know who have been attacked.[7]

Violence and Power   Yes, I'm talking about violence. But the violence did not originate with us. If we submit, evade, fight back directly or indirectly— no matter what we do we are responding to a violence that already is. Janet Koenig has described how the oppressor's violence

> becomes routinized and ritualized. It becomes so part of the environment, of the school, factory, prison, and family that it is barely perceived consciously. Ideology distorts the perception of violence. The source of violence now appears to be not the system but those who rebel against it.[8]

And Assata Shakur succinctly remarks:

> Women have been raped throughout history, and now when we fight back, now that we have the consciousness to fight back—they call us violent.[9]

To avoid this conceptual error, Ti-Grace Atkinson would call responsive violence, the violence of rebellion, by another name:

> When "violence" appears *against* "oppression," it is a *negation of institutionalized* violence. "Violence," these opening blows are a positive humane act—under such circumstances. Such acts are *acts of bravery* . . . It is a betrayal of humanity, and of hope, to represent such acts as shameful, or regrettable.[10]

Not to deny the horror of violence. Or to invalidate or mock the part in us that does not want to harm. We have an honorable past on this subject. Often life has been preserved solely because of our efforts to feed, wash, clothe, and keep our families in health. We have been active in movements to stop slavery, wars, imperialism, lynching, and abuse of all kinds.

It's hard to transform such concerns into a willingness to cut down another woman's son.

Nor am I saying violence should be leapt to lightly. But the situation is hardly light. I am saying only that using violence should be thinkable. And that the grounds on which we decide whether or not to commit violence against men be *our* grounds: *is it in our interest?*

Violence is an aspect of power. In a conflictual society, where power imbalance exists, so does the possibility of physical force to meet physical threat. "Women," Karen Hagberg points out,

> are called violent (indeed, we actually consider ourselves violent) whenever we assert ourselves in the smallest ways. One woman recently described the verbal challenging of men on the streets as an act of violence.[11]

This is absurd or tragic. Yet the piece of embedded truth is that any woman's challenge to male power—from a calm "I'm not interested" to an assertive "please turn down your stereo"—may be perceived as aggressive and met with violence. Most of us know we risk danger in even a mild confrontation with a man. Every male-female interaction assumes: *in a physical fight he will win.* Every man assumes this about every woman. This is the assumption behind rape. As Ellen Willis remarked in 1968, *Men don't take us seriously because they're not physically afraid of us.*

An Analog: African American Liberation from Slavery   Recent scholarship about African Americans in the South during and after the Civil War sheds intriguing light on the relationship between violence and freedom. When the war began, the great abolitionist and former slave Frederick Douglass

> immediately called for the enlistment of slaves and free blacks into a "liberating army" that would carry the banner of emancipation through the South. Within thirty days, Douglass believed, 10,000 black soldiers could be assembled. "One black regiment alone would be, in such a war, the full equal of two white ones. The very fact of color in this case would be more terrible than powder and balls. The slaves would learn more as to the nature of the conflict from the presence of one such regiment, than from a thousand preachers."[12]

But Northern white men were not so sure. As they debated the question of arming Blacks—slaves or freedmen—three fears were repeated. They feared slave insurrections against slaveholders who, though the enemy, were, after all, white. They feared Black incompetence; no less a personage than President Lincoln speculated that, if Blacks were armed, "in a few weeks the arms would be in the hands of the rebels." But perhaps the deepest and most revealing fear was that Blacks would prove competent. As one Union congressman noted,

> If you make him the instrument by which your battles are fought, the means by which your victories are won, you must treat him as a victor is entitled to be treated, with all decent and becoming respect.[13]

In the South, the same debate was much more anxiety-laden: would armed slaves turn on their masters? (The transparency of the "happy slave" myth is evident in these musings.) What would happen if distinctions were levelled? "The day you make soldiers of them is the beginning of the end of the revolution," warned General Howell Cobb. "If slaves will make good soldiers, our whole theory of slavery is wrong."[14]

In fact, Black soldiers were crucial to the North, and their performance in the Union army, by all accounts courageous and impressive as Douglass had predicted, revealed that "the whole theory of slavery" was more resilient than General Cobb had imagined, surviving as it did the institution of slavery itself. But whether violence is a tool, a back-up to power, a psychological release or an inevitable response to oppression,[15] *being able* to use violence may be a critical aspect of freedom. Listen to Felix Haywood, a former slave in Texas:

> If everymother's son of a black had thrown 'way his hoe and took up a gun to fight for his own freedom along with the Yankees, the war'd been over before it began. But we didn't do it. We couldn't help stick to our masters. We couldn't no more shoot 'em than we could fly. My father and me used to talk 'bout it. We decided we was too soft and freedom wasn't goin' to be much to our good even if we had an education.[16]

Couldn't shoot them. Soft. The definition of manliness that depends on murder may be the saddest comment on patriarchy anyone can dredge up. As W.E.B. Du Bois remarked with some disgust,

> How extraordinary, and what a tribute to ignorance and religious hypocrisy, is that fact that in the minds of most people, even those of liberals, only murder makes men. The slave pleaded; he was humble; he protected the women of the South, and the world ignored him. The slave killed white men; and behold, he was a man.[17]

What about the women? Slave women were vulnerable to sexual abuse by white and Black men alike, though solidarity between enslaved women and men appears to have been very strong.[18] Many women resisted, sometimes with violence. Rose Williams tells of taking a poker to the man chosen by her master for her to marry (i.e., breed with), and of capitulating only after her owner threatened her with a whipping.[19] Cherry Loguen used a stick to knock out a man armed with a knife who tried to rape her. Two women attacked by an overseer waited till he undressed and "pounced upon him, wrestled him to the ground, and then ran away."[20] It's likely that women were able to resist assaults and unwanted attention more forcefully from other slaves than from their owners, though Linda Brent's excruciating narrative of resistance to her owner's sexual demands demonstrates the lengths to which some women went to preserve their sexual integrity.[21]

Did women resist enslavement? During the Middle Passage, women, unlike men, were not chained or confined to the hold. While this freedom left them vulnerable to sexual abuse by the ship's crews, it also left them freer to rebel, and there are several reported instances of women inciting or assisting insurrections at sea.[22] On the plantations,

> Some murdered their masters, some were arsonists, and still others refused to be whipped. . . . Equipped with a whip and two healthy dogs, an Alabama overseer tied a woman named Crecie to a stump with intentions of beating her. To his pain and embarrassment, she jerked the stump out of the ground, grabbed the whip, and sent the overseer running.[23]

A Union official recorded several women entering the Union camp with marks of severe whipping. The whipper was caught and a male slave first lashed him twenty times, and then the women, one after another, gave him twenty lashes, according to the official, "to remind him that they were no longer his";[24] but maybe also because releasing rage where it belongs is one step towards healing.[25] There are also instances of women fighting against their men being taken away.[26]

The ability to defend oneself, one's people, one's dignity, to struggle for one's own liberation, is clearly a survival skill. As Robert Falls, former slave, summed it up: "If I had my life to live over, I would die fighting rather than be a slave again. . . ."[27]

Observations by Black and white, Southerners and Northerners indicate that the Black soldiery affected everyone strongly. Blacks felt pride. Whites felt fear. Both groups recognized that consciousness changed radically when the Black divisions marched through.

And not only consciousness. In New Orleans free Blacks formed two regiments for the Confederacy, in part to improve their status and esteem by learning firearms (though they were never called for combat duty).[28] We could argue the absurdity and tragedy of such a stance, not unlike the arguments that have swirled around Black police or military today. Yet Blacks understood that a Black soldiery might be fair, might protect them, would not automatically assume they were chattel and without rights. A Black soldiery gave Black—and white—people a vision of a differently ordered world: a hint that perhaps the whole theory of slavery was, indeed, wrong.

The analogy is suggestive. Women police officers, fire fighters, soldiers do challenge "the whole theory of slavery,"[29] as do women athletes and construction workers, as well as physicists. But particularly since physical domination so characterizes male-female relations under patriarchy, if women were to defend ourselves and other women, could avail ourselves of violence when needed; and if this potential for self-defense became an expectation, a norm, then patriarchal definitions of male and female would be shaken. Not only minds would change, but reality. Would men begin to wonder if *perhaps the whole theory of patriarchy is wrong?* Would women?

Fear of the Self/Fear of Our Power[30]

If in a patriarchal system violence is an aspect of power, if capacity for violence is a basis for resistance, it's obvious whose interests are served by *it won't work* and *it's wrong;* by the implied fear and horror.

Women often learn to see with the eyes of the dominant culture: male eyes. Especially middle-class heterosexual white women are taught to fear strong women, women with power, women with physical strength, angry women who express that anger forcefully. *It isn't ladylike. It isn't nice.* Even those of us who have long rejected these norms (or accepted our inability to live inside them) still may fear the explosiveness of anger—though this fear obscures the reason for our deep anger, which is our powerlessness. Instead of learning to cherish this rage and to direct it effectively, we often try to suppress it, in ourselves and in others. It's exactly as if we have an army we're afraid to mobilize, train, and use.

Yet we are not always victims. We can be violent. How have we managed to avoid noticing? The idea that men are inherently violent, women inherently non-violent, is dangerous, not only because it is a doctrine of biological superiority, and such doctrines have supported genocide.[31]

The idea that women are inherently non-violent is also dangerous because it's not true. Any doctrine that idealizes us as the non-violent sex idealizes our victimization and institutionalizes who men say we are: intrinsically nurturing, inherently gentle, intuitive, emotional. They think; we feel. They have power; we won't touch it with a ten-foot pole. Guns are for them; let's suffer in a special kind of womanly way.

Such an analysis dooms us to inappropriate kindness and passivity; overlooks both our capacity for and experience with violence; ignores in fact everything about us that we aren't sure we like, including how we sometimes abuse each other. Whatever we disapprove of, we call *theirs,* and then say, when women do these things—talk loud, use reason, fuck hard, act insensitive or competitive, ride motorcycles, carry weapons, explode with rage, fight—they are acting like men.[32]

But who defines "like men," "like women"? On what basis? Remember Sojourner Truth's challenge to restrictive definition: *ain't I a woman?* All women defined as deviant might well echo her words. We may be numerous enough to redefine the "norm." When we find many of us doing what only men are supposed to do, and nearly all of us expressing in some form what is supposed to be a male behavior, then maybe we need to enlarge our notion of who *we* are. The woman who is violent is not acting like a man. She may be announcing a host of contradictions: that her condition is intolerable; that she is or isn't afraid; that she feels entitled; that she has nothing to lose or something to protect; that she needs physical release; that she's a bully; that she has lost or given over or seeks control. But always, in addition, she announces that women are not who men say we are.

> TO SEE WOMEN'S VIOLENCE AS A FIELD INCLUDING:
> SLASHING YOUR WRISTS STANDING UP TO A THREATENING
> LANDLORD KILLING A RAPIST ATTACKING A WOMAN AT
> THE BARFIGHTING AN ABUSIVE HUSBAND PUNCHING
> YOUR LOVER PUNCHING A MAN WHO MOUTHS OFF AT YOU
> LEARNING KARATE KICKING A DOG SHOOTING UP
> WRESTLING FOR MONEY DRINKING TOO MUCH ALCOHOL
> WRESTLING FOR FUN BEATING YOUR CHILD KILLING
> ANOTHER WOMAN'S RAPIST

To see women's violence as a wide range of behavior which can serve, protect, endanger, or violate women and children—or be neutral.[33] To expose the taboo which clothes even our questions about violence. To admit that when we don't fight back against men's violence, it's not because we're passive, not even because we're good: but because we're afraid of what they'll do back.

And for good reason. Consider these words from two married women:

> Sometimes I get so mad I wish I could hit him. I did once, but he hit me back, and he can hurt me more than I can hurt him.

> When he's so much bigger and stronger, and you got four kids to take care of, what's a woman supposed to do?[34]

Consider the implications of the fact that in the late seventies a full 40% of the women imprisoned for homicide in Chicago's Cook County jail had killed men in response to physical abuse by these men.[35] Even though judges in some states have ruled to release women serving time on such convictions, many women still remain in prison.

The fact is, fighting back, even supporting women who fight back, can be dangerous. The wife who feigns sleep when her husband comes home drunk; the child who lies to avoid getting beaten; these are tactics based on experience. Sometimes evasion works better than confrontation. At least it has sometimes kept us alive.

We worry about making things worse. "If you do what I say, I won't hurt you," says the rapist, but the woman who trusts him forgets, in her desperation and terror, that he is, after all, a rapist: hardly a basis for trust. With the husband or mate, while appeasement may be plausible, it's hardly desirable as a way of life.

What happens to women who actively resist violence? The facts, especially about street violence, flatly contradict the usual police/male advice of "don't fight it." When a woman resists a rape *in any way*—saying NO like she means it, screaming, kicking, running, fighting—her chance of escaping ranges from 60–80%.[36]

Whereas *if she doesn't resist her chance of getting raped is 100%.*

Women and Guns

From my journal, 1978:

> For three or four years I've dreamed about rape regularly. The can't run dreams. The can't scream ones. Dreams where I'm being attacked and I have a knife in my pocket but I can't get it, or I'm afraid to use it. The dream that keeps extending into more complication, more danger, until there he is again, "my" rapist. I even had a dream where I'm sitting by a lake and a man swims up, sticks his head out of the water, and says: "I'm your rapist."

In many of these dreams, I don't recognize the danger early enough to respond.

Since I bought a gun and have learned to use it, my dreams have changed. Whatever the situation, whatever the form of attack, I simply whip out my gun. Sometimes I shoot. Sometimes I don't even need to shoot, I just aim and he is suddenly harmless. The man who called himself "my rapist "laughs at me when I draw my gun; he says, "The hospital can suck those bullets out in no time." But I know, and he doesn't, that it's a .38 I'm holding, and I shoot, confident that the bullets will do the job.

If resistance alleviates abuse and increases dramatically our chances of escape, how can we increase our ability to resist? The most certain way to refuse violation would be to keep a gun handy.

Many women immediately reject this option. Some call guns "masculine." Many are simply terrified of guns' murderous power. But aside from fears of legal repercussions or male retaliation, fears which are realistic and need to be addressed—is a gun really more dangerous than, for example, a car? Is owning a gun more dangerous than not owning one? Past the realistic fears is, I believe, a fear of our own selves.

I've talked with many women about getting a gun and learning to shoot.

R. tells me, "I'm afraid I'd kill my husband."

Not to dismiss killings that happen in rage because a gun is handy (though how many of these killings are committed by women?) But to recognize that in her mind she's protected against killing her husband only because she lacks the means.

K. says she's afraid she'd shoot the first man she saw acting like an asshole.

I ask what she means by "an asshole." She says, "Like some man beating up on some woman." Again, she is protected (from her best impulses) only by her inability to act.

N. says she's afraid she'd shoot her nose off.

As if a woman who has learned to cook, play the recorder, ride the subway, drive a car, and change a diaper couldn't learn to shoot.

H., B., C., E., many many women say, "I'm afraid if I have a gun it'll get used against me."

Of course this is exactly what men tell us. For example, in Boston in 1979, after the sixth Black woman in as many weeks had been killed, police still advised Black women against carrying weapons because they could be used against them. Yet what alternatives did the police offer?

In fact I've rarely heard of a real-life woman's weapon being used against her, though I've seen it happen over and over again on TV and in the movies. I've heard of a 14-year-old woman who shot her assailant with his gun, a 17-year-old who sliced her attacker's jugular vein with his knife, a mother who shot with his gun the policeman who threatened her child—she killed him and wounded his partner.[37] Maybe it's men who shouldn't carry weapons. But no one tells them that.

I also discover among my friends women who aren't afraid of guns. L., who teaches me to shoot, grew up around guns in rural Oregon. P. learned to shoot in the army. F.'s father hunted. M.'s grandfather was a gangster. Against the dominant experience of women—which is to have little acquaintance with deadly weapons—an alternative perspective emerges: that of women who were taught to shoot as girls; country women who'd as soon live without a knife in the kitchen as a gun in the bedroom; women who recognize a gun as a tool: useful, dangerous but controllable, like a book of matches.

The first time L. took me shooting with a handgun, I tried a .22 pistol for a while, practiced aiming again and again till it came easy. Then I tried the .38. Fire leaped from the barrel, my hand jumped. TV and movies lie about the sound of guns: it is unbelievably loud. The noise, even with earplugs, shook me. After the first round I sat down, took a deep breath, and said, "I feel like I can't control it."

"It feels like that," L. said, "you just have to get used to how it feels."

After a few minutes, I got up to try again. I started to hit the target.

A learning experience, like a million others in a woman's life. Yet so many of us consider ourselves tiny children when it comes to guns. We're afraid a gun—a source of possible protection—will be turned against us. This fear deprives us of strength, lest our strength benefit them, not us. We're afraid what we'd do *if we could*—which, again, keeps us powerless, lest we use our power badly.

To fear ourselves is to use them as model:

> *they abuse their power, therefore we would too*

is to imagine only helplessness keeps us in line:

> *the more choices we have, the worse we'll be*

is to insist in some hidden corner of the body:

> *we need oppression*

Like, *you can't take the law into your own hands.*
But what better hands to take the law into?

Our fear of ourselves then is fear of ourselves empowered. As we worry about what we'd do if we could, we are undermined in our attempts to end our oppression. We are partly afraid we can't be trusted with freedom.

NOTES

1. I want to acknowledge general indebtedness to the work that preceded or has accompanied the writing of this essay. The first feminist speak-out on rape, in New York City in 1971, was documented in Noreen Connell and Cassandra Wilson, *Rape: The First Sourcebook for Women* (1974). Susan Griffin, *Rape: The Power of Consciousness* (1979) includes her earlier essay, which is still one of the best discussions of the issue. Andrea Medea and Kathleen Thompson, *Against Rape* (1974) remains useful, as does Susan Brownmiller, *Against Our Will: Men, Women and Rape* (1975)—the classic, limited but essential. Early work on battering includes Erin Pizzey, *Scream Quietly or the Neighbors Will Hear You* (1974), Betsy Warrior, *Battered Lives* (1974) and Del Martin, *Battered Wives* (1976). Susan Schechter, *Women and Male Violence: The Visions and Struggles of the Battered Women's Movement* (1982) remains the best single text on battering to combine service-provider and activist consciousness. On incest, Florence Rush's early work is included in the Sourcebook noted above, and her book *The Best Kept Secret: Sexual Abuse of Children* (1980) contains the earliest discussion of how Freud suppressed information and revised his theory, based on his women patients' experience of incestuous abuse by male relatives, in favor of his oedipal theory that women fantasized this abuse. Sandra Butler, *Conspiracy of Silence: The Trauma of Incest* (1978) remains one of the clearest treatments built from women's experience, compassionate and politically savvy. Also, Judith Lewis Herman, with Lisa Hirschman, *Father-Daughter Incest* (1981). General books on violence against women: Andrea Dworkin's *Woman Hating* (1974) and *Our Blood* (1976); Kathleen Barry's *Female Sexual Slavery* (1979); and Frederique Delacorte and Felice Newman, eds., *Fight Back! Feminist Resistance to Male Violence* (1981). Pauline B. Bart and Patricia H. O'Brien, *Stopping Rape: Successful Survival Strategies* (1985), and Evelyn C. White, *Chain Chain Change: For Black Women Dealing with Physical and Emotional Abuse* (1985) are extremely useful.

   I want also to acknowledge general indebtedness to numerous conversations in the late seventies with Paula King and Michaele Uccella, and to the many thinkers and activists with whom I worked in the Portland, Oregon movement to stop violence against women. Many women have read pieces of this essay over the years and shared their responses with me: Gloria Anzaldúa, Margaret Blanchard, Sandy Butler, Chrystos, Irena Klepfisz, Helena Lipstadt, Fabienne McPhail-Grant, Bernice Mennis, Maureen O'Neill, Linda Vance, and Judy Waterman, in addition, of course, to Joan Pinkvoss, my editor and publisher at Aunt Lute. I alone am responsible for its weaknesses.

2. *Sourcebook*, note 1, 49.

3. Brownmiller, note 1, 363.

4. Interesting that in patriarchal western culture, revenge is considered practically a sacred duty for men, Hamlet and Orestes being only two of the more obvious examples (both sons avenging their fathers in part against their mothers). But women are not even supposed to entertain vengeful feelings.

5. Griffin, *Consciousness*, note 1, 21.

6. Phyllis Chesler, *Women and Madness* (1973), 292; see also M. F. Beal, *S.A.F.E. House* (1976) and Karen Hagberg, "Why the Women's Movement Cannot Be Non-Violent," *Heresies 6: Women and Violence* (1979), 44, from Nadia Telsey and Linda Maslanko, with the help of the Women's Martial Art Union, Self-Defense for Women (1974).

7. *The Women's Gun Pamphlet by and for Women* (1975), 3.

8. Janet Koenig, "The Social Meaning of Violence," *Heresies 6*, note 6, 91.

9. Assata Shakur, from an interview in *Plexus* by Women Against Prison, quoted in Beal, note 7, 111.

10. Ti-Grace Atkinson, *Amazon Odyssey* (1974), ccxlix. The term *violence* she reserves to represent "a class function," available as a *tactic* only to the oppressor class (200).

11. Hagberg, note 6, 44.

12. Leon Litwack, *Been in the Storm So Long: The Aftermath of Slavery* (1980), 65–66.

13. Litwack, note 12, 66.

14. Litwack, note 12, 43. What is being said here? First, the "whole theory of slavery" boiled down to an assumption of African inferiority, less-than-humanness. Second, military prowess dominated patriarchal notions of humanness: only competent soldiers, i.e., men who could act like "real men," were equal human beings. Consider that slaves were not an unknown people but the very people who not only performed necessary physical labor, but also raised white Southern children and tended the white Southern sick; obviously, tenderness, intelligence, caring, etc. did not challenge "the whole theory of slavery." See Deborah Gray White, *Ar'n't I a Woman: Female Slaves in the Plantation South* (1985).

15. Frantz Fanon, *The Wretched of the Earth* (1963), discusses the political implications of the oppressed's psychological need to release rage.

16. Litwack, note 12, 46.

17. W.E.B. Du Bois, *Black Reconstruction* (1935), quoted in Litwack, note 12, 64.

18. See Angela Davis, "The Legacy of Slavery: Standards for a New Womanhood," in *Women, Race, and Class* (1981), 3–29, and Linda Brent, *Incidents in the Life of a Slave Girl* (1973; 1st pub. 1861), which depicts extreme sexual harassment and abuse suffered by enslaved Black women from white men, and solidarity among Black women and men, both enslaved and free. Of course Brent was writing an abolitionist document.

    It appears that women employed all the forms of resistance used by men, direct and indirect. But unlike the men, the women had no access to the military, no institutional focus through which to transform capacity for violence into organized strength. And if "manliness," as Du Bois caustically remarked, meant murder, "womanliness" translated into what Black women were deprived of, the right to be protected by their men, and to raise their own babies.

19. White, *Ar'n't I a Woman*, note 14, 102–3, citing B. A. Botkin, ed., *Lay My Burden Down: A Folk History of Slavery* (1945), 160–62.

20. White, note 14, 78.

21. Brent, note 18.

22. White, note 14, 63–64.

23. White, note 14, 77–78.

24. Litwack, note 12, 65.

25. Toni Morrison's *Beloved* (1987) and Sherley Anne William's *Dessa Rose* (1986) both imagine permutations of violence from enslaved women.

26. Litwack, note 12, 76, 114.

27. Litwack, note 12, 46.

28. Litwack, note 12, 42.

29. Susan Brownmiller argued in *Against Our Will* for the critical importance of integrating by gender the military and the police. Though we have seen some signal changes as some gender integration occurs, and though women police and soldiers may improve their individual status, challenge stereotypes, and offer better

service or protection to women, it's no more an adequate solution to rape than Black soldiers were an adequate solution to racist violence. The missing link in Brownmiller's argument is the role of the army and police in the U.S., which is to safeguard the interests of the powerful at home and abroad. This means men. Until or unless male institutions truly serve our interest, we can't adequately fight for women through them. During the Civil War and Reconstruction the interests of northern capitalists uniquely coincided with the interests of the slaves.

30. An earlier version of part of this chapter appeared in *Fight Back,* note 1, coauthored by me and Michaele Uccella. The ideas emerged in our discussions; the actual writing was done by me.

31. Andrea Dworkin argued this in "Biological Superiority: The World's Most Dangerous and Deadly Idea," *Heresies 6,* note 6, 46.

32. "The belief that violence is somehow gender-linked is amazingly prevalent throughout all literature, even feminist literature. . . . Obviously it would be stupid and cruel to say that women are not brutally victimized, systematically, institutionally, across all age, class, and race barriers. Quite the contrary. But the assumption that women are inherently incapable of violence is something else. My own inquiry into the matter has shown me that this assumption is simply not true." Michaele Uccella, *Lesbian Violence,* presented at Goddard College and at the Montpelier (Vermont) Women's Center, September, 1978.

33. The theory that a woman's capacity for doing violence (however covert or unacceptable the expression) is also a capacity for resistance was developed by Michaele Uccella in *Lesbian Violence.*

34. Two women quoted in Lillian Rubin, *Worlds of Pain: Life in the Working Class Family* (1976), 117, 42.

35. C. McCormick, "Battered Women" (1977), cited by Schneider, Jordan, and Arguedas, "Representation of Women Who Defend Themselves," in *Heresies 6,* note 12, 100ff.

36. Police statistics from Portland, Oregon, 1976, indicated a 60% rate of escape for women who use some form of resistance. Considering that many women who get away don't bother to report to the police, the higher rate of 80% indicated by other studies seems plausible. (Of course many many women who don't escape also refuse to report to the police, perhaps as many as 90% of all women who get raped.) Bart, note 1, has compiled resistance strategies from women who escaped.

37. The first escape was recorded in the *Portland Oregonian* sometime in 1979; the second came from the *New York Post,* 1/31/79. Neither of these women was charged. Also note the following divine judgment: "An axwielding Portland youth was killed early Friday when he accidentally struck himself in the side of the neck while allegedly threatening two girls in the parking lot of a convenience market." *Oregon Journal,* 7/19/78.

55

EMINEM'S POPULARITY IS A MAJOR SETBACK FOR GIRLS AND WOMEN

JACKSON KATZ

Jackson Katz is internationally recognized for his groundbreaking work in gender violence prevention with men and boys, particularly in the sports culture and the military. He is cofounder of the multiracial, mixed-gender Mentors in Violence Prevention (MVP) program at Northeastern University's Center for the Study of Sport in Society. Katz also directs the first worldwide gender violence prevention program in the history of the United States Marine Corps. For more information, see www.jacksonkatz.com.

A couple of years ago I gave a speech about men's violence against women in a packed high school gymnasium in a town in the Midwest. The twelve hundred restless students in the stands were overwhelmingly white. Toward the end of my speech I decided to take a risk and criticize the superstar white rapper Eminem for the blatant woman-hating in his lyrics. I knew I would risk losing the support of some kids. After all, it was the height of his popularity, and it was safe to assume that many of them were fans of the white boy from the "wrong side of the tracks" in Detroit who had made it big in a hip-hop world previously dominated by African American artists. But I reasoned that as a man giving a speech about men's mistreatment of women, if I could not publicly challenge Eminem's misogyny, who could? There were audible moans and groans and whispered comments in response to my statements, but I still received a nice ovation when I finished. As the students filed out I was approached by at least twenty kids, most of whom were positive and supportive. But one small girl stood out. She waited for several minutes off to the side, an indication that she wanted to talk with me in private. She was shaking when she finally approached me. She introduced herself and told me that she was a junior. Then she told me she had been in an abusive relationship. She thanked me for coming, and she assured me that she had gotten out of the relationship and was getting help. Then she started to cry, and asked for a hug. I fought back a tear as she walked away. Twenty minutes later I was in the faculty lounge upstairs when a teacher walked in. She thanked me and then said that in anticipation of my visit, she had instructed her students to read a critical article I had written about Eminem. She was curious to hear how one particular student reacted to my speech. This student—a huge Eminem fan—had read my article and was furious with me, and had told the class that she was going to call me out for dissing her hero when I came to the school. I asked the teacher for the girl's name. It was the girl who had thanked and hugged me.

• • •

I realize that social and political critiques of the work of artists are fraught with peril. Artistic tastes vary widely, and so do people's opinions about the social and political responsibilities of art and artists. For example, many Americans believe that artists have an obligation only to be true to their artistic vision—not to be concerned with the social consequences of their art. According to this perspective, the expression of unpopular or disturbing ideas through art might make people uncomfortable, but that is not necessarily a bad thing. The purpose of art is not to make people feel good, but to give voice to the widest possible range of human experience and emotion. As the recording artist and feminist Tori Amos explains, "If you're singing songs that are about cutting women up, usually these guys (like Eminem) are tapping into an unconscious male rage that is real, that is existing—they're just able to harness it. So to shut them up isn't the answer . . . they're showing you what's happening in the psyche of a lot of people."[1] I would never say that it is necessary to "shut up" Eminem, but I do believe that it is imperative to explore the implications of his popularity. In fact, I do not think it is possible to talk about rape culture in this era and not talk about the man who has been called the "hip-hop Elvis."

If you followed the entertainment media over the past few years, you would get the impression that Eminem has moved beyond controversy and is now entrenched as a larger-than-life cultural force. He certainly experienced a more rapid and broad-based ascent into the mainstream than any black rappers ever have. But he has not been embraced by everyone. At the same time the white music/entertainment establishment was enthusiastically promoting Eminem as one of the most important artists of his generation, many people in the movements against domestic and sexual violence were appalled and profoundly disheartened. For decades, women and men in the field had maintained that rape and domestic violence thrive in a cultural environment where men's violence is not only tolerated but often encouraged. And then along came a charismatic white artist in a black musical genre whose lyrics consistently ridiculed and degraded women, and took images of homicidal misogyny to a new low: "Put anthrax on your Tampax and slap you til you can't stand." But instead of inspiring an anti-sexism backlash, Eminem's music was heralded by many as a brilliant, boundary-crossing contribution to lyrical performance and comic art. Instead of being condemned for stoking the fire of men's fury against women, the songwriter was lionized as an artistic voice for the ages—while his critics were dismissed as cultural rednecks and yahoos, or worse, opponents of artistic expression and free speech.

For people who are not familiar with Eminem's recordings, a sober reading of his lyrics—unadorned by the catchy tunes and infectious beats—can be an emotionally devastating experience.[2] One college professor I know told me that one of her students in a humanities class read aloud the lyrics to several Eminem songs as part of a class presentation. As she read the words, a number of female students began to cry; several got up and left the room. A number of the men in class looked uncomfortable and chagrined. In any assessment of art, it is important to remember that context matters. Critics who defend or excuse Eminem's misogyny often claim that his detractors do not understand his artistic intent when he gives voice to some of the most graphic homicidal rage against women ever captured on record.[3] For example, in one of his most famous songs, "Kim," Eminem presents a chillingly realistic narrative about a verbal confrontation and throat-slitting murder of his then-wife, who is named Kim in real life:

> Don't you get it bitch, no one can hear you?
>
> Now shut the fuck up and get what's coming to you
>
> You were supposed to love me
>
> (Kim choking)
>
> NOW BLEED! BITCH BLEED!
>
> BLEED! BITCH BLEED! BLEED!

It is possible that in this song and many others, Eminem uses his lyrical skills to transport the listener inside the mind of a murderer in a way that enlightens us about misogyny even as it entertains. It is possible, as Eminem's defenders assert, that his music contains multiple layers of meaning and that to take it literally is to miss its rich complexity. It is also possible that the very appeal of Eminem's music depends on widespread acceptance of violence against women as a cultural norm.

Whether you love him or loathe him, Eminem is unquestionably an impressive cultural player. He is a multitalented artist: a wildly inventive rap lyricist, a charismatic performer, and an effective actor (essentially playing a glorified version of himself in the 2002 Hollywood biopic *8 Mile.*). What *is* in question is the nature of Eminem's art and image, and its significance. Obviously his unprecedented mainstream success has much to do with his whiteness, and critiques of Eminem have typically centered on the racial politics of his initial rise to notoriety and then to the heights of pop-cultural fame. But there is another way to understand Eminem's popularity, which is that he has achieved success not *in spite* of his virulent misogyny and homophobic utterances—as many critics allege—but in part *because* of them.

Richard Goldstein argued in a brilliant piece in 2002 in the *Village Voice* that many of Eminem's male (and some female) fans take "guilty pleasure" in identifying with the aggressor—especially when the victims are women and gays. As Goldstein explains:

"At its hard core, Eminem's poetics is pornography, and it's accorded the same privileges. Just as we've declared the XXX zone exempt from social thinking, we refuse to subject sexist rap to moral scrutiny. We crave a space free from the demands of equity, especially when it comes to women, whose rise has inspired much more ambivalence than most men are willing to admit. This is especially true in the middle class, where feminism has made its greatest impact. No wonder Eminem is so hot to suburban kids . . . He's as nasty as they wanna be."[4]

Several years ago, Eminem was the target of protest from gay and lesbian activists who objected to his lyrical endorsement of violence against them. Other gays have embraced him in spite of this (most notably, and controversially, Elton John). But Eminem's homophobia is not simply a matter of specific lyrics. Rather, it is central to his constructed crazy/tough white guy image. For all of his vaunted "honesty" and presumed vulnerability, the misanthropically cartoonish "Slim Shady" persona that Marshall Mathers—aka Eminem—hides behind requires (at least publicly) a purging of anything that can be associated with femininity. Hence, you hear from Eminem—and his mentor, Dr. Dre—a steady stream of "bitch-slapping" misogyny peppered with anti-gay invective, all in the service of establishing their "hardness." "Now I don't wanna hit no woman but this chick's got it coming/Someone better get this bitch before she gets kicked in the stomach." The irony, of course, is that this hypermasculine posturing—so contemptuous and dismissive of women—produces its own homoerotic tensions, which then requires Eminem (and other rappers) to verbally demonstrate their heterosexuality by attacking gays. It is an embarrassingly predictable process. The popular hip-hop writer Touré provided further insight in this area in a widely circulated *Washington Post* article in 2004 about the sad state of women in hip-hop: "The love in hip-hop is over men, over love, crew love, brotherly love," he said. "It's very sort of ancient Greek. It really doesn't allow for a lot of room for women. Hip-hop at its essence is boys, not men, but boys talking about what they do for and with boys."[5]

Much of the mainstream cultural commentary about Eminem comes, understandably, from music critics and cultural commentators who write in major newspapers, magazines, and websites. Many of these people were initially critical of the misogyny and homophobia in Eminem's work. It was not uncommon to read strong criticism of this in their reviews of his early albums. But as he grew in popularity, criticism of the gender and sexual politics of his music became more muted. Richard Goldstein pointed out the evolution of *New York Times* critic/columnist Frank Rich's thoughts on Eminem in a November 2002 piece in the *Village Voice.* In 2000, Goldstein observed, Rich described Eminem as "a charismatic white rapper [who] trades in violence, crude sex, and invective roughing up heterosexual women, lesbians, and gay men." In 2001, Goldstein wrote, "Rich pondered whether 'racial crossover in the cultural market makes up for a multitude of misogynistic and homophobic sins'" By 2002, Goldstein reported, "Rich ended up slamming 'moral scolds' for dissing Em, while confessing, 'I've been fascinated with him ever since I first heard his songs at the inception of his notoriety.'"[6]

There is no doubt that as opinion-makers in the music world increasingly praised Eminem's talent, they made more excuses for his anti-woman lyrics. That is one definition of a rape culture: a society where sophisticated people routinely overlook or rationalize rape-supportive attitudes. In the case of Eminem, it is not just that his misogyny has been tolerated. He has been celebrated and honored in a way few artists ever have. He has won several Grammy awards. He even won an Oscar for best song in 2002, for his anthem, "Lose Yourself," from the *8 Mile* movie soundtrack. Can a society that heaps untold riches and praise on a man whose lyrics routinely brutalize women claim that it is serious about eradicating sexual and domestic violence? Consider this analogy. Could a society that claims to care about racism embrace and honor a white artist who glorified racism? Is it even remotely possible that a white artist who regularly rapped and joked about abusing and killing "niggers," "spies," and "kikes," would win critical acclaim—regardless of how artistically inventive he/she was?

The full stamp of cultural approval of Eminem came when the movie *8 Mile* was released in 2002. The Hollywood mythmakers Brian Grazer, Scott Silver, and Curtis Hanson (*8 Mile's* producer, screenwriter, and director, respectively) blatantly distorted the rapper's story in pursuit of box office glory. They left out the sexism and the homophobia. People who went to see *8 Mile* who had not heard or read the rapper's lyrics came out of the movie with a newfound appreciation for the talented white kid from a trailer park who had the courage to make something of his life. They were spared any exposure to the downside of Eminem's rise to fame, especially his—and his record company's—decision to attack women and girls in his lyrics with a vengeance that was truly breathtaking.

The cultural "meanings" of Eminem are sure to be the subject of debate for years to come. But so far, the national conversation about Eminem has taken place on the terms of fawning critics, flaks for the record and film industries, and lay prophets of the cultural Zeitgeist, all of whom have been incessantly hyping the bleach-blond rapper for the past several years. Give them credit. They have succeeded wildly—Eminem is now a full-blown cultural phenomenon and global merchandising cash cow. But it is time to expand the terms of debate. It is time to offer some counterbalance to the mythologizing distortions from the PR department of Eminem, Inc. In particular, it is time to consider with eyes wide open some of the potentially horrific effects of this art in a world already filled with misogynistic and violent men.

Eminem's Lyrics Help Desensitize Boys and Men to the Pain and Suffering of Girls and Women

Eminem's fans argue that his raps about mistreating, raping, torturing, and murdering women are not meant to be taken literally. I used to hear this regularly from young men and women when I asked them if they had any problems with the way the artist treated women in his lyrics. "Just because we listen to the music doesn't mean we're gonna go out and harass, rape, and murder women," they said. "We know it's just a song." Thoughtful critics of Eminem do not make the argument that the danger of his lyrics lies in the possibility that some unstable young man will go out and imitate in real life what the artist is rapping about. While possible, this is highly unlikely. (Although rare, it does happen. In December 2005, a twenty-one-year-old Eminem impersonator in London was sentenced to life in prison for beating a twenty-six-year-old woman to death and stuffing her body in a suitcase in a case that was widely reported as "life imitating art.")[7] Rather, one of the most damaging aspects of Eminem's violent misogyny and homophobia is how normal and matter-of-fact this violence comes to seem. Rapping and joking about sex crimes have the effect of desensitizing people to the real pain and trauma suffered by victims and their loved ones. The process of de-sensitization to violence through repeated exposure in the media has been studied for decades. Among the effects: young men who have watched/listened to excessive amounts of fictionalized portrayals of men's violence against women in mainstream media and pornography have been shown to be more callous toward victims, less likely to believe their accounts of victim-ization, more willing to believe they were "asking for it," and less likely to intervene in instances of "real-life" violence.

Let us not forget that the culture in which Eminem has become a huge star is in the midst of an ongoing *crisis* of men's violence against women. In the U.S., rates of rape, sexual assault, battering, teen-relationship violence, and stalking have been shockingly high for decades, far exceeding rates in comparable Western societies. Sadly, millions of American girls and women have been assaulted by American boys and men. Thousands of gays each year are bashed and harassed by young men. For these victims, this is not an academic debate about the differences between literalist and satirical art. It hits closer to home.

Girls Are Encouraged to Be Attracted to Boys and Men Who Don't Respect Women

What began as a tentative dance with the media has become a passionate embrace. After initially airing "misgivings" about featuring the woman-hating rapper, magazines with predominantly young female readership, like *CosmoGirl* and *Teen People,* now regularly feature "Em" on their covers, posed as a sex symbol, as an object of heterosexual female desire. This is not simply the latest example of the star-making machinery of mass media constructing the "bad boy" as desirable to women. It sends a powerful message to girls: He does not really hate and disrespect you. In fact, he loves you. He is just misunderstood. It is the hip-hop version of *Beauty and the Beast.* You know, underneath that gruff exterior, between the lines of those nasty lyrics, lies a tender heart that has been hurt, a good man who just needs more love and understanding.

This is a myth that battered women have been fed for centuries; that his violence is *her* responsibility, that if only she loved him more, his abuse would stop. This is one of the most damaging myths about batterers, and one of the most alarming features of Eminem's popularity with girls. Remember, Eminem is the same "lovable" rapper who wrote a chillingly realistic song ("Kim") about murdering his then-wife (whose real name is Kim), and putting her body in the trunk of his car, interspersed with loving references to their daughter Hallie (their real-life daughter is named Hallie). This is the same "cute" guy who angrily raps about catching diseases from "hoes": "All these bitches on my dick/That's how dudes be getting sick/That's how dicks be getting drips/Falling victims to this shit/From these bitches on our dicks" ("Drips"). This is the same "sexy" artist who raps: "Spit game, to these hoes, like a soap opera episode/and punch a bitch in the nose, 'til her whole face explodes/There's three things I hate: girls, women, and bitches/I'm that vicious to walk up, and drop-kick midgets." This is the same "adorable" man who constantly unleashes torrents of verbal aggression against women, even though he is so sensitive to the potential wounding power of words that he famously refuses to use the "n-word." Why is it not okay for a white rapper to diss "niggers," but it is okay for a man to express contempt for "bitches" and "hoes?"

His credulous female fans counter: He does not really hate women. How could he? He loves his daughter! For battered women's advocates, this is one of the most frustrating aspects of Eminem's popularity. "He loves his daughter" is one of the most predictable excuses that batterers give in pleading for another chance. The fact is, most batterers are not one-dimensional ogres. Abusive men often love the very women they are abusing. And let us not forget that when Eminem verbally abuses his daughter's mother, by extension he abuses his daughter.

We can gain important insight into one key aspect of the Eminem persona by studying both the behavior of men who batter, and people's responses to them. The man who is being lionized as one of this era's emblematic artists shares many character traits with men who batter. One glaring similarity is the folklore that Mathers has actively constructed about his famously difficult childhood. Narcissistic batterers frequently paint themselves as the true victims. It is *them* we are supposed to feel sorry for— not their victims (or the victims/targets of their lyrical aggression). It is well-known that many of Eminem's fans, male and female, reference his abusive family life to explain and rationalize his rage. But it is not as well-known that batterer-intervention counselors hear this excuse every single day from men who are in court-mandated programs for beating their girlfriends and wives. "I had a tough childhood. I have a right to be angry," or "She was the real aggressor. She pushed my buttons and I just reacted." The counselors' typical answer is, "It is not right or okay that you were abused as a child. You deserve our empathy and support. But you have no right to pass on your pain to other people."

Eminem's Popularity with Girls Sends a Dangerous Message to Boys and Men

Boys and young men have long expressed frustration with the fact that girls and young women often *say* they are attracted to nice guys, but end up with the disdainful tough guys who treat them like dirt. When I suggest in my college lectures that men need to find the courage to resist putting on the "tough guise" in order to prove their manhood, I frequently hear from sincere young men who approach me seeking advice. "Women want me to be their friend," they say. "But they want to go out with the alpha males. If I don't act hard I go to bed alone." What can I tell them? What are they supposed to conclude when 53 percent of the *8 Mile* audience on opening weekend was female?

What are men to make of *New York Times* columnist Maureen Dowd when she writes, uncritically, that a "gaggle" of her female baby-boomer friends are "surreptitiously smitten" with a certain thirty-year-old rapper whose lyrics literally drip with contempt for women?[8] What are boys to think of an online poll in *CosmoGirl* magazine in 2001 that found him to be the "sexiest musician"? That girls want to be treated with dignity and respect? Or that the quickest route to popularity with them is to be verbally and emotionally cruel, that "bad boy" posturing is a winning strategy to impress naïve (and self-loathing) girls? Surely most of Eminem's female fans would not want to be sending that message to their male peers—but they are.

People who have listened carefully to Eminem's actual lyrics—not just the hit songs or the sanitized movie soundtrack—know that many self-respecting girls who are conscious about the depths of our culture's sexism are repulsed by Eminem's misogyny and depressed by his popularity. Sadly, many of these girls have been silent, fearing they will be branded as "uncool" because they "don't get" the artist who is supposedly the voice of their generation.

There are women who like Eminem because (they say) he is complex and not easily knowable; they would argue that it is dismissive to characterize his art as sexist. But the burden is on them to demonstrate how—in a culture where so many men sexually harass, rape, and batter women—it is possible to reconcile a concern for women's physical, sexual, and emotional well-being with admiration for a male artist whose lyrics consistently portray women in a contemptuous and sexually degrading manner. Girls and women, even those who have been co-opted into Eminem worship, want to be treated with respect. They certainly do not want to be physically or sexually assaulted by men. They do not want to be sexually degraded by dismissive and arrogant men. But they cannot have it both ways. They cannot proclaim their attraction to a man who has gotten rich verbally trashing and metaphorically raping women, and yet reasonably expect that young men will treat them with dignity.

The Racial Storyline around Eminem Perpetuates Racist Myths

Eminem is popular with white audiences in large measure because the African American gangsta rap icon Dr. Dre and other hard-core black rappers with "street credibility" have conferred on him a certain legitimacy. Dre is Eminem's mentor and producer, signaling to black audiences as well that unlike previous white rappers such as Vanilla Ice, this white boy is for real. What is missing from this story is that Dr. Dre himself is one of the most misogynistic and homophobic figures in the history of rap music. He has produced and performed some of this era's most degrading songs about women. "Bitches ain't shit but hoes and tricks/How could you trust a hoe/Cuz a hoe's a trick/We don't love them tricks/Cuz a trick's a bitch" ("Bitches Ain't Shit"). In other words, Eminem and Dre are modeling a perverse sort of interracial solidarity that comes at the expense of women. It is an old story: sexism provides men with a way to unite across race and class lines. African American people who are happy to see Eminem earning rap greater legitimacy in white America might want to consider that this era's white artist most identified as a bridge to black culture has built that bridge on the denigration and undermining of black women—and all women.

Eminem's Success Has Unleashed a Torrent of Mother-Blaming

One element of Eminem's story of which all his fans are aware is that he and his mother do not get along. He claims that she was an unstable drug abuser who abused him emotionally. She sued him for defamation. Many people psychoanalyze him from a distance and argue that his problems with women stem from his stormy relationship with his mother. This may or may not be true, but it is an excuse that abusive men often make for their behavior. As Lundy Bancroft observes in his book, *Why Does He Do That? Inside the Minds of Angry and Controlling Men,* battered women themselves sometimes like this explanation, since it makes sense out of the man's behavior and gives the woman someone safe to be angry at—since getting angry at him always seems to blow up in her face. It is hard to say what percentage of Eminem fans relate to his often articulated rage at his mother, but consider this anecdotal evidence: I attended an Eminem concert in southern California during the Anger Management Tour in 2002. At one point, Eminem ripped off a string of angry expletives about his mother (something like "F-you, bitch!") after which a sizeable cross-section of the eighteen-thousand-person crowd joined in a violent chant repeating the verbal aggression against Ms. Mathers (and no doubt other mothers by extension). Why is this aspect of the Eminem phenomenon such a cause for concern? No one begrudges Eminem, or anyone else, the right to have issues—including in some cases being very angry with their mothers. However, it is not a great stretch to see that Eminem's anger can easily be generalized to all women and used as yet another rationale for some men's deeply held misogyny.

Considering Eminem's roots on the economic margins of "white trash" Detroit, class is also a critical factor here. Poor women—especially poor women of color—are easy scapegoats for many societal problems. Eminem's fans presumably know little about the context within which Debbie Mathers (who is white) tried to raise her children. Might we have some compassion for her as we are asked to for him? Why was she constantly struggling financially? How did educational inequities and lack of employment opportunities affect *her* life, her family experiences, her education level, her dreams, her ability to be a good parent? As a woman, how did sexism shape her choices? She became pregnant with Marshall (Eminem) when she was *fifteen*. What was her personal history, including her history with men? Was she ever abused? We know a lot of women with substance abuse problems develop them as a form of self-medication against the effects of trauma. What is the connection between Ms. Mathers's alleged (by her son) substance abuse and any history of victimization she might have? Further, if Eminem's father deserted him and the family when Marshall was young, why is so much of Eminem's verbal aggression aimed at his mother and at women? If you buy the argument that Eminem's misogyny comes from his issues with his mother, then considering his father's behavior, why doesn't he have a huge problem with men? Hint: the answer has to do with sexism. It is easy to blame struggling single mothers for their shortcomings; right-wing politicians have been doing this for decades. A more thoughtful approach would seek to understand their situations, and while such an understanding would provide no excuse for abuse or neglect (if that is what Eminem actually experienced), it would give it much-needed context.

Eminem Verbally Bullies Women and Gays and Then Claims, "I Was Just Kidding around"

Many of Eminem's fans claim that his Slim Shady persona and nasty anti-woman lyrics are just an act. But his misogyny comes out in interviews as well. In a *Rolling Stone* magazine interview in 1999, Eminem tried to explain his writing process:

"My thoughts are so fucking evil when I'm writing shit, if I'm mad at my girl, I'm gonna sit down and write the most misogynistic fucking rhyme in the world. It's not how I feel in general, it's how I feel at that moment. Like, say today, earlier, I might think something like 'coming through the airport sluggish, walking on crutches, hit a pregnant bitch in the stomach with luggage.'"

Elizabeth Keathley points out in a fascinating music journal essay entitled, "A Context for Eminem's Murder Ballads," that many journalists buy the argument that misogyny is a creative response warranted by certain circumstances in an intimate relationship, rather than a world view that informs a person's choices.[9] This rationalization allows them to "overlook" Eminem's misogyny and accept at face value his claim that's he's only kidding. Eminem's defenders—including a number of prominent music critics—like to argue that his ironic wit and dark sense of humor are lost on many of his detractors. This is what his predominantly young fans are constantly being told: that some people don't like the likeable Em because they don't get him, the personae he has created, his transgressive humor. In comparison, his fans are said to be much more hip, since they are in on the joke. As a non-fan, I would offer this response: "We get it, all right. We understand that lyrics are usually not meant to be taken literally. And we have a good sense of humor. We just don't think it is funny for men to joke aggressively about murdering and raping women, and assaulting gays and lesbians. Just like we don't think it is funny for white people to make racist jokes at the expense of people of color. This sort of 'hate humor' is not just harmless fun—no matter how clever the lyrics or spellbinding the backbeats. Music lyrics and other art forms can either illuminate social problems, or they can cynically exploit them. Eminem is arguably a major force in the latter category. Sorry if we don't find that funny."

Eminem's Rebel Image Obscures the Fact That Men's Violence against Women Is Not Rebellious

Eminem has been skillfully marketed as a "rebel" to whom many young people—especially white boys—can relate. But what exactly is he rebelling against? Powerful women who oppress weak and vulnerable men? Omnipotent gays and lesbians who make life a living hell for straight people? Eminem's misogyny and homophobia, far from being "rebellious," are actually extremely traditional and conservative. They are also clearly profitable, both for Eminem and Interscope records, for Nike, with whom Eminem has had a lucrative promotional contract, and with all of the other media that profit from his "controversial" act. As a straight white man in hip-hop culture, Marshall Mathers would actually be much more of a rebel if he rapped about supporting women's equality and embracing gay and lesbian civil rights. Instead, he is only a rebel in a very narrow sense of that word. Since he offends a lot of parents, kids can "rebel" against their parents' wishes by listening to him, buying his CDs, etc. The irony is that by buying into Eminem's clever "bad boy" act, one could argue that they are just being obedient, predictable consumers. It is rebellion as a purchasable commodity. But if you focus on the contents of his lyrics, the "rebellion" is empty. If you are a "rebel," it matters who you are and what you are rebelling against. The KKK are rebels, too. They boast about it all the time. They fly the Confederate (rebel) flag. But most cultural commentators would never dream of speaking positively about the KKK as models of adolescent rebellion for American youth because the *content* of what they advocate is so repugnant. Likewise Eminem would be dropped from MTV playlists and lose his record contract immediately if he turned his lyrical aggression away from women and gays and started trashing people of color, Jews, Catholics, etc. In that sense, Eminem's continued success makes a statement about how this culture regards women and gays. Sadly, it is a statement that many progressive, feminist, egalitarian, and nonviolent people in this era of white male backlash find quite deflating.

NOTES

1. The full text of Amos's remarks about Eminem can be found at www.mtv.com in an article entitled "Eminem's Fictional Dead Wife Spoke to Her." September 28, 2001.

2. For people who want to study Eminem's lyrics, there are countless websites that provide all of the lyrics to his songs at no charge. Just type in "Eminem lyrics" to any major search engine.

3. One talented and prominent music critic who repeatedly lavishes praise on Eminem and—to this reader—seems only slightly bothered by the white rapper's relentlessly misogynous lyrics is Robert Hilburn of the *Los Angeles Times*. For example, in a glowing concert review of a show on the 2002 Anger Management tour in southern California, Hilburn writes that "the ugly portrayal of women in such songs as the macho-minded 'Superman' is disheartening," and in a review of Eminem's 2004 release "Encore," he writes that if Eminem had "restrained himself to fifty minutes (instead of a bloated seventy-seven minute record), he could have left out moments of juvenile silliness and the further put-down of women that undercut some of the poignant reflection of 'Yellow Brick Road' and 'Mockingbird.'" Is it conceivable that a prominent music critic writing in a major metropolitan daily would describe as "disheartening" a white rapper who attacked people of color in his lyrics?

4. To locate the full text of Goldstein's article, see the bibliography. Here is one crucial paragraph: "There *is* a relationship between Eminem and his time. His bigotry isn't incidental or stupid, as his progressive champions claim. It's central and knowing—and unless it's examined, it will be free to operate. Not that this music makes men rape any more than the Klan-lionizing imagery in *Birth of a Nation* creates racists. The real effect is less personal than systematic. Why is it considered proper to speak out against racism and anti-Semitism but not against sexism and homophobia? To me, this disparity means we haven't reached a true consensus about these last two biases. We aren't ready to let go of male supremacy. We still think something central to the universe will be lost if this arrangement changes."

5. To locate the full text of the article, see Wiltz, 2004.

6. To locate the full article, see Goldstein, November 2002.

7. Here is a summary of a Reuters news report by Michael Holden on December 5, 2005: A British man, who was so obsessed with rapper Eminem that he dressed like him, had the same tattoos, and used to perform the same dance routines, was jailed for life on Monday for battering a woman to death.

   Christopher Duncan, twenty-one, forced his victim to undergo a torrid sexual ordeal before he beat her round the head with a metal baseball bat and, although she was still alive, crammed her into a suitcase where she died up to ninety minutes later.

   On the night of he murder, Duncan had met his victim in a London karaoke bar where the manager said he had been "aggressively" performing songs by Eminem, notorious for his violent and misogynistic lyrics.

   "You treat women as sexual objects and have a sadistic sexual fantasy life," Judge David Paget said as he ordered that Duncan should serve a minimum term of twenty-five years. "It may well be you pose such a danger to women it will never be safe to release you."

   Prosecuting lawyer Jonathan Laidlaw said Duncan's victim, twenty-six-year-old law student Jagdip Najran, a promising singer herself, had fallen for Duncan.

   "One of the tragic features of this case is the terrible misjudgment she made of him," Laidlaw told the Old Baily criminal court.

8. See Dowd, 2002.

9. See Keathley, Elizabeth, 2002.

REFERENCES

Bancroft, Lundy. *Why Does He Do That: Inside the Minds of Angry and Controlling Men.* New York: G.P. Putnam and Sons, 2002.

Dowd, Maureen. "The Boomers' Crooner." *New York Times,* November 24, 2002.

Goldstein, Richard. "The Eminem Shtick: What Makes a Bigot a Genius? Presiding Over Guilty Pleasures." *The Village Voice,* June 12–18, 2002.

Goldstein, Richard. "The Eminem Consensus: Why We Voted for Slim Shady." *The Village Voice,* November 13–19, 2002.

Hilburn, Robert. "Minus the Chain Saw, Eminem Seems a Bit More Mature." *Los Angeles Times,* August 9, 2002.

Hilburn, Robert. "With Encore, Eminem Melts: The Album Shows the Rapper to Have a Tender, Even Apologetic, Side." *Los Angeles Times,* November 8, 2004, p. E1.

Keathley, Elizabeth. "A Context for Eminem's Murder Ballads." *Echo: A Music Centered Journal,* Vol. 4, (No.2), Fall 2002.

Wiltz, Teresa. "Hip-Hop Nation: 30 Years of Rap, Ladies Last." *Washington Post,* December 31, 2004, p. C01.

56

PICTURES OF BOYHOOD

RICHARD HOFFMAN

Richard Hoffman's prose and verse have appeared in numerous journals, including *Agni, Ascent, Harvard Review, Poetry,* and in anthologies. Among numerous awards, the most recent is *The Literary Review's* Charles Angoff Prize. He is Writer-in-Residence at Emerson College and teaches at the University of Southern Maine's Stonecoast MFA program.

Richard Hoffman was sexually abused by Tom Feifel, his coach, prior to the incidents described here. A multiple offender who was finally brought to justice, Feifel died in prison in 1997. In this reading, Hoffman refers to a photo of himself with four of his baseball teammates.

The other boys in the photo are my teammates but not my friends. Of the four of them, I remember the names of only the two taller boys. I'll change them here and call them Kenny and Phil. It would not be improbable for either or both of them to have turned, immediately after this picture was taken, and thrown me to the ground right there on the asphalt parking lot, one or the other crying out, "Cherry belly!" while they sat on me and pulled out my shirtfront and smacked my stomach while I kicked and yelled until it was a mass of red welt. One or the other might finish by spitting down on my face, even saying, "What are you going to do about it?"[1]

I have talked to many men who remember both getting and giving these "cherry bellies" and who seem to have accepted them as a normal feature of boyhood. That these assaults, which happened to me frequently, were a kind of rape is borne out by an incident a couple of years after this photo was taken, in ninth grade, on the bus to an "away" baseball game.

I had been subjected to the usual bullying, I suppose, because I can recall very clearly that my right arm hurt that day, my "pitching arm" I would have called it, though I was by no means one of our main pitchers; in fact, Kenny and Phil were our starters. I can see each of them on the mound. Nobody ever threw more overhand than Phil. His was a bizarre windmill of a delivery, more like a pitching machine than a baseball player. Kenny was what we called a "sidewinder;" he had a wicked fastball that cut across your body from left to right if you were a right-handed batter.

I can recall that painful knot between elbow and shoulder from their once-again-refreshed mark on me, kept black-and-blue and sore by knuckle punches there at every opportunity. To soothe the bruise by touching or rubbing it was the signal that would invite a fresh punch there.

Some time into the ride I discovered my glove was missing. Kenny and Phil were sitting two seats behind me along the back bench of the bus.

"Hey, Hoffman. Where's your glove?" No way I was going to turn around. There was a lot of laughter. "Should we give him his glove back?"

Kenny's voice: "Can't you see I'm not finished with it yet?"

"Me next! Me next!" More laughter.

After a while my glove came flying at me, smacking the side of my face. Something wet, viscous on my cheek. At first I thought they had all spit in it.

Now I see that I was targeted in a different way. After Feifel's violation I seemed marked in some way that was visible to other boys. I'm reminded of that Far-Side cartoon of the two deer: one has a target of concentric circles on his chest and the other says, "Bummer of a birthmark, Hal." Boys do not walk up to other boys who are passive, cringing, and sad and ask what's the matter. Not the boys in this picture; not the boys, adjacent strangers, with whom I passed my boyhood. I had a target on me.

The boys in the back of the bus knew that the adults riding up in front—our freshman baseball coach and the assistant principal, a priest—would have to disapprove if their behavior came to light. They also knew that their aggression was congruent with a set of manly virtues, martial virtues, really, that they had learned, chief among them the ability to nullify empathy. "How would *you* like it?" the outraged question asked by a woman—in our case most often a nun—asking us to take some lesson from our transgression, would be missing from the response of the aging warrior who was our high command, sitting up next to the driver, talking to the priest, his boss, and studiously not turning round. In fact, his ignorance was dependable. From time to time, if things got too loud, he would bellow, "Don't make me have to come back there!" What would he have done had their cruelty and my ignominy been brought inescapably to his attention?

On the day this photo was taken, if Feifel had offered me a ride, I would have hesitated before saying no. I would have had to find another way to avoid Kenny and Phil, some way either to placate or elude them. Maybe this was the day, the day of this picture, when I was dragged to the creek and thrown in so that on my way home I had to make up a story about going deep for a fly ball in right field, running it down so intent on robbing the opposing batter of a home run that I kept right on going right over the retaining wall into the creek just as the ball smacked into the pocket of my glove. It seems I already understood how stories push against others' expectations, desires, needs: what they want to hear, not to mention how they might be made to take the shape of what I want to be true.

I don't know, can't know, whether I am imagining or remembering the sting of my own sweat in the corners of my eyes, the invisible cloud of heat when the big round trunk of the car is opened and the musical clinking and clonking of hickory baseball bats as the canvas duffel is thrown in, the fine brown dust in my nostrils as the trunk is closed—*whump*.

The park where this picture was taken was the closest thing I ever experienced to paradise. These days I go there when I return to Pennsylvania to visit my father. We walk his dog there. I have written about this already, about the creek, about the white roaring rapids above the bridge at 7th Street, the trout fanning in pools and eddies. Have I mentioned the benches along the creek, and the weeping willows' long fronds trailing on the surface of the cloud-capturing water? The red and blue damselflies we called matchsticks? The cool darkness under the bridge, the lacework of trembling light on its walls? The way that the echo there taught me that silence is sound stretched thin by time?

But paradise is a myth made necessary by its loss. Paradise was simply the world, the real one. By the time this photograph was taken, however, I could only enjoy it alone, and after a while I even started to believe that my love for these sensual things was unmanly, that I was wrong to find pleasure in them. Certainly in the shrunken world of boyhood's approved concerns there was no place for simple delight. Sneers were in ample supply.

All summer you could find Tom sitting in his car, a '51 Chevy, in the lot near the swimming pool, not far from where this picture was taken. The radio played—*Come on, let's twist again, like we did last summer*—while Tom sat, left arm out the window, aviator sunglasses on, watching. Watching. I think now that down below the angle of our vision he was stroking himself, recalling encounters with some of us, fantasizing—and planning—encounters with others.

The boy in this picture, the boy I was, hands covering his crotch, seems to be asking "Why me?" Psychologists who study the behavior of men like Feifel suggest that the world of such a person is both obsessive and opportunistic. Far from simply stumbling into temptation, those who assault children generally position themselves where they will have continual access to them, and their crimes are the result of a single-minded calculus.

Our uniforms, the finest of any team in town, came complete with those baseball undershirts, white with colored sleeves, and major league style baseball socks with the high thin stirrup of the big leaguers, not those two-tone, low-down Little League socks that the other teams wore and that looked like the kind of socks Ty Cobb or Roger Hornsby wore back in ancient times. Tom bought the uniforms, clothed us, with what he earned at his foreman's job at the nearby shirt mill. He bought our bats, balls, catcher's equipment. We were his team. We wore our hats with NE on them proudly, unaware that we had been bought, too. Every kid in town saw those uniforms and wanted to play for us. Parents, thankful that "somebody cares enough to do something for these kids," mistook Feifel's reticence, his lack of eye contact, for modesty, or as embarassment at their expressions of gratitude, and this meant to them that "his heart's in the right place," that he wasn't trying to make a reputation for himself, wasn't asking for their votes, their business, their money. "He does it for the kids." In our black-and-gold, spiffy uniforms ("your baseball suit" my mother called it) we flacked for Feifel as surely as the other teams who had the names of banks and beer distributors and bowling alleys stitched across the back of their shirts. The man knew his business, even if nobody else did.

Anna Salter, in her landmark study, *Transforming Trauma,* quotes one predator as saying,

> "I guess it's hard to, it's really hard to say how you decide what child is appealing to you because, say, if you've got a group of 25 kids, you might find nine that are appealing, well, you're not going to get all nine of them, but just by looking you've decided just from the looks what nine you want. Then you start looking at the family backgrounds. You find out all you can about them, and then you find out which ones are the most accessible, and eventually you get it down to the one that you think is the easiest target, and that's who you do."[2]

There is no question about it. I am, in the photo, hardly there. My posture shrinks from the camera's attention. I had contracted; somehow I no longer came all the way to my skin. I saw the world as if from deep within a cave. I was like a gangster who will sit only facing the door with his back to the wall. I mean this as a metaphysical position I'd assumed: call it mistrust, call it fear, call it alienation. I am hardly there. I had been emptied, gutted like a fish. I had forgotten myself. I had begun to assemble myself, piecemeal, as I would be thereafter, trying on this man's scowl, that man's walk.

As a boy, I loved the story of the child martyr Tarsisius. A Roman boy, he had been entrusted by the persecuted early Christian community to carry the consecrated Eucharist to a catacomb where, among the hidden faithful, the word made flesh would be consumed. On the way there, he was accosted by thugs who demanded to see what he was carrying under his cloak. "Next to his heart," the nuns said. The bullies beat him savagely but he would not surrender the tiny incarnation of the divine that had been entrusted to him.

I was trying to be good. I was devout in my prayers, obsessive in my observance of the liturgy (gilded pages of exquisite thinness, purple gros-grain ribbon, every single day with its feasts and prayers and colors of the priest's vestments and place in the seasons of the liturgical year) trying to be the best altarboy at St. Francis of Assisi school. "What are ya, buckin' for—sainthood?" my father would say, a locution that makes me smile but also opens the doors of history to me—the world of my parents, the scarred consciousness of their generation with its critical mass of trauma survivors, raised in the Great Depression, sent off to the butchery of World War II, ready on their return to settle for any rung in the hierarchy except the bottom-most, any drug for the pain, any empty promise about the future.

I remember my ninth-grade music teacher, a former bandleader in the Marines. One day when I was especially pleased with having mastered *The Merry Widow Waltz* on my trombone, he leaned into my face with his teeth gritted and a sneer curling his lip. "You think you're some pretty bird. Oh you're so smart! Oh you can do it all! You preen all day because you can sing. Because you think you can fly. Well let me tell you. Your song's the same as any other: you sing for your supper. And you aren't flying anywhere. You're right here in the cage. With the rest of us. Get it?"

I learned nothing the year this photograph was taken, not even the things that mattered to me, like how to throw a curveball or how to pop a wheely on my bicycle or the *Confiteor* and *Suscipe* in Latin that would qualify me to serve at the altar even though I knew I was unworthy. Nothing would stay in my head. There was nothing wrong with my eyes, but the world was out of focus. I was the kid walking down the street staring into the middle distance, waking when a carhorn warned me to snap out of it. I'm lucky I didn't get killed.

Worse, I could no longer play baseball. Oh, I could field all right, and throw; but at the plate I "stepped in the bucket," down the third-base line instead of into the pitch. To some extent I think my debilitating fear was in response to a physical injury, although my constant state of distraction may have been the cause of it. I'd been beaned was the problem. I hadn't been wearing a helmet and the ball hit me on the left cheek and I went down and then, oh, man! it hurt. It hurt like hell even with an icepack on it. So after that, no matter how many fantasy homers I hit in my backyard, no matter how much excited commentary I supplied for my imaginary triumphs—*And the crowd is on its feet! It's going . . . going . . . gone!*—I kept "stepping in the bucket," down the third base line, afraid; "bailing out" we sometimes called it, and I struck out over and over again. I went from the starting lineup to the bench and stayed there. Finally, I quit and joined a rag-tag team without uniforms run by the Police Athletic League.

Marty Romig was a cop, although I didn't know anything about him in that respect. I seem to recall something about his having had a motorcycle accident on a slick road and that's why he was no longer in uniform. Instead he ran—he was—the Police Athletic League, or PAL.

He spent Saturday mornings gathering us together from all over town, collecting bundles of old newspapers and rags in the process. It was a big, dark blue delivery truck with the PAL insignia on the side, a police badge with PAL inside it, the same badge sewn on the peaks of our caps. This ongoing paper drive was how the program bought balls and bats and caps. I remember the stamped metal floor of the truck, and how we spent all morning wrestling one another on its waffled surface as the space shrank, filling with bundles of newspapers and magazines.

Marty was no baseball player. I remember him pitching batting practice with no form or grace to speak of, no *oomph* on the ball, and not much control either. Marty was a bowler. His right forearm looked like Popeye's. That whole right forearm and hand were so hypertrophied that his left looked withered by comparison.

This was around the time that some kids were starting to throw a round-house curve, and it was humiliating when I ducked or stepped away from a ball that curved down and across the plate for a strike. I had had enough jeers. I was primed for self-hatred, and now I turned it on myself. I was a disgrace. I was a coward. I was a phony.

One day Marty asked me to stick around after practice. Just me. I remember I was bringing in second base. That was always the signal for the end of practice, when Marty would call out, "Okay, that's it; bring in the bags!"

He squeezed my shoulder. "Don't go anywhere. We're going to try something, just you and me."

I dropped the dusty base, picked it up, dropped my glove, bent to pick it up and tripped on the canvas strap hanging down from the base. My face was hot and dust was in my eyes.

"I can't, coach. I have to get home." My throat was tight as when I put my fingers down it to make myself throw up so my mother would let me skip school.

The next Saturday, he ended practice just as I was about to embarrass myself again at batting practice. "You stay," he said.

When the other boys had gone, he took me by the elbow, walked me to home plate. "Tell you what," he said. "Put the bat down a minute." Then he drew a line with the toe of his shoe. (He didn't wear baseball spikes, or even sneakers, just plain black oxfords and sagging trousers he stepped on at the heel.) "Now when I throw the ball, I want you to step down this line with your left foot. That's all. Just step. Ready?"

He backed up only about six or eight feet before he lobbed one past me. Underhand. Then another. And another. At first it was easy. I didn't look at the ball. I looked down at my foot. After a while I looked at the ball and still managed to step along the line, toward the pitcher, not the third-baseman. Marty backed up a little each time. Every 15 or 20 pitches I gathered up the balls and threw them back to him.

"Okay," he said. "Pick up your bat. Don't swing though. Not till I say. Just keep stepping along that line." The ball went by at nearly a normal speed. I stepped along the line. Again. Again. I wanted to swing so badly I could have screamed. Finally, he gave his permission.

"Crack!" I had forgotten how good it felt to hit the ball. Again, "Crack!"

I might easily have been left, if it were not for Marty, believing that adults all wanted something from me, no matter how they presented themselves, and that whatever I wanted or needed I was going to have to get for myself, without help, and probably at someone else's expense. I don't know anything about how he helped other kids, though I believe he must have. What I know for sure was that he cared about a frightened, eleven-year-old boy enough to help him overcome one fear that he knew about, and at least one other that he didn't.

That fall I showed up for football, of course. It was one thing to quit Tom's baseball team, quite another to quit his Downtown Youth Center Bears, perennial champs of the 110-lb. league. To lack the "balls" to stick it out on Tom's football team was a disgrace impossible to live down.

There was a drill most of us were unwilling to admit we dreaded called "bull-in-the-ring." Twelve or fifteen players would form a tight circle and count off. Then Feifel would call out a number and that boy would jog into the center of the circle. Then he would bark out another number and that boy would charge and try to knock the boy in the center down. As soon as one charge was over, sometimes as the boy was still getting to his feet, Feifel would call out another number and let another "bull" into the ring. The boy in the center would have to whirl and be ready or he would get slammed, blindsided. You were there, in the ring, until Feifel decided you'd had enough. Often, after he'd administered the coup de grace by calling the number of a particularly ferocious favorite positioned directly behind the player struggling to his feet, he would step into the ring and help the boy up, taking off the kid's helmet, grabbing him behind the neck and pulling him forehead-to-forehead with him. "Damn good job. Damn good. Ya all right? Good. Get your helmet back on."

Disgrace loomed over us, always. One flinch or cringe and Feifel was likely to blow the whistle. "You're done. You don't wanna play. Turn in your uniform."

"No, coach, please. Please, coach. Give me another chance!"

"All right then. Show me what you're made of. Get back in there."

On only one occasion do I recall a boy who decided for himself that he'd had enough. He staggered away with Feifel yelling after him, "You come back here now or don't come back at all! You hear me?" The boy kept walking, weaving and wobbly, until he sat down under a tree near the parking lot, took off his helmet, and put his head in his hands, waiting there, an emblem of shame for the rest of us, for his father to come and pick him up. We never saw him again.

By the time I became a high school senior, I had remade myself, or at least constructed a new version of myself that hid the target. Looking back, the process seems no more complex than the ten or twelve panels that made up the cartoon ad for the Charles Atlas chest-expander on the back of nearly every comic book (on the inside back cover were mail order offers for telescopes, sea-monkeys, Chihuahuas, genuine rattlesnake rattles, jumping beans, and ant farms.) The skinny guy with the rounded shoulders and concave chest is on a towel at the beach with a dazzling young woman in a two-piece bathing suit. The bully comes along and kicks sand in his face and unlike most of the women I have had the luck to know, the object of this poor scarecrow's affections sneers at him and goes off on the arm of the grinning, armor-plated Neanderthal. Of course you know the story: our antihero buys the Charles Atlas chest-expander and transforms himself in the space of two panels into a radiant beachboy with an adoring young woman on each arm.

Before you decide that deconstructing an ad on the back of a comic book is a silly exercise, know this: I believed it. I believed it as surely as my mother believed a television and screen actor named Ronald Reagan who flacked for the Chesterfields that killed her at the age of 55. I believed it as surely as I believed that our spiritual father, Pius XII, whom we would later learn had betrayed the Jews of Rome to the Nazi ovens, was the benevolent presence of Christ-like gentleness whose countenance graced every classroom I'd ever sat in. I believed it as surely as I believed that I was responsible for every sin and shame, for keeping my own soul pure and innocent, from the age of seven, as I was instructed in accordance with the Baltimore Catechism, 3rd edition, memorized and delivered flawlessly upon examination under threat of being cracked across the knuckles with a wooden stick.

For two years, from 15 to 17, I daily disappeared into the basement where, in what had been the coal-bin, I weight-lifted myself into an armored pose. My barbells were concrete poured into coffee cans, the bar between them a length of pipe. I constructed a system of pulleys to lift other cans of cement. I went at it with religious devotion. I gained forty pounds, all of it muscle.

In the final panels of the comic strip ad, the young man stands up to the cruel bully and regains his self-respect. Authenticated by a female caricature— "He's a REAL man!" she squeals—he beams with self-satisfaction. More often than not, however, the story unfolds differently.

Anybody who came out for the high school team for early practice in August and made it through the double workouts, the dozens of laps, the thousands of calisthenics, the blocking and tackling drills, the boot camp presided over by coaches riding the blocking sleds with whistles clenched between their teeth, growling at us that we were weaklings, queers, sissies, made the team. Anybody could wear the uniform of which we were so proud if he were simply tough enough to not quit.

I knew Teddy. He had once played, briefly, for Tom's football team, the Bears, but after having his lip cut open one day at practice, he quit. The word was that he'd needed stitches and wouldn't be back for a week or so, but that stretched out until it was clear he wasn't returning. Teddy was a chubby kid, knock-kneed, nervous; Feifel had always teased him mercilessly for having "titties."

"Sweat, you lard ass. You got titties like a sow. We're gonna buy you a brassiere for those titties."

I believe I was in college or had just graduated when my mother told me, on the telephone, that Teddy had taken his own life. "I don't know if you knew him. It said in the paper that he was on the football team the same year you were." I think I must have thought at the time that suicide was simply the final evidence of Teddy's cowardice or lack of character. I don't know, but I believe now that that is what I would have thought then. I don't remember having any feelings about it. Now I believe that he "came out" for football compromised by his having been a "quitter" and trying, as I was, to regain or recapture his self-respect and the respect of others. He was no good at football. He was not at all aggressive. He was soft and sweet. He simply refused, as a point of honor, to quit, no matter how many double-teamed tackles flattened him, no matter how many times he took a deliberate blow from someone's forearm to his Adam's apple that left him gasping and choking, no matter how disdained he was by the older members of the team. No doubt he consoled himself with the myth that he was simply being "hazed" by the upperclassmen on the team and that it was all a part of coming, eventually, to belong. But Teddy never belonged, and I believe now that the day when he found himself on the floor of the shower, pissed on by his teammates, the fuse of his ultimate despair was lit, a fuse that in his case was only a few short years long.

Too simplistic? Please, offer me another explanation. I pissed on that boy. I pissed on him to not be seen, to buy insurance, to not be him.

Could it be that every single one of us in the solitary storm of the shower felt the same need to not be the one victimized, each of us with a fear whose roar could drown out any scruples we might have had? Even Kenny, the cruelest among us? No. He was the instigator, but he was no more cruel than the rest of us. The evil, the ugliness, the cruelty arrived there that day carried by Kenny, our Lieutenant Calley, but we all took part.

Our collusion and our memories of the event, along with any questions about what it meant, or meant about us: about who we were, pretended to be, wanted to be, feared we were, coursed down the single drain in the center of our circular assault where now I remember Teddy sitting, face in his hands, sobbing as we left the showers, all of them, for him to turn off. "Last one out turns off the water!"

• • •

Looking at this photograph, one might think that these boys in their baseball uniforms, in front of a handball court, with a Chevrolet behind them, are emblematic of that golden age of America, the years of prosperity after the Second World War. Their uniforms are spiffy. It's summer. Their coach is taking their picture.

They are studying how to choke off empathy. They are getting the hang of hatred. They are dividing the world into victors and victims. They are running a phallic gauntlet. They are dying inside, of fear.

They are learning the national pastime.

NOTES

1. This essay first appeared in *The Literary Review*, Vol. 45, #4, Summer, 2002.
2. Salter, *Transforming Trauma* (Thousand Oaks, CA: Sage Publications, 1995), p. 63.

57

INJURY, GENDER, AND TROUBLE

LAURIE SCHAFFNER

Laurie Schaffner is an assistant professor of sociology at the University of Illinois at Chicago.

This reading is an excerpt from a study of 191 court-involved girls and 42 of the adults who work with them in detention centers, community agencies, drop-in centers, schools, after-school programs, residential facilities, and mental health facilities.

Mylen Cruz was Filipina American, sixteen years old, and in detention for stabbing a boy at her school. "I was in the office at my school, and this boy come up to me jus' to fuck with me. He was all, 'I'ma get me some of this shit, man.' He touched my butt! He thought we gonna be kickin' it or some shit! We got into a violent fight. I did a violent act. I don't know. I was mad. I couldn't deal with my anger; I couldn't hold it. I'm not a killer, but I would be able to do it. I hoped he wouldn't die, but I didn't want to go home. I wasn't scared to come to Juvey."

What did Mylen mean by "but I didn't want to go home"? It turned out that she was under brutal attack in her own house. In her file, I read that her mother was often homeless with Mylen and her little brother. Mylen continued: "My mom is there for me sometimes. She's always busy 'cause she has a lot of problems: the rent, money. We used to be close, but her stress affects me. I never ran away, but we always got evicted." One time her family was staying with another family, and her mother "had to serve the other family's father coffee and take a lot of shit, like she was the slave! I watched him treat her like shit!" Mylen was deeply affected by watching her mother be demeaned. She mentioned it in the interview and again when I went with her and her mother to an Ala-Teen meeting the following week.

Mylen became very upset during that first conversation and started crying. She said she felt that so many things were wrong with her life she couldn't figure out how to begin to fix it. "One of my mom's boyfriends molested me. It was the grossest thing in the world. Everybody knew and nobody would help. When I was twelve years old, I started hanging out with [a] guy from by my street, and he used to hit me all the time. He made me do gross shit to him, and then he even hit me!" Mylen also said she hated school and knew she shouldn't have gone the day she stabbed the boy. "I knew I was gonna go off on somebody."

Mylen's narrative was representative of the stories of most of the young women I met who were in detention facilities charged with violent offenses. They were simultaneously victims and perpetrators, and it was hard to know whether to console them or punish them. My contention . . . is that in court the biographies of Mylen and girls like her should play a significant role in determining their best interests—not as an excuse for physical assault, but as an aid to the court. The abuse that Mylen endured was sustained, chronic, and acute. The experience of abuse is gendered. For boys, abuse goes against what they are taught to expect from their position of superiority. Abuse of girls confirms their place in a gendered hierarchy. A distinct process needs to be enacted in order for girls to heal and to regain or achieve a sense of safety and psychological integrity. Thus, gender deeply affects how childhood abuse is processed and how recovery occurs. . . . Sexual violence is fundamentally gendered and racialized; it is experienced differently by girls than by boys, and among girls. Abuse plays a special role in the lives of many girls who come to the attention of authorities. This role must be theorized because its meaning cannot be determined empirically. Finally, the definitions of community and youth violence must be broadened in order to begin to capture the prevalence and significance of sexual violence in girls' lives.

Violence Against Girls Provokes Girls' Violence: Reconfiguring "Abuse"

Growing up female today includes sorting out and facing delicate sexual dilemmas. Pubescent and adolescent girls must learn to navigate the world of being feminine and attractive without getting raped. Girls constitute the majority of children who are traumatized in childhood both sexually and physically. Psychologists note that emotional responses to sexualized trauma unconsciously guide behavior. Girls in detention spoke of how, at home, their mothers' boyfriends, their fathers, and their stepfathers sexualized relationships with them. Girls recounted incidences of sexual degradation by neighborhood men and by cousins, brothers, friends, and strangers. Studies link girls' early sexual debut, as well as unhealed childhood injuries from sexual trauma, to unhealthy practices such as self-medicating with drugs and alcohol, striking out in aggression and violence, and seeking parental-type attention from adult men through romance and sexuality. Indeed, the range of choices that were available to young women were inextricably connected to and controlled by these varied sexual and gendered interactions.[1]

. . . Poverty and socioeconomic class influence girls' outcomes. Fewer alternatives and opportunities and thinner decisional avenues are available to poor girls than to their more affluent counterparts. Young women from disadvantaged communities are more vulnerable to predation by neighborhood men hanging around on street corners, are less likely to be protected by the law, and enjoy less access to resources that would help them heal from the trauma that occurs in their young lives.[2]

Child abuse—its study, measurement, prevention, treatment, and the punishment of offenders—has become a veritable cottage industry. Social work, psychiatry, psychology, and criminology have developed definitions, coursework, even diplomas. Legal experts make their cases and government officials win elections by focusing on attendant popular moral outrage. Meanwhile, young women across our nation are quietly dying from exploitation and injury. During the course of this research, I found it increasingly disturbing to witness celebrity indignation designed to increase Neilsen ratings and political rhetoric designed to boost voting popularity regarding prostitution, trafficking, and child abuse while vulnerable young women continued to be punished for the defense mechanisms they deployed in response to this onslaught against them. . . .

Anastasia Rudnik: To Witness Violence Is to Learn Violence

Anastasia Rudnik grew up in a chaotic house in California. Her mother emigrated from Russia while Anastasia was still a baby. When she was young, Anastasia lost a younger sibling in a devastating apartment fire. Anastasia was lanky and light-haired and sat hunched over her own body. The other girls told me her arms were "covered with scars" from cutting herself, and her files confirmed that they were. Anastasia's mother had been in a long-term relationship with a man who was physically violent with her often, and Anastasia witnessed the abuse. Anastasia moved around a lot, and her file noted, "When her mother can't handle her, she seems to 5150 her a lot" ("5150" is the California police term for a call regarding a person who appears to have a mental health—read aggressive—problem).

Anastasia says she has "too much problems—I have to care for all my brothers and sisters. My one sister is in a psych hospital. She is slow because my stepdad beat her and molested her. Then she got raped." Anastasia related these details in a deathly quiet monotone, as if we were talking about the weather.

> I know I'm a crime committer, but I'm human too. I just did it 'cause I have so much hatred for my stepdad, well my mom's boyfriend or whatever he is. Basically my only family was my PO [probation officer], but he retired. My new PO just leave me rot in here. I'm in here for assault and battery.
>
> When I was little, I got teased by all the kids and older people. I was in a psych ward when I was five [years old]. My brother died in a fire when I was seven—I almost died too! *Ooh* I'll never forget that smell of the fire. God! I was soo scared! We cried so much. I sort of remember.
>
> I was raised up in a not so good house. That asshole was always pushin' my mom around and making her cry. One time he

pushed her so hard she fell down! I hate him so much, I'd like to hit him with a 2 × 4! He's a pig!

My mom is pregnant now. Her boyfriend is a bad man. I got put in the ward for beating kids up. I am very violent. I been in trouble since I'm eight. I don't communicate a lot with girls because they talk too much, and I have to beat them up. I have a temper. I'm in here now 'cause I beat this girl in my group home.

In Anastasia's situation, her own assaultive behavior mimicked the family violence she witnessed. When she turned her hurt and fear outward and toward others, her aggression was an emotive response to the many stressors confronting her.

Broadening the Definition of Violence

Not until blood was spilled or police were called could the young women in this study "see" the community and family violence surrounding them. More than half—53 percent—of the young women reported being physically or sexually injured directly, and when asked whether they had ever witnessed their parents or other combinations of family and household members in physical battle, 71 percent answered in the affirmative. However, when asked whether they had ever witnessed abuse or whether they felt that there was violence in their homes, only a small portion framed abuse and fights as violence. A relationship between witnessing violence and subsequent offending was certainly suggested by these findings, but it was as if young women did not see the connection, and if they did, it was not that bad.

At first, the young women did not seem to have been disturbed by the chaos and violence they reported witnessing. Only when my follow-up questions signaled to the girls that I thought their feelings were crucial did they begin to unfurl details of powerful events that had made up just four- or five-word phrases in their files (and lives): "gfa [grandfather] raped her mo [mother] in her room one night," "was kidnapped and forced to watch pornographic sex acts before being released," and "was raped with a gun inserted into her vagina." After prompts such as "So, how do you feel about what happened that night?" "What do you think that means to you now?" girls reported feeling frozen with fear, terrified at seeing their mothers and siblings being hurt and unable to do anything to stop it, and panicked when recalling harm. Even though at least some of our discussion might have been prompted by my questioning, that to become disturbed about violent mistreatment would need probing was interesting in itself.

Some of the girls who insisted there was no connection whatsoever between their exposure to trauma and their current troubles seemed to disassociate themselves from the terror while they were recounting it. Many appeared a little bored by telling their stories over and over again to yet another social worker, which I believe is how I was often perceived. For example, one young woman related in a monotonous tone an account of watching her mother get raped by some men who stopped to "help" them when they had a flat tire on a Colorado highway one night. She knew it was an extraordinary experience, but I got the sense that it had become so normalized, made into a notation in her file, that she did not think it was of much importance or such an out-of-the-ordinary experience anymore. The girls' accounts in this research exemplify why definitions of community violence need to be broadened to include the abuse youths (meaning girls as well) see, face, and deal with all the time at home, at school, and out on the streets.[3]

Children are now considered invisible victims of domestic and community violence: "More than half of the police calls in many communities are for domestic disturbances, many of which are witnessed by children. Countless numbers of children whom one never hears about, and for whom the police do not receive calls, are exposed to physical and verbal abuse between their parents or caretakers several times a week."[4] In 1999, the California legislature signed into law a bill that provides for state assistance to victims and "derivative victims" of sexual abuse and domestic violence. Derivative victims include primary caretakers of minor victims of sexual or physical abuse and surviving family members of a victim who dies as a result of domestic violence. If witnesses in the family are later identified as in need of psychological counseling, state funds cover these expenses. In line with the reports of the court-involved girls in my study, the California policy demonstrates that witnessing family violence can have a long-term impact on the entire family structure.[5]

Although not expressly gendered, media exposure to violence can desensitize youth. Researchers claim that the average child is exposed to eight thousand television murders and more than one hundred thousand other violent acts by the time he or she enters seventh grade. Studies have found that Saturday morning programming for children contains twenty to twenty-five violent acts per hour. Exposure to violence in the media may result in young people becoming less sensitive to the pain and suffering of others, being more fearful of the world around them, and possibly behaving in more aggressive or harmful ways toward others. Directly witnessing or being a victim of violence has even stronger effects.[6]

Girls in juvenile corrections revealed that they witnessed an inordinate amount of violence on a regular, routine basis. They saw brothers, friends, cousins, fathers, and boyfriends being kicked, beaten, punched, knifed, shot, and killed. They witnessed their mothers being devalued and hurt physically by fathers, stepfathers, and boyfriends. Well over half the girls in my sample reported witnessing physical, sexual, or emotional abuse of others. Almost every girl could recount such events. Most recounted multiple events. Many intertwined tales of abuse and mistreatment with the regular stories of their daily lives:

> My mom drinks two cups of vodka every day. My dad was arrested
> for beating on my mom. They have six kids, but only my brother is

my real brother. I used to put my head under my pillow when
I was little so I wouldn't hear my brother cry when he got hit.
(Ilsa Davis, fourteen years old, simple assault)

My best friend's brother hanged himself. I found him there. . . . I'm
stressin' now because my friend Benito got killed in Bayview, and
they wouldn't let me go to the *funeraria*. See what happened is, um,
chiflaron y salió mucha gente. Luego lo mataron [they whistled and a
bunch of people came out of the house and then they killed Benito].
(Claudia Sereno, seventeen years old, assault, stringing various
events together)

I got cut off home detention 'cause I didn't go to school. I need to
stay at my boyfriend's [apartment) 'cause he lives nearby my
school, and I can just go from there. My mom's always goin' to jail.
> *For what?*
> For partyin'—I don't know what you call it. She freaked out
because my cousin got shot so my brother shot the people who shot
him and then *he* got shot. Me and my mom aren't getting along
ever since my brother died. I probably want to go to NA for crank
[Narcotics Anonymous for taking speed]—I been doin' like six lines
a day to forget about my problems. (Cheyanne McDerby, seventeen
years old, probation violation)

My daddy gets in jail a lot for drinking. I run away from
home because it is loud and noisy there—the music. It's hard to
concentrate. I've run from placements and hospitals too! My mom
and her boyfriend hit each other and hit me too. They give me
bloody lips. But I went to a hospital for cutting my arm. [File reads:
"Body covered with scars from cutting herself."] (Anastasia
Rudnik, fifteen years old, assault with a deadly weapon).

I came to consider the young women in this population as unnoticed,
mute witnesses of front-line violence in day-to-day urban life. Girls in my
study reported living in worlds tainted daily by aggression and assault.
Many adolescents experience power struggles with siblings and parents, but
for these girls common household conflicts such as not being able to use the
telephone or go out with friends, or discussions over their chores turned into
physically violent disputes.

For some people in some situations, violence becomes normalized, even
utilized as an emotional strategy and a psychological response to troubles
and frustrations. In my study, a certain routinization of violence in girls'
everyday lives was embedded in their decision making. Carina would talk
about throwing coffee cans, stabbing her brother, seeing her mother get hit,
and whacking a woman on the head in the street for her purse all in one
breath. She would explain how she would just go off—lose her temper, let

her frustrations build up, and then pour out violent expressions, as if that were normal. The social logic to her expressions of anger was that, unfortunately, they were a normal and natural part of day-to-day interactions.

Data from my interviews and observations made clear that factors such as witnessing sexual and physical trauma were salient when interpreting girls' violent offenses. Girls' troubles with juvenile authorities must be theorized within the contexts of the violence they suffer, including listening to fighting and watching brutal assaults.

> My dad was an abusive alcoholic, and the divorce helped him straighten up. But since their divorce, when I was eleven, all went downhill from there for me. I grew up in a bad household. I seen my dad pound on my mom. I can't blame it on my mom and dad but ever since my mom and dad got their divorce, I haven't got through it yet. I never thought it could happen to our family. Now I'm in here for jumping this girl and beatin' on her—I stole her chain too. It's jus' all bad for me. (Doris Montoya, fourteen years old, assault and battery)

> I even had to call the police on my own dad. He used to fight with my mom, with my uncle, even our neighbors! Fights: my dad taught me "If someone hits you then hit them back!" I don't know how many times he's been in jail for assault and battery! He taught me how to fight pretty good, well, not that good [laughs]. I lost the fight I'm in here for. (Joanne Billingsly, fifteen years old, assault and battery on school grounds)

Although girls' aggression and anger, as well as their parents' marital discord, were consistently related to offending behaviors, many criminology studies fall short of exploring the ways girls who grow up seeing their mothers beaten respond by being aggressive themselves. Research cannot definitively prove that witnessing or being victimized by brutality in childhood directly causes later offending behaviors, and it cannot predict which witness will become an offender, but plausible links among factors such as exposure to violence, girls' anger, and subsequent offenses, especially girls' involvement in violent crimes, became easy to verify by hearing the voices of girls who were locked up for violent offenses.[7]

Children are born into families where they learn their culture and family history, values, and how to love and work. Young people gravitate to safe and loving places in which to grow up. As one group of feminist scholars found in their work with urban girls, "'Homeplaces' can be broadly defined to include comforting, safe spaces in institutions such as schools or in social groups such as clubs, social movements, or gangs. Listening to young women's critiques of schooling, domestic spaces, gender relations, racial hierarchies, and social violence, we have learned that homeplaces, broadly defined, can also become constricting places from which they often try to break free."[8] As we saw, Anastasia's experience typifies how families can simultaneously offer girls and young women a home to grow up in but one sadly filled with violence, neglect, and abuse.

From Private to Public Injury

When we dig into the girls' accounts we see how their private anguish affects us as a public. In their families, friendships, neighborhoods, and schools, they were provoked into making an astonishing number of aggressive assaults. Their injuries were connected to their sexual misconduct as well. Their narratives revealed neither a simple structural determinism as a result of being poor or discriminated against nor any facile psychosexual dysfunction or pathology. Instead, girls' involvement in juvenile corrections resulted from the interplay among these forces and others, mediated often by an unprotective culture and punitive social stance.

Girls related relatively freely their sexual experiences as victims. Many court-involved girls sense that they may gain sympathy by sharing accounts of their victimization. Although the girls were comfortable presenting themselves as sexual objects, they seemed less comfortable sharing experiences of sexual agency. They were much more recalcitrant when it came to some aspects of their sexual choices—sex work, trading sex for favors and money, loving older men, and having desire for other girls. These narratives were difficult for them to share. They sensed that they had much to lose and could get into even more trouble if they told adults about much of their private lives. In addition, . . . the dual effects of growing up in families devoid of positive encouragement coupled with a hypereroticized popular culture led young women into problematic and, at times, illicit relationships.

NOTES

1. A considerable body of multidisciplinary research is devoted to documenting and understanding the sexual exploitation and traumatic injury of girl children. For claims made in this paragraph, see Charles Stewart Mott Foundation 1994; Costin, Karger, and Stoesz 1996; Eisenstein 1988; Elliott and Morse 1989; Finkelhor 1994; Gilgun 1986; Harway and Liss 1999; Herman 1992; Jacobs 1993; Ketterlinus et al. 1992; Lamb 2001; Phelps 1979; Pynoos and Eth 1985; Rich 1978; Sharpe 1976; Thompson 1995; Tolman 2002; Tolman and Higgins 1996; van der Kolk 1987; Widom and Kuhns 1996. See also Brumberg 1997; Eder 1997.

2. See Levine 2003; Rogers Park Young Women's Action Team 2003; Veysey 2003.

3. See also findings regarding the effects of family, community, and youth violence in Garbarino et al. 1992; Holden, Geffner, and Jouriles 1998; Jenkins and Bell 1997; Mohr 1997; Osofsky 1998; Zimring 1998.

4. Osofsky 1998, 97.

5. *California Government Code,* sec. 13965 (2000). See also Siegfried, Ko, and Kelley 2004.

6. Bell 1995; Dougherty 1998; Friedrich-Cofer and Huston 1986; Huesmann et al. 2003; John Murray 1997; Osofsky 1997; Singer et al. 1995.

7. A good deal of research across disciplines has been conducted connecting the effects of abuse with later troubling behaviors. See Cauffman 2004; Cauffman et al. 1998, Hennessey et al. 2004; Holden, Geffner, and Jouriles 1998; Obeidallah

and Earls 1999; Stein et al. 1997; Steiner, Garcia, and Matthews 1997; Teplin et al. 2002; Wood et al. 2002; van der Kolk and Greenberg 1987. For research supporting the victim-to-offender theory of girls' aggression, as well as considering that sequence within patriarchy, see, for example, Belknap and Holsinger 1998; Bernardez 1988; Brown, Chesney-Lind, and Stein 2004; Campbell 1994; Chesney-Lind and Belknap 2004; Herman 1981, 1992; Herrera and McCloskey 2001; Jacobs 1993; Tucker and Wolfe 1997; Wolfe and Tucker 1998.

8. Pastor, McCormick, and Fine 1996, 15. See also Furstenberg et al. 1999, a study that details ways that parents in disadvantaged communities and troubled urban environments have managed to provide loving and safe homes for their children.

REFERENCES

Belknap, Joanne, and Kristi Holsinger. 1998. "An Overview of Deliquent Girls: How Theory and Practice Have Failed and the Need for Innovative Changes." In Zaplin, *Female Offenders,* 31–64.

Bell, Carl. 1995. "Exposure to Violence Distresses Children and May Lead to Their Becoming Violent." *Psychiatric News* 6(8): 15.

Bernardez, Teresa. 1988. *Women and Anger: Cultural Prohibitions and the Feminine Ideal.* Wellesley, MA: Stone Center.

Brown, Lyn Mikel, Meda Chesney-Lind, and Nan Stein. 2004. *Patriarchy Matters: Toward a Gendered Theory of Teen Violence and Victimization.* Wellesley Centers for Women Working Paper 417. Wellesley, MA: Center for Research on Women, Wellesley College.

Brumberg, Joan Jacobs. 1997. *The Body Project: An Intimate History of American Girls.* New York: Random House.

Brydon-Miller, Mary. 2001. "Education, Research, and Action: Theory and Methods of Participatory Action Research." In Tolman and Brydon-Miller, *From Subjects to Subjectivities,* 76–89.

Campbell, Anne. 1994. *Men, Women, and Aggression.* New York: Basic Books.

Cauffman, Elizabeth. 2004. "A Statewide Screening of Mental Health Symptoms among Juvenile Offenders in Detention." *Journal of the American Academy of Child and Adolescent Psychiatry* 43(4): 430–439.

Cauffman, Elizabeth, S. Shirley Feldman, Jamie Waterman, and Hans Steiner. 1998. "Posttraumatic Stress Disorder among Female Juvenile Offenders." *Journal of the American Academy of Child and Adolescent Psychiatry* 37(11): 1209–1216.

Charles Stewart Mott Foundation. 1994. *A Fine Line: Losing American Youth to Violence.* Flint, MI: Charles Stewart Mott Foundation.

Chesney-Lind, Meda, and Joanne Belknap. 2004. "Trends in Delinquent Girls' Aggression and Violent Behavior: A Review of the Evidence." In Putallaz and Bierman, *Aggression, Antisocial Behavior, and Violence among Girls,* 203–222.

Costin, Lela, Howard Jacob Karger, and David Stoesz. 1996. *The Politics of Child Abuse in America.* New York: Oxford University Press.

Dougherty, Joyce. 1998. "Female Offenders and Childhood Maltreatment: Understanding the Connections." In Zaplin, *Female Offenders,* 227–244.

Eder, Donna, with Catherine Evans and Stephen Parker. 1997. *School Talk: Gender and Adolescent Culture.* New Brunswick, NJ: Rutgers University Press.

Eisenstein, Zillah. 1988. *The Female Body and the Law.* Berkeley: University of California Press.

Elliott, Delbert, and Barbara Morse. 1989. "Delinquency and Drug Use as Risk Factors in Teenage Sexual Activity." *Youth and Society* 21(1): 32–60.

Finkelhor, David. 1994. "Current Information on the Scope and Nature of Child Sexual Abuse." *The Future of Children: Sexual Abuse of Children* (David and Lucile Packard Foundation, Los Angeles) 4(2): 31–53.

Friedrich-Cofer, L., and A. Huston. 1986. "Television Violence and Aggression: The Debate Continues." *Psychological Bulletin* 100: 364–371.

Furstenberg, Jr., Frank, Thomas Cook, Jacquelynne Eccles, Glen Elder Jr., and Arnold Sameroff. 1999. *Managing to Make It: Urban Families and Adolescent Success.* Chicago: University of Chicago Press.

Garbarino, James, Nancy Dubrow, Kathleen Kostelny, and Carole Pardo. 1992. *Children in Danger: Coping with Consequences of Community Violence.* San Francisco: Jossey-Bass.

Gilgun, Jane. 1986. "Sexually Abused Girls' Knowledge about Sexual Abuse and Sexuality." *Journal of Interpersonal Violence* 1(3): 309–325.

Harway, Michele, and Marsha Liss. 1999. "Dating Violence and Teen Prostitution: Adolescent Girls in the Justice System." In Johnson, Roberts, and Worell, *Beyond Appearance,* 277–300.

Hennessey, Marianne, Julian Ford, Karen Mahoney, Susan Ko, and Christine Siegfried. 2004. *Trauma among Girls in the Juvenile Justice System.* Los Angeles: National Child Traumatic Stress Network.

Herman, Judith. 1981. *Father-Daughter Incest.* Cambridge, MA: Harvard University Press.

———. 1992. *Trauma and Recovery.* New York: Basic Books.

Herrera, Veronica, and Laura Ann McCloskey. 2001. "Gender Differences in the Risk for Delinquency among Youth Exposed to Family Violence." *Child Abuse and Neglect* 25: 1037–1051.

Holden, George, Robert Geffner, and Ernest Jouriles, eds. 1998. *Children Exposed to Marital Violence: Theory, Research, and Applied Issues.* Washington, DC: American Psychological Association.

Huesmann, Rowell, Jessica Moise-Titus, Cheryl-Lynn Podolski, and Leonard Eron. 2003. "Longitudinal Relations between Children's Exposure to TV Violence and Their Aggressive and Violent Behavior in Young Adulthood." *Developmental Psychology* 39(2): 201–221.

Jacobs, Janet L. 1993. "Victimized Daughters: Sexual Violence and the Empathic Female Self." *Signs* 19(1): 126–145.

Jenkins, Esther, and Carl Bell. 1997. "Exposure and Response to Community Violence among Children and Adolescents." In Osofsky, *Children in a Violent Society,* 9–31.

Ketterlinus, Robert, Michael Lamb, Katherine Nitz, and Arthur Elster. 1992. "Adolescent Nonsexual and Sex-Related Behaviors." *Journal of Adolescent Research* 7(4): 431–456.

Lamb, Sharon. 2001. *The Secret Lives of Girls: What Good Girls Really Do—Sex Play, Aggression, and Their Guilt.* New York: Free Press.

Levine, Kay. 2003. "Prosecution, Politics and Pregnancy: Enforcing Statutory Rape in California." PhD diss., School of Jurisprudence and Social Policy, University of California at Berkeley.

Mohr, Wanda. 1997. "Making the Invisible Victims of Domestic Violence Visible." *Domestic Violence Report* 2(6): 81–82.

Murray, John. 1997. "Media Violence and Youth." In Osofsky, *Children in a Violent Society,* 72–96.

Obeidallah, Dawn, and Felton Earls. 1999. *Adolescent Girls: The Role of Depression in the Development of Delinquency.* Research Preview. Washington, DC: National Institute of Justice.

Osofsky, Joy, ed. 1997. *Children in a Violent Society.* New York: Guilford Press.

Osofsky, Joy. 1998. "Children as Invisible Victims of Domestic and Community Violence." In Holden, Geffner, and Jouriles, *Children Exposed to Marital Violence.* Washington, DC: American Psychological Association, 95–120.

Pastor, Jennifer, Jennifer McCormick, and Michelle Fine. 1996. "Makin' Homes: An Urban Girl Thing." In Leadbeater and Way, *Urban Girls,* 15–34.

Phelps, Linda. 1979. "Female Sexual Alienation." In *Women: A Feminist Perspective,* edited by Joann Freeman, 18–26. Palo Alto, CA: Mayfield.

Pynoos, R., and S. Eth. 1985. "Developmental Perspective on Psychic Trauma in Childhood." In *Trauma and Its Wake,* edited by Charles Figley, 193–216. New York: Brunner/Mazel.

Rich, Adrienne. [1978] 1986. "Compulsory Heterosexuality and the Continuum of Lesbian Existence." In *Feminist Frontiers II: Rethinking Sex, Gender, and Society,* edited by Laurel Richardson and Verta Taylor, 120–141. New York: McGraw-Hill.

Rogers Park Young Women's Action Team. 2003. *"Hey Cutie, Can I Get Your Digits?" A Report about the Street Harassment of Girls in Rogers Park.* Chicago: Friends of Battered Women and Their Children, August.

Sharpe, Sue. 1976. *"Just Like a Girl": How Girls Learn to Be Women.* New York: Penguin Books.

Siegfried, Christine, Susan Ko, and Ann Kelley. 2004. *Victimization and Juvenile Offending.* Los Angeles: Juvenile Justice Working Group, National Child Traumatic Stress Network.

Singer, M., T. Anglin, L. Song, and L. Lunghofer. 1995. "Adolescents' Exposure to Violence and Associated Symptoms of Psychological Trauma." *Journal of the American Medical Association* 273(6): 477–482.

Stein, Nancy, Susan Roberta Katz, Esther Madriz, and Shelley Shick, special eds. 1997. "Losing a Generation: Probing the Myths and Realities of Youth and Violence." *Social Justice* 24(4).

Steiner, H., I. Garcia, and Z. Matthews. 1997. "Posttraumatic Stress Disorder in Incarcerated Juvenile Delinquents." *Journal of the American Academy of Child and Adolescent Psychiatry* 36(3): 357–365.

Teplin, Linda, Karen Abram, Gary McClelland, Mina Dulcan, and Amy Mericle. 2002. "Psychiatric Disorders in Youth in Juvenile Detention." *Archives of General Psychiatry* 59(12): 1133–1143.

Thompson, Sharon. 1995. *Going All the Way: Teenage Girls' Tales of Sex, Romance, and Pregnancy.* New York: Hill & Wang.

Tolman, Deborah. 2002. *Dilemmas of Desire: Teenage Girls Talk about Sexuality.* Cambridge, MA: Harvard University Press.

Tolman, Deborah, and Tracy Higgins. 1996. "How Being a Good Girl Can Be Bad for Girls." In *"Bad Girls/Good Girls": Women, Sex, and Power in the Nineties,* edited by Nan Bauer Maglin and Donna Perry, 205–225. New Brunswick, NJ: Rutgers University Press.

Tucker, Jennifer, and Leslie Wolfe. 1997. *Victims No More: Girls Fight Back against Male Violence.* Washington, DC: Center for Women Policy Studies.

van der Kolk, Bessel, ed. 1987. *Psychological Trauma.* Washington, DC: American Psychiatric Press.

van der Kolk, Bessel, and Mark Greenberg. 1987. "The Psychobiology of the Trauma Response: Hyperarousal, Constriction, and Addiction to Traumatic Re-exposure." In van der Kolk, *Psychological Trauma,* 63–88.

Veysey, Bonita. 2003. *Adolescent Girls with Mental Health Disorders Involved with the Juvenile Justice System.* Washington, DC: National Center for Mental Health and Juvenile Justice. http://www.ncmhjj.com.

Widom, Cathy Spatz, and J. Kuhns. 1996. "Childhood Victimization and Subsequent Risk for Promiscuity, Prostitution, and Teenage Pregnancy: A Prospective Study." *American Journal of Public Health* 86(11): 1607–1612.

Wolfe, Leslie, and Jennifer Tucker. 1998. *Report of the Summit on Girls and Violence.* Washington, DC: Center for Women Policy Studies.

Wood, Jennifer, David Foy, Carole Goguen, Robert Pynoos, and C. Boyd James. 2002. "Violence Exposure and PTSD among Delinquent Girls." In *Trauma and Juvenile Delinquency: Theory, Research, and Interventions,* edited by Ricky Greenwald, 109–126. New York: Haworth Press.

Zimring, Franklin. 1998. *American Youth Violence.* New York: Oxford University Press.

58

HOMOPHOBIA IN STRAIGHT MEN

TERRY A. KUPERS

Terry A. Kupers, M.D., a professor in the Graduate School of Psychology at The Wright Institute in Berkeley, California, practices psychiatry in Oakland. The author of *Public Therapy: The Practice of Psychotherapy in the Public Mental Health Clinic* (1981), and *Ending Therapy: The Meaning of Termination* (1988), he is married and has three young adult sons.

A few years ago I toured a high-security prison in the Midwest as an expert witness in litigation concerning the effects of prison conditions on prisoners' mental health. When I stepped into the main entry area of the prison, I saw a woman milling around with the men a short distance down one of the halls. She was blond, slim, very feminine—or so I thought on first glance. Actually, "she" was a young man, perhaps 21, dressed as a woman. Blond, blue-eyed, slight and sensuous, he played the part very well. He wore a flowing red gown that reached the floor, had a shawl draped across his chest in a way that did not permit one to assess the size of his breasts, wore make-up, and sported a very seductive female pose. I was surprised to see an attractive woman roaming around in a men's prison. One of the attorneys accompanying me on the tour told me with a wink that "she" was a he, and asked if I would like to talk to him.

The inmate told me he was not really gay, and certainly did not believe he would dress as a woman again after he was released, but on "the inside" it's the only way for him to survive unless he "locks up"; that is, asks for protective custody in a segregated section of the prison where inmates who do not feel safe on the "mainline" are housed, including those identified as "snitches" and child molesters. When this man arrived at the prison at 19 he was beat up and raped a number of times, and on several other occasions prison toughs fought with each other for the opportunity to use him sexually. He learned that it was safer to become the "woman" of a tough prisoner, that way he would not be beaten nor be the object of rivalries between prison toughs. He would become the passive sexual partner of one dominant man.

Later that day I met with a group of security officers. One mentioned the young man. I said I had met him. The officer asked if I'd like to hear the bit of advice he would have given that slight and fair young man if he had seen him when he entered the prison. Before I had a chance to answer, he blurted out:

> What you want to do is the first time you go out on the yard you break off a metal bed post and shove it down your trouser leg. Then, when a big guy comes up and pinches your ass or makes a lewd remark, you pull out the metal stick and smack him as hard as you can across the face. You'll both get thrown in the hole for ten days. Then, when you get out, everyone will respect you as a "crazy" and no one will hassle you for sex any more.

In prison, "butt-fucking" is the symbol of dominance. The strong do it, the weak must submit. Homosexual rape is a constant threat for those who cannot prove they are "man enough." According to Tom Cahill (1990), a survivor of prison rape: "We are victims of a system in which those who are dominated and humiliated come to dominate and humiliate others" (p. 33). Perhaps this explains why prisoners do so much body-building.

Free men do a lot of toughening, too. If it is not the physique it's the mind, or it's the reputation or the financial empire, but men are always building something that they believe will keep them off the bottom of the heap, out of range of those who would "shaft" them. This is not a complete explanation of men's competitiveness and defensiveness—competition is built into our social relations—but men's subjective dread of "being shafted" plays a part in sustaining those competitive social relations. The prison drama reverberates in the male psyche. It is as if men do not want to appear incapable of defending themselves against rape at any time. We stiffen our bodies when approached by other men who want to touch or hug and we keep men at a certain distance—where we can watch them and be certain that closeness and dependency will not make us too vulnerable.

REFERENCE

Cahill, T. (1990). "Prison Rape: Torture in the American Gulag." In *Men and Intimacy*, ed. F. Abbott. Freedom, CA: Crossing Press, 31–36.

59

THE ULTIMATE GROWTH INDUSTRY
Trafficking in Women and Girls

JAN GOODWIN

Jan Goodwin is the author of *Caught in the Crossfire* (1987) about Afghanistan and *Price of Honor: Muslim Women Lift the Veil of Silence on the Islamic World* (2003).

The California travel agency brochure could not be more blunt: "Sex Tours to Thailand, Real Girls, Real Sex, Real Cheap," it reads. "These women are the most sexually available in the world. Did you know you can actually buy a virgin girl for as little as $200? You could fuck a different girl every night for the rest of your life." There is even a prize for the man that has sex with the most girls during the tour. As for AIDS, the brochure continues, "Thailand is safe. And all the places we visit are police protected."

What the ad copy doesn't say is that these "virgin girls" are frequently children who have been kidnapped or sold into brothels. Forced into prostitution, sometimes even chained to their beds, they lead lives that are brutal, and frequently short. Averaging 15 customers a day, they work all but two days a month. They must perform any act demanded by their customers, most of whom refuse to wear condoms. If they object, the brothel owners beat them into submission. According to human rights activists working in Thailand, a large percentage of the prostitutes there are under 15, and girls as young as eight are sold into the industry. Within six months of being sold into the sex trade, a girl is commonly HIV-infected.

But you don't have to travel to Asia; sexual servitude can be found here in the U.S. too, as an 18-month undercover investigation by the Global Survival Network discovered. For example, women from the former Soviet Union can be found in brothels in New York, Bethesda, Maryland, and Los Angeles. Fleeing a collapsing economy at home, these women pay up to $3,000 in "processing fees" for what they are promised will be good jobs abroad; instead, they are sold into sexual slavery. The industry is tightly controlled by the Russian mafia, whose contacts with their own government and immigration officials facilitate the acquisition of the necessary visas and passports. Women trying to escape have been murdered, and the threat that family members back home will be beaten to death is also used to keep women in line.

According to GSN, which is based in Washington, D.C., every year trafficking in women and girls puts billions of dollars into the coffers of criminal syndicates worldwide—an amount rivaling their incomes from drugs and guns. And there is another plus in trading in human flesh: dope and weapons can only be sold once; a woman or girl can be sold again and again.

As the disparities in the global economy widen, girl children and young women are increasingly seen as currency and quick profits. The United Nations estimates that, around the world, some 200 million people are forced to live as sexual or economic slaves, the latter often involving sexual exploitation as well. In Southeast Asia alone, a reported 60 to 70 million women and children have been sold in the sex industry in the last decade. "Slavery is one of the most undesirable consequences of globalization," says a UN spokesman, adding, "We regret that this is not considered a priority by any country at the moment."

Nor is trafficking in women and girls limited to prostitution; it is also used to supply the forced-marriage industry. In China today, for example, there are now three males for every two females in the population over the age of 15. This as a result of the government's "one child, one couple" policy, combined with the traditional, and still powerful, requirement for a son. If the first child is a girl, the fetus may be aborted, or the infant abandoned or even killed. As a consequence, young women and girls are being sold into marriage, in a revival of a once-standard feudal practice. According to Chinese government reports, in the first 10 months of 1990 alone, trafficking in brides increased by 60 percent over the previous year. Either kidnapped or sold by impoverished families, the young women are purchased by potential bridegrooms for up to $600. The government's Office for the Eradication of the Kidnapping and Sale of Women acknowleges some 50,000 such kidnappings per year (although human rights organizations believe the real numbers are much higher). And the profits are enormous. In a five-year period from 1991 to 1996, Chinese police freed 88,000 women and children who had been kidnapped for this purpose.

Particularly disturbing is the violence to which these forced brides are subjected. The abducted women, who can be as young as 13 or 14, are frequently gang-raped by the slave traders before being sold, a practice that is intended to terrify them into passivity, and is no doubt effective in many cases. Those who try to run from their new husbands are violently punished, even maimed, by the traffickers in ways that are too sickening to be printed here.

In some cases, sex tours from the U.S. to the Third World are offered as a means by which lonely men can find a mate. Norman Barabash, who runs Big Apple Oriental Tours out of Queens, New York, views his tours as a social development program. Until recently, $2,200 bought 10 days and 11 nights of "paradise" in the Philippines; since last year, when Big Apple was banned from doing business in that country, Barabash has been sending American men to Thailand. Women in these countries have no jobs, and are dying to get American husbands, he says. "They are so set on landing one, they will do anything their conscience allows." According to Barabash, some 20 to 25 percent of his clients end up marrying women they meet on the tours.

Big Apple is only one of some 25 or 30 similar operations in the U.S. that ride on—and promote—the myth that "exotic oriental women are thrilled to meet American men, and know how to please and serve them," says Ken Franzblau, a lawyer for Equality Now, a human rights organization. Franzblau went underground for almost two years to investigate sex-tour companies in the U.S. "I posed as a shy man who felt insecure around women, and inquired about taking such a trip," he says. "I was told that all kinds of kinky sex would be available, and that the tour guides would negotiate prices for me with the pimps."

Franzblau points out that the operations demean women at both ends of their business. Reads one brochure: "Had enough of American bitches who won't give you the time of day, and are only interested in your bank account? In Asia you'll meet girls who will treat you with respect and appreciation, unlike their American counterparts." These operators insist that American women are unloving, feminist manhaters, he says. "At the destination end, sex tours create the ever-increasing demand to bring young women and girls into the sex industry."

In the Philippines and Thailand, prostitution is illegal. Here in the U.S., as well as in Germany, the Netherlands, Sweden, and Australia—all countries where sex tours originate—such "tourism" is likewise illegal, although in this country, the law applies only to traveling with the intent to engage in a sexual act with a juvenile, which is punishable for up to 10 years imprisonment. In the four years this law has been in force, however, there have been no prosecutions.

It is also illegal in virtually every state of America (including New York, where Big Apple operates) to promote prostitution, or knowingly profit from it. Yet sex-tour operators openly advertise in magazines and on the Internet, and the websites of many feature hardcore pornographic photographs of promised "delights." So, too, do the videos they send potential customers. An hour-long video sent to men interested in going on a Big Apple tour and viewed by *On the Issues* shows what is described as a wet T-shirt contest, but in reality is more a sex circus in which young women are stripped, and a mob of raucous overweight, aging American men suck on their nipples, perform oral sex, and otherwise explore their body cavities as they are passed around the crowd. The video also offers "daily introductions to the ladies of your choice who will be your companion for the night or around the clock." As two young women are shown cavorting naked in a jacuzzi, the voice-over cautions that if viewers don't take a tour, they will "miss an afternoon at a sex motel with two lovely ladies."

There is nothing subtle or obscure about the promotional video and its customer come-ons, but in a letter to Democratic Senator Catherine Abate last September, Queens County District Attorney Richard Brown wrote: "Our investigation [of Big Apple Oriental Tours], which has been quite extensive and included the use of undercover operatives as well as assistance provided by the FBI and the US Customs Service, has disclosed no provable violations of New York's criminal laws." At the time the decision not to pursue an indictment was made, the DA's office was in possession of the video.

After that ruling, Equality Now met with the DA, and offered additional evidence, including records of Franzblau's conversations with Big Apple's owner, and the reports of the two men who took the tours. The DA has subsequently reopened his investigation of the company.

Many other countries are also lax about cracking down on trafficking. The Japanese not only appear to condone the industry, they actively obstruct interference in it. Due to massive unemployment in the Philippines, even for those with college degrees, some 80,000 Filipinos work in Japan; 95 percent of them are women employed as "dance entertainers." Commonly, the passports of these "guest workers" are confiscated on arrival and their salaries withheld; according to Mizuho Matsuda, the director of HELP, the only shelter for abused migrant women workers in Tokyo, many are forced into prostitution. Japan's criminal syndicate, the Yazuka, is heavily involved in trafficking women for the country's sex-and-entertainment industry, and like their Russian counterpart, have contacts in the government, and therefore often enjoy its protection.

A grisly side of a grim industry is highlighted by the death of 22-year old Maricris Siosin, a graduate in modern dance. Five months after arriving in Tokyo, she was sent home in a closed coffin, with a death certificate stating she had died of hepatitis. When her family opened the coffin for the funeral, they discovered that she had been beaten and stabbed. An autopsy conducted by the Philippines National Bureau of Investigation and confirmed, at the request of Equality Now, by a leading pathologist in the U.S., showed that a double-edged sword had been thrust into her vagina.

In Japan, S&M has a long tradition, and extremely violent S&M comics are readily available. Many male commuters openly read them instead of newspapers as they travel to and from work. One theory is that Maricris was forced to participate in a "snuff" movie (a porno flick in which the woman is actually killed).

A Philippine government mission which was sent to Japan to investigate the murder was turned away by Japanese authorities. Similarly, Maricris' family has been denied access to medical documents and police records. Some 33 Filipino workers died in Japan the same year Maricris was killed. At least 12 of these deaths took place under "suspicious circumstances."

In other countries, local authorities facilitate sex trafficking. In the southern Thai town of Ranong, for example, brothels are surrounded by electrified barbed wire and armed guards to keep girls from escaping. The local police chief condones the practice, describing the brothels as an important part of the local economy. And while prostitution is illegal in Thailand, customers and owners alike have no fear of arrest. The police can be bought off, or accept payment in kind—free use of the brothels; a number of them also act as procurers for the traffickers.

The government periodically promises to crack down on the industry, but because of the amount of money it generates, invariably looks the other way. Of the five million annual visitors to Thailand on tourist visas, three out of four are men traveling alone, many of whom are from Europe, the Middle East, Japan, and the U.S. When raids are planned, the police often alert the brothels ahead of time. The only people arrested are the young prostitutes. Tragically, they are then frequently "recycled," often with the assistance of the local police, who resell them to agents of a different brothel. And so the tragic circle remains unbroken, until the girls become too sick to work, or die on the job, like the five young prostitutes on Phuket island, a popular vacation resort for foreigners in southern Thailand: When fire broke out in the brothel where they worked, they burned to death because they were chained to their beds and unable to escape.

Tourism in Thailand generates $3 billion annually, and the country's international image as a sexual paradise has made prostitution one of its most valuable economic subsectors. That international reputation is one even the U.S. Navy has recognized. The first port of call and liberty shore leave for much of the U.S. fleet after the Gulf War was Pattaya, a beach resort notorious as a center of Thailand's sex industry. This apparent reward for service was given despite the fact that at the time at least 50 percent of the prostitutes in the region were HIV-positive. Another major destination for sex traffickers is India, where an estimated 15 million women and girls, many of whom have been sold into it from impoverished Nepal, Bangladesh, and Pakistan, work in the sex industry.

"Women and girls are moved between a lot of different countries," says a spokesman for Human Rights Watch. Moreover, trafficking is not only a global phenomenon, it is a "hidden one." For example, the organization reported recently, the U.S. gives Thailand $4 million a year to control the traffic in narcotics, but no U.S. aid is aimed at curtailing sex trafficking there. It is imperative that the U.S. government "recognize the severity of the problem," says Human Rights Watch. "And the United Nations also needs to be very aggressive in fighting this modern form of slavery."

60

HOW SAFE IS AMERICA?

DESIREE TAYLOR

Desiree Taylor was a student at the University of Massachusetts-Boston completing an individualized major in gender, religion, and the arts when she wrote this essay.

I saw a picture in a magazine in which a woman is walking away from the collapsed World Trade Center towers covered in orange dust from head to toe. Her face is twisted into a shocked and horrifying expression and she is turned around slightly looking back at the photographer as she walks away from the scene. What strikes me about this picture is that I have never seen another like it, such an elegant and stylish depiction of war. The woman is so immaculately dressed, her hair so stylishly cut, that the whole scene looks like a clever fashion spread from an upscale magazine. This just couldn't be real, but it is. Looking at this picture, I try to really see the woman in it. I try to feel the horror of her experience, but as I do I can also see that she is not from my America. She is from an America that before September 11 was in many ways safer and freer than mine before or after that day.

On September 12, the day after the attack on the United States, I watched the media coverage and a very middle-class looking woman interviewed on the street said she "no longer felt safe in America." I was born and have grown up in this country. As a mixed race, half Black, half white woman born into poverty, I have never felt safe here.

In America, life within one class is nothing at all like it is in another. On September 11 thousands of people died in the collapsed World Trade towers. They were not alone. Every day in this country people die from exploitation that originates right here at home. Some who toil and slave in service to a system of wealth and prestige, who don't even earn a living for their trouble, slit their wrists out of desperation and pain. Some die used up and exhausted, in hospital beds with two dollars and eighty-five cents in their purse, like my own mother. Some people work two or more jobs and try to fit some kind of life in between, maybe an education, which gets harder and harder as they lose out on more and more sleep. The amount of safety one can truly feel in America is directly related to how much money you have.

Safety Depends on Money

I think about these people who were and are anything but safe here. I think about those who sweat out unappreciated labor to make the American Dream seem so real, to make the consumer culture function. I wonder if the woman in the picture ever looked as closely at the people who are dying in the class war here at home as I do at her.

It enrages me to hear people saying they no longer feel safe here. The United States that is being attacked is the one the woman in the picture belongs to. It is the prosperous, comfortable United States. It is not my United States. But all of a sudden we are all in it together. The flags are brought out and everybody sings, "I'm proud to be an American."

But it's impossible for me to suddenly forget that the United States empire was built upon and is still maintained by abuses against the poor and minorities. I think about those who will fight and die in this war. I think about all the poor, and often Black, students from my high school who enlisted in the armed services to earn money for college. I think about all the students who wouldn't have been caught dead joining the armed forces, kids for whom the military was not one of their few options to move out of poverty. I think about how many low-income families are worrying right now about the lives of their enlisted children. I wonder what proportion of persons who will fight in this war will be those who are not sharing in the "American Dream." I believe that it will be disproportionally high.

Poor Invisible to Mainstream

The plight of low-income people in this country is invisible to mainstream America. This invisible other America, the poor, enters through side and back doors of hotels, through the servants' entrances. They live in segregated neighborhoods, and work jobs in which they are unseen even though they are in plain view.

For example, I went to Walgreens the other day and was handed a receipt that read at the top: "I'm Laqueeta [name changed]. I'm here to serve you." The message continued on the next line: "with our seven service basics." A middle-class person in this corporation decided that Laqueeta should hand this message out on every one of her receipts. What made someone earning a good salary think that this was a good idea? We're not even told what those seven service basics are, and they don't really matter. What matters is that the plantation-type American Dream is being acted out here. I, as a consumer, am for a moment in the seat of power with someone to serve me. This is meant to register with me, but the server is not. She doesn't matter. If she did, she would be able to survive doing this kind of work.

I decided to inquire about a cashier's job at Walgreens. The pay rate, I was told, is $6.75 an hour in Boston. When I worked hourly wage jobs in retail stores I learned that employers would keep employees just under 40 hours a week, so that officially they were not full-time and therefore not entitled by law to benefits. I do not know if Walgreens does this, but the practice is widespread. For 39 hours of work at $6.75 an hour, that is $263.25 a week before taxes and $758.16 per month after taxes. After subtracting $35 for a subway pass and at least $460 a month for rent and bills (and for rent this low that means living in a hovel with probably four other people she doesn't know), that leaves Laqueeta just $65.79 a week for food, clothing, savings, entertainment, household expenses, healthcare, and any other expense that might come up, including saving for college and a computer. I hope she doesn't have a child. How safe is Laqueeta in America? Does anybody care? The appearance of America's bounty is maintained by the exploitation of people right here at home who are in positions to be easily misused.

The United States feels very much to me like several countries made up of separate social/economic classes, who don't and perhaps won't take the time to really look at each other; they can't feel each other's pains, cannot relate, and largely live in separate worlds. Now that we're at war with outside forces, we are supposed to come together within the United States. We are all supposed to feel the same hurts and the same threats. We are all supposed to feel each other's pain. We are all supposed to defend justice and freedom. During the past few weeks we have heard over and over again that these acts of terrorism are not only attacks on the United States, but on everything the country stands for. They tell us these are attacks on freedom and justice itself. But how is this possible when here at home justice, freedom, and the American Dream are denied to so many?

61

WIELDING MASCULINITY INSIDE ABU GHRAIB
Making Feminist Sense of an American Military Scandal

CYNTHIA ENLOE

Cynthia Enloe is research professor of international development and women's studies at Clark University. Her recent books include *Bananas, Beaches and Bases: Making Feminist Sense of International Politics* (2000), *Maneuvers: The International Politics of Militarizing Women's Lives* (2000), *The Curious Feminist: Searching for Women in A New Age of Empire* (2004), and *Globalization and Militarism: Feminists Make the Link* (2007).

In April, 2004, a year after the US government launched its massive military invasion of Iraq, a series of shocking photographs of American soldiers abusing Iraqi prisoners began appearing on television news programs and the front pages of newspapers around the world. American male and female soldiers serving as prison guards in a prison called Abu Ghraib were shown deliberately humiliating and torturing scores of Iraqi men held in detention and under interrogation. The American soldiers were smiling broadly. They appeared to be taking enormous pleasure in humiliating their Iraqi charges.

Most people who saw these photographs—people in Seattle and Seoul, Miami and Madrid, Bangkok and Boston—can still describe the scenes. An American male soldier standing self-satisfied with his arms crossed and wearing surgical blue rubber gloves, while in front of him, an American woman soldier, smiling at the camera, is leaning on top of a pile of Iraqi naked men forced to contort themselves into a human pyramid. An American woman soldier, again smiling, holding an Iraqi male prisoner on a leash. An American woman soldier pointing to a naked Iraq man's genitals, apparently treating them as a joke. American male soldiers intimidating Iraqi naked male prisoners with snarling guard dogs. An Iraqi male prisoner standing alone on a box, his head hooded, electrical wires attached to different parts of his body. An Iraqi male prisoner forced to wear women's underwear. Not pictured, but

Cynthia Enloe, "Wielding Masculinity Inside Abu Ghraib: Making Feminist Sense of an American Military Scandal" from *Asian Journal of Women's Studies* 10, no. 3 (2004). Reprinted with the permission of the author.

substantiated, were Iraqi men forced to masturbate and to simulate oral sex with each other, as well as an Iraqi woman prisoner coerced by several American male soldiers into kissing them.

What does a feminist curiosity reveal about the causes and the implications of the American abuses of Iraqi prisoners at Abu Ghraib? Few of the US government's official investigators or the mainstream news commentators used feminist insights to make sense of what went on in the prison. The result, I think, is that we have not really gotten to the bottom of the Abu Ghraib story. One place to start employing a feminist set of tools is to explain why one American woman military guard in particular captured the attention of so many media editors and ordinary viewers and readers: the twenty-one year old enlisted army reservist Lynndie England.

What proved shocking to the millions of viewers of the prison clandestine photos were several things. First, the Abu Ghraib scenes suggested there existed a gaping chasm between, on the one hand, the US Bush administration's claim that its military invasion and overthrow of the brutal Saddam Hussein regime would bring a civilizing sort of "freedom" to the Iraqi people and, on the other hand, the seemingly barbaric treatment that American soldiers were willfully meting out to Iraqis held in captivity without trial. Second, it was shocking to witness such blatant abuse of imprisoned detainees by soldiers representing a government that had signed both the international Geneva Conventions against mistreatment of wartime combatants and the UN Convention Against Torture, as well as having passed its own anti-torture laws.

Yet there was a third source of shock that prompted scores of early media commentaries and intense conversations among ordinary viewers: seeing women engage in torture. Of the seven American soldiers, all low-ranking Army Reserve military police guards, whom the Pentagon court-martialed, three were women. Somehow, the American male soldier, the man in the blue surgical gloves (his name was Charles Graner), was not shocking to most viewers and so did not inspire much private consternation or a stream of op ed columns. Women, by conventional contrast, were expected to appear in wartime as mothers and wives of soldiers, occasionally as military nurses and truck mechanics, or most often as the victims of the wartime violence. Women were not—according to the conventional presumption—supposed to be the wielders of violence, certainly not the perpetrators of torture. When those deeply gendered presumptions were turned upside down, many people felt a sense of shock. "This is awful; how could this have happened?"

Private First Class Lynndie England, the young woman military guard photographed holding the man on a leash, thus became the source of intense public curiosity. The news photographers could not restrain themselves two months later, in early August, 2004, from showing England in her army camouflaged maternity uniform when she appeared at Fort Bragg for her pre-trial hearing. She had become pregnant as a result of her sexual liaison with another enlisted reservist while on duty in Abu Ghraib. Her sexual partner was Charles Graner. Yet Charles Graner's name was scarcely mentioned. He apparently was doing what men are expected to do in wartime: have sex and wield violence. The public's curiosity and its lack of curiosity thus matched its pattern of shock. All three were conventionally gendered. Using a feminist investigatory approach, one should find this lack of public and media curiosity about Charles Graner just as revealing as the public's and media's absorbing fascination with Lynndie England.

Responding to the torrent of Abu Ghraib stories coming out of Iraq during the spring and summer of 2004, President George W. Bush and his Secretary of Defense, Donald Rumsfeld, tried to reassure the public that the graphically abusive behavior inside the prison was not representative of America, nor did it reflect the Bush administration's own foreign policies. Rather, the Abu Ghraib abuses were the work of "rogue" soldiers, a "few bad apples." The "bad apple" explanation always goes like this: the institution is working fine, its values are appropriate, its internal dynamics are of a sort that sustain positive values and respectful, productive behavior. Thus, according to the "bad apple" explanation, nothing needs to be reassessed or reformed in the way the organization works; all that needs to happen to stop the abuse is to prosecute and remove those few individuals who refused to play by the established rules. Sometimes this may be true. Some listeners to the Bush administration's "bad apple" explanation, however, weren't reassured. They wondered if the Abu Ghraib abuses were not produced by just a few bad apples found in a solid, reliable barrel, but, instead, were produced by an essentially "bad barrel." They also wondered whether this "barrel" embraced not only the Abu Ghraib prison, but the larger US military, intelligence, and civilian command structures.

What makes a "barrel" go bad? That is, what turns an organization, an institution, or a whole system into one that at least ignores, perhaps even fosters abusive behavior by the individuals operating inside it? This question is relevant for every workplace, every political system, every international alliance. Here too, feminists have been working hard over the past three decades to develop a curiosity and a set of analytical tools with which we can all answer this important question. So many of us today live much of our lives within complex organizations, large and small—work places, local and national governments, health care systems, criminal justice systems, international organizations. Feminist researchers have revealed that virtually all organizations are gendered: that is, all organizations are shaped by the ideas about, and daily practices of masculinities and femininities. Ignoring the workings of gender, feminist investigators have found, makes it impossible for us to explain accurately what makes any organization "tick." That failure makes it impossible for us to hold an organization accountable. Yet most of the hundred-page long official reports into the Abu Ghraib abuse scandal were written by people who ignored these feminist lessons. They acted as if the dynamics of masculinity and femininity among low-level police and high level policy-makers made no difference. That assumption is very risky.

A series of US Senate hearings, along with a string of Defense Department investigations tried to explain what went wrong in Abu Ghraib and why. The most authoritative of the Defense Department reports were the "Taguba Report," the "Fay/Jones Report" (both named after generals who headed these investigations) and the "Schlesinger Report" (named after a civilian former Secretary of Defense who chaired this investigatory team). In addition, the CIA was conducting its own investigation, since its officials were deeply involved in interrogating—and often hiding in secret prisons—captured Afghans and Iraqis. Moreover, there were several human rights groups and journalists publishing their own findings during 2004. Together, they offered a host of valuable clues as to why this institutional "barrel" had gone bad. First was the discovery that lawyers inside the Defense and Justice Departments, as well as the White House, acting on instructions from their civilian superiors, produced interpretations of the Geneva Conventions and US law that deliberately shrank the definitions of "torture" down so far that American military and CIA personnel could order and conduct interrogations of Iraqis and Afghans in detention using techniques that otherwise would have been deemed violations of US and international law.

Second, investigators found that an American general, Geoffrey Miller, commander of the US prison at Guantanamo Bay, Cuba, was sent by Secretary Rumsfeld to Iraq in September, 2003, where he recommended that American commanders overseeing military prison operations in Iraq start employing the aggressive interrogation practices that were being used on Afghan and Arab male prisoners at Guantanamo. Somewhat surprisingly, General Miller later was named by the Pentagon to head the Abu Ghraib prison in the wake of the scandal. Third, investigators discovered that the intense, persistent pressure imposed on the military intelligence personnel by the Defense Department to generate information about who was launching insurgent assaults on the US occupying forces encouraged those military intelligence officers to put their own pressures on the military police guarding prisoners to "soften up" the men in their cell blocks, thus undercutting the military police men's and women's own chain of command (which led up to a female army general, Janice Karpinski, who claimed that her authority over her military police personnel had been undermined by intrusive military intelligence officers). This policy change, investigators concluded, dangerously blurred the valuable line between military policing and military interrogating. A fourth finding was that non-military personnel, including CIA operatives and outside contractors hired by the CIA and the Pentagon, were involved in the Abu Ghraib military interrogations in ways that may have fostered an assumption that the legal limitations on employing excessive force could be treated cavalierly: We're under threat, this is urgent, who can be bothered with the Geneva Conventions or legal niceties?

Did it matter where the women were inside the prison and up and down the larger American military and intelligence hierarchies—as low level police reservists, as a captain in the military intelligence unit, as a general advising the chief US commander in Iraq? Investigators apparently didn't ask. Did it matter what exactly Charles Graner's and the other male military policemen's daily relationships were to their female colleagues, who were in a numerical minority in the military police unit, in the military interrogation unit and in the CIA unit all stationed together at Abu Ghraib? The official investigators seemed not to think that asking this question would yield any insights. Was it significant that so many of the abuses perpetrated on the Iraqi prisoners were deliberately sexualized? Was hooding a male prisoner the same (in motivation and in result) as forcing him to simulate oral sex? No one seemed to judge these questions to be pertinent. Was it at all relevant that Charles Graner, the older and apparently most influential of the low-ranking guards charged, had been accused of physical intimidation by his former wife? No questions asked, no answers forthcoming. Among all the lawyers in the Defense and Justice Departments and in the White House who were ordered to draft guidelines to permit the US government's officials to sidestep the Geneva Conventions outlawing torture, were there any subtle pressures imposed on them to appear "manly" in a time of war? This question too seems to have been left on the investigative teams' shelves to gather dust.

Since the mid-1970s, feminists have been crafting skills to explain when and why organizations become arenas for sexist abuse. One of the great contributions of the work done by the "Second Wave" of the international women's movement has been to throw light on what breeds sex discrimination and sexual harassment inside organizations otherwise as dissimilar as a factory, a stock brokerage, a legislature, a university, a student movement, and a military. All of the Abu Ghraib reports' authors talked about a "climate", an "environment," or a "culture," having been created inside Abu Ghraib that fostered abusive acts. The conditions inside Abu Ghraib were portrayed as a climate of "confusion," of "chaos." It was feminists who gave us this innovative concept of organizational climate.

When trying to figure out why in some organizations women employees were subjected to sexist jokes, unwanted advances, and retribution for not going along with the jokes or not accepting those advances, feminist lawyers, advocates and scholars began to look beyond the formal policies and the written work rules. They explored something more amorphous but just as, maybe even more potent: that set of unofficial presumptions that shapes workplace interactions between men and men, and men and women. They followed the breadcrumbs to the casual, informal interactions between people up and down the organization's ladder. They investigated who drinks with whom after work, who sends sexist jokes to whom over office email, who pins up which sorts of pictures of women in their lockers or next to the coffee machine. And they looked into what those people in authority did not do. They discovered that *in*action is a form of action: "turning a blind eye" is itself a form of action. Inaction sends out signals to everyone in the organization about what is condoned. Feminists labeled these webs of presumptions, informal interactions, and deliberate inaction an organization's "climate." As feminists argued successfully in court, it is not sufficient for a stock brokerage or a college to include anti-sexual harassment guidelines in their official handbooks; employers have to take explicit steps to create a workplace climate in which women would be treated with fairness and respect.

By 2004, this feminist explanatory concept—organizational "climate"— had become so accepted by so many analysts that their debt to feminists had been forgotten. Generals Taguba, Jones and Fay, as well as former Defense Secretary Schlesinger, may never have taken a Women's Studies course, but when they were assigned the job of investigating Abu Ghraib they were drawing on the ideas and investigatory skills crafted for them by feminists.

However, more worrisome than their failure to acknowledge their intellectual and political debts was those journalists' and government investigators' ignoring the feminist lessons that go hand in hand with the concept of "climate." The first lesson: to make sense of any organization, we always must dig deep into the group's dominant presumptions about femininity and masculinity. The second lesson: we need to take seriously the experiences of women as they try to adapt to, or sometimes resist those dominant gendered presumptions—not because all women are angels, but because paying close attention to women's ideas and actions will shed light on why men with power act the way they do.

It is not as if the potency of ideas about masculinity and femininity had been totally absent from the US military's thinking. Between 1991 and 2004, there had been a string of military scandals that had compelled even those American senior officials who preferred to look the other way to face sexism straight on. The first stemmed from the September, 1991, gathering of American navy aircraft carrier pilots at a Hilton hotel in Las Vegas. Male pilots (all officers), fresh from their victory in the first Gulf War, lined a hotel corridor and physically assaulted every woman who stepped off the elevator. They made the "mistake" of assaulting a woman navy helicopter pilot who was serving as an aide to an admiral. Within months members of Congress and the media were telling the public about "Tailhook"—why it happened, who tried to cover it up. Close on the heels of the Navy's "Tailhook" scandal came the Army's Aberdeen training base sexual harassment scandal, followed by other revelations of military gay bashing, sexual harassment and rapes by American male military personnel of their American female colleagues.

Then in September, 1995, the rape of a local school girl by two American male marines and a sailor in Okinawa sparked public demonstrations, new Okinawan women's organizing and more US Congressional investigations. At the start of the twenty-first century American media began to notice the patterns of international trafficking in Eastern European and Filipina women around American bases in South Korea, prompting official embarrassment in Washington (an embarrassment which had not been demonstrated earlier when American base commanders turned a classic "blind eye" toward a prostitution industry financed by their own male soldiers because it employed "just" local South Korean women). And in 2003, three new American military sexism scandals caught Washington policy-makers' attention: four American male soldiers returning from combat missions in Afghanistan murdered their female partners at Fort Bragg, North Carolina; a pattern of sexual harassment and rape by male cadets of female cadets—and superiors' refusal to treat these acts seriously—was revealed at the US Air Force Academy; and testimonies by at least sixty American women soldiers returning from tours of duty in Kuwait and Iraq described how they had been sexually assaulted by their male colleagues there—with, once again, senior officers choosing inaction, advising the American women soldiers to "get over it."

So it should have come as no surprise to American senior uniformed and civilian policy makers seeking to make sense of the abuses perpetrated in Abu Ghraib that a culture of sexism had come to permeate many sectors of US military life. If they had thought about what they had all learned in the last thirteen years—from Tailhook, Aberdeen, Fort Bragg, Okinawa, South Korea and the US Air Force Academy—they should have put the workings of masculinity and femininity at the top of their investigatory agendas. They should have made feminist curiosity one of their own principal tools. Perhaps Tillie Fowler did suggest to her colleagues that they think about these military sexual scandals when they began to delve into Abu Ghraib. A former Republican Congresswoman from Florida, Tillie Fowler, had been a principal investigator on the team that looked into the rapes (and their cover-ups) at the US Air Force Academy. Because of her leadership in that role Fowler was appointed to the commission headed by James Schlesinger investigating Abu Ghraib. Did she raise this comparison between the Air Force Academy case and Abu Ghraib? Did her male colleagues take her suggestion seriously?

Perhaps eventually the investigators did not make use of the feminist lessons and tools because they imagined that the lessons of Tailhook, the Air Force Academy and Okinawa were relevant only when all the perpetrators of sexualized abuse are men and all the victims are women. The presence of Lynndie England and the other women in Abu Ghraib's military police unit, they might have assumed, made the feminist tools sharpened in these earlier gendered military scandals inappropriate for their explorations. But the lesson of Tailhook, Okinawa and the most recent military scandals was *not* that the politics of masculinity and femininity matter only when men are the perpetrators and women are the victims. Instead, the deeper lesson of all these other military scandals is that we must always ask:

Has this organization (or this system of interlocking organizations) become masculinized in ways that privilege certain forms of masculinity, feminize its opposition and trivialize most forms of femininity?

With this core gender question in mind, we might uncover significant dynamics operating in Abu Ghraib and in the American military and civilian organizations that were supposed to be supervising the prison's personnel. First, American military police and their military and CIA intelligence colleagues might have been guided by their own masculinized fears of humiliation when they forced Iraqi men to go naked for days, to wear women's underwear and to masturbate in front of each other and American women guards. That is, belief in an allegedly "exotic," frail Iraqi masculinity, fraught with fears of nakedness and homosexuality, might not have been the chief motivator for the American police and intelligence personnel; it may have been their own home-grown American sense of masculinity's fragility—how easily manliness can be feminized—that prompted them to craft these prison humiliations. In this distorted masculinized scenario, the presence of women serving as military police might have proved especially useful. Choreographing the women guards' feminized roles so that they could act as ridiculing feminized spectators of male prisoners might have been imagined to intensify the masculinized demoralization. Dominant men trying to utilize at least some women to act in ways that undermine the masculinized self-esteem of rival men is not new.

What about the American women soldiers themselves? In the US military of 2004 women comprised 15% of active duty personnel, 17% of all Reserves and National Guard (and a surprising 24% of the Army Reserves alone). From the very time these particular young women joined this military police unit, they, like their fellow male recruits, probably sought to fit into the group. If the reserve military police unit's evolving culture—perhaps fostered by their superiors for the sake of "morale" and "unit cohesion"—was one that privileged a certain form of masculinized humor, racism and bravado, each woman would have had to decide how to deal with that. At least some of the women reservist recruits might have decided to join in, play the roles assigned to them in order to gain the hoped-for reward of male acceptance. The facts that the Abu Ghraib prison was grossly understaffed during the fall of 2003 (too few guards for spiraling numbers of Iraqi detainees), that it was isolated from other military operations, and that its residents endured daily and nightly mortar attacks, would only serve to intensify the pressures on each soldier to gain acceptance from those unit members who seemed to represent the group's dominant masculinized culture. And Lynndie England's entering into a sexual liaison with Charles Graner? We need to treat this as more than merely a "lack of discipline." We need to ask what were the cause and effect dynamics between their sexual behaviors and the abuses of prisoners and staging of the photographs. Feminists have taught us never to brush off sexual relations as if they have nothing to do with organizational and political practices.

Then there is the masculinization of the military interrogators' organizational cultures, the masculinization of the CIA's field operatives and the workings of ideas about "manliness" shaping the entire US political system. Many men and women—as lawyers, as generals, as Cabinet officers, as elected officials—knew full well that aggressive interrogation techniques violated both the spirit and the language of the Geneva Conventions, the UN Convention Against Torture and the US federal law against torture. Yet during the months of waging wars in Afghanistan and Iraq most of these men and women keep silent. Feminists have taught us always to be curious about silence. Thus we need to ask: Did any of the American men involved in interrogations keep silent because they were afraid of being labeled "soft," or "weak," thereby jeopardizing their status as "manly" men. We need also to discover if any of the women who knew better keep silent because they were afraid that they would be labeled "feminine," thus risking being deemed by their colleagues untrustworthy, political outsiders.

We are not going to get to the bottom of the tortures perpetrated by Americans at Abu Ghraib unless we make use of a feminist curiosity and unless we revisit the feminist lessons derived from the scandals of Tailhook, Fort Bragg, Annapolis, Okinawa and the Air Force Academy. Those tools and lessons might shed a harsh light on an entire American military institutional culture and maybe even the climate of contemporary American political life. That institutional culture and that political climate together have profound implications not only for Americans. They are being held up as models to emulate in Korea, Japan, the Philippines, Afghanistan and Iraq. That, in turn, means that the insights offered by feminist analysts from those societies who have such intimate experiences with this US institutional culture and this political climate are likely to teach Americans a lot about themselves.

SOURCES AND FURTHER READING

Simon Bowers, "Merrill Lynch Accused of 'Institutional Sexism, '" *The Guardian*, (London), June 12, 2004.

Ximena Bunster-Burotto, "Surviving Beyond Fear: Women and Torture in Latin America," in June Nash and Helen Safa, editors, *Women and Change in Latin America*, South Hadley, MA, Bergin and Garvey Publishers, 1985, 297–325.

Cynthia Enloe, *Maneuvers: The International Politics of Militarizing Women's Lives*, Berkeley and London, University of California Press, 2000.

Barbara Ehrenreich, "All Together Now," Op. Ed., *New York Times*, July 15, 2004.

Seymour Hersh, "Annals of National Security: Torture at Abu Ghraib," *The New Yorker*, May 10, 2004, 42–47.

Seymour Hersh, "Annals of National Security: Chain of Command," *The New Yorker*, May 17, 2004, 38–43.

Seymour Hersh, "Annals of National Security: The Gray Zone," *The New Yorker*, May 24, 2004, 38–44.

Human Rights Watch, *The Road to Abu Ghraib*, New York, Human Rights Watch, 2004.

Douglas Jehl, "Some Abu Ghraib Abuses are Traced to Afghanistan," *The New York Times*, August 26, 2004.

Insook Kwon, "Militarization in My Heart," unpublished PhD Dissertation, Women's Studies Program, Clark University, Worcester, MA, USA, 1999.

Neil A. Lewis and Eric Schmitt, "Lawyers Decided Bans on Torture Didn't Bind Bush," *New York Times*, June 8, 2004.

Catherine Lutz and Jon Elliston, "Domestic Terror" [re: domestic violence against US army wives at Fort Bragg, North Carolina], in Elizabeth Castelli and Janet Jackson, editors, *Interventions: Activists and Academics Respond to Violence*, New York, Palgrave, 2004.

The Miles Foundation, "Brownback/Fitz Amendment to S. 2400" [re: sexual assaults of American women soldiers by American male soldiers], email correspondence, June 14, 2004, from Milesfdn@aol.com.

Miles Moffeit and Amy Herder, "Betrayal in the Ranks" [a series on domestic abuse inside the US military], *The Denver Post,* May, 2004. Available on the Web at: http//www.denverpost.com.

Office of the Inspector General, US Department of Defense, *The Tailhook Report,* New York, St. Martin's Press, 2003.

Yuko Ogasawara, *Office Ladies and Salaried Men: Power, Gender and Work in Japanese Companies,* Berkeley and London, University of California Press, 1998.

Eric Schmitt, "Abuse Panel Says Rules on Inmates Need Overhaul," *The New York Times,* August 25, 2004.

Marjorie A. Stockford, *The Bellwomen: The Story of the Landmark AT&T Sex Discrimination Case,* New Brunswick, NJ, Rutgers University Press, 2004.

Antonio Taguba, "Investigation of the 800th Military Police Brigade," Washington, D.C., US Department of Defense, April, 2004.

Sandra Whitworth, *Men, Militarism and UN Peacekeeping: A Gendered Analysis,* Boulder, CO, Lynne Rienner Publishers, 2004.

62

THE PRIVATE WAR OF WOMEN SOLDIERS

HELEN BENEDICT

Helen Benedict is a professor of journalism at Columbia University. She is the author of four novels, four nonfiction books, and many essays.

As thousands of burned-out soldiers prepare to return to Iraq to fill President Bush's unwelcome call for at least 20,000 more troops, I can't help wondering what the women among those troops will have to face. And I don't mean only the hardships of war, the killing of civilians, the bombs and mortars, the heat and sleeplessness and fear.

I mean from their own comrades—the men.

Helen Benedict, "The Private War of Women Soldiers," from Salon.com (March 7, 2007). This article first appeared in Salon.com, at http://www.Salon.com. An online version remains in the Salon archives. Reprinted with permission.

I have talked to more than 20 female veterans of the Iraq war in the past few months, interviewing them for up to 10 hours each for a book I am writing on the topic, and every one of them said the danger of rape by other soldiers is so widely recognized in Iraq that their officers routinely told them not to go to the latrines or showers without another woman for protection.

The female soldiers who were at Camp Arifjan in Kuwait, for example, where U.S. troops go to demobilize, told me they were warned not to go out at night alone.

"They call Camp Arifjan 'generator city' because it's so loud with generators that even if a woman screams she can't be heard," said Abbie Pickett, 24, a specialist with the 229th Combat Support Engineering Company who spent 15 months in Iraq from 2004–05. Yet, she points out, this is a base, where soldiers are supposed to be safe.

Spc. Mickiela Montoya, 21, who was in Iraq with the National Guard in 2005, took to carrying a knife with her at all times. "The knife wasn't for the Iraqis," she told me. "It was for the guys on my own side."

Comprehensive statistics on the sexual assault of female soldiers in Iraq have not been collected, but early numbers revealed a problem so bad that former Defense Secretary Donald H. Rumsfeld ordered a task force in 2004 to investigate. As a result, the Defense Department put up a Web site in 2005 designed to clarify that sexual assault is illegal and to help women report it. It also initiated required classes on sexual assault and harassment. The military's definition of sexual assault includes "rape; nonconsensual sodomy; unwanted inappropriate sexual contact or fondling; or attempts to commit these acts."

Unfortunately, with a greater number of women serving in Iraq than ever before, these measures are not keeping women safe. When you add in the high numbers of war-wrecked soldiers being redeployed, and the fact that the military is waiving criminal and violent records for more than one in 10 new Army recruits, the picture for women looks bleak indeed.

Last year, Col. Janis Karpinski caused a stir by publicly reporting that in 2003, three female soldiers had died of dehydration in Iraq, which can get up to 126 degrees in the summer, because they refused to drink liquids late in the day. They were afraid of being raped by male soldiers if they walked to the latrines after dark. The Army has called her charges unsubstantiated, but Karpinski told me she sticks by them. (Karpinski has been a figure of controversy in the military ever since she was demoted from brigadier general for her role as commander of Abu Ghraib. As the highest-ranking official to lose her job over the torture scandal, she claims she was scapegoated, and has become an outspoken critic of the military's treatment of women. In turn, the Army has accused her of sour grapes.)

"I sat right there when the doctor briefing that information said these women had died in their cots," Karpinski told me. "I also heard the deputy commander tell him not to say anything about it because that would bring attention to the problem." The latrines were far away and unlit, she explained, and male soldiers were jumping women who went to them at night, dragging them into the Port-a-Johns, and raping or abusing them. "In that heat, if you don't hydrate for as many hours as you've been out on duty, day after day, you can die." She said the deaths were reported as non-hostile fatalities, with no further explanation.

Not everyone realizes how different the Iraq war is for women than any other American war in history. More than 160,500 American female soldiers have served in Iraq, Afghanistan and the Middle East since the war began in 2003, which means one in seven soldiers is a woman. Women now make up 15 percent of active duty forces, four times more than in the 1991 Gulf War. At least 450 women have been wounded in Iraq, and 71 have died—more female casualties and deaths than in the Korean, Vietnam and first Gulf Wars combined. And women are fighting in combat.

Officially, the Pentagon prohibits women from serving in ground combat units such as the infantry, citing their lack of upper-body strength and a reluctance to put girls and mothers in harm's way. But mention this ban to any female soldier in Iraq and she will scoff.

"Of course we were in combat!" said Laura Naylor, 25, who served with the Army Combat Military Police in Baghdad from 2003–04. "We were interchangeable with the infantry. They came to our police stations and helped pull security, and we helped them search houses and search people. That's how it is in Iraq."

Women are fighting in ground combat because there is no choice. This is a war with no front lines or safe zones, no hiding from in-flying mortars, car and roadside bombs, and not enough soldiers. As a result, women are coming home with missing limbs, mutilating wounds and severe trauma, just like the men.

All the women I interviewed held dangerous jobs in Iraq. They drove trucks along bomb-ridden roads, acted as gunners atop tanks and unarmored vehicles, raided houses, guarded prisoners, rescued the wounded in the midst of battle, and searched Iraqis at checkpoints. Some watched their best friends die, some were wounded, all saw the death and mutilation of Iraqi children and citizens.

Yet, despite the equal risks women are taking, they are still being treated as inferior soldiers and sex toys by many of their male colleagues. As Pickett told me, "It's like sending three women to live in a frat house." Rape, sexual assault and harassment are nothing new to the military. They were a serious problem for the Women's Army Corps in Vietnam, and the rapes and sexual hounding of Navy women at Tailhook in 1991 and of Army women at Aberdeen in 1996 became national news. A 2003 survey of female veterans from Vietnam through the first Gulf War found that 30 percent said they were raped in the military. A 2004 study of veterans from Vietnam and all the wars since, who were seeking help for post-traumatic stress disorder, found that 71 percent of the women said they were sexually assaulted or raped while in the military. And in a third study, conducted in 1992–93 with female veterans of the Gulf War and earlier wars, 90 percent said they had been sexually harassed in the military, which means anything from being pressured for sex to being relentlessly teased and stared at.

"That's one of the things I hated the most," said Caryle García, 24, who, like Naylor, served with the Combat Military Police in Baghdad from 2003–04. García was wounded by a roadside bomb, which knocked her unconscious and filled her with shrapnel. "You walk into the chow hall and there's a bunch of guys who just stop eating and stare at you. Every time you bend down, somebody will say something. It got to the point where I was afraid to walk past certain people because I didn't want to hear their comments. It really gets you down."

"There are only three kinds of female the men let you be in the military: a bitch, a ho or a dyke," said Montoya, the soldier who carried a knife for protection. "This guy out there, he told me he thinks the military sends women over to give the guys eye candy to keep them sane. He said in Vietnam they had prostitutes to keep them from going crazy, but they don't have those in Iraq. So they have women soldiers instead."

Pickett heard the same attitude from her fellow soldiers. "My engineering company was in the first Gulf War, and back then it had only two females," she said. "One was labeled a whore because she had a boyfriend, and the other one was a bitch because she wouldn't sleep around. And that's how they were still referred to all these years later."

In the current Iraq war, which Pickett spent refueling and driving trucks over the bomb-ridden roads, she was one of 19 women in a 160-troop unit. She said the men imported cases of porn, and talked such filth at the women all the time that she became worn down by it. "We shouldn't have to think every day, 'How am I going to go out there and deal with being harassed?'" she said. "We should just have to think about going out and doing our job."

Pickett herself was sexually attacked when she was training in Nicaragua before being deployed to Iraq. "I was sexually assaulted by a superior officer when I was 19, but I didn't know where to turn, so I never reported it," she told me.

Jennifer Spranger, 23, who was deployed at the beginning of the war with the Military Police to build and guard Camp Bucca, a prison camp for Iraqis, had a similar experience.

"My team leader offered me up to $250 for a hand job. He would always make sure that we were out alone together at the beginning, and he wouldn't stop pressuring me for sex. If somebody did that to my daughter I'd want to kill the guy. But you can't fit in if you make waves about it. You rat somebody out, you're screwed. You're gonna be a loner until they eventually push you out."

Spranger and several other women told me the military climate is so severe on whistle-blowers that even they regarded the women who reported rape as incapable traitors. You have to handle it on your own and shut up, is how they saw it. Only on their return home, with time and distance, did they become outraged at how much sexual persecution of women goes on. Having the courage to report a rape is difficult enough for civilians, where unsympathetic police, victim-blaming myths, and simple fear prevent 59 percent of rapes from being reported, according to the U.S. Bureau of Justice. But within the military, reporting is even more risky. Military platoons are enclosed, hierarchical societies, riddled with gossip, so any woman who reports a rape has no realistic chance of remaining anonymous. She will have to face her assailant day after day, and put up with rumors, resentment and blame from other soldiers. Furthermore, she runs the risk of being punished by her assailant if he is her superior.

These barriers to reporting are so well recognized that even the Defense Department has been scrambling to mend the situation, at least for the public eye. It won't go so far as to actually gather statistics on rape and assault in Iraq (it only counts reported rapes in raw numbers for all combat areas in the Middle East combined), but in 2006 the DOD did finally wake up to the idea that anonymous reporting might help women come forward, and updated its Web site accordingly.

The Web site looks good, although some may object that it seems to pay more attention to telling women how to avoid an assault than telling men not to commit one. It defines rape, sexual assault and harassment, and makes clear that these behaviors are illegal. The site now also explains that a soldier can report a rape anonymously to a special department, SAPR (Sexual Assault Prevention and Response), without triggering an official investigation—a procedure called "restricted reporting." And it promises the soldier a victim's advocate and medical care.

On closer scrutiny, however, the picture is less rosy: Only active and federal duty soldiers can go to SAPR for help, which means that neither inactive reservists nor veterans are eligible; soldiers are encouraged to report rapes to a chaplain, and chaplains are not trained as rape counselors; if soldiers tell a friend about an assault, that friend is legally obliged to report it to officials; soldiers must disclose their rank, gender, age, race, service, and the date, time and/or location of the assault, which in the closed world of a military unit hardly amounts to anonymity; and, in practice, since most people in the Army are men, the soldier will likely find herself reporting her sexual assault to a man—something rape counselors know does not work. Worse, no measures will be taken against the accused assailant unless the victim agrees to stop being anonymous.

The DOD insists on the success of its reforms, the proof being that the number of reported military sexual assaults rose by 1,700 from 2004 to a total of 2,374 in 2005. "The success of the SAPR program is in direct correlation with the increased numbers of reported sexual assaults," Cynthia Smith, a Defense Department spokeswoman, wrote to me in an e-mail.

In fact, as anyone familiar with sexual assault statistics knows, nobody can ever tell whether increases in rape rates are due to more reporting or more rapes.

My own interviewees and advocates on behalf of women veterans say these reforms are not working. They say there is a huge gap between what the military promises to do on its Web site and what it does in practice, and that the traditional view that reporting an assault betrays your fellow soldiers still prevails.

"Are soldiers who report sexual assaults in the military still seen as betraying their comrades?" I asked Smith.

"Our soldiers are being fully trained that sexual assault is the most under-reported crime," she wrote in reply. "In that training, not reporting a sexual assault is the betrayal to their comrades."

Back in real life, Pickett watched several of her friends try to report sexual harassment and assault since the 2005 reforms, and she said that none of them were sent a victim's advocate, a counselor or a chaplain. "These women are turning perpetrators in and they're not getting anyone to speak on their behalf," she told me. "There's no one sitting in that room with you, so you're feeling all alone." In the end, she added, it boils down to the woman's word vs. the man's, and he is the one with the advocate, not her.

Meanwhile, the studies I have cited, along with the other past and present studies of veterans, who feel freer to talk than soldiers because they are out of the military, show that women soldiers are suffering post-traumatic stress disorder as a consequence of military sexual abuse. All soldiers with PTSD come home to some combination of sleeplessness, nightmares, bursts of temper, flashbacks, panic attacks, fear and an inability to cope with everyday life. They often turn to drugs or alcohol for escape. Some become depressed, others commit suicide. Many are too emotionally numb to relate to their families or children. But those who have been sexually assaulted also lose their self-respect, feel they have lost control over their lives, and are particularly prone to self-destruction.

I have yet to meet an Iraq war veteran of either sex who does not suffer from some form of post-traumatic stress disorder, but officially the number of Iraq veterans with PTSD is estimated to be about 30 percent for those newly back from war, according to a 2004 study of combat veterans in the New England Journal of Medicine.

The extent and severity of PTSD in women who have had to cope with both combat and sexual assault in Iraq is still being studied, but as it is known that these are two of the highest predictors of PTSD, it is logical to assume that the combination is pretty bad. "When you are sexually assaulted by people who are your comrades, PTSD can be worse than in other circumstances," said Paula Shnurr, a research professor of psychiatry who conducted a new Veterans Administration study of therapy for women veterans with PTSD, published last week in the *Journal of the American Medical Association.* "You feel incompetent and helpless, like children feel when abused by the very people who are supposed to look after them," Schnurr told me. "The people you depend on have attacked you."

I am not claiming that sexual persecution is universal in the military, or that it is inevitable. Several soldiers I interviewed told me that if a commander won't tolerate the mistreatment of women, it will not happen, and studies back this up. Jennifer Hogg, 25, who was a sergeant in the Army's National Guard, said her company treated her well because she had a commander who wouldn't permit the mistreatment of women. But another National Guard soldier, Demond Mullins, 25, who served with the infantry in Iraq for a year from 2004–05, told me that a commander in his camp turned a blind eye to rape all the time. "One time a woman was taking a shower late, and guys went and held the door closed so she couldn't get out, while the others went in to rape her," he said. Some commanders not only turn a blind eye to assault and harassment but engage in it themselves, a phenomenon known in the military as "command rape." Because the military is hierarchical, and because soldiers are trained to obey and never question their superiors, men of rank can assault their juniors with impunity. In most cases, women soldiers are the juniors, 18 to 20 year old, and are new to the military and war, thus vulnerable to bullying and exploitation.

Callie Wight, a psychosocial counselor in women veterans' health in Los Angeles, has been treating women who were sexually assaulted in the military for the past 11 years. In all that time, she told me, she has only seen a handful of cases where a woman reported an assault to her commander with any success in getting the assailant punished. "Most commanders dismiss it," she said. A nine-month study of military rape by the Denver Post in 2003 found that nearly 5,000 accused military sex offenders had avoided prosecution since 1992.

At the moment, the most shocking case of military sexual assault is that of Army Spc. Suzanne Swift, 21, who served in Iraq in 2004. Swift was coerced into sex by one commanding officer, which is legally defined as rape by the military, and harassed by two others before she finally broke rank and told. As a result, the other soldiers treated her like a traitor for months.

Unable to face returning to the assailant, she went AWOL during a leave at home, and was arrested and put in jail for desertion. At first the Army offered her a deal: It would reduce her punishment if Swift would sign a statement saying that she had never been raped. She refused, saying she wouldn't let the Army force her to lie.

The Army court-martialed Swift, and stripped her of her rank. She spent December in prison and was then sent to Fort Irwin in the Mojave Desert, far away from her family. She must stay in the Army for two more years, and may face redeployment. The men who assaulted her received nothing but reprimanding letters.

Swift's mother, Sara Rich, has set up a Web site with a petition calling for her daughter's release: More than 6,700 veterans and soldiers have signed it, and 102 of them signed their names to stories of their own sexual persecution in the military.

Swift's case, and those of her petitioners, illustrate the real attitude of the military toward women and sexual assault, the one that underlies its fancy Web site and claims that it supports soldiers who've been raped.

The real attitude is this: If you tell, you are going to get punished. The assailant, meanwhile, will go free.

Which brings up an issue that lies at the core of every soldier's heart: comradeship.

It is for their comrades that soldiers enlist and reenlist. It is for their "battle buddies" that they risk their lives and put up with all the miseries of sandstorms, polluted water, lack of sanitation, and danger. Soldiers go back to Iraq, even if they've turned against the war, so as not to let their buddies down. Comradeship is what gets men through war, and is what has always got men through war. You protect your battle buddy, and your battle buddy protects you.

As an Iraq veteran put it to me, "There's nobody you love like you love a person who's willing to take a bullet for you."

So how does this work for women? A few find buddies among the other women in their squads, but for most there are no other women, so their battle buddies are men. Some of these men are trustworthy. Many are not.

How can a man who pressures you for sex every day, who treats you like a prostitute, who threatens or punishes you if you refuse him, or who actually attacks you, be counted on to watch your back in battle?

"Battle buddy bullshit," said García from the Military Police. "I didn't trust anybody in my company after a few months. I saw so many girls get screwed over, the sexual harassment. I didn't trust anybody and I still don't."

If this is a result of the way women are treated in the military, where does it leave them when it comes to battle camaraderie? I asked soldier after soldier this, and they all gave me the same answer:

Alone.

PART X

Health and Illness

Women and men face different challenges related to health and illness. Gender-linked illnesses correlate with both genetic/biological differences between women and men and with socialized differences in the form of masculine and feminine behavior. Thus, women don't get testicular cancer, and the vast majority of lung cancer patients were men before women earned the right to smoke.[1] The structure of sex-segregated work and the widely shared assumption that men should engage in risky physical behavior put many women and men at different risks for various injuries and illnesses. These differences probably explain why women live longer than men in the United States.[2] They probably also explain why women are more likely than men to become addicted to prescription drugs and are more likely to report feeling depressed.[3]

Even when women and men suffer from the same diseases, the causes and experiences of the disease may differ. For example, alcoholic women are more likely than men to hide their addictions, to be diagnosed later, to feel depressed and suicidal in the midst of the disease, and to feel low levels of self-esteem since addiction and femininity are typically not compatible.[4] Finally, they are more likely to be survivors of physical and sexual abuse than are male alcoholics.[5] There are close ties between masculinity and heart disease in public discourse as illustrated by the idea that men with Type A personalities (hard-working, competitive) were allegedly more prone to coronary heart disease, although this idea fell out of favor and heart disease is the most frequent cause of death in *both* men and women generally, and across all ethnic groups except Asian and Pacific Islander women, for whom cancer is the most frequent cause of death.[6]

Research suggests that environmental toxins affect male and female reproductive systems. Cynthia Daniels, who discusses health hazards among Vietnam veterans and their offspring in Part VIII also documents how work with toxic chemicals causes sterility in men and more frequent miscarriages in their partners.[7] Sterility can lead to high levels of stress as both women and men grapple with what it means for their identities as gendered beings.[8] (See Daniels for a discussion of this also.) Recent research on the link between ingredients in cosmetics and breast cancer suggests that the estrogenic effects of compounds such as parabens and phthalates could very likely help explain the high rates of breast cancer, the most common cancer in women.[9] An active campaign to make cosmetics and other body care products safer is underway. The European Union has banned several of the worst compounds, leading some companies to market different versions of their products in different parts of the world. These compounds are still allowed to be used in the United States because the U.S. Food and Drug Administration has no control over the ingredients that go into cosmetics before they are marketed. Breast Cancer

Action (http://www.bcaction.org/), and the Environmental Working Group (http://www.ewg.org/) are campaigning for safer cosmetics and full disclosure to consumers regarding potentially harmful ingredients in cosmetics and elsewhere in the environment. Consumers can get a safety rating on most body care products by going to the Cosmetic Data Base. Do you wonder how safe your deodorant or sun block or lipstick might be? Check them out at: http://www.cosmeticdatabase.com/index.php?nothanks=1. (See also Jeffreys, Part III.) The irony of using carcinogens in products and then sponsoring campaigns to raise money for cancer research is not lost on these consumer activists.

Other factors, such as sexual orientation and race, intersect with gender to put different groups at higher or lower risk for illness and injury. The AIDS epidemic, for example, thus far has affected primarily men in the United States, in part because the majority of early victims of this epidemic were gay men and intravenous drug users (unlike in Africa, for example, where AIDS has primarily been a heterosexually transmitted disease). Few lesbians, on the other hand, have contracted AIDS.[10] The faces of people with HIV infection and AIDS are changing, however, as the epidemic spreads (see Campo, this part). "The proportion of women among new HIV or AIDS diagnoses has increased dramatically—from 15% before 1995 to 27% in 2004."[11] About 75% were infected via unprotected sex with men, while two-thirds of men got the disease that way.[12] About 64 percent of new HIV cases occur among African American women although they represent only 12 percent of the U.S. female population. About 18 percent of new cases occur among Latina women, although they represent only 13 percent of the U.S. female population.[13] Research on Black men who have sex with men (MSM) shows that that group is at extremely high risk for HIV and AIDS. Among MSM, Black men have the highest incidence rates of HIV and the highest mortality from AIDS. Many factors contribute to this grim reality including homophobia, racism, high incarceration rates, low income, and limited access to effective treatment.[14]

Race interacts with gender to create vast disparities in the health issues of Blacks and whites in the United States. African American women face higher rates of violence and childbirth-related illness and death than do white women.[15] Both Black and white men die from homicide at higher rates than Black and white women. Although both Black and white men die in automobile accidents at similar rates, Black men are more likely than white men to die in other kinds of accidents.[16] Among young men, Black men aged 15–24 are six times more likely than white men to die of homicide, and homicide is the principal cause of death for Black men in this age group.[17] Men are more likely than women to commit suicide, and among both women and men, whites are twice as likely as Blacks to do so.[18] The suicide gap between Black and white teens is narrowing, however, as more Black male teens commit suicide. White men are much more likely than men of color to contract testicular cancer.[19] Black men are twice as likely as white men to die of prostate cancer.[20]

The kinds of discrimination and oppression described throughout this book are present in the health care system as well. People who deviate from a Caucasian able-bodied, male heterosexual norm are at higher risk for inadequate care. The Institute of Medicine, an independent research institute that advises Congress, released a report in March 2002 that addressed racial disparities in health care. Unlike most prior studies, this one looked only at people who had health insurance, and concluded that racial discrepancies in quality of care persist even when people have similar insurance coverage. The report lists a wide array of suggestions, including increasing the number of underrepresented health care professionals along with better education of consumers and especially professionals.[21] In addition to race and ethnicity, other factors affect health care. Women with disabilities, for example, are presumed by most doctors not to be sexual and not to want to be mothers.[22] Lesbians and gay men have health needs that many physicians fail to understand, including feeling uncomfortable with homophobic practitioners (and therefore avoiding health care) and protecting partners' rights in the face of illness or disability.[23] Disabled lesbians are hard pressed to find treatment facilities that can address their full array of medical needs when sexism, ableism, and homophobia intersect.[24] Trans liberationist Leslie Feinberg was ordered out of a hospital emergency room in the midst of a life-threatening illness when the physician discovered that although she appeared to be male, her body was female.[25] Fat women and men are frequently refused various kinds of treatment "until they lose weight," which is usually not feasible. The pressure on this group to take weight loss medication is high, with many women, especially, risking their health in an effort to get health care.[26]

Apart from differences in the kinds of health risks faced by various groups, the issue of access to health care is a major crisis in the United States. People who hold low-paying jobs without health insurance frequently cannot afford to buy it. Women are more likely than men to hold such jobs and are more likely than men to be the primary caretakers of children without coverage. A recent estimate put the number of uninsured people nationwide at 46.6 million in 2005.[27] Managed care is also interfering with health care in many cases, as doctors and patients must submit requests for treatment to third parties who do not know the individual patients involved. Without major structural reform of the health care system, this situation is very likely to worsen because individual and small collective efforts at empowerment cannot really change the system. A single payer health care plan—essentially an expanded version of Medicare—is being proposed by Physicians for a National Health Program (http://www.pnhp.org/).

The privacy and autonomy of pregnant women and girls continues to be an issue. Debates about abortion persist, as pro-choice advocates lobby to keep abortion easily accessible, safe, and legal (finally getting approval for Plan B in August 2006) and anti-choice advocates lobby for restricted access to abortion (illustrated by the Supreme Court's 2007 restriction on the so-called partial birth abortion procedure). Ironically, it appears that states with the strongest restrictions on abortions are less likely to provide resources for children in need than do states with stronger abortion access.[28] The privacy rights of pregnant women have also come under attack in recent years, leading to the arrest of pregnant women for behavior perceived as threatening to their fetuses. The Supreme Court rendered some of this policing activity illegal in March 2001, as it struck down a South Carolina statute that required drug testing of pregnant women at a public hospital and the subsequent arrest of those found to be using illegal drugs.[29] Advocates for children and women's health argue for supportive intervention and treatment when a fetus is allegedly placed at risk (for drug use, smoking, or alcohol use, for example), rather than arrest and incarceration. Women's studies professor Maia Boswell-Penc points out that there are many potential risks to fetal and infant health, including environmental toxins and the use of infant formula instead of breast feeding, yet those are not criminalized. It appears that racism, sexism, and elitism contribute to prosecuting poor women who use cocaine rather than: wealthy women who drink alcohol; men who drink, smoke, and use drugs; older men, whose offspring have higher rates of autism; or polluting corporations that have created a toxic environment for all living things.[30] In short, reproductive rights and reproductive freedom encompass many areas, not just the right to choose to terminate a pregnancy. See Jeanne Flavin, Part VI, for a discussion of some of these issues related to Black women.

The women's health movement has worked to address women's health concerns for the past 30 years. In the face of unresponsive health care systems, women have opened health clinics for women, have provided clandestine abortions when abortion was illegal, have lobbied for health-related legislation and research funding, and have written extensively about women's health. The success of the many editions of *Our Bodies, Ourselves* since it was first published in 1970 attests to women's need for straightforward information about their bodies. Various editions of *Our Bodies, Ourselves* have been translated into 17 languages, and a recent version in Spanish (*Nuestos Cuerpos, Nuestras Vidas*) has been revised to be more culturally appropriate for women in Latin America.[31] Organizations such as the National Asian Women's Health Organization (San Francisco, CA), the National Women's Health Network (Washington, DC), the National Black Women's Health Imperative (Washington, DC), the National Latina Health Organization (Oakland, CA), the Native American Women's Health Education Resource Center (Lake Andes, SD) and Sistersong Women of Color Reproductive Health Collective (Atlanta, GA) have all supported the movement for better health care for women via a wide range of health services, support, research, publications, education, and effective lobbying.

Women's health activism is illustrated by a recent article on hormone replacement therapy (HRT) by biologist and professor of women's studies Nancy Worcester at the University of Wisconsin-Madison. Worcester discusses the importance of caution in prescribing drugs to large numbers of women without adequate long-term research. HRT is a case in point, and its frequent use to treat normal menopausal symptoms has been called into question. Six million women on HRT learned in July 2002 that the drugs they were taking could increase their risk of heart disease. Further investigation showed that HRT did not even improve the "quality of life" or women's memory. The National Women's Health Network had been questioning HRT for more than a decade. Worcester sets this example in the context of other medical treatments that turned out to be disastrous.[32] The lesson seems to be that when women's normal bodily functions are treated as fields for medical intervention, the results can be much more damaging than whatever negative effects the normal bodily functions seem to produce (for example, hot flashes or miscarriages).

A new health controversy has emerged related to the vaccine designed to prevent some of the strains of the human papillomavirus (HPV) that cause cervical cancer. Cervical cancer is rare, ranking 13th in the list of cancer deaths.[33] Questions have emerged relating to the vaccination of millions of 11-year-old girls in the United States against a virus that occasionally leads to cervical cancer, raising questions about safety, health care priorities, and big profits for the pharmaceutical industry.[34]

Another current activist project addresses the need for human eggs for stem cell research. Both pro-choice and anti-choice women have supported an effort to educate young women about the risks of egg donation for research, which involves the infusion of hormones necessary to produce multiple eggs for extraction and the potential to lure poor women into risky egg donation. Check out Hands Off Our Ovaries at http://handsoffourovaries.com/.

Organizations for men, such as the former Prostate Cancer Action Network, have also lobbied for more attention to male-specific illnesses. Conflicting analyses over which gender has received more attention in health research has been the subject of much debate. Following an analysis of subjects in medical research published in a medical journal, the National Institutes of Health recently retracted a 1997 statement that "women were routinely excluded from medical research supported by NIH." Lobbying seems to have been effective in raising the number of women in clinical trials, and some critics argue that there was never a "gender gap."[35] (Specific information on health by gender is available from both the Centers for Disease Control and the National Institutes of Health.) Obviously, issues specific to all genders in all cultural/racial groups (plus people who are gay, lesbian, or bisexual or disabled) each need specific attention to ensure effective, humane, and accessible health care for everyone.

A growing literature explores gender socialization in relation to health and illness.[36] The readings in this part address several aspects of this large and growing field of study, focusing on men's health with many comparisons to women (Don Sabo); the need for health care reform (Catherine DeLorey); the importance of access to abortion for low-income women of color (Connie Chan); environmental toxins (Sandra Steingraber); AIDS (Rafael Campo); and health care for transgendered people (Kai Wright). The voices in this chapter make powerful pleas for decent health care for all people in a nontoxic world.

As you read these articles, you might want to think about your own health and that of people you know. Do all the people in your life have health insurance? Do the men and women you know seem to have any gender-related illnesses? Where do you stand on the debate about abortion? Have you ever thought about the potential toxicity of breast milk? What are your assumptions about the transmission of AIDS and who it affects? Do you know anyone who is transgendered? Do you know anyone who has experienced prejudice or discrimination in their search for health care?

NOTES

1. Ingrid Waldron, "Contributions of Changing Gender Differences in Behavior and Social Roles to Changing Gender Differences in Mortality," in Donald Sabo and David Frederick Gordon, eds., *Men's Health and Illness: Gender, Power, and the Body* (Thousand Oaks, CA: Sage, 1995), p. 27; Robert Weissman, "Women and Tobacco," *The Network News* (National Women's Health Network), March/April 2001, pp. 1, 4, 5.

2. Will H. Courtenay, "Behavioral Factors Associated with Disease, Injury, and Death among Men: Evidence and Implications for Prevention," *The Journal of Men's Studies* 9, no. 1 (Fall 2000): 81–142; Judith M. Stillion, "Premature Death among Males: Extending the Bottom Line of Men's Health," in Sabo and Gordon, *Men's Health and Illness*, pp. 46–67.

3. Regarding addictions, see "Addictive Behaviors from the Women's Health Data Book," reprinted in Nancy Worcester and Marianne Whatley, eds., *Women's Health: Readings on Social, Economic, and Political Issues,* 2nd ed. (Dubuque, IA: Kendall/Hunt, 1994), pp. 153–57. Regarding depression, see Marian Murphy, "Women and Mental Health," reprinted in Worcester and Whatley, eds., *Women's Health*, pp. 127–32.

4. Rokelle Lerner, "What Does Female Have to Do with It?" *Professional Counselor,* August 1995, p. 20.

5. Willie Langeland and Christina Hartgers, "Child Sexual and Physical Abuse and Alcoholism: A Review," *Journal of Alcohol Studies* 59, no. 3 (May 1998): 336–48.

6. Elianne Riska, *Masculinity and Men's Health: Coronary Heart Disease in Medical and Public Discourse* (Lanham, MD: Rowman & Littlefield, 2004). Center for Disease Control data on causes of death in men: http://www.cdc.gov/men/lcod.htm. Centers for Disease Control data on causes of death in women: http://www.cdc.gov/women/lcod.htm.

7. Cynthia R. Daniels, *Exposing Men: The Science and Politics of Male Reproduction* (NY: Oxford University Press, 2006), p. 121.

8. Yoram S. Carmeli and Daphna Birenbaum-Carmeli, "The Predicament of Masculinity: Towards Understanding the Male's Experience of Infertility Treatments," *Sex Roles: A Journal of Research* 30, no. 9–10 (May 1994): 663(15); Laura Hurd Clarke, Anne Martin-Matthews and Ralph Matthews, "The Continuity and Discontinuity of the Embodied Self in Infertility," *The Canadian Review of Sociology and Anthropology* 43, 1 (February 2006): 95(19).

9. Rita Arditti, "Cosmetics, Parabens and Breast Cancer," *Women's Community Cancer Project Newsletter*, Summer 2004, p. 1ff. Also available at: http://www.organicconsumers.org/bodycare/breastcancer090604.cfm.

10. Ruth L. Schwartz, "New Alliances, Strange Bedfellows: Lesbians, Gay Men and AIDS," in Arlene Stein, ed., *Sisters, Sexperts, and Queers: Beyond the Lesbian Nation* (New York: Plume, 1993), pp. 230–44.

11. *UNAIDS. AIDS Epidemic Update: Special Report on HIV/AIDS*. December 2006. Geneva: Joint United Nations Programme on HIV/AIDS and World Health Organization, 2006, p. 53.

12. *UNAIDS*, p.53.

13. DeAna Tucker, "The Feminization of HIV/AIDS: What Dick Cheney Needs to Know," *The Women's Health Activist* 30, no. 1 (January/February 2005): 3.

14. Gregorio A. Millett and John L. Peterson, "The Known Hidden Epidemic: HIV/AIDS Among Black Men Who Have Sex with Men in the United States," *American Journal of Preventive Medicine* 32 (4), Supplement 1 (April 2007): 31–33; Keith Boykin, *Beyond the Down Low: Sex, Lies and Denial in Black America* (New York: Carroll & Graf, 2005).

15. Paul Simao, "Pregnancy Death Highest for Black Women, US Study Shows," *The Boston Globe*; 11 May 2002, p. A27; Evelyn L. Barbee and Marilyn Little, "Health, Social Class, and African-American Women," in Stanlie M. James and Abena P. A. Buscia, eds., *Theorizing Black Feminisms: The Visionary Pragmatism of Black Women* (New York: Routledge, 1993).

16. Stillion, "Premature Death among Males," p. 52.

17. Jewelle Taylor Gibbs, "Anger in Young Black Males: Victims or Victimizers?" in Richard G. Majors and Jacob U. Gordon, eds., *The American Black Male: His Status and His Future* (Chicago: Nelson-Hall, 1994), p. 128.

18. Stillion, "Premature Death among Males," p. 53.

19. David Frederick Gordon, "Testicular Cancer and Masculinity," in Sabo and Gordon, *Men's Health and Illness*.

20. National Cancer Institute, *Cancer among Blacks and Other Minorities: Statistical Profiles* (Washington, DC: U.S. Department of Health and Human Services, NIH Publication #86-2785, 1986), p. 10.

21. Brian D. Smedley, Adrienne Y. Stith, and Alan R. Nelson, eds. *Unequal Treatment: Confronting Racial and Ethnic Disparities in Health Care* (Washington, DC: Institute of Medicine, 2002).

22. Carol J. Gill, "Editorial: When Is a Woman Not a Woman?" *Sexuality and Disability* 12, no. 2 (1994): 117–9; Carrie Killoran, "Women with Disabilities Having Children: It's Our Right Too," *Sexuality and Disability* 12, no. 2 (1994): 121–26.

23. Ann Pollinger Haas, "Lesbian Health Issues: An Overview," in Alice J. Dan, ed., *Reframing Women's Health: Multidisciplinary Research and Practice* (Thousand Oaks, CA: Sage, 1994), pp. 339–56.

24. Corbett Joan O'Toole, "Disabled Lesbians: Challenging Monocultural Constructs," *Sexuality and Disability* 14, no. 3 (1996): 221–36.

25. Leslie Feinberg, *Trans Liberation: Beyond Pink or Blue* (Boston: Beacon Press, 1998), p. 2.

26. Pat Lyons, "The Great Weight Debate: Where Have All the Feminists Gone?" *The Network News* (National Women's Health Network) 23, no. 5 (September/October 1998): pp. 1ff.

27. "The Number of Uninsured Americans Is at an All-Time High," Center on Budget and Policy, August 29, 2006. http://www.cbpp.org/8-29-06health.htm.

28. Jean Reith Schroedel, *Is the Fetus a Person? A Comparison of Policies across the Fifty States* (Ithaca, NY: Cornell University Press, 2000).

29. Lynn P. Paltrow, "South Carolina: Where Pregnancy Is a Crime," *The Network News* (National Women's Health Network) 25 (July/August 2000), pp. 3–4; Jean Reith Schroedel, *Is the Fetus a Person?*; Lyle Denniston, "Drug Test Ruling Backs Pregnant Women's Privacy," *The Boston Globe*, 22 March 2001, p. A3.

30. Maia Boswell-Penc, *Tainted Milk: Breastmilk, Feminisms, and the Politics of Environmental Degradation* (Albany: State University of New York Press, 2006), p. 58. Regarding effects of alcohol, drugs, and tobacco on sperm and offspring see Cynthia R. Daniels, *Exposing Men: The Science and Politics of Male Reproduction* (New York: Oxford University Press, 2006), 141–46. Abraham Reichenberg et al., "Advancing Paternal Age and Autism," *Archives of General Psychiatry*, 63, September 2006, pp. 1026–32.

31. For the most recent edition in English, see Boston Women's Health Book Collective, *Our Bodies, Ourselves: A New Edition for a New Era* (New York: Simon & Schuster, 2005). In Spanish: La Colectiva del Libro de Salud de las Mujeres de Boston, *Nuestos Cuerpos, Nuestras Vidas: La Guía Definitive para la Salud de la Mujer Latina* (Nueva York/New York: Siete Cuentos Editorial/Seven Stories Press, 2000). For an example of an early groundbreaking book in the women's health movement that was important enough to be republished 25 years later, see Barbara Seaman, *The Doctor's Case against the Pill, 25th Anniversary Edition* (Alameda, CA: Hunter House, 1995).

32. Nancy Worcester, "Hormone Replacement Therapy (HRT): Getting to the Heart of Politics and Women's Health" *NWSA Journal* 16, no. 3 (Fall 2004): pp. 56–69.

33. Holly L. Howe, et al., "Annual Report to the Nation on the Status of Cancer, 1975–2003, Featuring Cancer Among U.S. Hispanic/Latino Populations," *Cancer*, 107, Issue 8 (September 2006): 1711–42.

34. Adriane Fugh-Burman, "Cervical Cancer Vaccines in Context," National Women's Health Network, March/April 2007: http://www.nwhn.org/wha_marapr07_rxchange; Maryann Napoli, "How Vaccine Policy is Made: The Story of Merck and Gardasil, the HPV Vaccine," Center for Medical Consumers, 2007. http://www.medicalconsumers.org/pages/howvaccinepolicyismade.htm.

35. Cathy Young, "It's Time to End the Gender Gap in Health Care," *The Boston Globe*, 15 November 2000, p. A27.

36. For more information on women's and men's health, see Sabo and Gordon, *Men's Health and Illness* (Thousand Oaks, CA: Sage, 1995); Worcester and Whatley, eds., *Women's Health* (Dubuque, IA: Kendall-Hunt, 1994); Evelyn C. White, ed., *The Black Women's Health Book* (Seattle: Seal Press, 1990).

63

MASCULINITIES AND MEN'S HEALTH
Moving toward Post–Superman
Era Prevention

DON SABO

Don Sabo, Ph.D., is professor of sociology at D'Youville College in Buffalo, New York. His latest books include *Prison Masculinities* (2001); (with Leslie Heywood, Kathleen Miller, and Merrill Melnick) *Her Life Depends on It: Sport, Physical Activity, and the Health and Well-Being of American Girls;* (with Michael Messner) *Sex, Violence & Power in Sport* (1994); and (with Dave Gordon) *Men's Health & Illness: Gender, Power, & the Body* (1995). He directed the nationwide Women's Sports Foundation study *Sport and Teen Pregnancy* (1998).

M y grandfather used to smile and say, "Find out where you're going to die and stay the hell away from there." Grandpa had never studied epidemiology (the study of variations in health and illness in society), but he understood that certain behaviors, attitudes, and cultural practices can put individuals at risk for accidents, illness, or death. This chapter presents an overview of men's health that proceeds from the basic assumption that aspects of traditional masculinity can be dangerous to men's health (Sabo & Gordon, 1995; Harrison, Chin, & Ficarrotto, 1992). First, I identify some gender differences in relation to morbidity (sickness) and mortality (death). Next, I examine how the risk for illness varies from one male group to another. I then discuss an array of men's health issues and a preventative strategy for enhancing men's health.

Gender Differences in Health and Illness

When British sociologist Ashley Montagu put forth the thesis in 1953 that women were biologically superior to men, he shook up the prevailing chauvinistic beliefs that men were stronger, smarter, and better than women. His argument was partly based on epidemiological data that show males are more vulnerable to mortality than females from before birth and throughout the life span.

Don Sabo, "Masculinities and Men's Health." Portions of this selection previously appeared in *Nursing Care in the Community,* second edition, edited by J. Cookfair (St. Louis, Missouri: Mosby-Year Book, 1996). Reprinted by permission.

Mortality

From the time of conception, men are more likely to succumb to prenatal and neonatal death than females. Men's chances of dying during the prenatal stage of development are about 12% greater than those of females and, during the neonatal (newborn) stage, 130% greater than those of females. A number of neonatal disorders are common to males but not females, such as bacterial infections, respiratory illness, digestive diseases, and some circulatory disorders of the aorta and pulmonary artery. Table 1 compares male and female infant mortality rates across historical time. Though the infant mortality rate decreases over time, the persistence of the higher rates for males than females suggests that biological factors may be operating. Data also show that males have higher mortality rates than females in every age category, from "under one year" through "over 85" (National Center for Health Statistics, 1992). In fact, men are more likely to die in 9 out of the 10 leading causes of death in the United States. (See Table 2.)

TABLE 1   Infant Mortality Rate

Year	Both Sexes	Males	Females
1940	47.0	52.5	41.3
1950	29.2	32.8	25.5
1960	26.0	29.3	22.6
1970	20.0	22.4	17.5
1980	12.6	13.9	11.2
1989	9.8	10.8	8.8

Note: Rates are for infant (under 1 year) deaths per 1,000 live births for all races.

Sources: Adapted from Monthly Vital Statistics Report, Vol. 40, No. 8. Supplement 2, January 7, 1992, p. 41.

TABLE 2   Death Rates by Sex and 10 Leading Causes: 1989

	Age-Adjusted Death Rate Per 100,000 Population			
Cause of Death	Total	Male	Female	Sex Differential
Diseases of the heart	155.9	210.2	112.3	1.87
Malignant neoplasms	133.0	163.4	111.7	1.45
Accidents and adverse effects	33.8	49.5	18.9	2.62
Cerebrovascular disease	28.0	30.4	26.2	1.16
Chronic liver disease, cirrhosis	8.9	12.8	5.5	2.33
Diabetes	11.5	2.0	11.0	1.09
Suicide	11.3	18.6	4.5	4.13
Homicide and legal intervention	9.4	14.7	4.1	3.59

Sources: Adapted from the *U.S. Bureau of the Census: Statistical Abstracts of the United States: 1992* (112th ed., p. 84), Washington, DC.

Females have greater life expectancy than males in the United States, Canada, and postindustrial societies (Verbrugge and Wingard, 1987; Waldron, 1986). This fact suggests a female biological advantage, but a closer analysis of changing trends in the gap between women's and men's life expectancy indicates that social and cultural factors related to lifestyle, gender identity, and behavior are operating as well. Life expectancy among American females is about 78.3 years but 71.3 years for males (National Center for Health Statistics, 1990). As Waldron's (1995) analysis of shifting mortality patterns between the sexes during the 20th century shows, however, women's relative advantage in life expectancy over men was rather small at the beginning of the 20th century. During the mid-20th century, female mortality declined more rapidly than male mortality, thereby increasing the gender gap in life expectancy. Whereas women benefited from decreased maternal mortality, the midcentury trend toward a lowering of men's life expectancy was slowed by increasing mortality from coronary heart disease and lung cancer that were, in turn, mainly due to higher rates of cigarette smoking among males.

The most recent trends show that differences between women's and men's mortality decreased during the 1980s; that is, female life expectancy was 7.9 years greater than that of males in 1979 and 6.9 years in 1989 (National Center for Health Statistics, 1992). Waldron explains that some changes in behavioral patterns between the sexes, such as increased smoking among women, have narrowed the gap between men's formerly higher mortality rates from lung cancer, chronic obstructive pulmonary disease, and ischemic heart disease. In summary, it appears that both biological and sociocultural factors are involved with shaping patterns of men's and women's mortality. In fact, Waldron (1976) suggests that gender-related behaviors rather than strictly biogenic factors account for about three-quarters of the variation in men's early mortality.

Morbidity

Whereas females generally outlive males, females report higher morbidity rates, even after controlling for maternity. National health surveys show that females experience acute illnesses such as respiratory conditions, infective and parasitic conditions, and digestive system disorders at higher rates than males do; however, males sustain more injuries (Givens, 1979; Cypress, 1981; Dawson & Adams, 1987). Men's higher injury rates are partly owed to gender differences in socialization and lifestyle, such as learning to prove manhood through recklessness, involvement in contact sports, and working in risky blue-collar occupations.

Females are generally more likely than males to experience chronic conditions such as anemia, chronic enteritis and colitis, migraine headaches, arthritis, diabetes, and thyroid disease. However, males are more prone to develop chronic illnesses such as coronary heart disease, emphysema, and gout. Although chronic conditions do not ordinarily cause death, they often limit activity or cause disability.

After noting gender differences in morbidity, Cockerham (1995) asks whether women really do experience more illness than men—or could it be that women are more sensitive to bodily sensations than men, or that men are not as prone as women to report symptoms and seek medical care? He concludes, "The best evidence indicates that the overall differences in morbidity are real" and, further, that they are due to a mixture of biological, psychological, and social influences (p. 42).

Masculinities and Men's Health

There is no such thing as masculinity; there are only masculinities (Sabo & Gordon, 1995). A limitation of early gender theory was its treatment of "all men" as a single, large category in relation to "all women" (Connell, 1987). The fact is, however, that all men are not alike, nor do all male groups share the same stakes in the gender order. At any given historical moment, there are competing masculinities—some dominant, some marginalized, and some stigmatized—each with its respective structural, psychosocial, and cultural moorings. There are substantial differences between the health options of homeless men, working-class men, lower-class men, gay men, men with AIDS, prison inmates, men of color, and their comparatively advantaged middle- and upper-class, white, professional male counterparts. Similarly, a wide range of individual differences exists between the ways that men and women act out "femininity" and "masculinity" in their everyday lives. A health profile of several male groups is discussed below.

Adolescent Males

Pleck, Sonenstein, and Ku (1992) applied critical feminist perspectives to their research on problem behaviors and health among adolescent males. A national sampling of adolescent, never-married males aged 15–19 were interviewed in 1980 and 1988. Hypothesis tests were geared to assessing whether "masculine ideology" (which measured the presence of traditional male role attitudes) put boys at risk for an array of problem behaviors. The researchers found a significant, independent association with seven of ten problem behaviors. Specifically, traditionally masculine attitudes were associated with being suspended from school, drinking and use of street drugs, frequency of being picked up by the police, being sexually active, the number of heterosexual partners in the last year, and tricking or forcing someone to have sex. These kinds of behaviors, which are in part expressions of the pursuit of traditional masculinity, elevate boys' risk for sexually transmitted diseases, HIV transmission, and early death by accident or homicide. At the same time, however, these same behaviors can also encourage victimization of women through men's violence, sexual assault, unwanted teenage pregnancy, and sexually transmitted diseases.

Adolescence is a phase of accelerated physiological development, and good nutrition during this period is important to future health. Obesity puts adults at risk for a variety of diseases such as coronary heart disease, diabetes mellitus, joint disease, and certain cancers. Obese adolescents are also apt to become obese adults, thus elevating long-term risk for illness. National Health and Nutrition Examination Surveys show that obesity among adolescents increased by 6% during 1976–80 and 1988–91. During 1988–91, 22% of females of 12–18 years were overweight, and 20% of males in this age group were as well (*Morbidity and Mortality Weekly Report*, 1994a).

Males form a majority of the estimated 1.3 million teenagers who run away from home each year in the United States. For both boys and girls, living on the streets raises the risk of poor nutrition, homicide, alcoholism, drug abuse, and AIDS. Young adults in their 20s comprise about 20% of new AIDS cases and, when you calculate the lengthy latency period, it is evident that they are being infected in their teenage years. Runaways are also more likely to be victims of crime and sexual exploitation (Hull, 1994).

Clearly, adolescent males face a spectrum of potential health problems—some that threaten their present well-being, and others that could take their toll in the future.

Men of Color

Patterns of health and illness among men of color can be partly understood against the historical and social context of economic inequality. Generally, because African Americans, Hispanics, and Native Americans are disproportionately poor, they are more apt to work in low-paying and dangerous occupations, reside in polluted environments, be exposed to toxic substances, experience the threat and reality of crime, and worry about meeting basic needs. Cultural barriers can also complicate their access to available health care. Poverty is correlated with lower educational attainment, which, in turn, mitigates against adoption of preventative health behaviors.

The neglect of public health in the United States is particularly pronounced in relation to African Americans (Polych & Sabo, 1996). For example, in Harlem, where 96% of the inhabitants are African American and 41% live below the poverty line, the survival curve beyond the age of 40 for men is lower than that of men living in Bangladesh (McCord & Freeman, 1990). Even though African American men have higher rates of alcoholism, infectious diseases, and drug-related conditions, for example, they are less apt to receive health care, and when they do, they are more apt to receive inferior care (Bullard, 1992; Staples, 1995). Statistics like the following led Gibbs (1988) to describe young African American males as an "endangered species":

- The number of young African American male homicide victims in 1977 (5,734) was higher than the number killed in the Vietnam War during 1963–72 (5,640) (Gibbs, 1988:258).
- Homicide is the leading cause of death among young African American males. The probability of a black man dying from homicide

is about the same as that of a white male dying from an accident (Reed, 1991).

- More than 36% of urban African American males are drug and alcohol abusers (Staples, 1995).
- In 1993 the rate of contracting AIDS for African American males aged 13 and older was almost 5 times higher than the rate for white males (*Morbidity and Mortality Weekly Report,* 1994b).

The health profile of Native Americans and Native Canadians is also poor. For example, alcohol is the number-one killer of Native Americans between the ages of 14 and 44 (May, 1986), and 42% of Native American male adolescents are problem drinkers, compared to 34% of same-age white males (Lamarine, 1988). Native Americans (10–18 years of age) comprise 34% of inpatient admissions to adolescent detoxification programs (Moore, 1988). Compared to the "all race" population, Native American youth exhibit more serious problems in the areas of depression, suicide, anxiety, substance use, and general health status (Blum et al., 1992). The rates of morbidity, mortality from injury, and contracting AIDS are also higher (Sugarman et al., 1993; Metler et al., 1991).

Like those of many other racial and ethnic groups, the health problems facing American and Canadian natives correlate with the effects of poverty and social marginalization, such as dropping out of school, a sense of hopelessness, the experience of prejudice, poor nutrition, and lack of regular health care. Those who care about men's health, therefore, need to be attuned to the potential interplay between gender, race/ethnicity, cultural differences, and economic conditions when working with racial and ethnic minorities.

Gay and Bisexual Men

Gay and bisexual men are estimated to constitute 5% to 10% of the male population. In the past, gay men have been viewed as evil, sinful, sick, emotionally immature, and socially undesirable. Many health professionals and the wider public have harbored mixed feelings and homophobic attitudes toward gay and bisexual men. Gay men's identity, their lifestyles, and the social responses to homosexuality can impact the health of gay and bisexual men. Stigmatization and marginalization, for example, may lead to emotional confusion and suicide among gay male adolescents. For gay and bisexual men who are "in the closet," anxiety and stress can tax emotional and physical health. When seeking medical services, gay and bisexual men must often cope with the homophobia of health care workers or deal with the threat of losing health care insurance if their sexual orientation is made known.

Whether they are straight or gay, men tend to have more sexual contacts than women do, which heightens men's risk for contracting sexually transmitted diseases (STDs). Men's sexual attitudes and behaviors are closely tied to the way masculinity has been socially constructed. For example, real men are taught to suppress their emotions, which can lead to a separation of sex from feeling. Traditionally, men are also encouraged to be daring, which can lead to risky sexual decisions. In addition, contrary to common myths about gay male effeminacy, masculinity also plays a powerful role in shaping gay and bisexual men's identity and behavior. To the extent that traditional masculinity informs sexual activity of men, masculinity can be a barrier to safer sexual behavior among men. This insight leads Kimmel and Levine (1989) to assert that "to educate men about safe sex, then, means to confront the issues of masculinity" (p. 352). In addition to practicing abstinence and safer sex as preventive strategies, therefore, they argue that traditional beliefs about masculinity be challenged as a form of risk reduction.

Men who have sex with men remain the largest risk group for HIV transmission. For gay and bisexual men who are infected by the HIV virus, the personal burden of living with an AIDS diagnosis is made heavier by the stigma associated with homosexuality. The cultural meanings associated with AIDS can also filter into gender and sexual identities. Tewksbury's (1995) interviews with 45 HIV positive gay men showed how masculinity, sexuality, stigmatization, and interpersonal commitment mesh in decision making related to risky sexual behavior. Most of the men practiced celibacy in order to prevent others from contracting the disease; others practiced safe sex, and a few went on having unprotected sex.

Prison Inmates

There are 1.3 million men imprisoned in American jails and prisons (Nadelmann & Wenner, 1994). The United States has the highest rate of incarceration of any nation in the world, 426 prisoners for every 100,000 people (American College of Physicians, 1992), followed by South Africa and the former Soviet Union (Mauer, 1992). Racial and ethnic minorities are overrepresented among those behind bars. Black and Hispanic males, for example, comprise 85% of prisoners in the New York State prison system (Green, 1991).

The prison system acts as a pocket of risk, within which men already at high risk of having a preexisting AIDS infection are exposed to conditions that further heighten the risk of contracting HIV (Toepell, 1992) or other infections such as tuberculosis (Bellin, Fletcher, & Safyer, 1993) or hepatitis. The corrections system is part of an institutional chain that facilitates transmission of HIV and other infections in certain North American populations, particularly among poor, inner-city, minority males. Prisoners are burdened not only by social disadvantage but also by high rates of physical illness, mental disorder, and substance abuse that jeopardize their health (Editor, *Lancet,* 1991).

AIDS prevalence is markedly higher among state and federal inmates than in the general U.S. population, with a known aggregate rate in 1992 of 202 per 100,000 population (Brewer & Derrickson, 1992) compared to a total population prevalence of 14.65 in 100,000 (American College of Physicians, 1992). The cumulative total of American prisoners with AIDS in 1989 was estimated to be 5,411, a 72% increase over the previous year (Belbot & del Carmen, 1991). The total number of AIDS cases reported in U.S. corrections as of 1993 was 11,565 (a minimum estimate of the true cumulative incidence among U.S. inmates) (Hammett; cited in Expert Committee on AIDS and Prisons, 1994). In New York State, at least 10,000 of the state's 55,000 prisoners are believed to be infected (Prisoners with AIDS/HIV Support Action Network, 1992). In Canadian federal penitentiaries, it is believed that 1 in 20 inmates is HIV infected (Hankins; cited in Expert Committee on AIDS and Prison, 1994).

The HIV virus is primarily transmitted between adults by unprotected penetrative sex or by needle sharing, without bleaching, with an infected partner. Sexual contacts between prisoners occur mainly through consensual unions and secondarily though sexual assault and rape (Vaid; cited in Expert Committee on AIDS and Prisons, 1994). The amount of IV drug use behind prison walls is unknown, although it is known to be prevalent and the scarcity of needles often leads to sharing of needles and sharps (Prisoners with AIDS/HIV Support Action Network, 1992).

The failure to provide comprehensive health education and treatment interventions in prisons not only puts more inmates at risk for HIV infection, but also threatens the public at large. Prisons are not hermetically sealed enclaves set apart from the community but an integral part of society (Editor, *Lancet,* 1991). Prisoners regularly move in and out of the prison system. In 1989, prisons in the United States admitted 467,227 persons and discharged 386,228 (American College of Physicians, 1992). The average age of inmates admitted to prison in 1989 was 29.6, with 75% between 18 and 34 years; 94.3% were male. These former inmates return to their communities after having served an average of 18 months inside (Dubler & Sidel, 1989). Within three years, 62.5% will be rearrested and jailed. Recidivism is highest among poor black and Hispanic men. The extent to which the drug-related social practices and sexual activities of released or paroled inmates who are HIV positive are putting others at risk upon return to their communities is unresearched and unknown.

Male Athletes

Injury is everywhere in sport. It is evident in the lives and bodies of athletes who regularly experience bruises, torn ligaments, broken bones, aches, lacerations, muscle tears, and so forth. For example, about 300,000 football-related injuries per year require treatment in hospital emergency rooms (Miedzian, 1991). Critics of violent contact sports claim that athletes are paying too high a physical price for their participation. George D. Lundberg (1994), editor of the *Journal of the American Medical Association,* has called for a ban on boxing in the Olympics and in the U.S. military. His editorial entreaty, though based on clinical evidence for neurological harm from boxing, is also couched in a wider critique of the exploitative economics of the sport.

Injuries are basically unavoidable in sports, but, in traditional men's sports, there has been a tendency to glorify pain and injury, to inflict injury on others, and to sacrifice one's body in order to "win at all costs." The "no pain, no gain" philosophy, which is rooted in traditional cultural equations between masculinity and sports, can jeopardize the health of athletes who conform to its ethos (Sabo, 1994).

The connections between sport, masculinity, and health are evidenced in Klein's (1993) study of how bodybuilders use anabolic steroids, overtrain, and engage in extreme dietary practices. He spent years as an ethnographic researcher in the muscled world of the bodybuilding subculture, where masculinity is equated to maximum muscularity and men's striving for bigness and physical strength hides emotional insecurity and low self-esteem.

A nationwide survey of American male high school seniors found that 6.6% used or had used anabolic steroids. About two-thirds of this group were athletes (Buckley et al., 1988). Anabolic steroid use has been linked to health risks such as liver disease, kidney problems, atrophy of the testicles, elevated risk of injury, and premature skeletal maturation.

Klein lays bare a tragic irony in American subculture—the powerful male athlete, a symbol of strength and health, has often sacrificed his health in pursuit of ideal masculinity (Messner & Sabo, 1994).

Men's Health Issues

Advocates of men's health have identified a variety of issues that impact directly on men's lives. Some of these issues may concern you or men you care about.

Testicular Cancer

The epidemiological data on testicular cancer are sobering. Though relatively rare in the general population, it is the fourth most common cause of death among males of 15–35 years, accounting for 14% of all cancer deaths for this age group. It is the most common form of cancer affecting males of 20–34 years. The incidence of testicular cancer is increasing, and about 6,100 new U.S. cases were diagnosed in 1991 (American Cancer Society, 1991). If detected early, the cure rate is high, whereas delayed diagnosis is life threatening. Regular testicular self-examination (TSE), therefore, is a potentially effective means for ensuring early detection and successful treatment. Regrettably, however, most physicians do not teach TSE techniques (Rudolf & Quinn, 1988).

Denial may influence men's perceptions of testicular cancer and TSE (Blesch, 1986). Studies show that most males are not aware of testicular cancer, and even among those who are aware, many are reluctant to examine their testicles as a preventive measure. Even when symptoms are recognized, men sometimes postpone seeking treatment. Moreover, men who are taught

TSE are often initially receptive, but their practice of TSE decreases over time. Men's resistance to TSE has been linked to awkwardness about touching themselves, associating touching genitals with homosexuality or masturbation, or the idea that TSE is not a manly behavior. And finally, men's individual reluctance to discuss testicular cancer partly derives from the widespread cultural silence that envelops it. The penis is a cultural symbol of male power, authority, and sexual domination. Its symbolic efficacy in traditional, male-dominated gender relations, therefore, would be eroded or neutralized by the realities of testicular cancer.

Disease of the Prostate

Middle-aged and elderly men are likely to develop medical problems with the prostate gland. Some men may experience benign prostatic hyperplasia, an enlargement of the prostate gland that is associated with symptoms such as dribbling after urination, frequent urination, or incontinence. Others may develop infections (prostatitis) or malignant prostatic hyperplasia (prostate cancer). Prostate cancer is the third leading cause of death from cancer in men, accounting for 15.7 deaths per 100,000 population in 1989. Prostate cancer is now more common than lung cancer (Martin, 1990). One in 10 men will develop this cancer by age 85, with African American males showing a higher prevalence rate than whites (Greco & Blank, 1993).

Treatments for prostate problems depend on the specific diagnosis and may range from medication to radiation and surgery. As is the case with testicular cancer, survival from prostate cancer is enhanced by early detection. Raising men's awareness about the health risks associated with the prostate gland, therefore, may prevent unnecessary morbidity and mortality. Unfortunately, the more invasive surgical treatments for prostate cancer can produce incontinence and impotence, and there has been no systematic research on men's psychosocial reactions and adjustment to sexual dysfunction associated with treatments for prostate cancer.

Alcohol Abuse

Although social and medical problems stemming from alcohol abuse involve both sexes, males comprise the largest segment of alcohol abusers. Some researchers have begun exploring the connections between the influence of the traditional male role on alcohol abuse. Isenhart and Silversmith (1994) show how, in a variety of occupational contexts, expectations surrounding masculinity encourage heavy drinking while working or socializing during after-work or off-duty hours. Some predominantly male occupational groups, such as longshoremen (Hitz, 1973), salesmen (Cosper, 1979), and members of the military (Pursch, 1976), are known to engage in high rates of alcohol consumption. Mass media play a role in sensationalizing links between booze and male bravado. Postman, Nystrom, Strate, and Weingartner (1987) studied the thematic content of 40 beer commercials and identified a variety of stereotypical portrayals of the male role that were used to promote beer drinking: reward for a job well done; manly activities that feature strength, risk, and daring; male friendship and esprit de corps; romantic success with women. The researchers estimate that, between the ages of 2 and 18, children view about 100,000 beer commercials.

Findings from a Harvard School of Public Health (1994) survey of 17,600 students at 140 colleges found that 44% engaged in "binge drinking," defined as drinking five drinks in rapid succession for males and four drinks for females. Males were more apt to report binge drinking during the past two weeks than females: 50% and 39% respectively. Sixty percent of the males who binged three or more times in the past two weeks reported driving after drinking, compared to 49% of their female counterparts, thus increasing the risk for accident, injury, and death. Compared to non–binge drinkers, binge drinkers were seven times more likely to engage in unprotected sex, thus elevating the risk for unwanted pregnancy and sexually transmitted disease. Alcohol-related automobile accidents are the top cause of death among 16- to 24-year-olds, especially among males (Henderson & Anderson, 1989). For all males, the age-adjusted death rate from automobile accidents in 1991 was 26.2 per 100,000 for African American males and 24.2 per 100,000 for white males, 2.5 and 3.0 times higher than for white and African American females respectively (*Morbidity and Mortality Weekly Report,* 1994d). The number of automobile fatalities among male adolescents that results from a mixture of alcohol abuse and masculine daring is unknown.

Men and AIDS

Human immunodeficiency virus (HIV) infection became a leading cause of death among males in the 1980s. Among men aged 25–44 in 1990, HIV infection was the second leading cause of death, compared to the sixth leading cause of death among same-age women (*Morbidity and Mortality Weekly Report,* 1993a). Among reported cases of acquired immunodeficiency syndrome (AIDS) for adolescent and adult men in 1992, 60% were men who had sex with other men, 21% were intravenous drug users, 4% were exposed through heterosexual sexual contact, 6% were men who had sex with men and injected drugs, and 1% were transfusion recipients. Among the cases of AIDS among adolescent and adult women in 1992, 45% were intravenous drug users, 39% were infected through heterosexual contact, and 4% were transfusion recipients (*Morbidity and Mortality Weekly Report,* 1993a).

Because most AIDS cases have been among men who have sex with other men, perceptions of the epidemic and its victims have been tinctured by sexual attitudes. In North American cultures, the stigma associated with AIDS is fused with the stigma linked to homosexuality. Feelings about men with AIDS can be mixed and complicated by homophobia.

Thoughts and feelings about men with AIDS are also influenced by attitudes toward race, ethnicity, drug abuse, and social marginality. Centers for Disease Control data show, for example, that men of color aged 13 and older constituted 51% (45,039) of the 89,165 AIDS cases reported in 1993. Women of color made up 71% of the cases reported among females aged 13 and older (*Morbidity and Mortality Weekly Report,* 1994b). The high rate of AIDS among racial and ethnic minorities has kindled racial prejudices in some minds, and AIDS is sometimes seen as a "minority disease." Although African American or Hispanic males may be at a greater risk of contracting HIV/AIDS, just as yellow fingers do not cause lung disease, it is not race or ethnicity that confers risk, but the behaviors they engage in and the social circumstances of their lives.

Perceptions of HIV/AIDS can also be influenced by attitudes toward poverty and poor people. HIV infection is linked to economic problems that include community disintegration, unemployment, homelessness, eroding urban tax bases, mental illness, substance abuse, and criminalization (Wallace, 1991). For example, males comprise the majority of homeless persons. Poverty and homelessness overlap with drug addiction, which, in turn, is linked to HIV infection. Of persons hospitalized with HIV in New York City, 9–18% have been found to be homeless (Torres et al, 1990). Of homeless men tested for HIV at a New York City shelter, 62% of those who took the test were seropositive (Ron & Rogers, 1989). Among runaway or homeless youth in New York City, 7% tested positive, and this rate rose to 15% among the 19- and 20-year-olds. Of homeless men in Baltimore, 85% admitted to substance use problems (Weinreb & Bassuk, 1990).

Suicide

The suicide rates for both African American and white males increased between 1970 and 1989, whereas female rates decreased. Indeed, males are more likely than females to commit suicide from middle childhood until old age (Stillion, 1985, 1995). Compared to females, males typically deploy more violent means of attempting suicide (e.g., guns or hanging rather than pills) and are more likely to complete that act. Men's selection of more violent methods to kill themselves is consistent with traditionally masculine behavior (Stillion, White, McDowell, & Edwards, 1989).

Canetto (1995) interviewed male survivors of suicide attempts in order to better understand sex differences in suicidal behavior. Although she recognizes that men's psychosocial reactions and adjustments to nonfatal suicide vary by race/ethnicity, socioeconomic status, and age, she also finds that gender identity is an important factor in men's experiences. Suicide data show that men attempt suicide less often than women but are more likely to die than women. Canetto indicates that men's comparative "success" rate points toward a tragic irony that, consistent with gender stereotypes, men's failure even at suicide undercuts the cultural mandate that men are supposed to succeed at everything. A lack of embroilment in traditionally masculine expectations, she suggests, may actually increase the likelihood of surviving a suicide attempt for some men.

Elderly males in North America commit suicide significantly more often than elderly females. Whereas white women's lethal suicide rate peaks at age 50, white men age 60 and older have the highest rate of lethal suicide, even surpassing that rate for younger males (Manton et al., 1987). Canetto (1992) argues that elderly men's higher suicide mortality is chiefly owed to gender differences in coping. She writes,

> Older women may have more flexible and diverse ways of coping than older men. Compared to older men, older women may be more willing and capable of adopting different coping strategies— "passive" or "active," "connected" or "independent"—depending on the situation (p. 92).

She attributes men's limited coping abilities to gender socialization and development.

Erectile Disorders

Men often joke about their penises or tease one another about penis size and erectile potency ("not getting it up"). In contrast, they rarely discuss their concerns about impotence in a serious way. Men's silences in this regard are regrettable in that many men, both young and old, experience recurrent or periodic difficulties getting or maintaining an erection. Estimates of the number of American men with erectile disorders range from 10 million to 30 million (Krane, Goldstein, & Saenz de Tejada, 1989; National Institutes of Health, 1993). The Massachusetts Male Aging Study of the general population of noninstitutionalized, healthy American men between ages 40 and 70 years found that 52% reported minimal, moderate, or complete impotence (Feldman et al., 1994). The prevalence of erectile disorders increased with age, and 9.6% of the men were afflicted by complete impotence.

During the 1960s and 1970s, erectile disorders were largely thought to stem from psychological problems such as depression, financial worries, or work-related stress. Masculine stereotypes about male sexual prowess, phallic power, or being in charge of lovemaking were also said to put too much pressure to perform on some males (Zilbergeld, 1993). In contrast, physiological explanations of erectile disorders and medical treatments have been increasingly emphasized since the 1980s. Today diagnosis and treatment of erectile disorders should combine psychological and medical assessment (Ackerman & Carey, 1995).

Men's Violence

Men's violence is a major public health problem. The traditional masculine stereotype calls on males to be aggressive and tough. Anger is a by-product of aggression and toughness and, ultimately, part of the inner terrain of traditional masculinity (Sabo, 1993). Images of angry young men are compelling vehicles used by some males to separate themselves from women and to measure their status with respect to other males. Men's anger and violence derive, in part, from sex inequality. Men use the threat or application of violence to maintain their political and economic advantage over women and lower-status men. Male socialization reflects and reinforces these larger patterns of domination.

Homicide is the second leading cause of death among 15- to 19-year-old males. Males aged 15–34 years made up almost half (49%, or 13,122) of homicide victims in the United States in 1991. The homicide rate for this age group increased by 50% from 1985 to 1991 (*Morbidity and Mortality Weekly Report,* 1994c).

Women are especially victimized by men's anger and violence in the form of rape, date rape, wife beating, assault, sexual harassment on the job, and verbal harassment (Thorne-Finch, 1992). That the reality and potential of men's violence impact women's mental and physical health can be surely assumed. However, men's violence also exacts a toll on men themselves in the forms of fighting, gang clashes, hazing, gay-bashing, intentional infliction of injury, homicide, suicide, and organized warfare.

Summary

It is ironic that two of the best-known actors who portrayed Superman have met with disaster. George Reeves, who starred in the original black-and-white television show, committed suicide, and Christopher Reeve, who portrayed the "man of steel" in recent film versions, was paralyzed by an accident during a high-risk equestrian event. Perhaps one lesson to be learned here is that, behind the cultural facade of mythic masculinity, men are vulnerable. Indeed, as we have seen in this chapter, some of the cultural messages sewn into the cloak of masculinity can put men at risk for illness and early death. A sensible preventive health strategy for the 1990s calls upon men to critically evaluate the Superman legacy, that is, to challenge the negative aspects of traditional masculinity that endanger their health, while hanging on to the positive aspects of masculinity and men's lifestyles that heighten men's physical vitality.

The promotion of men's health also requires a sharper recognition that the sources of men's risks for many diseases do not strictly reside in men's psyches, gender identities, or the roles that they enact in daily life. Men's roles, routines, and relations with others are fixed in the historical and structural relations that constitute the larger gender order. As we have seen, not all men or male groups share the same access to social resources, educational attainment, and opportunity that, in turn, can influence their health options. Yes, men need to pursue personal change in order to enhance their health, but without changing the political, economic, and ideological structures of the gender order, the subjective gains and insights forged within individuals can easily erode and fade away. If men are going to pursue self-healing, therefore, they need to create an overall preventive strategy that at once seeks to change potentially harmful aspects of traditional masculinity and meets the health needs of lower-status men.

REFERENCES

Ackerman, M. D., & Carey, P. C. (1995). *Journal of Counseling & Clinical Psychology,* 63(6), 862–876.

American Cancer Society (1991). Cancer Facts and Figures—1991. Atlanta, GA: American Cancer Society.

American College of Physicians. (1992). The crisis in correctional health care: The impact of the national drug control strategy on correctional health services. *Annals of Internal Medicine, 117*(1), 71–77.

Belbot, B. A., & del Carmen, R. B. (1991). AIDS in prison: Legal issues. *Crime and Delinquency, 31*(1), 135–153.

Bellin, E. Y., Fletcher, D. D., & Safyer, S. M. (1993). Association of tuberculosis infection with increased time in or admission to the New York City jail system. *Journal of the American Medical Association, 269*(17), 2228–2231.

Blesch, K. (1986). Health beliefs about testicular cancer and self-examination among professional men. *Oncology Nursing Forum, 13*(1), 29–33.

Blum, R., Harman, B., Harris, L., Bergeissen, L., & Restrick, M. (1992). American Indian–Alaska native youth health. *Journal of American Medical Association, 267*(12), 1637–1644.

Brewer, T. F., & Derrickson, J. (1992). AIDS in prison: A review of epidemiology and preventive policy. *AIDS, 6*(7), 623–628.

Buckley, W. E., Yesalis, C. E., Friedl, K. E., Anderson, W. A., Steit, A. L., & Wright, J. E. (1988). Estimated prevalence of anabolic steroid use among male high school seniors. *Journal of the American Medical Association, 260*(23), 3441–3446.

Bullard, R. D., (1992). Urban infrastructure: Social, environmental, and health risks to African Americans. In B. J. Tidwell (Ed.), *The State of Black America* (pp. 183–196). New York: National Urban League.

Canetto, S. S. (1995). Men who survive a suicidal act: Successful coping or failed masculinity? In D. Sabo & D. Gordon (Eds.), *Men's health and illness* (pp. 292–304). Newbury Park, CA: Sage.

Canetto, S. S. (1992). Gender and suicide in the elderly. *Suicide and Life-Threatening Behavior, 22*(1), 80–97.

Cockerham, W. C. (1995). *Medical sociology.* Englewood Cliffs, NJ: Prentice Hall.

Connell, R. W. (1987). *Gender and power.* Stanford: Stanford University Press.

Cosper, R. (1979). Drinking as conformity: A critique of sociological literature on occupational differences in drinking. *Journal of Studies on Alcoholism, 40,* 868–891.

Cypress, B. (1981). Patients' reasons for visiting physicians: National ambulatory medical care survey, U.S. 1977–78. DHHS Publication No. (PHS) 82-1717, Series 13, No. 56. Hyattsville, MD: National Center for Health Statistics, December, 1981a.

Dawson, D. A., & Adams, P. F. (1987). Current estimates from the national health interview survey: U.S. 1986. Vital Health Statistics Series, Series 10, No. 164. DHHS Publication No. (PHS) 87-1592, Public Health Service. Washington, DC: U.S. Government Printing Office.

Dubler, N. N., & Sidel, V. W. (1989). On research on HIV infection and AIDS in correctional institutions. *The Milbank Quarterly, 67*(1–2), 81–94.

Editor. (1991, March 16). Health care for prisoners: Implications of "Kalk's refusal." *Lancet, 337,* 647–648.

Expert Committee on AIDS and Prison. (1994). *HIV/AIDS in prisons: Summary report and recommendations to the Expert Committee on AIDS and Prisons* (Ministry of Supply and Services Canada Catalogue No. JS82-68/2-1994). Ottawa, Ontario, Canada: Correctional Service of Canada.

Feldman, H. A., Goldstein, I., Hatzichristou, D. G., Krane, R. J., & McKinlay, J. B. (1994). Impotence and its medical and psychosocial correlates: Results of the Massachusetts Male Aging Study. *Journal of Urology, 151,* 54–61.

Gibbs, J. T. (Ed.) (1988). *Young, black, and male in America: An endangered species.* Dover, MA: Auburn House.

Givens, J. (1979). Current estimates from the health interview survey: U.S. 1978. DHHS Publications No. (PHS) 80-1551, Series 10, No. 130. Hyattsville, MD: Office of Health Research Statistics, November 1979.

Greco, K. E., & Blank, B. (1993). Prostate-specific antigen: The new early detection test for prostate cancer. *Nurse Practitioner, 18*(5), 30–38.

Green, A. P. (1991). Blacks unheard. *Update* (Winter), New York State Coalition for Criminal Justice, 6–7.

Harrison, J., Chin, J., & Ficarrotto, T. (1992). Warning: Masculinity may be dangerous to your health. In M. S. Kimmel & M. A. Messner (Eds.), *Men's lives* (pp. 271–285). New York: Macmillian.

Harvard School of Public Health. Study reported by Wechsler, H., Davenport, A., Dowdall, G., Moeykens, B., & Castillo, S. (1994). Health and behavioral consequences of binge drinking in college: A national survery of students at 140 campuses. *Journal of the American Medical Association, 272*(21), 1672–1677.

Henderson, D. C., & Anderson, S. C. (1989). Adolescents and chemical dependency. *Social Work in Health Care, 14*(1), 87–105.

Hitz, D. (1973). Drunken sailors and others: Drinking problems in specific occupations. *Quarterly Journal of Studies on Alcohol, 34,* 496–505.

Hull, J. D. (1994, November 21). Running scared. *Time, 144*(2), 93–99.

Isenhart, C. E., & Silversmith, D. J. (1994). The influence of the traditional male role on alcohol abuse and the therapeutic process. *Journal of Men's Studies, 3*(2), 127–135.

Kimmel, M. S., and Levine, M. P. (1989). Men and AIDS. In M. S. Kimmel & M. A. Messner (Eds.), *Men's lives* (pp. 344–354). New York: Macmillian.

Klein, A. (1993). Little big men: Bodybuilding subculture and gender construction. Albany, NY: SUNY Press.

Krane, R. J., Goldstein, I., Saentz de Tejada, I. (1989). Impotence. *New England Journal of Medicine, 321,* 1648–1659.

Lamarine, R. (1988). Alcohol abuse among Native Americans. *Journal of Community Health, 13*(3), 143–153.

Lundberg, G. D. (1994, June 8). Let's stop boxing in the Olympics and the United States military. *Journal of the American Medical Association, 271*(22), 1990.

Manton, K. G., Blazer, D. G., & Woodbury, M. A. (1987). Suicide in middle age and later life: Sex and race specific life table and cohort analysis. *Journal of Gerontology, 42,* 219–227.

Martin, J. (1990). Male cancer awareness: Impact of an employee education program. *Oncology Nursing Forum, 17*(1), 59–64.

Mauer, M. (1992). Men in American prisons: Trends, causes, and issues. *Men's Studies Review, 9*(1), 10–12. A special issue on men in prison, edited by Don Sabo and Willie London.

May, P. (1986). Alcohol and drug misuse prevention programs for American Indians: Needs and opportunities. *Journal of Studies of Alcohol, 47*(3), 187–195.

McCord, C., & Freeman, H. P. (1990). Excess mortality in Harlem. *New England Journal of Medicine, 322*(22), 1606–1607.

Messner, M. A., & Sabo, D. (1994). *Sex, violence, and power in sports: Rethinking masculinity.* Freedom. CA: Crossing Press.

Metler, R., Conway, G. & Stehr-Green, J. (1991). AIDS surveillance among American Indians and Alaskan natives. *American Journal of Public Health, 81*(11), 1469–1471.

Miedzian, M. (1991). *Boys will be boys: Breaking the link between masculinity and violence.* New York: Doubleday.

Montagu, A. (1953). *The natural superiority of women.* New York: Macmillian.

Moore, D. (1988). Reducing alcohol and other drug use among Native American youth. *Alcohol Drug Abuse and Mental Health, 15*(6), 2–3.

Morbidity and Mortality Weekly Report. (1993a). Update: Mortality attributable to HIV infection/AIDS among persons aged 25–44 years—United States, 1990–91. *42*(25), 481–486.

Morbidity and Mortality Weekly Report. (1994a). Prevalence of overweight among adolescents—United States, 1988–91, *43*(44), 818–819.

Morbidity and Mortality Weekly Report. (1994b). AIDS among racial/ethnic minorities— United States, 1993, *43*(35), 644–651.

Morbidity and Mortality Weekly Report. (1994c). Homicides among 15–19-year-old males—United States, *43*(40), 725–728.

Morbidity and Mortality Weekly Report. (1994d). Deaths resulting from firearm- and motor-vehicle-related injuries—United States, 1968–1991. *43*(3), 37–42.

Nadelmann, P., & Wenner, L. (1994, May 5). Toward a sane national drug policy [Editorial]. *Rolling Stone,* 24–26.

National Center for Health Statistics. (1990). *Health, United States, 1989.* Hyattsville, MD: Public Health Service.

National Center for Health Statistics. (1992). Advance report of final mortality statistics, 1989. *Monthly Vital Statistics Report, 40* (Suppl. 2) (DHHS Publication No. [PHS] 92–1120).

National Institutes of Health. (1993). Consensus development panel on impotence. *Journal of the American Medical Association, 270,* 83–90.

Pleck, J., Sonenstein, F. L., & Ku, L. C. (1992). In R. Ketterlinus, & M. E. Lamb (Eds.), *Adolescent problem behaviors.* Hillsdale, NJ: Larwence Erlbaum Associates.

Polych, C., & Sabo, D. (1996). Gender politics, pain, and illness: The AIDS epidemic in North American prisons. In D. Sabo & D. Gordon (Eds.), *Men's health and illness* (pp. 139–157), Newbury Park, CA: Sage.

Postman, N., Nystrom, C., Strate, L., & Weingartner, C. (1987). *Myths, men and beer: An analysis of beer commercials on broadcast television,* 1987. Falls Church, VA: Foundation for Traffic Safety.

Prisoners with AIDS/HIV Support Action Network. (1992). *HIV/AIDS in prison systems: A comprehensive strategy* (Brief to the Minister of Correctional Services and the Minister of Health). Toronto: Prisoners with AIDS/HIV Support Action Network.

Pursch, J. A. (1976). From quonset hut to naval hospital: The story of an alcoholism rehabilitation service. *Journal of Studies on Alcohol, 37,* 1655–1666.

Reed, W. L. (1991). Trends in homicide among African Americans. *Trotter Institute Review, 5,* 11–16.

Ron, A., & Rogers, D. E. (1989). AIDS in New York City: The role of intravenous drug users. *Bulletin of the New York Academy of Medicine, 65*(7), 787–800.

Rudolf, V., & Quinn, K. (1988). The practice of TSE among college men: Effectiveness of an educational program. *Oncology Nursing Forum, 15*(1), 45–48.

Sabo, D., & Gordon, D. (1995). *Men's health and illness: Gender, power, and the body.* Newbury Park, CA: Sage.

Sabo, D. (1994). The body politics of sports injury: Culture, power, and the pain principle. A paper presented at the annual meeting of the National Athletic Trainers Association, Dallas, TX, June 6, 1994.

Sabo, D. (1993). Understanding men. In Kimball G. (Ed.), *Everything you need to know to succeed after college,* (pp. 71–93), Chico, CA: Equality Press.

Staples, R. (1995). *Health and illness among African-American males.* In D. Sabo and D. Gordon (Eds.), *Men's health and illness,* (pp. 121–138), Newbury Park, CA: Sage.

Stillion, J. (1985). *Death and the sexes: An examination of differential longevity, attitudes, behaviors, and coping skills.* New York: Hemisphere.

Stillion, J. (1995). Premature death among males: Rethinking links between masculinity and health. In D. Sabo and D. Gordon (Eds.), *Men's health and illness,* (pp. 46–67), Newbury Park, CA: Sage.

Stillion, J., White, H., McDowell, E. E., & Edwards, P. (1989). Ageism and sexism in suicide attitudes. *Death Studies, 13,* 247–261.

Sugarman, J., Soderberg, R., Gordon, J., & Rivera, F. (1993). Racial misclassifications of American Indians: Its effects on injury rates in Oregon, 1989–1990. *American Journal of Public Health, 83*(5), 681–684.

Tewksbury, R. (1995). Sexual adaptation among gay men with HIV. In D. Sabo and D. Gordon (Eds.), *Men's health and illness* (pp. 222–245), Newbury Park, CA: Sage.

Thorne-Finch, R. (1992). *Ending the silence: The origins and treatment of male violence against women.* Toronto: University or Toronto Press.

Toepell, A. R. (1992). *Prisoners and AIDS: AIDS education needs assessment.* Toronto: John Howard Society of Metropolitan Toronto.

Torres, R. A., Mani, S., Altholz, J., & Brickner, P. W. (1990). HIV infection among homeless men in a New York City shelter. *Archives of Internal Medicine, 150,* 2030–2036.

Verbrugge, L. M., & Wingard, D. L. (1987). Sex differentials in health and mortality. *Women's Health, 12,* 103–145.

Waldron, I. (1995). Contributions of changing gender differences in mortality. In D. Sabo and D. Gordon (Eds.), *Men's health and illness* (pp. 22–45), Newbury Park, CA: Sage.

Waldron, I. (1986). What do we know about sex differences in mortality? *Population Bulletin of the U.N., No. 18-1985,* 59–76.

Waldron, I. (1976). Why do women live longer than men? *Journal of Human Stress, 2,* 1–13.

Wallace, R. (1991). Traveling waves of HIV infection on a low dimensional "sociogeographic" network. *Social Science Medicine, 32*(7), 847–852.

Weinreb, L. F., & Bassuk, E. L. (1990). Substance abuse: A growing problem among homeless families. *Families and Community Health, 13*(1), 55–64.

Zilbergeld, B. (1993). *The new male sexuality.* New York: Bantam.

64

HEALTH CARE REFORM—
A WOMAN'S ISSUE

CATHERINE DeLOREY

Catherine DeLorey, Dr. PH., is the director of the Women's Health Institute, which provides health information "to empower women to make their own wise health decisions." She is also the coordinator of Women's Universal Health Initiative in Boston, Massachusetts. She can be reached at Catherine@wuhi.org.

D issatisfaction with the cost and quality of the health care available in the United States is increasing. With the Democratic take-over of Congress in the November elections, there is new interest in changing the health care system, but little agreement on the best alternative for improving access to health care. Complicating this issue for women's health activists is the fact that—while women are often disproportionately affected by our health care system's problems—only fledgling efforts have been made to ensure that health care reform initiatives address women's concerns. It is important that current proposals consider women's health care needs, and for activists and advocates to support efforts that prioritize and recognize women's issues.

Access to Health Care Is a Women's Issue

The failures of our current health care system greatly affect women, especially women of color. Women constitute more than 52 percent of the U.S. population, and are the major consumers of health services, as well as the traditional caretakers of their families' health. Women have greater annual health care expenses than men ($2,453 vs. $2,316) and pay a greater proportion of their health care expenses out-of-pocket (19% compared to 16%). Women make 58% more visits each year to primary care physicians, and are more likely than men to take at least one prescription drug on a daily basis.[1]

Because women are disproportionately represented among low-wage workers and/or work in industries that do not offer benefits, they are more

Catherine DeLorey, "Health Care Reform—A Woman's Issue," from National Women's Health Network, *Women's Health Activist*, March–April 2007. www.nwhn .org/wha_marapr07_healthcarereform. Reprinted by permission.

likely to be uninsured or under-insured than men. In fact, women work in jobs that are 15 percent less likely to offer health care and, because of their low incomes and high health care costs, women are 20% more likely than uninsured men to have trouble obtaining health care.[2] Women are also more likely to be dependent on their spouses for coverage: they are more than twice as likely as men to receive employer-based health coverage as "dependents" through their spouses' insurance (26% vs. 11%). This dependent status makes women vulnerable to losing their coverage as a result of being divorced or widowed.[3] The predominance of employer-based insurance also hampers lesbians from accessing health coverage through their partners, since many companies do not recognize domestic partners and, of course, with limited exceptions, gay and lesbians cannot get married.

Although American women tend to live longer than men, this is not the case for uninsured women, compared to uninsured men. Women who are uninsured tend to forgo getting health care, especially preventive services, and they are more likely not to fill prescriptions than are women with insurance coverage. Of the 17 million uninsured women in America, more than 67 percent did not seek health care because they could not afford it.[4] The direct result of the way our health care system is structured is that women are more likely than men to be sick and to find health services unattainable.

Biological and physiological issues are not the only factors that influence women's concerns in health and health care. Other influences include women's social/cultural roles, and how we both use and are treated by the health care system. These other influences include inequities in health care that result in women traditionally not being included in clinical research studies on drugs and medical procedures; and not receiving the same rigorous care and treatment for cardiac problems as men do. In addition, important aspects of women's lives (such as pregnancy or menopause) are treated as medical conditions or diseases, rather than life experiences.

These problems—particularly access to health care—are magnified for women of color. Thirty-eight percent of Latinas and 23 percent of African American women are uninsured, compared to just 13 percent of White women.[5] Difficulties accessing health care are compounded for immigrant women who face both linguistic and cultural barriers to their receipt of health care. For undocumented women, the problems in accessing health care are compounded by State and Federal restrictions on their ability to use public health services.

Because women are more likely to be employed in industries that do not provide health insurance, and because they spend more time out of the workforce as caregivers and mothers, women are less likely to have adequate health insurance and more likely to face barriers in accessing care and other services. For these reasons, the fight for universal health care is a fight for equality and justice for all women. Only a system that guarantees access to affordable, comprehensive health care for everyone will resolve the health care disparities that women experience.

What Should Be Included in Women's Health Care?

There can be no health security for women without protection of the full range of women's reproductive needs that include, but are not limited to, abortion services. Comprehensive reproductive health care supports a woman's right to information and services that both prevent pregnancy and help her to become pregnant when she wants to; that support her during a healthy pregnancy; and promote healthy outcomes for pregnancy.

In addition to comprehensive reproductive rights, the following principles are central to health system change that meets women's needs:

- Universal access to quality health care,
- Comprehensive health benefits for all women, employed or not,
- Access to health services from a variety of providers,
- Access to health services provided in a variety of settings,
- Systems accountable to women and other consumers,
- Complete information for women to use to make their own health care decisions.

Making Women's Needs a Central Priority

The only way to achieve an adequate health system for women is for women to work together to have our voices heard. It is critical that women's health advocates come together to support initiatives that prioritize women's health care needs. The following organizations are among the many that are working on health care reform:

- The Avery Institute for Social Change, MergerWatch, and the National Women's Health Network are working together on an effort called "Women Lead on Health Care Reform." This effort mobilizes and unites advocates who are committed to achieving universal health care that meets women's comprehensive reproductive health care needs and works to ensure that any new system will meet women's comprehensive reproductive health care needs. More information is available on the organizational web sites.
- Women's Universal Health Initiative is a national organization dedicated to building diverse communities of women and work for health care reform. In addition, the organization publishes a quarterly electronic newsletter on women and health care reform.

These initiatives are a start, but we must ensure that our voices are heard by those who are making decisions about the future of health care in the U.S. Those of us who are working in health reform organizations must raise awareness of women's needs, and keep advocates focused on the issue of comprehensive reproductive rights. Those of us in professional organizations need to speak out and make sure health reform and women's needs are included in all of our efforts. And, in our own communities, we all need to communicate about the importance of health care reform, and inform others about efforts to enhance women's health.

NOTES

1. Lambrew, J., "Diagnosing Disparities in Health Insurance for Women: A Prescription for Change." New York: Commonwealth Fund, August 2001. Available online at: http://www.cmwf.org/publications/publications_show .htm?doc_id=221296.

2. Ibid.

3. Sered, S., "Seven Reasons Why Health Care Coverage is a Women's Issue." Boston: Center for Women's Health and Human Rights, Suffolk University, 2006. Available online at http://www.suffolk.edu/cwhhr/women_health_ coverage.html.

4. Salganicoff, A., "Diagnosing Women's Health Care," *National Council of Jewish Women Journal* 2006; 29(1): 1–4; Kaiser Family Foundation, "Women's Health Policy Facts: Women's Health Insurance Coverage Fact Sheet," Menlo Park, CA, November 2004; Kaiser Family Foundation, "Women's Health Policy Facts: Women's Health Insurance Coverage Fact Sheet," March, 2006.

5. Salganicoff, A., Ranji, U., Wyn, R. "Report: Women and Health Care: A National Profile." Kaiser Family Foundation: Menlo Park, CA, Summer, 2005. Available online at http://www.kff.orq/womenshealth/upload/Women-and-Health-Care-A-National-Profile-Key-Findinqs-from-the-Kaiser-Women-s-Health-Survev.pdf.

65

REPRODUCTIVE ISSUES ARE ESSENTIAL SURVIVAL ISSUES FOR THE ASIAN-AMERICAN COMMUNITIES

CONNIE S. CHAN

Connie S. Chan was born in Hong Kong, grew up in Hawaii, and now lives in Boston, Massachusetts. Bilingual and bicultural in her upbringing, she has experienced the world from a multicultural perspective. She is professor of human services at the University of Massachusetts Boston. Her research and publications focus on the intersection of gender, culture, and sexuality issues in Asian American women. She continues to work within Asian American communities to provide access to culturally appropriate health services. She is the author of *Depression: Reducing Your Risk* (1993).

When the Asian-American communities in the United States list their priorities for political action and organizing, several issues concerning basic survival are usually included: access to bilingual education, housing, health care, and child care, among others. Yet the essential survival issue of access to reproductive counseling, education, and abortions is frequently missing from the agenda of Asian-American community organizations. Why is the reproductive issue perceived as unimportant to the Asian-American communities? I think there are several reasons—ignorance, classism, sexism, and language barriers. Of course, these issues are interrelated, and I'll try to make the connections between them.

First, let me state that I am not an "expert" on the topic of reproductive issues in the Asian-American communities, but I do have first-hand experiences which have given me some insight into the problems. Several years ago, I was a staff psychologist at a local community health center serving the greater Boston Asian population. Most of our patients were recent immigrants from China, Vietnam, Cambodia, Laos, and Hong Kong. Almost all of these new immigrants understood little or no English. With few resources (financial or otherwise), many newcomers struggled to make sense of life in the United States and to survive in whatever fashion they could.

Connie S. Chan, "Reproductive Issues Are Essential Survival Issues for the Asian-American Communities" from *From Abortion to Reproductive Freedom,* edited by Marlene Gerber Fried, 1990. Reprinted with the permission of South End Press.

At the health center, the staff tried to help by providing information and advocacy in getting through our confusing system. I thought we did a pretty good job until I found out that neither our health education department nor our ob-gyn department provided *any* counseling or information about birth control or abortion services. The medical department had interpreted our federal funding regulations as prohibiting not only the performance of abortions on-site, but also the dissemination of information which might lead to, or help patients to obtain, an abortion.

Needless to say, as a feminist and as an activist, I was horrified. When I found out that pregnant women who inquired about abortions were given only a name of a white, English-speaking ob-gyn doctor and sent out alone, it seemed a morally and ethically neglectful practice. One of the nurse-midwives agreed with me and suggested that I could serve as an interpreter/advocate for pregnant women who needed to have abortions, or at least wanted to discuss the option with the English-speaking ob-gyn doctor. The only catch was that I would have to do it on my own time, I could not claim any affiliation with the health center, and I could not suggest follow-up care at the health center.

Not fully knowing the nature of what I was volunteering for, I agreed to interpret and advocate for Cantonese-speaking pregnant women at their appointments with the obstetrician. It turned out that over the course of three years I interpreted during at least a hundred abortions for Asian immigrant women who spoke no English. After the first few abortions, the obstetrician realized how essential it was to have an interpreter present, and began to require that all non-English-speaking women have an interpreter during the abortion procedure.

As a middle-class, educated, bilingual Asian-American woman, I was aware of the importance of having the choice to have an abortion, and the necessity of fighting for the right to choose for myself. I had been unaware of how the right to have an abortion is also a right to survival in this country if you are a poor, uneducated, non-English-speaking immigrant.

The women I interpreted for were, for the most part, not young. Nor were they single. They ranged in age from 25 to 45, with a majority in their late twenties and early thirties. Almost all were married and had two or more children. Some had as many as five or six children. They needed to have abortions because they had been unlucky enough to have gotten pregnant after arriving in this country. Their families were barely surviving on the low wages that many new immigrant workers earned as restaurant workers, garment factory workers, or domestic help. Almost all of the women worked full-time: the ones who had young children left them with older, retired family members or did piece-work at home; those with older children worked in the factories or hotels. Without fail each woman would tell me that she needed to have an abortion because their family could not afford another mouth to feed, that the family could not afford to lose her salary contribution, not even for a few months, to care for an infant. In some ways, one could not even say that these women were choosing to have abortions. The choice had already been made for them, and it was a choice of basic survival.

Kai Ling was one of the women for whom I interpreted. A 35-year-old mother of four children, ages 2 to 7, she and her husband emigrated to the United States from Vietnam. They had no choice; in their emigration, they were refugees whose village had been destroyed and felt fortunate to escape with their lives and all four of their children. Life in the United States was difficult, but they were scraping by, living with another family in a small apartment where their entire family slept in one room. Their hope was that their children would receive an education and "make it" in American society; they lived with the deferred dream for the next generation.

When Kai Ling found out that she was pregnant, she felt desperate. Because she and her husband love children and live for their children, they wanted desperately to keep this child, this one who would be born in America and be an American citizen from birth. Yet they sadly realized that they could not afford another child, they could not survive on just one salary, they could not feed another one. Their commitment was to the children they already had, and to keeping their family together.

When I accompanied Kai Ling to her abortion, she was saddened but resigned to what she had to do. The $300 that she brought to the clinic represented almost a month of wages for her; she had borrowed the money from family and friends. She would pay it back, she said, by working weekends for the next ten weeks. Their major regret was that she would not be able to buy any new clothes for her children this year because of this unexpected expense.

Kai Ling spoke very little English. She did not understand why she had to go to a white American doctor for her abortion instead of receiving services from her Asian doctor at the health center. She had no real understanding of reproductive rights issues, of *Roe v. Wade,* or of why there were demonstrators waving pictures of fetuses and yelling at her as we entered the clinic. Mercifully, she did not understand the questions they shouted at her in English, and she did not ask me what they had said, remarking only that the protesters seemed very angry at someone. She felt sure, I think, that they were not angry at her. She had done nothing to provoke anyone's anger. She was merely trying to survive in this country under this country's rules.

It is a crime and an injustice that Kai Ling could not receive counseling in her language and services from her doctors at the Asian neighborhood health center. It is a crime that she had to borrow $300 to pay for her own abortion, that her Medicaid benefits did not pay for it. It is a grave injustice that she had to have me, a stranger, interpreting for her during her abortion because her own doctor could not perform the procedure at her clinic. It was not a matter of choice for her to abort her pregnancy, but a matter of basic survival.

Kai Ling speaks no English. Kai Ling will probably never attend a march or a rally for choice. She will not sign any petitions. She might not even vote. But it is for her and the countless thousands of immigrant women like her that we need to continue to struggle for reproductive rights. Within the Asian-American communities, the immigrant women who are most affected by the lack of access to abortions have the least power. They do not speak English; they do not demand equal access to health care; their needs are easily overlooked.

Thus, it is up to those of us who are bilingual, who can speak English, and who can speak to these issues, to do so. We need to ensure that the issue of reproductive rights is an essential item on the Asian-American political agenda. It is not a women's issue; it is a community issue.

We must speak for the Kai Lings, for their children, for their right to survive as a family. We must, as activists, make the connections between the issues of oppression based upon gender, race, national origin, sexual orientation, class, or language. We can and must lead the Asian-American communities to recognize the importance of the essential issue of reproductive rights for the survival of these communities.

66

WHY THE PRECAUTIONARY PRINCIPLE?
A Meditation on Polyvinyl Chloride (PVC)
and the Breasts of Mothers*

SANDRA STEINGRABER

Sandra Steingraber, Ph.D., is currently on the faculty at Cornell University's Center for the Environment in Ithaca, New York. She is the author of *Living Downstream: An Ecologist Looks at Cancer and the Environment* (1997) and *Having Faith: An Ecologist's Journey to Motherhood* (2001).

Those of you who know me know that when I talk on these topics I usually speak out of two identities: biologist and cancer activist. My diagnosis with bladder cancer at age 20 makes more urgent my scientific research. Conversely, my Ph.D. in ecology informs my understanding of how and why I became a cancer patient in the first place: bladder cancer is considered a quintessential environmental disease. Links between environment and public health became the topic of my third book, *Living Downstream*, but since I have been given the task of speaking about the effect of toxic materials on future generations, I'm going to speak out of another one of my identities—that of a mother.

I'm a very new mother. I gave birth in September 1998 to my daughter and first child. So, I'm going to speak very intimately and in the present tense. You know it's a very powerful thing for a person with a cancer history to have a child. It's a very long commitment for those of us unaccustomed to looking far into the future. My daughter's name is Faith.

I'm also learning what all parents must learn, which is a new kind of love. It's a love that's more than an emotion or a feeling. It's a deep physical craving like hunger or thirst. It's the realization that you would lay down your life for this eight-pound person without a second thought. You would

---

*Remarks delivered at the Lowell Center for Sustainable Production's Workshop, Building Materials into the Coming Millenium, Boston, November 1998. Editor's note: References for toxicity in breast milk appear in Steingraber's book *Having Faith* on pages 251–253 and 259–60, among others.

pick up arms for them. You would empty your bank account. It's love without boundaries and were this kind of love directed at another adult, it would be considered totally inappropriate. A kind of fatal attraction. Maybe, when directed at babies, we should call this "natal attraction."

I say this to remind us all what is at stake. If we would die or kill for our children, wouldn't we do anything within our power to keep toxics out of their food supply? Especially if we knew, in fact, there were alternatives to these toxics?

Of all human food, breast milk is now the most contaminated. Because it is one rung up on the food chain higher than the foods we adults eat, the trace amounts of toxic residues carried into mothers' bodies become even more concentrated in the milk their breasts produce. To be specific, it's about 10 to 100 times more contaminated with dioxins than the next highest level of stuff on the human food chain, which are animal-derived fats in dairy, meat, eggs, and fish. This is why a breast-fed infant receives its so-called "safe" lifetime limit of dioxin in the first six months of drinking breast milk. Study after study also shows that the concentration of carcinogens in human breast milk declines steadily as nursing continues. Thus the protective effect of breast feeding on the mother appears to be a direct result of downloading a lifelong burden of carcinogens from her breasts into the tiny body of her infant.

When it comes to the production, use, and disposal of PVC (polyvinyl chloride), the breasts of breast-feeding mothers are the tailpipe. Representatives from the vinyl industry emphasize how common a material PVC is, and they are correct. It is found in medical products, toys, food packaging, and vinyl siding. What they don't say is that sooner or later all of these products are tossed into the trash, and here in New England, we tend to shovel our trash into incinerators. Incinerators are de facto laboratories for dioxin manufacturing, and PVC is the main ingredient in this process. The dioxin created by the burning of PVC drifts from the stacks of these incinerators, attaches to dust particles in the atmosphere, and eventually sifts down to Earth as either dry deposition or in rain drops. This deposition then coats crops and other plants, which are eaten by cows, chickens and hogs. Or, alternatively, it's rained into rivers and lakes and insinuates itself into the flesh of fish. As a breast-feeding mother, I take these molecules into my body and distill them in my breast tissue. This is done through a process through which fat globules from throughout my whole body are mobilized and carried into the breast lobes, where, under the direction of a pituitary hormone called prolactin, they are made into human milk. Then, under the direction of another pituitary hormone called oxytocin, this milk springs from the grape-like lobes and flows down long tubules into the nipple, which is a kind of sieve, and into the back of the throat of the breast-feeding infant. My daughter.

So, this, then, is the connection. This milk, my milk, contains dioxins from old vinyl siding, discarded window blinds, junked toys, and used I.V. bags. Plastic parts of buildings that were burned down accidentally are also housed in my breasts. These are indisputable facts. They are facts that we scientists are not arguing about. What we do spend a lot of time debating is what exactly are the health effects on the generation of children that my daughter belongs to. We don't know with certainty because these kids have not reached the age at which a lot of diseases possibly linked to dioxin exposure would manifest themselves. Unlike mice and rats, we have long generational times. We do know with certainty that childhood cancers are on the rise, and indeed they are rising faster than adult cancers. We don't have any official explanation for that yet.

Let me tell you something else I've learned about breast feeding. It's an ecstatic experience. The same hormone (oxytocin) that allows milk to flow from the back of the chest wall into the nipple also controls female orgasm. This so-called let-down reflex makes the breast feel very warm and full and fizzy, as if it were a shaken-up Coke bottle. That's not unpleasant. Moreover, the mouths of infants—their gums, tongues, and palates—are perfectly designed to receive this milk. A newborn's mouth and a woman's nipple are like partners in a tango. The most expensive breast pump—and I have a $500 one—can only extract about half of the volume that a newborn baby can because such machines cannot possibly imitate the intimate and exquisite tonguing, sucking, and gumming motion that infants use to extract milk from the nipple, which is not unpleasant either.

Through this ecstatic dance, the breast-fed infant receives not just calories, but antibodies. Indeed the immune system is developed through the process of breast feeding, which is why breast-fed infants have fewer bouts of infectious diseases than bottle-fed babies. In fact, the milk produced in the first few days after birth is almost all immunological in function. This early milk is not white at all but clear and sticky and is called colostrum. Then, from colostrum you move to what's called transitional milk, which is very fatty and looks like liquid butter. Presumably then, transitional milk is even more contaminated than mature milk, which comes in at about two weeks post-partum. Interestingly, breast milk is so completely digested that the feces of breast-fed babies doesn't even smell bad. It has the odor of warm yogurt and the color of French mustard. By contrast, the excretions of babies fed on formula are notoriously unpleasant.

What is the price for the many benefits of breast milk? We don't yet know. However, one recent Dutch study found that schoolchildren who were breast fed as babies had three times the level of PCBs* in their blood as

---

Editor's Note: 1.5 billion pounds of PCBs (polychlorinated biphenyls) were manufactured in the United States prior to being banned by the Environmental Protection Agency in 1977 due to their toxicity. They were used in many aspects of manufacturing including in electrical equipment, plastics, paint, rubber, carbonless paper, etc. They persist in the environment—and in our bodies—due to their longevity and stability and are defined by the EPA as "probable human carcinogens" based on animal studies and studies of workers exposed to PCBs (www.epa.gov/opptintr/pcb/).

compared to children who had been exclusively formula fed. PCBs are probably carcinogens. Why should there be any price for breast feeding? It should be a zero-risk activity.

If there was ever a need to invoke the Precautionary Principle—the idea that we must protect human life from possible toxic danger well in advance of scientific proof about that danger—it is here, deep inside the chest walls of nursing mothers where capillaries carry fat globules into the milk-producing lobes of the mammary gland. Not only do we know little about the long-term health effects of dioxin and PCB exposure in newborns, we haven't even identified all the thousands of constituent elements in breast milk that these contaminants might act on. For example, in 1997 researchers described 130 different sugars unique to human milk. Called oligosaccharides, these sugars are not digested but function instead to protect the infant from infection by binding tightly to intestinal pathogens. Additionally, they appear to serve as a source of sialic acid, which is essential to brain development.

So, this is my conclusion. Breast feeding is a sacred act. It is a holy thing. To talk about breast feeding versus bottle feeding, to weigh the known risks of infectious diseases against the possible risks of childhood or adult cancers is an obscene argument. Those of us who are advocates for women and children and those of us who are parents of any kind need to become advocates for uncontaminated breast milk. A woman's body is the first environment. If there are toxic materials from PVC in the breasts of women, then it becomes our moral imperative to solve the problem. If alternatives to PVC exist, then it becomes morally imperative that we embrace the alternatives and make them a reality.

67

DOES SILENCIO = MUERTE?
Notes on Translating the AIDS Epidemic

RAFAEL CAMPO

Dr. Rafael Campo teaches and practices internal medicine at Harvard Medical School and Beth Israel Deaconess Medical Center in Boston. He is the award-winning author of several books, including *The Poetry of Healing* (1997) and the collection of poems *Diva* (1999).

Palomita chatters in one of my clinic exam rooms in Boston, her strongly accented voice filling the chilly institutional chrome-and-vinyl space with Puerto Rican warmth. She's off on another dramatic monologue, telling me about her new boyfriend.

"Edgar, he loves me, you know, he call me *mamacita*. He want me to be the mother of his children someday, OK? I ain't no slut. *Mira,* I don't need to use no condom with him."

Even the way she dresses is a form of urgent communication—the plunging neckline of her tropically patterned blouse, whose tails knotted above her waist also expose her flat stomach, the skin-tight denim jeans, the gold, four-inch hoop earrings, and the necklace with her name spelled out in cursive with tiny sparkling stones. Her black hair is pulled back tightly, except for a small squiggle greased flat against her forehead in the shape of an upside-down question mark.

"People think bad of him 'cause they say he dealing drugs. I tell them, 'No way, you shut your stupid mouths. He good to me and beside, he cleaner than you is.' Sure, he got his other girls now and then, but he pick them out *bien* carefully, you know what I mean. That his right as man of the house. No way he gonna give me *la SIDA*. We too smart for none of that shit. We trust each other. We communicate. We gonna buy us a house somewhere *bien bonita.* Someday we gonna make it."

She is seventeen years old, hasn't finished high school, and cannot read English. I have just diagnosed her with herpes, and I am trying to talk to her about AIDS and "safer sex." Her Edgar, who is also a patient of mine, tested HIV-positive last week. It's clear they have not discussed it.

Rafael Campo, "Does Silencio = Muerte? Notes on Translating the AIDS Epidemic" from *The Progressive* 63, no. 10 (1999). Reprinted with the permission of *The Progressive* magazine, 409 East Main Street, Madison, WI 53703.

Latinos are dying at an alarming rate from AIDS. And for all our glorious presence on the world's stage—in music, literature, art, from MacArthur grants to MTV to *Sports Illustrated*—this is one superlative no one can really boast about. Few Latinos dare even to mention the epidemic. The frenetic beat of salsa in our dance clubs seems to drown out the terrifying statistics, while the bright murals in our barrios cover up the ugly blood-red graffiti, and that "magical realism" of our fictions imagines a world where we can lose our accents and live in Vermont, where secret family recipes conjure up idealized heterosexual love in an ultimately just universe unblemished by plague.

Here, loud and clear, for once, are some of the more stark, sobering facts: In the U.S., Latinos accounted for one-fifth of all AIDS cases reported to the Centers for Disease Control last year, while making up only one-tenth of the U.S. population; AIDS has been the leading cause of death since 1991 for young Latino men in this country; in areas with especially high numbers of Latinos, such as Fort Lauderdale, Miami, Los Angeles, and New York, AIDS deaths among Latina women were four times the national average since 1995. While the infection rate among whites continues to decline, today, and every day, 100 people of color are newly diagnosed with HIV infection. Behold our isolated and desperate substance users, the most marginalized of the marginalized, our forsaken impoverished, and our irreplaceable young people.

I do not have to wonder at the reasons for the silence among Latinos about the burgeoning AIDS epidemic that is decimating us. Though I stare into its face every day in the clinic where I work, there are times when even I want to forget, to pretend it is not happening, to believe my people are invincible and can never be put down again. I want to believe Palomita is HIV-negative, that Edgar will stop shooting drugs and someday return to get on the right triple combination of anti-viral medications. I fervently hope that César, a twenty-year-old Colombian man who keeps missing his appointments, is taking his protease inhibitors so that his viral load remains undetectable. I do not really know who pays for his drugs, since he is uninsured, but my thoughts do not dwell on it. In the end, I want to go home and rest after a long day in the clinic, to make love to my partner of fourteen years and feel that I'll never have to confront another epidemic. I want to look into his dark, Puerto Rican eyes and never have to speak of AIDS again.

But I know better. I know we must speak out—about the ongoing disenfranchisement of Latinos despite our much-touted successes, about the vicious homophobia of a *machista*, about Latino culture that especially fears and hates gay people whom it believes "deserve" AIDS, about the antipathy of the Catholic Church so many Latinos pray to for guidance they don't receive, about the unfulfilled dream of total and untainted assimilation for so many Mexicans, Dominicans, Cubans, and Puerto Ricans who came to America with nothing.

To break any of these silences is especially tempting, since together they allow me to blame most of the usual targets of my rage and frustration. Others are more difficult to penetrate, such as the persistent lack of access in

Latino communities to lifesaving information about AIDS. Still others make almost no sense to me at all. Rosa, another patient of mine, tells me she knows she should not have sex without condoms, but continues to do so anyway because she is afraid her drug-dealing boyfriend would think she no longer loves him. Yet she hardly imagines that he might be using drugs, or wonders whether he has other sexual partners.

Our silence, in all its forms, is killing us. I wince at the familiar ring of this realization. I can't help but remember my patient Ernesto in his hospital bed with his partner Jesús sitting quietly at his side, a tiny statue of the Virgin of Guadalupe keeping its mute vigil, no other family or friends around. Ernesto died years ago of AIDS. It is not passé or trite or irrelevant to ask why we remain silent. It is absolutely imperative. We must understand the causes of our *silencio.*

Most of the Spanish-speaking patients who come to my clinic do not much resemble Ricky Martin or Daisy Fuentes or Antonio Sabato Jr. They are "the working poor," janitors or delivery boys or hotel laundry workers or high school dropouts or dishwashers—people with jobs that pay subsistence wages and provide no health benefits. Still, they consider themselves fortunate because so many have no jobs at all.

Many of them are illiterate, and many more speak no English. They have come to Boston mostly from Puerto Rico, but some are from Cuba, the Dominican Republic, Mexico, Colombia, Guatemala, El Salvador, and Nicaragua. Some sleep on park benches when the weather is warm enough and in shelters during the winter. Some live in crowded apartments. Some are undocumented immigrants. Some have lost their welfare benefits, some are trying to apply for temporary assistance, and almost none have enough to feed themselves and their families.

Older couples too often have lost children to drugs, street violence, and AIDS. Young people too often blame their parents and their teachers for their problems. Some know very little about AIDS and fault homosexuals, injection drug users, and prostitutes for poisoning the community. Some view *la SIDA* with resignation and see it as inevitable, part of the price some must pay for a chance at a better life.

But the vast majority of Latinos in the U.S. remain shortchanged, despite the glittering success of a few. For every Federico Peña, many more anonymous "illegals" are deported to Mexico each day, never given the chance to contribute to our society at all. For every Sammy Sosa, a makeshift boat full of Dominicans is lost at sea. And even more noxious than the large-scale efforts to dismantle affirmative action or to deny basic social services (including health care) to undocumented immigrants are the daily insults and obstacles that prevent Latinos from sharing fully in our nation's life. Lack of economic opportunities pushes Latinos toward criminal activities as a means to survive. Discrimination and rejection breed the kind of despair that drug use and unsafe sex only temporarily ameliorate. The despair and the apathy, heightened by what the very few who are successful have achieved, numb the soul.

It's a common litany, yet I can't help but see how this imposed demoralization is manifest in the behavior of so many of my patients. Why leave an abusive relationship, they say, when all that awaits is the cold streets? Why insist on a condom when it's so much easier not to and the reasons to go on living are not so clear anyway? It doesn't seem farfetched to me that this cumulative hopelessness is fueling the AIDS epidemic.

But these causes, the subject of so many lefty social work dissertations, do not get at the entire problem. We remain ourselves a culture in which men treat women as icons—or as powerless objects of our legendary sexual passions. Our wives must be as pure as we believe our own mothers to be, and yet we pursue our mistresses with the zeal of matadors about to make the kill. Brute force is excused as a necessary means by which Latino men must exert control over weak-willed women, and it is by no means secret that in the shadow of the AIDS epidemic lurks another senseless killer, the domestic violence that too often goes unreported.

Could Palomita and Rosa fear more then just losing the financial support of their boyfriends? For Yolanda, another patient of mine with HIV infection, it was the beatings from her husband that finally drove her onto the streets, where prostitution soon became her only means of making a living. Now she is dying.

Sexism's virulent *hermano* is homophobia. AIDS has long been considered a disease exclusively of homosexuals—especially in Spanish-speaking communities, where not only is HIV strongly associated with gayness, it is further stigmatized as having been imported from the decadent white world. Since we cannot speak calmly and rationally of homosexuality, we certainly cannot bring up AIDS, perhaps the only affliction that could be worse.

Latinos are allowed to be gay only outside the confines of their families and old neighborhoods. Indeed, many Latino men who have sex with men would never even consider themselves "gay" at all, a derogatory term that they would apply only to those whom they consider to be their "passive" partners. Even those who take pride in their homosexuality are not immune to this hatred. I have many gay Latino friends whose parents will not allow their partners to visit during holidays, friends who go to great lengths to (literally) "straighten out" their homes when family is coming to visit by creating fictitious separate bedrooms and removing anything suggestive of homosexuality (which can get difficult, when one gets down to the joint Andy Garcia fan club application, the Frida Kahlo shrine, or the autographed and framed Gigi Fernandez poster).

Hand in hand with both sexism and homophobia goes Catholicism. Latinos are overwhelmingly Catholic, and the Catholic hierarchy remains overwhelmingly not only anti-gay, but also opposed to the use of condoms as a means to prevent HIV transmission. (The only time I have ever heard AIDS mentioned in a Catholic church was at a wedding service, when it was invoked as a reminder of what punishments lay in store for the fornicators and homosexuals who scorned marriage.) While on the one hand preaching about the sanctity of life, our religious leaders have abetted the deaths of countless Latinos by refusing to endorse the use of condoms as a means to prevent AIDS transmission.

No one disagrees with the monotonous message that abstinence is the safest sex of all. Yet in today's ascendant moment, when young Latinos must party—we drink our Cuba libres followed by café con leche, dance the merengue provocatively with shiny crucifixes dangling around our necks, and later engage in sultry, unsafe sex, even if always (supposedly) with partners of the opposite sex—such teaching is utterly impractical.

Then there are the people like me, the Cuban doctors and Chicano lawyers, the Nuyorican politicians and the displaced Argentine activists— those who mean well but who have allowed the silence to engulf us, too. The thick warm blanket of our insularity and relative power comforts us. We are a small, tightly knit group; we work hard and hope to send our children to Harvard or Stanford or Yale, praying that they stay out of trouble. We increasingly vote Republican, elated that George W. Bush tosses out a few words in a halting Spanish, and fearing that a liberal government might take away too much of what we have struggled to make for ourselves—and might allow too many others in for a share of our pie. We would hardly acknowledge Palomita and Edgar if we passed them in the street, and we might even regret their very existence, the way they bring all of us down by their ignorance and poverty. Full of our quiet self-righteousness, gripping our briefcases just a bit more tightly, we might not even feel sorry for them if we knew they were being afflicted with AIDS.

Mario Cooper, a former deputy chief of staff for the Democratic National Committee, knows first-hand about a community's indifference to AIDS. Black, gay, and HIV-positive, he spearheaded an initiative sponsored by the Harvard AIDS Institute called Leading for Life. The summit brought together prominent members of the African American community to talk frankly about their own AIDS epidemic—just as uncontrolled, just as deadly, and until last year's summit, just as silent as the one ravaging Latinos.

"The key is to make people understand this is about all of us," Cooper says, as we brainstorm a list of possible invitees to another meeting, to be called *Unidos para la Vida*. Inspired by his past success in Boston, where the likes of Marian Wright Edelman, Henry Louis Gates Jr., and Dr. Alvin Poussaint eventually heeded his call to action, Cooper is now intent on tackling the same issue for Latinos.

"What came out of the Leading for Life meeting was incredible," he says. "Suddenly, everyone was paying attention, and things started happening for young African Americans. They started to learn more about AIDS." He is beaming, and we add Oscar de la Renta, Cristina, and Edward James Olmos to the list. "We have the chance to do the same thing here."

But after a few weeks of working on the project with him and others at the Harvard AIDS Institute, it became clear to us that we might be facing even greater obstacles than those he encountered in the black community. We had hardly even gotten started when conflicts over terminology almost sank the entire effort. "Latino" competed with "Hispanic," while all of us felt that neither term fully articulated the rich diversity and numerous points of origin of those who undeniably formed some kind of a community. Some of us secretly questioned whether a shared vulnerability to AIDS was itself enough to try to unify us. Was a Puerto Rican injection drug user in Hartford, Connecticut, really facing the same issues as a Salvadoran undocumented immigrant selling sex in El Paso, Texas? Was loyalty to the Venezuelan community, or Nicaraguan community, imperiled by joining this larger group? At times, we saw evidence of the kind of pecking-order mentality (in which certain nationalities consider themselves superior to others) that has since the days of Bolívar interfered with efforts to unify Spain's colonies in the New World.

If these mostly suppressed internal divisions were not enough to surmount, we also battled the general lack of interest in AIDS—yesterday's news, no matter how loudly we shouted the latest statistics, no matter how emphatically we pointed out the lack of access for Latinos to the new treatments.

"Don't they have a cure for that now?" remarked one person I called, exemplifying precisely the sort of misinformation we were working to correct, her breathy laugh further revealing both the kind of distancing from— and absence of comfort with—the entire issue that surely reinforced her lack of knowledge.

Others were simply fatalistic. "You can't change the way these kids think and behave," said one person who declined the invitation to attend the summit, "so why bother?"

"Tell them to stop having sex," came one memorably blunt response, before the phone crashed down on the other end.

"I pray for them," said another pious woman. "I pray that they will renounce their wicked ways and find peace in Christ." She then regretted to inform me that she would be unable to attend the summit.

The special insight I thought I could bring to the effort, as a gay Latino poet doctor who writes both poems and prescriptions, seemed to be of less and less use, as more and more "no" answers, accompanied by their usually polite excuses, filtered back to us. Weeks later, when the situation grew bleakest, Cooper only urged us to redouble our efforts. "We're dealing with a situation that is almost unfathomable to most of these people," he said. "It's an epidemic no one wants to believe exists. Latinos are supposed to be the rising stars of the next millennium, not the carriers of a disease that could wipe out humanity." What was on one level a glaring public health crisis had to be understood more radically. "We have to ask ourselves why this message isn't getting out. We're kidding ourselves if we think we're the magic solution. In fact, we may be part of the problem."

The work of Walt Odets, the Berkeley psychologist who shook up the safer sex establishment, immediately came to mind. Odets observed young gay men at the height of the AIDS epidemic in San Francisco, noting a pervasive hopelessness in the face of a belief that infection with HIV was inevitable. Behind the apathy and denial, might not the same thing exist in this second-wave epidemic among inner-city Latinos? The stupidity of our early efforts at sloganeering, which tried to encapsulate a myriad of complex issues under a single bright banner, suddenly became utterly apparent to me. What faced us was not simply a matter of speaking out, of breaking a silence so many Latinos already living with HIV had already renounced. What we had to do was learn to speak their language, to incorporate in our every effort an entirely new mode of expression.

I knew right then that we had a lot more work to do.

Palomita's mood is decidedly less cheerful today. She is three-and-a-half-months pregnant, but that's not why she starts to cry. It's the end of January, and my office is just as cold as ever. A thin crust of ice is gradually forming on everything outside. Last week, while Palomita's HIV test was being run, a storm knocked out power to most of New England. My heart feels as empty and dark as one of the houses caught in the blackout now that I've read out her result.

"I don't believe you. You mean, I'm gonna die of AIDS?" A leaden moment passes before the inevitable next question. "And what about my baby?"

Looking at Palomita, I wonder again at how AIDS does not get prevented, how it seems to have a terrible life of its own. I want to answer her questions, explain to her that AZT lowers the risk of maternal fetal transmission, that the new triple combination anti-retroviral regimens, if she takes them exactly as prescribed, could buy her many years with her child. But I can't. Instead I keep thinking about her name, which means "little dove," and trying to imagine the innocence her parents must have seen in her tiny face when they named her, trying to feel that boundless joy at the earliest moment of a new life. I am looking at Palomita as she cries, framed by a window from which she cannot fly. I am imagining peace. In her beautiful brown face, mirror of a million souls, I try to envision us all in a world without AIDS.

68

TO BE POOR AND TRANSGENDER

KAI WRIGHT

Kai Wright is a freelance journalist in Bed-Stuy, Brooklyn. His work explores the politics of sex and race, with a particular focus on the implications for public health. Wright is the author of *Soldiers of Freedom: An Illustrated History of African Americans in the Armed Forces* (2002) and *The African-American Archive: The History of the Black Experience Through Documents* (2001).

Sharmus has been a sex worker for about five years. She started after breaking up with a boyfriend who was supporting her while she was out of work. It was quick money, and, as with many of her transgender friends, she didn't believe there were many other jobs out there for her.

"You have your good nights, and your bad nights," says Sharmus, thirty-five. "There are no fringe benefits. Summer time is the best time; the winter is hard," she explains, casually ticking off the pros and cons of being a prostitute. "It's just hard getting a job. Nobody really wants to hire you, and when they do hire you they give you a hard time."

Sex work was not in her plans back when she transitioned from male to female at age twenty-one. "Sometimes I regret it," she sighs. "My lifetime goal was to be a schoolteacher."

Her uncertainty is to be expected. Our culture depicts people whose discomfort with gender norms goes beyond being tomboys or feminine men as mere curiosity items for trash TV ("Your woman is really a man!" episodes of *Jerry Springer*). This collective ignorance leaves people like Sharmus without much guidance. Many go through puberty and into adulthood without meeting people like themselves. The resulting high rates of depression, drug use, violence, and suicidal thoughts are unsurprising.

"One of the greatest agonies one can experience is gender dysphoria," says transgender activist Jessica Xavier. "When your anatomy doesn't match who you are inside, it's the worst feeling in the world."

Sharmus and Xavier are part of a group whose existence challenges normative gender. They include drag performers, heterosexual cross-dressers, and people from all walks of life who live permanently in a gender other than that assigned at birth. They range from individuals who have had

Kai Wright, "To Be Poor and Transgender" from *The Progressive*, 65, no. 10 (2001). Reprinted with the permission of *The Progressive* magazine, 409 East Main Street, Madison, WI 53703.

thousands of dollars worth of reconstructive surgery to people who simply style themselves in a way that feels comfortable.

Around the nation, a growing cadre of activists is working to build bridges between all of these populations and to encourage the formation of an umbrella community called "transgender." What the members of this latest American identity group share is a far more practical understanding of gender politics than that of the ethereal, academic world to which it is often relegated. From employment to health services, transgender folks, particularly those in low-income environments, face enormous barriers when navigating even the most basic aspects of life—all because of their gender transgressions.

"We continue to be one of the most stigmatized populations on the planet," says Xavier, the former director of a national coalition of transgender political groups called It's Time!—America. Xavier recently cajoled the local health department into financing a survey of around 250 transgender people in D.C. Forty percent of respondents had not finished high school, and another 40 percent were unemployed. Almost half had no health insurance and reported not seeing a physician regularly. A quarter reported being HIV-positive, and another 35 percent reported having seriously considered suicide.

Xavier's was the latest in a series of such studies done in cities where relatively emboldened trans activists have pushed local officials to begin considering public policy solutions to their health care concerns. Across the board, they have found largely the same thing: higher rates of just about every indicator of social and economic distress. "And all because of the stigma," Xavier concludes.

One problem that stands out, Xavier and others say, is the need for accessible counseling and medical supervision for those who are in the process of gender transitioning. Most medical professionals require certain steps, outlined in a set of protocols dubbed the "Benjamin Standards of Care." First, a therapist must diagnose you with "Gender Identity Disorder," which the American Psychiatric Association established in 1979. In adults, the diagnosis essentially confirms that your "gender dysphoria" is profound enough that the drastic step of making physiological alterations to God's plan is an acceptable treatment.

The diagnosis clears you for reconstructive surgery and hormone therapy. Hormone use for gender transitioning is strictly off-label, but select doctors will nevertheless prescribe a particular hormone and simply file paperwork for one of its approved usages. While there is disagreement within the trans community about how this process should be altered, most unite around frustration with the gatekeeping nature of it all—the notion that one must first ask permission, then be declared insane, before being allowed to violate our gender rules.

For Angela (a pseudonym), this means choosing between the career she's spent ten years building and her recent decision to live as a male. Angela, twenty-eight, gained security clearance while serving in the Marines. Despite having climbed to officer rank, she fled the forces when it became clear they were going to throw her out for being a lesbian.

As a civilian, her clearance allowed her to land a well-paying job at an aerospace engineering firm. The position has afforded her partner of four years a comfortable life, and even occasionally helps support her partner's budding acting career. But all of that will be jeopardized once a gender-identity-disorder diagnosis is placed in Angela's medical records. Technically, it's a mental health problem, and that would likely prompt the revocation of her clearance when it next comes up for review. So Angela and her partner are again searching for new ways she can use her skills.

Middle class professionals like Angela have options. The barriers to a legal and safe gender transition are surmountable, if profound. But for people like Sharmus, the whole discussion is absurd.

Sharmus has never had "body work" done, but she's taken some hormones in the past. In her world, spending thousands of dollars on therapy, surgery, and hormone treatments is impossible, but a hyper-feminine appearance is still highly valued—not only for personal aesthetics, but also for professional development. So a thriving black market has developed. In D.C., for $200 to $300, you can have silicone injected into your chest to create breasts. Thirty bucks will get you around 100 hormone pills, though injections are usually cheaper.

"When I was taking the hormone shots, my girlfriend was shooting me," Sharmus explains. "You get a knot in the breasts first, then your skin gets soft. After about two months, my breasts started forming."

With hormones, often someone who has taken them before supplies and mentors a curious friend. Similar arrangements develop with silicone, but just as often there's a dealer in town who also injects clients. The silicone is not encased, as it would be with an implant, but rather injected with large syringes directly into varying body parts. In some cases, the materials injected are not even silicone, but substitutes made from more readily available things such as dishwashing liquid or floor wax. Similarly, some men wanting estrogen will simply take birth-control pills. Testosterone is harder to improvise, but even the real thing can irreparably damage internal organs when taken improperly. All of this can result in fatalities.

"I have known several people that passed," Sharmus sighs. She steers clear of silicone and stopped taking unsupervised hormones. A couple of years ago, she started working with an organization called Helping Individual Prostitutes Survive, or HIPS. She conducts outreach for HIPS, offering information on how to protect against HIV and other sexually transmitted diseases, and encouraging colleagues to leave the silicone alone.

Omar Reyes, whose drag persona is former Miss Gay America, works for La Clinica del Pueblo, a D.C. clinic serving the city's ballooning Latino community. Reyes uses his male birth name and male pronouns but considers himself transgender because of his drag work and his discomfort with male gender "norms." In his monthly transgender support group and in conversations with other *dragas* he meets at his weekly show, Reyes harps on the *malas noticias* about silicone. But he recognizes why it's attractive: It's cheap, and it's fast.

"They put silicone in their face and their bodies and, in just a very short period, they can look like a woman," he says. This is particularly important for drag performers and sex workers, whose income may depend on how exaggeratedly feminine they look. "We have to deal with the fact that they want to look like a woman, and this is the short-term way to do it."

Reyes and Xavier want to see someone in D.C. start a low-cost clinic devoted to counseling and treatment for people who are transitioning. Gay health centers in Boston, Los Angeles, New York City, San Francisco, and Seattle all have such clinics already and are developing their own sets of protocols for how the process should work. Earlier this year, San Francisco became the first jurisdiction in the United States to include sex reassignment surgery and related treatments in its health plan for civil servants. This is the kind of thing Xavier says we need to see more of.

But even if the services were there, getting people into them would take work. Most transgender people tell horrifying stories of the treatment they have experienced in health care settings. In one of the most high-profile cases nationally, a trans woman named Tyra Hunter died in 1995 when D.C. paramedics refused to treat her wounds from a car accident. After removing her clothes at the scene of the accident and discovering her male genitals, a paramedic allegedly ceased treating Hunter and began shouting taunts. She died at the hospital later. Following a lengthy court battle, Hunter's family won a suit against the city.

There are many less prominent examples. From the hospital nurse who gawks when helping a trans woman into her dressing gown to the gynecologist who responds with disbelief when a trans man comes in for a checkup, the small indignities act as perhaps the greatest barriers to health care.

"They feel like when you go for services, people are going to give attitude," Reyes says. "Therefore, you find that they don't even think about going for help when they really need it."

Tanika Walker, who goes by Lucky, is your standard eighteen-year-old hard ass: short-sighted, stubborn-headed, determined to be the toughest guy in the room. Born and raised in rough-and-tumble southeast Washington, D.C., Lucky has a mop of dreadlocks, light mustache, tattoos, and brands—including the name of a deceased sibling spelled out in cigarette burns. These all send one message: I'm the wrong dude to mess with.

Like Angela, Lucky is in the process of transitioning genders to become a young man. It's an emotional journey she began when she was fourteen years old. Along the way, she's been yanked out of school and tossed out of her home. She's also been involved in a lot of disastrous relationships, marred by violence, often her own.

"I know that I'm homosexual, that I'm a lesbian," Lucky says, groping to explain her feelings. "But at the same time, it's like, I look so much like a boy. I act so much like a boy. I want to be a boy."

So far, however, Lucky's transition is primarily stylistic. She still uses her birth name and answers to female pronouns, but she describes her gender as "not anything." She uses only the men's bathroom because she's had too many fights with women who thought she was a Peeping Tom in the ladies' room. And she'd much rather her friends call her "dawg" than "girlfriend." Among African American lesbians, Lucky fits into a category of women often dubbed "doms," short for dominant.

"I never had chests," Lucky brags. "Never. Around the time you're supposed to start getting chests, I didn't get any. So I was like, am I made to be like this? I was the little girl all of the other little girls couldn't play with 'cause I was too boyish."

The dyke jokes started early, sometime in middle school. She settled on a violent response to the taunting just as early. Her fighting became routine enough that by her sophomore year the school suggested counseling for her "identity crisis." She balked and, instead, came out to her mom, who promptly threw her out of the house. "I was like, how am I having an identity crisis? I know what I am," Lucky remembers. "My mom said I had to go."

Lucky enrolled herself in the Job Corps and by the time she was seventeen had her GED. She came back to D.C., moved in with her godsister, and began dating a thirty-two-year-old woman.

But the relationship quickly turned violent, and the godsister put Lucky out as well. She turned to one of her brothers and started dating someone her own age. But it was a stormy relationship, and Lucky battered her partner. After one of their more brutal fights, the young woman called the police and Lucky wound up in jail for a month for aggravated assault. That was this April. In May, she started dating another young woman, and she believes this relationship will work out. She's also started hanging out at the Sexual Minority Youth Assistance League (SMYAL).

One urgent lesson she's trying to learn is that violence isn't her only option when conflict arises. But she dismisses the severity of her problem. "I would be, like, 'Go away and leave me alone, '" she says, describing how the fights started. "And she would just keep hitting me in the arm or something. But it didn't really affect me; it would just be real irritating. She used to do stupid stuff like that to aggravate me. So I just hit her. And when I hit her, I blacked her eye out or something."

She sums up her life in a gigantic understatement, saying, "It's just some things I've been through that a normal eighteen-year-old female wouldn't have been through."

Twenty-year-old Vassar College senior Kiana Moore began transitioning at seventeen. She is articulate and engaging, has never been in trouble, and is studying to become a clinical psychologist. As the only transgender person on her campus, she comes out to the entire first-year class every term during one of the school's diversity programs. She spent this summer interning at SMYAL, counseling Lucky and fifteen to twenty other mainly black transgender youth. What these young folks need, she says, are more role models.

"I am here at SMYAL working as an intern, but where else can you go around this country and see a trans intern? Where can you see a trans person who's in college?" Moore asks. "And so you don't really have anyone to connect to or know about. So if they are at high risk [for social problems], that's why. Because there's nothing there for them at all."

Moore has what Xavier calls "passing privilege." She's a beautiful and confident black woman most people would never assume is transgender. That's something usually achieved only by those with significant resources.

And once trans people have found they can pass—usually middle class whites living in the suburbs—they don't want to ruin it by becoming an activist or a role model.

"You lose something if you help, because then you put yourself in the spotlight. And if you are a pretty, passable female, you don't want to do that," Moore explains. "We don't want to be advocates, because then we're Kiana the transsexual instead of Kiana the new neighbor."

And thus the activists trying to build a transgender community and social movement face much the same battle gay activists confronted for years: Those with the resources to help have too much to lose.

But Moore sees promise in the youth she spent the summer with. "Every time I talk to them I always give them a big hug before, during, and after the session, because that's the only way I can say I'm here and I think you're stronger than me," she says. "They deal with their problems, and they come in here, and they smile, every day. And they take care of each other."

PART XI

A World That Is Truly Human

In the introduction to this book, Gerda Lerner calls for "a world free of dominance and hierarchy, a world that is truly human." A democratic society depends on equal access to the rights and benefits of the social order. It requires a system in which people born tied down by ropes of oppression are given the means to untie themselves and are offered equal opportunities once they are free. In a truly human world, the ropes would not exist. Our social, political, and economic systems do not provide such opportunities, so individuals, groups, and communities are left on their own to devise empowerment strategies.

As many authors in this book have said or implied, altering the gender system, entrenched as it is in many structural arrangements, requires change at many levels—in individuals, in relationships, in families, in communities, in all social institutions, in national alliances, through legal reform, and through global policy and action. Recall Elizabeth Janeway's conclusion, reported in the introduction to this book, that disempowered people can become empowered only after we question the truth of the ideas of those in power. Janeway argues that disbelief, the first stage of empowerment, needs to be followed by action, both individual and collective.

A current strategy used to address gender injustice is to call for the treatment of women's rights as human rights. As mentioned in the introduction, this call harks back to an early women's movement definition of feminism: feminism is the radical notion that women are human. Human rights activist and scholar Charlotte Bunch, director of the Center for Women's Global Leadership at Rutgers University, argues that gender-related abuse "offers the greatest challenge to the field of human rights today."[1] She reports that women and girls are subjected to a wide range of abuse not perpetrated on men and boys, such as abortion of female fetuses, restricted nutrition, women's and girls' lack of control over their bodies (as reflected in high death rates from illegal abortions and female genital mutilation), and overt violence against them of the types described earlier in this book by Melanie Kaye/Kantrowitz, Jan Goodwin, Laurie Schaffner, and others. Bunch concludes, "Female subordination runs so deep that it is still viewed as inevitable or natural, rather than seen as a politically constructed reality maintained by patriarchal interests, ideology, and institutions."[2]

Bunch recommends four approaches to alleviating these injustices. Attention to *political and civil rights* would focus, for example, on the sexual abuse of female political prisoners and female refugees. Attention to *socioeconomic rights* would address the right to food, shelter, health care, and employment. Attention to *legal rights* would protect women against sex discrimination. And finally, a *feminist transformation of human rights* designed to explicitly focus on violations in women's lives would address other ways in which women are oppressed such as battering, rape, forced marriage, lack of reproductive rights, compulsory heterosexuality, and genital mutiliation.[3] A case in point is the disarmament, demobilization, and reintegration of girl soldiers following involvement in armed conflict. In addition to facing many of the concerns faced by boy soldiers (such as rejection by communities and families that they may have brutalized), many must deal with the trauma of sexual abuse, sexual slavery, forced marriages to their commanders, and the stigma of being "unclean" as presumed carriers of HIV/AIDS which leaves them unfit for marriage in their home communities.[4] Rita Arditti (this part) lays out a clear case for addressing women's rights as human rights. In fact, most of the issues addressed in this book are human rights issues.

A new approach to peace—the "culture of peace" perspective—addresses gender in the context of violence. Analyzing the gendered nature of war and warriors, critics of world violence have dissected masculinity with the goal of changing how masculine identities and behaviors are developed and expressed, both at the microlevel in interpersonal relationships and at the international level as expressed in wars.[5] They have also examined women's roles and their potential for helping to create a more peaceful world.[6] Although many women have struggled to actively intervene in the interest of peace (see, for example, Gila Svirsky, this part), political scientist Cynthia Enloe believes that we have a long way to go before women can make a serious impact on moving the world away from militarization and toward peace: "At the opening of the new century, militarization continues to rely on women located in different social, economic, ideological, and cultural locations remaining uninformed about, unconnected to, or even hostile toward one another. The experiences of fragmentation have provided an incentive for some current feminists to expend more intellectual and organizing energy in understanding those differences and reducing the hostilities they can foment."[7]

Given the power of gender oppression and the other oppressions addressed in this book, there is no way to create a humane world unless many women and men are able to work within and across groups to fight for change that will benefit the largest number of people. Educators Rita Hardiman and Bailey Jackson have proposed a theory of stages of social identity development that helps me to think about this issue at both a personal and a collective level.[8] They argue that in order to struggle against oppression, people first need to have a critical analysis of oppressive aspects of the social order. Next, they need to gather with members of their own groups to solidify their identities independent of the systems of oppression. For people with privilege—who Hardiman and Jackson call agents—this means identifying their privilege and understanding how it contributes to the oppression of others. For people without privilege—who Hardiman and Jackson call targets—this means understanding how oppression has affected them, both externally and as internalized subordination. Given that most people experience a mix of privilege and oppression, and are therefore a combination of both targets and agents, the development of one's identity is a complex process.

Ultimately, Hardiman and Jackson suggest that once people have gained enough confidence in their awareness of their identities, having embraced both the privileged and the oppressed aspects of themselves, they will be in a position to work for social justice across the boundaries of identity and special interests. Instead of focusing only on the needs of their own group(s), they will be able to begin working in broad-based movements for social justice, understanding how others are oppressed, and building coalitions that have political clout. Oppression against anyone contributes to an unequal world. The writers in this book would ask us to use our sociological imaginations to understand the dimensions of oppression, work on our identities, become clear about using our privileges in ways designed to share the privilege, root out our internalized oppression, solidify our sense of pride and empowerment, and go about working creatively with other women and men to create peace in a world that is truly human.

In the preceding readings, we have heard from many people calling for change in specific areas. In this final section, we hear from several people working toward a more human world across various differences and in various ways. First is the Statement of Principles of the National Organization for Men Against Sexism. Next, Mark Anthony Neal calls for Black men to get on board with feminism. Then Daisy Hernández and Pandora Leong discuss the participation of young feminists of color in the women's movement. This is followed by Eisa Nefertari Ulen's call for a serious look at Islam from the perspective of a Black U.S. Muslim woman. This section closes with a description on women's peace activism in Israel by Gila Svirsky and a plea to treat women's rights as human rights by Rita Arditti.

In relation to this final set of readings, I suggest that you consider these questions: What, if anything, do you personally think should be done about the array of challenges presented in this book? Do the authors in this section offer any suggestions or approaches that make sense to you? Finally, as you think about the array of issues you have encountered in here, consider this question: If a human rights framework were to inform our approach to gender inequality, and if policy, law, and disciplinary action were brought to bear on violators of human rights, which of the gender inequalities addressed in this book might diminish or even disappear?

NOTES

1. Charlotte Bunch, "Women's Rights as Human Rights: Toward a Re Vision of Human Rights," in Charlotte Bunch and Roxanna Carrillo, *Gender Violence: A Development and Human Rights Issue* (New Brunswick, NJ: Center for Women's Global Leadership, 1991), p. 3.
2. Bunch, "Women's Rights," p. 7.
3. Bunch, "Women's Rights," pp. 10–13.

4. Susanna Kim, "Weary from War: Child Soldiers in the Congo," *Harvard International Review* 27, no. 4 (Winter 2006): 7–8.

5. Ingeborg Breines, Robert Connell, & Ingrid Eide, eds., *Male Roles, Masculinities and Violence: A Culture of Peace Perspective* (Paris: UNESCO, 2000).

6. Ingeborg Breines, Dorota Gierycz and Betty Reardon, eds., *Towards a Women's Agenda for a Culture of Peace* (Paris: UNESCO, 1999).

7. Cynthia Enloe, *Maneuvers: The International Politics of Militarizing Women's Lives* (Berkeley: University of California Press, 2000), p. 295.

8. Rita Hardiman and Bailey Jackson, "Conceptual Foundations for Social Justice Courses," in Maurianne Adams, Lee Ann Bell, and Pat Griffin, eds., *Teaching for Diversity and Social Justice: A Sourcebook* (New York: Routledge, 1997).

69

STATEMENT OF PRINCIPLES

NATIONAL ORGANIZATION FOR MEN AGAINST SEXISM

National Organization for Men Against Sexism www.nomas.org.

The National Organization for Men Against Sexism is an activist organization of men and women supporting positive changes for men. NOMAS advocates a perspective that is pro-feminist, gay-affirmative, and committed to justice on a broad range of social issues including race, class, age, religion, and physical abilities. We affirm that working to make this nation's ideals of equality substantive is the finest expression of what it means to be men.

We believe that the new opportunities becoming available to women and men will be beneficial to both. Men can live as happier and more fulfilled human beings by challenging the old-fashioned rules of masculinity that embody the assumption of male superiority.

Traditional masculinity includes many positive characteristics in which we take pride and find strength, but it also contains qualities that have limited and harmed us. We are deeply supportive of men who are struggling with the issues of traditional masculinity. As an organization for changing men, we care about men and are especially concerned with men's problems, as well as the difficult issues in most men's lives.

As an organization for changing men, we strongly support the continuing struggle of women for full equality. We applaud and support the insights and positive social changes that feminism has stimulated for both women and men. We oppose such injustices to women as economic and legal discrimination, rape, domestic violence, sexual harassment, and many others. Women and men can and do work together as allies to change the injustices that have so often made them see one another as enemies.

One of the strongest and deepest anxieties of most American men is their fear of homosexuality. This homophobia contributes directly to the many injustices experienced by gay, lesbian, and bisexual persons, and is a debilitating restriction for heterosexual men. We call for an end to all forms of discrimination based on sexual–affectional orientation, and for the creation of a gay-affirmative society.

We also acknowledge that many people are oppressed today because of their race, class, age, religion, and physical condition. We believe that such injustices are vitally connected to sexism, with its fundamental premise of unequal distribution of power.

Our goal is to change not just ourselves and other men, but also the institutions that create inequality. We welcome any person who agrees in substance with these principles to membership in the National Organization for Men Against Sexism.

70

NEW BLACK MAN

MARK ANTHONY NEAL

Mark Anthony Neal is associate professor of black popular culture in the Program in African and African-American Studies at Duke University. He is a regular commentator on NPR, and his blog can be found at *newblackman.blogspot.com*. He is author of *What the Music Said* (1999), *Soul Babies* (2002), and *Songs in the Key of Black Life* (2003) and co-editor of *That's the Joint: The Hip-Hop Studies Reader* (2004).

Why write a book like *New Black Man*? What's to be gained by calling forth a generation of pro-feminist, anti-homophobic, nurturing black men? Scholars all have an intellectual project, a basic issue that they seek to address during the course of their careers. My goal has always been to address the concept of black community. Although many have interpreted the fissures and crevices within the so-called black community (particularly in the post–civil-rights era) as evidence of weakness, I believe that a diversity of ideas and identities actually strengthens our communities. I've been committed to doing work that highlights the value of those who have been marginalized in our communities, including but not limited to black youth, black women (and black feminists in particular), and black gays and lesbians.

I've been equally committed to using my work and my civic voice to challenge the real violence—physical, rhetorical, and emotional—that we inflict on those marginalized bodies in our communities. It's not enough to close ranks around those who we marginalize; we need to take aim at the very forms of privilege that allow folks to continue to be marginalized. As a heterosexual black man in my late thirties, I have access to modes of privilege within black communities and the larger society, namely patriarchy and social status. These are privileges that many of those marginalized within our communities simply don't possess. *New Black Man* is my attempt to talk openly and honestly about those privileges, especially black male privilege, and to think out loud about the ways that black men can develop relationships with their mothers, daughters, sisters, friends, and colleagues that are pro-feminist and anti-sexist. There's no doubt in my mind that Black America must address sexism, misogyny, and homophobia at this point in our history. Below are just a few things for us to think about when pursuing the life of a *New Black Man*.

Understanding Black Male Privilege

Too often when I discuss black male privilege with black men, they fall back on defense mechanisms that highlight the effects of racism and unemployment in the lives of black men. There's no question that these issues are real challenges to black men, but just because black men are under siege in White America, it doesn't mean that they don't exhibit behaviors that do real damage to others, particularly within black communities. What many of these young men want to do is excuse the behavior of black men because of the extenuating circumstances under which black manhood is lived in our society. What they are suggesting is that black male behaviors that oppress women, children, and gays and lesbians in our community are understandable given the amount of oppression that some black men face from White America. This is unacceptable because one form of oppression cannot be used to justify another. Furthermore, it neglects the fact that others, some black women, for example, are also oppressed by White America because of their race and gender.

Countless conferences, books, pamphlets, articles, and online discussions are devoted to the crises that black men face, and the violence that is manifested against them, but there is comparatively little discussion of the very violence that black men often wield against black women. In fact, conversations about black male violence against black women and children are often interpreted as being part of the very racism that black men face. Those who speak out about black male violence are seen as traitors. We must get to a point where black male violence against black women, children, gays, and lesbians is openly challenged for what it is—behavior that is deeply harmful to the entire black community—and not just in the cases where the culprit is some young black male of the hip-hop generation. It has been too easy to blame the indiscretions and crimes of hip-hop generation figures like R. Kelly, Mystikal, or Tupac on the moral failings of the hip-hop generation, when we should be owning up to the fact that their behavior might have been influenced by their perceptions of how black male privilege operates in our communities.

Black Feminism Is Not the Enemy

One of the main attributes of black male privilege is the unwillingness or incapability to fully understand the plight of black women in our communities. Yes, there are acknowledgments of incidents where black woman are affected by blatant racism, but fewer when black women are affected because they are *black women* as opposed to being simply black people. Black feminism has sought to address this issue, creating a body of writings and activist events that highlight the conditions of black women globally. For example, it was not surprising that during the vice-presidential debate in October 2004 neither Vice-President Dick Cheney nor Democratic nominee John Edwards were aware that for black women between the ages of twenty-five and thirty-four,

HIV disease was the largest cause of death. Tellingly, the debate was hosted by television journalist Gwen Ifill, an African-American woman. Black feminism has sought to make such information available and a topic of conversation, especially among the black political leadership.

Much of the violence against black women happens close to home, so it shouldn't be surprising that black men come under close scrutiny and criticism by black feminism. Yes, some of the criticism is very angry, and admittedly not all of it is constructive (as with criticisms of white racism), but it is absolutely necessary in a society where black women's critical voices are so often silenced. For those black men who don't understand the anger that many black women feel toward them, it might be helpful to think about the amount of anger that many blacks still harbor toward whites, given the history of racism in this country. Indeed, some black men have oppressed black women in ways that closely resemble the historical oppression of blacks by whites in American society.

Very often those black men who are critical of feminism simply have not done their homework. They are responding to hearsay they've heard on call-in talk shows or read online, rather than actually reading any black feminist writings themselves. These men should check themselves, and check out a book by Audre Lorde, June Jordan, Barbara Christian, Pat Parker, Cheryl Clarke, Barbara Smith, Patricia Hill-Collins, Jewelle Gomez, Beverly Guy-Sheftall, Johnetta Cole, Cathy Cohen, Sharon Patricia Holland, Gwendolyn Pough, Joy James, and Alice Walker, Sonia Sanchez, Nikki Giovanni, and Masani Alexis DeVeaux—just a few of the women who have contributed to the body of literature known as Black Feminist Thought. Black feminism is wide ranging, and is concerned not only with dealing with violence against black women and girls, but also pressing issues of patriarchy, black women's healthcare, sex, and sexuality, black women's education, and racism. We do no justice to the legitimate issues that these women and others have raised if we don't seriously engage their work.

Black men also need to be serious about finding out the issues that affect the black women in their lives. For example, some studies have shown that eighty percent of black women in the United States will suffer from some form of fibroid disease and yet most black men are unaware of the fact, largely because they view it, like menstrual cycles, as simply a "woman's issue." Could we ever imagine a malady that affected eighty percent of all black men in the United States that the majority of black women would be unaware of? Of course not.

Real Black Men Are Not Homophobes

The prevailing notion on the ground is that real black men ain't "fags." This concept not only goes against any notion of community, it also simply isn't true. Black gay men have been valuable contributors to all aspects of black life in the United States. The same faulty logic that suggests real black men ain't "fags" also suggests that black women are lesbians because black men have failed to live up to some "Strong Black Man" ideal, as if black lesbians were solely motivated by their displeasure with black men as opposed to their own social, cultural, and sexual desires. In either case, the presence of black gays and lesbians is often interpreted as a sign of failed black masculinity.

It's time that we start championing a movement where "real black men are not homophobes," given the damage that homophobia does in our community. Such a movement would encourage black men to forcefully challenge homophobia wherever they encounter it, whether it's expressed as heterosexist jokes on the *Tom Joyner in the Morning Show,* BET's *Comic View,* or in the kinds of homophobic violence, rhetorical and literal, that circulate regularly in our churches, on college campuses, in barbershops, within hip-hop, and other institutions within black communities. It's not enough for us to simply eradicate homophobia in our own lives, we need to make the message loud and clear that homophobia is not welcome in our communities. We also need to think differently about black masculinity and understand that black men exhibit a range of attitudes and behaviors that don't always fit neatly into some mythical notion of a "Strong Black Man." We do incredible damage to ourselves and to those around us by submitting to an idea that there is some little box that all black men must fit into. We are bigger than that.

Real Black Fathers Are Loving Fathers

It has long been believed that the only responsibilities black men have in relation to their families are to provide financially and to dispense discipline. Although these are important aspects of parenting, this model of fatherhood does not allow black men to be emotionally available to their children and wives as nurturers. The idea that black men can be nurturers is often viewed skeptically, as evidence of some kind of weakness. Therefore, many black men who are unable to find work often think that they aren't good fathers because the only model of fatherhood they know is one where black men are, above all else, providers. I suspect this thinking can be directly correlated to the number of black men who have chosen to be involved in the illicit underground drug economy.

This narrow view of fatherhood can take men away from their sons and daughters by means of incarceration or worse, death, and it can prompt men to leave their families because they feel unfit as fathers if they fall upon hard times. We need black men to be there for their children, not just financially, but physically and emotionally. So it is crucial that we establish new rules of fatherhood that allow black men to be good fathers regardless of their temporary economic status.

Rethinking black fatherhood goes hand-in-hand with rethinking black masculinity. We need to applaud black fathers who see themselves as partners in the full range of parenting activities, and who take seriously their roles as nurturers. We need to build a model of black feminist fatherhood, one in which black men aren't just the protectors of their daughters, but also seriously consider how black girls and black women live in the world and the challenges and dangers that they are liable to face. In a world where young black girls are so often silenced and invisible, black fathers have a responsibility, along with black mothers, to create the spaces where the plight of black girls is taken seriously. This also requires sensitizing young black boys, both our sons and those that we come in contact with on a regular basis, to the importance of black girls and black women.

Hip-Hop Is Not the Enemy, but It Is a Problem

Like it or not, hip-hop is the soundtrack of black youth. It's been so easy to point to the moral failings of the hip-hop generation, particularly in relation to the sexism, misogyny, and homophobia that circulates in some of the music and videos, but those moral failings are often just a reflection of how the larger society and black communities think about black women, children, gays, and lesbians. Many criticisms of hip-hop simply deflect attention from equally disturbing practices within more traditional and acceptable black institutions. Too often, the criticisms of hip-hop are done without a real understanding of how ideas, knowledge, language, emotions, and relationships are cultivated by the hip-hop generation. It's not as if the hip-hop generation is beyond scrutiny, but if our elders are going to hold us accountable, they should at least make an effort to understand our worldview and the reasons why we make the choices we make. The world that the post–civil-rights generation(s) inhabits is fundamentally different from the one that produced the freedom movement of the 1950s and 1960s, and our elders need to acknowledge that fact. Our demons are not their demons, and our elders do us no good pretending that our current dilemma is somehow the product of our moral failings and our inability to pay homage to the freedom fighters who came before us. That said, the hip-hop generation also needs to appreciate the sacrifices made by our elders and accept that there are worthwhile lessons to be learned from their examples.

Just as hip-hop has been used to help politicize the hip-hop generation, it must also be used to create better gender relationships within the hip-hop generation. We need to make language available to young men in hip-hop that will help them rethink their gender politics. Young men often see hip-hop as a haven to articulate their frustrations with women—girlfriends, mothers, baby-mamas, groupies—but they are rarely capable of turning the critique upon themselves in order to interrogate their own roles in creating and maintaining dysfunctional relationships with women. The dialogue with young men is beginning in the work of black feminists of the hip-hop generation—Gwendolyn Pough and Joan Morgan come immediately to mind—and it is valuable work that I hope will continue to engage hip-hop music and those who listen and produce it, so that an honest conversation takes place, not just scolding and finger-wagging.

Young black women, of course, are also learning about and expressing their gender and sexuality through hip-hop. Talk about women and hip-hop, or hip-hop and gender, is often reduced to issues of misogyny and homophobia. Although these critiques *must* be made, the conversation typically remains focused on how men portray women in their lyrics and music videos. Rarely do we discuss how women use hip-hop to articulate their view of the world, a view that may or may not be predicated on what the men in hip-hop (or their lives) might be doing. For example, many black women hip-hop artists, scholars, and journalists speak about "desire" (sexual and otherwise) and the ways that women artists articulate desire in their art. Unfortunately, these issues are rarely discussed in mainstream discussions about hip-hop. Perhaps some of the critical energy focused so much on what black men in hip-hop are saying about women would be better spent by learning to listen to the voices of black women themselves.

Becoming a New Black Man

I am a man of my times, but the times don't know it yet!

Erik Todd Dellums as Bayard Rustin in *Boycott*

Finally, it is important the readers remember that I am not *the* New Black Man, but rather that the New Black Man is a metaphor for an imagined life—a way to be "strong" as a black man in new ways: strong commitment to diversity in our communities, strong support for women and feminism, and strong faith in love and the value of listening. I struggle, and often falter, to live up to these ideals every day of my life. It's a challenge, but one I know is well worth facing for myself, for my wife, and for my beautiful daughters. After reading these words, I hope you will join me, men and women, in making the New Black Man the man of our times.

71

FEMINISM'S FUTURE: YOUNG FEMINISTS OF COLOR TAKE THE MIC

DAISY HERNÁNDEZ • PANDORA L. LEONG

Daisy Hernández is *ColorLines* senior writer. Her writing focuses on race, gender, sexuality, and other issues affecting young women of color. She is the coeditor of *Colonize This! Young Women on Today's Feminism* (2002).

Pandora L. Leong directs the teen health initiative at the New York Civil Liberties Union. Her publications include "Living outside the Box" in *Colonize This! Young Women of Color on Today's Feminism* and "Virulent Virginity" (*ColorLines*, Winter 2005).

When San Jose State University senior Erika Jackson tried to recruit fellow women of color for a new feminist group on campus, the overwhelming reply was the sneer: "white women." Those words were code for another term: racist.

Many women of color, like their Anglo counterparts, eschew the term "feminism" while agreeing with its goals (the right to an abortion, equality in job hiring, girls' soccer teams). But women of color also dismiss the label because the feminist movement has largely focused on the concerns of middle-class white women. This has been a loss for people of color. Likewise, it's a loss for the movement if it expects to grow: the U.S. Census projects that the Latino and Asian-American population is expected to triple by 2050.

The "browning" of America has yet to serve as a wakeup call for feminist organizers. Attempts to address the racism of the feminist movement have largely been token efforts without lasting effects. Many young women of color still feel alienated from a mainstream feminism that doesn't explicitly address race. One woman of color, who wishes not to be identified and is working with the March for Women's Lives, put it this way: "We're more than your nannies and outreach workers. We're your future."

Progressive movements have a long history of internal debates, but for feminists of color the question of racism and feminism isn't about theories. It's about determining our place in the movement. As the daughters of both the civil rights and feminist movements, we were bred on grrlpower, identity politics, and the emotional and often financial ties to our brothers, fathers,

Daisy Hernández and Pandora L. Leong, "Feminism's Future: Young Feminists of Color Take the Mic," from *In These Times* 28, no. 12 (April 21, 2004): 32–33. Reprinted by permission.

aunties, and moms back home, back South, back in Pakistan, Mexico or other homelands. We live at the intersections of identities, the places where social movements meet, and it's here that our feminism begins.

Organizations as Obstacles

Feminism in the United States has stagnated in part because it has largely neglected a class and race analysis. Feminism can't survive by helping women climb the corporate ladder while ignoring cuts to welfare. Family and medical leave only matter if we have jobs with benefits. Feminism has to recruit beyond college campuses.

"If the message doesn't get broader, [communities of color] aren't going to open their arms," says Sang Hee Won of Family Planning Advocates in Albany, New York. "These issues don't resonate with an immigrant woman on the streets of New York City. I'm first generation. When I think of my parents, they have so many other things to think about. People are struggling with daily lives and it's especially hard to connect [traditional feminist] issues with their situation."

The priorities of national feminist organizations often are secondary to our daily struggles. Reproductive freedom has to include access to affordable healthcare and the economic opportunities to provide for the children some of us do want to have. Likewise, it's jarring to see the word "policing" on a feminist Web site and be directed to information on gender equity in police departments without mention of police brutality.

For feminists of color to identify with the mainstream movement, national organizations need to address race explicitly. Women of color always have participated but largely have remained ignored. Organizations purport to be aware but don't hire, promote, or recognize women of color as leaders. Affinity groups and special projects remain ghettoized add-ons.

"[Feminist organizations] try and are well-intentioned," says Lauren Martin, a New York activist. "They talk a lot but don't do a lot. Organizations I've worked with talk a lot about being anti-racist. [There would be] lots of trainings and in-services, but [racist] incidents that occurred would be brushed under the rug."

"Their attitude is, 'I'm going to empower you. I'm going to teach you,'" says Alma Avila-Pilchman, program manager at ACCESS, a reproductive rights organization in Oakland, California. "When the truth is we already have that power. We need to use it. We need to be listened to."

Change in Leadership

The young feminists of color we interviewed called for the inclusion of women of color and low-income women in national campaigns—when the agenda is being set.

"Forming a real coalition means starting from the very beginning rather than the 'add and stir' approach," Martin says. "The beginning is when issues are defined. It doesn't work to tack our perspective on at the end and call it 'outreach.'"

Khadine Bennett, a board member of Third Wave Foundation, which supports the activism of young women, says that feminist organizations need to share their power. "Sometimes your organization is not the best one to carry out the work," she says. "Part of the mandate from funders should be to work with people of color organizations."

More than 30 years after the first charges of racism against the movement, these young feminists believe progressive women of color need to be the leaders of national feminist groups. That the executive directors of these organizations and senior staff still are overwhelmingly white testifies to the movement's division. The professionalization of the nonprofit world has deepened this divide by internalizing corporate expectations and marginalizing the involvement of women who can't afford to work for free. In pursuit of mainstream acceptance, organizations are losing touch with the grassroots that could revive feminism. There needs to be a commitment to leadership development among women of color and low-income women that includes mentoring and training.

Seeking Common Cause

The movement also should consider models already practiced by younger activists who actively seek out coalitions. "The people I know are working around anti-violence including sexuality and antiwar work and anti-globalization," says Mina Trudeau, of Hampshire College's Civil Liberties and Public Policy Program. "Our feminism is about social justice."

Election years are good moments to broaden an organization's agenda. Last fall, Erika Jackson's feminist campus group organized against Proposition 54, which would have eliminated racial classifications in California. They were the first student organization to tackle the issue, and they didn't debate whether it was a feminist issue.

"Like with public health, we talked about how it affects women of color," she says. A lack of racial classifications would hide the higher rate of low birth weight babies born to women of color. The measure was defeated in the November 2003 state election.

Leah Lakshmi Piepzna-Samarasinha, a Toronto-based spoken-word artist, sees race as a central part of the work she did in counseling women who have suffered from sexual abuse and racism. "You can't deal with the abuse and not the colonialism," she says of her work with Native American women. Healing, she adds, can often mean reconnecting to cultural pride.

Avila-Pilchman has talked to women of color "who've given up on working with white women." However, she doesn't fall into that category.

"I don't think that all white women don't want to work with us. I can't think that. But how is it going to happen? When?"

These are questions the mainstream feminist movement must answer, and some are hopeful.

Trudeau observes, "There is new visioning. Maybe this happens at all different points but at this time, we're conscious of our history and of where we want to go. I think there's some back and forth, an internal dialogue that will hopefully take us to a better place."

72

TAPPING OUR STRENGTH

EISA NEFERTARI ULEN

Eisa Nefertari Ulen responded to September 11 with "Muslims in the Mosaic," which originally appeared in *Essence* magazine and was anthologized by Robert Atwan in *America Now*. Her essay "Tapping Our Strength" was included in Lee Gutkind's Living Issue Project on CreativeNonFiction.org. Other essays have appeared in several anthologies, and Eisa has contributed to the *Washington Post, Ms., Health,* and *Azizah*. A member of the English department faculty at New York City's Hunter College, she was awarded a 2004 Presidential Award for Teaching. Eisa lives with her husband in Fort Greene, Brooklyn.

I walk with women draped in full-length fabric. We swirl through the delicate smell of incense and oil filling air around the mosque. Even as the mad Manhattan streets overflow with noise, we sisters rustle past the crisp ease of brothers in pressed cotton tunics and loose-fitting pants, past tables of over-garments and woven caps, Arabic books, and Islamic tapes. Our scarves flap and wave in bright color or sober earth tones above an Upper East Side sidewalk that is transformed, every Friday, into a bazaar— the sandy souk reborn on asphalt.

Worshippers walk through a stone gate, along a path, and into a room unadorned yet filled with spiritual energy. Women and men lean to remove their shoes where rows of slippers, sandals, heels, and sneakers line the entrance hall. White walls bounce light onto the high ceiling. Men sit in rows along the carpeted floors, shifting in silence as we file past them, up the stairs and to a loft where other women sit and wait. "As salaam u alaikum." "Wa alaikum as salaam." "Kaifa halak—how are you, sister?" "Al humdilillah—praise be to God—I am well."

Soon the imam's voice begins to resonate in the hushed rooms. Contemplative quiet focuses communal piety. The cleric speaks in Arabic, then in English, building ideas about a complete way of life. About an hour later, when he concludes, a chanting song, lyrical poetry, calls the Muslims to prayer. We women stand tall, shoulder to shoulder, forming ranks, facing Mecca, kneeling down and then forward in complete submission to Allah, our faces just tapping the prayer rug.

And our ranks are growing. Islam is the second most popular religion in the world, with over one billion Muslims forming a global Umma (community) that represents about 23 percent of the world's population. In virtually every country of Western Europe, Islam is now the second religion after Christianity. There are approximately six million Muslims in the U.S. today, and about 60 percent or so are immigrants. About 30 percent of the remaining American-Muslim population are African-American, with U.S.-born Latinos and Asian-Americans making up the 10 percent difference. There are now more Muslims in the U.S. than Jews, and the numbers of new shahadas and Muslim immigrants continue to rise. Islam is even changing the way the United States sounds, as the azan converges with church bells, calling Muslims to prayer five times a day. Words of worship are filling the air with Arabic all across America. This country will increasingly need to explore gender, generation, politics, and plurality from an Islamic perspective. The veiled lives of American Muslim women, so often garbled into still passivity, pulsate with social ramifications.

So how will pluralistic America shift and groan under the weight of this new diversity? What happens when uber-girrrl in spiked heels and spiked hair turns the corner on her urban street and peers into the wide eyes of a woman whose face is covered with cloth? What happens when uber-girrrl's daughter brings home a friend who has two mommies—and one daddy? Under what terms do we launch that dialogue of encounter? Are women who insist on wearing hijab unselfconsciously oppressed, or—particularly in the land that gave birth to wet T-shirt contests—are they performing daily acts of resistance by covering their hair? In the West, where long blond tresses signify a certain power through sexuality and set the standard for beauty, are veiled women the most daring revolutionaries? In workplaces, where anything less than full assimilation is dismissed, are women who quietly refuse to uncover actually storming the gates for our own liberation? Is liberation possible within the veil? American feminists would do well to engage these and other questions, and then again to engage what may seem the easy answers.

I am peering outward, clustered with sisters in scarves. And I am also aligned with women sporting spikes. I am a Muslim woman. I am also a womanist, a feminist rooted in the traditions of Sistah Alice Walker. I run those mad Manhattan streets, contribute my own voice to the cacophony; I also sit in focused silence, shifting space to embrace the presence of my many-hued sisters. I celebrate the sanctity of varicolored flesh, of difference, that is celebrated in Islam. And I am also an ardent advocate of Black Empowerment, of Uplift, of Pride—I am a Race Woman.

When non-Muslims ask how a progressive womanist sistah like me could convert to Islam, I tell them Muslim women inherited property, participated in public life, divorced their husbands, worked and controlled the money they earned, even fought on the battlefield—1,400 years ago. When Muslims ask how a woman who submits to Allah like me could still be feminist, I tell them the same thing and add that modern realities too often fall short of the Islamic ideal. The Qur'an was revealed because Arabs were burying their newborn daughters in the sand, because Indians were burning their wives for dowry, because Europeans were keeping closet mistresses in economic servitude, because Africans were mutilating female genitals, and because the Chinese word for woman is slave. Obviously, these forms of violence against women continue, very often at the hands of Muslim women and men. The presence of patriarchal, sanctioned assaults against women and girls anywhere in the global Ummah horrifies me, particularly because I recognize these atrocities as anti-Islamic.

Contrary to popular opinion among non-Muslims, the Qur'an rejects the sexist propaganda that Eve is the first sinner who tempted Adam and led him to perdition. Both are held responsible for their exploits in the garden. Muslims believe Islam is the perpetuation—the refinement—of monotheistic religion and admonishes the persecution of people on the basis of gender, race, and class. Non-Muslims often confuse sexist individuals or groups with an entire religious system—and a cross-racial, multicultural swath of the world's population gets entangled in the inevitable stereotypes.

This political irresponsibility is dangerous especially because Islam is the sustenance more and more women feel they need. Indeed, while American women were publicly calling for more foreplay a few decades ago, Islam sanctioned equal pleasure in spouses' physical relationship—again, 1,400 years ago. Muslim men actually receive Allah's blessing when they bring their wives to orgasm.

Knowing many Muslim women are cutting their daughters, I celebrate Islam and teach to raise awareness about the culturally manifested, pre-Islamic practice of female genital mutilation, which is falsely considered an Islamic practice worldwide. I feel the same passionate need for widespread truth and empowerment when I read about women across this country knifing their breasts and hips and faces in the name of Western-inspired beautification. Fellow feminists too often allow difference to impede a coalition based on these virtual duplications, on this cross-cultural torture. My Muslim sisters too often think feminism is a secular evil that would destroy the very foundations of our faith. This is all a waste. While we allow difference to divide us, women everywhere are steadily slicing into their own flesh—and into the flesh of emergent women around them.

Any concerted efforts to link and liberate on the part of American feminists must proceed from factual knowledge of the veiled "other." Immigrant Muslim women must begin to align themselves with non-Muslim-American women, even as they maintain their *deen* (religion) and their home culture. Increasing conversion in this country demands U.S. citizens interested in women's freedom begin to understand why women like myself have chosen Islam.

I became Muslim because the Qur'an made sense, because my mind and spirit connected. Islam is a thinking chick's religion. Education is more than just a privilege in Islam; it is a demand. Qur'anic exhortations to reflect and understand highlight each Muslim's duty to increase in knowledge, a key component of this *deen,* this religion, where science especially supports a better understanding of spirit. Islam makes no distinction between women and men and access to knowledge, though some men would deny women's Islamic right to education, just as men in America have historically denied women the opportunity to learn.

The more I think about feminism and Islam, the more compatibility emerges from the dust of difference, and the more potential I see. I want to reconcile the great gulf that all my sisters—American non-Muslims who can't get past the *hijab* and American Muslims who can't get past secularism—see when they peer (usually past) "the other." I understand my Muslim sisters' trepidation, because first wave feminism's relationship with African-Americans lacked a cohesion born of acute commitment and fell victim to white supremacist techniques. Likewise, second wave feminism fell victim to the science of divide and conquer. Daring individuals pushed past division, though. They leaped over the great gulfs system controllers contrived to separate abolition and suffrage, Black Power and Women's Lib, and embraced a decidedly universal freedom. I am still slightly shocked when Muslims and non-Muslims claim I can not be both Muslim and feminist. I am leaping the great abyss dividing submission (to Allah) and resistance (to patriarchy) in this increasingly complex place called America. We must build bridges.

We must build cross-cultural, multi-ethnic bridges. Now, especially now, I ask my African-American sistahs to remember our legacy of domestic terrorism, of white sheets streaking by on horseback, of strange fruit, of Black men burned alive, of four little girls. Now, more than ever, we must remember the centuries of domestic terrorism in this country, but we must also remember this: that countless white women were our sisters in fighting the horror and pain their fathers and brothers wrought. We must remember this, too: We must remember the white men appalled by the terrorism of white supremacists, the white men who battled their own souls. We must allow these memories to help form a link connecting non-Muslims with Muslims in the country today. I am asking women to remember today. I am asking you.

I am ready to do this important new work. Islam fuels my momentum. I empower myself when I wash and wrap for prayer. I transform out of a space belonging to big city chaos and into a space conjuring inner peace. I renew. With the ritual Salaat, I generate serenity. I can create and channel strong energy as I pray.

Although I only cover for prayer, I deeply admire women who choose to outwardly manifest their connection to the Divine within. I want more non-Muslims to understand veiled Muslim women and respect them for celebrating Islamic creed, for resisting overwhelming economic forces in this country, for not succumbing to the images captured in high fashion gloss. By living in constant alignment with faith, they challenge the misogynist systems that compel too many Western women and girls to binge, purge, and starve themselves. For these pious sisters, plain cloth is the most meaningful accessory they could ever wear. To me, American Muslim women who choose to cover undeniably act out real life resistance to the hyper-sexualization of girls and women in the West. In the context of consumerist America, women who cover express power of intellect over silhouette, of mind over matters of the flesh.

Because I move in non-Muslim circles, I hear too many of my fellow feminists focus on *hijab,* urging complete unveiling as the key to unleashing an authentic liberation. For them, scarves strangle any movement toward Muslim women's emancipation. I ask them to just imagine 1,400 years—generations—of women moving without bustles, hoops, garters, bustiers, corsets, zippers, pantyhose, buckles, belts, pins, and supertight microminis. The way I see it, Western men wear comfortable shoes and slacks while women are pinned, underwired, heeled, and buttoned to psychological death. We American women still strangle ourselves every day we get up and get dressed for work.

Ah, you say—but even in their loose garb, Muslim women are still, so, so . . . passive. But Muslim women are not silent, not sitting still. We do not require American pity. We take the very best America has to offer. We are moving our bodies. As American women wow the world with unleashed athletic excellence in the WNBA, women's soccer, bob sledding, and pole vaulting, Muslim-American women are running and kicking along that mainstream—in full *hijab* or not. For Muslim immigrants who hail from nations that denied women access to physical movement, this country has freed them to pilot their own bodies. Many American Muslims are destroying the cultural forces that chained them while remaining true to the essence of Islam.

I remember hearing Sister Ama Shabazz, a bi-racial Muslim educator and lecturer (her mother is Japanese-American and her father is African-American) urging a large group of Muslim women to take swimming classes and learn CPR to satisfy the Shariah (Islamic law) not to defy it. (Anecdotes can be so helpful sometimes.) A friend of mine, whose mother immigrated to this country from Colombia, wears long loose clothing to the gym three days a week, then washes to cover and go home. An African-American girlfriend of mine rollerblades through her Bedford Stuyvescent neighborhood, full *hijab* blowing through her own body's wind.

These women fiercely assert Islam even though they have felt American hands tug at their clothing, especially since 9/11. They are obviously Muslim even though non-Muslims hurl offensive epithets or gestures at them.They do not cower. "It takes a warrior to be a Muslim woman," says another friend, a New Yorker born and bred Dominican. I agree with her.

Yet there is so much promise in the future: I know two Muslim high school students of mixed Iraqi/Indian heritage who play tennis in traditional whites and have earned black belts in karate. One even coaches the boys' basketball team. Interestingly, their immigrant mother could not wear blue jeans because her father forbade it. Certainly some men are still using women to assert a political agenda via Islam. I recoil when I see young Muslim girls in full *hijab* while their brothers skip beside them in shorts and t-shirts. I think about the women I know who cover themselves and their daughters for the wrong reason, and then I remember I know some women who wear push up bras for the same wrong reason: to please men.

We must recognize that the similarities in our oppression as women far outweigh the differences in the ways that oppression manifests. And to do that we must fuse our stories. Like African-American women who have fought to wear locks and braids and naturals on the job—or have fought to use relaxers without the ultra-righteous disparaging them as loser sell-outs—Muslim women have had to fight to wear *hijab* here. For everything from job security to an American passport photo, Muslim women have been asked to uncover. At root, we are all denied our right to represent an authentic self by these predominant cultural and social forces.

The last place we women of all faiths need to suffer the indignity of judgment based solely on outward appearance is in the company of other women. Right now, half of American non-Muslim women encourage other women to be free by being naked, and the other half desperately tries to get women and girls to cover up. Meanwhile, the men simply get dressed in the morning. Likewise, Muslim women who wear *hijab* are automatically considered unhappy, while men who wear turbans and long loose clothing are just considered Muslim.

Non-Muslim women need to stop telling Muslim women their traditional Islamic garb symbolizes oppression. Muslim women need to open themselves to coalitions with women in mini-skirts. Only then will we work successfully toward a world where all women can truly wear what they feel. Ultimately, societies grant men much more freedom in clothing. Perhaps this is the point from which our discussion should launch.

We must begin to think more critically, and honestly, about media representations of all women. While Muslim immigrants need to reconsider the East's portrayal of American women as loose and wild, feminists need to check their sweeping generalizations about the seemingly inherent violence and suppression the media projects as Islam.

Since the 1970s America has slowly shifted evil empire status from the former Soviet Union to the site of underground power, where black, slick, liquid energy fuels America's Middle East policy. Americans have been taught to fear the Arab world so that America can easily justify killing Arabs. Images of Middle Eastern men in the state of *jihad* demonized the people of an entire region. But the only legitimate Islamic war is a war waged in self-defense—the other guy must be the clear aggressor. And the direct translation of *jihad* is struggle, while the primary focus of that struggle is within. We must remember this as we watch our evening news, as we watch bombs fall from U.S. planes. We must remember this as we vote.

American feminists should not join the Pentagon and media in denigrating veiled women and our faith as archaic, out-of-touch, regressive. This is part of the propaganda of fear America needs to perpetuate in order to maintain world dominance. This country takes the very universal problem of sexism and often presents it as if it were exclusively a Muslim issue, as when non-Muslims degrade Islam for allowing men to marry up to four wives, even as American men practice their own kind of polygamy—via mistresses, madams, and baby's-mammas. Who are we to judge? After all, while the United States has never had a woman president, Pakistan, Turkey, and Bangladesh—all Muslim countries—have had female heads of state.

Of course, as Jane Smith of the Hartford Seminary says, "I think you'd have to be blind not to see things going on in the Islamic world—and in the name of Islam—that are not Islamic." Muslim women would do well to remember that the Hadith (sayings of Prophet Muhammad) have been interpreted to give men powerful social advantages over women, and that there are men, and women complicit in their own oppression, who use Islam as justification for misogyny.

Certainly the 9/11 attacks were not Islamic. Islam means peace. We greet each other with peace. Islam is no more violent than Christianity. Yet there have been American Christian networks formed to throw bombs—at abortion clinics. When have you ever heard the term Christian terrorist? We Americans do not profile white men with crew cuts, but a white man in a crew cut bombed the federal office building in Oklahoma City. Certainly we should not denigrate Christianity—and Christians—because of the few who would use their faith as a justification for violence. Why has it been easy for white Americans to turn on their own darker brothers?

Maybe we simply need to understand each other. Certainly America needs to begin the work necessary to understand Islam. El Hajj Malik El Shabazz said in his letter from Mecca, "America needs to understand Islam, because it is the one religion that erases from its society the race problem." Back at the Islamic Cultural Center in Manhattan, when the congregational Jummah prayer concludes, chatter fills the once hushed room as women and men prepare to leave. They step off the carpet, slip on their shoes, and the women readjust their *hijabs*. Vari-colored Indian and Pakistani sisters toss beautifully brilliant cloth sari-style. Olive-skinned Arab sisters check the pin securing the cotton scarves underneath their chins. Deep brown African sisters toss oversized lightweight cloth in their handbags, revealing their artfully wrapped gelees. And some women—of all colors and nationalities—take their *hijab* off completely, now that prayer has ended. This dynamic diversity might just be what the next wave of American feminism needs.

Muslim women and men are active forces in many different struggles, just as Western feminists struggle against misogynist forces. As a Muslim brother of mine once reminded me, race is just a smokescreen. Gender is just a smokescreen. Religion is just a smokescreen. These are tools of the oppressor used to separate and slay as he takes.

We have so much work to do. I chose Islam for the wonder of the word, because I believe in the five pillars of the faith, because I love Allah and justice. I have been blessed to bear witness to women's realities in what people think of as two different worlds, and I have seen that those realities are essentially the same.

I bear witness to the woman beaten by her lover in the street outside my Brooklyn apartment—and to the woman tied to a Nigerian whipping post. I bear witness to the woman forced to strip to survive in Atlanta—and the woman forced to cover to survive in Afghanistan. I bear witness to the ever-increasing legions of women caught in this country's prison industrial complex, often because of their associations with husbands and male lovers—and I bear witness to the women struggling against inequity in interpretations of the Shariah in Islamic courtrooms. How do we measure a veiled woman's pain? Does it weigh more or less than the trauma in an American woman's eyes? Should we compare and contrast the horror, brutality, and hard smack against a woman's cheek?

I simply ask that we warrior women, Muslim and non-Muslim, stand shoulder to shoulder, forming ranks, bending forward to carry all our sisters, Muslim and non-Muslim, tapping our collective strength.

73

THE WOMEN'S PEACE
MOVEMENT IN ISRAEL

GILA SVIRSKY

Gila Svirsky is a veteran peace and human rights activist in Israel and has headed some of the major peace and human rights organizations there. She has been a member of Women in Black since its inception and is cofounder of the Coalition for Peace, which engages in dramatic acts of resistance to end Israel's occupation of the Palestinian territories. She is the recipient of several peace prizes. http://www.gilasvirsky.com/.

> *We are having a terrible day today. While we were demonstrating at our regular Women in Black square (30–40 people in all), we were bombed on both sides. It felt like being targeted from up close. We had to abandon the vigil and look for shelter. We came back 20 minutes later and completed the vigil on time. As we were traveling home, there was a second attack and we had to stop the car and look for shelter . . . [Now] I am off to our daily demonstration of Women Against War in front of the Foreign Office and the foreign press. We will not be silenced.*
>
> E-MAIL FROM *HANNAH SAFRAN, JULY 21, 2006*

The women's peace movement in Israel has always been marked by dramatic actions, but those undertaken to end the Lebanon War in 2006 were extraordinary. In the midst of shelling and a brick wall of Israeli support for the war, the women of the peace movement were loud, outspoken, and gutsy. "Children in Beirut and Haifa ALL want to live" was a slogan we commonly used. "May all your children be killed in the war!" was the response of more than one passerby.

The Israeli women's peace movement pulls together and works in unison during extreme circumstances, such as the Lebanon War or the siege of Gaza, both in 2006. But during days of "normal" conflict with the Palestinians, the movement spans a wide variety of creative efforts for ending the occupation and achieving peace.

Gila Svirsky, "The Women's Peace Movement in Israel" (2007). Reprinted with the permission of the author.

A Profusion of Activities

The Coalition of Women for Peace is composed of ten different women's peace organizations in Israel, each with its own strategy and target audience (http://coalitionofwomen.org/home). The Coalition speaks for the women's peace movement as a whole and has its own range of activities: It conducts mass rallies and demonstrations; it organizes bus tours of the occupied territories, urgent-action e-mail lists, and trilingual websites to mobilize international opinion; and it participates in direct action in the Occupied Territories.

Much of the Coalition's nonviolent resistance has included acts declared illegal by the authorities, such as "laying siege" to the Israeli Ministry of Defense. Some actions are carried out together with mixed-gender peace organizations, such as rebuilding Palestinian homes that the Israeli army demolished or removing blockades and filling in trenches intended to constrain Palestinian travel. Women have blocked bulldozers with their bodies, chained themselves to olive trees, and confronted soldiers in efforts to prevent further destruction of Palestinian homes and property. Much joint work has also been done with Palestinian women to prevent construction of the so-called security wall. Some of the Coalition's actions have ended in arrests, and many ended in injury to protesters at the hands of Israeli forces.

The women's peace movement has also engaged in humanitarian aid as a political statement: helping Palestinian families with the olive harvest; providing school supplies, infant food, sanitary napkins, and other needs. Sadly, we generally have to struggle with the Israeli army to allow aid to enter the Palestinian areas.

The Coalition has also held some dramatic public actions within Israel. Three months after the current Intifadah began in fall 2000, 5,000 Israeli and Palestinian women marched together from the Israeli to the Palestinian side of Jerusalem under the banner "We Refuse to be Enemies." We held a concert for peace, featuring Israeli and Palestinian women performing works that express our common longing for peace. We organized a cavalcade of cars that drove through Israel bearing signs like "The Price of the Occupation is Too High!" We staged a mass "die-in" in Tel Aviv: 1,000 women dressed in black lying flat out on the hot summer pavement under the banner "The Occupation is Killing Us All." We have held "walking exhibitions," holding blown-up photos of the carnage in Gaza for theatergoers to see as they stand in line to buy tickets. As the violence continues, we wrack our brains to come up with new ways of waking up other Israelis.

One new and promising strategy is a campaign we call "Reframing Security." This campaign aims to broaden the understanding of security in Israel to include all aspects of "human security"—a society that cares for its poor, reduces violence, protects its natural resources, and co-exists in peace with its neighbors. Indeed, this campaign seeks to instill the understanding that "peace is the best way to promote security." The Reframing Security campaign reflects a shift of strategy for us, as we invest our best efforts in outreach to populations that do not share our views, engaging them in ways we hope will change their minds.

A Broad Social Vision

Ideologically, the organizations of the Coalition of Women for Peace hold a broader social vision than that of the mixed-gender peace organizations. We view the conflict as integrally related to social, economic, and gender issues. Indeed, the conflict with the Palestinians directly affects both gender inequality and oppression of the poor. Regarding gender inequality, in a society at war—where it is predominantly the men who are risking their lives in army service and making military and political decisions—men and their views become valued and privileged over women and our views. This entrenches inequality for women, leaving us at a disadvantage in competing for jobs, political office, and social status. The conflict also deepens poverty, as Israel sinks vast resources into illegal settlements and the military occupation at the expense of housing, education, health, care for the elderly, and other social needs inside Israel. And since women are more likely to find themselves among the poor, they become the first victims of unemployment and recession.

While ending the conflict is important for its own sake—to protect men and women on both sides—it is also important for the sake of the equality of women and allowing Israel to address all the socio-economic and environmental issues that have been marginalized in the face of the conflict.

Four Mothers

The most successful peace movement ever in Israel was a women's organization—the Four Mothers Movement. This group, founded in 1997 by four women whose sons served in the Israeli occupation of southern Lebanon, sought to mobilize the Israeli public to demand that Israel withdraw its troops from Lebanon on the grounds that Israel's prolonged presence there served no security purpose and jeopardized the lives of soldiers. The movement was initially met with scorn from senior military officers. "What do women know about security?" they jeered. Indeed, at the heart of the Four Mothers' strategy was the leveraging of their status as mothers. This was effective in a society that may disrespect professional women, but honors its mothers. The Four Mothers Movement never used civil disobedience but rather held small demonstrations and vigils that highlighted the sincerity of their plea as law-abiding women, not activists or politicians. Their status as mothers who had sons serving in combat units gave them the right, in the eyes of the public, to challenge Israeli policy in Lebanon. They demanded— and were accorded—meetings with the highest government officials, whose inadequate answers were then magnified through the well-run media work of this group. The mother-oriented nature of this movement, and its dissociation from partisan politics, struck an empathetic nerve among the Israeli public. The deaths of Israeli soldiers were on the increase in Lebanon, and the message of the Four Mothers fell on attentive ears, feeding public dismay over the seemingly endless body bags. When some generals weighed in on the mothers' side, the tide was reversed. Within three years of the start of the movement, the Israeli army withdrew from Lebanon.

The Four Mothers Movement disbanded in 2000 upon the Israeli evacuation of its troops from Lebanon. Avowedly non-feminist and non-radical, the women in this movement successfully exploited the traditional role of motherhood to buttress their emotional appeal. And yet, scratching the surface reveals that a large proportion of the activists were themselves feminists, progressives, and professional women—and highly skilled at using the media. The apparent success of this movement deserves careful analysis: The peace movement may have paid a high price for exalting women as mothers rather than thinkers and doers. Is it possible that women, a group that often includes people particularly skilled at bridge-building, will continue to be kept away from the peace negotiation tables around the world because we exploit our maternal image?

Pariahs or Prophets?

The women's peace movement in Israel has consistently articulated progressive positions—well before the mixed-gender peace movement adopted them. Women advocated a two-state solution, sharing Jerusalem, and returning to Israel's 1967 border long before other peace movements reached these conclusions. These views are today rapidly approaching consensus within Israel, but when we first uttered them, we were branded "pariahs"—the title of the only article in an Israeli magazine that ever featured our movement.

The women's peace movement continues to assume unpopular positions: encouraging young people to refuse to serve in an army of occupation, labeling as "war crimes" some military actions, advocating against the so-called "security fence," refusing to go along with the prevalent military culture. Our actions are often imaginative and original in a relentless effort to arouse media interest and win public sympathy. Women have also proven to be steadfast activists, maintaining the Women in Black vigil every single week for some 20 years.

Women constitute the majority of participants even in the mixed-gender peace movement, though they rarely become the decision-makers in these groups. And I would be remiss if I did not also mention that lesbians are disproportionately represented throughout the peace and human rights community.

Above all, women in both Israel and Palestine have crossed the great divide, forging a peace agreement decades before the Rabin-Arafat talks and maintaining their links with each other despite the Palestinian suicide-bombings, the Israeli bombardments, and all the lives lost and destroyed. The feminist principles of an egalitarian world and the nonviolent resolution of conflict have been at the core of our commitment, enabling Israeli and Palestinian women to sustain our alliance for peace despite the bitter reality outside and the pressures within our own societies.

74

WOMEN'S HUMAN RIGHTS
It's about Time!

RITA ARDITTI

Rita Arditti is professor emerita of the Graduate College of the Union Institute and University. She was born and grew up in Argentina and lives in the United States. She has been active in the women's movement since the late sixties and learned about human rights doing support work for the Argentine human rights movement in the eighties. She is the author of *Searching for Life: The Grandmothers of the Plaza de Mayo and the Disappeared Children of Argentina* (1999).

> *The advancement of women and the achievement of equality between women and men are a matter of human rights and a condition for social justice and should not be seen in isolation as a women's issue. They are the only way to build a sustainable, just and developed society. Empowerment of women and equality between women and men are prerequisites for achieving political, social, economic, cultural and environmental security among all peoples.*
>
> PLATFORM FOR ACTION, ARTICLE 41,
> FOURTH WORLD CONFERENCE ON WOMEN, BEIJING, 1995.

At the first meeting of a five-day seminar on Women and Human Rights that I was leading for doctoral students, one of the two men attending expressed deep skepticism about the need to discuss Human Rights through the lens of women's experiences. Didn't the Universal Declaration of Human Rights apply to everybody? Didn't Article 1

Rita Arditti, "Women's Human Rights: It's about Time!" (2005). Reprinted with the permission of the author.

of the Declaration state that "All human beings are born free and equal in dignity and rights?" So, what was the fuss all about? Why was Women and Human Rights even a topic worthy of exploration? As far as he was concerned, we would be wasting our time.

When I recovered from my surprise at his attitude I offered a "yes, but . . ." answer, that got me more or less intact through that first session. For the rest of the seminar, however, his questions stayed with me, forcing me to clarify, expand, examine, and connect in new ways each single topic discussed. By the end of the seminar, I was happy to hear that he had changed his mind. He found the seminar to be a mind expanding experience and expressed his appreciation for the new insights he gathered. I believe that the shock I had because of his bluntness at the beginning of the seminar forced me to dig deeper and do a better job. For that, I thank him.

I hope that this article will be useful to others who, like him, have questions about the relevance of the topic and to those who already believe that women's rights must be an integral part of the human rights paradigm and want to convince others to join them in this belief.

The Universal Declaration of Human Rights

The Universal Declaration of Human Rights, adopted in 1948 by the United Nations starts by asserting that freedom, justice, and peace in the world depend upon the recognition of human dignity and the rights of all members of the human family.[1] It then goes on to spell out a variety of political, civic, social, cultural and economic rights in its 30 articles. Political and civic rights have received most of the attention in the West, while economic, social, and cultural rights have been seen with suspicion, as if not fully qualifying as human rights. For people in the global South, however, this distinction does not make sense and it is because of their unrelenting insistence that now official UN circles have started more and more to pay attention to those rights.

According to the Declaration, all human beings have "inherent dignity," are "born free and equal," are "endowed with reason and conscience," and are "entitled to all the rights and freedoms set forth in this Declaration." Rights are not earned or conferred; they are part and parcel of the human condition. We have those rights by the very fact of our existence, simply because we are born, and the respect for those rights is considered essential to create a free, just, and peaceful world. Moreover, human rights are seen as indivisible and interdependent—they constitute a whole where each right is linked to the others and necessary for the full realization of the principles embodied in the Declaration.

Yes, my learner was right, the Declaration (and later UN documents since 1948) in its final written form, applies to all human beings. However, since its inception, the Declaration has struggled with the issue of women and its inclusion in the human rights framework.[2] Language was one of the first important issues that needed to be addressed. Originally article 1 read *"All men are brothers . . ."* Hansa Mehta, a legislator from India and a member of the Human Rights commission working on the Declaration, fought against the use of exclusionary language and warned the commission that the wording in article 1 would be construed so as to exclude women.[3] She eventually convinced her colleagues and in 1948, at the last meeting of the Commission, *"All human beings"* was the term accepted, though strangely enough the rest of the Declaration remains written in non-inclusive language ("man," "brotherhood," "his," "him").

Indeed, a brief history of the rights of women in the United Nations reveals that though equality between the sexes was asserted in the basic human rights documents, in practice women's rights were marginalized and not considered part of the human rights paradigm.[4] It was not until 1979, when the United Nations adopted the Convention on the Elimination of All Forms of Discrimination Against Women (CEDAW), that the rights of women were finally enshrined in the transnational human rights perspective.

Feminists from around the world were of course interested in the human rights conversation at the international level and participated and followed it attentively from its beginning. There is now a vast literature on women and human rights from legal and activist perspectives at the international and local levels. In this article I can simply mention a few of the many contributions that I have found especially useful because of the clarity with which they express the author's viewpoints and because they seem representative of many of the discussions held through the years.

Are Human Rights Only for Men?

When feminists started to question the lack of attention to women's rights in the human rights paradigm and asserted that women's rights were not those of a "special" interest group but belonged at the center of the human rights conversation, they identified at least three themes that threw some light on this critical issue. One was the separation between public and private life which is considered "normal" in most societies; the second was the hidden issues associated with the power differential that permeate the relations between men and women in the great majority of cultures; and the third was the gap between the ideals of the UN documents[5] and its practical implementation by a largely male establishment.

The separation of the public and private spheres is a given in patriarchal societies and ensures the control of women by men within different groups and at all levels. The male, as head of the household rules home life and the individual *right to privacy*, an important human right, is often interpreted as if in the familial sphere there should **not be** governmental or community interference. The *right to privacy*, which includes the right to choose with whom one associates and deals with all reproductive decisions, becomes instead the right of men to control their "private" families. In other words, the human rights of women are not protected in the home with the result that the intimate relations between men and women follow a rigid hierarchical pattern and are left out of the human rights framework.[6] As for the public sphere, civil and political rights, which are concerned with the right to life, seem primarily directed at the protection of men in public life. As such they do not address the many life-threatening situations that women encounter all over the world, like infanticide, malnutrition, reproductive health hazards, illegal abortion, less access to health care, trafficking, forced prostitution and many other forms of violence.[7]

The second theme, that of the power differential between men and women, manifests itself in the persistent discrimination against women in practically all spheres of life, in the violence aimed at maintaining women in a subordinate role, and in the dismissal of that pattern as a private or cultural matter. Charlotte Bunch, among others, saw violence against women as a political issue which resulted from the "structural relationships of power, domination and privilege between women and men in society" (491). Bunch located women's bodies as the physical territory of this political struggle, as demonstrated by the resistance to allow control of women's bodies to women and the plethora of laws and regulations that ensure the physical subjugation of women to men.[8]

And on the topic of implementation of women's human rights by the international law-making institutions that developed and support the traditional human rights framework, feminists pointed out that these institutions are very male-dominated "rendering suspect the claim of the objectivity and universality of international human rights law" (103).[9] For instance, the International Court of Justice, (also known as the World Court) in The Hague, the principal judicial organ of the UN, with 15 elected judges, has only one woman member as of 2004. And the International Law Commission, established by the UN General Assembly in 1947 to promote the progressive development of international law and its codification, with 34 members, elected its very first woman member only in 2001. As for the UN Secretariat, which carries on the day-to-day work of the organization, women hold 32.7 percent of the positions at the senior level. All in all, there is an over-representation of men, which extends also to the committees that monitor the implementation of human rights treaties.[10] Implementation is an especially important issue in order to make declarations and treaties truly effective in the lives of women.

Recognizing that women's rights are human rights is an ongoing and arduous process and an agenda for struggle. New themes and areas of activism continue to arise as a result of this awareness and contribute to deepen and widen the human rights conversation in the near and far future. In the next section I address some of the activism that has both propelled and emerged from the women's human rights agenda.

Women's Transnational Organizing

For the past 25 years women activists from all over the world, but particularly from the global South, have played an increasingly important role in the recognition of the rights of women as part of the human rights framework. The *First United Nations Decade for Women* which took place in 1976–1985 marked an explicit commitment to women's issues and in the midpoint of the decade, in 1979, the General Assembly adopted the *Convention for the Elimination of All Forms of Discrimination Against Women* (CEDAW).[11] This Convention expressly addresses violations of the human rights of women and it represents a truly major step in the struggle for the recognition of women's rights as human rights. Its preamble and 30 articles are widely and rightly seen as an international bill of rights for women. Its first article sets the tone of the document by defining discrimination against women as

> "any distinction, exclusion, or restriction made on the basis of sex, which has the effect or purpose of impairing or nullifying the recognition, enjoyment or exercise by women, irrespective of their marital status, on a basis of equality of men and women, of human rights and fundamental freedom in the political, economic, social, cultural, civil, or any other field."

From this first article flows the rest of the document, specifying concrete steps to end discrimination against women and requiring action in all fields to advance women's human rights. Significantly, the Convention is the "only human rights treaty which affirms the reproductive rights of women and targets culture and tradition as influential forces shaping gender roles and family relations."[12] Just to give an idea of some of its salient points: CEDAW requires the end of traffic in women and the exploitation of prostitutes; mandates equal rights of women and men regarding their nationality and that of their children; demands equal access for women to family benefits, credit, bank loans, sports and cultural life; focuses on the problems of rural women; guarantees equality before the law and equal access to administer property; requires steps to ensure equality in marriage and family relations, etc. CEDAW should be read in its entirety to fully appreciate its comprehensiveness. CEDAW has been ratified by 179 countries as of October 2004.[13]

Since the 1975 UN World Conference on Women in Mexico City, marking International Women's Year, women activists from all over the planet have converged not only at the UN Women's conferences in Copenhagen (1980), Nairobi (1985), and Beijing (1995), but also at the UN World conferences on Environment and Development (Rio de Janeiro, 1992), Human Rights (Vienna, 1993) and Population and Development (Cairo, 1994), pressing for the recognition of women's rights as human rights in all spheres of life. Many voices have convincingly argued that thanks to the persistent work of these activists, the UN global conferences have successfully incorporated gender analysis into areas previously considered "gender-neutral" and that this "gendering the agenda"[14] has greatly contributed to the recognition of women's rights. In other words, gender has now become part and parcel of the important global conversations in all spheres of life, such as war, peace, health, development, militarism, security, globalization, etc.

In 1995, twenty years after the first Women's conference, 3,000 women participated in the official UN Fourth World Conference on Women in Beijing, China, and over 30,000 attended the parallel NGO (non-governmental organizations) forum. Out of this conference emerged another significant document, the Platform for Action (PfA), which acknowledges the continual barriers to women's empowerment and calls on governments, NGOs and the private sector to take action. It highlights 12 critical areas of concern which are interrelated, interdependent, and considered "high priority."[15] They are worth listing because they present a succinct summary of the main issues that impede the incorporation of women as full members of society all over the world and provide a map that helps inspire us and remind us of what still needs to be done. They are:

- The persistent and increasing burden of poverty on women
- Inequalities and inadequacies in and unequal access to education and training
- Inequalities and inadequacies in and unequal access to health care and related services
- Violence against women
- The effects of armed or other kinds of conflict on women, including those living under foreign occupation
- Inequality in economic structures and policies, in all forms of productive activities and in access to resources
- Inequality between men and women in the sharing of power and decision-making at all levels
- Insufficient mechanisms at all levels to promote the advancement of women
- Lack of respect for and inadequate promotion and protection of the human rights of women
- Stereotyping of women and inequality in women's access to and participation in all communication systems, especially in the media
- Gender inequalities in the management of natural resources and in the safeguarding of the environment
- Persistent discrimination against and violation of the rights of the girl child.

The Beijing conference was also the scenario of the emerging backlash that the success of the transnational women's movement has generated. Well-organized conservative right-wing groups from various countries (including the United States) framed women's rights as threats to family, nation, and God.[16] This countermovement objected to issues such as reproductive rights and LGBT rights, and engaged in a vigorous defense of traditional marriage and family arrangements. Women's rights were portrayed as an attempt to discount and take over national and religious values. In spite of this backlash, the conference managed to produce the PfA, which was signed by more than 180 governments although several countries expressed reservations about language that seemed to support abortion or alternative family structures.

Furthermore, in addition to this backlash, globalization and the huge influence of the United States in the international scene have allowed for direct impact on the lives of women all over the world, making more necessary than ever the transnational organizing for women's rights. Consider for instance, the Global Gag Rule. President Bush's first action when he took power in 2001 was to stop all United States financing to the United Nations Population Fund (UNPF) allegedly because the Fund "promotes" abortion. This was undoubtedly an attempt to impose conservative U.S. policies on the rest of the world and is in direct violation of women's reproductive and sexual health as explicitly addressed in the UN Conference on Population and Development in Cairo in 1994. The Global Gag Rule "denies health organizations in countries that receive US family planning monies the right to use their own, non–U.S. funds to perform abortions (even where legal), provide abortion counseling or referrals or advocate to change abortion laws."[17] This has had huge consequences for the health and lives of women in the poorest parts of the world and has prompted a solidarity campaign started by two women in the United States, Lois Abraham and Jane Roberts, to raise $34 million, one dollar at a time, to make up the funds that have been denied to the UNPF.[18]

One encouraging example of women's transnational organizing has been the case of the International Criminal Court (ICC) based in The Hague. The Rome Statute, the creating document for the ICC, raised the standards of responding to crimes against women by recognizing rape, sexual slavery, enforced prostitution, forced pregnancy, enforced sterilization and sexual violence as war crimes and crimes against humanity. Of the 18 judges elected last year, seven are women. This is an unprecedented proportion in international law circles and reflects the successful work of the Women's Caucus for Gender Justice whose mission is "strengthening advocacy in Women's Human Rights and international justice."[19]

Women's Rights and Cultural Relativism

The debates about the universality versus relativism of human rights have been going on since the UN started to work on the Declaration. Are human rights truly universal or are they relative to culture/religion/or nation? In fact, even before the Universal Declaration of Human Rights had been adopted by the UN, the American Anthropological Association wrote to the Human Rights Commission expressing concern about the limitations of a "statement of rights conceived only in terms of the values prevalent in the countries of Western Europe and America."[20] Much work has taken place around this issue with contributions by historians, philosophers, activists, and public intellectuals from many different cultural and religious backgrounds.

However, the central themes of the Declaration, based on the dignity and common humanity of all people, have generally held strong while allowing for differences in implementation and emphasis. This has been reinforced by the 1993 UN Vienna Declaration on Human Rights which states that human rights "must be considered in the context of a dynamic and evolving process of international norm-setting, bearing in mind the significance of national and regional particularities and various historical, cultural and religious backgrounds."[21] At the same time, the Vienna conference became the focus for organizing the worldwide Global Campaign for Women's Human Rights which brought to the international scene the idea that "women's rights are human rights." As a result, the *Vienna Declaration and Programme of Action* states that "The human rights of women and of the girl-child are an inalienable, integral and indivisible part of universal human rights."[22]

It seems though that in practice, over and over again the universality of human rights is particularly challenged when applied to women. The resistance to women's rights often takes the form of adopting a cultural relativism viewpoint and claiming that women's position in the private sphere leaves women outside the human rights framework. Specific abuses of women such as sexual slavery, genital mutilation,[23] forced marriage, systematic rape, violence in the home, discrimination at many levels, etc., continue unabated worldwide.

Many factors come into play in the discussion of universality and relativism particularly because of the history of Western colonialism, national resistance movements, and the role of women in transmitting culture. Women are seen in most societies as the bearers and reproducers of culture and as such they carry a special weight in terms of maintaining tradition and group identity. Equating women with culture often manifests itself in traditional legal systems (sometimes referred as "customary laws") that discriminate against women in family life—i.e. divorce, inheritance, marriage, child custody, property ownership, etc. How to deal with the tension between women's rights as articulated in CEDAW and various cultural and religious systems can be a frustrating matter and as such it has been the focus of intense discussions. One thing that has emerged from these conversations is the need to avoid the "arrogant gaze" of the outsider (i.e. the West) and be extremely aware of the strategies used when trying to modify or eradicate cultural practices that harm women.[24]

I will illustrate the complexity of the issue by looking at a particular situation that was useful to me because it allowed me to think and learn about these issues in a concrete fashion. In March 2002, Amina Lawal, a poor Muslim woman in her early thirties was sentenced to death by stoning by a lower

Shari'a court in the Katsina state of northern Nigeria, allegedly because of adultery. Married at age 14, she was divorced and at a later stage she became pregnant and had a baby daughter.[25] This case attracted considerable international attention. Petitions to the president of Nigeria, Olusegun Obasanjo, and the Minister of Justice, Kanu Godwin Agabi, were circulated and gathered millions of signatures asking that the death penalty be suspended. I signed several of these petitions and encouraged others to do so.

However, in May of 2003, BAOBAB for Women's Human Rights in Nigeria (a HR organization working on the case in Nigeria) posted a letter on the Internet asking people to stop the international Amina Lawal protest letter campaigns. The reasons for this request were many and varied, including the fact that many of the letters in circulation were inaccurate and could even damage Amina Lawal's situation because of the backlash they could create. They pointed out that in a similar case some time ago, a sentence of flogging was carried out illegally and with no notice, deliberately to defy international pressure. A clear example of letters being inaccurate was a letter stating that Amina Lawal was set to be stoned on a certain date, August 27, 2003, (which was the date of her appeal) and that the Nigerian Supreme Court had upheld her sentence. BAOBAB clarified that the Amina Lawal case was still being appealed at the State Shari'a Court of Appeal and that if the appeal was not successful she would appeal to the Federal Shari'a Court and if that was also unsuccessful it would go to the Supreme Court of Nigeria. In other words, there was no imminent threat of executing the sentence and the appeal process had not been exhausted. Moreover, BAOBAB pointed out that they had never lost an appeal process and that it is the lower courts that are the most conservative and repressive in Nigeria. They explained that when petitions with inaccurate information are circulated, they damage the credibility of the local activists because everyone assumes that they have provided the information to the international networks. Furthermore they pointed out that the strategy they were pursuing through an appeal strengthens the local groups, sends the message that people have a right to appeal and challenge injustices successfully, and makes clear that the conviction should not have been made in the first place. They also argued that a successful appeal is more powerful than a pardon because a pardon means that the person was guilty but the state is willing to forgive them.

Another problem with some of the letters was/is that often the international media presents Islam as being incompatible with human rights and this helps foster racism and support right-wing and conservative elements in the West. The petitions may be seen as fostering those attitudes also. Condemning a whole faith because of the behavior of some extremist factions does not help local progressive movements and gives license to these factions which can seriously threaten the life and safety of the victims and those who support them. Vigilante groups are a real problem in Nigeria and can act quickly when they have an excuse to do so and Western criticism may provide such an excuse. BAOBAB and other local groups asked for international solidarity and respect for the wishes of the local activists involved with the issues on the ground and that those interested in supporting cases like the Amina Lawal case get in touch with them to discuss strategies of solidarity and support. They welcomed resources, in terms of expertise, exchanges of information, knowledge of similar situations and money to support the victims and to pay for the expenses of the appeal process. Eventually Amina Lawal's sentence was overturned by the Shari'a Federal Court and the charges against her dropped.[26]

This experience was an eye-opener for me and an opportunity to increase my sensitivity to and understanding of how to work on international issues and be able to offer support from a more informed position. As a result I now feel that caution and in-depth research about local activism will be my first concern before I leap into action when I learn about situations in countries and cultures with which I am unfamiliar. In the Amina Lawal case, I stopped signing petitions and instead sent money to BAOBAB to support their work. In retrospect I marvel about my own naivete. Thanks to the Internet, I regularly read news about Argentina both in the Argentine and U.S. media, which keeps me in touch with my country of origin. I know all too well how differently news is portrayed in each country and how the lack of historical and cultural perspectives distorts the news, even in the case of well intentioned observers. The distortions range from egregious errors over simple facts to cultural assumptions and generalizations which are frequently laughable.

Clearly, cultural beliefs, attitudes, and values have often been used to justify the oppression of women. Justifications such as "this is how we do things, this is part of our culture," negate the fact that cultures are dynamic entities, that what is acceptable today is different from what was acceptable 100 years ago (i.e., slavery, foot-binding, widow-burning, etc.). Resistance to cultural change is hard to overcome but we cannot give up and accept practices that deny women basic human rights. Furthermore, extremist positions often present themselves as the "true" bearers of culture in spite of the fact that there are different ideologies and deep contradictions within the cultures themselves. Supporting local activists to engage in "internal dialogue," since women do not speak with only one voice, followed by external dialogue with the transnational women's movement, seems a prudent strategy, though at times admittedly a slow and frustrating one, in furthering the recognition of women's rights.

Bringing Beijing to the U.S.

What about the U.S. and women's human rights? The concept of human rights is still foreign to the majority of the population in this country and a poll in 1997 showed that 92 percent of people interviewed had never heard of the Universal Declaration of Human Rights.[27] Many people think that violations of women's human rights take place only abroad and discount the necessary and continuous work that hundreds of organizations perform locally everyday to uphold women's human rights in the United States. As Loretta Ross, founder of the Atlanta-based National Center for Human Rights Education has perceptively said:

"Most people still think of Human Rights as letter-writing campaigns to help free political prisoners. Few people realize that women's movements, the anti-war and anti-poverty movements, disability rights and even the environmental justice movement have supporting language in the Universal Declaration of Human Rights."[28]

In the United States, violence against women takes place in both private and public spheres and is compounded by other factors such as race, ethnicity, class, sexual orientation, disability, and age. Violence against women manifests itself in sexual harassment in school and workplace, sexual abuse, forced prostitution, battering, marital rape, and domestic violence. Domestic violence has gained some attention because of the work of committed activists who have brought the issue into the open.[29] But is domestic violence the only form of violence we should worry about? If we focus exclusively on that issue and do not look also at the social context it is easy to forget that domestic violence takes place in a society that systematically discriminates against women economically, legally, and culturally.

Clearly, in the United States as in the rest of the world, we must look at all the aspects in the culture that erode women's human rights. So, when we talk about women and violence we need to remember the violence against women in prison in the form of rape, sexual assault, groping during body searches, shackling during childbirth and general medical neglect.[30] We need to be aware of the control of women's sexuality and reproductive choice, which affects particularly poor women, and of the increased vulnerability of women to the AIDS epidemic because of the refusal of men to wear condoms. And most glaringly, we need to examine the total impunity for the perpetrators of these actions. In fact, often, the reactions to many of these abuses is to "blame the victim" and to ostracize and shame those who have the courage to speak up about the abuses that they have suffered.

Introducing the human rights framework in the United States will allow us to have an integrated perspective within which any violation of women's human rights will be seen as part of the larger denial of humanity to women. Such a perspective will end the fragmentation and separation of the various types of human rights abuses. It will take us out of the "single-issue" focus and enable coalitions and multi layered campaigns to emerge, zeroing in on the denial of women's dignity in its many manifestations, and fostering transnational connections and a better understanding of the global forces that affect women's rights in the United States.[31]

In the case of women's reproductive and sexual health rights, for instance, it is becoming increasingly clear how these rights, locally and internationally, are connected to economic justice and that they must be linked to grassroots organizing and a campaign to end poverty. Otherwise they remain abstract and unattainable.[32] Another prime example which powerfully illustrates the intersection of various forms of human rights violations in the United States is that of women on welfare, where gender, race, and poverty come together to ensure that poor single mothers of color are blamed and punished for their situations. In 1996, under President Clinton, the PRWORA (Personal Responsibility Work Opportunity Reconciliation Act) known as "welfare reform" was passed and the welfare system known as Temporary Assistance for Needy Families (TANF) was established. Practically all the critical areas listed in the Beijing Platform for Action are violated by this "welfare reform."

The majority of people currently on welfare are poor mothers of color. Study after study shows that family homelessness and hunger have continued to increase and that the low-wage work available for women with limited education leaves them in an extremely vulnerable situation.[33] The act punishes young single mothers, is based on a patriarchal view of the family which promotes marriage as the solution, and contains especially harsh measures against legal immigrants. As Gwendolyn Mink points out, TANF fosters women's dependency on individual men "by sanctioning mothers with mandatory work outside the home if they remain single. Mothers who are married do not have to work outside the home, even though they receive welfare, for labor market work by only one parent in a two parent family satisfies TANF's work requirements."[34] TANF requires mothers to "reveal the identity of her child's father and must pursue a child support order against him." It also pressures women to open their families to biological fathers and promotes their involvement, regardless of poor mothers' understanding and judgement of what is best for themselves and their children. TANF also lets states who have "family cap" policies withhold benefits from children born to mothers on welfare. By dismissing women's caregiving work, forcing women into the labor market and increasing their dependence on men, TANF reduces poor mothers on welfare to creatures who are denied any opportunity for growth or nourishment that would help them on their path to strength, freedom, and independence.

Not surprisingly, the movement for the recognition of economic rights as human rights continues to grow in the United States and organizations like the Kensington Welfare Rights Union in Philadelphia, founded in 1991, have received well deserved national and international attention for their organizing efforts. The inspired leadership of their founder, Cheri Honkala, has taken their case to the Organization of American States and to the UN accusing the U.S. government of human rights violation on the issues of welfare, health care, and housing. They have used for their education campaigns: articles 23, (right to desirable work and to join trade unions), article 25 (right to an adequate living standard) and article 26 (right to education) from the Universal Declaration to shift the attention from scarcity to greed: "We say that scarcity is not the issue—greed is."[35]

Finally, and furthermore, the United States has an extremely poor record in terms of ratification of the international treaties that provide the legal framework for the application of the rights articulated in the Universal Declaration. The United States has voted against the creation of the International Criminal Court (ICC), and has not ratified the Covenant on Economic, Social and Cultural Rights (ICESCR), or the Convention on the Elimination of All Forms of Discrimination Against Women (CEDAW), or the Convention on the Rights of the Child (CRC) as well as other important treaties. As a result of this inertia, social activists have started pursuing the possibility of local treaty implementation, bypassing the mammoth federal bureaucracy and harsh resistance of archaic legislators, who keep yawning at the mention of treaty ratification. The city of San Francisco adopted CEDAW in 1998 and codified it into law raising the eyebrows of the political establishment nationwide. In 2003, San Francisco finished its five-year implementation plan and one of its accomplishments has been a "gender analysis" of selected city departments and legislation turning the Commission on the Status of Women into a permanent city department. Obstacles remain regarding implementation, compliance, and analysis of the intersectionality of gender with other forms of discrimination, due to race and class. But there is a general sense that the local understanding of human rights has increased and the creation of a five-year Action Plan in 2003 calls for establishing an anti-discrimination committee reporting directly to the local authorities, advocating for resources and acting as liaison with similar efforts elsewhere.[36]

Inspired by the San Francisco experience, the Human Rights Initiative was born in New York City in 2002 attempting to obtain local ratification for CEDAW and for CERD (Convention on the Elimination of All Forms of Racial Discrimination). A broad coalition of progressive groups is at the heart of the coalition and the hope is to introduce legislation by 2005. When passed, the Initiative is expected to counteract discrimination against women of color, the most marginalized population in the city. And yet another local effort has recently been started in Massachusetts, the Mass CEDAW Project.[37]

Much remains to be done. Education about human rights in the United States is at the beginning stages. The resistance to the application of the human rights framework to problems in the United States, (sometimes called "U.S. exceptionalism") has been hard to overcome, but there are hopeful signs on the horizon. A plethora of groups has emerged in the last ten years or so, trying to connect the local with the global, understanding that fragmentation and isolation are convenient tools for the maintenance of privilege and injustice.[38]

Local initiatives for ratification of treaties, human rights education in schools and universities, and a growing interest from activist groups to integrate the human rights framework in their work give me reasons for optimism. One of the women responsible for the introduction of the city ordinance in San Francisco, Krishanti Dharmaraj, who is also one of the founders of the Women's Institute for Leadership Development for Human Rights, has said: "I do not know how else to do social change in this complex world but to do human rights."[39] Her phrase summarizes well the hope and promise of the human rights framework. It simply reasserts the original and powerful insights first articulated in the Universal Declaration. It continually reminds us of the indivisibility and interdependence of human rights so that truly ALL women will be included in the struggles against discrimination, exploitation, and violence. Linking the local to the global will strengthen our movement for justice for all and put human dignity at the forefront of the struggle.

Like the quote at the beginning of this article from the Beijing Platform of Action states, the advancement of women and the full recognition of our humanity is the only way to build a sustainable, just and developed society. So, let's get to work!

NOTES

1. The work of Eleanor Roosevelt, as chair of the Human Rights committee which drafted the Declaration, was instrumental for its adoption by the UN General Assembly. See Glendon, Mary Ann. 2001. *A World Made New: Eleanor Roosevelt and the Universal Declaration of Human Rights.* Random House: New York. The book includes various drafts of the Declaration and the final version.

2. Ibid. See pages 90–93; 111–112; 153–154; 162; 164; 177.

3. Ibid. See page 90.

4. Reanda, Laura. Spring 1981. "Human Rights and Women's Rights: The United Nations Approach." *Human Rights Quarterly* 3, No. 2: 11–31.

5. The Universal Declaration is simply that, a declaration, and it is not legally binding. Two UN Covenants were eventually drafted to implement the principles of the Declaration: the Covenant on Civil and Political Rights and the Covenant on Economic, Social and Cultural Rights. Nations that ratify these covenants are legally bound to enforce the implementation of the human rights listed in the covenants.

6. Eisler, Riane. Spring 1987. "Human Rights: Toward an Integrated Theory for Action." *Human Rights Quarterly.* 25–46. See also Gerda Lerner. 1986. *The Creation of Patriarchy.* Oxford University Press: New York, NY.

7. Charlesworth, Hilary. 1995. "Human Rights as Men's Rights." In *Women's Rights, Human Rights: International Feminist Perspectives,* edited by Julie Peters and Andrea Wolper. 103–113. Routledge, New York, NY. Women, though, have also taken leadership roles in the movement for the protection of civic and political rights worldwide. See for instance, Bouvard, Marguerite Guzman. 1996. *Women Reshaping Human Rights: How Extraordinary Activists Are Changing the World and Revolutionizing Motherhood: The Mothers of the Plaza de Mayo.* 1994. Both published by Scholarly Resources, Wilmington, Delaware; Arditti, Rita. 1999. *Searching for Life: The Grandmothers of the Plaza de Mayo and the Disappeared Children of Argentina.* 1999. Berkeley: University of California Press; Clements, Alan. 1997. *The Voice of Hope: Conversations with Aung San Suu Kyi.* New York: Seven Stories Press; and many others.

8. Bunch, Charlotte. 1990. "Women's Rights as Human Rights: Toward a Re-Vision of Human Rights." *Human Rights Quarterly* 12, No. 4: 486–498.

9. See note 7, p 103.

10. Charlesworth, Hilary. 2002. "The Hidden Gender of International Law." *16 Temp.Int'l & Comp. L.J.* 93.

11. In 1976, the United Nations Development Fund for Women (UNIFEM) was created to provide financial support for innovative projects mainly directed at rural and poor urban women in developing countries. For CEDAW, see Tinker, Catherine. Spring 1981. "Human Rights for Women: The UN Convention on the Elimination of All forms of Discrimination Against Women" *Human Rights Quarterly* 3, No. 2: 32–43.

12. www.un.org/womenwatch/daw/cedaw/cedaw/htm.

13. Many states that have ratified the Convention have done so with "reservations," some of which are quite substantial and compromise the integrity of the convention. For more on this important point see Cook, Rebecca, "Reservations to the Convention on the Elimination of All Forms of Discrimination Against Women," 1990. *Va.J. Int'l L.* 30: 643–716.

    An interesting addition to CEDAW is the "Optional Protocol," a separate treaty which countries that have ratified CEDAW can also sign. It allows a woman whose rights have been violated to bring her claims to the U.N. and her government will have to answer her claim at the international level; 39 countries have signed on to the Optional Protocol.

14. Friedman, Elizabeth Jay. 2003. "Gendering the Agenda: The Impact of the Transnational Women's Rights Movement at the UN conferences of the 1990s." *Women's Studies International Forum* 26, No. 4: 313–331.

15. www.un.org/womenwatch/daw/beijing/platform.

16. See note 14 and Butler, Jennifer. 2002. "New Sheriff in Town: The Christian Right Shapes U.S. Agenda at the United Nations." *The Public Eye.* XVI, No. 2: 14–22.

17. Petchesky, Rosalind. 2004, June. www.radiofeminista.net./junio04/notas/cairo+10-ing3.htm. Washington, Joi. "The U.S., Rowing Against the Tide." *National Women's Health Network.* 29, Issue 3: 3.

18. www.34millionfriends.org.

19. The Women's Caucus for Gender Justice has changed its name to "Women's Initiatives for Gender Justice" and their web address is: www.iccwomen.org. For more info on the ICC go to: www.icc-cpi.int and www.iccnow.org.

20. American Anthropological Association, "Statement on Human Rights," 49 *American Anthropologist* 539 (1947). Quoted in Glendon, Mary Ann, see note 1, p. 222.

21. Quoted in Steiner, Henry J. and Philip Alston. 1996. *International Human Rights in Context: Law, Politics, Morals.* New York: Oxford University Press. 235.

22. Ibid. 928.

23. The term "genital mutilation" covers a wide range of practices which vary in extent and severity involving women's genitals. Other terms used are "female circumcision," "female genital cutting," and "female genital surgery." Some Western feminists's views on the issue gave rise to a public debate raising issues of colonialism, racism, and simplistic constructions regarding women in the countries where these practices are carried on. See *Genital Cutting and Transnational Sisterhood: Disputing U.S. Polemics.* 2002. Edited by Stanlie M. James and Claire C. Robertson. Urbana and Chicago: University of Illinois Press. Note especially the Prologue, a "Position paper on Clitoridectomy and Infibulation"

drafted by the Women's Caucus of the African Studies Association (first appeared in 1983) and Cheryl Chase's essay "'Cultural Practice' or 'Reconstructive Surgery'? Genital Cutting, the Intersex Movement and Medical Double Standards." See also Nahid Toubia's work, *Female Genital Mutilation: A Call for Global Action.* 1993. Women Ink, and visit www.rainbo.org, the webpage of Research, Action and Information for the Bodily Integrity of Women, an African led international non-governmental organization.

24. Coomaraswamy, Radhika, 2002. "Are Women's Rights Universal? Re-engaging the Local." *Meridians: feminism, race, transnationalism.* 3, No. 1, 1–18. Abdullahi Ahmed An-Na'im. 1994. "State Responsibility Under International Human Rights To Change Religious and Customary Laws" in *Human Rights of Women: National and International Perspectives,* edited by Rebecca J. Cook. Philadelphia: University of Pennsylvania Press.

25. Currently in some states in Northern Nigeria new Shari'a-based penal codes, which apply only to Muslims, have been introduced. According to these laws, pregnancy out of marriage amounts to adultery. The man supposedly responsible for the pregnancy denied having sex with Amina and charges against him were dropped.

26. For a more detailed discussion of this case see "Please Stop the International Amina Lawal Protest Letter Campaigns" at www.whrnet.org/docs/action-03-05-07.html. Arditti, Rita. *Amina Lawal-To Sign or Not To Sign.* www.umb.edu/human_rights/issues/index. September 25, 2003. Also visit the webpage of Women Living Under Muslin Laws, an international solidarity network: www.wluml.org

27. Hart Survey on Attitudes and Knowledge of Human Rights/Adults. 1997. At www.hrusa.org/features.shtm

28. *Close to Home: Case Studies of Human Rights Work in the United States.* 2004. A Ford Foundation Report. Also at: www.fordfound.org/publication/recent_articles.

29. U.S. Department of Justice, Office of Justice Programs, 2000. "Extent, Nature, and Consequences of Intimate Partner Violence: Findings from the National Violence Against Women Survey." Battered Mothers' Testimony Project at the Wellesley Centers for Women. November 2002. *Battered Mothers Speak Out: A Human Rights Report on Domestic Violence and Child Custody in the Massachusetts Family Courts.*

30. Davis, Angela Y. and Cassandra Shaylor. 2001. "Race, Gender, and the Prison Industrial Complex: California and Beyond" in *Time to Rise: US Women of Color—Issues and Strategies. A Report for the UN World Conference Against Racism, Racial Discrimination, Xenophobia, and Related Intolerance.* Edited by Maylei Blackwell, Linda Burnham, and Jung Hee Choi. Women of Color Resource Center. Berkeley, CA.

31. Mallika Dutt. 1994. *With Liberty and Justice for All: Women's Human Rights in the United States.* Center for Women's Global Leadership. Douglass College, New Brunswick. NJ.

32. Petchesky, Rosalind Pollack. 2000. "Human Rights, Reproductive Health and Economic Justice—Why they are Indivisible." *Reproductive Health Matters,* 8, No. 15. Also at http://urban.hunter.cuny.edu/~respet/RHMedit00.htm.

33. Burnham, Linda. 2002. "Welfare Reform, Family Hardship, and Women of Color" in *Lost Ground: Welfare Reform, Poverty, and Beyond* edited by Randy Albelda and Ann Withorn. Boston: South End Press.

34. Mink, Gwendolyn. 2002. "Violating Women: Rights Abuses in the Welfare Police State" in *Lost Ground,* see note above.

35. See note 28.

36. Ibid.

37. For information on the NYC Human Rights Initiative contact cedawcerdnyc@ yahoo.com; for information on the Mass CEDAW Project contact MassCEDAW@ yahoo.com.

38. *Something Inside so Strong: A Resource Guide on Human Rights in the United States.* Distributed by the U.S. Human Rights Network. www.ushrnetwork.org. This resource guide was drawn from the Second Leadership Summit on Human Rights in the United States held in July 2002.

39. See note 28.

NAME INDEX

SUBJECT INDEX